A PHILOSOPHICAL COMMENTARY

NATURAL LAW AND
ENLIGHTENMENT CLASSICS

Knud Haakonssen
General Editor

Pierre Bayle

NATURAL LAW AND
ENLIGHTENMENT CLASSICS

A Philosophical Commentary on These Words of the Gospel, Luke 14.23, "Compel Them to Come In, That My House May Be Full"

Pierre Bayle

Edited, with an Introduction, by
John Kilcullen and Chandran Kukathas

LIBERTY FUND

Indianapolis

This book is published by Liberty Fund, Inc., a foundation established
to encourage study of the ideal of a society of free and responsible individuals.

𒄑𒂼𒄀

The cuneiform inscription that serves as our logo and as the design motif for
our endpapers is the earliest-known written appearance of the word
"freedom" (*amagi*), or "liberty." It is taken from a clay document written
about 2300 B.C. in the Sumerian city-state of Lagash.

09 08 07 06 05 C 5 4 3 2 1
09 08 07 06 05 P 5 4 3 2 1

Frontispiece and cover (detail) photo credit:
Réunion des Musées Nationaux/Art Resource, NY

Library of Congress Cataloging-in-Publication Data
Bayle, Pierre, 1647–1706.
[Commentaire philosophique. English]
A philosophical commentary on these words of the Gospel, Luke 14.23:
"Compel them to come in, that My house may be full"/Pierre Bayle;
edited and with an introduction by John Kilcullen and Chandran Kukathas.
p. cm.   (Natural law and enlightenment classics)
Includes bibliographical references.
ISBN-13: 978-0-86597-494-4 (alk. paper)
ISBN-10: 0-86597-494-2 (alk. paper)
ISBN-13: 978-0-86597-495-1 (alk. paper: pbk.)
ISBN-10: 0-86597-495-0 (pbk. alk. paper)
1. Religious tolerance.   I. Kilcullen, John, 1938–   II. Kukathas, Chandran.
III. Title.   IV. Series.
BR1610.B3913 2005
61.7′2—dc22   2005044290

LIBERTY FUND, INC.
8335 Allison Pointe Trail, Suite 300
Indianapolis, Indiana 46250-1684

CONTENTS

A PHILOSOPHICAL COMMENTARY
on These Words of the Gospel, Luke 14.23,
"Compel Them to Come In, That My House May Be Full"   1

Appendixes

INTRODUCTION

Liberalism makes it a matter of moral principle not to use coercive means, threats, and inducements to impede the spread of ideas we reject, even when they seem not only wrong but dangerous. In Bayle's time many Christians believed that God himself had commanded the use of such means to prevent the spread of religious error, but even apart from this theological opinion it will seem natural to many people to block the spread of dangerous ideas by force, if that is the most effective way. Coercive methods may often be ineffective, but the liberal believes that even when they are effective, or might be, they are wrong. The earliest and still perhaps the most persuasive argument in favor of this basic tenet of liberalism is Pierre Bayle's *Philosophical Commentary on these words of the gospel (Luke 14.23), "Compel them to come in, that my House may be full."*

Bayle's Life

Pierre Bayle, the second son of a Protestant pastor, was born on 18 June 1647 in Le Carla (now Carla-Bayle) in the Compté de Foix, at the foot of the Pyrenees. With his brothers, Jacob and Joseph, he learned to read and write in the town's only school, and furthered his education with the help of his father, who introduced him to Latin and Greek as well as to the various books found in his own library and those of his colleagues living nearby. Jean Bayle's modest circumstances made it impossible for him to send his younger son to secondary school until Jacob had finished his theological studies, and Pierre was twenty-one when he set out for the academy at Puylaurens. Already in love with books and learning but disappointed by the school's low standards, Pierre left three months later for Toulouse and was accepted as a day-pupil in a Jesuit college, where he was instructed in Aristotelian philosophy and logic. Unable, as a young country scholar, to defend his Protestant faith against the arguments of his teachers, on 19 March 1669 he converted to Catholicism, to the dismay of his Huguenot family.

Bayle's conversion did not last long. By the time he stood to defend his Master's thesis in August 1670 he had become thoroughly disaffected with Catholic practice and was no longer satisfied intellectually by its doctrine. But if abandoning his Protestant faith had taken considerable moral courage, abjuring Catholicism—even for the religion of one's birth—was positively dangerous, since under French law "relapsed heretics" incurred heavy penalties. Nonetheless, Bayle converted again and fled to Geneva, never to see his parents or younger brother again.

In Geneva Bayle also abandoned his Aristotelian views and, under the influence of his fellow students at the Academy, Jacques Basnage (1653–1723) and Vincent Minutoli (1640–1710), became a follower of Descartes's philosophy. After two years as tutor in a noble family near Geneva, Bayle returned to France to other tutorships, going under the name Bèle to avoid being identified as a lapsed Catholic. In 1675 he competed for and won the chair in philosophy at the Protestant Academy of Sedan.

At the Academy Bayle formed a close friendship with the professor of theology and Hebrew, Pierre Jurieu (1637–1713), and enjoyed the benefits of his patronage and of his extensive library. In Sedan he read Malebranche (1638–1715) and Spinoza (1632–77), and began to produce writings of his own. This academic life was disrupted by political developments. The religious toleration the Huguenots had enjoyed since the 1598 Edict of Nantes was slowly eroded during the reign of Louis XIV (1638–1715). In 1681 the Academy at Sedan was abolished by royal decree, and Bayle and Jurieu moved to the École Illustre in Rotterdam to take up chairs in philosophy and theology respectively, Bayle carrying with him the manuscript of *Various Thoughts on the Occasion of a Comet*.

That work was first published anonymously under the title *Letter on the Comet* in March 1682 and gained substantial public attention, not only because Bayle attacked superstition but also because he argued that a society of atheists could endure, contrary to the widespread belief at the time that belief in God is necessary to social cohesion. But it was the publication in

May that year of Bayle's reply to Louis Maimbourg's (1620?–1686) anti-Huguenot tract, *History of Calvinism,* that brought about greater controversy. Bayle's *General Criticism of M. Maimbourg's History of Calvinism* was well-received among Protestants and some Catholics, going into a second edition in November 1682, but it incurred the wrath of the authorities. The consequences were disastrous for Bayle. The burning of the book by the public hangman in Paris in March 1683 served only to increase sales; but the imprisonment of Jacob Bayle was another matter. Unable to capture the author of the *General Criticism,* the authorities incarcerated his only remaining relative; Jacob died in his cell on 12 November 1685.

The other unhappy consequence of Bayle's publication of his *General Criticism* was that it cast his colleague Jurieu's own response to M. Maimbourg's *History* in poor light, leading to a jealousy on the part of the theologian that would turn their friendship into a bitter enmity. In 1685 Bayle began work on several enterprises, including his *Philosophical Commentary.* The work was presented as an anonymous translation from the English of a work by "Mr John Fox of Bruggs." Bayle concealed his identity to avoid controversy with Jurieu, with whom he sought to maintain good relations. Nonetheless, Jurieu attacked the work, though pretending not to know the author. While Bayle had been led to a deep conviction that religious persecution was indefensible, Jurieu held to the traditional Calvinist belief that persecution was warranted if undertaken in defense of the true faith against the false. While Bayle called for toleration, Jurieu preached holy war, encouraged by the success of the Protestant William of Orange in taking the English throne from his Catholic father-in-law, James II. The ensuing battle of pamphlets further soured relations between the two men. In 1693 Jurieu succeeded in persuading the municipal council of Rotterdam to suppress Bayle's post at the École Illustre.

By this time Bayle had already commenced work on his most ambitious project, the *Historical and Critical Dictionary.* Relieved of his post by the municipal council and assured of a small annuity from his friend and publisher, Reinier Leers, he was now free to devote himself to his writing. The *Dictionary* was published in December 1696 and was an immediate success. The first edition sold out within months, and Bayle promptly began work on a second. But the work also provoked controversy and attracted the attention of the Walloon Consistory in Rotterdam, anxious about several entries thought scandalous to the faithful—because obscene, unduly tolerant of atheists, skeptics, and Manicheans, and insufficiently respectful of King David, on whose crimes and failings Bayle had dwelt at length in the *Dictionary*'s most controversial entry. The second edition, published in December 1701, toned down several of the articles and included four "clarifications" to mollify the authorities.

Bayle's last years were devoted to scholarship, and he produced several more works, including his four-volume *Reply to the Questions of a Provincial* (1703–7), in which he continued his battle with those who, in his view, offered facile solutions to the problem of evil and implausible arguments to reconcile reason and faith. Though he often had visitors because of his now considerable reputation, he died alone, after a prolonged illness, on 28 December 1706, surrounded by his books and papers.

Bayle's writings at once prefigured and did much to shape the European Enlightenment. When his *Dictionary* eventually found its way back to France, it became one of the most widely read works of the eighteenth century, and the one most readily found in private libraries. Voltaire and Diderot declared their indebtedness to it, while Thomas Jefferson included it in the one hundred books to form the basis of the Library of Congress. Leibniz felt compelled to respond to Bayle in his *Theodicy*, while Benjamin Franklin was moved to defend Bayle's thesis that atheists could form a coherent society, a thesis also defended by Bernard Mandeville. Early in the eighteenth century the *Dictionary, Thoughts on the Comet,* and *Philosophical Commentary* were translated into English, and the *Dictionary* and *Thoughts on the Comet* were translated into German. Herder, Hume, Lessing, Montesquieu, and Rousseau studied and discussed Bayle's work, which was well known to philosophers and poets as well as to some politicians and monarchs. His influence was immense.

Religious Conflicts of the Times

To understand Bayle's thought and its impact, it is important to see it not only from the perspective of later thought, but also in relation to the political and intellectual circumstances of early modern Europe. Politics and philosophy at this time were dominated by questions of religion.

Bayle was born four years after Louis XIV became king. Louis saw himself as God's representative in France, with the right to appoint bishops and abbots. He would bow to the pope in matters of faith and morals, but the French clergy were bound to the king in matters of state. The king's claims were supported by the "Gallican" party among the Catholic clergy. The Ultramontanes, members of the clergy who asserted the absolute authority of the pope, were in the minority. The Catholic clergy were further divided over the conflict between the Jesuits and the Jansenists.

Reluctant to concede anything to the temporal authority of the papacy, Louis was even less willing to tolerate the presence in France of dissenting religious sects. Lutheran works first appeared in Paris in 1519. By the mid-1530s the ideas of John Calvin, a French exile in Geneva, began to spread. Calvinist (commonly called "Huguenot") pastors trained in Geneva entered the country in large numbers, and by 1562 there were 2,000 Calvinist churches in France. Catherine de Médicis, ruling through her young son, Charles IX (1560–74), abandoned the policy of repression and, with the chancellor, Michel de L'Hospital, attempted to bring about religious compromise and offer the Calvinists a measure of toleration. The violent Catholic reaction, led by François, Duke de Guise, led to a civil war that lasted nearly forty years. The most famous incident was the massacre of Huguenots on the eve of the feast day of St. Bartholomew on 24 August 1572. Eventually, because of the death of the Catholic heir to the throne, the Huguenot leader Henry of Navarre became the legitimate heir and, after further fighting, became king as Henry IV (1589–1610). To secure his position, he converted to Roman Catholicism, but on 13 April 1598 he promulgated the Edict of Nantes, which granted the Huguenots a considerable measure of religious toleration. The Edict guaranteed the Huguenots freedom of conscience and the right to practice their religion publicly in certain areas of the country, and it also gave them a number of fortresses as surety against attack. Huguenots were made eligible to hold some public offices formerly available only to Catholics and to attend schools and universities. During the time of the Frondes (civil disturbances that almost brought down the monarchy) the Huguenots remained loyal to Louis XIV, who publicly thanked them.

There was good reason why many Huguenots were likely to be loyal subjects. An important element of Calvin's teaching was that subjects should obey the secular authority without resistance. This idea became more difficult for Huguenots to accept after the St. Bartholomew's Day Massacre, and the theory of justifiable rebellion against tyrannical rule for a while acquired a greater following. However, when a more tolerant attitude among Catholics was expressed by the "Politique" Party, led by Chancellor L'Hospital, who thought the Huguenots should be tolerated in the interests of peace, the Huguenots returned to Calvin's doctrine of nonresistance. Pierre Bayle himself always believed that the temporal authority of the king could not rightly be resisted.

In 1660 an assembly of the French clergy asked that the king close the Huguenots' colleges and hospitals and exclude them from public offices. In 1670 it suggested that, at seven years of age, a child be deemed capable of abjuring Protestantism, and that those who did abjure be taken from their parents. The clergy subsequently called for mixed marriages to be annulled and for the children of such unions to be considered illegitimate. Louis XIV gradually acceded to the demands of the clergy. The 1670s and '80s thus became decades of increasingly severe repression for Huguenots. By 1670 Huguenots were forbidden to establish or maintain colleges; attempted emigration was punishable by imprisonment and loss of property; and those caught helping would-be emigrants were sentenced to life in the galleys. A fund was established to pay Huguenots to convert to Catholicism, and there were hefty punishments for lapsed converts.

Between 1682 and 1685 most of the remaining Huguenot churches were closed or torn down. Worshippers discovered among the ruins were severely punished as enemies of the state. In 1681 the minister of war, Louvois, suggested to Louis that the Huguenots should be coerced through the practice of lodging troops in private homes at the expense of owners (dragonnade or "dragooning"). The soldiers' excesses included looting, rape, and beating their hosts, and the terror they provoked led even Louis to condemn their violence. But it continued at the insistence of the minister of war, who tried to keep news of violence from the king. Spreading through France, the dragonnades brought about many conversions, but hundreds of thousands left France. In October 1685 the Edict of Nantes was revoked, Louis declaring it unnecessary now that France was again entirely Catholic. For the Huguenots who were left, the dragonnades continued, and some historians have concluded that the holy terror of 1685 was worse than the revolutionary Terror of 1793. Of the 400,000 "converts" who were made to attend Mass and receive the Eucharist, those who refused the consecrated wafers were punished, often cruelly. Men were imprisoned, and women sent to convents, and children were taken from their parents, baptized as Catholics, and sent out for adoption.

The horror of the repression goes some way to explaining Bayle's passion in the *Philosophical Commentary*. He was well aware that his brother's fate was one shared by many French Protestants. Though the 400,000 Huguenots who managed to leave France were generously received throughout Europe, only a minority of French Catholics condemned the massacres of the Revocation, even in private. Such luminaries as Bossuet, Fénelon, and La Fontaine, among others, praised Louis for his courage and resolve. Arnauld wrote privately that "if even half of what is reported about the coercion of the Huguenots is true it is deplorable" and likely to make the Catholic religion odious—but what he deplored was the use of coercion without adequate provision for instruction. It was left to Bayle to advance the view that violence against the dissenters could not be Christian and could not be justified.

In this he found few supporters even among his Calvinist coreligionists. Calvin himself had argued vigorously in support of persecution, notably in his writings following the execution of Michael Servetus, who was burned as a blasphemous heretic in Geneva in October 1553 for propounding doctrines that questioned received beliefs about the Trinity and denied that Christ was the Eternal Son. Some of Servetus's views associated him with the Anabaptists, a sect whose rejection of civil authority had led to their being regarded as dangerous fanatics deserving of suppression. Protestant thinking was divided on the question of suppressing even the Anabaptists, and the prosecution of Servetus, led by Calvin, caused great uneasiness among the various Swiss churches, in Basle, Berne, Geneva, and Zurich. It was only Calvin's zeal that ensured Servetus's execution, but the distress and soul-searching it provoked led to Calvin's most concerted attempt to show that it was the duty of the Christian magistrate to suppress heresy and punish heretics. The most difficult philosophical question Calvin had to confront here was one raised by Sébastian Castellion (1515–63):

if highly complex theological doctrines had been debated for thousands of years and yet remained unsettled, with none having proven demonstrably true, how could men justify killing one another for their differences in opinion on these matters? Calvin answered that this contention implied that nothing could be known and brought into question everything, even belief in God. But he went further, anticipating the objection that authorizing the civil magistrate to suppress heresy by force would justify Catholic suppression of Protestants. His reply was that Catholic persecution was impermissible because Protestants were in the right.

The Argument of the *Philosophical Commentary*

Whether possession of the truth justifies religious persecution is the question Bayle confronted in the *Philosophical Commentary.* French Catholics, for the most part, were in no doubt that it does and that they possessed the truth. But the Calvinists saw matters the same way but in reverse; their objection to the persecution against them was that it was perpetrated by heretics against the innocent followers of the true faith, Calvinism. For Bayle this stance was morally untenable. Bayle's *Commentary* is a critique of *all* coercion in religious matters, as being inconsistent with reason. To the extent that the *Commentary* is further intended to demonstrate that persecution is incompatible with Christianity, it also turns into an argument about the philosophical basis of theology, and indeed about the sovereignty of reason. His thesis is that natural law must guide the interpretation of religious doctrine. In the very first chapter of the *Philosophical Commentary* Bayle makes his stand:

> Thus the whole Body of Divines, of what Party soever, after having cry'd up Revelation, the Meritoriousness of Faith, and Profoundness of Mysterys, till they are quite out of breath, come to pay their homage at last at the Footstool of the Throne of Reason, and acknowledg, tho they won't speak out (but their Conduct is a Language expressive and eloquent enough) That Reason, speaking to us by the Axioms of natural Light, or metaphysical Truths, is the supreme Tribunal, and final Judg without Appeal of whatever's propos'd to the human Mind. Let it ne'er then be pretended more, that Theology is the Queen, and Philosophy the Handmaid;

for the Divines themselves by their Conduct confess, that of the two they look on the latter as the Sovereign Mistress: and from hence proceed all those Efforts and Tortures of Wit and Invention, to avoid the Charge of running counter to strict Demonstration. Rather than expose themselves to such a Scandal, they'l shift the very Principles of Philosophy, discredit this or that System, according as they find their Account in it; by all these Proceedings plainly recognizing the Supremacy of Philosophy, and the indispensable obligation they are under of making their court to it; they'd ne'er be at all this Pains to cultivate its good Graces, and keep parallel with its Laws, were they not of Opinion, that whatever Doctrine is not vouch'd, as I may say, confirm'd and register'd in the supreme Court of Reason and natural Light, stands on a very tottering and crazy Foundation. (pp. 67–68)

It is Bayle's intention in the *Philosophical Commentary* to examine closely the case for righteous persecution by the light of reason, to show how sorely it is wanting. The theory he proposes as an alternative is a doctrine of mutual toleration, under which those who disagree on matters of faith are entitled to try to persuade each other of what each takes to be the truth, but not entitled to force an opponent's alleged erring conscience to convert to an alleged true faith.

In the Gospel according to Luke, Jesus offers a parable of the man who prepared a great feast but found that the many people he had invited refused his invitation. Angry, this lord commanded his servant, "Go out into the highways and hedges and compel them to come in, that my house may be filled" (Luke 14:23). From St. Augustine (354–430) on, Christian apologists had appealed to this verse to justify forcible conversion. Bayle's contention, however, is that this interpretation cannot be correct. His commentary on the passage is "philosophical," not historical or literal. Instead of entering into discussion of its literal sense, Bayle argues that Christ cannot have intended in these words to command anything contrary to what the natural light of reason reveals to us about right and wrong. Bayle argues that the natural light shows that the use of force to obtain conversion is morally wrong and that therefore, whatever the correct literal interpretation of the text may be, Christ cannot have intended it as a command to persecute.

The *Commentary* is divided into four parts. Part I establishes the case

Bayle wishes to put against the alleged literal interpretation of Luke 14:23. It begins with his statement in Chapter 1 that the principles of reason must govern all our interpretations of Scripture. In succeeding chapters he argues that the alleged literal sense is contrary to the natural light of reason; that it is contrary to the spirit of the gospel; that it causes a confusion of vice and virtue, to the ruination of society; that it gives infidels a pretext for expelling Christians from their dominions; that it leads inevitably to crimes; that it deprives the Christian religion of an important argument against Mohammedanism; that it makes the complaints of the first Christians against their pagan persecutors invalid; and that it exposes Christians to continual oppression without any hope of ending the disputes between persecutors and the persecuted.

Part II of the *Commentary* replies to a series of objections. Here Bayle responds to those who might think his case exaggerates the violence implicit in the doctrine of compulsion, fails to recognize that force was condoned by the laws given by God to the people in the Old Testament and by the teachings of the Fathers of the Church, threatens, by excessive toleration, to throw the state into confusion, and neglects the fact that the literal reading of "compel" authorizes only violence in defense of truth. Bayle's replies answer these various objections, but also work toward the construction of his own positive doctrine of toleration as a viable alternative to the theory of righteous persecution and to the ideas of the "half-tolerationists" who think that general toleration is absurd. The erroneous conscience, Bayle tries to show, has the same rights as an enlightened one. Those who are mistaken are entitled to no less respect than those blessed with insight, if they are sincere in their belief in the rightness of their convictions. The dispute between persecutor and persecuted cannot be resolved by invoking the superior rights of truth—since what is the truth is precisely what is at issue. Each therefore has an equal claim to the tolerance of the other. Since, however, one of them must be in error, we can only conclude that the claims of an erroneous conscience are equal to those of an enlightened one.

At the center of Bayle's doctrine is a theory of the morality of conscience. An act is never more sinful than when it is undertaken with the conscious belief that it is wrong. On the other hand, an innocent mistake on a point of fact may excuse: a woman who sleeps with a man she mistakes for her husband does not sin if the mistake is an honest one. These points were generally accepted, but Bayle goes further, and argues that an innocent mistake over moral principle or religious doctrine may also excuse, and that an act done in error is not sinful and may be praiseworthy. If an error is the result of sinful negligence or self-deception, the sin is in the negligence or self-deception, not in the actions that result from the error.

On the other hand, there is no greater wrong than forcing a person to perform an act he believes to be wrong. To force conscience is to force a person into a state of sin, for it means causing a person to act contrary to what he believes is the voice of God. Indeed, even tempting a person to act against conscience by making threats or offering inducements is wrong. In the end, God will judge us not by the real qualities of our actions but by our intentions—by our purity of heart. All God requires is that people act on what seems to them to be the truth, after as much inquiry as seems to them appropriate. This doctrine lies at the center of Bayle's theory of toleration and is the point that must bear the greatest critical weight.

Parts I and II were published together in 1686. Part III of the *Commentary,* published in 1687, offers a critical commentary on passages from St. Augustine included in a book published recently on the orders of the Archbishop of Paris, entitled *The Conformity of the Conduct of the Church of* France *for reuniting the Protestants, with that of the Church of* Africk *for reuniting the Donatists to the Catholick Church.* Commenting on these passages, Bayle takes Augustine to task for the weakness of his defense of the persecution of the Donatists, applying and reinforcing the arguments of Parts I and II. What is striking about this part of the work, however, is the vigor with which Bayle pursues Augustine, a figure revered by all the various Christian denominations—from the Jesuit Molinists to the Jansenists, Arminians, and Calvinists. In answering Augustine, Bayle is taking on arguments advanced, or at least accepted, by his fellow Huguenots, following the line of Calvin's reasoning in his defense of the execution of Servetus. While individual chapters take St. Augustine to task for a variety of failings, from misinterpreting biblical passages and drawing implausible conclusions from Old Testament stories to reasoning poorly and begging questions, one concern dominates Bayle's attack. He wants to show, again and again, that the principle of persecution always rebounds upon the orthodox. If the case for persecution is sound, it may be used with equal warrant by heretics. The consequence of St. Augustine's position, if accepted, would simply be to arm all sects against each other.

Part IV, the "Supplement" to the *Philosophical Commentary,* published in 1688, is a fragment of a much longer, otherwise unpublished reply to criticisms of the earlier Parts advanced by Jurieu in his *Rights of two sovereigns in matters of religion, conscience and the prince; to destroy the dogma of the indifference of religion and universal tolerance, against a book entitled "Philosophical Commentary."* In this part Bayle develops in detail an argument already sketched in Part II, Chapter 10, and in Part III, that if Christ had commanded true believers to persecute, then, since as God he must have been able to foresee that Christians would disagree about what is the truth, he would have commanded an unending war between sects; since this would be contrary to divine goodness, he cannot have intended to give such a command. In Part IV he also refutes in detail the Augustinian idea that error in religious and moral matters is a punishment for original sin leading to further punishable sins: Bayle argues that even apart from sin, resolving the doctrinal disputes that divide Christians is beyond the capacity of ordinary people, perhaps of anyone. Sin, original or personal, therefore does not explain the differences of opinion among Christians.

However, it seems to follow from Bayle's principles that persecutors themselves do no wrong, and may even act meritoriously, if they sincerely believe that they ought to persecute. Bayle offers three replies. The first is that for persecutors to be excused by sincerity their beliefs must really be sincere, the product of an honest search for the truth rather than negligence and "criminal Passion," which is unlikely. Second, in persecuting, persecutors will stir up in themselves passions of hatred and anger which in themselves involve sinning, and they would then invariably be tempted into further sinful actions—thereby strengthening the presumption that they err not out of sincerity. Third, Bayle points out that, even if persecutors are sincere in their belief in the rightness of persecution, we must endeavor to correct their error (which is the aim of Bayle's book) and meanwhile restrain them from actions so pernicious to human society. We must not persecute would-be persecutors, but we may and must take precautions against their ever having power to act on their intolerant convictions.

The Influence of the *Philosophical Commentary*

The *Philosophical Commentary* is not as well known as Locke's *Letter concerning toleration,* published shortly after Bayle's much longer treatise. But Bayle's work offers an account of the case for toleration that is more comprehensive, and in many ways deeper, than Locke's. Whereas Locke takes as his main premise the notion going back to Marsilius of Padua that the state is concerned only with the protection of this-worldly interests, a premise that would never have been conceded by the people Locke needed to convince, Bayle's premises are ones that even Christians most inclined to persecute would have had to accept. As he often says, arguments are of no value if they "beg the question," i.e. somehow assume what they are supposed to prove. The distinctive mark of Bayle's intellectual style is his energetic effort to argue from "common principles" acceptable to people to whose practices he was most deeply opposed. As a champion of rational argument, Bayle is hard to match, and it is not surprising that he exerted the influence he did on the philosophers of the Enlightenment. Since Augustine's time, European thought has struggled with the question of toleration in religion, and more recently with similar questions of tolerating diverse views in politics and morality; all these questions have become urgent again at the present time. Much can be learned from a careful study of Bayle's engagement in the *Philosophical Commentary* with problems that remain very much alive.

Sources

On Bayle's Life and Times

Allen, J. W., *A History of Political Thought in the Sixteenth Century* (London: Methuen, 1961).

Labrousse, Elizabeth, *Bayle,* trans. Denys Potts (Oxford: Oxford University Press, 1983).

MacCulloch, Diarmid, *The Reformation: A History* (New York: Penguin Viking, 2004).

On Bayle's Thought

Bayle, Pierre, *Various Thoughts on the Occasion of a Comet,* translated with notes and an interpretive essay by Robert C. Bartlett (Albany: State University of New York Press, 2000).

Brush, Craig, *Montaigne and Bayle: Variations on the Theme of Skepticism* (The Hague: Martinus Nijhoff, 1966).

Kilcullen, John, *Sincerity and Truth: Essays on Arnauld, Bayle and Toleration* (Oxford: Clarendon Press, 1988).

Lennon, Thomas, *Reading Bayle* (Toronto: University of Toronto Press, 1999).

Mori, Gianluca, *Bayle Philosophe* (Paris: Champion, 1999).

Rex, Walter, *Essays on Pierre Bayle and Religious Controversy* (The Hague: Martinus Nijhoff, 1965).

Tinsley, Barbara Sher, *Pierre Bayle's Reformation: Conscience and Criticism on the Eve of the Enlightenment* (Selinsgrove, Pa.: Susquehanna University Press, 2001).

A NOTE ON THE
PRESENT TRANSLATION

This edition of the *Philosophical Commentary* is an amended version of the first English translation, which appeared in London in 1708. The author of the translation, which remains the only complete rendering of the *Commentary* into English, is unknown. A more recent translation by Amie Godman Tannenbaum was published in 1987, but it omits Part III and the Supplement.[1]

We have checked the text of the 1708 translation against the French text (from http://gallica.bnf.fr/) and made silent changes to correct omissions, misprints, and mistranslations and to clarify places where change in the meaning of English words would make the translation unintelligible or misleading to the modern reader.[2] We have also implemented the corrigenda of the 1708 edition. We have not tried to make the translation more literal; in our judgment it is rather free (in the manner of the time), but substantially very faithful, and lively. The pagination of the 1708 edition is indicated inside angle brackets.

We have identified and supplied details for Bayle's various references and translated passages quoted in foreign languages, unless Bayle himself supplies a translation or paraphrase. We have left the titles of works referred to in the original language unless the title illustrates Bayle's argument, and then we have translated it. In notes and appendixes we have provided information needed for reading the work with reasonable comprehension. Footnotes of the 1708 edition are indicated by asterisk, dagger, etc. Notes

---

1. Amie Godman Tannenbaum, *Pierre Bayle's Philosophical Commentary. A Modern Translation and Critical Interpretation* (New York: Peter Lang, 1987).
2. See "Alterations to the 1708 Translation," in the Appendixes.

supplied by the present editors are numbered. Material we have added to the 1708 footnotes is enclosed in square brackets.

We are grateful to Professor Gianluca Mori for help in identifying some of Bayle's references; see notes 129, 193, 195, 199, and the reference to Josephus (p. 143, note). We are grateful also to Greg Fox for help in transliterating some passages in Greek, and to Guy Neumann for help with a difficulty in the French text. The web sites of the Bibliothèque nationale de France have been of great assistance.

ABBREVIATIONS USED IN REFERRING TO BAYLE'S WORKS

CG *Critique générale de l'histoire du Calvinisme de Mr Maimbourg,* OD, vol. 2.

CP *Commentaire philosophique sur ces paroles de Jésus-Christ, "Contrain-les d'entrer,"* OD, vol. 2.

CPD *Continuation des Pensées diverses,* OD, vol. 3.

DHC *Dictionnaire historique et critique* (various editions, and English translation, London, 1734).

EMT *Entretiens de Maxime et de Thémiste,* OD, vol. 4.

NL *Nouvelles lettres de l'auteur de la Critique générale de l'histoire du Calvinisme,* OD, vol. 2.

OD *Oeuvres diverses* (La Haye, 1727, reprint Hildesheim: Olms, 1966).

PD *Pensées diverses à l'occasion de la comète,* OD, vol. 3.

RQP *Réponse aux questions d'un provincial,* OD, vol. 3.

S *Supplément du Commentaire philosophique,* OD, vol. 2.

*A Philosophical Commentary on These Words
of the Gospel, Luke 14.23, "Compel Them to
Come In, That My House May Be Full"*

A <i>

Philosophical Commentary

ON

These Words of the Gospel,

Luke XIV. 23.

Compel them to come in, that my House
may be full.

In Four Parts.

I. Containing a Refutation of the Literal Sense of this
Passage.
II. An Answer to all Objections.
III. Remarks on those Letters of St. Austin which are
usually alledg'd for the compelling of Hereticks, and
particularly to justify the late Persecution in *France*.
IV. A Supplement, proving, That Hereticks have as much
Right to persecute the Orthodox, as the Orthodox them.

Translated from the *French* of Mr. Bayle,
Author of the Great *Critical and Historical Dictionary*.

In Two Volumes.

LONDON, Printed by *J. Darby* in *Bartholomew-Close*, and sold
by *J. Morphew* near *Stationers-Hall*. 1708.

Advertisement of the *English* Publisher. <ii> <iii>

When the two first Tomes of the following Work were publish'd in Holland, *they were pretended to be* translated from the English of Mr. *John Fox of Bruggs. The Reason of Mr.* Bayle *'s feigning this Original, as 'tis observ'd in his* LIFE, *lately translated from a* French *Manuscript, and printed at the End of the Second Volume of his* Miscellaneous Reflections, *was,* 1. *Because the way of Reasoning in it resembl'd that Depth and strenuous Abstraction, which distinguishes the Writers of* England. *And,* 2. *Because he wou'd not be suspected* <iv> *for the Author; for which end he disguis'd his Stile, making use of several obsolete or new-coin'd Words.*

The Reader need not be surpriz'd, if he find the Author does not always keep so strictly to the Part he personates of an English *Writer, particularly where he gives such an account of the Anabaptists, as agrees rather to* Holland *than* England.

A Character of this Work, as well as his other Writings, need not be given here, that being already so well perform'd in the LIFE *above-mention'd. And for this Translation, it must speak for it self.*

THE CONTENTS
OF THE WHOLE WORK

<v>

[1708 Translation].

The Preliminary Discourse.

Contents of the First Part.

The Second Part.

<xvii> The Third Part.

IV. *St.* Austin's *Words.*

If a Man saw his Enemy ready to throw himself down a Precipice in the Paroxisms of a raging Fever, wou'd it not be rendring him evil for evil to let him take his own way, rather than with-hold and bind him hand and foot? Yet this frantick Person wou'd look on such an Act of Goodness and Charity only as an Outrage, and the Effect of Hatred for him: But shou'd he recover his Health and Senses, he must be sensible that the more Violence this mistaken Enemy exercis'd on him, the more he was oblig'd to him. How many have we even of the *Circoncellions,* who are now become zealous Catholicks, and who had never come to themselves, if we had not procur'd the Laws of our Emperors to bind 'em hand and foot, as we do Madmen?

V. *St.* Austin's *Words.*

You'l tell me, there are those on whom we don't gain an inch of ground by these Methods; I believe it: but must we forgo the Medicine, because there are some incurable Patients?

VI. *St.* Austin's *Words.*

Did we only lift the Rod over 'em, and not take the pains to instruct 'em, our Conduct might justly appear tyrannical; but on the other hand, did we content our selves with instructing 'em, without working on their Fears, they'd ne'er be able to surmount a kind of Listlessness in 'em, contracted by Use and Custom.

VII. *St.* Austin's *Words.*

All those who sooth and spare us are not therefore our Friends, nor all who chastize us our Enemys: *Faithful are the Wounds of a Friend, but the Kisses of an Enemy are deceitful.* The Severitys of those who love us are wholesomer than the soft Addresses of those who deceive us; and there's more Charity in taking a man's Bread from him, be he ever so hungry,

VIII. *St. Austin's Words.*

To bind one in a Phrensy, or awake one in a Lethargy, is vexatious indeed; yet it's friendly at the same time. God loves us with a truer Love than any Man can do; yet he joins the salutary Terrors of his Threats to the Lenity of his Counsels, and we find that he thought fit to exercise the most religious Patriarchs by a Famine. 301

<xx> *The Question is not, whether we may love those we chastise, but whether 'tis just to deprive a Man of his Goods and Liberty because of his Belief.* 301

God's chastising his Servants includes nothing in favor of St. Austin. 302

The sad Consequences to the Clergy of France, *if their King shou'd exercise 'em in the same manner as God did the Patriarchs.* 302

IX. *St. Austin's Words.*

You are of opinion, that no one shou'd be compel'd to do well; but have you never read, that the Father of the Family commanded his Servants to compel all they met with to come in to the Feast? Han't you seen with what Violence *Saul* was forc'd by *Jesus Christ* to acknowledg and embrace the Truth? . . . Don't you know, that Shepherds sometimes make use of the Rod to force their Sheep into the Fold? Don't you know that *Sarah,* according to the Power committed to her, subdu'd the stubborn Spirit of her Servant by the harshest Treatment, not from any hatred she bore to *Agar,* since she lov'd her so far as to wish that *Abraham* wou'd make her a Mother, but purely to humble the Pride of her Heart? Now you can't be ignorant, that *Sarah* and her Son *Isaac* are Figures of spiritual, and *Agar* and *Ishmael* of carnal things. Notwithstanding, tho the Scripture informs us that *Sarah* made *Agar* and *Ishmael* suffer a great deal; St. *Paul* does not stick to say, that 'twas *Ishmael* persecuted *Isaac,* to signify, that tho the Catholick Church endeavors to reclaim carnal Men by temporal Punishments, yet it is they persecute her, rather than she them. 303

X. *St.* Austin's *Words.*

The Good and the Bad do and suffer very often the same things; nor ought we to judg of the nature of their Actions by what either does, or what either suffers, but from the Motives on which they act or suffer. *Pharaoh* oppress'd the People of God with excessive Labor: *Moses,* on the other hand, punish'd the Transgressions of the same People by the most severe Punishments. The Actions of each side were much alike, but their Ends very different: One was an errant Tyrant, bloated with Pride and Power; the other a Father fill'd with Charity. *Jezabel* put the Prophets to death, and *Elias* the false Prophets; but that which put Arms into the hands of one and t'other, was no less different than that which drew on the deaths of each. In the same Book, where we find St. *Paul* scourg'd by the Jews, we find the Jew *Sosthenes* scourg'd by the *Greeks* for St. *Paul;* there's no difference between 'em if we only look at the Surface of the Action, but there's a great deal if we look at the Occasion and Motive. St. *Paul* is deliver'd to the Jailor to be cast into Irons, and St. *Paul* himself delivers the incestuous *Corinthian* to Satan, whose Cruelty much exceeds that of the most barbarous Jailors; yet he delivers this Man to Satan, only that his Flesh being buffeted his Soul might be sav'd. When the same St. *Paul* deliver'd *Philetus* and *Himeneus* to Satan to teach 'em not to blaspheme, he did not intend to render Evil for Evil, but judg'd it an Act of Goodness to redress one Evil by another.   309

XI. *St.* Austin's *Words.*

If the being persecuted were always a sign of Merit, *Jesus Christ* wou'd only have said, *Blessed are they who are persecuted,* and not have added, *for Righteousness sake.* In like manner, if persecuting were always a Sin, David wou'd not have said, *Psalm* 101. 5. *Whoso privily slandereth his Neighbor, him will I persecute.*

XII. *St.* Austin's *Words.*

The wicked have never left persecuting the Good, nor the Good the Wicked: but these act unjustly herein, and only to do mischief; those charitably, and so far as the necessity of correcting requires. . . . As the Wicked have slain the Prophets, so the Prophets have sometimes slain the Wicked; as the Jews were seen with Scourge in hand against *Jesus Christ,* so *Jesus Christ* was seen with Scourge in hand against the Jews. Men deliver'd the Apostles to the earthly Powers, and the Apostles deliver'd Men to the infer-<xxiii>nal Powers. What then ought we to consider in all these Examples? only this, which Side acts for the Truth and Righteousness, and which for Iniquity and a Lye; which acts only to destroy, and which to correct.

XIII. *St.* Austin's *Words.*

But, say you, it no where appears from the Gospel, or from the Writings of the Apostles, that they ever had recourse to the Kings of the Earth against the Enemys of the Church. True; but the reason is because this

Prophecy, *Be wise now therefore, O ye Kings; be instructed, ye Judges of the Earth: Serve the Lord with Fear, and rejoice with Trembling;* was not as yet accomplish'd.   323

This is in effect to say, that if the first Christians did not take up Arms against the Pagans, 'twas because they were too weak.   323

XIV. *St.* Austin's *Words.*

As it is not impossible, but that even among those Christians, who have suffer'd themselves to be seduc'd, there may be some of the true Sheep of *Jesus Christ,* who soon or late shall come back to the Fold, tho ever so far gone astray; for this reason we mitigate the Severitys appointed against 'em, and use all possible Lenity and Moderation in the Confiscations and Banishments which we are oblig'd to ordain, in hopes of making 'em enter into themselves.   325

Allowing Persecution, the greatest Punishments are lawful against the erroneous.   325

XV. *St.* Austin's *Words.*

There is not a Man among us, nor yet among you *(Donatists)* but approves the Laws of the Emperors against the Sacrifices of the Pagans; yet these Laws ordain much severer Punishments, and punish those <xxiv> with Death who are guilty of these Impietys: whereas in the Laws enacted against you, it's visible they have study'd much more how to recover you from your Errors, than how to punish your Crimes.   326

St. Austin's *Contradictions.*   326

There may have been predestin'd Souls among Pagans, as well as among Hereticks.   327

St. Austin *not the most human nor best-natur'd Man.*   328

Blunder of the Sieur Brueys.   328

Strange Idea which the Clergy form of Moderation.   329

XVI. *St.* Austin's *Words.*

As to the solliciting the Emperors to make Laws against Schismaticks or Hereticks, or to enforce 'em, and enjoin their being put in Execution; you'l be pleas'd to remember the Violence with which the other *Donatists* egg'd on, not only the *Maximinists, &c.* but above all, you won't forget how in the Petition, by which they implor'd the Authority of the Emperor *Julian* against us, they tell this Prince, whom they knew to be an

XVII. *St.* Austin's *Words.*

By this time you must, I'm sure, be sensible, that we ought not so much to consider, whether People are forc'd, as what they are forc'd to; that is, whether to Good or to Evil. Not that any one becomes a better Man by mere Force; but the dread of what People are loth to suffer, makes 'em open their Eyes to the Truth.   333

XVIII. *St.* Austin's *Words.*

I cou'd instance you not only in private Persons, but intire Citys, which of *Donatists,* as they formerly \<xxv\> were, are become good Catholicks, and detest the diabolical Sin of their old Separation; who yet wou'd never have bin Catholicks, but for the Laws which you are so displeas'd with.   334

XIX. *St.* Austin's *Words.*

Ought I to prevent the confiscating what you call your Goods, while you with impunity proscribe *Jesus Christ?* The barring you the liberty of disposing 'em by your last Testament, according to the Roman Law, while you by your slanderous Accusations tread under foot the Testament which God himself has made in favor of our Fathers, *&c?*   336

XX. *St.* Austin's *Words.*

If there be any among us who abuse the Laws which the Emperors have enacted against you (*Donatists*) and who make 'em a handle for exercising their private Spite, instead of employing 'em as an Instrument and Means of Charity to rescue you from Error; we disapprove their Proceedings, and think of 'em with Grief. Not that any Man can call this or that thing his Property, at least unless intitled to it by a divine Right, by the which all belongs to the Just; or by a Right founded on human Laws, and which depends on the Pleasure of the temporal Powers: so that you, for your parts, can call nothing your own, because not entitled to it, as being of the number of the Just, and because the Laws of the Emperors deprive you of all: consequently you can't properly say, *This thing is ours, and we have got it by our Industry;* since it is written, *Prov.* 13.22. *The Wealth of the Sinner is laid up for the Just.* Notwithstanding, when under color of these Laws Men invade your Possessions, we disapprove the Practice, and it troubles us exceedingly. In like manner, we condemn all those who are mov'd more <xxvi> by Avarice than Zeal, to take from you, either the Funds for your Poor, or the Places of your Assemblys; tho you enjoy neither one nor t'other but under the Notion of the Church, and tho only the true Church of *Jesus Christ* has an unalienable Right to these things.

XXI. *St.* Austin's *Words.*

But tho you will always be complaining of this kind of Treatment, you find it a hard matter to prove it upon any one; and tho you shou'd, it is not always in our Power to correct or punish those you complain of, and we are sometimes oblig'd to tolerate 'em.

XXII. *St.* Austin's *Words.*

When *Nebuchodonosor* ordain'd, That whoever blasphem'd the Name of the God of the *Hebrews,* shou'd be destroy'd with his whole House; had any of his Subjects incur'd the Punishment, by the violating this Law, cou'd they have said, as these (*Donatists*) do now, that they were righteous, and alledg'd the Persecution by the King's Authority, as a Proof of their Innocence?

<xxvii> XXIII. *St. Austin's Words.*

Was not *Hagar* persecuted by *Sarah?* Yet she that persecuted was holy, and she who suffer'd Persecution was wicked. 347

Difference between Sarah's *Persecution of* Hagar, *and that for Religious Opinions.* 347

XXIV. *St. Austin's Words.*

If the Good may not persecute, and if they are only to suffer Persecution, he was neither a good Man nor a Saint, who speaks thus in the 17th Psalm, *I will persecute mine Enemys, I will pursue them and attack them and will give them no Rest &c.* 348

Misapplication of this Passage of David. 348

Sophism in exaggerating the Fury of the Donatists, *and the moderate Chastisements of the Catholicks.* 349

XXV. *St. Austin's Words.*

The Service which Kings perform to God as they are Men, is one thing; and that which they perform as Kings, is another. As Men they serve him, by leading Lives as becomes the truly Faithful: but as Kings they serve him, only by enacting righteous Laws, which tend to the promoting Good, and punishing Evil; and by maintaining these Laws with Firmness and Vigor. 350

Definition of Just Laws, and of Good and Evil, being laid down, St. Austin's *Thought becomes favorable to Toleration.* 350

XXVI. *St. Austin's Words.*

One must be void of common Sense, to tell Princes, Take no thought whether People trample upon, or whether they revere, within your Dominions, the Church of him whom you adore. What, they shall take care to make their Subjects live according to the Rules of Vertue and Sobriety, without any one's presuming to say, that this concerns 'em not; and yet they shall presume to tell 'em, that it is not their business to take cognizance within their Dominions, whether Men observe the Rules of the true Religion, <xxviii> or whether they give themselves over to Profaneness and Irreligion? For if from hence, that God has given Man a Free-will, Profaneness were to be permitted, why shou'd Adultery be punish'd? The Soul which violates that Faith which it has plighted to its God, is it therefore less criminal than the Wife which violates the Faith she owes her Husband? And tho Sins, which Men thro Ignorance commit

against Religion, are punish'd with less Severity; must they therefore be
suffer'd to subvert it with Impunity?   351

XXVII. St. Austin's Words.

We must own, that Children who are drawn by Gentleness and Love, are
much the best; but these don't make the greatest number: there are
incomparably more of another sort, whom nothing will work upon but
Fear. Accordingly we read in Scripture, *Prov. 29. 19. That a Servant will
not be corrected by words; for tho he understand he will not answer:* which
supposes a Necessity of employing some more powerful Means. It
informs us in another place, that we must employ the Rod, not only
against evil Servants, but untoward Children. It is true, the Scripture says
again, *Prov. 23. 14. Thou shalt beat him with a Rod, and shalt deliver his
Soul from Hell:* and elsewhere, *Prov. 13. 24. He that spareth his Rod, hateth
his Son;* <xxix> *but he that loveth him, chasteneth him betimes.*   356

XXVIII. St. Austin's Words.

Jesus Christ himself exercis'd Violence on St. *Paul,* and forc'd him to
believe: let these Men then never say more, as the custom is, *Every one is
at liberty to believe or not to believe.*   359

XXIX. St. Austin's Words.

Why shou'd not the Church have the Privilege of employing Constraint
for recovering her lost Children, and bringing 'em home into her bosom;

when these wretched Children make use of the same means for bringing
others into Perdition? 360

Examples don't authorize Sin. 360

XXX. *St. Austin's Words.*

Shou'd we, for example, see two Men in a House that we knew was ready
to fall down about their Ears, and that whatever pains we take to warn
'em out, they shou'd obstinately resolve to abide in it; wou'd it not be a
degree of Cruelty, not to drag 'em out by main force? 361

Their Preservation depends not on their Consent, as in the Case of
Conversion. 361

XXXI. *St. Austin's Words.*

As to what they say, that we have a design upon their Estates, and wou'd
fain have the fingering of 'em; let 'em turn Catholicks, and we assure 'em
they shall not only enjoy what they call their own Estates, but also come
in for a share of ours. Passion has blinded 'em to such a degree, that they
don't perceive how they contradict themselves. They reproach us with
exerting the Authority of the Laws for constraining 'em into our
Communion, as if it <xxx> were the most odious Action: And shou'd
we take this pains, if we had a design upon their Estates? 362

Those who put Kings upon confiscating the Goods of Sectarys, are acted by
Avarice. 362

XXXII. *St. Austin's Words.*

The *Canaanite* shall ne'er rise in judgment against the People of *Israel,*
tho these drove them out of their Country, and took away the Fruit of
their Labor; but *Naboth* shall rise up against *Ahab,* because *Ahab* took
away the Fruit of *Naboth's* Labor. And why one, and not the others?
Because *Naboth* was a just Man, and the *Canaanites* Idolaters. 363

That Hereticks seizing the Goods of Catholicks commit a Sin, and Catholicks
seizing the Goods of Hereticks perform a good Work, is Jesuitical Morality. 363

The more Orthodox a Man is, the more he is oblig'd to be equitable to all
Men. 363

XXXIII. *St. Austin's Words.*
Letter 164. *to* Emeritus.

If the Temporal Powers stretch forth their hand against Schismaticks, 'tis
because they look on their Separation as an Evil, and that they are
ordain'd by God for the Punishment of Evil-doers, according to that
Saying of the Apostle, *Whosoever therefore resisteth the Power, resisteth the*

Ordinance of God; and they that resist, shall receive to themselves Damnation: For Rulers are not a terror to Good-works, but to the Evil, &c. The whole Question then lies here, whether Schism be an Evil, and whether you have not made the Schism; for if so, you resist the Powers, not for any Good, but for Evil. But, say you, no one shou'd persecute even bad Christians. Allow they ought not; yet how can this secure 'em against the Powers ordain'd by God for the Punishment of Evil-doers? Can we cancel that Passage of St. *Paul,* which I have just now cited?   365

St. Austin's *Explication of this Passage leads to an impious Falshood, in charging all the Martyrs, Confessors* <xxxi> *and Apostles with Rebellion against God.*   365

In what sense 'tis to be understood.   365

This Passage, Do good to all, but especially to the Houshold of Faith, *is a sufficient Answer to St.* Austin *and the Bishop of* Meaux; *since it excludes Hereticks and Schismaticks from the number of Evil-doers.*   369

XXXIV. *St.* Austin's *Words.*
Letter 166. *to the Donatists.*

Must not he be abandon'd to all shame, who won't submit to what Truth ordains by the Voice of the Sovereign?   371

This can't be apply'd but to a Man, who being persuaded 'tis Truth, refuses to submit to it.   371

XXXV. *St.* Austin's *Words.*
Ibid.

If the care we take to rescue you from Error and Perdition be what inflames your Hatred so much against us, you must lay the blame upon God, who has given this terrible Reproof to the slothful Pastors, *Ye have not brought back the Stray or looked for what was lost.*   371

In what sense this Passage is to be understood.   371

According to St. Austin's *sense, those Pastors of the Roman Church who have bin the most violent Persecutors, wou'd yet be culpable before God of Connivance and criminal Laxity.*   372

XXXVI. *St.* Austin's *Words.*
Letter 204. *to* Donatus.

If you think it unlawful to constrain Men to do good, pray consider that a Bishoprick is a good Office, since the Apostle has said as much; yet there are a great many on whom Violence is actually exercis'd to oblige 'em to accept of it. They are seiz'd, they are hurry'd away by main force, they are shut up and confin'd till they are forc'd to desire this good thing.   373

From what Opinion they acted who refus'd Bishopricks.   373

Essential Differences between a Man, made Bishop as 'twere by force, and another constrain'd to abjure his Religion.   374

<xxxii> XXXVII. *St.* Austin'*s Words.*
Ibid.

We well know, that as nothing can damn Men but an evil Disposition of Will; so nothing but their good Will can save 'em: But how can the Love, which we are oblig'd to bear our Neighbor, permit our abandoning such numbers to their own wicked Will? Is it not cruel to throw, as I may say, the Reins loose on their Necks; and ought we not, to the utmost of our Power, prevent their doing Evil, and force 'em to do Good?   375

'Tis a Contradiction to force any one to do Good.   375

XXXVIII. *St.* Austin'*s Words.*
Ibid.

If we must always leave an evil Will to its natural Liberty, why so many Scourges and piercing Goads to force the Children of *Israel,* in spite of all their Murmurings and Stiffneckedness, to move forward toward the Land of Promise? *&c.*   376

Difference between Actions to which a good Will is requir'd, and those to which it is not; between Actions which we know will displease God, and those by which we think to please him.   376

Solomon'*s advising Fathers to correct their Children, is not for Opinions in Religion.*   377

Difference between the Violence in hindring a Man who wou'd kill himself out of Conscience, and that done to make him abjure his Religion.   378

XXXIX. *St.* Austin'*s Words.*
Ibid.

While *Jesus Christ* was upon Earth, and before the Princes of the World worship'd him, the Church made use only of Exhortation; but ever since those days she has not thought it enough to invite Men to Happiness, she also forces 'em. These two Seasons are prefigur'd in the Parable of the Feast: The Master of the Family was content, for the first time, to order

his Servants to bid the Guests to his Dinner; but the next time he
commanded 'em to compel 'em <xxxiii> to come in.   379

Confutation of this contain'd in the two first Parts of this Commentary.

XL. *St.* Austin's *Words.*
Letter 167. *to* Festus.

If any one will compare, what they suffer thro our charitable Severity,
with the Excesses to which their Fury transports 'em against us; he'l easily
judg which are the Persecutors, they or we. Nay they might justly be
denominated such with regard to us, without all this; for be the Severitys
which Parents exercise over their Children, to bring 'em to a sense of
their Duty, ever so great, yet they can never properly be call'd Persecution: whereas Children, by following evil Courses, become Persecutors of
Father and Mother, tho possibly they mayn't be guilty of any personal
Violence against 'em.   380

We ought not to punish the Innocent with the Guilty.   380

*Parents, in many Instances, wou'd deserve the name of Persecutors, with
respect to their Children.*   380

The Fourth Part, or Supplement.

<1>

A
Preliminary Discourse,
Containing some Remarks of a
distinct Nature from those in
the Commentary.

A *French* Gentleman, whom I had known in my Travels in *France* about seven or eight Years ago, having fled for Refuge into *England* soon after the Expedition of the Dragoons; told me, as we often discours'd on the Subject, That among all the Cavils with which the Missionarys (and under this name he comprehended Priests, Monks, Evidence for the King, Judges, Intendants, Officers of Horse and Foot, and others of all Conditions and Sexes) had pester'd him, none appear'd to him more sensless, and yet at the same time more thorny and perplexing, than that drawn from these words of JESUS CHRIST, *Compel 'em to come in,* in favor of Persecution, or, as they term'd it, the charitable and salutary Violence exercis'd on Hereticks, to recover 'em from the Error of their Ways. He let me know how passionately he <2> desir'd to see this Chimera of Persecutors confounded: And fancying he observ'd in me not only an extreme Aversion to persecuting Methods, but something too of a Vein for entring into the true Reasons of things; he was pleas'd to say, he look'd on me as a proper Person for such an Undertaking, and urg'd that, succeeding in it as he expected, I shou'd do great Service to the Cause of Truth, and indeed to the whole World. He added that he had a Translator ready at hand who would put what I wrote in my Language, if not into good French, at least into a quite intelligible Style.

I answer'd him, That I had not the Vanity to think my self equal to such an Undertaking; and that I had still a worse Opinion of Convertists, whom I look'd on as utterly irreclaimable, to such a pitch did their wild Prepossession in this point over-bear 'em: in general, that Books were but an

Amusement; so that Authors, after taking a deal of pains with 'em, had this new Mortification to boot, of seeing that what they promis'd themselves the greatest things by, had little or no good effect upon the World. As he's a Man of a fiery Spirit, which he has sufficiently discover'd in a small Pamphlet of his, entitled, *A Review of* France *intirely Catholick under the Reign of* Lewis *the Great;*[1] he press'd me unmercifully, as oft as ever I fell in his way, without the least regard to my Excuses. At last, as well to deliver my self from his Importunity, as to try my hand upon a Subject which on one side appear'd to me very evident, yet leading on the other to Consequences somewhat harsh, unless thorowly explain'd; I promis'd him to form a Philosophical Commentary on those Words of the Parable of the Wedding, which Convertists, that's to say Persecutors, do so much pervert. <3> For *Convertist,* henceforward, and *Villain,* and *Persecutor,* and fouler Language, if any be, shall mean the same thing, and I shall accordingly use the Terms indifferently; which 'twas but fit I shou'd signify in the Entrance.

It has happen'd with the word *Convertist* much as with those of *Tyrant* and *Sophist.* The word *Tyrant* in the beginning had no other meaning than that of King, nor *Sophist* than that of Philosopher: but because many of those who exercis'd the Sovereign Power, abus'd it to wicked and cruel purposes, and many who profess'd Philosophy fell into fallacious ridiculous Subtletys, design'd to obscure the Truth, their Names became odious, and convey'd only the Idea of the worst of Men; and respectively signify'd Blood-suckers and Oppressors, Whifflers and Cheats. Here's the true Image of the Fate of the word *Convertist:* It imported originally a Soul sincerely zealous in propagating the Truth, and undeceiving those in Error; but for the future it shall signify only a Mountebank, only a Counterfeit, only a Pilferer, only a Maroder, a Soul void of Pity, void of Humanity, void of natural Equity, only a Man who proposes by tormenting others to expiate for his own Leudness past and to come, and for all the Irregularitys of a profligate Life; or, shou'd it happen that all these Characters don't exactly fit every Convertist, let's try in fewer words to settle its just and proper Sense

1. This is one of Bayle's own anonymous works: *Ce que c'est que la France toute Catholique sous le Regne de Louis le Grand* (What wholly Catholic France is like under the reign of Louis the Great), 1686, against Catholic persecution of Protestants.

for the time to come. It shall mean a Monster, Half-Priest and Half-Dragoon, who like the Centaur of the Fable, which in one Person united the Man and the Horse, confounds in one Actor the different Parts of a Missionary <4> who argues, and a Foot-Soldier who belabours a poor human Body, and rifles a Cottage. They say there are Taverns already in some parts of *Germany* with the Sign of the Convertist, dress'd up by the Model of some Cuts of *Bernard de Galen,* Bishop of *Munster,* in which he's represented with half Mitre half Helmet round his Temples; with a Cross in one hand, a Sabre in t'other; half Rochet, and half Cuirass about his Loins, and so on; commanding to sound to Horse in the middle of his Mass, and a Charge at the place where he shou'd give the Benediction. 'Twas by this Model they say, *mutatis mutandis,* that the Sign of the Convertist to some Inns or Taverns in certain famous Imperial Towns was drawn. Judg then whether Mr. *Arnaud*[2] deserves any Answer on his making so much of what the agreeable Author of the *Politicks of the Clergy*[3] has said by way of Elogy on the Protestants, *That they came not into this World on the foot of Convertists.* It's strange our *Dutch* Artists shou'd let the *High-Germans* run away with this Whim.

Having thus resolv'd to form a Commentary of a new kind, on the famous words, *Compel 'em to come in;* I thought it wou'd be best to draw the Convertists out of their own ground: I mean out of their old beaten common Places, and propose 'em Difficultys, for which they have not yet had leisure enough to find out Evasions. For here's the main drift of the Writers of this Party; they apply themselves much less to the proving their Point, than to the eluding the Arguments with which they are press'd; like those false Witnesses, *Greeks* by Nation, whose <5> Picture *Cicero* has drawn to the life: *Nunquam laborant quemadmodum probent quod dicunt, sed quem-*

---

2. Antoine Arnauld, *Apologie pour les catholiques contre les faussetés et les calumnies d'un livre intitulé La Politique du clergé de France* (Defence of the Catholics against the falsities and calumnies of a book entitled "The policy of the French clergy"), 1681.

3. Pierre Jurieu, *La politique du clergé de France . . . sur les moyens dont on se sert aujuourd'huy pour destruire la religion protestane dans ce royaume* (The policy of the French clergy . . . on the means being used today to destroy the Protestant religion in this kingdom), 1681.

admodum se explicent dicendo.[4] Accordingly I foresee, that if they attempt to answer me, they'l pass over all my principal Difficultys, and only endeavor to find whether I have not contradicted my self in some part or other of the Work; whether I have not made a trip in my Reasonings; whether my Principles are not attended with some absurd Consequences. If this be all they do, I declare to 'em before-hand, that I shan't look on it as an Answer, nor on my Cause as less victorious in the main; for the Cause is not lost, because perhaps its Advocate does not always reason justly, because his Notions in one place do not perhaps nicely fall in with his Notions in another; because he pushes his point too far at some times, and loses himself in the chase. All this may possibly have befallen me: but because notwithstanding all these Failings, which are purely those of the Advocate, and not of the Cause, I persuade my self I have said enough to prove my point incontestably; I declare once more, that if the Convertists design to justify their Proceedings, they must answer all that's reasonable and solid in my Argument, and not think to get off as their Controvertists commonly do, if they can only discover that an Author has perhaps cited a Passage wrong, or employ'd a particular Argument sometimes to one purpose, sometimes to another, and which perhaps may be retorted,[5] or committed some other Over-sights of this kind; since there never was a Book, how strong and forcible soever, which may not be answer'd at <6> this rate. One that can pick up some faults of this kind, or separate a Proof here and there from that which in other parts of the Works does sufficiently support it, and from the true end and purpose to which the Author design'd it, fancies he makes a fine Answer to the best Book; which shall triumph in the Judgment of those who don't compare the two Pieces with Exactness, and freedom from Prejudice. Hence we meet with Answers to every thing; tho, properly speaking, this is not confuting, but rather making the Errata of an Adversary's Book, and leaving the Merits of the Cause upon the Tenters: And for my part, if my Adversarys do no more than this, I shall look on my self as the Victor.

4. "They never trouble to prove what they say but only to make a display of themselves by talking"; Cicero, *Pro Flacco,* iv.10, translated Louis E. Ford, Loeb Classical Library, 1977, Cicero, vol. 10, p. 377.
5. See Appendixes, "Bayle's Use of Logic," p. 581 ("retorted").

As I wrote it at the instance of a *French* Refugee, and on occasion of the late Persecution in *France,* and with a design of having it translated into *French;* I have forbore quoting any Books, but such as are perfectly well known to the *French* Convertists. Were it not for this, I might often have refer'd my Reader to very excellent Pieces written in the *English* Tongue upon the Point of Toleration.[6] No Nation can be suppos'd to afford more Arguments on this Subject than ours, by reason of that Variety of Sects among us, harass'd for so long a time by the establish'd Religion. The very Papists in this Country are the first to cry out, That nothing is more unjust than vexing Men on the score of Conscience. A ridiculous Maxim in their mouths; and not ridiculous only, but perfidious and insincere in them, Qualitys inseparable from their Nature for so many Ages past: since it's certain they wou'd <7> not forbear three years, nor fail bringing those to the Stake who did not go to Mass, had they once more the Power in their own hands; and had others the Baseness of those Court-Parasites and Pensioners, Men unworthy of the Name of Protestants, tho outwardly professing it, who endeavor the Subversion of that fundamental Barrier of our Security, which ballances the Royal Authority.[7] Tho I don't doubt but there are still brave Spirits enough left among us, worthy Patriots, and sincere Protestants, to correct the evil Influences of the Complaisance of these false Brethren, and by God's Blessing to preserve to us that Tranquillity we enjoy, tho under a Catholick Sovereign.[8] The Calamitys of our Brethren of *France* will, in all probability, turn to our advantage. They have awaken'd us to a prudent Distrust of Popery; they have convinc'd us that this false Religion is not to be mended by length of time, that she's still animated as much as ever with a Spirit of Cruelty and Fraud, and in spite of all the Civility and Politeness which reigns in the Manners of the Age, still savage and intractable. Strange! All that was rough and shocking in the Manners of our Ancestors is quite worn off; to that rustick and forbidding Air of former times, there has succeeded an universal Gentleness and exceeding Civility, all

6. On English seventeenth-century writings on toleration see W. K. Jordan, *The development of religious toleration in England* (London: Allen and Unwin, 1936–).

7. That is, Parliament, which, according to their opponents, the court party attempted to "subvert."

8. James II.

Christendom over. Popery alone feels no Change; she alone keeps up her antient and habitual Ferocity. We of *England* began to think the Beast was grown tame and tractable; began to think that this Wolf, this Tiger had forgot her savage Nature: but, God be thank'd, the *French* Convertists have undeceiv'd us, and < 8 > we now know what we must trust to, shou'd it ever be our lot to fall into her clutches. *Nunquam bona fide vitia mansuescunt,*[9] is chiefly applicable to the Vices of Religion. God grant that we may more and more profit by the Calamitys of our Brethren, and always stand upon our Guard.

Nor can this Fierceness of Popery be computed, as some undertook to do about a year ago, by a Parallel between the Growth of the Politeness of this Age, and the Diminution of the Punishments which it has of late made use of for converting. We affirm, there's as much Barbarity in Dragooning, Dungeoning, Cloistering, *&c.* People of a contrary Religion, in such a civiliz'd, knowing, genteel Age as ours; as there was in executing 'em by the hands of the common Hangman, in Ages of Ignorance and Brutality, before People had purg'd off the Manners of their Ancestors, *Goths* and *Vandals, Scythians* and *Sarmatians,* who formerly overspread the *Roman* Empire, and founded all the Empires and States in the Western *Europe.* Where Men have not purg'd off the Barbarousness of their Race, nor are inur'd to new Opinions, 'tis not so much in them to put those to death who profess 'em, as in those who are intirely quit of the Rust of their first Origin, who are polish'd by an Improvement of the Sciences and nobler Arts, who have liv'd all their Lives in the same Towns, in the same Conversation, in the same Partys of Pleasure, very often with those of the Reform'd Religion, carry'd Arms together for the same Cause; and bin in the same Interests with 'em, to prosecute, disquiet, torment, and vex 'em in < 9 > their Persons and Estates, as has lately been practis'd in *France.* This is our Rule for computing the just Proportion between the Crueltys of antient and modern Persecutions; nay, sometimes the slow Pain seem'd to us to cast the Scale: tho capital Punishment, or Death by the hand of the Hangman, not being inflicted in this last Persecution, must have hinder'd most People's thinking it equal to those of former Ages, unless they compensated the want of Rigor

9. "Their vices are never really tamed," Seneca, *Epistulae morales,* LXXXV.8.

in this last Scene, with the Excesses of Ignorance and Barbarity in former times. But setting aside all Compensations of this kind, here's a certain Rule for finding the true Proportion between the one sort of Persecution and the other: Let any one compare 'em upon the square, and abstracted from all Circumstances of more or less Politeness of Times, and he shall find 'em equal, at least since the Declaration of *July* last, which forbids, upon pain of Death, the Exercise of any other Religion in *France* except the Romish; and which is executed without delay upon all who have the Courage to contravene it in the least. If the Reform'd of *France* were as zealous in these days as in those of *Francis* I and *Henry* II or as the *English* in the Reign of Queen *Mary;* we shou'd see as many Gibbets in these days as in those of old. Let's think of this, and consider what Miserys betide us, shou'd we let Popery grow up again in these happy Climates. I don't say this with a design of stirring up People to retaliate upon the Papists; no, I detest such Imitations: I only desire they may be kept from ever having it in their power to execute on us what they have the will to do. <10>

When I say the Protestants ought not to reprize themselves when they may, it is not from any such pitiful Reason as a *French** Author gives us in a Book lent me since my *Commentary* was printed. 'Tis a reason so impertinent, that I cou'd scarce think they'd make use of it, and therefore did not propose it as an Objection. I was wrong tho in believing any thing too absurd for these Gentlemen; one wou'd imagine they had resolutely taken up the Character of being as ridiculous in their Apologys, as terrible in their Exploits: and one can never enough admire, that in a Country where there are so many good Pens, so many vile Justifications shou'd be suffer'd to pass. 'Twere much better not say a word, than defend themselves so wretchedly. Here's this pleasant Author's Thought. He introduces some Persons apprehending, that the Violences exercis'd on the Protestants in *France* may be prejudicial to the Catholicks in other Countrys.

Still it is to be fear'd, say some sort of People, that the Protestants, seeing how their Brethren are treated at this time in France, *may think themselves war-*

---

* *The Conformity of the Conduct of the Church of* France *with that of* Africk. [Goibaud-Dubois, *Conformité de la conduite de l'église de France pour ramener les protestans avec celle de l'église d'Afrique pour ramener les donatistes à l'église catholique,* 1686.]

ranted to treat the Catholicks in the same manner wherever they are Masters. But one must be abandon'd to all shame to pretend, that People, who have gone out of the Church within less than two hundred Years, and in a manner which all the World knows; People who have no kind of Authority but what they bestow on themselves, and what any one, who has a Mind to separate this hour, may give himself with altogether as <11> much color, shou'd be entitul'd to the same Privileges as the Catholick Church; which being founded by JESUS CHRIST *and the Apostles, has continu'd in an uninterrupted Succession of all Ages, and shall abide to the end of the World in spite of all the Malice and Artifices of Sects and Schisms, and all their Endeavors to get her disown'd. . . . Once more then, he must be lost to all Shame who'l pretend, that rebellious Children have the same Power over their Mother which she has over them, or that they can take the same Methods for bringing those into their Communion who were never of it, as the Church has a right to take to reduce those to its Communion who cannot disown their going out from it. For which reason we have no Cause to apprehend, that what passes now in* France *can ever be drawn into a Rule in favor of Protestants. They may do the same thing in the Countrys where they are uppermost; but that which in the Church is a holy and regular Discipline, because founded on a lawful Authority, wou'd in them be a tyrannical Oppression, because destitute of a like Authority. As Kings punish those with Death who are taken in Arms against 'em, so Rebels have sometimes treated the faithful Servants of their Kings the same way when they have fall'n into their Hands. Whence comes it then, that the same Action is an Act of Justice with regard to the Sovereign, and a Violation of Right and Justice with regard to them? From hence, that of one side it's done by a lawful Authority, and of the other without Authority. The Case is the same, when those who have revolted from the Church will force the Catholicks to come into their Communion, by the same Methods which the Church makes use of to bring them into hers.* <12>

I ask my Reader's pardon for troubling him with so long a piece of Impertinence. What! will these People ever be playing the fool? will they never leave arguing like Children, how great Abilitys soever they may have in other Matters? Shall we never beat it into 'em, that nothing in nature is more ridiculous than reasoning by always assuming the thing in question?[10]

---

10. See Appendixes, "Bayle's Use of Logic," p. 580 ("petitio principii").

The Dispute between them and us is, whether the Church of *Rome* be the true Church: Common Sense requires, that we on our parts shou'd prove from common Principles, and not from a bare Pretension, that she is not; and that they on their part prove she is the true Church, not by a bare Pretension (for that's unpardonable in a School-boy) but from Principles common to them and us. This we have represented to 'em a thousand and a thousand times over; we have done it sometimes in a serious way, sometimes by turning 'em into ridicule: but nothing will open their Eyes; still they come about to their old Cant, We are the Church, you are the Rebels, therefore we have a right of chastising you, but you have none of returning us like for like. What stock of Patience is sufficient for such stuff?

There are some among 'em who tell us with the same compos'd Look, and with the same grave Air of Impertinence, that to find whether the *Hugonots* have just Cause to complain, we ought to consider what Judgment the *Gallican* Church makes of 'em; to wit, that she looks on 'em as rebellious Children, over whom she retains a right of Punishment, in order to reclaim 'em from their Disobedience. I own I can't comprehend how these Men do to pick up all this <13> wretched Trumpery (give me leave to use this word to represent Impertinences, too ridiculous and vile to be fully exprest). Are they so blind as not to see, that the Pretensions of the Protestants, once suppos'd, give them a far more plausible Pretext for persecuting Popery, than that which Popery borrows from the Pretensions which it makes.

The Protestants pretend,[11] that the Church of *Rome,* far from being that Spouse of JESUS CHRIST which is the Mother of all true Christians, is really an infamous Harlot, who has seiz'd the House, by the Assistance of a band of Ruffians, Cut-throats, Hell-hounds; who has turn'd the Father and Mother out o' doors, has murder'd as many of the Children as she cou'd lay her hands on, forc'd others to own her for lawful Mistress, or reduc'd 'em to live in exile. These exil'd Children, these who are not able to bear the Infamy of living in a feign'd Obsequiousness for a Mother, whom they look upon as a Strumpet who has expel'd their true Mother, and slain their Brethren; these are the Protestants, or at least pretend to be.

11. See Appendixes, "Obsolete or Unusual Words or Meanings," p. 579 ("pretend").

On one side then we see a Church which pretends to be the Mother of the Family, and that all who own her not as such are rebellious Children; and on the other side, Children pretending she is only an abominable Harlot, who has seiz'd upon the House by downright force, and turn'd out the true Mistress and the true Heirs, to make room for her Lovers, and the Accomplices of her Whoredom. To consider only the respective Pretensions of both Partys, the Rigor is more natural and more reasonable on the side of the Protestants than on that of the <14> Church of *Rome:* For the Church of *Rome,* by supposing her Pretensions, ought to preserve the natural Tenderness of a Mother for the Protestants, and make use only of moderate Chastisements to recover 'em to their Duty. We know how *David* commanded that they shou'd spare the Life of his Son *Absalom,* tho in Arms against him, and tho he had carry'd his Rebellion to the greatest Extremity;[12] and there are very few Mothers who won't put up the Affronts and Insolences of their Children, rather than arraign 'em before the criminal Judg, when they think their Lives may be in danger. So that the terrible Punishments which the Church of *Rome* has inflicted on Hereticks for so many Ages past, are a Rigor so much the more unnatural and monstrous, the more strongly one supposes her Pretensions.

But by supposing the Pretensions of the Protestants, their most extreme Rigors are in the order of human things. For when the case is no less than the revenging a Mother impiously turn'd out of her own House by a Strumpet, and resettling her in her Right, Nature does allow her Children to act with all imaginable Vigor and Vehemence; nor can it be thought hardly of, if they have no Mercy upon this wicked Prostitute who had usurp'd her place, or upon her Favorers and Adherents.

The Reader will easily perceive the Ridiculousness of the Passage which I have cited, without my taking it to task Period by Period; and comprehend, that nothing is more reasonable than the Apprehensions of *some sort of People,* did the Protestants think fit to imitate the Church of <15> *Rome.* Let any one but reflect a little on the State in which the two Religions liv'd together about twenty Years ago, supposing always their respective Pretensions. The Church of *Rome,* believing her self the true Mother of all Chris-

12. 2 Samuel 18:5.

tians, thought it expedient for the good of those Children who did own her, not to exercise her Right over those who persisted in their Disobedience. The Protestant Church, believing the Romish an Adulteress, who in prejudice of her Rights acted the Mistress in the Family, suffer'd her for peace sake to injoy the finest Apartments in the House, and suspended her Right of punishing the Favorers and Accomplices of her Adultery. Here was a kind of Truce; the Church of *Rome* comes and violates this Truce, and prosecutes her Pretensions, constraining all those of *France,* who were of her Rival's Party, to come over to her own. Who sees not that the Protestant Church has all the right in the World, on the foot which we suppose, to prosecute the Punishment of the Whore's Accomplices? So that the Church of *England* might now reasonably tell all the *English* Papists; *I hitherto suspended the Punishment due to you for continuing in the Interest of a Harlot, who had expel'd me my House; me, who am the true Mother of the Family: but since she begins to treat my faithful Children cruelly, I shall no longer delay your deserv'd Punishment.*

Pray mind what this Author advances twice in a Breath, *That one must be abandon'd to all shame to pretend, that rebellious Children have the same Right over their Mother which she has over them.* But who told him, the Protestants are rebellious Children? only a humor of always supposing the <16> thing in question. To be a little more exact he shou'd have stated the Question thus, *One must be abandon'd to all shame who pretends, that Children who do not wish to recognise as their Mother a Woman they believe is only a rapacious Adulteress prostituted to all Comers, have as much Right of punishing her, as a Mother has to punish those, who she pretends are her Children.* The Question being thus propos'd, to pretend this, is so far from being a Sign that one is lost to all shame, that not to pretend it, one must have lost all his Senses; for what Right can be more reasonable than a Right in Children to expel a wicked Woman out of their House, who is a Dishonor to the Family, and to the Memory of their Father, who deprives the Mother of her Dowry, and of all the Provision for her Widowhood, and consumes their Substance on a pack of dissolute Wretches, and Servants whom she has seduc'd? To continue in her Interest, even after the injur'd Mother has bin reinstated in her House, as God be thank'd she is in *England,* is much the same as continuing in *Cromwel*'s Interest after the Restoration of King

Charles II. Nor let it be pretended, that there's a difference between the two Cases, because *Cromwel*'s Usurpation lasted but 9 or 10 Years; for we are all agreed in this common Principle, that there's no Prescription against the Truth: so that tho the dethroning the Successors of *Hugh Capet,* for example, might be an unjust Attempt in the Descendants of *Charlemagne,* were there any of his Line in being, so very long a Possession having rectify'd the Injustice done to the Family of *Charlemagne* by Hugh; yet it can be no Injustice, after a thousand, two thousand Years, or any longer Prescription of Falshood, to restore the Truth, <17> and reinstate it in all its inalienable Rights.[13] And by this we overthrow, and have overthrown so often that we are even asham'd to repeat it, all the Common-places of Papists on the uninterrupted Succession, *&c.* Nothing they can possibly say will hinder the Principle that Falshood may not usurp the place of Truth; and therefore we are to examine whether the Case has really happen'd as the Protestants alledg. We are to examine which side is right, and which wrong in fact; for if we talk of the bare Pretension only, and if Pretension be a sufficient ground for persecuting, all the World will persecute; each Party will say that they persecute righteously, and are very unrighteously persecuted: and till such time as God shall decide this great Claim at the last Day, the Strong will always oppress the Weak without controul. Are not these rare Principles?

It's plain then, that a Right of Persecuting cannot be contested to Protestants upon the ridiculous Reason which this Author assigns, nor upon any other but that which I have establish'd in this Work, and which equally and universally takes this Right from all Religions.

I shan't say any thing in particular to his alledg'd Example of a King who punishes his rebellious Subjects, and of Rebels who sometimes serve their Prisoners of the King's side in the same kind; because the Application is one of the common Impertinences of the Party. Be it known to him, that the Protestants look on themselves as those who fight under the Banner of

---

13. Prescription gives rights by lapse of time. There is, Bayle says, no prescription against the truth, though there is in some other matters, e.g. property and government. In 987 a French assembly decided not to recognize as king the heir descended from Charlemagne and instead elected Hugh Capet as king. Hugh's descendants ruled France until the end of the monarchy.

the lawful Queen, and on the Papists as rebellious Subjects, who had depriv'd her of almost <18> all her Dominions, and who still usurp the most considerable part of them; persisting obstinately in the Interests of an Adulteress, most justly repudiated, and still continuing her Prostitutions.

I must now offer a word or two in answer to an Objection which may be made, upon the Laws of this Kingdom's excluding Papists from all Places, and exacting from 'em the Oath of Supremacy. Is not this, say they, tempting Men? Is not this the ready way to make the Ambitious betray their Consciences, when a fair Employment presents for the Reward of their Hypocrisy? I answer, according to my Principles, That no doubt there is a defect in these Laws, in that they don't equally exclude all the new Converts; for did they exclude 'em for Life, and their Children who had not abjur'd Popery before they were fully bred up and instructed in it, nothing in my opinion cou'd be more reasonable or more necessary than these Laws: not that I think the false Religion of Papists, consider'd simply as such, a just ground for making Laws against those who profess it. No, it certainly is not. I take the Justice of these Laws to be founded wholly on their having Principles, such as that Hereticks must be compell'd to come in, that Heretick Kings should not be obey'd, &c., inconsistent with the publick Safety of the State where they themselves are not uppermost: for tho I shou'd suppose that there were here and there a Papist who believ'd the paying Obedience to a Heretick King no Sin, yet there's no Papist but must believe the Doctrine right in the main, as it is better relish'd at *Rome,* and more agreeable to the Sense of several Councils <19> than the contrary Doctrine. And this alone is a sufficient Reason for never trusting Popish Subjects but upon special Security: the rather, because they clandestinely introduce Monks, and other Emissarys of the Church of *Rome,* who study all occasions of embroiling the State, and devolving the Crown on Heads of their own Religion; wherein if they succeed, presently they talk of nothing else but crushing the infernal Hydra of Heresy, and sacrificing all their Oaths and Assurances to the Interests of Religion. The Reign of Queen *Elizabeth,* and that of her Successor (to say nothing of the two following) have shewn to what excesses they can carry their Attempts against Sovereigns of a contrary Religion: So that 'twere the most inexcusable Imprudence in this Nation, not to take all just Precautions against this Party, by excluding it from all Trusts and Employments, which 'tis plain it wou'd only make use of for the better executing the black and horrible Maxims of Persecution, its favorite Doctrine. And as to the Oath of Supremacy, for my part I think our Legislature has bin very weak, and done Papists too great an Honor, to believe it any Security against 'em. For that Man who thinks it lawful to *compel to come in,* as in the Romish Communion they do, where 'twere no less than Heresy to maintain the contrary, after it has been so often enjoin'd by Popes and Councils; may as well believe that the Decalogue was ne'er intended for those who are occupy'd in propagating Religion, but that as they are dispens'd with in the Breach of the Command against Murder and Stealing, so they are by a Parity of Reason in the Breach of that <20> against false Swearing: so that there's no reckoning upon any such thing as Oaths with them. It's a jest to say, the Council of *Constance* boggled at declaring, That Faith was not to be kept with Hereticks. Is it not enough that Papists think themselves oblig'd to kill and extirpate 'em? For by this, it's plain, they think themselves freed from the Obligation of not committing Murder: now no body will say that the Obligation is less in this case, than in that of performing Vows and Promises. But I insist not on this Point here; the Reader will find it amply treated in the *Commentary.*[14]

So abominable a Doctrine is that which authorizes the forcing Men to embrace a Religion, that with all the Aversion I have to Non-Toleration, I think it were a thing highly displeasing to God, to suffer Papists to get the Power into their hands of compelling Men: and therefore Prudence indispensably obliges us to banish 'em from all Places where there may be the least ground of Umbrage from 'em; and displace Ministers of State, Magistrates, and all Persons in any Trust or Employment, the moment they are convicted of Catholicity. I always except the Persons of Kings, because the Royal Dignity, and sacred Unction of their Character, dispenses with the most general Laws in their favor; and therefore it may be lawful for them to turn Papists, if they please, Jews, Turks, Infidels, without the least danger of forfeiting what they have a Right to by their Birth. But as for all others,

14. See p. 96 and p. 192.

they ought to be immediately oblig'd to break ground, or utterly depriv'd of all means of endangering the State. <21>

'Twere to be wish'd from the pure Motives of wise Policy, that Policy which aims at the general Good of Mankind, that all the Christian Princes who are not Papists wou'd unite in a solemn League, to take away that Reproach which Christianity lies under, on account of the horrible Persecutions exercis'd by it from time immemorial. If such a League shou'd not be thought sufficient, let's hope for the Addition to it of all the Infidel Nations of both Continents, till we make up a Body capable of bringing Popery to reason; Popery, that sore Disgrace of Christianity, and Bane of Human kind! Such a League wou'd be altogether as just as a League against the Rovers of *Barbary:*[15] And as it were very reasonable to exact all manner of Assurances from these, that they wou'd never cruise more, nor disturb the Trade of the World by their infamous Piracys; so nothing were more reasonable than exacting from Popery a Promise never to persecute more, and obliging it to annul all the Decrees of Councils, all the Bulls of Popes, and all the Decisions of Casuists authorizing Persecution. But because there wou'd still be ground enough to apprehend, that she wou'd flinch from all Engagements as soon as the danger was over; to obviate this Inconvenience, 'twere necessary to demand Hostages from her, and impose such heavy Penaltys on every default, that she shou'd never more presume to violate the Treaty. These indeed are Projects fitly calculated for sparing the World many and great Desolations, yet they are never the less chimerical; and, as the Author, who has occasion'd the writing this Commentary,[16] has very justly re-<22>mark'd, Popery is too necessary an Instrument in the hands of an incens'd Providence (which to punish Human kind effectually, must decree it both miserable and ridiculous) to expect that any thing shou'd ever deliver the World from it. And I know a Man of a great deal of Wit, who querying whether there shou'd be a Romish Church in Hell, that is, a Body of Men govern'd by the furious and detestable Maxims of this Re-

15. The papacy had taken part with various European powers in several "leagues" aimed at destroying the Barbary Pirates, Muslim pirates operating out of North Africa. See Robert Wild, "Holy Leagues of the Sixteenth Century," http://europeanhistory .about.com/library/weekly/aa083101c.htm.

16. See above, p. 36, note 1.

ligion; answers in the affirmative, and for this reason, Because without it there wou'd something still be wanting to compleat the Misery of those who are consign'd to the darksom Abodes.

I took the Infidel Nations of both Continents into my imaginary Scheme, and not without good reasons; because tho they have not so immediate an Interest in the abolishing the impious Maxims of Persecution as we, yet they all have a concern in it more or less remote, according as they are more or less distant from the places into which the Missionarys riggle themselves; especially that dark and dreadful Machine which stretches out its Arms as wide as *China*. There's no room to doubt but the Pope, and his Imps, have a design of reducing the whole World under their Yoke. They are prompted to this by the Interest of Lording it far and near, and heaping up Riches, and of preventing that Confusion with which the Protestants cover 'em, as often as they shew how ridiculous their Pretences are to the Title of Universal Church, when there are so many Nations in the World which have never as much as heard of it. Now to gratify their Ambition and their Avarice, and to spare <23> themselves the shame of never being able to answer pertinently to this Objection of the Protestants; there's no manner of doubt but they will introduce their dear and well-beloved Handmaid, the constraining to sign a Formulary, as soon as they have power enough among the Infidels. The Jesuits[17] have themselves own'd, during the Life of their Founder, that they had made use of Constraint in the *Indies*. In their Letters written from this Country we are inform'd, that the *Brachmans* being nonplus'd in a Dispute, stood it out upon this single Reason, That they follow'd the Doctrines of their Ancestors; and persisted to such a degree of Obstinacy, that no Arguments, of what force soever, cou'd make the least Impression on 'em: Whereupon the Vice-Roy, to shorten the Dispute, and drive one Nail with another, publish'd a Law, whereby they who wou'd not turn within the space of forty days, were condemn'd to Banishment; on pain, if they did not depart the Country in that time, of forfeiting all their Substance, and being sent to the Gallys. *Scioppius* is the Man who reproaches the Jesuits with this, in his Criticism

17. "Jesuit": a member of the Catholic religious order the Society of Jesus, founded by Ignatius of Loyola.

on *Famianus Strada;*[18] where there are several other very honest Remarks to the same purpose, but which stand to the worst advantage imaginable in this Author, because he himself had bin a mere Firebrand in his former Writings; his *Classicum Belli Sacri,* printed in 1619,[19] being stuff'd with the most execrable Maxims relating to the Excision of those who are call'd Hereticks. However, he had ground enough for censuring the Uncertainty and Variations of the Jesuits Tenets, on their publishing a Work in *Germany* about seven <24> years ago, intitled, *Justa Defensio,*[20] in which they laugh at a set of Monks, who pretended to maintain, that no Arms but the Apostolical ought to be employ'd for the Conversion of those in Error: that's right, say they, with regard to Infidels, but not with regard to Hereticks, nothing will do with these but Menaces and Blows. Why then will they make use of the same means for converting the Pagans in the *Indies?*

The truth is, they who take on 'em the odious task of vindicating Persecution of any kind, are hard put to it to trim the Matter. If they persecute only Hereticks, and the Conduct of the Apostles be alledg'd against 'em, they answer, That this Example wou'd be a Rule indeed if they had to deal with Infidels as the Apostles had; but that Hereticks being rebellious Children, the Church retains more Right over them than over Pagans. They don't perceive, that this is furnishing Jews and Pagans with Arms against those among them who embrace the Gospel; and furnishing these Arms in such a manner, that shou'd the new Converts pretend to constrain those who persisted in the Religion of their Fathers, they may presently speak out, *That one must be abandon'd to all shame who pretends, that rebellious Children have the same Right over their Mother which she has over them.* If they persecute and constrain infidels, as has bin practis'd thro both the *Indies* in a manner, the very Accounts of which are enough to chill one's Blood, then they are necessarily forc'd to turn the Tables; they alledg the Practice of the antient Christian Emperors (who, unacquainted with the modern Distinction between the Me-<25>thods to be taken with Hereticks

18. Possibly: Gaspar Scioppius, *Comitis clatae vallae Infamia Famiani,* 1658.

19. Possibly: *Consilium regium, in quo, a duodecim regibus et imperatoribus, catholico Hispaniarum regi demonstratur quibus modis omnia bella feliciter profligare possit. Accessit Stemma augustae domus Austriae . . . Item Classicum belli sacri,* 1619.

20. Not found.

and Infidels, condemn'd the Pagans to Death) and interpret the Parable in its utmost Import, without any manner of Restriction. So that they have such or such Principles, according to the Exigency and Occasions, nothing fixt, but staring Contradictions at every turn, as any one may see, who takes the Pains of reading what Pope *Gregory* the Great, and his new Historian* *Maimbourg,* have said upon the Methods of converting the Jews and others. To shew that these Gentlemen have time-serving Principles, I shall cite *P. Maimbourg* writing at a time when the forcing Men to communicate was not as yet practis'd in *France,* and highly disapproving this Constraint; for he tells us, that by forcing the Jews *to receive Baptism against their Opinion, there were as many Profanations of so holy an Ordinance, and as many Acts of Sacrilege as there were Jews baptis'd.* By condemning these forc'd Baptisms, he necessarily condemns all forc'd Communions. At that very time he approv'd all the other Methods made use of against the Reform'd; but because this of constraining to communicate was not yet in vogue, and consequently needed no Apology, and he did not foresee that it wou'd need any, he condemns it peremptorily. As Matters are order'd since, he must bethink himself of some new come-off.

Mr. *Diroys,*† whom I have cited in the Body of my *Commentary,* must needs be strangely out of Countenance, because it follows from what <26> he has advanc'd in his reasonings on these Points, that his own Religion is good for nothing. Observe how he cuts down Mahometism, without considering, that he strikes Catholicism to the heart at every stroke.

The fourth Character of Falshood, says he, *in this Religion of* Mahomet, *is, That whereas the true Religions, as those of the Jews and Christians, admit no body as a Member of 'em, unless he appears persuaded of their Truth, Hypocrisy serving only to enhance their Guilt; that of* Mahomet *does in many Cases exact an outward Profession from Persons who inwardly detest it. If a*

---

* *Hist.* of Greg. *p.* 241, &c. *of the* Holl. *Edit.* [Louis Maimbourg, *Histoire du Pontificat de S. Grégoire le Grand* (History of the pontificate of St. Gregory the Great), Paris, 1686, La Haye, 1687.]

† Preuves de la Relig. Chret. *l. 6. ch. 6.* [François Diroys, *Preuves et prejugez pour la religion chrétienne et catholique, contre les fausses religions et l'athéisme* (Proofs and presumptions in favor of the Catholic Christian Religion, against false religions and atheism), 1683.]

Man has had the Misfortune unwittingly, or even in drink, to give any external Mark of his [Dis]Approbation;[21] *if he has hapned to speak of it with Contempt, if he has struck a Mahometan tho in his own defence, if he debauches a Woman, or marrys one of this Religion; there's no way left for him of expiating these real or pretended Crimes, but by making external Profession of this Religion, altho the Reluctance with which he does it sufficiently testifys, that he is not in the least persuaded of its Truth.*

We have shewn, continues he, *in discoursing of the Religion of the Gentiles, that the extorting the Profession of a Religion, which one is not in conscience persuaded of, is an evident Proof of its being govern'd by a Spirit at Enmity with Truth and Holiness; since nothing can be more repugnant to Truth, to Vertue, and to solid Piety, than the outward Profession of a Religion, which one believes to be false. The Jews, before the coming of* JESUS CHRIST, *and sometimes the Christians since, have indeed punish'd Crimes committed against their Religions with Death, but the embracing it was never made the Condition of Pardon. And therefore no-<27>thing but the Love of God, and a firm Persuasion of its Truth, cou'd incline these Offenders to bewail their Crime, and confess that Religion which they had once blasphem'd.* So far Monsieur *Diroys.*

O what fine Divisions might a Body run upon this Passage! but there's no great need of discanting on it; I leave it to every Reader to do this of himself, and apply to the present Methods of *France* so much as comes to its share in this Discourse. I shall only observe, that this learned Doctor of the *Sorbon* is of my Mind in the *Commentary,* to wit, that they who condemn Hereticks to Death with a Proviso of Pardon in case they abjure their Heresy, do much worse than if they condemn'd 'em without Mercy. The *Spaniards* and *Portuguese,* who give a horror to all true Christians with their detestable *Autos de fe,* which our Gazets ring with yearly, act very honestly, the first Demerit once suppos'd, I mean the capital Crime of a poor Jew, in not giving him his Life on condition he declares himself a Christian; and wou'd act still better if they did not mitigate his Punishment by changing it for strangling, because in all probability the dread of being burnt alive is what extorts this feign'd Conversion.

I wou'd willingly know how Mr. *Diroys,* if sent a Missionary into *China,*

---

21. Apparently an error in the French text.

cou'd look a *Chinese* in the Face, who shou'd read this Book of his, after having first read over the Accounts which the Protestants might and ought to furnish 'em of the Exploits of Popery in *Europe, America,* and the *Indies.* Wou'd not they tell Monsieur the Missionary, that by his own Principles, the extorting a Profession by Violence is Evidence enough, that the Religion which requires it, is < 28 > *led by a Spirit at enmity with Truth and Holiness?* This he cou'd not deny. Wou'd not they likewise tell him, that the Religion which he now preach'd to them had very lately extorted forc'd Professions in the Kingdom of *France,* and even constrain'd those to communicate who were first constrain'd to sign; and threatned those with the Gallys if they recover'd, who refus'd the Sacrament in their Sickness, or with having their dead Bodys drawn on a Sledg in case they dy'd in such a Refusal? He durst not deny it, if he found that the Protestants took care to transmit the *French* King's Edicts to *China;* or if he were only an honest Man, as we are willing to suppose him. The Conclusion on the whole is unavoidably this; Therefore the Religion, which you, Mr. *Diroys,* a Doctor of the *Sorbon,* come to preach up among us, is led by a Spirit at enmity with Truth and Holiness; whereupon all well-minded Men, Christians or not Christians, ought to cry out, εὖ καὶ ὑπέρευ, *belle, optime, nihil supra.*[22] And here I can't but greatly wonder, that the ease of confuting Mr. *Diroys* on his applying to the Church of *Rome,* exclusive of all other Churches, the Characters of the Truth of the Christian Religion, has never tempted any one to undertake it. Did I, unworthy I, take up the Cudgels against him, I dare say, I shou'd quickly make appear, that all his Arguments on this Head are purely a begging the Question,[23] or palpable Paralogisms and fallacious Reasoning.

Some of my Acquaintance were strangely surpris'd at the Edicts for drawing on Sledges the dead Bodys of those who refus'd the Communion, and for putting those to Death who shou'd exer-< 29 >cise any Function of the Reform'd Religion in *France,* and all Ministers who shou'd come into the Kingdom without a Licence, with large Rewards to the Discoverers, and Penaltys on those who shou'd harbor 'em; the Fate precisely of the

---

22. "Well done, the best, nothing better."
23. See Appendixes, "Bayle's Use of Logic," p. 580 ("petitio principii").

Proscrib'd in *Rome* during the Triumvirate.[24] These Gentlemen told me, they cou'd never have believ'd, that in an Age so clear-sighted and so civiliz'd as ours, a Nation which passes for very polite, cou'd ever come to such cruel Extremitys. I soon chang'd the Object of their wonder, by letting 'em see there was much more reason to be surpriz'd at the Church of *Rome*'s chaffering so long, and trifling away so much time without coming to Blood; that as this was her natural Element, and the Scene she most delighted in, and the Mark which her truest Arrows oftnest hit, she ought by the course of nature, and by the tendency of human things, to have struck the Blow much sooner, and lodg'd her Arrow, which was not the four nor the five hundredth she had let fly at Hugonotism in the very midst of the Mark. And as to what they mention'd concerning the Civility of the Age, I let 'em know, that false Religions are always excepted out of the number of those things whose Nature may be humaniz'd. Cruelty is their indelible Character; they have the Power of effacing from the Hearts of Father and Mother those Sentiments of Love and Tenderness for their Infants, which Nature has so deeply imprinted upon 'em. They have had the Power of making Parents stand the broiling and sacrificing these innocent Creatures before their Eyes. <30>

> *Aulide quo pacto Triviai Virginis arma*
> *Iphianassai turparunt sanguine foede*
> *Ductores Danaum delecti prima virorum.*[25]

Why then shou'd they boggle at the Lives of their Enemys? The Church of *Rome* is now in the very Posture which becomes her best, and sets her off to the greatest Advantage; all she had bin hitherto transacting in *France* might well have had the Substance and full Effect of the extremest Cruelty, but the Pomp of it was wanting: This she has at last compass'd with great

---

24. The triumvirs (Octavian, Anthony, and Lepidus) controlled Rome after the assassination of Julius Caesar. The proscriptions were lists they published of people to be killed without trial. See Appian, *Civil War,* IV.ii, Loeb Classical Library, p. 146 ff.

25. Lucretius, *De rerum natura,* I.85: "As when at Aulis the altar of our Lady of the Crossways was foully defiled by the blood of Iphianassa, shed by the chosen leaders of the Danai, chieftans of the host." Translated W.H.D. Rouse, Loeb Classical Library, 1975, p. 11.

Glory; and after having turn'd herself often round her resting-place, you see her lolling at full length, and perfectly at her ease.

It remains that I offer a Word or two in answer to those who pretend, that Toleration creates endless Confusions in a State, and prove it too by the Advice which *Mecenas* gives *Augustus* in the 52*d* Book of the History of *Dion Cassius: Worship the Gods,* says he to him, *at all Seasons, and in all the ways of Worship which the Religion of your Ancestors prescribes, and take care, that your People, do the same; shew your Abhorrence of those who cause the least Innovations in religious Matters, and restrain 'em by your Authority, not only from a Reverence to the Gods, but also from a Regard to your own Dignity, in as much as these Innovators, by introducing new Worships, divide the Body of the People, whence naturally spring Factions, Cabals, Seditions, Conspiracys, things of very pernicious Consequence in a State.*[26] These words taken in gross, and as coming from a Pagan Politician, have an appearance of excellent reason; but nothing in nature can be <31> more ridiculous, than applying 'em as the Roman Catholicks eternally do, to the instigating Christian Princes to persecute different Communions: because in the first place, by virtue of this Advice *Augustus* and his Successors were oblig'd to persecute the Jews and Christians; and the Emperors of *Japan, China,* &c. to oppose those with all their Might who mention Christianity in their Dominions, which the Pope and his Adherents will never allow: and therefore they must change the general Maxim of *Mecenas* into this particular Maxim; *Worship God in the way of your Ancestors, where it shall appear that they worship'd God aright; oppose all Innovations except they be for the better:* And then it's a mere indefinite Sentence, which decides nothing.

In the second place, The Maxim of *Mecenas* was much more reasonable in his times than it wou'd be at present, because the *Romans,* granting a full Liberty of Conscience to all the Sects of Paganism, and frequently adopting the Worships of other Countrys, it might justly be presum'd, that a Man who did not find his Account in a Religion so large and comprehensive, but affected Noveltys, cou'd have no other design than that of making himself the Head of a Party, and forming political Cabals under a Pretence of worshipping the Gods. But this Presumption does not easily

26. Dio's *Roman History,* LII.36, Loeb Classical Library, 1968, p. 173.

reach a Christian, as well because he is persuaded, that JESUS CHRIST has left us a standing Rule which we are strictly to follow, as because the Church of *Rome* imposes a necessity of believing all her Decisions; in which case he who is persuaded, that she has not Reason of her side, is bound in conscience, as he wou'd avoid <32> the Guilt of Hypocrisy, to withdraw from her Communion.

To shew the Absurdity of those who pretend that Toleration causes Dissensions in the State, we need only appeal to Experience. Paganism was divided into an infinite number of Sects, which paid the Gods several different kinds of Worship; and even those Gods which were supreme in one Country, were not so in another: yet I don't remember I have ever read of a Religious War among the Pagans, unless we give this name to the War enter'd into against those who attempted to pillage the Temple of *Delphos.* But as for Wars undertaken with a design of compelling one Nation to the Religion of another, I find not the least mention of any such in the Heathen Authors. *Juvenal* is the only Author who speaks of two Citys of *Egypt* which had a mortal Aversion to one another, because each maintain'd its own were the only true Gods.[27] Every where else there was a perfect Calm, a perfect Tranquillity; and why? but because the Partys tolerated each others Rites. It's plain then, as I have shewn in my *Commentary,*[28] that Non-Toleration is the sole cause of all the Disorders which are falsly imputed to Toleration. The different Sects of Philosophy ne'er disturb'd the Peace of *Athens,* each maintain'd its own Hypothesis, and argu'd against those of all the other Sects; yet their Differences concern'd matters of no small moment, nay, sometimes it was over Providence, or the Chief Good. But because the Magistrates permitted 'em all alike to teach their own Doctrines, and never endeavor'd by violent Methods to incorporate one Sect into another, the State felt <33> no Inconvenience from this Diversity of Opinions; tho, 'tis probable, had they attempted this Union, they had thrown the whole into Convulsions. Toleration therefore is the very Bond of Peace, and Non-Toleration the Source of Confusion and Squabble.

I shall conclude this Preliminary Discourse with a Remark, which may

27. Juvenal, *Satire* XV.33–38, Loeb Classical Library, pp. 290–91.
28. See p. 200.

serve to illustrate what I have said touching the evil effects of Constraint in Religion. I took notice, that Persons intirely persuaded of the Truth of what they abjure with their mouths, sink under the Violence of Pain and Torment. We have a memorable Example of this in the Christians of the first Century, when accus'd of the Fire of *Rome* under the Reign of *Nero*. This wicked Emperor was himself the Incendiary; and was generally thought so. He did what he cou'd to remove the Suspicion from himself, but all in vain; at last he bethought himself of laying it on the Christians, and had 'em put to the most exquisite Tortures. Some own'd the Fact, and accus'd a very great number of their Brethren; yet they were all perfectly innocent: but as their Executioners undoubtedly signify'd, that the Design of these Torments was only to make 'em confess themselves the Authors of the Crime, and name a great many Accomplices (for *Nero* hop'd by this means to acquit himself) they readily gave into the noose, overcome by the Extremity of Pain. Which shews how very difficult it is for a body not to lye, when expos'd to the trial of the sharpest Sufferings. What's remarkable herein, is, that the Martyrology celebrates all these first Christians, who were tormented on this occa-<34>sion, as Martyrs; as well those who had the Weakness to tell a lye by owning themselves guilty, and accusing their Brethren of an Action very infamous to the Christian Name, as those who resisted the Temptation. *Igitur primo correpti qui fatebantur,* says *Tacitus* in B. 15. of his Annals, *deinde indicio eorum multitudo ingens haud perinde in crimine incendii quam odio humani generis convicti.*[29]

When a body considers the Effects of violent Methods on these first Christians, who ought to have bin fill'd with the greatest Ardor which a nascent Religion is able to inspire, when sustain'd by so many visible and fresh Marks of the Divinity of its Founder; when one considers besides, the Success that all those have had who have persecuted to the Rigor, he can't but conceive a Contempt, mixt with Indignation, for those *French* Writers, who deafen us with their vile Flatterys, while they pretend that the Extirpation of Calvinism in *France* was a Work reserv'd for the greatest and

---

29. Tacitus, *Annals,* XV.44: "First, then, the confessed members of the sect were arrested; next, on their disclosures, vast numbers were convicted, not so much on the count of arson as for hatred of the human race." Translated J. Jackson, Loeb Classical Library, pp. 283–85.

most accomplish'd Monarch that ever came into the World, meaning *Lewis* XIV. One of these Scriblers, a Preacher by Trade (which I observe not to heighten, but to diminish my Reader's Surprize) pronounc'd a Panegyrick in a full *Sorbon* last year,[30] in which he told his Hearers, there was a necessity of a Concurrence of several extraordinary Circumstances to extinguish Hugonotism; A solid Peace with the neighboring Powers, the Glory of a Prince spread to the uttermost parts of the Universe, the Terror of his Name transmitted to distant Countrys, a mighty Power, a deal of Lenity, *&c.* He adds, that *Lewis* the <35> Great was blest with all these Advantages; that the Kings his Predecessors had employ'd Fire and Sword to destroy the Heresys of their Times, some with good Success, and some to no purpose: *but that his Majesty, without making use of these lawful means, had triumph'd over Heresy by his Gentleness, by his Wisdom, and by his Piety.* This is exactly the Language of a world of other Authors, even those who are neither Haranguers nor Sermon-mongers. And now who cou'd forbear laughter, did the Miserys of his Neighbor allow his laughing at things the most ridiculous in themselves? 'Twas necessary, say they, that his Glory shou'd be spread to the utmost parts of the Earth, the Terror of his Name convey'd to foreign Nations, and a mighty Power: And why all this? Only to convert Hereticks, *by his Gentleness, by his Wisdom, and by his Piety.* Did ever any one hear such Extravagance? This Terror, this Power, this Glory, were proper enough, I own, for constraining Men to return into the Bosom of the Church, who were most averse to it, and to extort the signing of a Formulary; but where a Prince resolves to employ only Gentleness, and Wisdom, and Piety, as this *Abbe Robert* says in his Panegyrick the King did, I can't see of what use it was to render himself terrible to all *Europe.* But to pass over this Contradiction, to pass over all the Remarks which may be made on these mercenary Declamations; as their saying on one hand, he had accomplish'd the Work by Methods of Gentleness, and on the other hand that it was necessary to strike a terror into Strangers, and be sustain'd with mighty Forces; which shews at least that there was a Design of working upon the Fears <36> of People, and employing Force against those who wou'd not be con-

---

30. See Journ. des Sav., 10 Dec. 1685, extract from a panegyric preached by l'Abbé Robert. [Author's note in the French edition.]

verted by fair means: to pass over, I say, all these Remarks, I shall content my self with maintaining, that there was so little need of acquiring a mighty Reputation, such as the King of *France* has got by the Success of his Arms, in order to constrain his Subjects by the methods which have bin practis'd to make 'em abjure, that the meanest Monarch of the first or second Race might have done as much, had he to deal with Subjects under such Circumstances as the *Hugonots,* dispers'd over a vast Kingdom, without a Head, without Fortresses, without Magazines, surrounded and every where beset by Popish Subjects and arm'd Troops. Chuse me out any Nation of Men that you please, and of what Religion you please; scatter 'em all over *France,* exactly as those of the Reformation lay, and I'l chuse my King the despicablest and meanest that ever wore a Crown, but with plenty of Dragoons and Foot-Soldiers at his beck: let him give 'em orders to treat their Landlords as the pretended Hereticks were lately treated in *France,* I'l pawn my Life, and I dare say any sober Man, who considers the matter ever so little, will be of my opinion, that these People will almost every Mother's Son of 'em change their Religion. But how comes it then, that neither *Charles* IX nor *Henry* III cou'd compass the Ruin of this Sect? Not because either of 'em was void of the personal Qualitys which meet in the Prince who is now on the Throne, but because the *Hugonots* were then arm'd, and in a condition to repel Force by Force; besides that, generally speaking, they were in those days extremely zealous in their <37> Religion. Had these Princes found the Reformation in that Declension to which it was reduc'd about ten years ago, they had certainly accomplish'd its Ruin as effectually as others have now. I say then, that its Declension in Power being once suppos'd, which is principally due to *Lewis* XIII, there was no need of a formidable Glory among Strangers, nor of any extraordinary personal Qualitys to finish its Ruin; there was nothing more requisite to this end, than on one hand a Capacity in the Prince of looking with a dry and unrelenting Air on the sacking of one part of his Subjects, and the Captivity or Exile of so many Familys, and on the other a great many Soldiers accustom'd to Barbaritys: nothing more was requisite for the so much boasted Exploit. The *Chilperic's* and the *Wenceslaus's*[31] had bin altogether as well

31. There were two kings named Chilperic in French history, the first famous for

qualify'd for such a Work in the foremention'd Circumstances, as the *Charlemagn's*.

Which more and more exposes the *French* Panegyrists want of Judgment, who can't say three words together with any Justness, or without cutting themselves down. I'm amaz'd, that among so many Refugees as write upon the present State of their Religion, not one of 'em shou'd think of making Extracts of all that the *French* Catholicks say of this kind in their Books. One shou'd find in 'em such a Chaos of jarring and incoherent Thoughts, as can no where be parallel'd. I'm told, they design to intreat Mr. *Colomies* to give himself this trouble.[32]

I can scarce make the primitive Church an Exception to the general Rule. I know 'twas the Purpose of Providence, that it shou'd prevail without the Assistance of the Secular Power, and <38> in spite of all the Opposition of the World; and for this end God inspir'd the Faithful of these first Days with an extraordinary Zeal: yet I can't but think that the intervals of Peace and Respite which they enjoy'd, sometimes for many years together, contributed mainly to the establishing the Christian Religion. It's certain, all our Accounts of the ten Persecutions are deliver'd by Historians none of the most exact, and that they are all stuff'd with Declamation and Hyperbole. Christianity had undoubtedly perish'd, without a continual course of Miracles for the three first Centurys, if all the Pagan Emperors had apply'd themselves in good earnest to the extinguishing it: but God was pleas'd to entertain 'em with other Thoughts and other Affairs, which oblig'd 'em to let the Christians live in Peace. And the great Progress of the Christian Church is as much owing to this, as to its Patience under Sufferings.

I can't conclude without a short Reflection on these words of the Panegyrick of the *Abbé Robert,* Great Penitentiary of the Church of *Paris; That his Majesty chose not the lawful means, to wit, Fire and Sword, which his Ancestors had frequently employ'd against the Hereticks of their times.* Pray

---

quarrels and murders, the second for his weakness; it is difficult to know which Bayle had in mind. Wenceslaus is probably not the saint, but the "Holy Roman Emperor" deposed for neglect in 1400.

32. See DHC, art. "Colomies, Paul."

observe his Language in the presence of a full *Sorbon*,[33] the Language of Popery in general: Fire and Sword are wholesom and warrantable Methods with all who are not Orthodox. If so, pray how cou'd the Duke of *Guise*, who was murder'd by *Poltrot*,[34] pronounce with so much Emphasis the Saying which is ascrib'd to him, and mention'd so much to his Honor? The Story is this: That at the Siege of *Roan* a Hugonot <39> Gentleman being brought before him, who had conspir'd his Death, and who own'd he was not prompted to it from any Hatred to his Person, but purely from the Instincts of his own Religion, and because he thought his Death might be of service to it; the Duke releasing him, said: *Go, Sir, if your Religion enjoins you to assassinate those who have never injur'd you, mine obliges me to give you your Life, tho I might justly take it away; and now judg you which of the two is best.* This were a truly Wise and Christian Saying, from any one but a Catholick, at the head of a persecuting Army: but when one considers that the Person who speaks thus is a Persecutor on the score of Religion, he can't but despise him, as acting an unnatural part, and turning Religion into Grimace; one who out of rank Pride and a Bravado pardons a private Person who deserves Death, while at the same time he exercises the most savage and horrible Crueltys on a whole Body of innocent People. Was not this very Duke of *Guise* of the same Religion as *Francis* I and *Henry* II? Had not he approv'd and advis'd the Edict of *Chateau-Briant*, and that of *Romorantin*, which first decreed the Protestants to death? Did not he labor with all his might to settle the Inquisition in *France?* which, strictly speaking, had bin setting up a Slaughterhouse for Men, a Court of Fire and Faggot, beset and continually surrounded with Bloodhounds. Was not he the principal Promoter of all the Measures which were broken by the precipitate Death of *Francis* II for marching Troops thro all the Provinces of the Kingdom, to force <40> every living Soul to sign a Formulary, on pain of Banishment and Confiscation of Goods (which was the gentlest Treatment). For how many, alas, must they have put to death! Last of all, Was not this the very Duke, who had suffer'd his Troops to massacre a whole

---

33. The Sorbonne was the (Catholic) Theology faculty of the University of Paris.

34. Guise was murdered by Poltrot. Some days elapsed between the attack and Guise's death.

Congregation of *Hugonots* at *Vassi,* only because they were assembled at their Prayers in a Barn? In a word, the Obstinacy of this single Person, and his persisting to have these poor People inexorably punish'd with Death, was it not the cause of all the Civil Wars on the score of Religion; which *France* had never felt, if these People had bin suffer'd to worship God in their own way? And did not he do all this out of a Zeal for Religion? Had he done any thing like it, if he had bin a Pagan? Wou'd not he have tolerated Protestants as well as Papists? Was not all this Conduct of his approv'd by Pope and Clergy? How then cou'd he pretend that his Religion taught him to pardon those who had injur'd him, since it oblig'd him to murder and torment, by a thousand exquisite ways, a world of poor People, who never had done him the least prejudice, and who had no other demerit, but that of serving God according to the Light of their Consciences? Observe the horrible Turpitude and Kind of Farce, which mixes with those Religions that persecute, and *compel to come in.* A Man of such a Religion will make no difficulty of protesting he's ready to pardon one of a different Religion all private Offences committed against himself; yet he'l truss him up to a Gibbet, or send him to the Gallys, because he wants the true Faith, even tho he had receiv'd <41> kind Offices from him. In good truth, this Duke did not think before he spake, when he durst make a comparison of the two Religions, and give his own the Preference in point of Charity. The Gentleman, who had conspir'd his Death, upon a persuasion of its being for the Interest of the Protestant Religion, was a Stranger to the true Principles of this Party; for there's no Protestant Divine, but says, and preaches, and maintains, that Assassination is an unlawful means of promoting the Interest of Religion: but the Duke, conformably to a Doctrine approv'd and enjoin'd a thousand times over in his own Religion, gave his Opinion in Council for the enacting of sanguinary Laws against a world of innocent inoffensive People; nor was there a Pulse in his Body, that did not beat high for the extirpating Protestants by the most violent methods. And, with such Dispositions as these, was it not mocking the World to glory in being of a Religion which enjoins Forgiveness? I wish the Convertists would think a little of this. They are got into such Circumstances, that all the fairest Maxims of Christian Morality are mere Ironys, Farce, and unaccountable Jargon in their mouths. For can they have the face to say, that they sacrifice their Resentments for the Love of JESUS CHRIST, forgive Injurys, and seek peace with all Men? Can they have the face to say this, when we may so justly reproach 'em, that by constraining Conscience, which they believe a Christian Duty, they are under a necessity of pillaging, smiting, imprisoning, kidnapping, and putting to death a world of People, who do no prejudice to the <42> State, nor to their Neighbor; and who are guilty of no other Crime, than that of not believing, from a sense of their Duty to God, what others do believe from a sense likewise of their Duty to God?

The Age we live in, and, I'm apt to think, the Ages before us, have not fallen short of ours; is full of Free-Thinkers and Deists. People are amaz'd at it; but for my part, I'm amaz'd that we have not more of this sort among us, considering the havock which Religion has made in the World, and the Extinction, by an almost unavoidable Consequence, of all Vertue; by its authorizing, for the sake of a temporal Prosperity, all the Crimes imaginable, Murder, Robbery, Banishment, Rapes, &c. which produce infinite other Abominations, Hypocrisy, sacrilegious Profanation of Sacraments, &c. But I leave it to my *Commentary*, to carry on this matter.

A   <43>
Philosophical COMMENTARY
On these Words of the Gospel
according to St. *Luke,*
Chap. XIV. ver. 23.

And the Lord said unto the Servant, Go out into the Highways and Hedges, and COMPEL THEM TO COME IN, *that my House may be fill'd.*

Containing a Refutation of the Literal Sense of this Passage.

PART the First.

ʊʊ CHAPTER I ʊʊ

That the Light of Nature, or the first Principles of Reason universally receiv'd, are the genuin and original Rule of all Interpretation of Scripture; especially in Matters of Practice and Morality.

I leave it to the Criticks and Divines to comment on this Text in their way, by comparing it with other Passages, by examining what goes before and what follows, by descanting on the Force of the Expressions in <44> the Original, the various Senses they are capable of, and which they actually bear in several places of Scripture. My design is to make a Commentary of an uncommon kind, built on Principles more general and more infallible than what a Skill in Languages, Criticism, or Common-place can afford. I shan't even inquire, why Jesus Christ might make choice of the Expression *Compel,* how soft a Construction we are oblig'd to put on it, or whether there be Mysterys conceal'd under the Rind of the Expression; I shall content my self with overthrowing that literal Sense which Persecutors alledg.

To do this unanswerably, I shall go upon this single Principle of natural Reason; *That all literal Construction, which carries an Obligation of committing Iniquity, is false.* St. *Austin* gives this as a Rule and Criterion for discerning the figurative from the literal Sense.[35] Jesus Christ, says he, declares that unless we eat the Flesh of the Son of Man, we cannot be sav'd. This looks as if he commanded an Impiety; it's therefore a Figure which enjoins our partaking of the Lord's Death, and bearing in continual remembrance to our exceeding Benefit and Comfort the crucifying and wounding his Flesh for us. This is not the place to examine, whether these words prove St. *Austin* was not of the opinion of those of the Church of *Rome,* or whether he rightly applies his Rule: It's enough, that he reasons on this fundamental Principle, this surest Key for understanding Scripture, *That if by taking it in the literal Sense we oblige Men to commit Iniquity, or,* that I may leave no room for an Equivoque, *oblige 'em to commit Actions which the Light* <45> *of Nature, the Precepts of the Decalogue, or the Gospel Morality forbid; it's to be taken for granted, that the Sense we give it is false, and that instead of a Divine Revelation, we impose our own Visions, Prejudices, and Passions on the People.*

God forbid I shou'd have a thought of stretching the Rights of natural Reason; or of the Principles of Metaphysicks, to such a length as your *Socinians,* who pretend that all Sense given to Scripture, not agreeable to this Reason or to these Principles, is to be rejected; and who in virtue of this Maxim refuse to believe the Trinity and Incarnation. No, this I can't come up to, without boundary and limitation. Yet I know there are Axioms against which the clearest and most express Letter of the Scriptures can avail nothing: as, *That the Whole is greater than the Part; That if from equal things*

---

35. Augustine, *De doctrina Christiana,* book 3. [Author's note in the French edition. See III.xvi.24, Migne, *Patrologia Latina,* vol. 34, col. 74.]

we take things equal, the remainder will be equal; That 'tis impossible Con-
tradictorys shou'd be true; or, that the Accidents of a Subject shou'd subsist after
the Destruction of the Subject. Shou'd the contrary be shewn a hundred
times over from Scripture, shou'd a thousand times as many Miracles as
those of *Moses* and the Apostles be wrought in confirmation of a Doctrine
repugnant to these universal Principles of common Sense; Man, as his Facultys are made, cou'd not believe a tittle on't, and wou'd sooner persuade
himself either that the Scriptures spoke only by Contrarys, or only in Met-
aphors, or that these Miracles were wrought by the Power of the Devil,
than that the Oracles of Reason were false in these Instances. This is such
a Truth, that those of the Church of *Rome,* as much interested as they are
to sacrifice their <46> Metaphysicks, and render all Principles of common
Sense suspect, confess that neither Scripture, nor Church, nor Miracles, are
of any force against the clear Light of Reason, against this Principle, for
example, *The Whole is greater than its Part.* We may consult *P. Valerien
Magni,* a famous *Capucine,* on this point, in the 8th and 9th Chapt. of the
first Book of his *Judgment concerning the Rule of Faith of Catholicks.*[36] And
lest it be objected, that this is but one Doctor's Opinion, and to avoid citing
a vast number of other Catholick Authors, I shall take notice in general,
that all the Controvertists of this side deny that Transubstantiation is repugnant to sound Philosophy; and frame a thousand Distinctions, a thousand Subtletys, to shew it does not overthrow the Principles of Metaphysicks. The Protestants, in like manner, will ne'er allow the *Socinians,* that
the Trinity or Incarnation are contradictory Doctrines; they alledg and
maintain that this cannot be prov'd upon 'em. Thus the whole Body of
Divines, of what Party soever, after having cry'd up Revelation, the Mer-
itoriousness of Faith, and Profoundness of Mysterys, till they are quite out
of breath, come to pay their homage at last at the Footstool of the Throne
of Reason, and acknowledg, tho they won't speak out (but their Conduct
is a Language expressive and eloquent enough) That Reason, speaking to
us by the Axioms of natural Light, or metaphysical Truths, is the supreme
Tribunal, and final Judg without Appeal of whatever's propos'd to the human Mind. Let it ne'er then be pretended more, that Theology is the

36. Valerianus Magnus, *Judicium de catholicorum regula credendi* (Prague, 1641).

Queen, and Philosophy the Handmaid; for the Divines themselves <47> by their Conduct confess, that of the two they look on the latter as the Sovereign Mistress: and from hence proceed all those Efforts and Tortures of Wit and Invention, to avoid the Charge of running counter to strict Demonstration. Rather than expose themselves to such a Scandal, they'l shift the very Principles of Philosophy, discredit this or that System, according as they find their Account in it; by all these Proceedings plainly recognizing the Supremacy of Philosophy, and the indispensable Obligation they are under of making their court to it; they'd ne'er be at all this Pains to cultivate its good Graces, and keep parallel with its Laws, were they not of Opinion, that whatever Doctrine is not vouch'd, as I may say, confirm'd and register'd in the supreme Court of Reason and natural Light, stands on a very tottering and crazy Foundation.

If we inquire into the true reason hereof, 'tis this, that there being a distinct and spritely Light which enlightens all Men the moment they open the Eyes of their Attention, and which irresistibly convinces 'em of its Truth; we must conclude, it's God himself, the essential Truth, who then most immediately illuminates 'em, and makes 'em perceive in his own Essence the Ideas of those eternal Truths contain'd in the first Principles of Reason, or in the common Notions of Metaphysicks. Now why shou'd he act thus with regard to these particular Truths; why reveal 'em at all times, in all Ages, and to all Nations of the Earth, provided they give but the least Attention, and without leaving 'em the liberty of suspending their Judgment: why I say, shou'd he thus deal with Mankind, but to give him a standing Rule <48> and Criterion for judging on all the Variety of other Objects, which are continually presenting, partly false, partly true, sometimes in a very obscure and confus'd, sometimes in a more clear and distinct manner? God, who foresaw that the Laws of the Union of the Soul and Body, wou'd not permit the special Union of the Soul with the Divine Essence (an Union which appears real to thinking and attentive Minds, tho perhaps not distinctly conceiv'd) to communicate all sorts of Truths with the clearest Evidence, and be a thorow Preservative against Error, was pleas'd to provide her an Expedient for infallibly distinguishing Truth from Falshood; and this Expedient is no other than the Light of Nature, or the general Principles of Metaphysicks, by which, if we examine the particular

Doctrines occurring in moral Treatises, or deliver'd by our Teachers, we shall find, as by a Standard and original Rule, which are current and which counterfeit. Whence it follows, that we can never be assur'd of the truth of any thing farther than as agreable to that primitive and universal Light, which God diffuses in the Souls of Men, and which infallibly and irresistibly draws on their Assent the moment they lend their Attention. By this primitive and metaphysical Light we have discover'd the rightful Sense of infinite Passages of Scripture, which taken in the literal and popular Meaning of the Words, had led us into the lowest Conceptions imaginable of the Deity.

Once more I say, Heavens forbid I shou'd have a thought of straining this Principle to such a degree as the *Socinians* do: yet I can't think, whatever Limitations it may admit with respect to <49> speculative Truths, that it ought or can have any with regard to those practical and universal Principles which concern Manners; my meaning is, that all moral Laws, without exception, ought to be regulated by that natural Idea of Equity, which, as well as metaphysical Light, *enlightens every Man coming into the World.* But as Passion and Prejudice do but too often obscure the Ideas of natural Equity, I shou'd advise all who have a mind effectually to retrieve 'em, to consider these Ideas in the general, and as abstracted from all private Interest, and from the Customs of their Country. For a fond and deeply-rooted Passion may possibly happen to persuade a Man, that an Action, which he dotes on as profitable and pleasant, is very agreeable to the Dictates of right Reason: The Power of Custom, and a turn given to the Understanding in the earliest Infancy, may happen to represent an Action as honest and seemly, which in it self is quite otherwise. To surmount both these Obstacles therefore, I cou'd advise whoever aims at preserving this natural Light, with respect to Morality, pure and unadulterate, to raise his Contemplations above the reach of private Interest, or the Custom of his Country, and to examine in general, *Whether this or that Practice be just in it self; and whether, might the Question now be put for introducing it in a Country where it never was in vogue, and where it were left to our choice to admit or reject it; whether, I say, we shou'd find upon a sober Inquiry, that it's reasonable enough to merit our Suffrage and Approbation?* I fancy an Abstraction of this kind might effectually disperse a great many Mists which swim between the Eyes of our

Understanding, and that <50> primitive universal Ray of Light which flows from the Divinity, discovering the general Principles of Equity to all Mankind, and being a standing Test of all Precepts, and particular Laws concerning Manners; not excepting even those which God has afterwards reveal'd in an extraordinary way, either by speaking immediately to Men, or by sending 'em inspir'd Prophets to declare his Will.

I am verily persuaded, that Almighty God, before ever he spoke by an external Voice to *Adam,* to make him sensible of his Duty, spoke to him inwardly in his Conscience, by giving him the vast and immense Idea of a Being sovereignly perfect, and printing on his Mind the eternal Laws of Just and Honest; so that *Adam* thought himself oblig'd to obey his Maker, not so much because of a certain Prohibition outwardly striking upon his Organs of Sense, as because that inward Light which enlighten'd his Conscience e'er God had utter'd himself, continually presented the Idea of his Duty, and of his Dependance on the Sovereign Being: Consequently it may be truly affirm'd, with regard even to *Adam,* that the reveal'd Truth was subordinate to the natural Light in him, and from thence was to receive its Sanction and Seal, its statutable Virtue, and Right to oblige as Law. And by the way, 'tis very probable, that had not the confus'd Sensations of Pleasure, excited in the Soul of our first Parent upon proposing the forbidden Fruit, drown'd the eternal Ideas of natural Equity (which must ever happen by reason of that essential Limitedness in created Spirits, rendring 'em incapable of immaterial Speculations, and of the lively and hurrying Sen-<51>sations of Pleasure at one and the same time). It is, I say, very probable he had never transgrest the Law of God; which ought to be a continual Warning to us, never to turn away our Eyes from that natural Light, let who will make Propositions to us of doing this thing or that with regard to Morality.

Shou'd a Casuist therefore come and inform us, he finds from the Scriptures, that 'tis a good and a holy Practice to curse our Enemys, and those who persecute the faithful; let's forthwith turn our Eyes on natural Religion, strengthen'd and perfected by the Gospel, and we shall see by the bright shining of this interior Truth, which speaks to our Spirits without the Sound of Words, but which speaks most intelligibly to those who give Attention; we shall see, I say, that the pretended Scripture of this Casuist is only a bilious Vapor from his own Temperament and Constitution. In a word, 'twill afford us an Answer to the Example which the Psalmist furnishes him, to wit, that a particular Case where God interposes by a special Providence, is by no means the Light by which we must walk, and derogates not from the positive Command propos'd universally to all Mankind in the Gospel, of being meek and lowly in heart, and praying for those who persecute us; much less from that natural and eternal Law which discovers to all Men the Ideas of Honest, and which discover'd to so many Heathens, that 'twas a glorious part, and highly becoming the Dignity of human Nature, to forgive those who have offended us, and to return 'em Good for Evil. <52>

But that which is highly probable with regard to *Adam* in a state of Innocence, to wit, his discovering the Justice of God's verbal Prohibition, by comparing it with his previous Idea of the Supreme Being, was become indispensably necessary after his Fall: for having experienc'd, that there were two kinds of Agents, which concern'd themselves in directing him what to do, 'twas absolutely necessary he shou'd have a Rule to judg by, for fear of confounding what God shou'd outwardly reveal to him, with the Suggestions or Inticements of the Devil disguis'd under the fairest Appearances. And this Rule cou'd be nothing else than natural Light, than the Conscience of Right and Wrong imprinted on the Souls of all Men; in a word, than that universal Reason which enlightens Spirits, and which is never wanting to those who attentively consult it, especially in those lucid Intervals when bodily Objects possess not the whole Capacity of the Soul, either by Images of their own, or by the Passions they excite in the Heart.

All the Dreams of old, all the Visions of the Patriarchs, all Discourses which strike the Sense as utter'd by God, all Appearances of Angels, all Miracles, every thing in general must have pass'd the Test of natural Light; otherwise how cou'd it appear, whether they proceeded from that evil Principle which had formerly seduc'd *Adam,* or from the great Creator of Heaven and Earth? 'Twas necessary, that God shou'd mark whatever came from him with some certain Character, bearing a Conformity with that interior Light which communicates it self immediately to all Spirits, or which at least shou'd not ap-<53>pear repugnant to it; and this once ascertain'd, all the particular Laws of a *Moses* suppose, or any other Prophet, were entertain'd with Pleasure, and as coming from God, altho they might have ordain'd things indifferent in their own nature.

Moses himself, we know, enjoin'd the *Israelites* on the part of God, not to believe every Worker of Miracles, nor every Prophet; but examine his Doctrines, and receive or reject 'em according as they were consonant or contrary to the Law which was given by God. There was this difference then between the Jews after the days of *Moses* and the antient Patriarchs, that these were oblig'd to compare the Revelations made to them with natural Light alone, those with the Light of Nature, and with the positive Law. For this positive Law, once vouch'd by the natural Light, acquir'd the Quality of a Rule and *Criterion,* in the same manner, as a Proposition in Geometry once demonstrated from incontestable Principles, becomes it self a Principle with regard to other Propositions. Now as there are certain Propositions, which one wou'd be easily inclin'd to admit, were they not attended with harsh and pernicious Consequences, but which are rejected with horror as soon as these Consequences appear; so that instead of saying, *These Consequences are true because they arise from a true Principle; This Principle,* say we, *is false, because such false Consequences follow from it:* So there are those, who without reluctance wou'd believe, that some things might have bin reveal'd by God, did they not consider the Consequences of 'em; but when they see what these things lead to, they conclude, they are not from God: and this Argument *a posteriori* <54> for them has the value of the strictest Demonstration.

Thus about the beginning of the *Saracen* Empire several Jews renounc'd their Religion, and dedicated themselves to the Pagan Philosophy,[37] pretending they had discover'd in the ceremonial Law of *Moses* a world of unprofitable or absurd Precepts, which they perceiv'd not to be founded on any solid Reasons of their Institution or Prohibition, and thence concluding, that such a Law cou'd not be given by God. Their Consequence without doubt was fairly drawn, but they suppos'd amiss: They had not consider'd the incontestable Proofs which God himself had given of *Moses*'s Divine Mission, Proofs which will bear the strictest Trial at the Bar of

---

37. William of Paris, *De legibus.* [Author's note in the French edition. Guilielmi Alverni *Opera omnia* (Paris, 1674), vol. 1, p. 24b.]

the pure and living Ideas of natural Metaphysicks, in virtue of which each particular Law of *Moses* implicitly carrys a good Reason with it. Besides, they had not Strength enough or Compass of Judgment, to comprehend the drift of the ceremonial Laws, which, with regard to the Character of the Jewish Nation, and their Proneness to Idolatry, or as they were Figures and Types of the Gospel, were all founded on solid Reasons. Thus they were in an Error as to the point of Fact; and tho the Consequence follow'd justly and necessarily from their false Principle, they were wrong nevertheless. But by this example we see of what importance it is, that natural Light shou'd find nothing absurd in any thing propos'd as Revelation; for that which might otherwise appear most certainly reveal'd, will cease to appear so, when once found repugnant to that primitive, universal, and mother <55> Rule of judging, and of discerning Truth from Falshood, Good from Evil.

Every Philosophical attentive Mind clearly conceives, that this lively and distinct Light which waits on us at all Seasons, and in all Places, and which shews us, *That the whole is greater than its part, that 'tis honest to be grateful to Benefactors, not to do to others what we wou'd not have done to our selves, to keep our Word, and to act by Conscience;* he conceives, I say, very clearly, that this Light comes forth from God, and that this is natural Revelation: How then can he imagine, that God shou'd afterwards contradict himself, and blow hot and cold, by speaking to us outwardly himself, or sending his Messengers to teach us things directly repugnant to the common Notions of Reason? An *Epicurean* Philosopher reasons very justly, tho he applies his Principles badly, when he says, that since our Senses are the first Rule of Knowledg, and the original Inlet to Truth, it cannot be suppos'd they are subject to Error.[38] He's wrong in making the Report of the Senses the Rule and Touchstone of Truth; but this once suppos'd, he's in the right to conclude, they ought to be the Judges of our Controversys, and decide in all our Doubts. If therefore the natural and metaphysical Light, if the general Principles of Sciences; if those primitive Ideas, which carry their own Conviction with 'em, have bin afforded us as a means to judg rightly upon

---

38. Lucretius, book 4. [Author's note in the French edition. Lucretius, *De rerum natura*, IV, 469–521.]

things, and to serve as a Rule for our Decisions, they must of necessity be the Sovereign Judg, and we must submit to their Decisions in all Differences about obscure points of Knowledg: so that shou'd it enter into any one's head to maintain, that <56> God has reveal'd a moral Precept directly contrary to the first Principles, we must deny it, and maintain in opposition to him, that he mistakes the Sense, and that 'tis much more reasonable to reject the Authority of his Criticisms and Grammar, than that of Reason. If we don't fix here, farewel all Faith, according to the Remark of the good Father *Valerian:** *If any one will pretend,* says he, *that we must captivate our Understanding to the Obedience of Faith, so far as to call in question, or even to believe that Rule of judging which Nature has afforded us, false in some Instances; I affirm, he does by this very Attempt necessarily subvert the Faith, because it is absolutely impossible to believe, upon any Credit whatsoever, without a previous reasoning, which concludes, that the Person on whose Testimony we do believe, is neither deceiv'd himself nor deceives: which kind of reasoning, we see, is of no force, unless we admit that natural Rule of judging which has bin hitherto explain'd.*

And here we shall find all the pompous Discourses of Roman Catholicks against the Way of Reason, and for the Authority of the Church, terminate in the end. Without thinking on't, they only take a larger Circuit to come home at last to the very same point, which others make by a strait Course. These say plainly, and without going about the Bush, that we must keep to that Sense which appears to us the justest: But they tell us, we must have a care of that, because our own Lights may possibly deceive, and Reason is all Darkness and Illusion; we must therefore rest in the Judgment of the Church. What is this but coming a round way about to our own Rea-<57>son? For he who prefers the Judgment of the Church to his private Judgment, must not he do this in virtue of this reasoning, *The Church has greater Lights than I, she's therefore more to be believ'd than I?*

Thus we see every one's determin'd by his own private Lights; if he believe any thing as reveal'd, it's because his good Sense, his natural Light, and his Reason inform him, that the Proofs of its Revelation are sufficient. But what will become of us, if every private Person must distrust his Reason

* Ubi supra. [See p. 67.]

as a dark and illusive Principle? Must not he in this Case distrust it, even when he says, *The Church has greater Lights than I, she's therefore more to be believ'd than I?* Must not he be afraid, that his Reason is deceiv'd here, both as to the Principle and as to the Consequence he draws from it? What will become of this reasoning too? *All that God says is true; he tells us by* Moses, *that he created the first Man, therefore this is true.* If we had not a natural Light afforded us, as a sure and infallible Rule for judging upon every thing that can fall under Debate, not excepting even this Question, *Whether such or such a thing is contain'd in Scripture;* might not we have ground to doubt of the Major[39] of this Argument before us, and consequently of the Conclusion? As this wou'd therefore introduce the most fearful Confusion, the most execrable Pyrrhonism imaginable, we must of necessity stand by this Principle, *That all particular Doctrines, whether advanc'd as contain'd in Scripture, or propos'd in any other way, are false, if repugnant to the clear and distinct Notions of natural Light, especially if they relate to Morality.* <58>

❧ CHAPTER II ❧

First Argument against the literal Sense of the Words, Compel 'em to come in, *drawn from its Repugnancy to the distinctest Ideas of natural Light.*

Having dispatch'd these Preliminary Remarks, which I thought fit to present my Reader, in a way of Universality; I come now to the particular Subject, and special Matter of my *Commentary,* on the Words of the Parable, *Compel 'em to come in:* and thus I reason.

The literal Sense of these Words is repugnant to the purest and most distinct Ideas of natural Reason.

It's therefore false.

The Business now is only to prove the *Antecedent;* for I presume, the Consequence[40] is sufficiently demonstrated in the foregoing Chapter. I say then,

---

39. See Appendixes, "Bayle's Use of Logic," p. 580 ("syllogism").
40. Ibid. ("consequence," "antecedent").

I. That by the purest and most distinct Ideas of Reason, we find there is a Being sovereignly perfect, who rules over all things, who ought to be ador'd by Mankind, who approves certain Actions, and rewards 'em, and who disapproves and punishes others.

II. By the same way we understand, that the principal Adoration due to this supreme Being, consists in the Acts of the Mind; for if we conceive, that an earthly King wou'd not look on the falling down of a Statue in his Presence, either by chance, or by a violent Blast of Wind, as a homage to his Person, or on the Figure of Pup-<59>pets plac'd before him in a kneeling posture; by a much stronger reason ought we to believe, that God, who judges of all things by their real Worth, receives not as an Act of Worship and Submission what's only perform'd to him in outward shew. We must grant then, that all external Acts of Religion, all our costliest Sacrifices, all our Expenses in erecting Temples and Altars, are approv'd by God only in proportion to the internal Acts of the Mind from whence they proceed.

III. Hence it plainly follows, that the Essence of Religion consists in the Judgments which our Understanding forms of God, and in those Motions of Reverence, of Fear and of Love, which the Will feels for him; insomuch that it's possible a Man may fulfil his Duty towards God by this part alone, without the Exercise of any outward Act. But as Cases of this kind are rarely found, we shall chuse to say, that the inward Disposition, in which consists the Essence of Religion, is brought forth into outward Act by bodily Humiliations, and by sensible Expressions discovering that Honor which the Spirit pays to the Majesty of God. However it be, 'tis still true, that those Expressions in a Person void of all Feelings for God; I mean, who has neither the sutable Judgments, nor Motions of the Will with regard to God; are no more an Honoring or Adoration of God, than the Fall of a Statue, by a chance puff of Wind, is an Act of Homage from the Statue.

IV. It's evident then, that the only reasonable way of inspiring Religion, is by producing in the Soul certain Judgments with relation to God, <60> and certain Motions of the Will. Now as Threats, Jails, Fines, Banishment, Cudgelling, Torturing, and in general whatever is comprehended under the literal signification of *Compelling,* are incapable of forming in the Soul those Judgments of the Will in relation to God, which constitute the Essence of Religion; it's evident that this is a mistaken way of establishing a Religion, and consequently that JESUS CHRIST has not enjoin'd it.

I don't deny but the ways of Constraint, over and above the outward Movements of the Body, which are the ordinary Signs of inward Religion, produce also in the Soul certain Judgments, and certain Motions of the Will: yet these same have no relation to God; they only regard the Authors of the Constraint. The Partys judg of 'em, that they are a sort of Men much to be dreaded, and they dread 'em indeed; but they who before were void of right Conceptions of the Divinity, and of that Reverence, and Love, and Fear, which are due to the supreme Being, acquire neither these Conceptions, nor these Motions of the Will, by the practice of the outward Signs of Religion, which the Methods of Constraint had extorted. They who before had form'd certain Judgments of God, and who believ'd that he ought to be worship'd only in one certain manner, opposite to that in favor of which the Violences are exercis'd; change no more than the others, as to their inward State towards God: Their new Sentiments do all terminate in a Dread of their Persecutors, and in a Desire of securing those temporal Goods, which they threaten to rob 'em of. Thus these Compulsions <61> do nothing for God: for as to the inward Acts they produce, these are by no means refer'd to him; and as for the outward Acts, 'tis manifest they can't be consider'd as belonging to God, farther than as attended by those inward Dispositions of the Soul, wherein consists the Essence of Religion: Which has led me to sum up the whole Proof.

The Nature of Religion is, its being a certain Persuasion in the Soul with regard to God, which in the Will produces that Love, and Fear, and Reverence, which this supreme Being justly deserves, and in the Members of the Body Signs sutable to this Persuasion and this Disposition of the Will: insomuch that if these outward Signs exist without that interior State of the Soul which answers to 'em, or with such an inward State as is contrary to 'em; they are Acts of Hypocrisy and Falshood, or Impiety and Revolt against Conscience.

If therefore we wou'd act according to the nature of things, or according to that Order which right Reason, and the sovereign Reason of God himself does consult; we shou'd never make use of means for the propagating a Religion, which, incapable on one side of informing the Understanding, or imprinting the Love and Fear of God on the Heart; is most capable, on the other, of producing in the Members of the Body those external Acts, which are not infallible Indications of a religious Disposition of Soul, and which may be Signs directly opposite to the true inward Disposition.

Now so it is, that Violence is incapable on one hand of convincing the Judgment, or of <62> imprinting in the Heart the Fear or the Love of God; and most capable, on the other, of producing in our Members some outward Signs void of all inward Sincerity, or Signs perhaps of an interior Disposition most opposite to that which we really are in: that's to say, external Acts which are Hypocrisy and Imposture, or a downright Revolt against Conscience.

'Tis notoriously then contrary to good Sense, to the Light of Nature, to the common Principles of Reason; in a word, to that primitive original Rule of distinguishing Truth from Falshood, Good from Evil; to exercise Violence for the inspiring a Religion into those who profess it not.

As the clear and distinct Ideas therefore we have of the Natures of certain things, convince us irresistibly, that God cou'd not make any Revelation repugnant to these things (for example, we are most thorowly assur'd, there cou'd be no such divine Revelation, as, That the Whole is less than its Part; That it's honest to prefer Vice to Virtue; That one shou'd value his Dog more than his Parents, more than his Friends, or his Country; That to go by Sea from one Country to another, one must ride full-speed on a Post-horse; That to prepare the Ground for a plentiful Crop, the best way is never to turn it) it is evident that God has not commanded us in his Word to cudgel Men into a Religion, or use any other ways of Violence to make 'em embrace the Gospel; and therefore if we meet with any Passage in the Gospel which enjoins Compulsion, we must take it for granted, that it's meant in a metaphorical, <63> and not in a literal Sense: just as if meeting with a Passage in the Scripture which commanded us to be very well skill'd in Languages, and in all other Facultys, without studying, we shou'd conclude that it ought to be understood in a Figure; We shou'd rather believe that the Passage was corrupted, or that we did not understand all the Senses of the Terms in the Original, or that 'twas a Mystery which concern'd not us, but another sort of Men perhaps which were to arise hereafter, and which shou'd not be made just as we are; or in short, that 'twas a Precept deliver'd after the manner of the Oriental Nations in Emblems, or under symbolical and enigmatical Images: We shou'd believe, I say, any thing of this kind, rather than persuade our selves that God, wise as he is, shou'd enjoin his Creatures of the Human kind, in a strict and literal sense, to be profoundly learned without studying.

The only thing to be alledg'd against what I offer, is this: They don't pretend that Violence shou'd be exercis'd, as a direct and immediate means of establishing a Religion, but as a mediate and indirect means. That is, They agree with me that the proper and natural way of propagating Religion, is enlightning the Mind by sound Instructions, and purifying the Heart by inspiring it with a Love of God; but that to put this means in practice, it is sometimes necessary to force People, because without some degree of Violence they'l neither apply to be instructed, nor endeavor to deliver themselves from their Prejudices; that thus Constraint is <64> only made use of to remove Obstacles to Instruction: and these once remov'd, they employ the proper Methods, they re-enter into order, they instruct, they proceed by that primitive Light which I preach up as the sovereign Tribunal, or rather as the Commissary General, whose business it is to pass in review all Revelations, and discard those which want its Livery.

I shall adjourn the Confutation of this Exception to another place: 'Tis an ingenious Illusion, and a very handsom *Chicane;* but I promise my self to confute it so fully, that for the future it shall be made over to the Underspur-leathers, to those Missionarys of the Village, who never blush to produce the same Objections over and over, without taking the least notice of the Answers, which have ruin'd 'em to all intents and purposes.

∞ CHAPTER III ∞

Second Argument against the Literal Sense, drawn from its Opposition to the Spirit of the Gospel.

Before I propose my second Argument, I must desire my Reader to remember what I had laid down in the first Chapter;[41] *That a positive Law, once vouch'd by natural Light, acquires the Force of a Rule or Criterion, in the same manner as a Proposition in Geometry, demonstrated by incontestable Principles, becomes it self a Principle with regard to other Propositions.* The reason of my re-<65>peating this Remark is, that I am in this Chapter about to prove the Falshood of the literal Sense of the words, *Compel 'em to come in,* by shewing that it is contrary to the whole Tenor and Spirit of the Gospel. Were I to write a Commentary merely as a Divine, I shou'd not need to take the Argument higher; I shou'd o' course suppose, that the Gospel is the first Rule of Manners, and that deviating from the Gospel-Morality is, without further proof, the being in a state of Iniquity: but writing as a Philosopher, I'm oblig'd to go back to the original and mother Rule, to wit, Reason or natural Light. I say then, that the Gospel being a Rule which has been verified by the purest Ideas of Reason, which are the primary and original Rule of all Truth and Rectitude; to sin against this Gospel, is sinning against the primary Rule it self, or which is the same thing, against that internal still Revelation, by which God discovers to all Men the very first Principles. I add this Consideration too, That the Gospel having more fully explain'd all the Dutys of Morality, and having carry'd the Idea of Honest farther than God had originally reveal'd by natural Religion, it follows, that every Action in a Christian, which is not agreeable to the Gospel, is more unjust and more enormous, than if simply contrary to Reason; for the more any Rule of Justice or Principle of Manners is open'd, explain'd, and enlarg'd, the more inexcusable is the Transgression. So that if Constraint in matters of Religion be found contrary to the Spirit of the Gospel, this will be a second Argument more forcible than the first, that this Con-

41. See above, p. 72.

straint is unlawful, and opposite to the pri-<66>mary and original Rule of Equity and Reason.

But not to leave the least Rub in our way, let's bestow one word or two upon a difficulty which here presents. They'l tell me that, by the Principle laid down in the first Chapter, the Gospel cou'd ne'er have bin receiv'd as a Divine Revelation; because if we compare its Precepts by my original Rule, they'l not be found agreeable to it: for nothing is more agreeable to natural Light than defending one's self when assaulted, than revenging an Injury, than caring for the Body, &c. and yet nothing more opposite to the Gospel. Might we therefore conclude, that a Doctrine, pretended to be given from Heaven, was not divine, unless conformable to natural Light, the primary, perpetual, and universal Revelation of the Divinity to Mankind; we must reject the Doctrine of JESUS CHRIST as false, and the Gospel had not now bin a second standing Rule collated with the Original: and consequently, I shou'd prove nothing in my way, by proving that Compulsion is opposite to the Gospel-Morality.

I answer, that all the moral Precepts of the Gospel are such, as when weigh'd in the ballance of natural Religion, will certainly be acknowledg'd Sterling: And JESUS CHRIST having, over and above this, wrought a vast number of Miracles, so that only the Repugnancy of his Doctrine to some evident Truths of natural Revelation, cou'd give the least ground for doubting the Divinity of his Mission; we may rest intirely satisfy'd as to this point. The Miracles he wrought were in confirmation of a Doctrine, which, far from being opposite to the first No-<67>tices of Reason, and to the purest Principles of natural Equity, did really but perfect 'em, enlarge, unfold, and explain 'em; he spoke then on the part of God. Does not natural Light distinctly inform every Soul which attentively consults it, that God is just, that he loves Virtue, disapproves Vice, merits our utmost Regard and Obedience; That he's the Source of our Felicity, and that 'tis to him we ought to apply our selves for every thing needful for us? Does not this Light inform all, who contemplate it duly, and who raise themselves above the sable Clouds with which the Passions and earthy Vapor of the Body overcast the Understanding, that 'tis honest and praise-worthy to forgive Enemys, to moderate our Resentments, and subdue our Passions? Whence shou'd all those shining Maxims flow, with which the Writings of Heathens abound, but from a natural Revelation of these things, communicated without respect of Persons to all Mankind? This being the case, 'twas easy to perceive that nothing cou'd be more reasonable, or more agreeable to Order, than enjoining Meekness of Heart, Forgiveness of Injurys, Mortification, and Charity. For our Reason clearly comprehending that God is the sovereign Good, relishes and approves those Maxims which unite us to him. Now nothing is more fitted to unite us to God than a Contempt of this World, and the Mortification of the Passions. Reason then finds the Gospel-Morality agreeable in every Instance to Order: And this Morality, far from inclining it to doubt whether the Miracles of JESUS CHRIST manifested his Divinity, becomes on the contrary a thorow Confirmation of <68> it. We can't say so much of the Morality they claim to find in the words, *Compel 'em to come in:* For did, they import, *Employ the Whip, Prisons, Tortures, to force those into the Christian Religion, who won't freely come in;* our Reason, our natural Religion might have ground to entertain the shreudest Suspicions, and look at JESUS CHRIST as an Emissary of Satan, coming under the fairest Appearances of a severe and spiritualiz'd Morality, and supported by mighty Prodigys, to infuse the deadliest Poison into the Hearts of Men, and to render the World a wild and never-changing Scene of Blood, and of the most execrable Tragedy. But let's propose this second Argument in form.

Every Interpretation of Scripture, repugnant to the Spirit of the Gospel, must needs be false.

The literal Sense of the words, *Compel 'em to come in,* is directly repugnant to the Spirit of the Gospel.

The literal Sense therefore of these words must needs be false.

I may reasonably presume that the Major in this Argument needs no farther Proof: So I am only to prove the Minor.[42]

To this end I shall first observe, That the Excellency of the Gospel above the Law of *Moses* consists in this among other things, that it spiritualizes Man's Nature, that it treats him more as a reasonable Creature, as arriv'd at a Maturity of Understanding, and no longer as a Child who stood in need of being amus'd by Shew and Ceremony, and outward Splendor, and

---

42. See Appendixes, "Bayle's Use of Logic," p. 580 ("syllogism").

wheedled from the Pagan Idolatry. From hence it follows, that the Gospel <69> most peculiarly requires we shou'd embrace it from a Principle of Reason; that its first and principal purpose is to enlighten the Understanding by its Truths, and afterwards attract our Zeal and Esteem; that it's far from the Mind of the Gospel, that either the Fear of Men, or the Apprehension of temporal Misery, shou'd engage us to the outward Profession of it, when neither the Heart is touch'd, nor the Reason persuaded. It is not the mind of the Gospel then, that we shou'd force any one; this were treating Man as a Slave, and applying him like a brute Instrument, or mere Machine: As sometimes in handicraft servile Operations, where it's no matter whether he work with a good will or no, provided he works; whereas, in the business of Religion, so far is it from being perform'd, when gone about with an ill will, that it were infinitely better to stand idle than to work by Force. Here the Heart must be in exercise, with a thorow Knowledg of the Cause; and the more any Religion requires the Heart, the Good-will, a Persuasion thorowly enlighten'd, and a reasonable Service, as the Gospel does, the farther it shou'd be from any kind of Constraint.

I observe in the second place, that the principal Character of JESUS CHRIST, and, if I may say it, the reigning Qualitys of his Soul, were Humility, Meekness, and Patience: *Learn of me,* says he to his Disciples, *for I am meek and lowly in heart.* He's compar'd to a Lamb led to the slaughter, which opens not its mouth: *Blessed,* says he, *are the Meek, and the Peacemakers, and the Merciful. When he was revil'd, he revil'd not again, but committed himself to him who judgeth* <70> *right.* He'l have us bless those who curse us, and pray for those who persecute us; and far from commanding his Followers to persecute Infidels, he won't allow 'em to oppose their Persecutions, otherwise than by Flight: *If they persecute you,* says he, *in one City, fly to another.* He does not bid 'em stir up the People against the Magistrates, call to their aid the Citys which are in their interest, lay formal siege to that which had persecuted 'em, and compel 'em to believe: No, *Go forth from thence,* says he, *and remove to another place.* He does indeed, in another place, order 'em to protest in the Streets against those who should not hear 'em; but this is the utmost he allows, and after that commands 'em to depart. He likens himself to a Shepherd who goes before his Sheep; *And they follow him, for they know his Voice.* These words are very emphatical: He does not say that he drives the Flock before him with Rod or Whip, as forcing 'em into grounds against their will; no, he goes before 'em, and *they follow him, because they know his Voice:* which signifies his leaving 'em at full liberty to follow, if they know him, or go astray, if they know him not; and his accepting no other than a voluntary Obedience, preceded by and founded upon Knowledg.

He opposes his own Mission to that of Thieves and Robbers, who break into the Fold, to carry off the Sheep by force which don't belong to 'em, and which know not their Voice. When he sees himself forsaken by the Multitude, he does not arm those Legions of Angels, which were always as it were in his pay, nor send 'em in pursuit of the Deserters, to bring 'em back <71> by force: far from it, he asks his very Apostles, who had not yet forsaken him, whether they had not a mind to do like the rest; *And will ye also go away?* to let 'em, as 'twere, understand that he was not for keeping any of 'em in his service against their inclination. When he ascends into Heaven, he commands his Apostles to go and convert all Nations; but then 'tis only by Teaching and by Baptizing: his Apostles follow'd the example of his Meekness, and they exhort us to be Followers of them and of their Master. One must transcribe almost the whole New Testament, to collect all the Proofs it affords us of that Gentleness and Long-suffering, which constitute the distinguishing and essential Character of the Gospel.

Let's now sum up the Argument thus: The literal Sense of this Gospel-Text, *Compel 'em to come in,* is not only contrary to the Lights of natural Religion, which are the primary and original Rule of Equity, but also to the reigning and essential Spirit of the Gospel it self, and of its Author; for nothing can be more opposite to this Spirit, than Dungeons, Dragoons, Banishment, Pillage, Gallys, Inflictions, and Torture. Therefore this literal Sense is false.

I don't think it possible to imagine any thing more impious, or more injurious to JESUS CHRIST, or more fatal in its Consequences, than his having given Christians a general Precept to make Conversions by Constraint. For besides that a Maxim so opposite to good Sense, to Reason, to the common Principles of Morality, might induce one to believe, that he who vents it speaks not on the part of the same God, <72> who has given another antecedent Revelation, quite different from this, by the Oracles of natural Light; on the part of God, I say, who is incapable of contradicting himself so grosly: Besides all this, what Notion must we form of the Gospel, if we find in it on one hand so many Precepts of Gentleness and Clemency, and on the other a general Order authorizing all the ways of Violence, all the Craft and Cruelty which Hell can inspire? Who cou'd forbear thinking it a very odd medly of contradictory Conceits, and that the Author had not got his Lesson by heart, or did not know his own mind? Or rather, who wou'd not suspect that he knew his Lesson but too well, and that the grand Enemy of Mankind seducing him, had borrow'd his Organs to introduce into the World the fearfullest Deluge of Misery and Desolation; and the better to succeed, had made him play his game under a counterfeit beguiling Moderation, on a sudden to let fly the terrible Sentence of compelling all Nations to profess Christianity? Into such Abysses do the infamous Patrons of the literal Sense plunge themselves; who better deserve the Title of Directors-General of the Slaughter-House and Shambles, than that of Interpreters of Scripture. A certain Father of the Oratory, by name *Amelote,* writing about the Differences of the *Jansenists,* has this Saying,* *That were there in the Question of Fact concerning* Jansenius, *such an Evidence as there is by Sense, or by the first Principles of Reason, they whose Eyes were so far* <73> *enlighten'd might reasonably take umbrage at the Diligence and Faithfulness of the Pope and Bishops, and justly demand an express Revelation from those who wou'd oblige 'em to sacrifice their Opinion, and submit against Knowledg.* And that Evidence which is founded on Sense, or on the first Principles, he calls an *impregnable Post.* From this Principle of his, I make bold to conclude, that the least a Man shou'd do to convince us of the literal Sense of the words, *Compel 'em to come in,* so opposite to the Lights of Reason and of the Gospel, wou'd be to prove, by a new and most evident Revelation, that he interprets this Passage aright. And yet I'm of opinion, that except in some special cases, in which God may dispense with his own Laws, we ought not to give heed to a Revelation of this kind, tho ever so evident and express. My meaning is, that shou'd a Prophet, working Miracles in confirmation of the literal Sense of the Text, draw it into a general Precept, no way limited by any particular Circumstance, as in the Case of *Phineas;*

* *See his Treatise of Human Faith,* p. 1. c. 17. [Not found.]

this very thing wou'd be ground enough to take him, with all his Miracles, for an Impostor. <74>

⚙ CHAPTER IV ⚙

The Third Argument against the Literal Sense, drawn from its cancelling the Differences of Justice and Injustice, and its confounding Vertue and Vice, to the total Dissolution of Society.

But it's amusing the Court, to dwell so long upon Proofs, which are only passably good, when compar'd with what we have to offer: Let's strike home then, and henceforward cut at the very root of the literal Sense of the Parable.

That literal Sense of Scripture is necessarily false, which overturns all Morality, whether Human or Divine; which confounds Vertue and Vice, and thereby opens a door to all kind of Confusion.

Now this is what the literal Sense of the words, *Compel 'em to come in,* must do.

It's therefore necessarily false.

The Major is so evident, that 'twere ridiculous to go about to prove it: let's proceed then to the proof of the Minor, which at first sight looks like a Paradox.

I'm so fair as to allow the Convertists of *France,* that by supposing JESUS CHRIST to have enjoin'd the converting Men by force, they only obey'd the Will of God, in compelling the Reform'd, by quartering of Soldiers, by Prisons, and by other ways of Violence, to turn Catholicks; and consequently, that these Violences <75> were by no means criminal in them, but that they were very righteous doings. Yet I desire to ask 'em one Question, Whether the only Reason which renders these Actions good, is not their being perform'd for the Interest of the Church, and from a design of enlarging the Kingdom of JESUS CHRIST? I don't think they'l deny me this: for shou'd they pretend, that a King so absolute as that of *France* may quarter Soldiers on whom he pleases, allow 'em such and such Libertys, take 'em off where the Party merits this distinction by signing a Formulary;

and therefore that the reason why these Violences are not criminal, is their being lawful for a King in his own Dominions: Shou'd they, I say, pretend to give me this Answer, I think it were no hard matter to weather it.

For I shou'd ask 'em again, Whether, on a supposition that what the King of *France* now does, he did without any other reason, or from any other Motive or View, than just to divert himself by a capricious Exercise of his Power, it had not bin very unjust; and whether God might not most justly have punish'd him for it? I can't conceive there's a Man alive, either Flatterer or stupid enough to tell me, No: It follows then, that a King who vexes a Party of his Subjects at this rate, by giving their Goods to the Spoil, by forcing Children from their Parents, and Wives from their Husbands, by imprisoning some, and cloistering others; by demolishing their Houses, cutting down their Inclosures, and permitting the very Soldiers to abuse and buffet their Hosts; ought to have some other reason for his so doing, besides that of his <76> sovereign Will and good Pleasure: else all the World will condemn it, as an unjust and tyrannical Abuse of the Regal Power.

They'l tell me perhaps, that these Vexations are founded on one Party's refusing to conform to the King's Edicts: Now a King can justly punish such of his Subjects as conform not to his Edicts. But this Answer not only goes upon a false Supposition, to wit, that none were punish'd by quartering, except those who had not obey'd the Royal Edicts (because it's certain this quartering preceded the Revocation of the Edict of *Nants,* or the time at least which this Edict allow'd for the Protestants to instruct themselves) but is likewise too indefinite to be satisfactory. For to render a Punishment just, which is inflicted for Non-compliance with a King's Injunctions, it's necessary these Injunctions be founded on some good reason: else a King might justly punish those of his Subjects who had not blue Eyes, a Roman Nose, and fair Hair, those who lik'd not certain Dishes, who lov'd not Hunting, Musick, Books, *&c.* He might punish 'em, I say, very justly, supposing he had publish'd his Orders before-hand, enjoining 'em to have blue Eyes within such a time, *&c.* and to take pleasure in Books, *&c.* But who sees not, that as these Injunctions are unreasonable, so the Punishment of the Transgressors wou'd be likewise unjust? And therefore to vex Subjects in a way of Justice, it is not sufficient to say in the general they have disobey'd Edicts; but it must be shewn in particular, that they have disobey'd Edicts which were just in themselves, or at <77> least such as cou'd not be disobey'd, but thro an unreasonable and perverse Neglect.

They'l tell me, the Edicts of *Lewis* XIV are all of this kind. I shan't dispute it. But then they'l grant me, that the only Reason which render'd the treating his Subjects of the Reform'd Religion as he did, no Injustice, was his treating 'em so for the advantage of the Church of *Rome,* in his Judgment the only true Church in the World. This we must come to: and everything comes back to this Foundation, to wit, that the Methods in *France* against the Reform'd had bin unjust, if mov'd, not for any advantage of the true Religion, but to make 'em profess, for example, that they were persuaded the Earth turns round, that the Heat we ascribe to Fire is only a Sensation in the Soul, that such a Sauce is better than such a Sauce; but forasmuch as no Violence was exercis'd on the Hereticks, to make 'em acknowledg Truths of this kind, but only those Truths which are reveal'd to Christians, the Treatment they met with was very just, as being agreeable to the Command of JESUS CHRIST.

They'l add, that it's abusing the Terms, to call this Treatment Persecution. Nothing is properly Persecution, but bearing hard on the Faithful. Violences exercis'd on Hereticks, are Acts of Kindness, Equity, Justice, and right Reason. Be it so: Let's agree then, *That what might be unjust, if consider'd as not being done in favor of the true Religion, becomes just by being done for the true Religion.* This Maxim is most evidently contain'd in the words, *Compel 'em to come in,* supposing JESUS CHRIST meant 'em in a literal Sense; for they import, *Smite, scourge, im-*<78>*prison, pillage, slay those who continue obstinate, rob 'em of their Wives and their Children; it's all right, when done in favor of my Cause: In other Circumstances these might be Crimes of the blackest dye; but the Good resulting from 'em to my Church, expiates and sanctifies these Proceedings.* Now this, I say, is the most abominable Doctrine that ever enter'd into the Heart of Man: And I question whether there be Spirits in Hell wicked enough to wish in good earnest, that Mankind shou'd be govern'd by such Maxims. So that to attribute 'em to the eternal Son of God, who came into the World only to bring Salvation, and to teach Men the most holy and most charitable Truths, is offering him the most outragious Affront and Injury imaginable. For,

Consider, I pray, what Horrors and Abominations trail after this exe-crable Morality; since all the Barriers which separate Vertue from Vice, be-ing hereby remov'd, all Actions, be they ever so infamous, must become Acts of Piety and Religion, if tending to the Extinction of Heresy. So that shou'd a Heretick by his good Sense, by his Eloquence, and by his sober Life, confirm others in their Heresy, or persuade some among the Faithful that they are deceiv'd, presently assassinating, poisoning, blasting his Rep-utation by the wickedest Calumnys, and suborning false Witnesses to prove 'em upon him, is all fair play. People may shake their heads, and say, it's hard and unjust; the Answer is ready: *It might be so in other cases; but the Interest of the Church interfering, nothing is more just.* Every one sees, with-out my entring into the hideous Detail, that there's no kind of Crime which does not become <79> an Act of Religion; Judges might conscientiously give the most unjust Decrees against Hereticks; others rob 'em with im-punity, break Faith with 'em in the most important Affairs, force away their Children, stir up false Witnesses against 'em, debauch their Daughters, in hopes the shame of a big Belly might humble 'em into the true Religion: In a word, they might insult and outrage 'em all manner of ways, and Vi-olence and Fraud play by turns, in a prospect of wearying 'em out of their lives, and obliging 'em at last to change Religion; and all this while persuade themselves, that acting from this holy Motive, they committed no Injustice. Can any thing be more horrible!

Nor are they the only Party privileg'd by the Result of this fine Man-agement: all others wou'd think themselves authoriz'd to take the same methods, because each Sect looks on it self as the only true Religion, or at least much the truest; and looking on all others as Enemys to God, or im-perfect at best, imagine they shou'd do great service to Truth by bringing about their Conversion. I shan't in this place examine, whether all have an equal Right, supposing only a sincere Persuasion in all to endeavor the Ex-tirpation of what they believe false: but this at least is plain, that JESUS CHRIST must have foreseen how his Command might prompt all sort of Christians to exercise Violence on those who were out of their own Com-munion, which wou'd be an inexhaustible Source of Iniquity, and an *Iliad* of Miserys to those of the really true. Now it's not to be conceiv'd, but a bare prospect of the many Mischiefs to which his express Command might

<80> give birth, and for which it might be a very plausible Excuse, wou'd have hinder'd him from delivering it, tho he had not bin otherwise abundantly bar'd by the essential and inherent Injustice of Persecution on the score of Religion.

Tho I don't design to enter into a Detail of the abominable Confusions which might spring from hence, that the most unjust Actions become just by their Subserviency to the Extirpation of Error; yet I can't but observe this grand Inconveniency arising from it among others, That Kings and Sovereign Princes cou'd never be safe when their Subjects were of a different Persuasion. Their Subjects wou'd think themselves oblig'd in Conscience to depose and expel 'em, unless they abjur'd their Religion; and still believe it a very justifiable Action: for in fine, say they, the Gospel will have us *Compel to come in;* and accordingly we must compel our King to turn, we must refuse our Obedience till he conforms; and if he obstinately persists, we must depose, and confine him a while to a Cloyster. It may be, the sense of so many temporal Afflictions will incline his Heart to Instruction, and deliver him from his Prejudices: Be that as it will, we shall however promote the Interest of Religion, by dethroning a Prince who's an Enemy to it, and placing one in his room who'l be a Father and Defender. This Circumstance suffices to render Actions Just, which without it wou'd be exceeding Criminal. Let's depose therefore, or even put to Death our heretical King, because, tho an infernal Parricide, when perpetrated from any other Motive, it's yet a good Work if done for the Interest of the true <81> Religion. Thus Sovereigns and Subjects might conscientiously persecute one another by turns; those compel their People of a different Religion by main force to abjure; and these, when they had the Power, do as much for their Prince: each in the mean time religiously obeying the Command of the Son of God. Shou'd not we be mightily oblig'd to JESUS CHRIST for taking our Nature upon him, and submitting to the Death of the Cross for our sakes, if by these three or four words, *Compel to come in,* he had depriv'd us of those small remains of natural Religion, which were sav'd from the Shipwreck of the first Man; if he had confounded the Natures of Vertue and Vice, and destroy'd the Boundarys which divide the two States, by making Murder, and Robbery, and Felony, and Tyranny, and Rebellion, and Calumny, and Perjury, and all Crimes generally, when practis'd against a heterodox Party, lose the Character of Evil, and become Vertues of a most necessary Obligation? The drift of which must be the dissolving all civil Societys, and consigning Men to Dens and Caves of the Earth, for fear of meeting with any of their own kind, the most dangerous Beasts in the Forest.

What's very absurd in a great many Roman Catholicks, and particularly the *French,* is their insisting on one hand, that JESUS CHRIST has enjoin'd Constraint, and yet denying, that this Command extends to Kings, or that the Church has any Right to depose 'em.[43] This is in the last degree pitiful. They are satisfy'd, that Kings, by virtue of this Passage, are authoriz'd by God to destroy their heretical Subjects, imprison, dragoon, hang, and burn 'em; but they won't allow, that the same Passage gives <82> Subjects a right, whenever the Pope or a General Council shall judg it a proper Season, to drive out an heretical King, and set up an orthodox Person in his room. Where's the sense of this? Wou'd they have JESUS CHRIST enjoin Constraint in all, excepting the single Case, where it may be of the greatest Advantage to the Church, by the Destruction of just one Man? For who sees not, that the Downfal of one heretical bigoted Monarch may prevent more Mischiefs to the opposite Religion, than the Ruin of a hundred thousand Peasants or Mechanicks? So that granting the words, *Compel 'em to come in,* did signify in general, strip, smite, imprison, hang, break upon the Wheel, till no one dare boggle at signing; I can't see the reason of laughing at *Suarez, Becan,*[44] and a great many more, for saying, that in the words, *Feed my Sheep,* there's a Power imply'd of treating heretical Kings as Shepherds do Wolves, which they are to destroy, *Omni modo quo possunt,*[45] to wit, the shortest way.

They'l tell me, God expresly declares, that *'tis by him Kings reign;* and that resisting their Ordinances is resisting the Ordinance of God. And what

---

43. This was the opinion of the Gallicans. See Appendixes, p. 590, "Church and State."

44. Francisco Suarez, S.J., possibly: *Defensio fidei Catholicae et apostolicae adversus Anglicanae sectae errors* (Defence of the Catholic and apostolic faith against the errors of the Anglican sect), 1613. Martin Becan, S.J., possibly: *Manuale Controversiarum* (Manual of controversies), 1623. The Jesuits were "ultramontanes."

45. "In whatever way they can."

then? Is it not as plain, that Murder, Calumny, Robbery, and Perjury, are expresly forbidden by God? Yet, if notwithstanding the Prohibition, these Actions become righteous, when perform'd for the Good of the Church; mayn't we say the same of every other prohibited Action, not excepting even that of deposing Kings? And the truth is, these very Men, who express such an Abhorrence of deposing Principles, when their Kings are orthodox, contradict themselves in practice, when they happen to be <83> otherwise, as was seen with a witness in *France,* in the days of the League. So natural a Consequence is it of the literal Sense that I refute, and so necessary not to spare even Crown'd Heads, or any thing else upon Earth, when put into the Ballance with the Prosperity of the Church.

I wish my Readers wou'd weigh these Reasons a little; and I assure my self they'd be convinc'd, that a Command, which (as the World is made) must naturally be attended with such a horrible train of Impietys, and so total an Extinction of the first Principles of Equity, which are the eternal and immutable Rule, cou'd never proceed from the Mouth of him who is the essential Truth. That literal Sense therefore, which I contend against, is utterly false.

∞ CHAPTER V ∞

The Fourth Argument against the literal Sense, drawn from its giving Infidels a very plausible and very reasonable Pretence for not admitting Christians into their Dominions, and for dislodging 'em wherever they are settl'd among 'em.

I said I did not design to enter into a Detail of the mischievous Consequences which might follow from the Principle I confute; yet upon second thoughts I find it necessary to lay open a few of 'em, the better to discover the Horribleness and strange Enormity of the Command so <84> injuriously ascrib'd to the Son of God. 'Twere wronging the Cause of Truth wholly to decline this; I shall therefore touch upon certain Heads, which to me appear the most considerable. And thus I argue:

That literal Sense of Scripture which gives Infidels a just and reasonable ground for denying the Preachers of the Gospel, either Admittance, or an Abode in their Dominions, must needs be false.

Now the literal Sense of these words, *Compel 'em to come in,* gives Infidels this handle.

'Tis therefore false.

No one will dispute the Major: for where's the sense of requiring on one hand, that all Men wou'd be converted to the Truth, and yet laying Obstacles in the way to render their Conversion impracticable? Wou'd not this be trifling cruelly with Mankind, and frustrating the ends of Providence, which aims at rendring Men inexcusable, unless they lay hold of the Opportunitys God is pleas'd to afford 'em?

Let's therefore endeavor to prove the Minor.

Let us suppose for this purpose, that a Set of Missionarys from the Pope shou'd now for the first time present themselves in the great Empire of *China* to preach the Gospel, and that they were sincere enough to answer honestly to some Questions which might naturally be propos'd to 'em. At the same time I suppose a Principle, which, if rightly consider'd, can't well be deny'd me, to wit, That every Man living, having experienc'd his own Proneness to Error, and that he sees, or fancys he sees, as Age comes on, the Falshood of a thousand things which had pass'd on him for true, <85> ought to be always dispos'd to hearken to those who offer'd him Instruction, even in Matters of Religion. I don't except Christians out of this Rule; and I'm persuaded, shou'd a Fleet now arrive here from Terra Australis,[46] with Persons aboard, who hearing we had entertain'd erroneous Opinions about the Nature and Worship of God, desir'd a Conference with us on these points, that it wou'd not be amiss to hear 'em out, not only as this might be a means of delivering them from the Errors we shou'd certainly think 'em in, but also because it is not impossible, that we shou'd benefit by their Knowledg; since we ought to entertain so vast and worthy an Idea of Almighty God, as to expect he will increase our Knowledg infinitely, and by an infinite Variety of Degrees and Methods. Now as we are all persuaded, that the People of Terra Australis wou'd be oblig'd to hear our Missionarys on their bare general Proposition of undeceiving 'em in matters of Religion, so we ought to think our selves under the same Obligation, with re-

---

46. Terra Australis, the South Land, the then undiscovered continent on the opposite side of the globe from Europe, was the setting for various imaginary travel books. See Bayle, DHC, art. "Sadeur."

gard to Persons coming from Terra Australis: For the Obligation on their side cou'd not be bas'd on the Expectation that our Missionarys wou'd bring them the Truth, since I suppose 'em oblig'd to hear by virtue of a general Offer, antecedent to any proof of the Truth of the Matters to be preach'd, and before they had entertain'd the least Doubt of their own Opinions. I mean in this place, a distinct and determinate Doubt, not an implicit, unfixt, and general Mistrust, which seems inseparable from every Man, who has Sense enough to make these Reflections: *I have firmly believ'd a thousand things in some part of my Life, which I am far from believing at present;* <86> *and what I now believe, a great many others I see of as good Sense as my self, believe not a tittle of: My Assent is often determin'd, not by Demonstrations which appear to me cou'd not be otherwise, and which appear so to others, but by Probabilitys which appear not such to other Men.* If the People then of Terra Australis wou'd be oblig'd to give ear to our Missionarys, before any particular Prejudice had determin'd 'em to doubt of their antient Religion, or to dream, that these new Men were the Messengers of Truth; it's plain their Obligation must be founded on a Principle obliging universally, to wit, a Duty in all of embracing all Occasions of enlarging their Knowledg, by examining those Reasons which may be offer'd against their own, or for the Opinions of others.

But not to perplex my Matter, let's quit these Reflections: There's no great need of Arguments to prove, that the *Chinese* wou'd be under an Obligation of hearing the Pope's Missionarys. Let's therefore represent both Partys in their first Conversation: We'l suppose, that the Emperor of *China* orders these good Fathers to appear before him in Council, and there desires in the first place to know, what mov'd 'em to undertake so long a Voyage. They'l answer without doubt, to preach the true Religion, which God himself had reveal'd by his only Son; and hereupon they'l tell him a thousand fine things of the Morality of JESUS CHRIST, of the Felicity he promises the Faithful, and of the Dishonor done to God by the Pagan Religions. Possibly this Prince might answer them as our King *Ethelred* answer'd the Monks sent by St. *Gregory* the Great, as Missionarys into this Country, That 'twas all very fine, provided <87> 'twere but true; and that he cou'd with all his heart give into it, if he found not more Certainty in what he had receiv'd from his Forefathers; that they who believ'd it true, might with his free leave make open Profession of it. But let us suppose the Chinese Council wise enough to put this hard Question to the Missionarys; *What course do you take with those, who having heard your Sermons a hundred times over, can't bring themselves to believe a word of what you say:* and the Monks, sincere enough, as before suppos'd, to answer, We have a Command from our God, who was made Man, to compel the obstinate, that is, those, who after hearing our Doctrines shall refuse Baptism; and in consequence of this Command, whenever we have the Power in our hands, and when a greater Evil may not ensue, we are oblig'd in conscience to imprison the idolatrous *Chinese,* to bring 'em to Beggary, curry 'em with Cudgels into our Churches, hang some for an Example to others, force away their Children, give 'em up to the Discretion of the Soldiers, them, their Wives, and their Goods. If you doubt whether we are bound in conscience to do all this, lo here's the Gospel, here's the plain and express Precept, *Compel 'em to come in;* that is, make use of whatever Violence you deem most proper for surmounting the obstinate Oppositions of Men.

We may easily conceive, that this Sincerity, which I suppose in the Missionarys, is but a Chimera; however, I may be allow'd to make the Supposition, since it's only to lead my Reader more commodiously to the point I drive at. Now what do we think wou'd the Privy-Council think and say upon this occasion? Either they <88> must be Counsellors void of common Sense and common Prudence and Thought, mere speaking Machines; or else they must advise the Emperor to order these Men immediately out of his Dominions, as profest publick Pests, and charge his Subjects at their peril never to admit 'em more: for who sees not that granting 'em a liberty to preach, is laying the foundation of a continual Butchery and Desolation in Town and Country? At first they wou'd do no more than preach, than instruct, wheedle, promise a Paradise, threaten a Hell; they'l gain over a great many of the People, and have their Followers in all the Citys and Ports of the Kingdom: but in time they'l come to downright Violence against those who persist in their old Religion, either by calling in a foreign Power, or by stirring up their new Disciples against 'em. Perhaps these won't easily bear being ruffled in places where they are yet strong enough to defend themselves; so the Partys come to downright blows, they kill one another like so many Flys; and so many Christians as die in the Conflict, so many

Martyrs in the Language of the Missionarys, provided they lose their lives in executing the express Command of JESUS CHRIST, *Compel 'em to come in.* Is there a Soul Popish or Monkish enough not to shiver at the thoughts of this dreadful Tragedy? Yet this is not all; the Emperor himself must soon or late have a lift, if he has not force enough to keep his Christian Subjects at bay. For,

As I have already observ'd, 'twere absurd to think JESUS CHRIST had enjoin'd Constraint with regard to an ordinary Burgher, a poor Peasant or Mechanick, whose Conversion is of little <89> importance to the enlarging the Borders of the Church; and not enjoin'd it with regard to Kings, whose Authority and Example is so useful for spreading a Religion. Therefore, the literal Sense that I reject once suppos'd, the first thing the Missionarys ought to do, after they had gain'd over a Party among the *Chinese,* considerable enough to be fear'd by the State, wou'd be to let the Emperor understand, that unless he turn'd Christian they shou'd obey him no longer, they'd do him all the mischief they cou'd, call in Crusades from the West to deprive him of his Crown, or chuse themselves another King, who shou'd be a faithful Son of the Church; and having increas'd their Numbers by the methods of Constraint, thrust him into a Cloister, or shut him in between four Walls all the days of his Life, unless he embrac'd their Religion. Nay, shou'd he bring an Army into the Field, to repel Force by Force; and having the good fortune to conquer his Christian Subjects, oblige 'em to take a new Oath of Fidelity, and promise to do no further Violence on anyone; yet he cou'd not rely upon this Oath or Treaty, because he must be sensible, that the Law of Christianity, since it makes Robbery, Murder, and Rebellion, all lawful when tending to the Interest of Religion, wou'd equally authorize the Violation of Promises and Oaths; so as he might justly apprehend, that the moment he withdrew his Armys, his Christian Subjects wou'd revolt anew, in contempt of all their Oaths, which, by a tacit Condition, they constantly postpone to the enlarging the Borders of the Church. Thus he must never expect to see himself or his Kingdom at peace, while there were <90> such Disturbers in its Bowels; whom nothing is strong enough to bind, and who judg every thing lawful, and even a Duty, provided it tends to the Interest of their Religion.

Consequently, all kind of Reasons engage him to order the Missionarys out of his Dominions after the first two hours Audience; and by this means he must with Reason and Justice continue for ever in his false Religion. A horrible Consequence! and which arising naturally from the literal Sense, shews it to be false, impious, and abominable.

I say, he may with Reason and Justice expel these Missionarys; because in the first place Reason and Justice require, that a Prince, who sees Strangers come into his Dominions, to preach up a new Religion, shou'd inform himself of the Nature of this Religion, and whether it reconciles the Fidelity which Subjects owe their Sovereign with their Duty to God: Consequently this Emperor of *China* ought to examine the Nature of their Doctrine in the very first Conversation, whether it be consistent with the publick Good, and with those fundamental Laws, which constitute the Happiness of Sovereigns and Subjects. I make no scruple to say, that a King who neglected this, wou'd sin against the eternal Laws of Justice, which require his watching for the publick Welfare of the People committed to his Charge.

Be this then agreed to, that he's bound in Prudence and Justice, and as he tenders the publick Peace, to interrogate the Missionarys, as to their Proceedings against those they shou'd account obstinate. Now as he must at first dash discover a Principle in 'em which gives Horror, which is contrary to natural Equity, destructive of the <91> Peace of his Subjects, and dangerous to his Throne: as, I say, he must discover this before he is let into any such degree of Knowledg, as obliges a Man to embrace Christianity; 'tis plain, that of the two Obligations we may represent him under successively, one of endeavoring to preserve the publick Peace, the other of professing Christianity, the former precedes; and consequently, he most justly banishes the Christians out of his Dominions, and will never hear 'em more: Whereupon the second Obligation can never take place, because it's a Contradiction that a Prince shou'd be oblig'd to turn Christian, before he's instructed in the Christian Religion, or that he shou'd be instructed according to the ordinary course of things, without having several Conferences with Christians. Let's remember this Maxim of a modern* Author,

* Nichole, Pret. Ref. convaincus. [Pierre Nicole, *Les prétendus Réformés convaincus de schisme* (The self-styled Reformed convicted of schism), 1684.]

That not to be a Schismatick, it is not sufficient the Church we separate from be false, but there must in addition be a well-grounded Certainty of the Falseness of that Church. In like manner, that the Emperor of *China* might with Justice depart from his own Religion, 'tis not enough that he embraces the Christian, which is the true, but he must moreover be assur'd, by sound and well-weigh'd Informations, that it is the true; else his embracing it is only a Caprice, and an Act of Temerity, to which God can have no regard. It's plain then, Christianity obliges only those who clearly perceive its Divinity, or those who have had opportunitys of being instructed. They therefore who have bin depriv'd of these Opportunitys, by being oblig'd to banish those who were <92> qualify'd to instruct 'em, are excusably out of the Pale. Whence we may more and more discover the Enormity of the literal Sense, from the fatal Consequences which flow from it.

I maintain in the second place, that this Emperor can't reasonably be condemn'd for judging from this first Interview, that the Religion of these Missionarys is ridiculous and diabolical: Ridiculous, as being founded by an Author, who on one hand requires all Men to be humble, meek, patient, dispassionate, ready to forgive Injurys; and on the other hand, bids 'em drub, imprison, banish, whip, hang, give up as a Prey to the Soldiers, all those who won't follow him. And Diabolical; because, besides its direct Repugnancy to the Lights of Reason, he must see that it authorizes all kind of Crimes, when committed for its own Advantag; allows no other Rule of Just and Unjust, but its own Loss and Gain; and tends to change the whole World into a dreadful Scene of Violence and Bloodshed.

Last of all, I affirm, that if this Emperor believes there's a God, as it's certain all the Pagans do, he's oblig'd from a Principle of Conscience, the eternal Law and Rule antecedent to all Religions of positive Institution, to banish all Christians out of his Dominions. Thus I prove it. He must find by these Missionarys, that the forcing Men by Torture and Violence to the Profession of the Gospel, is one of the fundamental Laws of the Christian Religion, and one of the plainest and most express Commands of the Son of God. Now this method, humanly speaking, is inseparable from a world of Crimes and Trespasses against the first and most indispensable of <93> all Laws; and consequently of a blacker nature, and more provoking to God, than any Attempts against Christianity misunderstood. Every Prince then is in Conscience oblig'd to prevent the introducing such Maxims into his Dominions; and one can scarce think how God shou'd call 'em to account for not tolerating Christians, when they plainly perceive 'em to be a morally necessary Cause of an endless Complication of Crimes: for every one that fears God ought, with all his Authority, to prevent the Commission of Crimes; and what Crimes are there, which they ought to prevent with greater care, than religious Hypocrisys, Acts against the Instinct and Lights of Conscience? Now these the Maxims arising from the literal Sense do infallibly produce. Ordain Punishments for all who practise the Rites of any one Religion, and who refuse to practise those of another; expose 'em to the Violence of the Soldiery, buffet 'em, thrust 'em into noisom Dungeons, deprive 'em of Employments and Honors, condemn 'em to the Mines or Gallys, hang up those who are impertinent, load others with Favors and Rewards who renounce their Worship: you may depend upon't, a great many will change, as to the outward Profession, from the Religion they esteem the best, and make profession of that which they are convinc'd is false. Acts of Hypocrisy and High Treason against the Divine Majesty, which is never so directly affronted, as when Men draw near to his Worship in a way which their Consciences, I mean even the most erroneous Consciences, represent as dishonorable to him. So that a Prince who wou'd prevent, as much as in him lies, the Depravation of his Subjects, and their <94> being guilty of that Sin, which of all Sins is the most provoking to Almighty God, and the most certainly Sin, shou'd take special care to purge his Dominions of all Christians of persecuting Principles.

Nor let any one pretend 'tis an Error of Fact in him; for absolutely, universally, and in the eternal Ideas we have of the Divinity, which are the primary, original, and infallible Rule of Rectitude, it's a most crying Iniquity to pretend to turn Christian, when Conscience remonstrates that the *Chinese* Religion, which we outwardly abjure, is the best: And therefore this Emperor cou'd not avoid banishing these Missionarys, without exposing his Subjects to the almost insurmountable Temptation of committing the most heinous of all Sins, and hazarding his own Conscience. For as no one can be assur'd that a new Religion, now to be propos'd, shall appear to him true; and that a King once reduc'd to the Alternative either of losing his Crown, or of professing a Religion which he believes to be false, ought in reason to dread his sinking under the Temptation; his Love of Truth, and of the Deity shining upon his Conscience, altho he's in an erroneous Belief, oblige him indispensably to prevent these Dangers, by the Expulsion of those who carry 'em about 'em, wherever they go, in that pretended Gospel-Rule of theirs, *Compel 'em to come in.*

I don't think there needs any thing more in proof of the second Proposition of my Syllogism;[47] for who sees not that a Prince who expels the Christian Missionarys, expels 'em with all the Reason and Justice in the world? <95>

1. Because his Kingly Office obliges him; Eternal and Immutable Order requiring that he shou'd keep off every thing which threatens Confusion, Civil Wars, Seditions, and Rebellion in his Dominions.

2. Because natural Religion, and all the Ideas of pure Morality oblige him; Eternal and Immutable Order requiring that all, but especially Kings, shou'd endeavor to avert whatever destroys the Boundarys of Vertue and Vice, and changes the most abominable Actions into Acts of Piety, when design'd to extend the Borders of Religion.

3. Because the Rights of Conscience, which are directly those of God himself, oblige him; Eternal and Immutable Order requiring, that he shou'd to the utmost of his power prevent all Conjunctures which bring Men into a near prospect, and into an almost unavoidable danger of betraying their Conscience and their God.

There's no need, after what has bin said, of proving in particular, that any Pagan Prince, who shou'd find a Generation of Christians settled in his Dominions, either thro the Negligence of his Ancestors, or because he had conquer'd their Country, might justly expel 'em because of these pernicious Maxims.

The only thing to be alledg'd against me is, That the Emperor of *China* might want the Pretext I furnish him, because there's no necessity of letting him know at first word that JESUS CHRIST had commanded Constraint. But beside that I have prevented this Objection, by shewing how he and his Council wou'd be guilty of a very criminal Neglect, if they did not ex-<96>amine these new Comers about the nature of their Religion with re-

---

47. See Appendixes, "Bayle's Use of Logic," p. 580 ("syllogism").

gard to Princes and Subjects who shou'd not comply; which Question once propos'd, our Missionarys must explain themselves roundly, or be a pack of Knaves: besides this, I say, who sees not 'tis confessing that the literal Sense of the Parable imports a Doctrine they are asham'd of, that 'tis tricking in Religion, and being guided in the preaching of the Gospel by the Spirit of *Machiavel;* the very thought of which gives horror, and were alone enough to make Christianity detested as an execrable Cheat? What, wou'd they think it fair to riggle themselves into the Kingdom of *China* under the appearances of great Moderation, and as so many Foxes, to turn Tygers and Lions in due time, and worry these good People whom they had bubbled by a shew of exceeding Charity and Meekness? No, this can never pass; nor wou'd any thing more effectually discredit the Morality of JESUS CHRIST, than supposing he had commanded his Disciples to use Violence when they might without danger to themselves, and in the mean time to beware babling, to keep it as a Mystery among themselves, which shou'd break out in due time, when they were manifestly the strongest side, and to hide it under the appearance of the perfectest Moderation and the most theatrical Patience, that no body shou'd have the least suspicion of the matter: like a Ruffian, who hides his Dagger in his sleeve, and strikes his Man only when he's sure of the blow. For my part, if this be the case, I can't see why the Christian Religion mayn't justly be liken'd to one who raises himself step by step to the highest Dig-<97>nitys, like the *Tartuffe* in *Moliere,* by a Contempt of Injurys, by an Austerity of Life, by his Submission, by the most popular Civility; but when he has gain'd his point, throws off the mask all at once, and becomes the Scourge of Mankind by his Cruelty and tyrannical Insolence. If the Historian might liken the *Roman* Empire to Man in the several Stages of Life, who can hinder our carrying the comparison forward to the several States of Christianity? Its Infancy and early Youth were exercis'd in forcing its way thro all the Obstacles of Fortune; it acted the meek and the modest, the humble and the dutiful Subject, the charitable and the officious: and by these Virtues it struggled up from the lowest Cusp of Misery, ay marry, and rais'd it self to a pretty fair pitch: but having once fully compass'd its ends, it quitted its Hypocrisy, authoriz'd all the ways of Violence, and ravag'd all those who presum'd to oppose it; carrying Desolation far and wide by its Crusades, drenching the new World in Crueltys which give astonishment, and now at last endeavoring to act 'em over in that remnant of the Earth which it has not yet stain'd with Blood, *China, Japan, Tartary,* &c. We can't stop the mouths of Infidels, or hinder their charging Christianity with these things, since they may find 'em in our Historys; and the Church of *Rome,* which has had the whip-hand for so many Ages past, can't hinder the Sects which have separated, from laying all these Reproaches at her door. But if we can't save Christianity from this Infamy, at least let us save the Honor of its Founder, and of his Laws; and not say, that all this was the consequence of his express Com-<98>mand to compel the World: Let's rather say, that Mankind very rarely acting according to its Principles, Christians have happen'd not to act by theirs; and that they exercis'd Violences, at the same time that they preach'd Meekness. Thus we shall acquit our Religion at the expence of its Professors: but if we say that all the Violences which Popery has exercis'd, were the genuine and natural Consequence of that Precept of JESUS CHRIST, *Compel 'em to come in;* this will turn the Tables, and we shall save the Honor of Christians, at the expence of their Religion, and its adorable Founder. Now how abominable wou'd it be, to impute to JESUS CHRIST all the Crueltys of Popes, and of Princes, who have own'd him as Head of the Church? And yet there's no avoiding this, if we admit the literal Sense of the Parable. All their Violences and Barbaritys must be so many reputed Acts of Piety, and of filial Obedience to the Son of God. We are constrain'd then to affirm, that the literal Sense is not only a false Interpretation of Scripture, but an execrable Impiety to boot. <99>

∞∞ CHAPTER VI ∞∞

The Fifth Argument against the literal Sense, drawn from the Impossibility of putting it in execution without unavoidable Crimes. That it's no Excuse to say, Hereticks are punish'd only because they disobey Edicts.

We have by this time partly seen how very odious this pretended Precept of JESUS CHRIST must needs render his Religion to all the World: I shall now, from what has bin said in the former Chapter, draw a new Argument in the matter before us.

All literal Sense of Scripture including an universal Command, which cannot be practis'd without a Complication of Crimes, must needs be false.

Now the literal Sense of the Words, *Compel 'em to come in,* is of this kind:

It's therefore false.

The major Proposition carries its own Evidence; so that 'tis needless insisting on proof. Let's proceed then to the second Proposition, tho there's no need of dwelling long upon this, because 'tis partly clear'd already by the several Proofs advanc'd in the former Chapters, and that, properly speaking, it's only a branch of my general *Medium.* It won't trouble me, if I am accus'd of multiplying my Proofs without necessity; I'l rather bear this reproach, than leave several Faces of my general Argument shaded and in-<100>volv'd. 'Twill certainly have the greater force, if every Part is considered separately.

The greatest Patrons of Persecution will own, that the Order of *Compelling* has not bin committed to the discretion of every private Person: So that shou'd I reproach 'em with the sad Disorders which are apt to spring from their Principle thro popular Tumults, or thro the blind Zeal of a giddy Curate, or Portrieve of a Town, who as often as the maggot bites might raise the Mob upon all the Sectarys within his Jurisdiction; they'l tell me, they have quite a different Notion of the matter: Their Sense of it, they'l say, is, that JESUS CHRIST directs the Command only to those who have the power of the Sword in every Country, and who are entrusted with the Civil Authority, to whom the Spiritual Guides are to apply themselves, when 'tis expedient, to compel Hereticks. Let's see then whether with this Limitation, which strikes off the whole Article of popular Fury, and private Violence at once, there still remains not a strange Complication of Crimes in the regular way, according to our Adversarys, of executing this Order of JESUS CHRIST. I shall even carry my Complaisance for 'em so far, as not to alledg those sanguinary wholesale Executions which History furnishes; but confine my self to that which they reckon the most orderly and most moderate of the kind, to wit, the present Persecution in *France.*

Good God! What Iniquity, what Crime has bin uncommitted in the course of this regular Persecution? How many Orders of Council, void of all Sincerity and good Faith? How many Decrees of Parliament contrary to the establish'd <101> Rules? How many Subornations of Witnesses?

How many vexatious Prosecutions? Nor can it be pretended that these are personal Faults in those who have the Executive part, since they are the natural and unavoidable Consequences of the literal Sense they give to the Parable. In effect, this Sense importing, as they pretend, a general Right of Compelling, it's left to the Discretion and Zeal of the Prince in each Country, to make choice of that method of Compulsion which to him seems properest. The method they begun with in *France,* was by Proceedings against the Ministers and Temples, and by Civil Actions against private Partys. Here's a Choice founded upon the words of JESUS CHRIST: it follows then, that the ways devis'd for compelling under this Head, are Dependances on the first Choice; and if these be so far necessary, that without 'em there cou'd be no Compulsion, it's plain they are the natural and regular Consequences of the Command of JESUS CHRIST, and not any personal Obliquity in him who executes the Command. For it's plain, this Method had bin too gentle and unoperative, were the Rules of Equity and upright Dealing observ'd in the Courts of Law. And yet a compulsive Virtue in it being absolutely necessary to answer the Intention of the Command, 'twas consequently necessary to mingle all the Arts of Fraud and Collusion, that the temporal damage done the Protestants by the Wager of Law might constrain 'em to turn Catholicks.

Now what a train of Crimes besides hangs after this method, which we suppose chosen in execution of the Command of God? For can <102> any one doubt but this must raise a thousand Passions in the Souls of those who suffer, and in the Souls of those who are the Authors of their Sufferings? Must not this exasperate the Spirits of both sides, kindle a deadly Hatred to one another, force 'em to traduce and slander each other, and become mutually wickeder and worse Christians than they were before? Supposing Popery the true Religion, must not these Proceedings tempt the Hereticks, who suffer, to blaspheme it in their Heart, to detest it, and thereby bring 'em under a proximate Occasion of sinning and stiffning in their Heresy? Wou'd People but think a little of this, I persuade my self they'd agree that nothing tends more to the banishing from the Hearts of Men that Gospel-Peace of Heart, that Calm of the human Passions which is the surest Foundation of a Spirit of Piety, and the proper Soil of all Christian Vertues.

Yet this is nothing in comparison of that Deluge of Iniquity which in the issue overspread the Kingdom, when they proceeded to force the Protestants, by the quartering of Soldiers, to renounce their Religion. For on the one hand, what Insolences, what Outrages did not these Soldiers commit; and on the other, how much Hypocrisy, how much Profaneness were the Protestants guilty of who sign'd? What Intemperance, what Rapines, what Blasphemys did these Soldiers stick at; what Injurys and Crueltys to their Neighbor? Must we place the Disorders committed by 'em to the account of the Persecution or no? I wou'd fain know how a Confessor behaves himself, when a Dragoon confesses he has buffeted his Hugonot Landlord. If the Father <103> looks not on this as a Sin, he falls into the Absurdity I have spoke to sufficiently already, to wit, *That an Action, which might be a Crime in any other case, ceases to be so, when committed against one of a false Religion, with a design of bringing him over to the true:* An Absurdity, which opens a door to the fearfullest State 'tis possible to imagine. If the Confessor accounts it a Sin, as in reason he ought, it follows, that the late Persecution has necessarily and unavoidably oblig'd the Soldiers to commit an infinite number of Sins; since it was absolutely necessary to distress their Landlords either in Body or Goods, else there had bin no Constraint, nor had the Command of the Son of God bin obey'd. Whether the Dragoon confess the Injury he did his Neighbor or no, it's all one; his Action is equally opposite to another Gospel-Command, of not doing wrong to our Neighbor.

The Question may possibly be here ask'd, Whether a Dragoon, in executing the Orders of his Prince, may not innocently drub his Landlord; as he might innocently have hang'd him, if duly appointed to be the Executioner? To this I answer, (1.) Be that how it will, still the Insolences of these Soldiers are Sins in him who authorizes 'em; so that the number of Crimes is still the same. In the second place, there's as much certainty as we can have of any human thing, that all the Abuses and ill Treatment committed to the discretion of these Soldiers will become Sins in them, because they'l undoubtedly execute their Orders with pleasure, and even exceed 'em. A Hangman who executes a Criminal innocently, when he only acts in obedience to the <104> Sentence of Justice, sins manifestly against Charity and against his Duty towards his Neighbor, if he takes pleasure in performing his Office, if he be glad of the occasion, and studies how to aggravate the Sufferings of a dying Man: Accordingly, it is not to be doubted, but the Dragoon becomes exceeding criminal, by executing his Orders with joy, and with a thousand base inhuman Passions; whence it follows that all their Disorders are Sins not only in him who commands or permits 'em, but in themselves also. And yet these Disorders being necessary for compelling Hereticks to come in, it must likewise follow, according to our Doctors, that JESUS CHRIST has commanded a method of Constraint, which is necessarily attended with a Complication of infinite Sins. What flesh alive can forbear shivering, to hear such Doctrine?

But how much worse will it sound, if to the Villanys of the Soldiers we add in all the intermingled Frauds, both on the part of the Priests, and on that of the Persecuted? The Churchmen came and pretended they'd be satisfy'd with general Professions of Faith, and in reality admitted a great many to Abjuration upon these terms. Then they told a thousand lyes to those who stood it out either in Prison, or in the Cloisters, that such and such had actually sign'd; and shook the Constancy of several by these Wiles, who they found were to be influenc'd by the Examples of others. This was the common and general Cheat, together with that of promising Pensions, Grants, and Employments; which yet they never intended to perform, at least not to that value, or for so long a time as they made believe. But the poor < 105 > Persecuted were drawn into still a wickeder piece of Imposture, by outwardly renouncing a Religion, which in their Souls they were more firmly persuaded of than ever. What Groanings of Conscience succeeded hereupon? What Remorses, what Imbitterment of Life, what Distraction of Mind! sometimes how to save themselves by flying into foreign Countrys, at the hazard of begging their bread; then thinking, shou'd they escape themselves, they must leave their Children in the pit of Destruction! But with regard to the Church of *Rome,* what Profanations of its most august Sacraments has it bin guilty of? How edifying, where a Person refus'd to communicate in the Article of Death, to see 'em abuse his dead Body, for an Example to others? Isn't it a pretty thing, to see the Body of the Son of God cram'd down Peoples throats who are unwilling to receive it; and that which is the Death of the Soul to him who is not duly prepar'd by Faith and Affections, serv'd upon those who they know have no Faith for it, and who they know are under an invincible inward Prepossession for what they reproach as Heresy? It's plain it can't be Zeal which prompts 'em to Actions of this nature, but pure Vanity, on finding themselves impos'd on, and after all their pains for the Triumphs of Popery, bubbled by sham Renunciations.

I can't conceive how some Persons of good Understandings, who were his most Christian Majesty's Accomplices in the design of letting loose his Dragoons to make the Hugonots abjure, have bin able to support the thought of that frightful Complication of Crimes, which must <106> necessarily arise in the execution. They are too clear-sighted not to have foreseen 'em; How then cou'd they take on themselves all the brutal Insolences of the Dragoons, all the Falshoods and Frauds the Missionarys must practise, all the Hypocrisys of those who might sink under the Temptation; the sacrilegious Communions, and Profanations of Sacraments which they must get over, all the Sighs and Groanings of tender Consciences, all the Yearnings of Bowels in those sequester'd from their Children and Habitations; in a word, all the Passions of Hatred, Resentment, Vanity, and Insult, respectively operating in the Persecutors and the Persecuted? To say, after all this, that JESUS CHRIST is the Author of a Design of this nature, and of a Compulsion tack'd to such a train of the blackest and foulest Crimes, is Blasphemy in the highest degree.

But here it will be proper to prevent Objections. 1. They'l tell me, they had not the Gift of foreseeing all these Consequences; and that JESUS CHRIST, who foresaw all the Mischiefs his Gospel has occasion'd, did nevertheless command his Apostles to preach it to all Nations. 2. That the great Benefits redounding to the true Church compensate for all these Disorders. 3. That Kings being supreme in their own Dominions, and having the executive Power in their own hands, may punish, as they see fit, all who slight or disobey their Injunctions; let the People beware then, and conform to their King's Religion.

To the first Difficulty I answer, That tho Men indeed have no certain knowledg of the Future, yet the Conjectures they are able to make upon <107> some Cases, are attended with a moral Certainty sufficient to regulate their Designs and Actions; so that when Conjectures highly probable, and manifestly convincing, tell 'em they shall be the occasion of a great many Crimes, if they give such and such Orders, they are inexcusably guilty if they issue 'em. Now I maintain, that the Persecutors of *France* are in the present case: One must be downright stupid and ignorant of the most obvious matters, not to know that Soldiers quarter'd on the Hereticks, with Orders to teaze, and even ruin 'em, unless they renounc'd their Religion, must commit infinite Disorders and Violences, and force a world of poor People to yield; that is, to turn Hypocrites, and Profaners of the Mysterys. The Consequence being thus most apparent and morally unavoidable, they cou'd not act as they did, without partaking in the Iniquity: and had JESUS CHRIST commanded 'em to act so, he had oblig'd 'em to the Commission of it. It's manifest then, they are in a most damnable Error, by believing he has commanded 'em to compel Hereticks to the Catholick Religion. No one will deny, that one of the Qualitys which renders the Devil so very odious in the sight of God, is that of a Tempter: he must therefore sin in a grievous manner, when he leads us into Temptation, tho he knows the Success of his Temptation no otherwise than by Conjecture. Accordingly he who from a bare Conjecture only knows he shall extort a great many false Abjurations thro a dread of Misery and an insolent Soldiery, is fairly in for the Character of a Tempter. The Mission of the Apostles to preach the Gospel, had nothing in't of this <108> nature; they were only to teach, to instruct, and to persuade: and nothing's more innocent than this. If their Preaching happen'd to set the World in flames, and occasion'd a thousand Disorders, 'twas intirely the World's fault, the Gospel was only the accidental Cause. —It left all who wou'd not embrace it in the quiet Enjoyment of their Goods, Honors, Houses, Wives, and Children; and consequently never tempted 'em to Acts of Hypocrisy: It ne'er enjoin'd its Followers to tell a lye, to baptize the Obstinate; it only desir'd they wou'd instruct. It can't therefore be justly charg'd with the Misdemeanors of Convertists, nor the Rage of the opposing Heathens. But 'tis quite otherwise in the case before us; the Convertists have had Orders to abuse Men, to spoil their Goods, tear away their Children, and thrust themselves into Prison, &c. Thus the Violences of Convertists are directly enjoin'd, and the Temptation of signing hypocritically put directly in their Way.

The second Difficulty scarce needs an Answer, after what has bin already said: For who sees not, if we once judg of the nature of an Action by the benefit which accrues to the Church, that we have no Boundarys left to separate Vertue and Vice; that Calumny, Murder, Adultery, and in general whatever can be conceiv'd most horrible, become pious Deeds when practis'd against Hereticks? In good truth, we have to deal with Men who have a clever knack this way; they have made all the Hereticks of *France* disappear in the turning of a hand. All the Crimes then of our Dragoons, all the Profanations of Sacraments, are finely juggled into good Works. <109> *Scelera ipsa nefasque hac Mercede placent,*[48] was the saying of old to flatter *Nero*. How many *French* Men say the same in our days: Since all this long train of Crimes has purchas'd our invincible Monarch the Glory and Satisfaction of seeing only one Religion in his Dominions, 'tis all right, 'tis all just, and infinitely fit they shou'd have been committed; *Scelera ipsa nefasque hac Mercede placent.* It's a Maxim of some standing in the Church of *Rome,* that by compelling the Fathers to turn Hypocrites, they make sure of their Children at least. Cursed, detestable Thought! and if this be right, pray why don't they send their Corsairs in full Peace, to cruise for Children on the Coasts of *England, Turkey, Greece, Holland,* and *Sweden?* Why will they condemn those who compel'd the Jews to baptize their Children? Why not assassinate those Ministers, who by their Sermons obstruct the Church's bringing in all the ignorant Peasantry? Oh, say they, this is not our way; we don't intend to dye our hands in Blood; Prisons and Fines are the farthest we can go, we detest your Persecutors by Wheel and Gibbet. Good Creatures! and yet you are under a mighty Illusion; and I shall shew you in due time, that Compulsion of any kind once authoriz'd, there's no fix'd point to stop at, no Center of rest, because the same Reasons which prove it lawful to imprison for matter of Heresy, prove much stronger, that a Man may be hang'd and drawn for it.

There remains a third Objection, the Common-place, and old beaten Argument of *French* Flatterers; a Set of Men, of whom we may say, without an overflowing of Gall, that a Spirit of servile <110> Flattery, unworthy a Christian, unworthy the vilest Eves-dropper under the ten or twelve first *Roman* Emperors, has infatuated to such a degree, that they are not in the least sensible of their giving all *Europe* new and daily occasions of turning

---

48. Lucan, *Civil War,* I.38: "Even such crimes and such guilt are not too high a price to pay." Translated J. D. Duff, Loeb Classical Library, 1977, p. 5.

'em into ridicule. They fondle their Prince day and night with such Elogys as these; That he converts his Subjects by Methods of Love, and by the most manifest Justice of his Edicts. Wou'd you know the meaning of this? It is, that if any Rigor has bin exercis'd, 'twas only on those who had disobey'd his Majesty's Edicts, particularly the Declaration made by the common Cryer, in every Town and Village, before Billets were distributed to the Dragoons, *That the King for the future wou'd have but one Religion in his Kingdom,* and wou'd let those, who comply'd not with his Intentions, feel the Effects of his Power. He had a right to punish 'em, say they, by Banishment, by Confiscation of Goods, by Loss of Liberty, by denying 'em the Exercise of any Trade or Calling, in case they persisted in their Heresy. They have persisted; Is it not very just then, that the Soldiers shou'd make 'em suffer the Penaltys incur'd by their Disobedience? This Objection deserves to be confuted, the rather, because many well-meaning People, Enemys to Persecution, as they suppose, and great Assertors of the Rights of Conscience, imagine, that tho Sovereigns can't indeed punish those of their Subjects who are under the Power of a certain Belief, yet they may forbid 'em the publick Profession and Exercise of it under certain Penaltys; and if they still persist, punish 'em, not as tinctur'd with such or such Opinions, but as Infringers of the Laws. But <111> this is coming pitifully about by a long and vain Circuit, to strike against the same Rock which others steer directly upon. For,

If nothing cou'd denominate a Man a Persecutor, but his punishing Sectarys before a Law were enacted against 'em, the Sovereign might easily commit the cruellest Violences without coming in the least under the Notion of a Persecutor: The whole Mystery wou'd lie in forbearing a while, till an Edict were thunder'd out, enjoining 'em to assist, for example, at divine Service in such a certain Church, upon pain of the Gallows; and after a short Ceremony of this kind, then find out all those who had not assisted, and hang 'em for a parcel of Rebels. Now as 'twere mocking the World to pretend, this was not a Persecution strictly speaking; so it's plain, that Edicts previously publish'd and promulgated, alter not the Case, nor hinder, but the Conscience is violated, and the Punishment inflicted unjust.

I cou'd wish these fulsom Scriblers wou'd read their own St. *Thomas* a little, or the Treatise of *Human Faith,* publish'd by the Jansenists.[49] There they might find, in the 8*th* Ch. of the 1*st* Part, *That a Law unjust in it self, is* ipso facto *null; nor partakes of the force of a Law, any farther than it's agreeable to Justice* ——— *That it ought to be possible in the Nature of things, necessary, useful, regarding the Publick Good, and not any private Interest.*[50] For, as the same Authors tell us a little lower, *Ecclesiastical Laws ought to respect the particular Welfare of those on whom they are impos'd; it not being allowable in the Church, to do private Persons any wrong, under a pretence of promoting the Good of the Publick.* Whether all these Conditions <112> be requisite or no, and for my part I don't think they always are, in order to a private Person's submitting (for when the Question is concerning a temporal Interest only, a Man may act wisely in submitting to an unjust Law) I insist, according to the Remark already laid down, in Chap. IV,[51] that to prove a Prince punishes his Subjects justly, 'tis not sufficient to alledg in general, they have disobey'd his Injunctions; but it must likewise appear, they might in Honor and Conscience comply. For shou'd a Prince, who was but a vile Poet, have a humor of enjoining all his Subjects by an Edict, to give under their hands, that they were verily persuaded, his Verses were incomparably fine, and this on pain of being condemn'd to Banishment; and shou'd several of his Subjects happen to be of such a stubborn Mold as *Philoxenus,* who cou'd ne'er be brought to praise *Dionysius* the Tyrant's Poetry; wou'd any one think their Banishment just? Nevertheless, it's founded on their disobeying an Edict. Wou'd any one think it reasonable to fine Folks for not believing, that the Earth turns round, that Colors don't subsist in the Objects, that Beasts are mere Machines; supposing a previous Law, that all who believ'd not these three Articles, shou'd be fin'd in such a Sum? Or rather, wou'd any one think it just, that a King shou'd enjoin all his Subjects, under certain Penaltys, to love Books, Perfumes, Fish, certain Sauces, have blue Eyes, a brushy Beard, *&c?* Wou'd it not be downright study'd Tyranny, to send Dragoons to live at discretion upon those

49. Pierre Nicole, *De la Foi humaine,* 1664.
50. Cf. Thomas Aquinas, *Summa theologiae,* 1–2, q. 95, a. 3 and q. 96, a. 4 (http://www.ccel.org/a/aquinas/summa/home.html).
51. See above, p. 87.

who comply'd not with Edicts of this kind? It's the grossest Stupidity then, or rather the most ridiculous Flattery, to <113> pretend, the Treatment the Reform'd met with was just, because they obey'd not a verbal Order, enjoining 'em, a little before the Billets were given out, to conform to the King's Religion. For as to an Edict issu'd to this purpose, and authentickly notify'd, for my part, I know of none before the Dragoons were let loose upon one quarter of the Kingdom: and I have already observ'd, that the Edict of Revocation allow'd 'em a certain limited time to consider what to do; tho I know at the same time, 'twas one of the most grosly perfidious Cheats that e'er was put upon a People.

Since therefore, from the Subjects not conforming to the Sovereign's Will, we are not universally to infer, that they justly suffer the Punishments with which he threaten'd the Delinquents; we ought to examine into the special Nature of the Laws disobey'd, when we wou'd discover, whether the Partys were justly expos'd to the Pillage and Discretion of the Soldiery. Now this Inquiry, if made, wou'd satisfy us, that the Laws, for the Nonobservance of which it's pretended, the *French* Protestants merited dragooning, are intrinsecally evil and unequitable; consequently the Punishments annex'd to 'em, and inflicted on those who obey'd 'em not, *ipso facto* and by their Nature unjust. This shift therefore will not serve to elude the force of my Argument, whereby I prove, that JESUS CHRIST cou'd not have enjoin'd Constraint; since this, as appears from the late Persecution in *France,* was impracticable without a Complication of Iniquity.

To shew in a few Words the Injustice of the verbal Declaration made the Protestants, that the King for the <114> future wou'd have but one Religion in his Kingdom, and that all who wou'd not conform to this his Pleasure, shou'd feel the Rigors of his Justice; to shew, I say, the Injustice of this Declaration, I might cite the Edict of *Nants,* and the many other solemn Promises to the same effect; but that these are only trifles in the Account of Kings: Solemn Assurances, Oaths, Edicts, are Makeshifts they must make use of on occasion, but brush thro 'em like so many Cobwebs, when once they have gain'd their point. I return to my primary and essential head of Argument.

All Law, enacted by a Person who has no right to enact it, and which exceeds his Power, is unjust; for, as *Thomas Aquinas* has it, To the end a

Law be just, it's requisite among other Conditions, *That he who makes it have Authority so to do, and exceed not this Authority.*[52]

Now so it is, that all Laws obliging to act against Conscience, are made by a Person, having no Authority to enact it, and who manifestly exceeds his Power.

Therefore every such Law is unjust.

To shew the truth of my second Proposition, I am only to say, that all the Power of Princes is deriv'd, either immediately from God, or else from Men, who enter into Society on certain Conditions.

If it be deriv'd from God, it's plain, it can't extend to the making Laws, which oblige the Subject to act against Conscience: for if so, it wou'd follow, that God cou'd confer a Power upon Man, of commanding to hate God; which is absurd, and necessarily impossible; the hatred <115> of God being an Act essentially wicked. If we examine this Matter ever so little, we shall find, that Conscience, with regard to each particular Man, is the Voice and Law of God in him, known and acknowledg'd as such by him, who carrys this Conscience about him: So that to violate this Conscience is essentially believing, that he violates the Law of God. Now to do any thing we esteem an Act of Disobedience to the Law of God, is essentially, either an Act of Hatred, or an Act of Contempt against God; and such an Act is essentially wicked, as all Mankind acknowledg. Commanding therefore to act against Conscience, and commanding to hate or contemn God, is one and the same thing; and consequently, God being uncapable of conferring a Power which shou'd enjoin the Hatred or Contempt of himself, it's evident he cou'd not have confer'd a Power of commanding to act against Conscience.

For the same Reason it's evident, that no Body of Men, who enter into Society, and deposite their Libertys in the hands of a Sovereign, ever meant to give him a Power over their Consciences; this were a Contradiction in terms: for unless we suppose the Partys to the original Contract errand Ideots or mad Men, we can't think they shou'd ever entrust the Sovereign with a Power of enjoining 'em to hate God, or despise Laws, clearly and distinctly dictated to their Consciences, and engraven on the Tables of their Heart. And certain it is, that when any Body of Men engage for them and

52. Cf. Thomas Aquinas, *Summa theologiae,* 1–2, q. 90, a. 3.

their Posterity to adhere to any particular Religion, they do this on a Supposition somewhat too lightly entertain'd, that they and their Posterity shall for ever <116> be under the Power of the same Conscience as guides 'em at present. For did they but reflect on the Changes which happen in the World, and on the different Sentiments which succeed one another in the human Mind, they ne'er wou'd engage farther than for Conscience in general, that is, promise for them and their Posterity, never to depart from that Religion they will deem best; but by no means confine their Covenant to this or that Article of Faith. For how are they sure, that what appears true to 'em to day, will appear so to themselves thirty Years hence, and much more to People of another Age? Such Engagements therefore are null and void in themselves, and exceed the Power of those who make 'em; no Man being able to engage himself for the future, much less others to believe what may not appear to 'em true. Princes therefore deriving no Power, either from God or Man, of enjoining their Subjects to act against Conscience; it's plain, all Edicts publish'd by 'em to this effect, are null in themselves, a mere Abuse and Usurpation: and consequently, all Punishments appointed by virtue of 'em for Non-conformity, are unjust.

From hence I draw a new and demonstrative Argument against the literal Sense of the Parable; because, were this the genuin Sense, 'twou'd confer a Right upon Princes, of enacting Laws obliging their Subjects to the Profession of a Religion repugnant to the Lights of their Consciences; which were the same as giving Kings a Right of enacting Laws, enjoining the Hatred and Contempt of God. But as this were the most extravagant Impiety, it follows, that the words, *Com-*<117>*pel 'em to come in,* do not mean what is claim'd; because if they did, it wou'd above all be to Princes that they were address'd, to the end that they might first ordain severe Laws against all Differences in Religion, and afterwards inflict the Punishments appointed by these Laws.

I shall take another Opportunity to examine the Illusion they are under, who say, that Princes pretend not to enact Laws for making Men act against Conscience, but for recovering 'em from an erroneous Conscience by Threats and temporal Inflictions. But here I'l venture to affirm, that if they may justly do this, 'tis not by virtue of the Command in the Parable, but from Reasons of State, when it happens that any Sect is justly obnoxious, with regard to the publick Good: and in this case, if they believe their Dis-affection proceeds from the Principles of their Religion, and find, that the proper and natural Methods of converting by friendly Conferences, by Books, and familiar Instructions, have no effect; they may very justly, if they conceive it expedient for the Peace of the State, oblige 'em to seek for Settlements elsewhere, and take their Goods and Familys fairly away with 'em. But to proceed as they did in *France,* where they wou'd neither suffer 'em to go out of the Kingdom, with or without their Substance, nor stay without the publick Exercise of their Religion, worshipping God after their own way in Chambers or Closets only; but reduce 'em to this Alternative, either of going openly to Mass, or being devour'd by Dragoons, and teaz'd to death by a thousand vexatious Devices: This, I say, is what can never be <118> justify'd, and what refines upon all the most extreme Violences we have any Accounts of.

I ask these Gentlemen, who tell us, that since the King of *France* only inflicts the Punishments he had fairly threatned on the Infringers of his Edicts, they ought not to tax him with Injustice, but own themselves guilty of Obstinacy and Disobedience to their lawful Prince; I ask 'em, I say, whether this ben't maintaining, that Punishments are always justly in-flicted, where the Party has disobey'd the Prince's Injunctions. For if these Punishments were just in certain limited Cases only, their Answer wou'd be illusive, and bring us under the Perplexity of discussing whether the Punishments of the *Hugonots* in particular, be in the number of just Pun-ishments; which wou'd only bring about the Dispute upon the main Ques-tion between us. If therefore they wou'd answer pertinently, they must lay it down as a general Position; and in this case, what will become of the Punishment of the Jewish Children, who were cast into the fiery Furnace? Must not we say, 'twas just? Were not they fairly warn'd and threaten'd by a Law, unless they kneel'd before the King's Image? I ask these Gentlemen once more, what they wou'd think on't, shou'd *Lewis* the Great make a Law for all his Subjects to kneel before the Statue, which the Duke *de la Feuillade* has lately erected him. I don't here enter into the Conjectures of idle People, who talk, that if Affairs go on as they have done for fifteen or twenty years past, one of these three things must necessarily happen; either the Court of *France* will enjoin publick Worship to be paid this Statue; or shou'd the

Court be coy, the People < 119 > will fall down before it of their own accord; or if these too shou'd be backward, the Clergy will lead the Dance by their Processions and Apostrophes from the Pulpit. What God pleases; for my part I'm too much employ'd at present to examine these airy Speculations on Futurity.

> *Prudens futuri Temporis exitum*
> *Caliginosa nocte premit Deus,*
> *Ridetque si mortalis ultra*
> *Fas trepidat: quod adest memento*
> *Componere aequus, caetera fluminis ritu feruntur.*[53]

But shou'd this really happen, I mean; shou'd the King enjoin his Subjects to invoke this Statue, burn Incense, fall prostrate before it, on pain of a Fine at discretion, or corporal Punishment; I desire to know whether fining the Catholicks, who refus'd to comply (some I don't doubt wou'd, especially of the Laity) were not very unjust, and the punishing 'em very criminal? Neither *Maimbourg,* nor *Varillas,* nor *Ferrand,* dare even at this day affirm the contrary.

We read of *Basilides,* Great Duke of *Muscovy,* that he enacted very hard Laws, and enforc'd 'em with capital Punishments: he commanded one of his Subjects to cross a River half frozen over; another to bury himself stark naked in the Snow; another to leap into a Fire of live Coals; a fourth to bring him a Glass of his Sweat in a cold frosty Morning, a thousand Fleas fairly counted, as many Frogs, and as many Nightingals. He was the wildest Tyrant upon Earth; yet if you consider it rightly, he did not enjoin things more < 120 > impossible than the believing this or that in matters of Religion, according as some Mens Minds are made. There are those who shou'd run you down with Sweat in a Bed of Snow, extract Wine and Oyl from their Skin and Bones, sooner than such or such an Affirmation from their Soul. I own the difficulty is not near so great as to the Hand and Mouth;

---

53. Horace, *Odes* III.xxix.29; "With wise purpose does the god bury in the shades of night the future's outcome, and laughs if mortals be anxious beyond due limits. Remember to settle with tranquil heart the problem of the hour! All else is borne along like some river." Translated C. E. Bennet, *Horace. The Odes and Epodes,* Loeb Classical Library, 1978, p. 275.

for a Man may easily say with his Tongue, and sign with his Hand, that he believes so and so, and put his Body into all the Postures that the Convertist demands: But this is not what a King, who wou'd preserve any thing of the Substance of Religion, ought to demand. He shou'd not require 'em to say, or to sign any thing till the Soul were inwardly chang'd; this inward Change, these Affirmations and Negations of the Soul, are what a King, who enacts Laws for the Conversion of his Subjects, ought in the first place to enjoin. Now this, I say, is altogether as impossible, and even more so than the Sweat which the Great Duke of *Muscovy* demanded. For if we consider, that no one believes things but when they appear to him true, and that their appearing true depends not on the human Mind, any more than their appearing black or white depends on it; we must allow, that it's easier to find Fleas and Sweat in Winter, than mentally to affirm this or that, when we have bin train'd up to see the Reasons which produce a Dissent, when we are accustom'd to hold the Negative from a Duty to God, and our Minds prepossest with a religious Shiness for all the Reasons which incline to the Affirmative. I'm not insensible, that the Mind suffers it self to be sometimes corrupted by the Heart; and that in things <121> of a dubious nature, the Passions and Affections win the Soul's Assent, where perhaps she has but a confus'd View. Yet even thus it were a horrible Wickedness to desire, that a Man shou'd determine his Choice of a Religion by a cheat upon his own Understanding; which besides is scarce possible with regard to some particular Doctrines, which People are accustom'd to look upon as absurd and contradictory: for example, that a Man shou'd eat his God; that Rats and Mice shou'd sometimes eat him; that a human Body is in a thousand places at one and the same time, without occupying any space. In a word, as it depends not on our Passions to make Snow appear black; but it's necessary to this end, either that it be tinctur'd black, or that we be plac'd in a certain Situation, and with a certain kind of Eyes, which might cause such Modifications in the Brain as black Objects usually do: so it's necessary, in order to make us affirm what we formerly deny'd, that the Matter be render'd true with regard to us, which depends on a certain Proportion between the Objects and our Facultys, and is a Circumstance not always in our own power.

But now for a few Comparisons less invidious than those of *Nebuchad-*

nezzar and *Basilides.* What wou'd the World have said of *Alphonso* King of *Castile,* had he sent his Soldiers about thro all the Towns, and Boroughs, and Villages of his Kingdom, to declare 'twas his Royal Will and Pleasure, that all his People shou'd be of his Opinion as to the Number of the Heavens, the Epicycles, Cristalins, *&c.* and that whoever refus'd to subscribe his Belief of these things, shou'd <122> be ruin'd by the quartering of Soldiers? What wou'd the World have said, if Pope *Adrian* VI who lov'd Gudgeon,[54] and whose Example had so vitiated the Tast of his Court, that this which was look'd on as a very ordinary Fish before, bore a topping price under his Pontificate, to the great laughter of the poor Fishermen; had bethought him of enjoining, not as he was Pope, but as Prince of the Ecclesiastical State, that every one for the future shou'd comply with his Tast, upon pain of Imprisonment, or Fine, or quartering of Soldiers? There's no reasonable Man but must condemn this Conduct as ridiculous and tyrannical. Yet take it all together, and 'twou'd not be near so ridiculous as saying, in a Country of different Religions, We will and ordain, that every one declare he is from henceforward of the Court-Opinion in all matters of Religion, upon pain of Imprisonment or Confiscation of Goods: I say, this Order wou'd be more unreasonable than either of the former, because it is harder for a Protestant to believe that JESUS CHRIST is present in his human Nature on all the Altars of the Catholicks, than to believe *Alphonso*'s System; and easier to reconcile one's Palat to certain Dishes, than the Understanding to certain Opinions, especially where there's a Persuasion that these Opinions hazard a Man's eternal Salvation.

Every honest Roman Catholick will own, if he reflect a little, that he cou'd much easier bring himself to relish the vilest Ragoos in *Tartary,* and believe all the Visions of *Aristotle* or *Descartes,* than believe it's an Impiety to invoke the Saints; which yet he must be oblig'd to sub-<123>scribe here, if the Papists were treated among us as the Protestants are in *France.* Away then, away all ye wicked or sensless Divines, who pretend that Kings may command their Subjects to be of such or such a Religion. The most they can do, is commanding 'em to examine or inform themselves of a Religion;

---

54. Jovius, *De piscibus.* [Author's note in the French edition. Probably: Paulus Jovius, *De romanis piscibus libellus,* 1531.]

but 'twere as absurd commanding, that what appears true to them shou'd appear so to their Subjects, as commanding that their Features and Constitution shou'd be exactly alike. *Grotius** cites two fine Passages from *Origen* and St. *Chrysostom,* shewing, that of all our Customs, there is not any so hard to be chang'd as those in favor of Religious Tenets. He likewise cites *Galen* in the same place, saying, No Itch so hard to be cur'd, as the Prejudice for a Sect.

∽ CHAPTER VII ∽

The Sixth Argument against the literal Sense, drawn from its depriving the Christian Religion of a main Objection against the Truth of Mahometism.

This Chapter shall be much shorter than the foregoing, because a certain Doctor of the *Sorbon,* call'd Mr. *Dirois,* has lately wrote a Treatise intitled, *Proofs and Prejudices in favor of the Christian Religion:* [55] wherein he fully shews the Falsity of all idolatrous Religions, and of the <124> Mahometan in particular, from their extorting Professions by main force, and from their being built upon persecuting Principles: to which he opposes the Manner in which Christianity was establish'd: gentle, peacable, bloodi'd by Persecution suffer'd, not inflict'd. 'Tis by this Topick we baffle all the Cavils of Libertines, when we urge the mighty Progress of the Christian Religion, and its spreading far and wide in so short a time, as a Proof of its Divinity. They answer, That this, if a good Argument in any Case, will be as strong on the side of the Mahometan, as the Christian Religion: since it's well known that Mahometism over-spread numberless Countrys in a small space of time. But this, we reply, is not so strange, because *Mahomet* and his Followers employ'd Constraint; whereas Christianity prevail'd and triumph'd by Sufferings, in spite of Violence and Artifice, and all Endeavors to extinguish it. There's nothing in all this Dispute that is not very reason-

---

* De Jure Belli & Pac. l. 1. cap. 20. art. 50. [Hugo Grotius, *De jure belli ac pacis* (Concerning the law of war and peace), 1631.]

55. See above, p. 52, note.

able and convincing on the side of Christians: but if once it be prov'd that JESUS CHRIST has injoin'd Constraint, nothing will be weaker than our making it an Objection against Mahometism. Whence I argue thus:

That literal Sense which deprives the Christian Religion of one of its strongest Arguments against false Religions, is false.

The literal Sense of these words, *Compel 'em to come in,* does this.

Therefore it's false.

What have you to say against the Violences of Pagans and Saracens? Dare you reproach 'em, as Mr. *Dirois* does, *That a forc'd Adoration, an* <125> *evident Hypocrisy, a Worship notoriously against Conscience, and purely to please Men, were the Characters of Piety and Religion among them?* Will you tell 'em, *That their Gods, and their Worshippers demanded no more Religion than just what might serve to destroy the true, since they were as well satisfy'd with a forc'd as with a sincere Adoration?* But can't you see they'l laugh at you, and send you home to *France* for an Answer to your Charge? Don't you see they'l reply upon you, that they do no more than JESUS CHRIST himself has expresly commanded; and instead of allowing that his first Disciples are more to be admir'd than those of *Mahomet,* tell you quite contrary, that these discharg'd their Duty much more faithfully, having trifled away none of their time, but immediately fallen to the short and effectual way appointed by God? They'l tell you, the Christians of the three first Centurys were either Contemners of the Orders of JESUS CHRIST, or a pack of Poltrons, who had not a Spirit to execute his Commands; or Simpletons, who knew not the hundredth part of their own Power: Whereas the *Mahometans* took their Orders right from the first hint, and executed 'em gallantly; very zealous in the Execution of a Law, which can't but be very just, since we are oblig'd to own 'twas deliver'd by JESUS CHRIST. And as to the swift Progress of their Religion; if on one hand we diminish the Merit of it on account of their great earthly Power, they'l enhance it on the other, by saying, that God gave a visible Blessing to that Zeal and Courage which they manifested, without loss of time, in propagating the Divine Religion of his Prophet, by <126> methods which we our selves revere as holy, and expresly enjoin'd by God.

ಿಲ್ CHAPTER VIII ಿಲ್

The seventh Argument against the literal Sense, drawn from its being unknown to the Fathers of the three first Centurys.

This Argument might be binding upon those of the Church of *Rome,* were they Men of fixt Principles: But alas, they are not, they are *Proteus's,* who get loose by a thousand slippery tricks, and under all kind of Forms, when one thinks he has 'em fastest. They'l teach us in all other Instances, that where a Dispute arises concerning the Sense of any Scripture-Passage, we must consult Tradition, and hold by the Sense of the Fathers: So that let any Exposition of Scripture be ever so reasonable, yet if it be new, they'l tell us it's not worth a straw, it comes too late, and there's Prescription against it. To reason upon this Principle, all Arguments for Persecution drawn from the Gospel, in the days of *Theodosius* and St. *Augustin,* ought to be rejected; because 'twas giving the Gospel a Sense intirely new, which came too late, and which there was Prescription against. But our Adversarys are not to be stun'd with such Trifles; they'l say, the Authority of the Fathers is valid, not where themselves happen to differ about any point of Doctrine, but where they unanimously agree: And for this Reason, the great <127> Lights of the fourth Century not falling in with some former Opinions concerning Persecution, the more antient Fathers are not a sufficient Authority for the Doctrine I maintain. When we press 'em by saying, that all the Fathers are not agreed in any one point, they wriggle themselves out by some other Loop-hole, and are not asham'd to maintain the literal Sense; tho by their own Confession, the unanimous Consent of the Fathers, that indispensable mark of Truth, be wanting. However, this shall not hinder my going on with my Argument in the following manner.

It is not probable, had JESUS CHRIST ordain'd the making Christians by force, that the Fathers of the three first Centurys had constantly reason'd, as Men verily persuaded, that all Constraint is inconsistent with the Nature of Religion: for with regard to all points of Gospel-Morality, or as to any Precept, or Counsel (call it so) of JESUS CHRIST, none were fitter to know the Sense of the Scriptures than they; and shou'd God have conceal'd from 'em the meaning of a Precept of this importance, so far as to let 'em run on in false Reasonings, and in a Supposition of its being impious, there's no Christian but might justly be shock'd and scandaliz'd at their Ignorance. Once more then, I say, it's manifestly against Reason, against all the Appearances of Truth, that JESUS CHRIST shou'd enjoin compelling the Jews and the Gentiles to Baptism; and yet the Apostles either not comprehend him, or if they did, not caution their chief Disciples to be reserv'd in condemning Violences, lest by condemning 'em in general, they shou'd advance <128> an Heterodoxy, and directly contradict JESUS CHRIST, at least put Arms into the hands of those whom the Christians might one day use violence to, and give 'em a handle for crying out upon the shameful difference between the Christianity of the first, and that of the latter days. This was the least cou'd be expected from the Apostles and their first Disciples, the trustiest Depositarys of Tradition: If it was not seasonable or prudent to execute the Order of JESUS CHRIST in those earlier days, by compelling to come in; at least they shou'd have hinted, that a Day wou'd come, when this might be very piously practis'd, and in the mean time beware branding this Doctrine with the Character of Falshood. Yet this the Fathers have done in the strongest terms, and even in the fourth Century, when the *Arians* first began to persecute. *This alone,* says St. *Athanasius, is a plain Argument, that they have neither Piety nor the Fear of God before their Eyes. 'Tis the Nature of Piety not to constrain, but to persuade; after the Example of* J. CHRIST, WHO CONSTRAINING NONE, *left it to every one's Discretion, whether they wou'd follow him or no. For the Devil's part, as he has not the force of Truth on his side, he comes about with Sledges and Iron Crows to burst open the Doors of those who are to receive him: but so meek is our Lord and Saviour, that tho he teaches in such a Stile as this,* If any one will come after me; He that will be my Disciple; *yet he compels none; knocking only at the Door, and saying,* My Sister, my Spouse, open unto me; *and entring when it's open'd, and departing if they tarry and are unwilling to receive him: for it is not* (mark well these words, ye Gentlemen of the Council of Conscience to *Lewis* XIV most Chris-<129>tian King of *France* and *Navarre*) WITH SWORD AND SPEAR, NOR WITH SOLDIERS AND ARM'D FORCE, THAT TRUTH IS TO BE PROPAGATED, BUT BY COUNSEL AND

SWEET PERSUASION.[56] Isn't this the plainest Proof, that the Apostles knew nothing of this pretended Mystery of Persecution, contain'd in the Parable; and that JESUS CHRIST intended, not only that it shou'd be unknown to the first Ages of Christianity, but condemn'd also and stigmatiz'd as a cruel and diabolical Impiety? which wou'd look very absurd, if at the same time he had enjoin'd Persecution. For how can we conceive, that he shou'd suffer a Point of Morality of such Consequence to be traduc'd and anathematiz'd by the holiest and purest part of Christianity for some Ages together; and these Anathema's intended to refute the Enemys of Truth, by showing, that JESUS CHRIST taught his Disciples to constrain no one? They said so much not only before the Christian Emperors made use of Violence, but for a long time after. Our venerable* *Bede* speaking of King *Ethelred,* in whose Reign St. *Gregory* Pope of *Rome* mission'd the Monk *Augustin,* with some others, to convert our Island, mentions expresly, that this King being converted to the Christian Faith, *constrain'd none of his Subjects to follow his Example, and only distinguish'd those by his Favors, who* <130> *became Christians; having learn'd,* says he, *from his Doctors and Instruments of his Salvation, that the Service of* JESUS CHRIST *ought to be voluntary, and not constrain'd.* This Notion, to wit, that JESUS CHRIST has ordain'd only Instruction, Persuasion, a voluntary Service, and by no means Violence, is so deeply engrav'd in our Minds, that we vend it as indubitable, whenever there is not an actual design of flattering, or not provoking Princes who persecute, or when the justifying Persecutions is not the present Subject of one's Book. In *France* there are Treatises daily printed, in which this Notion is plainly exprest, which renders the Popish Writers of that Kingdom extremely ridiculous; because sometimes in the very Books where they say it's

---

* Ut nullum tamen cogeret ad Christianismum, sed tantummodo credentes arctiori dilectione quasi concives Regni coelestis amplecteretur, didicerat enim a doctoribus auctoribus suae salutis servitium Christi voluntarium non coactitium debere esse. *Bed. l.* 1. *c. 26.* [Bede, *Historical Works,* Loeb Classical Library, vol. 1, p. 114.]

56. Athanasius, *Epistula ad solitarios.* [Author's note in the French edition. Athanasius, *History of the Arians* (formerly called "letter to the solitaries"), Part IV, ch. 33, in *Nicene and Post Nicene Fathers,* ed. Schaff and Wace, series 2 (Oxford: Parker, 1890), vol. 4, p. 281.]

lawful to compel, having in view the Dragoonerys for forcing the Protestants, they drop unawares, that the Gospel is a Law of Meekness and Gentleness, which accepts no Offerings but what are voluntary: the Reason is, that they forget for that moment their principal Theme of palliating and flattering, and so long the Notions of the Heart and Understanding take place. Add to this, that they deny their King has made use of Violence, which is in some measure acknowledging the Falsity of the literal Sense.

I don't cite those Passages of the Fathers, which condemn in the general all manner of Persecution and Violence on the score of Religion: they are notorious to all the World. *Grotius* has collected a good many; and even the mercenary *French* Apologists for Persecution can't dissemble these Authoritys of the Fathers, as may be seen in a Book written by one *Ferrand,* a Barister at Law among 'em. <131>

∽ CHAPTER IX ∽

The eighth Argument against the literal Sense, drawn from its rendring the Complaints of the first Christians against their Pagan Persecutors all vain.

The Argument in the foregoing Chapter does not seem to me near so convincing as some of the rest, tho consider'd *ad hominem,*[57] it might well silence those who talk only of Tradition, and the Rule of Prescription. However it has a close Connection with what I'm next to offer, and therefore I shall not be so long upon the principal Matter of this Argument as upon the Accessorys. Here goes then:

That literal Sense which renders the Complaints of the first Christians against their Pagan Persecutors vain, is false.

Now such is the literal Sense of the words, *Compel 'em to come in.*

It's therefore false.

The Minor I prove in this manner. I'l suppose the primitive Christians had sent their Deputys to Court to present their Apology, and complain, how they were imprison'd, banish'd, expos'd to wild Beasts, tortur'd. I'll

---

57. See Appendixes, "Bayle's Use of Logic," p. 580, note 3.

suppose too, that the literal Sense in question was known to Pagans as well as Christians, both having read this Passage in the Gospel according to St. *Luke,* which the Pagans might have Copys of if they pleas'd. I'l <132> suppose in the third place, that some great Person, commission'd by the Emperor, had entred into a Conference with these Christian Deputys, and having heard out their Allegations, answer'd 'em, *Gentlemen, what do you complain of? You are treated no worse than you wou'd treat us if you were in our place: you ought to approve our Prudence, and complain of the Season only, and not of us. This is our Day, we are the strongest side: common Prudence requires, that we shou'd lay hold of the Opportunity Fortune presents us of extinguishing a Sect, which strikes not only at our Temples and Gods, but at our very Lives and Consciences. Your God has commanded you to compel all that fall in your way to follow him; what then cou'd you do less, if you had the power in your hands, than put all those to death who cou'd not resolve on be-traying the Lights of their Conscience to worship your crucify'd God?* To this they must answer, if they have the least Sincerity, and be of the Principle which I confute: *It's true, my Lord, if we had the power in our hands, we shou'd not leave a Soul in the World unbaptiz'd; and herein wou'd appear our Charity and great Love towards our Neighbor: we believe all are eternally damn'd who are not of our Religion, 'twere very cruel then in us not to employ some means of Constraint. But still we shou'd not use those Methods which you Pagans make use of towards us; we shou'd only take care, that those, who did not turn, shou'd never carry any Cause in our Courts; we shou'd start strange Cavils upon 'em, hinder their religious Meetings; and if this did not make their Lives uneasy enough, we shou'd send Dragoons to quarter upon 'em, to eat 'em out of House and Home, and drub 'em into the Bargain: We shou'd hinder their flying into foreign Parts;* <133> *and if we found 'em fleeing, send 'em away to the Gallys: we shou'd put their Wives and Children under Sequestra-tion; in a word, we shou'd leave 'em but this Alternative, either to pass their whole Life in the gloom of a Dungeon, or get themselves baptiz'd. But as to taking away their Lives, God forbid we shou'd be guilty of it: now and then perhaps a Soldier exceeding his Orders, might lay one of 'em on so as he shou'd never recover it; but this wou'd seldom happen, and be seldomer countenanc'd.* It's plain, that instead of poisoning this Answer, I couch it in the mildest and most moderate terms our Adversarys themselves can propose; since I form it upon the Plan of the present Persecution in *France,* the most regular in their Opinion, and the most Christian Scheme of Evangelick Compulsion, that ever yet was known. I was at liberty to regulate this Answer upon the Inquisition, upon the Crusades of St. *Dominick,* upon the Butcherys of Queen *Mary,* upon the Massacres of *Cabrieres,* of *Merindol,* and of the Valleys of *Piemont;* upon the Tortures under *Francis* I and *Henry* II and upon the Slaughter of St. *Bartholomew:* but I soften the matter as much as it will bear. Let's see now what the Pagan Emperor's Minister wou'd reply.

Upon my word, Gentlemen (says he without doubt) you are very admirable Folks; you reckon it a mighty piece of Charity, not to dispatch a Man all at once, but keep him in a lingring Torture all his Life, whether he resolve to rot in a Dungeon, or has the weakness to pretend he embraces what his Conscience tells him is a detestable Impiety. Go, go, Gentlemen; beside that this mock Charity wou'd scarce restrain you from the <134> Methods we take, that is, from inventing exquisite Torments when time and place requir'd (for your Master commands you only in general to constrain, and leaves it to your Discretion, to chuse the way; vexatious Prosecutions, and quartering of Soldiers, when you deem these properer than Massacres and the sharpest Deaths; and these again when you judg 'em more expedient than Fines, and Querks of Law, or Insults of the Soldiery) Beside this, I say, you are a parcel of merry Fellows to recommend your selves upon a politick Fetch, in not spilling the Blood of your Subjects, when the only Motive of sparing was, that you might not weaken your temporal Power by the loss of too many Lives; and at the same time boast you had done more without the Wheel or Gibbet, than others had ever done with 'em. Take it by which handle you please; we shan't be Sots enough, if we have the Power to prevent it, to let you grow to a head, and put you in a condition of doing Mischief; resolve therefore to suffer: The Emperor, my Master, owes this Sacrifice to his own Repose, and to that of his Posterity, to whom you may one day become a Scourge.

The Rules of Probability won't allow me to make the Deputys speak a word more; for after the Answer I have already made for 'em, there's no likelihood they shou'd long be allow'd any kind of Liberty: however, that my Reader may the better comprehend what I aim at, I shall suppose a Reply on the Deputys part.

Pray pardon us, my Lord, if we yet presume to inform you, that our holy Doctrine has bin all along misrepresented to you by our Enemys; it's <135> only by mere chance, and with the greatest regret in the world, that we shou'd proceed to rough Methods. We shou'd first endeavor by our Instructions to convince Men of the Truth; we shou'd employ all the sweetest and most endearing Arts: but if 'twere our misfortune to light upon perverse obstinate Spirits, who stood it out against all the Lights we cou'd furnish their Understandings; then indeed, tho much against the grain, and from a charitable Asperity, we shou'd be oblig'd to make 'em do that by force, which they wou'd not do voluntarily; and even have the Charity not to exact a Confession from 'em, that their signing was a downright force upon 'em. This were a Monument of Shame to themselves, and to their Children, and to us too; we shou'd rather oblige 'em to give under their hands, that 'twas their own voluntary Act and Deed. Besides, my Lord, it does not follow from our having a Right to constrain, that you have the same Right too: We speak in the Cause of Truth, and therefore are allow'd to exercise Violence on Delinquents; but false Religions have no such Privilege, such Methods in them wou'd be downright *Barbarian* Cruelty; in us it's all Divine, being the Fruits of a holy Charity.

If I have broke the Rules of Probability, by supposing, that these Deputys wou'd be allow'd to reply, I shou'd do so much more by suggesting a Rejoinder on the High Commissioner's part, or any other Answer than ordering 'em the Strapado by the hands of the common Beadle; saving notwithstanding, and reserving to the Gibbet or Amphitheatre all its Rights and Privileges, where no doubt they'd be expos'd on the very next occasion. <136> However, let's suppose him phlegmatick enough not to fly into a Rage at such nonsense; let's suppose this, I say, the better to lead the Reader to the design'd end. There's no manner of doubt then but he wou'd tell 'em in this Case:

Good People, your Maxims have only this one Fault, that they are wrongfully apply'd; no Religion but that of my Master's can talk at this rate, because it's the only true Religion: I undertake on his part, that none but the obstinate among you shall be ill treated; get your selves instructed, and be converted; you shall find the Effects of his Clemency: otherwise you'l provoke him to your Ruin, and with Justice; whereas, shou'd you exercise any Violence against a Religion establish'd for so many Ages, you must be guilty of a crying Iniquity.

One that were an Enemy to all Persecution, and had any thing of a Talent in reasoning, might add as follows, addressing himself to these Deputys:

After all, what you say seems very odd to me, that your proceeding to Violence shou'd be purely accidental: For since your Master enjoins you to compel People by main Force, your business is, not only to enter those into your Religion whom you have fairly convinc'd, but those likewise who are convinc'd your Religion is false. Now, if your direct end concerns those, it must naturally and directly include all the means which lead to it, to wit, Force and Violence; and consequently, it is not by mere accident that you vex Men but by a necessary and natural Consequence of your Scheme.
<137>

Perhaps there's some room for a Cavil here, tho I'm persuaded the Reason is good at bottom; and from it I draw this new Argument against the literal Sense of the Parable:

If any thing cou'd excuse the Violences imply'd in the Command of making all Men Christians, 'twere saying, they are only accidentally included in it.

Now it's false that they are included in it only by accident.

Nothing therefore can excuse 'em.

The Major is not evident enough to Understandings, which the Passions, and an unhappy Education in the Principles of a Religion, which properly speaking are only Nature in its corruptest state, lurking under the shew of God's Worship; have miserably blur'd, and encompass'd with thick Darkness: let's therefore endeavor to set it in the clearest light.

I affirm then, that Persecutions, directly and absolutely included in the means of converting Men, are wholly inexcusable: and this I prove from that Order which God has establish'd in the Operations of our Mind, whereby Knowledge precedes Love, and the Light of the Understanding all Acts of the Will. This Order appears to be a necessary and immutable Law: for we have no greater Evidence that two and two make four, than we have, that to act reasonably a Man must doubt of what appears to him doubtful, deny what appears to him evidently false, affirm what appears evidently true, love those things which appear to him good, and hate what appears evil. These things are so consonant to Order, that we all agree a Man acts rashly, and even commits <138> a Sin, when he swears a thing is so or so, which really is, but which he believes to be otherwise: and we can't doubt but the Love even of Vertue wou'd be a Violation of this Order, in a Person sincerely persuaded 'twas evil, and forbidden by a lawful Authority. This being the Case, a Man is not justify'd to Order when he embraces the Gospel, unless previously convinc'd of its Truth: All Designs therefore and Means of making a Man embrace the Gospel, who is not persuaded of its Truth, swerve from the Rules and Course of that Eternal Order, which constitutes all the Rectitude and Justness of an Action. Now all Designs leading directly and point-blank to Violences on those who don't freely convert to the Gospel, tend directly to make even those embrace it who were not persuaded of its Truth; every such Design therefore must swerve from the Rules and Course of Order, and consequently be naught. It's plain, there can be no Intention of directly forcing a Man, without a direct Design of making him comply, even where he has a Repugnancy; it's therefore plain, as I have already said, that whoever shou'd employ Force to get People to subscribe the Apostles Creed, and employ it as the direct Means to this End, must have a direct design of making even those subscribe who believ'd it false. And since this Design wou'd be manifestly against Order, it follows, that no Violence, directly included in the means of converting, can be lawful; and consequently, the only thing in excuse must be saying, that the Violence enters indirectly, and by accident, into the Scheme of converting. And thus I think the *Major* is clearly prov'd. Now for the *Minor*. <139>

I desire my Adversarys to answer me this Question; Whether the Design of travelling includes a Ship by it self, or by accident. They'l answer, without doubt, and very rightly, that a Ship is a thing purely accidental to Travelling. But if instead of keeping to the general Notion of Travelling, I descend to this particular Case, that such a one has a design to travel from *France* into *England;* won't it then be true, with regard to this design, that a Ship is no longer a thing accidental, but a means naturally necessary? Let's apply this to the Design of converting Mankind to the Christian Religion.

Either you have such a Design indefinitely and in general, or else you propose to your self some particular means. If you have only the Design at large, all particular Measures are accidental: but if you descend to the particular Design of making all the World Christians, either by fair or by foul means, it's evident you directly and truly include Violence in your Design; because in case of Opposition, you are resolv'd to surmount it by Force. I grant your Violence is but a conditional Ingredient; that is, you wish you cou'd accomplish your Design by fair means, but still with this reserve, that if these won't do, you'l proceed to foul. Hence I affirm, that Violence enters into your Design, not by mere Accident, but by a proper Choice and secondary Destination. For as they who dread the Sea wou'd be very glad there were no occasion for Ships, yet if they resolve to pass from *France* into *England* they directly and properly design to make use of a Ship; so he who'd be glad he cou'd convert Men by preaching only, may wish he may <140> never come to Violence: yet if he's resolv'd to convert, even where preaching is in vain, he directly and properly wills Persecution. In a word, where we are intirely at liberty to pursue or to quit a Design, and it happens that we encounter certain Obstacles; it's plain, that if we pursue it in this case, we shew that we properly will this Pursuit; and that all the means indispensably leading to it, are the proper matter of our Choice and Consent. They don't therefore belong to such a Design by Accident, in that sense which this Term imports, when it's pleaded in excuse of the Consequences of an Affair, or the Faults of a Person.

There's no need of proving that JESUS CHRIST must come under the present case, since 'twas purely at his own election, whether he wou'd force People or no; nor to prove by a hundred Reasons, that the Man, who wou'd willingly bring about his Ends by one method preferably to all others, but is firmly resolv'd to attain 'em by another sort of means, if he fail in the first, does properly and culpably (if he be a free Agent, and the Matter sinful) will this other means. From whence it wou'd follow, that Violence is included in the Design of converting Men to the Gospel, directly, and by the Destination of JESUS CHRIST: so that his Intent must be constru'd thus; *My will is, that Men be persuaded to believe the Gospel, and that they make profession of it; but if they are not to be fairly persuaded, I intend nevertheless they shall profess it.* Now I affirm and maintain, that such a Design shocks the Eternal Law of Order, which is an indispensable Law to God himself; and consequently, that it is impossible JESUS CHRIST <141> cou'd have form'd it. All the Cavils that can possibly be started from the Distinction of *being by accident*, can't prevent the Minor's being demonstrated as fully as matters of this nature will bear. But be that how it will, the general Position in this Chapter seems to me sufficiently prov'd, to wit, That the Complaints and Remonstrances of Christians, who must have confess'd, that were they in the place of the Pagans, they shou'd hardly be behindhand with 'em in Persecution, were vain and ridiculous.

∞ CHAPTER X ∞

The Ninth and Last Argument against the Literal Sense, drawn from its tending to expose true Christians to continual Violences, without a possibility of alledging any thing to put a stop to 'em, but that which was the ground of the Contest between the Persecutors and the Persecuted: And this, as 'tis but a wretched begging the Question, *cou'd not prevent the World's being a continual Scene of Blood.*

We have already seen in two several places, to wit, in the fifth and the foregoing Chapters, the Mischiefs, which a Command of exercising Violence on those who refus'd to be converted, wou'd do to the true Religion: And it's certain, that this alone, consider'd in gross and in the general, forms a very plausible Preju-<142>dice against it. For how is it to be imagin'd, that God shou'd enjoin his Church such a Practice, as must render all its Complaints in the midst of Oppression ridiculous, and give Princes and States a very just pretence for extinguishing it? Had St. *Austin* but remember'd his own excellent Lesson, in his Treatise *de Genesi ad Literam,* he had ne'er embroil'd himself, as he did, in defending the Cause of Persecutors; for there he tells us, that 'tis shameful, dangerous, and extremely indiscreet in a Christian, to speak of things according to the Principles of his Religion in the presence of Infidels, and in such a manner, that they can't forbear laughing. How came he not to see that he shou'd expose himself to the Derision of Pagans, when he maintain'd that God had in his Holy Word authoriz'd Persecutions on the score of Religion? Certainly nothing's more sensless than blaming those Actions in others which we canonize in our selves; nothing more absurd, than to take it ill, that a Prince, who believes the Pagan Religion true, and that God commands him to watch for the publick Welfare, shou'd not tolerate a Sect, which by its Principles must ravage the World, if once it had the Power. But that which is no more than a Prejudice, when consider'd in the gross, becomes a solid Argument, when we take the pains to unfold and examine it accurately. This is what we have partly endeavor'd to perform already in the two foremention'd Chapters, and what we shall continue to do in this, to the best of our power. Here then is our last Argument. <143>

That literal Sense, which tends to throw all the different Partys of Christians into a never-ceasing War, without admitting any possible Remedy to stop so great an Evil, but the Sentence which shall be pronounc'd upon the Cause of each at the last Day; cannot be the true Sense.

Now such is the literal Sense of the words, *Compel 'em to come in.*

It's therefore not the true Sense.

The first Proposition seems to me evident enough of it self: for tho God has not spoke to us in his reveal'd Word after a manner perfectly fitted to prevent all Differences among Christians, yet we must believe, that if on one hand he has permitted Divisions in his Church, he has on the other provided a certain Rule, and certain Principles common to all, sufficient to keep the disagreeing Partys in some order, and prevent their worrying one another like so many wild Beasts. The obscure parts of Scripture are chiefly concerning speculative Points: Doctrines of Morality being more necessary for the Welfare of Societys, and for hindring the utter Extinction of the little Vertue that's left, are propounded there much more intelligibly to all the World. But whether these be quite clear enough or no, to prevent their being wrested to a false Sense, and to ill Purposes; this at least is certain, that the Intention of the Holy Spirit must have bin holy, just, and innocent, and very far from giving a handle and plausible excuse for confounding the World. Now this is what cou'd not be affirm'd, were it true that JESUS CHRIST had given his Followers a Command to persecute. <144>

I pass over all the Disorders likely to happen in the World from the use which Infidels might make of seeing Christians authorize Violence: I won't affirm, that they wou'd turn all the Arguments of Christians for the tormenting of those who differ from 'em in Opinion, upon themselves; I shan't insist on this: I'l only consider what wou'd happen between Sect and Sect among Christians themselves. It's plain, that if JESUS CHRIST had meant Persecution in a strict sense, and the constraining Men to sign a Formulary, when he exprest the words, *Compel 'em to come in;* the Orthodox Party wou'd have a Right of forcing the Erroneous as much as they judg'd convenient: There's no doubt of this. But as each Party believes it self the Orthodox, it's plain, if JESUS CHRIST had commanded Persecution, that each Sect wou'd think it self oblig'd to obey him by persecuting all the rest with the utmost rigor, till they constrain'd 'em to embrace their own Profession of Faith: And thus we shou'd see a continual War between People of the same Country, either in the Streets or in the open Field, or between Nations of different Opinions; so that Christianity wou'd be a mere Hell upon Earth to all who lov'd Peace, or who happen'd to be the weaker side.

But what's most ridiculous in all this, is, that the Oppress'd could have no just ground for the Reproaches and Complaints which yet they wou'd certainly make against the oppressing persecuting Party. For shou'd they say; *It's true,* JESUS CHRIST *has commanded his Disciples to persecute, but this gives no Right to you, who are a Heretick; the executing this Command belongs only* <145> *to us, who are the true Church:* These wou'd answer, that they are agreed in the Principle, but not in the Application; and that they alone having the Truth undoubtedly of their side, have the sole Right to persecute. Whereby it's plain the Persecuted cou'd not justly blame their Persecutors, either for imprisoning, or fining 'em, or taking away their Children, or letting the Dragoons loose on 'em, or for any other Violence; because instead of examining the Facts by any common Rule of Morality, to know whether just or no, they must begin from the bottom of their Controversys to find which Party is right, and which wrong, in their respective Confessions of Faith. Now this is a tedious business, as every one knows: We never see the end of such a Dispute; and no Judgment being to be pronounc'd upon the Violences in question, till the issue of the Dispute, and till a definitive Sentence upon their Controversys be pass'd, the Power must remain by a kind of Sequestration in the hands of the victorious Party: The suffering Party pining in the mean time, and spending it self in a fruitless Vye and Revye of its Controversys one by one, without having the wretched pleasure of saying, *I'm unjustly us'd;* but by supposing the thing in dispute, and saying, *I am the true Church.* To which the opposite will presently reply, *You are not the true Church, therefore you are justly treated: you have not prov'd your Pretensions as yet, we still deny; forbear your Complaints then, till the Cause is decided.* <146>

I can't conceive a more melancholy State among Men, and at the same time more expos'd to the Mockery of all the Profane, of all Libertines, and even of all Mankind, than this. 'Tis pleasant enough, and very glorious to the Christian Name, to compare the Griefs of the Orthodox, and their Complaints against the Pagan and Arian Persecutions, with their Apologys for persecuting the *Donatists.* When one reflects on all this impartially, he'l find it amount to this rare Principle; *I have the Truth on my side, therefore my Violences are good Works: Such a one is in an Error, therefore his Violences are criminal.* To what purpose, pray, are all these Reasonings? Do they heal the Evils which Persecutors commit, or are they capable of making 'em enter into an Examination of the way they have bin bred in? Isn't it absolutely necessary, in order to cure the Frenzy of a Zealot, who turns a whole Country upside down, and give him a Sense of his doings, to draw him out of his particular Controversys, and bring him to Principles which are common to both Partys, such as the Maxims of Morality, the Precepts of the Decalogue, of JESUS CHRIST and of his Apostles, concerning Justice, Charity, refraining from Theft, Murder, Injurys to our Neighbor, &c? This therefore were one great Inconvenience in the pretended Command of JESUS CHRIST, that it wou'd deprive Christians of their common Rule of judging whether an Action be good or evil. Nor wou'd it be a less Evil, that Christians of all Denominations might claim a Right by it of persecuting all who were not of their <147> own Communion; which must needs draw on a thousand Violences on one side, and a thousand Hypocrisys on the other. A third and main Inconvenience wou'd be, that Christians of all Sects might maintain, with like reason on their side, that their persecuting all other Christians is just; whence it wou'd follow, that persecuting the very Truth wou'd be a pious Action. For as the Precepts of honoring our Father and Mother, of not defiling our selves with the Lusts of the Flesh, of not killing, not robbing, of loving our Neighbour as our selves, loving God, and forgiving our Enemys, concern *Arians, Nestorians,* and *Socinians,* as much as they do the Reform'd, the Catholicks, and the very Flower of Predestination; so the Precept of Compelling may be said to be indifferently addrest to all Christians: or if you restrain it to the Orthodox only, why won't you also limit the Command of being sober, chast, charitable, to them alone? Now if the Command of Compelling, in the literal Sense, be addrest to all who believe the Gospel; each Sect shou'd take it as addrest to themselves, and execute it in favor of the Tenets which they take for Gospel, in favor of that Religion they think the true; otherwise they formally disobey the Orders of their Creator: they therefore are oblig'd to persecute in duty to God. A new Proof of the Falsity of this Precept, since it implies God's giving a Command, by the obeying of which the greatest part of Christians must be not only guilty of a Crime, but likewise of a direct Attempt to destroy the Truth. But we shall speak more <148> fully in another place to the Right which the Unorthodox may claim from the words of the Parable.

A

Philosophical COMMENTARY
On these Words of St. *Luke,*
Chap. XVI. ver. 23.
COMPEL 'EM TO COME IN.

The Second PART.

Containing a full Answer to all the Objections which may be rais'd against what has bin before demonstrated.

⁊ CHAPTER I ⁊

First Objection, That Violence is not design'd to force Conscience, but to awaken those who neglect to examine the Truth. The Illusion of this Thought. An Inquiry into the Nature of what they call OPINIATRETÉ.[58]

To shew how frivolous an Excuse this is, I shall only endeavor to prove the two following Points: First, That the Means these Gentlemen propose for examining the Truth, is the most unreasonable in the World; Next, That it can be of almost no service in a manner to their Cause, while they <150>

---

58. Opiniatreté: Being opinionated, being stubbornly unwilling to change one's mind.

keep to those Terms which they seem fully resolv'd to abide by. Let's explain both these Considerations severally.

All the reasonable part of Mankind, and those who have made the best Observations on the nature of things, and on that of Man in particular, are agreed, that one of the greatest Obstacles in a Search after Truth, is that of the Passions obscuring and disguising the Objects of our Understanding, or making a perpetual diversion of the Forces of the Mind. Hence they so earnestly recommend the getting an intire Command over our Passions, so as to be able to silence and dismiss 'em at pleasure: Hence they suppose it the Duty of a righteous Judg to hear the Reasons o' both sides in cool blood, and free from all Passion; and even believe him incapable of dispensing exact Justice, without this Disposition. Even Pity and Compassion, Qualitys very useful in Religion and civil Life, they suppose capable of blinding the Judgment, and giving a wrong Biass. It's certain, where the Mind is calm, and preserving an even and steddy frame, is able to look fixedly on a miserable Object, without those Emotions of Pity, which intender the Soul; 'tis much more capable of sifting out the Truth thro all the Disguises of Artifice and Counterfeit; 'tis plac'd in the true Point of Sight for perceiving the Merits of the Cause. For after all, the Wretch whose melancholy Figure moves Pity, and makes our very Bowels yearn, may have committed the Fact he stands accus'd of: and shou'd there be any thing of a shuffle or slight in the Management, which a dispassionate Judg might be able to see thro, by the Penetration of <151> his Genius; yet he's utterly disabled, when Pity operates and possesses him with a favorable Opinion of the Accus'd. In a word, nothing is truer than this Maxim of the *Roman** Historian; *That it behoves those who consult upon things of a doubtful nature, to be free from Hatred, Friendship, Anger and Compassion; for the Mind can't readily discern the true state of things, where these interfere.* I cou'd furnish out twenty Pages with Sentences of the same kind, did I only consult the *Polyanthea.* But who sees not already how unreasonable the Objection is, which I'm about to confute in this Chapter? It's not our Intention, say the

---

* *Sallust. de Bell. Catilin.* Omnes homines qui de rebus dubiis consultant, ab odio, amicitiâ, irâ, atque misericordiâ vacuos esse decet, nam animus haud facilè verum providet ubi illa officiunt. [Sallust, *Bellum Catilinae*, LI.1–2, Loeb Classical Library, p. 89.]

Convertists, that any one shou'd violate the Lights of his Conscience, to be deliver'd from the Uneasiness we give him: All our aim and all our hopes is, that a Love for the Comforts of Life, and a Dread of Misery will rouze him from his slumber, and put him upon an Examination of the two Religions; being confident that a fair Review can't fail of discovering to him the Falseness of his own, and the Truth of ours. That is, the business being to pass judgment in a Question of mighty importance, as well with regard to the Reasons o' both sides, as to the Consequences of a good or a bad Choice; we'l have Men enter upon the Merits of it, not in a state of clear and undisturb'd Reason, when their Passions are calm'd; but under the disadvantage of all those Mists and thick Darkness, which a Conflict of several violent Passions must <152> needs produce in the Soul. Can any thing be more absurd? Were there a difference between two Footmen about three Half-crowns, no body wou'd think it reasonable, that one who was an Enemy to either of 'em, or who fear'd or expected any thing from either, shou'd be the Umpire between 'em: and yet here, where the Glory of God is at stake, and the eternal Salvation of mens Souls, 'tis thought reasonable that the Judges who are to decide between Catholick and Protestant, who is right, and who wrong, shou'd come with Souls full of Resentment, full of worldly Hopes and Fears. It's thought reasonable, that a Man who is to weigh the Reasons of both sides, instead of applying the whole force of his Facultys in the Inquiry, shou'd be distracted on one hand with the approaching prospect of a Family ruin'd, exil'd, or encloister'd; of his own Person degraded and render'd incapable of all Honors and Preferments, buffeted by Soldiers, and thrust into a loathsom Dungeon; and on the other hand, by the prospect of several Advantages for himself and Family. The Man, you see, is in a fair way of making a right judgment; for if he be strongly persuaded of the Truth of his own Religion, and fears God enough to find a reluctance to the professing a Religion he thinks naught, he'l be but the more confirm'd in his own, by the prejudice he must needs conceive against the other, from the tyrannical methods it employs against him. If he loves the World more than his God or his Religion, one of these two things will undoubtedly follow; either he'l blind himself the best he can, to introduce a dislike of his own Religion; or else <153> quit it abruptly, without troubling his head to examine whether t'other Religion be better or no: he'l determine himself by the temporal Advantages which this offers, and by the Persecutions which that might expose him to. All this is so just, and so obvious to any Man who will but examine himself, and who knows the imperious Sway of our Passions, that I'm afraid People will complain I insist too long upon the proofs of a Point which no body can deny.

But without fearing this Reproach, let's omit nothing, if possible, which may contribute to render this Truth palpable, and cut off the Convertists from all their Starting-holes. Do they indeed believe, that a Man who compares two Reasons together, one of which is supported by the hopes of temporal Advantage, the other weaken'd by the dread of temporal Misery, is in a good way for finding out either the just Poise, or the true and natural Inclination of the Scale? Do they believe, that were the Reasons really equal on both sides, he wou'd not be determin'd to that which is attended with temporal Advantage? Do they believe, that if the Ballance of Evidence, with respect to him, lies on the side of that Reason which is weaken'd by the fear of temporal Evil, he won't often counter-ballance with the temporal Advantages accruing from the opposite side? Do they believe, that the Corruption of the Heart is incapable not only of counterpoising that Overmeasure of Evidence which appears on one side, but even of making it dwindle, and totally disappear by degrees? Can they believe, that this Counterballancing does not take place more or less in proportion to <154> the Covetousness or Ambition of the Man: so that if three degrees Overballance of Evidence on one side yield to a Counterballance of two hundred Crowns with regard to a Man not immoderately covetous; six degrees Overballance of Evidence shall do the same with regard to a Man of a great measure of Avarice and Vanity, when put into the Scale with a profitable and glorious Employment? If they believe nothing of what I here suppose as highly probable, I'm at a loss to know what Country they have liv'd in, what Books they have read, and what kind of Understandings they have got about 'em; and truly shou'd be for treating 'em according to the Maxim, *Adversus negantem Principia non est disputandum.*[59]

---

59. "One should not dispute with one who denies the basic principles": J. Hamesse (ed.), *Les Auctoritates Aristotelis* (Louvain: *Publications Universitaires,* 1974), p. 140. See also Thomas Aquinas, *Summa theologiae,* 1, q. 1, a. 8.

But it is not likely they'l deny the Principles I suppose, and from which I necessarily conclude, that nothing cou'd be more wrong, nothing more untoward, nothing more unworthy even of a moderate Understanding, than ordaining, as a reasonable means for discovering the Truth, that the Party enter upon the examination at the precise time when several Passions were excited in the Soul, and when he must have known, that in case he found one side of the Question true, he shou'd be expos'd to the last degree of Infamy and Misery; in case he found the other, honor'd and rewarded with sundry Favors. All our Ideas of Order, all the Maxims of good Sense, all that Judgment which the Experience of human Affairs bestows, revolt against this Management; and had JESUS CHRIST appointed that Method of Constraint suppos'd in this Objection, we shou'd not know how to justify his having proportion'd things aright, or adapted the Means to their Ends: An <155> Impiety never to be suggested! The examining two Religions under such Circumstances cou'd only breed Perplexitys and Distraction in the minds of some, new Engagements to their own Religion in others, and a Determination to that which has temporal Advantages of its side, whether it has Falseness to boot, or whether it has not, in all those who are possess'd by the Love of this World.

This is further confirm'd by the following Consideration; to wit, That all the Discourses of JESUS CHRIST, and his Apostles, tending to prepare us for Tribulations in this World, for the Cross, for a continual Exercise of Patience amidst a froward and perverse Generation; it's natural for a good Soul, a Soul not to be determin'd by any thing but the Fear of God, to believe that the Truth lies on the suffering side, and not on that which threatens and afflicts 'em if they persevere, and which offers a thousand earthly Advantages if they go over to it. I cannot see that one can find any Obscurity in this Hypothesis, if we consider it well. So that if we suppose a truly Christian Spirit in those who are to enter upon an Examination of the two Religions, the surest way to frustrate their Inquiry, and rivet 'em in their Error, is to tell 'em they must expect Persecution unless they embrace the opposite Faith; for the very thoughts of Persecution will become an Argument, or a very strong Prejudice at least, of their being in possession of that Evangelick Truth which the Scripture has foretold shou'd be hated and persecuted in this World. Thus we see, that the Means which these

Gentlemen propose, as ordain'd by JESUS CHRIST for finding out the Truth, only tend on one hand to confirm in Error (and that from a <156> regard to the Predictions of CHRIST himself) every good Soul, which sincerely prefers what it believes to be the Truth before any Conveniences of Life; and on the other hand, to tear every weak Soul, and such as are wedded to the World by some strong Passion, from the bosom of Truth, as to the outward appearance at least: whence I conclude, that this Method is stark naught, and that it never was ordain'd by God.

Let's now proceed to the second Point. I desire the Gentlemen-Convertists to tell me, whether they are in earnest, when they say they don't mean to force Conscience, but only to put People upon examining both Religions; which they neglected to do, so long as their not examining was of no prejudice to 'em. It's plain, if this be their whole Intention, that the Penaltys of their Edicts ought to have bin only minatory; that is, they ought only to threaten some Punishment on those, who within a prefix'd time did not get instructed (for if they proceed to actual Execution on those, who at the expiration of the term shall declare, that they have had themselves well instructed, that they are not one jot less persuaded of the Truth of their own Religion than they were before) it's manifest they originally design'd to violate Conscience, and to force even those to an outward Profession, who upon a thorow Examination had not bin able to change Belief. Now see where our Gentlemen are driven, into a Defilee between the two lowring horns of the following terrible Dilemma.[60]

Either they mean, that their Constraint shall be limited to the care of getting instructed, or that it shall fall at long run upon Conscience. <157>

If the first, they mean no more than that People shan't continue in their Religion merely from Habitude and Custom, without examining whether it be true, and comparing it with theirs; but that they shall enter into a nice Examination, and very serious Discussion of both. But when this is done, they can have nothing farther to say against a Man, who having listen'd to their Conferences and Instructions, and having read over their Books, declares at the foot of the account, that tho he is not able to give 'em a satisfactory Answer to all their Objections, yet he remains inwardly convinc'd

60. See Appendixes, "Bayle's Use of Logic," p. 580 ("dilemma").

that they are in a very bad way, and that the Truth is of his own side. Thus all their minatory Edicts are hung upon the tenters without further Virtue or Vigor; the Intention of the Legislator being answer'd and satisfy'd by a careful Examination of the Reasons o' both sides. Whence it appears, that upon this supposition our Gentlemen recede from the literal Sense of the words, *Compel 'em to come in,* because in reality they wou'd constrain none; for the Constraint now in question is not that of obliging to dispute, to read, and to meditate.

If they mean the second, they plainly renounce their Objection; they own above-board that they are for forcing Conscience: and then all my Arguments return upon 'em with the same force they were in before they cast up this wretched Intrenchment.

There remains, I think, nothing to be offer'd on their side but this, That the Penaltys which, I say, cou'd be only minatory in their first design, as a kind of Essay to try what Examination might produce, are afterwards justly inflicted, <158> when it appears, that all the Conferences, Missions, Disputes, Books, and Instructions imaginable, han't bin sufficient to bring a Man to reason: for this is a sign, he's under a prodigious degree of Opinionatedness and Obstinacy; and tho he mayn't be justly punish'd for not being of the true Religion, yet he may as an opinionated and obstinate Person. But who sees not how miserable a Come-off this is? Upon the very same grounds* *Antiochus* put a great many Jews to death, looking on 'em as guilty of a sensless Obstinacy, because the Threats of a terrible Punishment cou'd not oblige 'em to eat Swines Flesh; a thing in its own nature perfectly lawful. On the same grounds *Pliny* put a great many Christians to Death.† *I ask'd 'em,* says he, *whether they were Christians; and when they confess'd, I ask'd 'em again a second and a third time, with Threats of the severest Punishment, which I order'd to be actually inflicted on 'em when I saw they persisted in confessing. I was satisfy'd, were the Matter never so inconsiderable which they confest, that their Obstinacy and inflexible Stiffness was a just Cause of Punishment.*

---

* Josephus, *in his Treatise of the Government of Reason.* [Josephus, *Opera Omnia*, Paris, 1528, fol. 325ff, especially 326 (not an authentic work).]

† Ep. 2. l. 10. [Pliny, *Epistulae*, X.xcvi.3. Loeb Classical Library, vol. 2, p. 286.]

We see already, that this is but a mere childish Illusion, and a wretched Pretence with which the Pagans wou'd cover over their Barbaritys. But let's sound this Matter a little deeper. What do People mean when they say, that a Man, who might otherwise challenge some regard, forfeits all Pretence[61] to it when he shews himself an errand Opiniater? Do they only mean, that a Man, <159> who persists in his Errors after it's made appear to him that they are gross Errors, and when convinc'd in his Conscience they are so, deserves no quarter? Truly I am of their mind: I am no Advocate for such a Man's Toleration, who in reality deserves none; for if he persist in his Opinion, contrary to the Dictates of his Conscience, it's an infallible Argument, that there's Caprice and Malice in the case, and that his only Aim is to do despite to his Neighbor, and insult his Superiors while they are taking the pains to convert him. But how can they be assur'd, that they have convinc'd this Man of his Errors? Is the Convertist sharp enough to read in the Book of Conscience? Is he a Sharer with God in the incommunicable Attribute of *Searcher of Hearts?* 'Twere the most extravagant Impertinence in the World to pretend this: and therefore so long as a Man, whom he has instructed to the best of his Skill, shall say, he's still persuaded in his Conscience, that his own Religion is the best, the Convertist has no ground to say, he has convinc'd him inwardly and evidently of his Errors; and so long he can't be reputed an Opiniater, nor obnoxious to the Punishments due to a stubborn Spirit: so that where, after two Months time, or four, or five, according to the term prescrib'd by the Prince for the Work of Instruction, with minatory Clauses of Penaltys on those, who after the Expiration of the term limited, shall persist in their Errors, the Partys declare they are the same they were before, as much persuaded of the Truth of their own Religion as ever, there the Convertist must leave 'em, or proceed to a direct and immediate Force <160> upon Conscience; which is what he wou'd avoid by this Objection, and consequently the vain Pretext of his being an Opiniatre won't do.

The Convertist will certainly answer (for these Gentlemen are in possession of all the false reasoning) that tho he is no Searcher of Hearts, yet

61. See Appendixes, "Obsolete or Unusual Words or Meanings," pp. 577, 579 ("pretend," "challenge").

he is not without a reasonable Assurance, that the Man is under those Circumstances of Obstinacy which we are speaking of, that is, under such a Malignancy as to profess his antient Doctrines, even where he has bin fully convinc'd they are false. He's thorowly satisfy'd of this, he'l say, because he cou'd not answer the Objections against his own Religion, no nor his very Minister, who was by, and who had not a word to say for himself; beside, that the Truths of the Church are so evident, that 'tis but considering 'em a little without Prejudice, and a Man must needs feel their Divinity, and the Falseness of the Calvinist Opinions for example. Now here are the two ways of knowing that one has enlighten'd a Man's Intellectuals, tho he dissembles it with his Lips; first, that there had bin Objections made to himself, or to his Minister, which neither of 'em cou'd solve; and next, that the Reasons given to them are as clear as Noon-day. But 'twill be no very hard Task to confute both these ways.

There needs no more to confound these Gentlemen, as to the first, but asking 'em, whether they believe, that a Peasant, a Shopkeeper, or Roman Catholick Gentlewoman, engag'd in an Argument of Religion with a Bishop of *Lincoln*,[62] a Doctor *Stillingfleet,* a *Du Moulin,* a *Daillé,*[63] wou'd be able to answer all the Objections made 'em. I consent too, that these ignorant People be as-<161>sisted by the Curate of the Parish, or by his Vicar, or by a Monk, or any other Convertist. Can any one be assur'd in such a Case, that all the Objections propos'd by a learned Protestant, who comes prepar'd, and has cull'd out the knottiest, shall be clearly solv'd; or that the Defendants shall never be at a loss what to offer for themselves, with any color of Reason? One must never have consider'd things, one must be utterly unacquainted with the human Mind, to entertain such a thought; for it's well known, that in all Disputes, he who has a ready Wit, a voluble Tongue, a subtle Head, improv'd by Logick, and a great Memory, shall always get the better in problematick matters of a Man learn'd indeed, but who wants Utterance, who does not express himself in apt words, who is distrustful of himself, and has neither a Presence of Mind, nor good Mem-

---

62. Robert Sanderson (1587–1663), Anglican theologian, writer on casuistry.
63. Protestant controversialists. For their lives and works see *Biographisch-Bibliographisches Kirchenlexikon,* http://www.bautz.de/bbkl/.

ory. To conclude from hence, that he who happens to be foil'd defends the bad Religion, is risking one's own Cause, and falling into an absurd Consequence, that all Religions are false, or that the same Religion is true in one place, and false in another: since it may happen, that a Minister, disputing in one Chamber with a Monk, may put him to a Nonplus; and a Monk, disputing with another Minister in the next Chamber, may get the better of him: as in Duels with several Seconds, where there happen to be Victors and Vanquish'd o' both sides. We must therefore clash with all the Rules of good Sense, or agree, that it's no Mark of Falshood in any Religion, that all who profess it, are not able to answer every Difficulty which a learn'd Controvertist of the opposite side may suggest: <162> and therefore a Protestant, who has found, that neither he, nor his Minister, had given full Satisfaction to some subtle Questions, and which he may even suspect as mere Cavils when coming from a Missionary, may yet be far from believing on this score, that his Religion is false. 'Tis rash judging then to say, that he's convinc'd in his Conscience of the Falseness of his Religion, when he affirms, that these Disputes have not shock'd him in the least.

In a word, if this first Means of knowing when a Man is convinc'd, were just, there's no ignorant Catholick, but might be suspected of violating his Conscience, after he had once bin in a Conference with any of our learn'd Divines: for it's certain, he wou'd not know what to answer to several Points; and that many a Monk wou'd be as much at a loss as he. No Man shou'd be so imprudent as to make his Religion depend on the Address, the Memory, and the Eloquence of his Minister. 'Twou'd alter the case indeed, if any Minister that we cou'd name, disputing with any Papist that can be nam'd; the most learn'd of all our Ministers, with the most ignorant of all the Papists (not quite so low neither, let it be with the most ignorant of all the Monks) were continually so baffl'd, as not to have a word to say for himself: in this case I own, a Man might be tax'd of inexcusable Obstinacy, if he had not some mistrust of his own Religion; but as this case has never hapen'd, and 'tis impossible it ever shou'd, it's nothing at all to the purpose.

The second Means of knowing when a Man is convinc'd in his Conscience, is not a jot bet-<163>ter than the former: for beside that 'tis going too far, to say Matters of Controversy are clear and evident as Noon-day, every one knows, or ought to know, that Evidence is a relative Quality; and therefore we can't answer, except with regard to common Principles, that what appears evident to our selves, must likewise appear so to others. That Evidence which we perceive in certain Objects, may proceed from the Situation and particular View by which we consider 'em, or from a proportion betwixt them and our Organs, or from Habitude, Education, or any other Cause: so that there's no arguing from our own case to our Neighbor's, because another may not consider things by the same View that we do, has not his Organs form'd exactly like ours, has not had the same Education, &c. Several Persons shall look at a piece of *Raphael,* and make a thousand different Judgments of it. He who stands in the true point of Sight, and is a Judg, thinks it admirable; others who look at it from another point, and who have no tast nor notion of Painting, see nothing extraordinary in't. The Man of Skill may laugh at their Ignorance, or pity it as much as he pleases; but 'twere ridiculous to tax 'em of a Lye, or of a malicious design of running down the Piece, whilst convinc'd of its Excellence. Oh, but the Beauty of this Piece is so visible, that there's no room for not seeing it! Who told you so? and even you, Sir, who perceive this so plainly, do you perceive the Beauty and Goodness of some Stones, which a Jeweller pretends must strike every Body's Sense? You think Canary perhaps so good a Wine, that you believe it's only being born with a Palat to find out <164> its Goodness; yet how many Men are there of as good a Tast as you, who can't abide it? It's therefore the grossest Ignorance of the World, and of Man in particular, to make a Judgment of the Perceptions of others by our own.

But the Missionarys will reply, This had all bin very right, if it had come before our Instructions; but those we have given are so clear to every Point, that it's not possible to resist 'em. I answer, That 'tis but just we shou'd have an ill Opinion enough of most of these Gentlemen, to believe they are sincere, when they talk at this rate of the Nature of their Instructions; 'twere doing 'em a greater honor than they deserve, to think they are free enough from the rusty Shackles of their Prejudices, to perceive that their Commonplaces are wretched stuff, or that they have bin a thousand times solidly confuted. Let's believe then, that they themselves find 'em very evident, since they say so; but let 'em not pretend, that others, who have bin tinctur'd and educated in different Principles, who see things by a different Light, and have not the same Conceptions with them, shou'd perceive the same

Evidence in their Instructions. Whence it appears, that to know certainly when a Man is in a state of Obstinacy and Opinionatedness, that is, when he persists in a Profession after he's fully convinc'd of its Falseness; or has a formal design of not applying his Thoughts to the Reasons which oppose, for fear of discovering its Falseness; one must be a Searcher of Hearts, that is, he must be God himself: for it's an extravagant Presumption, to say, that a Man persists in his Religion after several Conferences with the Missionarys, only because he refuses to apply his <165> Mind to the Consideration of their Arguments, for fear he shou'd find 'em reasonable; or having found 'em solid and convincing, that he'l rather betray his Conscience, than give the Convertists the Satisfaction of gaining their Point: This, I say, is an extravagant Pesumption, since there are so many opposite and very probable grounds to believe, that the Missionarys Arguments have not appear'd convincing, either thro a want of Understanding, or thro the involuntary Prejudices of those whose Conversion is endeavor'd. I say, and insist, that none but God alone can judg of the Measures of our Understanding, and the Degrees of Light which are sufficient to each; its Proportion varying infinitely, or at least incomparably more than the Proportions of sufficient Food, with regard to our Bodys. The quantity of Food which suffices one Man, is either too much or too little for another, yet varys not in such a latitude, or within terms so extensive, as the degrees of Light sufficient for the Conviction of such a one, and such a one, &c.

The only Means remaining to convict a Man of Opinionatedness, is, by saying in general, that all Reluctance to the Truth sufficiently explain'd, is downright Opinionatedness. But how shall we make the Application of this Definition? Is not this revolving into two inexhaustible Disputes? The first upon the ground of the Differences, for each Party pretends to have the Truth of its own side; so that before either is pronounc'd opinionated according to this Definition, it has a Right to demand a further Proof of what it refuses to believe as Truth: And when shall we ever see an end of this? <166> The second is upon the Competency of the Explication: for no body having a distinct Idea of Minds, not even of his own; it's as absurd to say, that such an Explication is a Competency for the Conviction of such an Understanding, as to say, that such a quantity of Food is a Competency for the Man in the Moon, whom we know nothing of. It's plain, this whole

Matter in an imply'd meaning amounts to this, *The Reasons of the strongest side are ever best; the Right is of my side because I'm the Lion:* and that it's reducing Men to the ridiculous Controversy of saying by turns, *You are very opinionated, since the Truth is of my side,* without any common Rule to draw us out of this Strife of Words, this Childrens-play, of ever tossing the Ball backwards and forwards. You see what a fine pass we are brought to by these Gentlemens Principles, left without any Criterion to distinguish Constancy from Opinionatedness, but by begging the Question, or because we are pleas'd to bestow fine names on whatever belongs to our selves, and names of Reproach on what belongs to others. <167>

☞ CHAPTER II ☜

Second Objection, The literal Sense appears odious, only by our judging of the ways of God from those of Men. Tho the State that Men are in, when they act from Passion, seems likely to lead 'em to wrong Judgments, it does not follow but God, by the wonderful Issues of his Providence, may accomplish his own Work. The Fallacy of this Thought, and what are the ordinary Effects of Persecution.

Before I proceed to Objections of greater Importance, it's fit I take notice of a Challenge, which may arise upon my saying, that our Saviour had very ill adapted the Means to the Ends, had he appointed the exciting several Passions in the Soul, in order to its discerning the true Religion from the false. They'l tell me, shou'd a Man go this way to work, 'twou'd indeed be very wrong in him; but that the ways of God being not our ways, JESUS CHRIST might very well have prescrib'd such a Method. When he wou'd open the Eyes of a blind Man, he did the very thing which in all probability must have put out his Eyes, if they had not bin out before, yet he gave him his Sight by a means so seemingly improper: And why not as easily administer the Influence of his Holy Spirit, to a Review of the two Religions in a storm of worldly Hopes and Fears? Let's scan this Cavil. <168>

In the first place I observe, that the Proposition, *The ways of God are not our ways,* being incapable of this general meaning, *God never operates by the same means which Men make use of,* since there are a hundred Instances to the contrary; nothing can be concluded from it in favor of the meaning contended for in the words, *Compel 'em to come in,* till it be first made appear from other Heads, and by direct Proofs, that we ought to understand 'em in the literal Sense, and that no absurd Consequences hinder our understanding 'em so. If once it were clearly prov'd, that JESUS CHRIST enjoins Constraint, I own indeed we might justify this Command from the Sovereign Prerogative of God, which makes him sometimes take measures very opposite to those which we shou'd take. But as long as the literal Sense of this Passage is disputed by numberless Reasons, and some of 'em drawn from the very Spirit and Tendency of the Gospel; to plead this Maxim, *The ways of God are not our ways,* is in truth a degree of Dotage; and what's worse, 'tis resolving all human Knowledg and divine Revelation into downright detestable Pyrrhonism. For there's not a Text in Scripture, which by this Rule might not have a Sense given it directly opposite to the ordinary meaning of the words. I might say, for example, that when JESUS CHRIST promises he'l reward our good Works in Heaven, his meaning is, that he'l damn Men for their good Works; for the ways of God not being our ways, he ought not to speak as we do, but have a meaning to his words quite contrary to what we impose. So that there wou'd be no proving of any thing from Scripture, nor in-<169>deed from Reason; because it might still be alledg'd, that the Principles of Reasoning, which are the Rule of Truth and Falshood when deliver'd by a Father to his Son, ought not to be reputed such when coming from God, who is suppos'd to run counter in every thing to the ways of Man. Away then with these Extravagancys, which our Adversarys are driven to for Objections.

In the second place, I say, that the Example of the Clay made use of for opening blind Eyes, carrys in it two essential Differences: One, that it is a particular Action of JESUS CHRIST, which we don't read, that either he or his Disciples had ever repeated, whereas the Command of compelling is deliver'd in general terms; and the other, that Matter having no repugnancy to one Motion more than another, or to one Figure more than another, may very aptly be employ'd in the hands of God to the producing any kind of Effect; but the Soul of Man, guiding it self by Reason, and by a certain scale or gradation of Thought, Order requires, that God shou'd accommodate himself to this Scale. So that if the thought of Danger, for example, or any other Passion, be follow'd with Darkness in the Judgment and Precipitation in the Will, God shall surely never ordain, that the Season for distinguishing Truth from Falshood shou'd universally be that of this Darkness in the Soul, and this Precipitation in the Will.

Will they have infinite Examples of the Conformity of the ways of God with those of Men? let 'em only read the Gospel; so many Verses almost as they read, are so many Instances of it, since it is evident, God speaks there after the manner of a Master instructing his Disciples. A Master <170> speaks; he makes use of terms which are current in the Country, and understood by his Hearers: these are the ways of Man when he teaches. And are not these the ways of God too? Does not he speak the Language of those he addresses himself to; and does not he most commonly use words in the same Sense that others do? But I have other Examples at hand, which are still nearer my purpose.

When God had a design of converting the Pagan World, 'tis certain he made use of Instruments very different from those which Men wou'd have employ'd in such a Work; yet a great many human Means interven'd, Instructions by living Discourse, and by Writings, Censures, Disputes, and other like ways by which Men instruct one another. Nor have we a single Example of any Peoples being converted without the Means of Preaching, any more than we have an Example of a Scholar's believing all *Plato* has said, without ever hearing of *Plato*. The natural and human order is, that a Man be first acquainted with *Plato*'s Doctrines, either by reading his Works, or by Conversation with those who have. And God so constantly pursues the same methods, that never was it heard, that any Man had known there was such a Person as JESUS CHRIST, but by reading the Gospel himself, or by the Testimony of others. Don't imagine, that e'er the People of the *Terra Australis* shall become Christians, till Christian Preachers come among 'em to preach the Gospel. I say further, that after the Holy Spirit has converted a Man to Christianity, he still strikes in with his natural Temper; whence it comes to pass, that there's always a Tincture of the Dis-<171>position and natural Temper in the religious Conversation and Actions of every Man: an evident Argument, that God overturns not the Order establish'd upon the Union of Soul and Body, when Religion's in the

Case. Since therefore this general Law of the Union of Soul and Body forms such a Chain or Gradation of Thoughts in the Soul, that the Apprehension of a temporal Evil is follow'd by a Perturbation, which obscures the Lights of the Judgment, weakens the use of the Free-will, and inclines the Soul to that side which promises it Deliverance (I say the same of all the other Passions) it's reasonable to believe, that God does not thwart this natural Series of the Thoughts: and for my part, I don't doubt, when he converts a Sinner in an extraordinary way, as he converted St. *Paul,* but he falls in with the stream of his Thoughts by one side or other, and afterwards follows their natural drift. I don't deny, that he often makes use of the Passions of the Soul to draw us towards him, and to disengage us from the World; but 'tis in such a manner, that he forbids us to do that Evil to our Neighbor, which yet his Providence makes an occasion of his Salvation. For example, there's no doubt but God, for the Conversion of a young Rake, may make use of a Blow, which has crippled him; of a Fraud, which has brought him to Beggary; of a Calumny, which ruins his Reputation, and obliges him perhaps to quit this World, and think upon things above: yet the salutary Uses, which God knows how to draw from these Disgraces, lessen not the Sin in him who cripples, or defrauds, or calumniates this Person. Accordingly, shou'd I allow, that Persecutions <172> oblige a great many to examine their Religion, and quit it for the true, yet they are criminal nevertheless, and consequently forbidden by God; so far from being commanded by the Words, *Compel 'em to come in.*

This single Remark is in my Opinion decisive; for since Fraud, Mutilation, Calumnys, Imprisonment, and such like Practices, wou'd be criminal, if employ'd against these young Rakes, who transgressing no politickal Law of the State, are not justly punishable by the Magistrate: since, I say, these Practices wou'd be criminal, notwithstanding God might draw out of 'em the Repentance and Amendment of the Sufferers; it must be allow'd, that ruining a Man, ordering him to be beaten, imprison'd, tormented, is exceeding criminal in Sovereigns, notwithstanding that God, by the invisible Springs, and incomprehensible Dispensations of his Grace, may make use of those Evils for the enlightening a Man's Understanding. Whence we can't but see the gross Illusion that Persecutors are under in believing they are quit of all their Iniquitys, by supposing that God reaps the Advantage of 'em towards the enlightening those who are in Error. But pray wou'd not he reap the same Advantage from their doing the like to a Gamester, to a Whoremonger, to a Drunkard? Wherefore then don't they think it lawful to quarter a Troop of fifty Dragoons on a Gamester, to spoil him of his Goods, his Wife, his Children, to suborn false Witnesses against him, to brand him with publick Infamy? Is it not because we have a Law of God, prescribing and stating our Dutys, without permitting the Practice of the contrary, under any <173> pretence of God's drawing out of 'em the Manifestation of his own Glory, and the Salvation of the Elect? Why won't they apply this to their persecuting on the score of Religion?

But how will this look, if I shew in the third place, that, very far from God's making use of Persecutions as a means of bringing Men to the knowledg of the Truth, we have all the Experience in the world to the contrary, and all the ground to believe they are of no effect this way: which ought to convince us, that God has not establish'd Violence as an occasional Cause of his Grace. Yet this is what Persecutors must suppose, to give their second Objection the least weight. They ought to say, that Violences consider'd in themselves, and in their own nature, are unjust and forbidden by God: but as the Water of Baptism, incapable in its own nature of sanctifying our Souls, has bin exalted by the Institution of God to the Quality of a moral, at least an occasional, Cause of Regeneration; so Violences have bin exalted, by the appointment of God, to the Quality of instrumental and occasional Causes of the Illumination of Hereticks. And at this rate they must be consider'd as a kind of Sacrament, transubstantiated by the virtue of these Sacramental Words, *Compel 'em to come in;* and trans-elemented from unjust, as they were by nature, into perfectly holy Actions, and perfectly divine.

Upon this I have two or three things to offer: 1. That it does not seem possible, that an Action repugnant to natural Equity, to the Law, and to the Gospel, evil from an intrinsick Turpitude, and from the Interdiction of God, shou'd be <174> pitch'd on by JESUS CHRIST for the Instrument of the Salvation of Men, apply'd and put in Execution by the very same Men to whom it is most peculiarly forbidden. Were Persecution a thing purely indifferent in its own nature, as Water, which morally speaking is neither good nor evil, I shou'd not talk at this rate. 2. That were such an Action chosen by God for the instrumental Cause of the Illumination of those in error, it might be expected that the Revelation of it shou'd be made in the clearest and most express Terms, the freest from all Equivoke, and the least liable to any exception; it might be expected, that God shou'd have prevented all our Doubts upon this head, satisfy'd all our Scruples, and reconcil'd all the apparent Contradictions in this Revelation to the general Tenor and Spirit of the Gospel. But so far is he from having reveal'd it in such a manner, that we find but one small Sentence tending this way in the whole Gospel, and that a piece of a Parable too, with the word *Compel* at the tail on't; a Word which on a hundred other occasions signifies the pressings of Civility and Kindness to keep a Friend, for example, to dine with us. And this Sentence being only ascrib'd to the Master of the Family, does not directly imply the Constraint of those without, or of Infidels; which yet 'twas but reasonable it shou'd, in a case so inconsistent with the Spirit of JESUS CHRIST, and his divine Doctrine. In a word, I say, the Experience of all Ages convinces us, that Violences lose not their nature by being employ'd in the service of the true Religion; for they have the very same Effects and Consequences in this, as in all other Cases. <175>

Let's suppose for a moment, that the Church of *Rome* is the true Church; and take a view of the Consequences of Compulsion to it, and compare 'em with the Consequences of compelling to any other Religion. As long as the King of *France* did only alarm his Protestant Subjects, did only publish Edicts to clip their Privileges, and deprive 'em of several common Advantages; did only threaten those who persisted in their Heresy with the roughest Treatment; what came of it? Why only this, that these People, excepting a very few here and there, grew more zealous in their Religion than ever. Nothing was to be seen among 'em but continual Fastings, extraordinary Humiliations, retrenching in Luxury and Superfluity: the last thought that cou'd ever enter into their Souls, was believing God afflicted 'em on account of a false Religion; quite contrary, they were eternally imputing the Evils which fell, or were ready to fall on 'em, both in their Sermons and serious Conversations, to their want of Zeal for this Religion, to their Lukewarmness in its Services, to their disrelish for those Truths which their Ministers preach'd to 'em; and confessing that the only means of averting the Judgments, and appeasing the Wrath of God, was a Change of Life, and a ferventer Zeal in the Protestant way. This is very far from what the Convertists pretend, that Violences open a Man's eyes to see his Heresys. I'm verily persuaded, shou'd a Protestant Prince treat his Roman Catholick Subjects the same way, that they wou'd just so have recourse to extraordinary Prayers to God and to the Saints, as believing 'em displeas'd only at their Indifference and want <176> of Zeal for their own Religion; and thus become more Popish than they were before. The Turks, in like manner, wou'd but grow more zealous and obstinate in Mahometism; the Jews in Judaism, and so on.

Let's now take a view of what happen'd, when the King of *France* let loose his Dragoons, and left his Protestant Subjects only the hard Alternative, either of going to Mass, or leading the Remainder of their Life in a long and almost infinite Complication of Miserys: They sunk almost all under the Temptation, some more persuaded than ever that their own Religion was the true, and the Romish detestable; others by bringing themselves by little and little to an Indifference for all Religions, and believing they might be sav'd in a false one, by not embracing its wicked Worship at heart. Such of 'em as play'd the Bigots, and even Persecutors of their Brethren, were still some degrees worse than the rest: the greatest part acting only from Vanity and Avarice; they wou'd not have it suspected, that their Change was from any other Motive than Conviction; they aspire to Pensions and Benefices, and this in plain *English* means that they won't believe in God, but upon an Inventory of what he's worth. These Consequences are very deplorable, and far from enlightning the Soul, serve only to plunge it into a worse state than the former, supposing the former a Heresy in good Faith. Nothing of what I here suppose concerning the Dispositions of the Lapsed, can be justly deny'd, because we see so few of 'em go to Mass with a good will, and that there's a necessity of keeping strict guards on all the Fron-<177>tiers and Sea-ports, to prevent their flying out of the Kingdom; and of publishing terrible Edicts against those who refuse the Sacrament in their Sickness: not a day passes but their dead Bodys are drag'd on Sledges, and deny'd Christian Burial. There's no doubt but a Protestant Prince, who took the same methods with his Popish Subjects, must produce the same effects by his Dragoons; most of 'em wou'd sign whate'er was tender'd, but with a deeper horror for Calvinism than ever, and perhaps

some Seeds of Atheism; a great many wou'd hope to be sav'd by their In-
vocations of the Virgin in secret, by their Pocket Images, and by the Confessions and clandestine Communions from Priests in masquerade; very
few enlighten'd. So that now supposing the Reform'd Religion the truest,
Persecutions wou'd avail it very little to the making sincere Converts, and
propagating the Truth. The persecuting Turks, Jews, Pagans, or their persecuting one another, can have no other effect; Hypocrisys and Irreligion,
and nothing more. God perhaps does not suffer Infidels to get ground by
their Persecutions. But History abounds with Examples to the contrary:
Pliny writes to his Emperor, that several Christians, whom he had summon'd, having at first confess'd they were Christians, deny'd it soon after;
professing they had bin so once, but never wou'd again. He adds, that the
Pagan Religion, which was in a manner lost in *Bythinia,* began to take
heart.[64] Which shews, that the Dread of Punishment had made a great
many Apostates. It's astonishing to think what multitudes of Christians fell
away under the Emperor *Decius;* read *Cyprian*'s ac-<178>count of it.[65] It's
well known, what numbers the *Saracens,* Disciples of *Mahomet,* pluck'd
out of the Christian Church. Let's conclude then, that Compulsion never
loses its natural tendency, which is that of confirming Men in their Opinions, or teaching 'em to dissemble thro Fear, Vanity, Ambition, or leading
'em to an Indifference for all Religions. Let's now confound our Adversarys
by their own Maxims.

Don't they say, that the Severity of our *Harry* VIII was the cause why
most of his Subjects renounc'd the Pope's Supremacy? Don't they say, that
the pretended Reform'd Religion had never bin establish'd in *England* under *Edward* VI if the Secular Arm had not bin employ'd against the Catholick? Don't they say, that after Queen *Mary* had effectually restor'd the
Church of *Rome, Elizabeth* cou'd ne'er have re-establish'd Heresy, had she
forbore Constraint, and not issued the most severe Injunctions, and enacted
penal Laws against Papists? Don't they still believe, as appears by the favorable Construction they wou'd put upon *Coleman*'s Plot,[66] discover'd by

64. See above, p. 143, note.
65. For example, Cyprian, "Of the Lapsed," chs. 6–9, *Ante-Nicene Christian Library,*
ed. A. Roberts and J. Donaldson (Edinburgh: Clark, 1867–), vol. 5.
66. Edward Coleman was accused by Titus Oates and executed as a traitor.

Letters under his own hand, that were there a free Exercise of the Popish Religion allow'd in *England,* and the Penal Laws repeal'd, the whole Kingdom wou'd quickly be of that Religion? Don't they object against the Truth of the Protestant Religion, that it has bin establish'd by Arms and Violence? They won't, I suppose, pretend to dispute any of these Facts. And therefore I shall make bold to conclude for 'em, that Constraint and threaten'd Punishment have the very same effects against the true, as against a false Religion. So that 'tis extremely imperti-<179>nent to suppose that God gives his Blessing only to the Compulsion of Hereticks: for if so, the Lot of the persecuted Orthodox wou'd not resemble that of persecuted Hereticks; and even this Absurdity follow, that the Orthodox wou'd be abandon'd of God under their Persecutions, and Hereticks receiv'd into his Arms; the Sheep driven out of the Fold, those who were nurtur'd and bred up in it, and Strangers made to come in. The Successes of the *Mahometan* Compulsions are enough to confound our Missionarys.

But if we consider only the Consequences of Persecutions between Christian and Christian, we shall find reasons enough to convince us that God cou'd not have establish'd 'em as an occasional Cause of enlightning Grace. The reason is this: Had he constituted 'em such by the Efficacy of the words, *Compel 'em to come in;* every Christian Sect that had sense enough to take the Intention of the Son of God aright, and Zeal enough to observe it, must persecute the rest, in hopes that God wou'd convert 'em by this means. And thus God might order it so, that the Means of Grace shou'd be much oftner employ'd in favor of Falshood than Truth, and yet have no reasonable ground, it seems, neither for taxing Hereticks with their Abuse of Persecution; because as it is no sin in a Heretick to give an Alms in obedience to God's Command, so it were no sin in him to *compel* in obedience to the Command of JESUS CHRIST. Nor can it be pretended that this Command is given, not to promote the Interests of Error, but those of Truth; and that therefore a Heretick who executes the Or-<180>ders which JESUS CHRIST has given in his Parable, commits a Sin: for by the same rule it might be prov'd, that a Heretick does very ill in giving Alms to any of the Poor of his own Sect, because this hinders their applying to the Overseers of the Poor among the Orthodox, who might thereby have an opportunity of bringing 'em over by the hopes of Bread.

From hence it wou'd likewise follow, that praying and living soberly and vertuously in a heretick Society, wou'd be downright Sin; because this Devotion and good Life promote the Interests of Error. So that the nature of all Christian Dutys wou'd hereby be chang'd and confounded, and the Precepts of the Gospel, addrest to all Christians in general, wou'd concern only the Orthodox, and the obeying 'em be sin in the rest of the World. Was ever so monstrous a Notion fram'd of moral Dutys?

Cou'd there be any ground for a plausible Murmur against the most wise and most adorable Providence of God, 'twou'd surely be his permitting those of the true Religion to be expos'd to Temptations so hard to be resisted, as Tortures and acute Pain; very few Souls are proof against 'em, and few who in the extremity of Suffering won't betray Conscience. 'Tis true, the Rack is appointed by the Justice of several Countrys, yet all don't approve it; because the Pain often forces the Party to confess what he ne'er was guilty of, and accuse others who are suspected, and whom it's design'd he shou'd accuse. *Montagne* talks very judiciously upon this: *It's a dangerous Invention,* says he, *this of the Rack, and looks like a proof of Patience rather than Truth.* <181> *He who is able to bear it, hides the Truth, and he who is not. For why shou'd Pain force me to confess what I do know, and not force me to confess what I know nothing of? On the other hand, if he who is not guilty has patience enough to support the Torment, why shou'd not he who is; so sweet a Reward as Life being propos'd him? . . . To say the truth, it's an Experiment of great uncertainty and danger. What won't a Man say, what won't he do, to avoid so exquisite a Torture?* Etiam Innocentes cogit mentiri Dolor: *Whence it often happens, that he who condemns him to the Rack, for fear of making him die innocent, makes him die both innocent and rack'd.*[67] These are truly the ordinary Effects of those cruel Pains, which a Man is put to by the racking of his Limbs. Will they have him say, he does not believe what he really does; that he is not a Christian, when he is in his Soul? he'l tell 'em, not able to bear the Pain, he's no Christian. Will they have him say, he believes what he really cannot; that he's a good Papist, tho he's a Calvinist, suppose, or Lutheran; or that he's a good Calvinist, tho in his Soul he's a

67. *Essais,* l. 2. [Author's note in the French edition. Montaigne, *Essais,* book 2, ch. 5, "De la conscience."]

Papist? he'l tell 'em he is; overcome by the Torment, and finding that his Dissimulation and Lying will be a present Relief. Monsieur *St. Mars,* who was beheaded at *Lyons* for conspiring against Cardinal *Richlieu,* died with a deal of Constancy, and shew'd a perfect Contempt of Death; but under such a dread of the Question[68] at the same time, that it's probable had they given it him, he wou'd have confess'd what they pleas'd, and perhaps things most opposite to those Notions of Honor which were dearest to him. <182>

Now if this be what our Reason can't well reconcile, that the same God, who in uniting the Soul to the Body, ordain'd it shou'd be sensible of such a degree of Pain, whenever this Body was strain'd to such a pitch; shou'd permit this Body to be subject to the Rage of Persecutors, who put us to the most exquisite pains, but with this condition, that they'l immediately deliver, and load us with Favors, provided we'l declare our Assent to things which we disbeliev'd before: If, I say, the bare permitting this be hardly reconcilable to Reason, what wou'd it be shou'd JESUS CHRIST himself have positively ordain'd these Tortures, and under such a Condition? For my part I can't see, if he had, what cou'd be offer'd, with the least color of Reason, to quiet the Murmurs of a Man, who shou'd go about to reject all reveal'd Religion: whereas by supposing that the Law and declar'd Will of God to Men is this, That they do no wrong to their Neighbor; we may easily reconcile his not forcing 'em to do good by a positive Act, and against their Inclination. Whence it follows, that he may, consistently with his Justice and Holiness, permit 'em to proceed to Persecution: in which case he supports the Faithful by his special Grace, or suffers 'em to yield, that he may raise 'em up again with greater Glory by Repentance.

What I have bin observing about the Rack, may be apply'd in a due proportion to all other Trials; such as those which the *French* Protestants were put to, when expos'd, beaten, eaten up by Dragoons, and brought into such distress, that they had nothing before their eyes but Dun-<183>geons and Distress on Distress, in case they made the least discovery of the firm Persuasion of their Soul. They say, the Millers were forbad, in some Provinces, to grind Corn for the new Converts; and the Bakers to sell 'em Bread, unless they brought an authentick Certificate of their Catho-

---

68. That is, the rack.

licity. So that they were put to the hard Choice of starving, they and their Children, or taking the Sacrament; not daring to make their escape out of the Kingdom, on pain, if they were taken, of tugging at an Oar all the rest of their Life. Every reasonable Body will allow, that the Gnawings of Hunger which a Mother suffers, and which she sees her Children suffer before her eyes, are altogether as sharp as the Pains of the Rack, and sharper perhaps in some Complexions than the Rack it self; which if the Party undergoes without confessing, he's sure of being out of the clutches of the Law.

But if there's no room to believe that JESUS CHRIST has enjoin'd Persecution, because by enjoining it he becomes the immediate Cause of all the Evils which Hereticks might bring upon the Orthodox, and the mediate Cause of all the Hypocrisys which these might be forc'd to, in the same manner as he is the immediate Cause of the Alms which Hereticks bestow on their Neighbor, in obedience to the Gospel, and the mediate Cause of all the natural Consequences of these Alms: if, I say, this be incredible from that reason, it's no less so from this; to wit, that there being intrepid resolute Spirits in all Sects, and strongly persuaded of the Truth of their own Religion, each must have its Martyrs in case of Persecution. Now these Martyrs are the su-<184>rest Support in the world of any Religion, by confirming their Brethren in a persuasion, that they die for the Truth. And therefore if JESUS CHRIST had commanded Constraint, he had himself left a mighty Obstacle in the way of Truth, because the inflexible Temper of some Men, and their Courage in dying for their Errors, had confirm'd the rest of the Sect more and more in the Belief of 'em. A *French* Historian has observ'd very justly, that the Martyrdom of *Anne du Bourg unsettled more mens Minds, than a hundred Ministers cou'd have done with all their Sermons.*[69] I know what's commonly said, that it is not the Suffering, but

69. Mézerai, *Abr. chron.,* t. 6, p.m. 413. [Author's note in the French edition. Probably: François Eudes de Mézerai, *Abrégé Chronologique de l'Histoire de France* (Chronological summary of French History), 1674. Anne du Bourg, counselor of the Parliament of Paris, expressed opposition to the punishment of Protestants. He was arrested on suspicion of heresy, and after a trial and various appeals over a period of six months was executed on December 23, 1559. See "Bourg, Anne du," *The Oxford Encyclopedia of the Reformation* (New York: Oxford University Press, 1996), vol. 1, p. 206.

the Cause, which makes the Martyr. But pray how is this to the purpose? Is it not a bare Dispute about words, or begging the Question? However, without insisting, that the intrepid Joy with which a Man dies for his Religion, may have a retrospective effect upon his Tenets, to the persuading those of their Truth who believ'd 'em most false before; there being no Argument for moving the People like Spectacles of this kind, nor no such Testimony of Sincerity: without insisting, I say, upon this, is it not at least incontestable, that those of the same Religion for which he dies, will reckon him a true Martyr, persuaded, as we suppose they are, of his dying for the Cause of Truth? We are at the same Childrens-play with regard to the nature of Martyrdom, as with regard to a thousand other things. We dispute about mere Words; each Sect supposing, that only they who die in its own Cause are worthy of the name of Martyr. And now, I may presume, the pretended Institution of Violences, as <185> an occasional Cause of Grace, is as fully confuted as any reasonable Reader can desire. So I shall pass to a new Objection.

১৩৩ CHAPTER III ১৩৩

Third Objection: They aggravate the matter maliciously, by representing the Constraint enjoin'd by JESUS CHRIST, *under the Idea of Scaffolds, Wheel, and Gibbet; whereas they should only talk of Fines, Banishment, and other petty Grievances. The Absurdity of this Excuse; and supposing the literal Sense, That capital Punishments are much more reasonable than the Law-Quirks, Pillorys, and Captivitys made use of in* France.

Your Reasoning, they'l tell me, is very disingenuous; you eternally suppose, that to obey the Precept, *Compel 'em to come in,* we must set up a Gibbet in every street, and study the most exquisite Torments. This is not our way of understanding it: tho we think it but reasonable, that a King in whom the whole Legislative Power is vested, shou'd distinguish those of his own Religion by his Favors, and discountenance others; nay threaten, if they obstinately refuse to be instructed, that he shall be forc'd against his Inclination to lay on extraordinary Taxes, exact all the Dutys of Vassalage, quarter his Troops on 'em, &c. <186>

I answer, 1. That they might easily see I did not make the most odious Crueltys, or the most crying in the judgment of the world, my Standard; and for the most part, that I have gone upon the Persecution which our Adversarys wou'd fain have accounted the gentlest that ever was, to wit, the late Persecution in *France*. 2. That I had a right to guide my self by what is actually practis'd in all the Countrys where the Inquisition is settled, and by what the Popish Princes have ever done at the instigation of the Pope and his Emissarys, as here among our selves under the Reign of Q. *Mary,* and in *France* under that of *Francis* I and *Henry* II. Fire, and Faggot, and Gibbet was the way then; I suppose they won't deny this.

But my most significant Answer is this, That the Constraint allegedly enjoin'd by JESUS CHRIST being impracticable without the Commission of Actions evil in their nature, if the Appointment of JESUS CHRIST, and the Benefit accruing from 'em to the Church did not rectify; it follows, that in order to judg whether any particular Species of Constraint be unjust, we ought to consider these two things: 1. Whether prohibited by God. 2. Whether unfit to promote the Good of the Church. And if it lie under neither of these Defects, it evidently follows from the Principles which I impugn, that it is just. If neither the Wheel then, nor any other cruel Punishment, be under either of these cases, it follows they may be very justly employ'd against Sectarys. Now it's easily prov'd, that they lie under neither.

1. Nothing can be pretended from God's having <187> forbidden 'em; because we must by a necessary Consequence allow, that no other way of constraining to the true Religion, by Fine, Banishment, Dungeons, and quartering of Soldiers, is warranted by God. It's evident, these are all prohibited and sinful in other circumstances; but our Gentlemen pretend, that in case they are made use of for bringing Men over to the true Religion, they become lawful, and warranted, and good: consequently the general Reason, That God has forbidden Murder, and detests the shedding of innocent Blood, does not hold against the burning a Heretick; because by the same rule it wou'd hold against the imprisoning him, or bringing him to Beggary: it being evident, that one is as much forbidden by God as the other. If therefore the general Command against oppressing the Innocent ceases with regard to Hereticks; the Command against shedding of inno-

cent Blood must cease with regard to the same Hereticks, unless God himself declares the Exception to his own Law, when he enjoins *the compelling to come in.* But it's manifest he makes no such Exception, since he only expresses it simply and absolutely, *Compel 'em to come in.* There can be no reason then which, in paying obedience to this Command, dispenses with the Breach of another Command, *Thou shalt not steal,* but shall equally dispense with the Breach of, *Thou shalt do no murder.* The Command of constraining is general, it must therefore either derogate from no Law of the second Table, or derogate from all; nor can it ever be shewn, why it shou'd dispense with the Transgression of any one, and not dispense with the Transgression of all the rest. This I have <188> urg'd in another place.[70] Since JESUS CHRIST therefore has no where distinguish'd upon the kinds of Constraint, he has left the choice of 'em to the pleasure and discretion of the proper Powers; and it can't be pretended, that Wheel and Gibbet have had an exclusion.

They'l tell me perhaps, that the Analogy of Faith makes us easily perceive what kind of Constraints are disallow'd by JESUS CHRIST; and that as the Spirit of the Gospel is that of Gentleness and Patience, common Sense must tell us, when JESUS CHRIST dispenses with this Gentleness, that he still means we shall keep as near it as possible, and avoid all those barbarous Punishments which Cruelty inspires. This, in my opinion, is the most reasonable thing they can offer, and yet there's nothing at all in it.

For were we to set bounds to our Constraint by the Analogy of the Gospel Spirit, we shou'd never go beyond lively and pathetick Exhortations, and the pressing in season and out of season the Promises of a future Life, and the Pains of Hell; or at most, not beyond the diminishing some Privileges, when we saw Men make an ill use of their Liberty. We shou'd never think it allowable to depart from the Gentleness of the Gospel so far, as to separate Husbands from their Wives, Fathers and Mothers from their Children, expose 'em to the Pillage of the Soldiery, thrust 'em into Dungeons, and deprive 'em of all means of subsisting. And tho there's perhaps less Cruelty and Barbarity in Punishments of this kind, than in impaling a Man 'nointed with a bituminous matter, and then setting him in a blaze, or stov-

70. See above, Part I, Chapter 4, p. 86.

ing him in *Phalaris*'s brazen Bull; yet it <189> is certain, there's Inhumanity and Injustice enough to convince us that JESUS CHRIST does not approve 'em. Else we must say, he forbids only Crimes of the most heinous, and not those of a lower kind; whereas he condemns the very Thought and Look of Inhumanity and Injustice. Shou'd they say, it's out of charity that they torment People with their Dragoons, it's to save 'em so as by Fire; who sees not that as much may be said in behalf of the cruellest Punishments? For what can hinder their answering, that they break a Heretick upon the Wheel out of an excess of Christian Charity, either in hopes that the Dread of the Punishment will make himself comply, or the Example strike a terror into the whole Sect? But we shall speak more fully to this in another place. What I have said, suffices to shew that the first of the two things I suppos'd, to wit, that taking the Parable in the literal Sense, it can't be pretended the cruellest Punishments are unlawful.

2. The next thing I advanc'd was, that Punishments of this kind are not improper towards promoting the Good of Religion; that is, towards adding to the number of those who profess it. All Constraint is indeed in different respects proper and improper for this end; for there are those who stiffen in their Opinions by being teaz'd about 'em, and on whom the Blood of Martyrs, be they true or false, makes a wonderful impression: but there are many more on the other hand, generally speaking, who stagger, and at last sink under Persecution. It's hard to lay down any general Rule in this case, because the Effects of Persecutions vary according to the Circumstances of <190> Time and Place, and according to the Dispositions of the Perse-cuted. The surest I think is this, That if a gentle Persecution can add to a Church, a smart Persecution shall add much more; and therefore tho per-secuting by Fine, Prison, and Dragoon, be less estrang'd from the Spirit of the Gospel, than persecuting to the life, as in the Reign of *Dioclesian,* yet it were more expedient, take one thing with another, to persecute in this last way than the first; because that which on one hand might be less Evan-gelick in this way, wou'd be abundantly compensated by the Overplus of Advantage to Religion. The better to comprehend this, let us examine what Advantages the Convertists pretend to reap from their mitigated Violences; that is, from Prisons, Banishment, and Confiscation.

1. Say they, These rouze Men from their slumber in a false Religion, such as live in it only because they were born in it, without ever considering the Reasons o' both sides; and oblige 'em seriously to examine their own Religion: and in this Examination they will meet with the Truth.

But I ask any reasonable Man, whether they shan't be much better rouz'd by threatning 'em with the Galleys, than by threatning only with a Fine; by threatning 'em with perpetual Imprisonment, than by threatning with double Taxes; in a word, by threatning 'em with the Wheel, than by threatning with Banishment. I don't think any will deny this; and consequently, that they advance more by the most violent Persecutions, than by the less violent, with regard to the obliging the Incurious, who are of such a Religion only from Custom and <191> Education, to examine wherefore they are of it.

2. They say, the Fear of pinching Want, and slight temporal Affliction, inclines 'em to examine the Reasons without prejudice; it weans from a Fondness for their native Sect, it slackens the Bands of inveterate Habits, to think it may be much for their advantage, shou'd they get thorow this Examination undeceiv'd of their Opinions, and firmly persuaded that the Church which threatens is better for this Life, as well as for that which is to come. Now this happy Disposition is a good step to the finding out the true Church.

But let me ask any reasonable Man in my turn, Whether, if the Fear of a slight Punishment be able to break the Charm of inveterate Habits, and the Power of Prejudices, and inspire a predisposing Desire or implicit Wish, that what the Party had all along believ'd false, might now upon the inquiry be found true: I ask, I say, whether if the Fear of a slight Punishment be able to produce such Effects, the Fear of the Wheel, Gibbet, or Galley, won't produce 'em much quicker. They who have a mortal hatred for Convertists, need only wish 'em ridiculous enough to answer, No.

3. Say they, Threatning a Forfeiture of Goods and Honors, makes the Ambitious and Covetous quit their Heresy; and tho they shou'd not be inwardly chang'd, not even by habitually going to Mass, which they are oblig'd to do, still their Children and Posterity are gain'd.

But once more, won't they gain all this, and much more securely, by

threatning Hereticks with Death? Won't they conquer their Obsti-
<192>nacy much the sooner, the more terrible the threatned Punishments
are? How many Men wou'd submit to pay a heavy Fine yearly, to be redeem'd from the Mass, who yet wou'd not redeem themselves at the price
of Life; so that they are sure of gaining the more Children, the more they
aggravate the Penaltys? In a word, we need only trace this last Persecution
from the beginning to the end, to find that it never produc'd its effects to
any considerable degree, till it put Men upon the Alternative, either of
starving, dying of lingring Deaths in Dungeons, the Sport and May-game
of an insolent Soldiery; or else signing the Formulary. All the Preludes to
it by Quirks at Law and vexatious Prosecutions, scarce quitted the Cost of
signing, sealing, and registring the Edicts: They must either have bin baffled
and lost all their labor, or put the Persecution upon a foot, which if rightly
consider'd, was more rigorous than Death it self. Here then is a fresh Example confirming what I had said before, to wit, that the sharper the Persecution, the more it increases the persecuting Communion, generally
speaking.

4. Say they, The Church is secur'd from the Scandal of having dy'd its
hands in Blood, when they content themselves with a Persecution *a la mode
de Lewis* XIV. Now the being freed from this Reproach is no small gain;
the rather, as it preserves the Lives of many who become good Catholicks
by Custom and Acquaintance.

I answer, (1.) That as to the Glory of Christianity, I see no great matter
in its being rescu'd from the blackest Reproach. To set up for Merit, it is
not enough that it fall short of the <193> extremest Point of Evil: its Reputation is low enough, if it be confessedly very bad, tho 'twere possible to
be worse. (2.) That the Protestants expostulate in their Writings, that they
wou'd rather be persecuted in *Francis* I's or *Dioclesian*'s way, than *a la mode
de Lewis* XIV. And therefore these pretendedly mitigated Persecutions can
no more hinder their crying out against the *Gallican* Church, than if she
had actually dy'd her hands in Blood. (3.) That if on one hand it be an
advantage to spare the Lives of Hereticks under the appearance of good
Catholicks, because in effect they sometimes become such; it is pernicious
on the other, because they may corrupt their Children, and instruct 'em

privately in their Heresy: whereas if the Fathers and Mothers were all knock'd o' the head, they might afterwards reckon upon the Children. (4.) That it's pure Vanity, or Reasons of State, which hinder their putting Hereticks to death, and make 'em chuse to dragoon 'em into compliance. 'Tis because they wou'd find matter for their fulsom Panegyricks and Poems, and boast that his Majesty had done more without Fire and Faggot, than all his Ancestors with 'em. 'Tis because they are afraid this kind of Punishment might mar the Design, as it did in the days of *Francis* I, *Henry* II, *Charles* IX, &c. Beside that the Death of a Subject is a detriment to the State.

Nothing in nature is more to be pity'd than the Writings of the *French* Authors against the *Spanish,* upon their methods of supporting the Catholick Church. The *Spaniards* glory in their Inquisition, and reproach the *French* on their tolerating Calvinists. The *French* (I mean those <194> who wrote before the late Persecution) say a thousand handsom things in answer, cite the antient Fathers thick and threefold, to prove, that we must not force Conscience, and say as severe things against the Inquisition as any Protestant. They'l still cry it down, and reproach the *Spaniards,* that their Faggots and bloody Tribunal of the Inquisition are a Scandal to Christianity; and that if they must persecute, they ought to follow the methods which were taken in *France.* I hope I shall live to see some able *Spanish* Doctor expose the Absurdity and Ridiculousness of this Distinction; for in reality, here's the fairest occasion in the World for mocking the bitter Invectives of the *French* Writers against the *Spanish* Inquisition: not that at bottom they condemn'd it in it self, but purely because not establish'd among themselves; for were it once introduc'd, you shou'd have Panegyricks upon the Inquisition stuck up at the Corner of every street. The truth is, nothing can be more agreeable than the Inquisition to the literal Sense of the Words, *Compel 'em to come in,* if you only except some want of Formality in the Indictment; nothing more just or more laudable, than putting Hereticks to death, as the *Spaniards* do; if once it be suppos'd, that JESUS CHRIST commands to force 'em in. How horrible that some Christians shou'd hold a Doctrine, which once suppos'd, must make the Inquisition the most holy Institution that ever was upon Earth!

It's possible the greatest part of my Readers may not have consider'd these things thorowly enough, to agree to all I have now said; yet I am persuaded, they can't but allow what follows. <195>

That the same Reasons which authorize the Dragoon Crusade, and the other Methods in vogue with the *French* Government, being sufficient to authorize Wheel and Faggot, the Question is only this, to know at what Seasons, and in what Places the first kind of Constraint is preferable to the latter: and after this, in order to know, whether the *Spanish* Inquisition be a more proper way than the *French* Dragooning, 'twere requisite to know, which of the two methods is best fitted to the Genius of the Subjects upon whom they are serv'd; for to say, that the Inquisition puts People to death, whereas the Dragoonery only ruins 'em, is saying nothing. The *Spaniards* will presently reply, that they have to deal with a sort of People, who are never to be reclaim'd but by broiling; whereas the *French* have to do with more tractable Spirits, and there's an end of that Dispute: each Nation employs the means which they deem properest; shou'd either be wrong, it is not out of any Disregard to the Command of JESUS CHRIST, but for want of a thorow Acquaintance with the Character of the *Spanish* Nation, or from a juster Knowledge of that of the *French*. Now it's but a slight Fault in the sight of God, and a very low degree of Vertue, to be more or less ignorant of the Genius of a Nation; and as for the Judgment of Men, the *Spaniards* are under no pain about it, because they find their own Account in the Tribunal of the Inquisition, they preserve Unity by it as near as possible, and therefore may very well applaud themselves in having wisely adapted the means to the ends. And in case it did happen, that a Prince, in obeying the Command, *Compel 'em to come in,* <196> shou'd chuse amiss, as the Duke of *Alva* in the *Low Countrys,* when he chose the bloody way of Executions with those People; yet 'twere no hard matter to justify him in the thoughts of all equitable Persons, by only saying, that we must not judg of things by the Event, and that those means which in human Prudence are thought the fittest, have very often an unprosperous Issue. One might even insist, that the King of *Spain* had hit, in the Temper of the Duke of *Alva,* upon the true means for extinguishing the Reformation in the Low Countrys, had he but the Patience to let him continue for a few Years; and there's good ground to believe, if *Philip* made a wrong step in

sending such a Man into *Flanders,* that he made much a worse step in re-
calling him. He ought either never to have employ'd him there, or have let
him go on in his own way. The Convertists of those times, such as were
the least unreasonable of the Tribe, wish'd undoubtedly something, not
unlike the illustrious* *Roman*'s Wish touching the Union of *Cesar* and
Pompey. A world of People, and especially the *French,* talk and exclaim to
this Day, against *Charles* V as tho, thro his Remisness, in not vigorously
exerting his Arms early enough against Lutheranism, he had bin the Cause
of its taking root in *Germany,* where, say they, he might easily have crush'd
it, if he had bestir'd himself betimes. By this they confess, that generally
speaking, there's no such sure way of duly fulfilling the Precept of the Parable as extreme Severity. <197>

From hence I think it very plainly appears, that the literal Sense which
I reject is justly chargeable with Wheel, Gibbet, Tortures, *Phalaris*'s Bull,
and in general, with the most inhuman Executions; since it calls for 'em by
a just and very natural Consequence, wherever the less rigorous Methods
are judg'd insufficient to the end.

And here I can't forbear exposing the Conceit of a modern *French* Monk,
who, *after*† *having shewn from Scripture and Ecclesiastical History,* that the
Council of *Lateran* was right, *in delivering over Hereticks,* the *Albigenses* for
example, *to the Secular Arm, to be punish'd with temporal Punishments;* adds,
*that the Clemency of Princes, who treat 'em by gentler Methods, to recover 'em
from their Errors and incline them to be instructed, is notwithstanding more
to be prais'd, and more conformable to the Spirit of the Church: what our great
Monarch* (Louis XIV) pursues he, *practises with so much Wisdom and Gentleness.* The whole ground of this Monk's Moderation was this: He saw the
way with the Calvinists of *France* was, not punishing with Death, but tormenting 'em sundry other ways; this was Demonstration to him, that the
Practice was more praise-worthy, and more agreeable to the Spirit of the
Church; since else he must have fallen into this capital Heresy, that what
is practis'd in *France* is not more agreeable to the Spirit of God which

---

* Utinam, Cn. Pompeii, cum C. Cesare Societatem, aut nunquam coisses, aut nunquam diremisses. *Cicero Philip.* 2. [Cicero, *Philippics.* II.x.24: "I wish, Pompey, that you
had never allied with Caesar, or never broken with him."]

† Journal des Savans *of the* 19*th of* Feb. 1685. *speaking of a Book of* Natalis Alexander.

governs the Church, than what is practis'd in the Countrys under the Inquisition. But what wou'd this Monk mean by saying, that a Conduct,
opposite to Scripture, and to Ecclesiastical Histo-<198>ry, is more to be
commended, and more agreeable to the Spirit of the Church? This is
strange Jargon. Can the Spirit of the Church be opposite to Scripture, and
to the History of the Church? And when a Prince won't do what's recommended in Scripture and Church-History, can he merit greater Praises,
and be more conform'd to the Spirit of the Church than when he does?
After all, is it not overthrowing the Authority of Councils to say, it's more
praise-worthy to treat Hereticks, as they have bin treated in *France* for
twenty years past, than to obey the Council of *Lateran,* which ordains the
exterminating 'em?

See what a Lock our Doctors of the Romish Communion are got into.
Their Councils have ordain'd Persecution to death, yet a great many Authors dare not condemn those Princes who keep within some Bounds of
Moderation; and they who maintain the literal Sense of the Precept, *Compel 'em to come in,* are yet constrain'd to own upon several occasions, that
'tis more agreeable to the Spirit of the Church, not to compel by temporal
Inflictions. This we plainly see in that Passage of the *Jacobin*[71] just now
cited. He proves from Scripture, and doubtless he cou'd not have over-
look'd the Parable in question, that the Council of *Lateran* was very right;
and yet the King of *France,* who for three years past has neither obey'd the
Council of *Lateran,* nor the Scripture approving that Council, was more
to be prais'd, and more led by the Spirit of the Church, than if he had
conform'd to the Council of *Lateran,* which, according to this Author, was
most exactly conformable to Scripture and Tradition. 'Tis not amiss to observe, that <199> the words of the Parable, taken in the literal Sense, don't
import a bare Permission only of compelling, but a most express Command; so that one is oblig'd, in pursuance of it, to force to the utmost of
his Power.

I have met with another hitch of this kind, and which has a near relation
to these matters, in a Treatise of *Justus Lipsius.* This Man having bin ruin'd
in his Fortune by the Wars in the *Low Countrys,* fled to *Leyden,* where he

71. Dominican, member of the Order of Preachers.

found an honorable Retreat; and was chosen a Professor, making no great scruple of outwardly abjuring Popery. During his stay there, he publish'd some Pieces concerning Government, in which he advanc'd among other Maxims, That no State ought to suffer a Plurality of Religions, nor shew any Mercy towards those who disturb'd the establish'd Worship, but pursue 'em with Fire and Sword; it being better, one Member shou'd perish rather than the whole Body. *Clementiae non hic locus, ure, seca, ut membrorum potius aliquod quam totum Corpus corrumpatur.*[72] This was very unhandsom in a Person kindly entertain'd by a Protestant Republick, which had newly reform'd its Religion; since it was loudly approving all the Rigors of *Philip* II, and the Duke *d'Alva*. And besides, 'twas a prodigious piece of Imprudence, and an execrable Impiety: since on one hand it might be infer'd from his Book, that none but the Reform'd Religion ought to be tolerated in *Holland;* and on the other, that the Pagans were very right in hanging all the Preachers of the Gospel. He was attack'd on this head by one *Theodore Cornhert,* and put into some disorder; <200> for we find him oblig'd to tack about, and declaring, that these two words, *Ure, Seca,* were only Phrases borrow'd from Chirurgery, to signify, not literally Fire and Sword, but some smart Remedy. All these Doubles are to be met with in his Treatise *de una Religione.* It is truly the very worst Book he ever wrote, except his impertinent Legend, and silly Poems written in his old Age, upon some Chappels of the Virgin; his Mind beginning about this time to be moap'd, as heretofore *Pericles*'s, so far as to suffer himself to be trick'd out Neck and Arms with Amulets, and old Womens' Charms; being perfectly infatuated to the Jesuits, into whose Arms he threw himself, when he found the vile little Book we are now speaking of, began to be censur'd in *Holland:* this was it that made him sneak away privately from *Leyden.* To return to this little Book, it's a wretched Medly of Passages, authorizing all the Pagan impious Maxims on which their horrible Persecutions of the primitive Christians were founded, and of a great many other Passages directly contrary. And as the Author does not avow his two words, *Ure, Seca,* in their full force, he has recourse to some pitiful Distinctions, amounting to this,

72. Lipsius, Civil. doctr. IV.3. [Author's note in the French edition. Justus Lipsius, *Politicorum, sive civilis doctrinae libri sex,* 1589.]

that Hereticks shou'd be put to death but rarely, and then too very privately; but as for Fines, Banishment, Marks of Infamy, Degradation, there shou'd be no stinting 'em in these. All these Doctrines fall flat to the ground before the Reflections already made.

It's certain, there are a great many Roman Catholicks, who approve the inflicting capital Punishments on other Christians, and undoubtedly they reason more consistently; but the prettiest <201> Conceit I have met with on this head is that of one *Ferrand,* a modern *French* Author, that they who put Hereticks to death do well, but not quite so well as they who don't carry it so far as capital Punishment. This is extravagant; for if a Heretick deserves death, 'tis either because JESUS CHRIST has commanded to compel all Straglers to come in, or because the Heretick blasphemes in saying, for example, that the Priest has no more than a piece of Wafer in his hands, and that instead of the Son of God, he adores and swallows a bit of Bread. If he's worthy of death by virtue of the Command of JESUS CHRIST, it's as great a Sin to let him live, as it had bin in the Jews to let a Sorcerer live, whom God expresly commanded to be put to death. If he be worthy of death on the score of his scandalous Blasphemys, it's an Impiety to spare him three days, for so long he only repeats his Blasphemys; whereas, if he were cut off quick, 'twou'd prevent the Danger of his infecting others. *Nullus hic Clementiae locus,* quoth *Lipsius* very justly, *Ure, Seca;* there's no room for Mercy here, burn, broil, break on the Wheel incessantly, and without trifling time. See where the abominable Maxims of our Convertists lead; they can alledg nothing in favor of their pretendedly mollify'd Persecutions, in reality crueller than a quick Death, which does not necessarily infer an Obligation of dispatching a Heretick altogether as soon as a Highwayman, provided always he refuse to abjure his Tenets.

I remember a Dilemma that *Tertullian* makes use of against *Trajan's* Instructions to *Pliny* the younger, by which he orders him not to promote In-<202>formations against the Christians; but if Accusers voluntarily impeach'd and convicted 'em by due course of Law, in such case to put 'em to death. *Tertullian* looks on this Order as absurd: for says he, If Christians recognized as such deserve Death, strict inquiry shou'd be made to find 'em out; and if they merit a Suspension of this inquiry, they ought not to be put to death when detected. *O. sententiam,* says he, *necessitate confusam!*

negat inquirendos ut innocentes, & mandat puniendos ut nocentes. Parcit &
saevit, dissimulat & animadvertit. Quid teipsum censura circumvenis? Si dam-
nas, cur non & inquiris? Si non inquiris, cur non & absolvis?[73]

All things rightly consider'd, Persecutions which put Men to death are
best of all, especially where they don't spare the Lives of those who abjure:
for to promise a man Life who is sentenc'd to die; to promise it, I say, on
condition he abjures his Religion, is a dangerous Snare, leading to Acts of
Hypocrisy, and the grievousest Sins against Conscience: Whereas were
there nothing to be gain'd by dissembling, every one wou'd know what he
must trust to, and resolve to die for what he believes the Truth. And there's
no doubt but he who is sincere in his Error, dies a Martyr for the Cause of
God; since 'tis to God, as revealing himself to his Conscience, that he offers
himself in Sacrifice; I say, in a voluntary Sacrifice, tho it is not in his choice
either to live or die. It fares in this case much as when a Man commits a
Rape on a Woman: He does her less injury than if he tempted her Vertue,
and brought her to yield by his Wheedles, because the Consent makes her
a sharer in <203> the Guilt; whereas his forcing her Body leaves not the
least stain on the Purity or Innocence of her Soul in the sight of God. These
are the good Fruits of your Persecutions which give no quarter; which,
upon the Confession of such a Faith, sentence you to death, and dispatch
you, even tho you profess'd you change your Opinion. But your teazing
knavish Persecutions, which promise on one hand, which threaten on another, which tire you out of your life with Dispute and Instruction; which,
in fine, whether you change inwardly, or whether you do not, will have it
under your hand before they have done with you, or never expect a moment's Comfort of your Life: these Persecutions, I say, are diabolical Temptations, which extort the Sin, as the Presents, the Flatterys, and Wheedles,
work Women to yield to their Lovers vicious Desires.

I remember I have read that *Mahomet* II, intending to get rid of *David*

---

73. Tertullian, *Apologeticum,* II.8: "What a decision, how inevitably entangled! He
says they must not be sought out, implying they are innocent, and he orders them to be
punished, implying they are guilty. He spares them and rages against them, he pretends
not to see and punishes. Why cheat yourself with your judgment? If you condemn them,
why not hunt them down? If you do not hunt them down, why not also acquit them?"
Translated T. R. Glover, Loeb Classical Library, 1977, p. 11.

Emperor of *Trebizond,* and his Children, gave 'em their Choice either of Death or of the Alcoran. Of nine Children which he had, there was one Son and one Daughter incapable, by reason of their tender Age, of chusing between these two Extremes; so they fell a Prey to *Mahometism:* but *David* and seven of his Sons chose Death, which they all suffer'd with a great deal of Constancy. This was a glorious Martyrdom, and by so much the more, as 'twas in their power to redeem their Lives, by abjuring the Christian Faith; and therefore with respect to them, and considering the Success, 'twas better that the Sultan left 'em the liberty of chusing. But on the other hand, what a violent Temptation did he lay 'em <204> under by promising Life? and therefore with regard to him the Order was much more malicious, than if he had simply condemn'd 'em to death; tho even in this case the Sacrifice had bin voluntary: just as in Sickness, when a Man sees he cannot recover, and makes a free Act of Resignation to the Will of God, he does that which shall be constru'd a voluntary Sacrifice of his Desires to those of his Creator.

Judg now, whether Persecution ben't very execrable; since the only way to render it less evil, is its being made inexorable Death.

✂ CHAPTER IV ✂

The Fourth Objection: We can't condemn the literal Sense of the words, Compel 'em to come in, *but we must at the same time condemn those Laws which God gave the Jews, and the Conduct of the Prophets on several occasions. The Disparity, and particular Reasons for giving the Old Law, which don't take place under the Gospel.*

Before I propose this Objection, I think my self oblig'd to say a word or two upon a Scruple which may arise in the minds of some People. It looks, say they, as tho you wou'd maintain that there are but two ways to be taken with Hereticks, that of putting 'em to death, or that of abandoning 'em to their Errors, without troubling your head, whether you go the <205> first way to work, or whether you take the second, with the thoughts of converting 'em to the true Church. This, add they, is what you plainly insinuate, when you say, that where Hereticks are condemn'd to death, it's better not to offer, than offer 'em their Lives on condition they abjure. I answer, that my opinion is, all imaginable care shou'd be taken in endeavoring to convert those who are suppos'd to be in error, by Instructions, by charitable and calm Reasonings, by clearing up their Doubts, by Prayers to God in their behalf, and by all the Demonstrations of a Zeal truly Christian: but if all this will not work upon 'em, far from pressing 'em to change their Religion, we ought to let 'em know that they wou'd do very ill to change it, as long as their Minds are not enlighten'd. We ought to send up our Prayers to God for 'em, but still take care not to act the part of a tempting Angel, by promising 'em great Advantages if they change, or by threatning 'em with Death if they refuse. And here's the true reason why of two Evils, to wit, that of condemning a Man to death unless he change his Religion, or condemning him whether he be willing to change or no; I shou'd be of the mind to chuse the latter as the least, because it does not expose the Man to the dangerous Temptation of sinning against Conscience, and puts him in a way, when he sees there's no remedy, of sacrificing himself by a serious Act of Resignation to the Love of Truth: for it's impossible a Man shou'd lay down his Life chearfully for what he believes the Truth, tho possibly it may be an Error, without a sincere Love of Truth. Let's now consider this fourth Objection. <206>

It seems to be drawn from hence, that the Law of *Moses* allow'd no Toleration for Idolaters or false Prophets; that it punish'd with Death; and from the Prophet *Elias*'s putting the Priests of *Baal* to death, without sparing a Soul.[74] Whence it happens, that all the Reasons I have bin laying out in the First Part of this *Commentary* prove nothing; because they prove too much, to wit, that the literal Sense of some of the Laws of *Moses* wou'd by the same Rule be impious and abominable. Now since God might, without a breach upon Order, have commanded the Jews to slay the false Prophets among them, it evidently follows, he may enjoin the putting Hereticks to death under the Gospel.

I don't perceive I'm yet infected enough with the Spirit of Controversy, to bully this Objection, or look down on it with an air of Scorn and Con-

74. 1 Kings 18:40.

tempt, as generally those do, who find themselves at a loss for a satisfactory Answer: I freely own the Objection is strong, and seems to be one pregnant Instance, that God has a mind we shou'd know scarce any one thing with certainty, by his having left so many Exceptions in his Word to almost all the common Notions of Reason. I even know those, who have not any greater difficultys against believing Almighty God Author of the Law of *Moses,* and of those Revelations which have occasion'd such slaughters of Men, than to see that this is repugnant to the purest Ideas of natural Equity: for in fine, say they, our common Notions being the primary Revelation, the original and mother Rule of every thing that falls under our cognizance, what reason is there to imagine that God shou'd <207> on one hand reveal to us, by natural Light, that Conscience ought not to be forc'd; and on the other, by the mouth of *Moses* or *Elias,* that we must slay all those who are not of such or such a Persuasion in matters of Religion? We must believe then, say they, that *Moses* acted in this from a mere human Spirit, and from Principles of pure Policy, such as he judg'd the fittest for the Preservation of that Commonwealth which he founded. It's a rule with great Politicians, never to suffer any Innovations in Religion, and to appoint the grievousest Punishments for those who shall attempt the introducing any Change in this particular. Here, say they, is the foundation of *Moses*'s Laws in that point. Now the particular Notions of any one Man not being the Rule of Equity, there's no ill Consequence in rejecting whatever *Moses* might have ordain'd from a private Judgment. With regard to *Elias,* these *Free Thinkers* wou'd have us likewise believe, that his Zeal transported him too far, and that he made use of some pious Fraud, from a good Intention, to make the Fire descend upon his Victims. But God forbid, that to get over this Objection, we shou'd ever adopt a Thought so dangerous and impious as these. I'm of opinion, we may give a reasonable Solution, upon a supposition, as no doubt it's true, of the Inspiration of *Moses* and *Elias.*

To ground this Solution on the Principles I have made use of from the beginning of this Work, it's fit I demonstrate that there's no real Contradiction between that Revelation which God vouchsafes to all attentive Minds by the pure Ideas of good Sense, and that particular Revela-<208>tion communicated to *Moses* for the exterminating all Idolaters who shou'd rise up among the Jewish People. For were there a real Contradiction between the first Revelation and the Laws of *Moses,* 'twou'd follow from my Principles, that this were ground enough, *a posteriori,* to reject *Moses* either as a wilful Impostor, or as a Person seduc'd by some invisible Genius attempting to oppose the Orders of God. Let's make it appear then, that there's no real Contradiction in the case.

To this end, I reclaim my Readers to this Idea, which Reason and Experience do both confirm: That a Being can't be said to contradict it self when it ordains several Laws, the Observation of one of which is sometimes inseparable from the Non-observance of others. For example, no body will say that God has contradicted himself in commanding Children to honor their Fathers, and commanding to do no murder; yet it is in some cases impossible to obey both these Laws at the same time, supposing there were Fathers who commanded their Children to take away a Man's Life. If the Opinion of some modern Philosophers be true, it is God who moves all Matter by certain general Laws, and among others by these; That all Motion shall be made in a right line, and if an invincible Obstacle hinders, the moving Body shall turn off to one side. It's evident, that in consequence of these two Laws, Motion shall often be made in a circular line. Will any one therefore say that God overthrows his first Law? 'Twere the grossest Ignorance to fancy so. Good Sense teaches us, that one of these two Laws is subordinate to <209> the other, and that the requisite Conditions presenting for the executing of one of 'em, the Legislator, to maintain an Uniformity, must abandon the other Law, and execute this, to execute that other in its turn as soon as the Conditions to which it is annext present. The same thing happens between the Laws of the Union of Soul and Body; by one of which, according to the same Authors, it's ordain'd, that as often as the Soul desires to move an Arm, the animal Spirits shall flow to the Muscles which serve for moving the Arm. Yet a Paralytick may wish long enough, and desire to move his Arm; it won't do. Is it that God forgets his first Law? No; What then is the reason? 'Tis this, that before the animal Spirits arrive at the Muscles of the Arm, they meet with a rub or obstruction by the way; which, in consequence of another Law between Bodys, reflects or turns 'em aside. This Law cannot be executed, without the other being suspended; God complying with each in its turn, and postponing one when the juncture for the other presents; the observing of which must inevitably cross the Execution of that.

Accordingly to conclude, that such or such a Command cannot come from God, it is not sufficient that it be repugnant to the pure Ideas of Reason, and that we cannot obey it without shocking natural Light; but we must moreover be assur'd that this Command is not the necessary Consequence of a Law, which God has in reality establish'd: for if once it appears to be a necessary Consequence from such a Law, we ought not any longer to think it strange, that it's ex-<210>pedient in some cases not to obey a particular Law of Nature: just as we don't think it strange, that it's sometimes expedient to disobey that most natural Law of obeying the Will of those to whom we owe our being, because we see this Disobedience is a necessary Consequence of other Laws establish'd by God, which we perceive by common Sense to be very just; such as those of not killing nor defrauding our Neighbor. From hence it's easily conceiv'd, how when the Jews heard *Moses* give a Law for immediately putting any Man to death, who shou'd rise up among 'em, and teach Doctrines opposite to the Fundamentals of their Religion, the only true Worship of that God who had brought 'em out of the House of Bondage; it's, I say, easily conceiv'd how there shou'd be no room for their suspecting, that this Law did not come from God, upon the pretence of any Contradiction in it to the purest Ideas of Equity, which require that every one shou'd follow the Dictates of his Conscience: This, I say, is easily conceiv'd, and from this Reason.

That every Man, who contemplates the Idea of a Being sovereignly perfect, must distinctly conceive, that God may communicate himself to a People in a particular manner, and by an oral Revelation declare, he will chuse 'em for his peculiar Inheritance, and be not only a God, but also a King to 'em, and Head of their temporal Government. And therefore when *Moses* on the part of God declar'd to the Children of *Israel,* that God remember'd the Promise which he had made to *Abraham,* that he wou'd deliver 'em by a mighty Hand and an out-stretch'd Arm <211> from their *Egyptian* Bondage, and bring 'em into the Land of *Canaan;* in a word, that he wou'd be their God, and they shou'd be his People: 'twas natural for 'em to believe these words of *Moses,* and not have the least distrust of their being true, after all the mighty Wonders and Miracles he had wrought to justify his Mission. Here then we find this People rationally persuaded that the sovereign Lord of all things, the infinitely perfect Being, is its God, and its King properly and immediately; and from henceforward, their obeying particular Laws, which God enjoins 'em, shall be not only a Duty of Religion, but that also of a good Subject, who observes the politickal and fundamental Laws of the Government under which he lives: and Disobedience to the Laws of God, shall for the future be punishable not only at the Bar of Conscience, but at the Tribunal of Civil Justice also; forasmuch as the Laws of God are those of the temporal Sovereign, and political Head of the State. Now as the Basis and fundamental Law of this State, is that of having no other God but him who brought 'em out of the Land of *Egypt;* as this is the first Covenant betwixt God and the People of *Israel;* betwixt God, I say, consider'd not simply as Creator, but as supreme and temporal Lord of the Jewish Commonwealth: it's plain, all Idolatry was punishable by Death, and that any one who preach'd or intic'd to the Service of other Gods, and to the Religion of the Nations round 'em, was as liable to capital Punishment, as he wou'd be, who shou'd at this day exhort the People of *London* to take an Oath of Allegiance to the King of *France* or *Spain.* So that <212> whoever was but the least attentive to that natural Light, which informs that we ought not to force Conscience, might easily have conceiv'd upon the first hearing the Laws of the 13th of *Deuteronomy,* that they were righteous and just; and that they might flow from the same God, who tells us in general by the Oracles of common Sense and Reason, that no Man shou'd be forc'd by temporal Punishments to the Profession of this or of that Religion.

There was no more difficulty in reconciling these two things, than in reconciling the Disobedience of a Son, order'd by his Father to commit a Murder, with the fifth Command of the Decalogue. For as that which makes the neglect of the fifth Commandment in this case no Transgression, is, that its non-Observance is a necessary Consequence of the Observance of another Command; so that which made the forcing of Conscience among the Jews no Violation of natural Right in the Case specified in *Deuteronomy* Chapter 13, was its depending as by a necessary Consequence on the Observance of the fundamental Laws of their Commonwealth. Since therefore one Law may hinder the Execution of another, and yet no reason to suspect that both are not given by the same Legislator; the Jews cou'd have no ground to doubt whether the Laws of the 13th of *Deuteronomy* came from the same God, who by the Oracles of natural Light ordains, that there shall be no forcing of Conscience. But wherefore, will some say, why put a Man to death for persuading his Neighbor to worship another Divinity, which in his Judgment he believes to be the true? Because, by that particular Form of Government, and in that <213> Theocracy under which the People of *Israel* liv'd, this was an overt Act of High Treason; 'twas an Attempt of Rebellion against the Sovereign Magistrate. Now since Order Eternal and Immutable confers a Power on the Magistrate of punishing Treason and Rebellion, and whatever else tends to the overthrowing the Constitution; it's plain, that God being once constituted Head of the Jewish Commonwealth, whoever shou'd afterwards alienate his own Allegiance, or endeavor to draw away others, deserv'd to die as a Traitor and Rebel: nor will it avail him, that in so doing he follow'd the Light of his Conscience, this being a singular Case, in which God by an extraordinary Appointment, to wit, that of a Theocratical Government among the Jews, derogates from the Immunitys of Conscience.

The Crime in this case becomes punishable by the Secular Arm, in quality of Treason and Rebellion against the State, and not as it is simply a Sin against the moral and metaphysical Obligation Men are under of worshipping the only true God. Whence it follows, that there's no Consequence to be drawn from this Case to that of the Gospel, because the Precepts of the Gospel are not the political Laws of the State, except in some chief Instances without which human Society cou'd not subsist; for example, the forbidding Murder, and False Witness, and Robbery, is at the same time a Political and Evangelical Law: whence it happens, that shou'd a Man commit Murder or Robbery from the Dictates of his Conscience, he is nevertheless punish'd by the Secular Authority, because the Magistrate <214> loses not his inherent Right of cutting off from the Commonwealth whatever necessarily destroys the Security of its Members, and tends to dissolve the Society; he loses not this Power, I say, tho a Man shou'd by chance be found, who committed Murder and Robbery from an Impulse of Conscience.

The Conduct of *Elias* is not near so considerable an Objection as the thirteenth Chapter of *Deuteronomy,* because it is only a particular Example not propos'd to our Imitation by any Command of God; whereas the Law of *Moses* is general with regard to the Jews, and deliver'd absolutely and without any restriction to Time or Place. Upon this particular Case of the Priests of *Baal* put to death by the Prophet's Command, we have only one of these two things to offer; either that God, who may dispense with his own Laws in certain Cases, thought fit that these false Priests shou'd be put to death at that time, because the natural Impression made by such an Adventure on the Machine of the Body, and on the Spirits of those who shou'd hear or see it, might be fruitful in thousands and thousands of very considerable Combinations physical and moral: or what seems to me more probable, that *Elias* had a Revelation that these Priests were insincere at heart, and maliciously abus'd the Credulity of the People for filthy Lucre. Now in this case we declare that no Heretick has right to a Toleration; and we freely consent that Minister and People be condemn'd to the Gibbet, if we know certainly that they preach Errors and Heresy, to them known as < 215 > such, from mere Malice and worldly Interest. In this case let 'em all be truss'd up.

I might here alledg, with *Spencer* a learned Man of our own Nation, that God had ordain'd several things among the Jews, which are no farther reasonable, than as, consider'd with regard to the Situation of that People, to their perverse Inclinations and absurd Prejudices, they were capable of preventing great Evils, or procuring indirectly some Good: and in this number I might reckon that Law which condemns false Teachers to death, but I have no need of this Remark.

Let's now examine the Difference between the literal Meaning of the Precept, *Compel 'em to come in,* and the objected Examples of the old Law.

1. The Jews had no Orders to send forth Preachers for the propagating their Religion, and instructing all Nations in it. They confin'd themselves to their own Country, without almost any Commerce with other People; so that the Command of putting those to death, who conform'd not to their Religion, concern'd only those of their own Nation, who shou'd attempt changing the God of *Abraham* for any of the Pagan Divinitys round 'em. Now it was morally impossible that a Jew, bred up in Judaism, shou'd attempt this Change from any Motive of Conscience, or from any other Principle than that of a Spirit of Rebellion, Libertinism, or mere Malice, in which case he justly deserv'd to die; and there's a very notable difference between this and that Constraint which the Convertists speak of: for Chris-

tians being oblig'd by their Master's Commands to instruct all Nations, they must of <216> necessity have to do with People educated in Principles different from their own, and under the power of Prejudices which must needs destroy their taste for the Gospel. So that to say Christians shou'd make use of Constraint, is saying that they ought to force People who are sincerely persuaded they can't forsake their own Religion with a good Conscience.

2. In the second place, the Proceedings against Seducers under the Law of *Moses,* might indeed be severe enough; yet they left their Consciences intirely free. This Law did not force Men to abjure what they believ'd true, it did not tempt 'em by the hopes of Life to act a part; in a word, they dy'd in the full Enjoyment of all the Principles of their Conscience, if they had any, and were never constrain'd to live in Anxiety and Remorse, by Promises of Life if they comply'd with the publick Worship. Death was their certain Lot, without the Alternative of Death or Renunciation. On the contrary, our Convertists will have Men threaten'd in the first place, and this Condition annex'd, that they who abjure shall be quit of all Prosecution, and stand fair for Rewards; and that their Threats may work the more efficaciously, the Craftiest have a way of threatning such Deaths as are attended with slow and exquisite Torments, or depriving People of all means of flying, or subsisting at home. This constrains a world to betray the Lights of their Conscience, and live afterwards under an Oppression of Spirit, which disorders, and at last drives 'em to despair. What can be more cruel? The Law, which is thought so hard, was a Honey-moon in comparison of such a Gospel. <217>

3. Besides, the Severitys under the antient Law were limited to certain particular Cases; as when *Elias,* for example, from a prophetick Impulse upon his Spirit, acted by a dispensing Power, and even from a Knowledg of the Heart of those false Prophets whom he slew, and of their obstinate fraudulent Malice; or else to certain Doctrines tending to subvert the fundamental Constitution of the Commonwealth, as that for example, of not acknowledging God, the God of *Abraham* and *Isaac,* who was become the sovereign Lord of the Jews in a more especial manner by Covenant and formal Contract. Nothing of this nature can be pleaded in behalf of the present Convertists. They pretend that JESUS CHRIST has commanded

Violence simply and absolutely; and in reality there's no Restriction in the words either to Time, or Place, or Doctrine. No body under the present Dispensation can tell, whether a Heretick be sincerely or maliciously in Error. Christians are under no Theocratical Form of Government; they have a Discipline, and Canon Law distinct from the Civil: Christianity is not the fundamental Constitution of the State, in such a manner that a King is supreme in his Dominions only by virtue of being Christian; for *Constantine* and *Clovis* acquir'd not a tittle of Right by being baptiz'd, beyond what they enjoy'd in a state of Paganism: and *Julian* the Apostate reign'd not less rightfully than if he had bin a Christian. For which reason Magistrates shou'd commit the Care of punishing Hereticks to God alone, so long as they disturb not the publick Peace; I mean, so long as they obey the Laws, since purely as they are Hereticks they offend not against <218> those things which Magistrates have a right to impose.

4. Last of all, the Jews tolerated all the different Sects which were form'd on the various Interpretations of the Law of *Moses,* and punish'd only those who subverted the Foundation, by quitting the Religion of their Country for good and all, to go after strange Gods. They even tolerated the most detestable Heresys, and which by consequence destroy'd all Religion; such as the Sect of the Sadduces, who deny'd the Immortality of the Soul, and the Resurrection of the Body: but forasmuch as they talk'd not of renouncing the true God to worship *Baal* or any other Idol, they not only suffer'd 'em patiently, but we even don't find that J. CHRIST ever blam'd their Conduct in this; nor is it to be doubted but he had reproach'd the Pharisees with it, if he had thought their tolerating 'em unjustifiable. If the Convertists of these days wou'd square themselves by the Practice under *Moses*'s Law, they ought to punish only such as turn'd Jews, Pagans, or Mahometans, and bear with all the different Opinions which might be rais'd on such or such a Passage of Scripture. But very far from this, they have those among 'em, who say that the Church of *Rome* has a hundred times more right to compel and persecute dissenting Christians than mere Infidels.

I have shewn elsewhere,[75] that Princes cannot establish their own Religion by a politickal Law, obliging their Subjects to the Profession of it under

75. See above, pp. 112–13.

pain of High Treason and Rebellion. God alone had a power to do this, by declaring it immediately to *Moses,* and confirming this Pur-<219>pose by incontestable Miracles: so that Princes may ordain what they please in matters of Religion, their Subjects may lawfully dispense with their Submission, provided they can in truth and sincerity alledg that famous Saying of St. *Peter's,* said before him by a* Heathen; *It's better to obey God than Men.* And if they proceed to Constraint, they are guilty of the same Sin as those who were Persecutors of the Apostles: for the Heathen Emperors who establish'd Paganism in their Dominions by a Law, had not hereby acquir'd a jot the more right to persecute the Apostles.

I must conclude this Chapter by observing, that natural Light, the primary and original Rule of Equity, can never acknowledg Compulsion, which is directly repugnant to it, as divine; unless it appear to be the necessary Consequence of some Law, known by another Means to come from God. Now Compulsion under the Gospel can be the necessary Consequence of no other Law known by another Means to come from God; and nevertheless it directly contradicts the Rule of natural Equity. We must therefore conclude from the irrefragable Lights of right Reason, that JESUS CHRIST has not ordain'd Constraint. Let's answer on this occasion to those who alledg *Moses,* much the same as JESUS CHRIST answer'd those who alledg'd him in favor of Divorce: 'Twas because of the Hardness of Heart <220> and incorrigible Proneness of the Jews to Idolatry, Murmuring, and Rebellion, that *Moses* ordain'd Death for all those who shou'd not conform to the Religion of the Country; but from the beginning it was not so. We must therefore resolve things to their first Origin, and regulate 'em by that natural Law which irradiates the human Mind, before any positive Law is propos'd.

---

* Veremur vos Romani, & si ita vultis etiam timemus: sed plus veremur & timemus Deos immortales. *Lycortas Achaeorum Praetor, ap. Liv. l. 39.* [Livy, XXXIX.xxxvii.17: "Indeed we respect you, Romans, and, if you wish it so, we even fear you; but still more do we both respect and fear the immortal gods." Translated E. T. Sage, Loeb Classical Library, 1965, p. 338–39. Cf. Peter, Acts 5:29.]

⚇ CHAPTER V ⚇

The Fifth Objection: Protestants can't reject the literal Sense of the Parable, without condemning the wisest Emperors and Fathers of the Church, and without condemning themselves; since they in some places don't tolerate other Religions, and have sometimes punish'd Hereticks with Death: Servetus *for example. The Illusion they are under who make this Objection. Particular Reasons against tolerating Papists.*

Ever since the Court of *France* has bin infatuated with the Spirit of Persecution, we have had the Lord knows how many Parasites, mercenary Scriblers, bigotted Flatterers, employ'd in compiling with the exactest care all the Laws publish'd of old by the Christian Emperors against Arians, Donatists, Manicheans, and other Sectarys; the Emperors, I say, egg'd on by the Zeal and Importunitys of their Clergy, and extol'd for it to the skys by some of <221> the Fathers of the Church; particularly St. *Austin,* who has written the Apology of Persecution with more Intenseness of Thought, than *Tertullian* that of the Christian Religion. We shall keep this Father's Dole in reserve for him to another place. At present I shall only say a word or two in answer to what is objected from the Example of *Constantine, Theodosius, Honorius,* &c. that if their Actions were the Rule of Right, there's no Crime but might be justify'd by it. So that it's making a mock of Folks, when the Question being concerning a Point of moral Right, they come and alledg, that such an Emperor and such an Emperor has authoriz'd it. *Quid tum?* What's this to the purpose? Is the way of the Court the Rule of Equity? Is this the School where we are to learn what is just and unjust? Is it not well known, that temporal Greatness is the chief End of Princes and their Counsellors, and that they sacrifice every other Consideration to their Interest, especially when Persons acted by an indiscreet Zeal bait it with Promises of earthly and celestial Glory? I shou'd think my time very ill bestow'd, shou'd I spend a quarter of an hour, in discussing the particular Reasons which mov'd these Emperors to publish very severe, and even sanguinary Laws, against the Sects of their times. The shortest way is saying, there's no Consequence to be drawn from what they have done, to what right Reason requires shou'd be done, and that our Convertists will never be able to shew this Consequence. Had we the secret Historys of all their Courts, as we have that of *Justinian*'s; had we all the Remonstrances, and <222> all the Accounts which they call Libels, all that the Pagans and Sectarians had remark'd on their Conduct; we shou'd see 'em in a light that wou'd be none of the favorablest to them. But 'tis their good fortune, that we scarce have any Memoirs of them, but from the hands of Flatterers, or Persons prepossess'd in their favor. Yet there's enough, did we duly weigh the Circumstances, to perceive that they little consulted the eternal Ideas of unalterable Order, but issu'd their Injunctions just as they came, according to occasions, and according to the Views of temporal Advantage which were suggested to 'em. Oh! but the Fathers have applauded their Zeal. *Quid tum?* Indeed! And what if they did? Were not the Fathers, as well as the Ecclesiasticks of these days, almost ever ready to make the present Advantage their measure of Right and Wrong? Is it not a scandal to Christianity, that the Fathers shou'd declaim with so prodigious force against the persecuting Pagans and Arians, and by and by praise with all their force the persecuting Emperors, and sollicit severe Edicts? 'Tis true, they made a great difference as to Words, for they wou'd by no means have the Rigors on their own side call'd Persecution; they laid up all the odious Names for the opposite Partys. But even this is ridiculous, and moves our Pity. The truth is, we ought never to mention the Maxims on which they reason'd in different conjunctures; it's much better to hide their Weakness, and the little care they had taken to fix any general Principles; living as 'twere from hand to mouth, and arguing like Weather-cocks, sometimes on one side and some-<223>times on another, as time and occasion serv'd. Let's stir this Matter no more, but content our selves with demanding from the Convertists a Proof of the Consequence[76] of this Enthymeme.[77]

The Fathers applauded the Emperors who persecuted Hereticks:

Therefore the persecuting Hereticks is just and highly pleasing to God.

I don't see why this Argument shou'd have any more weight with us now,

---

76. See Appendixes, "Bayle's Use of Logic," p. 580 ("consequence").
77. Ibid. ("enthymeme").

than another of the same stamp, which will possibly be thus advanc'd a hundred years hence.

The Bishops of *France,* the Jesuits, and the Monks have extol'd the Methods by which *Lewis* XIV destroy'd Calvinism, as being perfectly holy and divine:

Therefore these Methods were perfectly divine and holy.

I can't forbear representing, by one memorable Instance, to what an Excess the Fathers carry'd their unjust Prejudices.

There was a Village in the *East* call'd* *Callicin,* in which the Jews had a Synagogue, and the *Valentinian* Hereticks a Meeting-house. A Procession of Hermits passing by one day with their Votarys, happen'd to receive some Insult from these Villagers. Immediately the noise of it spread, and reach'd to the Bishop's Ears, who stir'd up his People with such Success, that they immediately went along with the Hermits, and laid the Jewish Synagogue, and Heretick Conventicle in Ashes. This was a manifest Invasion of the <224> Prince's Authority; for surely 'tis to him, or to his Lieutenants, that Bishops ought to have recourse for Reparation of Injurys, and not revenge themselves off-hand by Seditions stir'd up among a giddy Populace.

He who commanded in the *East* under *Theodosius,* understood his Duty, and was jealous enough of his Master's Authority, not to fail giving an Account of all that pass'd; and the Emperor, upon notice of it, order'd the Bishop to rebuild the Synagogue at his own Expence, and the Incendiarys to be punish'd. Nothing cou'd be more equitable than this Decree, nor farther from excessive Severity; for in fine, the Conventicle and Synagogue had both stood in that place by the Prince's Authority, and cou'd not be remov'd but by his Orders: and all popular Commotions are so much the more punishable, as those who foment 'em have not the least shadow of Right, or pretence for so doing; and such we may suppose Bishops, a Set of Men notoriously culpable, if they exhort not Christians to the forgiving of Injurys, and to all kinds of Moderation. But as gentle as this Punishment appears, the Eastern Bishops were delicate enough to find it insupportable; and as St. *Ambrose* was within reach of the Court, and a proper Person to represent their pretended Grievances, they charg'd him with this Affair.

* Paulin in vita Ambros. [Migne, *Patrologia Latina,* vol. 14, col. 34, cap. 22.]

Matters not permitting St. *Ambrose* to go to Court in Person, he* wrote to *Theodosius,* and represented that his Decree had laid a Bishop under the necessity, either of disobeying his Prince, <225> or betraying his own Ministry, and tended to make him, either a Martyr or Prevaricator; that *Julian* the Apostate, having attempted to rebuild the *Jewish* Synagogues, Fire fell from Heaven on the Builders, and that could well happen again; that *Maximus,* some days before he was abandon'd by God, had issu'd the like Edict. In fine, St. *Ambrose,* after he had, in terms of Duty and Respect, exhorted the Prince to recal his Order, let him understand, that if his Letter had not the desir'd effect, he shou'd be oblig'd to remonstrate from the Pulpit. The Emperor made him no favorable Answer; and St. *Ambrose,* one day in his Sermon, to be as good as his word, address'd† himself to the Emperor as on the part of God, and lectur'd him pretty roundly. At which the too good and over-easy Emperor was not at all offended, but on the contrary, promis'd the Preacher, as he was descending from his Throne, that he wou'd give Orders to recal his Decree. Some of the Lords who were present insisted, that at least, to save the Honor of his Imperial Dignity, so unworthily affronted by the Rabble, he wou'd order the Hermits, who were Authors of this Riot, to be chastis'd; but St. *Ambrose* reprimanded 'em with such a Spirit, that they durst not say a word more of the Matter: so the Edict was revok'd.

This shews, that the Reign of *Theodosius* was perfectly Priestridden, and that he was deliver'd, bound hand and foot, to the Mercy of the Clergy; which cou'd not chuse but bring a Deluge of Woes upon the Nonconformists. Is not this a <226> strange thing, that a Man who passes for a Saint, shou'd have bin so violent an Advocate for a Seditious Bishop, and for all the Furys of a mutinous Rabble; and that he shou'd pretend 'twere better submit to death than give some Mony in obedience to the Emperor's Order, for the rebuilding a Structure, demolish'd in open Contempt of the Emperor's Authority? What wonder after this, that the Worship the Pagans paid their Divinitys, *more majorum,*[78] shou'd be punish'd with death, and

---

* Ambros. Ep. 29. [Migne, *Patrologia Latina,* vol. 16, col. 1101, epistula XL.]
† Vide Paulin. in vita Ambros. [Migne, *Patrologia Latina,* vol. 14, col. 35, cap. 23.]
78. "In the ancestral way."

declar'd High-Treason, by this* same Emperor? Did the Pagan Emperors do more against the Christians? and if they spill'd more Blood than he, is it not because the Pagan Votarys had not the same Constancy as Christians, to maintain their Belief at the expence of their Lives?

But what Answer shall we make for those Protestants, who won't allow Liberty of Conscience to other Sects? This we are next to speak to.

I say then, that there are some Distinctions necessary to be premis'd: for either they won't allow other Sects from abroad to come and settle among 'em; or if they spring up among themselves, they take care to prevent their Growth; or last of all, they disperse and expel 'em after they have bin form'd and establish'd. These different Circumstances excuse their Non-Toleration more or less: tho if we consider this matter impartially, and by that Light in which right Reason shews it, it cannot be absolutely excus'd unless in cases where it's purely political, and indispensably necessary for the publick Safety of the <227> State. To explain my self.

Not to tolerate those who entertain certain particular Opinions in Matters of Religion, and who infuse 'em into others, implys certain Penaltys on those who infuse 'em, and that these Penaltys be ordain'd by the Authority of the Magistrate. To this end it were necessary that Princes shou'd have a Right of enjoining the Belief of certain things on their Subjects, and of restraining 'em to such a Conscience, rather than any other; since without such a Right it's plain, they cou'd not impose Penaltys on those who had not the same Notions of things as they themselves have. Now if it appear, that they have no such Right, it follows, they can appoint no such Punishments; and yet all who are against the tolerating certain Sects impose Penaltys on 'em: they act therefore without any Justice or Reason, and consequently Non-Toleration is repugnant to Reason and Justice; since from what we have said before, it's manifest, that those who enact Laws obliging Conscience, exceed their Power, and overstrain their Authority: whence it follows, that those Laws are actually null and void in themselves.

However, there is an Exception to be made, which manifestly arises from

---

* Leg. 12. de pag. Cod. Theo. [Theodosian Code, XVI, 10, 12, ed. Mommsen, Berlin, 1962, p. 900; tr. C. Pharr, New York, 1952, p. 473.]

the Remarks laid down in another place,[79] to wit, That Sovereigns, having an essential and unalienable Right of enacting Laws for the Preservation of the State and Society over which they are plac'd, may ordain, that all, without distinction, who endanger the publick Peace by Doctrines tending to Sedition, Rapine, Murder, Perjury, &c. be punish'd according to the Nature of their Crimes; <228> accordingly any Sect, which strikes at the Foundation of human Society, and bursts the Bands of the publick Peace and Amity, by exciting Seditions, by preaching up Rapine, Murder, Calumny, Perjury, deserves to be immediately cut off by the Sword of the Magistrate: but so long as the Principles of any Sect overthrow not those Laws which are the Foundation of the Security of Individuals; so long as they preach Submission to the Magistrate, and the chearful Paying of Taxes and Subsidys impos'd by him; and maintain, that no Man ought to be disturb'd in the Possession of his Right, or in the peaceable Enjoyment of his Goods, moveable or immoveable, of his Reputation, Life, &c. I don't think there can be any just ground for vexing 'em on the score of their not obeying any particular Law enjoining such a certain Belief, or such a particular form of Divine Worship: for as I have already observ'd, a Magistrate, who enacts Laws of this kind, and enforces the Observation of 'em under pain of Death, Prison, Galley, &c. manifestly exceeds his Power.

If any one therefore wou'd know my Opinion in particular, concerning those Protestant States which allow but one Religion; I answer, That if they act purely from a regard to the suppos'd Falseness of the Opinions of other Religions, they are wrong; for who has requir'd this at their hands? Is Falshood to be overcome by any other Arms than those of Truth? Is not attacking Errors with a Cudgel, the same Absurdity as attacking Bastions with Syllogism and Harangue? Sovereigns therefore who wou'd discharge their Duty aright, ought not to send forth their Soldiers, their Hangmen, their Tipstaffs, their Life-<229>guard-men, their Pursuivants, against those who teach Doctrines different from their own; but slip their Divines, their Ministers, their Professors at 'em, and order 'em to endeavor with all their Might, the Confutation of the obnoxious Doctrines: but if these Means are not sufficient to silence their Adversarys, or bring 'em over to the Religion of the Country, they shou'd e'en let 'em be quiet, and for the rest,

79. See above, p. 180.

content themselves with their obeying the Municipal and Politickal Laws of the State. So much for what concerns those Doctrines which Protestants consider simply as false; this Falseness gives 'em not the least Right of treating their Subjects ill.

But the case is not the same with regard to those Opinions which they look upon not only as false, but also as tending directly, and in the Nature of 'em, to the Disturbance of the State, and the endangering the Sovereign's Authority: for as to all such Doctrines, I pronounce 'em unworthy of a Toleration; and for this Reason I think it but just, that all those States, which have shaken off the Yoke of Popery, shou'd make the most severe Laws against its Re-admission; and that those who have Papists still in their Bosom, shou'd keep 'em chain'd up like so many Lions or Leopards, that is, deprive 'em of the Power of doing Mischief, by the severest Penal Laws, and those duly put in Execution against 'em, that there may be no room for apprehending any thing from their restless Contrivances. Yet I shou'd never be for leaving 'em expos'd to Insults in their Persons, or for disturbing 'em in the Enjoyment of their Estates, or the private Exercise of their Religion, or for doing 'em any <230> Injustice in their Appeals to Law, or for hindring 'em to breed up their Children in their own Faith, or to retire with their Effects, and after the Sale of their Estates, as often and as many of 'em as pleas'd, to any other Country: much less for constraining 'em to assist at the Exercises of a Religion which their Consciences condemn'd, or recompensing those who did; this being properly the Part and Office of a tempting Demon, and tending to make all those who lov'd worldly Honors and Dignitys betray the Lights of Conscience. I shou'd be for a Law, excluding new Converts from all the Privileges and Favors of which they were made incapable by their former Religion; because thus we might be assur'd, that their Conversion proceeded purely from Conviction, and that they did not play the Hypocrites. But as the keeping this sort of Men to strict Discipline is only intended with regard to a temporal Good; I shou'd not disapprove, where there may be particular and weighty Reasons against having any jealousy, the granting 'em a greater Liberty, and even as great as the Interest of the State will permit: for, as I have already said, the Falseness of Opinions is not the true Rule of Toleration or Non-Toleration, but their Influence with regard to the publick Peace and Security.

If those of the Church of *Rome* will impartially consider it, they must allow, that I don't here destroy what I had bin establishing thro-out this *Commentary,* against the Compulsion allegedly enjoin'd by JESUS CHRIST: for the Laws which I propose to be made against them, are not with a design of forcing 'em to <231> change Religion, but purely as a Precaution against all Attempts on their part; and to prevent their having it in their power to force the Conscience of their Fellow-Subjects, and even the Sovereign himself. I don't pretend, by confuting the literal Sense of the words, *Compel 'em to come in,* to condemn Sovereigns, who for just causes may keep a strict Rein over some of their Subjects. I don't blame the King or Republick of *Poland* for being upon their guard against the bold Attempts of the *Cossacks,* or the King of *France* for building Citadels and Forts in Citys which have bin subject to revolt. And therefore what I have bin saying just now cannot be turn'd upon my self, since that kind of Constraint which I allow against Papists in Protestant States does not affect their Consciences, nor has any other aim than to prevent their disturbing the State, which the Principles of their Religion directly lead to.

In effect, their Councils and their Popes having a thousand times approv'd Persecution, and injoin'd it on Princes upon the severest Penaltys; their Princes having exercis'd in all Ages all manner of barbarous Crueltys on Hereticks, or reputed Hereticks; and never having kept their Promises of letting 'em live in quiet, tho ratify'd by the solemnest Oaths, but breaking thro 'em without the least scruple, whenever they had a fit occasion: Their Bishops, the rest of their Clergy, and their Popes always egging 'em on to this Breach of Faith, and extolling and blessing 'em for it, as a most holy, most pious, and most divine Action; as may be seen in the Briefs of *Innocent* XI and his Harangue to a full Con-<232>sistory in praise of *Lewis* XIV and by infinite Panegyricks, with which the Pulpits ring all over *France:* In a word, it being the current and avow'd Doctrine of the Church of *Rome,* that Hereticks, of whom they form a more hideous Idea than of any Monster, may and ought to be punish'd, and compel'd to come in, according to the Command of JESUS CHRIST, which they expound literally, and never tolerated while there's a possibility of preventing it. All these things, I say, rightly weigh'd, Prudence and common Sense require that we shou'd consider Papists as a Party of Men who look on all Government in the hands of Protestants with an evil eye, and with the sharpest regret; who omit no means to wriggle themselves into power, to recover the Churches and Benefices they were once possess'd of, and to extirpate what they call Heresy; which they think themselves oblig'd to, by the Command of JESUS CHRIST, and by the Spirit of their Church; a Spirit in their persuasion infallible. I pass over what the more devoted to the Pope pretend, that he has a power of absolving Subjects from their Oaths and Allegiance, and depriving Kings of their Dominions, and deposing 'em when not obsequious enough to the See of *Rome;* and content my self with insisting as before, and saying in one word, that Protestant Princes have the very same Reasons not to tolerate Papists, as an Emperor of *China* might have for banishing the Popish Missionarys, shou'd they frankly own that, as soon as they had the power in their hands, they'd force all People to receive Baptism. I have said so much of this in the fifth <233> Chapter of the first Part, that 'twill be enough to make an Application of it here to those of the Church of *Rome;* forasmuch as if they were sincere in the point, they must answer, to whoever shou'd ask 'em, in case they were uppermost, whether they wou'd grant Protestants a Toleration, that in truth they never wou'd, but oblige 'em to go to Mass by fair or by foul means. I shan't here insist in particular upon another Remark, That whoever thinks it lawful to force Conscience, must by a natural Consequence believe the greatest Crimes become Acts of Piety in his hands, provided they tend to the destroying of Heresy: I insist not, I say, on this point here, and only desire my Reader to remember I have bin full enough on it elsewhere,[80] and apply it to those of the Church of *Rome.* And now, to shorten this Article, I offer this one Argument, which deserves to be consider'd.

That Party which, if uppermost, wou'd tolerate no other, and wou'd force Conscience, ought not to be tolerated.

Now such is the Church of *Rome.*

Therefore it ought not to be tolerated.

Nor let any one say, it follows from hence that Protestants cou'd not be entitled to a Toleration from the Church of *Rome;* nor pretend to prove it by saying, that on this very score, because the Protestants wou'd not tolerate her if they were uppermost, she is oblig'd not to tolerate them when it is

---

80. See above, p. 88.

her turn: let no one, I say, reason thus, because there is this material difference between her and us, that Non-Toleration on our part is depriv'd of
that fearful Sting, that most odious and most criminal Quality <234> which
it has from Popery, to wit, the forcing Conscience by the most violent
Temptations into Acts of Hypocrisy and deadly Remorse; whereas Protestants allow People a liberty of removing with their Effects, or serving God
privately in their own way. So that the Major of my Syllogism cannot be
retorted, there being a Clause in it which concerns not Protestants. In the
mean time I shall observe one thing, which is of weight against the literal
Sense of the Precept.

That by an odd Counterstroke it furnishes a pretence of persecuting even
against those who might naturally be most inclin'd to tolerate: for in effect,
if Prudence, and even Religion require, that a Prince shou'd remove from
his State any thing that might bring Persecution upon it, which must naturally draw on all the Horrors and Villanys set forth in the fifth Chapter
of the first Part;[81] the Church of *Rome* might justly suspect, that if Protestants were uppermost, they wou'd not grant her a Toleration: for fear then
of coming under such a misfortune one day, she thinks her self oblig'd to
prevent and crush them. So that this literal Sense cannot be embrac'd by
either Party, but by a Counterstroke it sets the other upon Persecution, how
great soever its natural Aversion might be to the thing. Whence it appears
that this pretended Precept, *Compel 'em to come in,* by its natural Action
and Re-action, must be a continual and insatiable Principle of Horrors and
Abominations over the face of the Earth. An evident Argument it never
was the Meaning or Intention of JESUS CHRIST. <235>

Yet if we judg equitably of things, we are oblig'd to say, that the fear of
a Retaliation warrants not the Church of *Rome*'s anticipating the Persecution of Protestants: 1. Because, as I have already observ'd, Non-Toleration
among them has lost its sting. 2. Because in the places where they are tolerated they behave themselves like good and faithful Subjects, having never
taken up Arms till control'd in their Liberty of Conscience; which shou'd
be a sufficient Security to their Governors, that they never will give 'em any
disturbance, so long as they are allow'd to serve God in their own way.

81. See above, Part I, Chapter 5, pp. 103–107.

3. Because in Countrys where the Government is Protestant, they treat Papists with a great deal of Tenderness, as long as they see 'em conform to the Laws of the Land, in any degree becoming good Subjects; in *Holland,* for example, and in the Dutchy of *Cleves,* and here in *England* under the late Reign. Whereas the Roman Catholick Princes and States persecute without end and without measure, either in effect or intention; so that when they don't oppress their Subjects of a different Religion, it is not for want of Good-will, but because their Interest won't permit. The House of *Austria, Poland, Savoy,* are pregnant Examples. *France* has bin the greatest Example of Toleration that the Church of *Rome* can shew; and how did this happen? Was it from any sense of Equity, or any regard to the Dictates of right Reason, which so clearly discover to us, and which had discover'd to so many of the antient Fathers of the Church, that no Man shou'd be forc'd in the Worship of God? No, *Lewis* XIV in his Preamble to the Edict of Re-<236>vocation, lets all *Europe* understand that he, his Father, and Grandfather, had all along a design of repealing that of *Nantes,* if other Affairs had not interven'd.[82] He ought to know his own thoughts best; and as to what he says of his Father, 'tis probable enough, if the Protestants of the Kingdom had had as much patience under his Reign, as they have shewn of later years, he had left but little for his Successor to do. But as to *Henry* IV, he'l give us leave to believe he had no intentions of revoking the Edict of *Nantes* the next day after it was register'd by his own Orders or even during his Reign. He was naturally too honest a Man, and had bin too long of the true Religion, to fall in seven or eight years time into all the abominable Maxims and knavish Counsels, that a Confessor of the Society of *Jesus* is capable of suggesting.

So much for Toleration, with regard to those of the Romish Communion. Let's now proceed to that which Protestants are oblig'd to allow those of other Religions, whose only Ambition is Liberty of Conscience, and whose Principles are not destructive of the municipal and politickal Laws. And with regard to these, I shan't spare to say, that those States which refuse 'em a Toleration do very ill; but their Iniquity varying according to the

82. For the text of the Revocation of the Edict of Nantes, see http://www.fordham.edu/halsall/mod/1685revocation.html.

degrees of more or less, it's fit we shou'd consider it with regard to the following Rule, or fixt point of Liberty: *That it is the Duty of Superiors to use their utmost endeavors, by lively and solid Remonstrances, to undeceive those who are in error; yet to leave 'em the full liberty of declaring for their own Opinions, and serving God according to the Dictates of their Conscience,* <237> *if they have not the good fortune to convince 'em: neither laying before 'em any Snare or Temptation of worldly Punishment in case they persist, nor Reward if they abjure.* Here we find the fixt indivisible Point of true Liberty of Conscience; and so far as any one swerves more or less from this Point, so far he more or less reduces Tolerance. For any thing further, I don't think the having publick Churches, or walking in Processions thro the streets, essential to Liberty in Religion. This may contribute to the outward Pomp, or *melius esse;* but the ends of Religion are sufficiently answer'd, if they be allow'd to assemble to perform divine Service, and to argue modestly in behalf of their own Persuasion, and against the opposite Doctrine, as occasion requires.

The first step of Variation from this Rule might happen, shou'd we suppose the People of any Country, perfectly united in the Profession of one and the same Religion, enact this as a fundamental Law, That no Person of a different Religion shou'd ever be suffer'd to come in or sojourn among 'em, or vend his Opinions within their borders. This Law seems very reasonable and innocent at first sight, yet it is not without its Inconveniences: for supposing such a Law in force among the *Gauls,* in *Spain, Arabia* or *Persia,* upon the first preaching of the Gospel; the Apostles, and their Disciples, had bin excluded by virtue of it: and shou'd they declare in the open streets that 'twas better to obey God than Men, and to preach his Gospel rather than conform to the Laws of the Land, they had bin punish'd as seditious Persons, and Infringers of the Laws of the State. This had bin unjust, and <238> the Law consequently unjust. Such a Law excludes the Preachers of Truth, as well as those of false Doctrines: Shou'd all the Pagan and Mahometan Countrys at this time enact such a Law, how shou'd we send forth Missionarys with any hopes of Success? Let's agree then, that a true Liberty of Conscience is inconsistent with such a Law, especially when put in execution against those who shou'd run the hazard, and come into a Country, in spite of such a Prohibition, with a design to convert it.

A second step of Variation from this Rule wou'd be; if, together with the above-mention'd Prohibition, another Law shou'd be enacted, forbidding any Inmate or Native of the Country to innovate in matters of Religion, on pain of Banishment. It's evident, the enacting such a Law is forging Chains for Conscience; because, shou'd a Man, upon examining his Religion, find, or fancy he finds something amiss in it; shou'd he be convinc'd in his Judgment, that it were fit to teach so and so, to reform such and such Abuses, he shall be restrain'd by the fear of Banishment, and his Conscience undergo a conflict between the Love of his Country and that of Truth; and if bound to the former by prevailing Considerations, he's in a fair way of playing the Hypocrite. I own, he's much to blame if he does not chuse to run the hazard of Banishment rather than stifle the Motions of his Conscience; but still it's a hardship upon the Man: And as such a Law might have occasion'd the banishing a *Roman,* or a *Gaul,* in the days of the Apostles, who in his Travels abroad, or by Epistles at home, had bin instructed in the Gospel; < 239 > it's plain, that in such a case it had bin very unjust; and is no less so now, with regard to an Indian, Turk, or Moor, who having bin instructed in Christianity by the same means, shou'd have a desire of preaching it in his own Country. Sure I am, that if any one considers the Mind of Man, and his Attainments in Knowledg, and compares 'em with the Historys of former times, he shall plainly see, that there's no one so persuaded of the Truth of what he believes, but may have ground to think he may alter his Opinion as to some matters; and therefore we shou'd never refuse to hear those who have any thing new to propose: for how know we, but it may still be better than what we have hitherto sincerely believ'd the best? This has often happen'd before: The *Indians,* who hear a New-comer speak of JESUS CHRIST, and change their antient Belief for what this new Man tells 'em, find their account in it: The Jews and Gentiles, who embrac'd the new Doctrines of the Apostles, were infinitely satisfy'd in 'em: They who hearken'd to *Luther* and *Calvin,* and were converted to their Opinions, thought themselves happy in so doing. And can we, after so many Examples, imagine it's impossible at this day, that any one shou'd teach us things profitable to Salvation? This, on the whole, shews that all Laws restraining any further Inquiry or Progress in Knowledg, human and divine, are violent. What wou'd have become of us, if such Laws had bin duly put in execution for two or three thousand years past?

The third degree of Variation happens, when a Law is enacted, ordaining, that whatever Per-<240>son, whether a Stranger or born in the Land, teaches any thing contrary to the establish'd Religion of the State, shall be oblig'd to retract, and declare publickly, that he believes as the rest of the Country do, upon pain of Fire, Wheel, digging in the Mines, Galley, dark and noisom Dungeon, &c. Here we find the last and highest degree of Violence; but with this discretion, that to know whether Punishment by Fire be worse than that by Galley or Dungeon, we must consult the Temper of the Patient: for there be those who wou'd much rather get off by a quarter of an hour's smart Pain, than tug at an Oar for thirty or forty years together; which however hinders not but Death in the ordinary gradation of Punishments exceeds Prison and perpetual Galley.

From hence it follows, that Non-Toleration on the part of Protestants is a Variation from the Rule only in the lowest and nearest degree; since the utmost Punishment they inflict on a Subject who turns Papist, does not exceed Banishment: and as for a Stranger, who may be surpriz'd in the clandestine Exercise of some Religious Function, if he be punish'd with Death, 'tis not so much on the score of Religion, as on that of his being a Fryar or Monk in masquerade, and a Presumption that he's come to burn, poison, play the Spy, or carry on some hellish Conspiracy; of which there have bin a hundred Examples.

But, say they, the Punishment of *Servetus*[83] is demonstration that Protestants will carry Persecution as high as Papists. I answer, very far from it: The Punishment of *Servetus,* and of a very small number besides of the same stamp, <241> erring in the most fundamental Points of the Christian Religion, is look'd on at this day as a horrid Blot upon the earlier days of the Reformation, the sad and deplorable Remains of Popery: and I make no doubt, were there such another Process before the Magistrates of *Geneva* at this day, but they wou'd be very cautious of coming to such extremitys.

---

83. John Calvin had Michael Servetus tried as a heretic and burnt at the stake in 1553 for denying the doctrine of the Trinity. See Joseph Lecler, *Toleration and the Reformation,* translated T. L. Westow (London: Longmans, 1960), vol. 1, pp. 325–32.

∞ CHAPTER VI ∞

Sixth Objection: The Doctrine of Toleration can't chuse but throw the State into all kinds of Confusion, and produce a horrid Medly of Sects, to the scandal of Christianity. The Answer. In what sense Princes ought to be nursing Fathers to the Church.

It must be own'd, that the Condition of Man, among a thousand other Infirmitys, is subject in particular to this, of scarce ever knowing any Truth but by halves: for if it happen that he is able to prove a thing from clear and demonstrative Reasons *a priori,* immediately he finds himself hamper'd with absurd, or at least very difficult Consequences, arising from what he reckon'd upon as demonstrated; which is no small balk upon his Spirits: Or if he has the good fortune not to be shackled with Absurditys flowing from his Opinions, he has the mortification, on the other hand, of having only <242> very confus'd Notions, and but insufficient Proofs of his Position. They who maintain either the infinite Divisibility of Matter, or *Epicurus's* Doctrine of Atoms, can answer for the truth of this. For my part, I am sincere enough to own, that if the Opinion I have bin hitherto defending has any flaw at all, it is on the side of its Consequences. The direct Proofs which support it are admirable, the Consequences of the contrary Opinion monstrous; so far all's right: but when we turn to the Consequences of my Hypothesis, things don't look altogether so well. One wou'd think, that Almighty God, to humble the human Understanding, had decreed it shou'd find no sure footing o' this side Heaven, but Rubs and Perplexitys of what side soever it turns it self. I have however this Comfort, that all the frightful Consequences from my Opinion may very well be resolv'd. We shall see.

There is not, say they, a more dangerous Pest in any Government than Multiplicity of Religions; as it sets Neighbor at variance with his Neighbor, Father against Son, Husbands against their Wives, and the Prince against his Subjects. I answer, that this, far from making against me, is truly the strongest Argument for Toleration; for if the Multiplicity of Religions prejudices the State, it proceeds purely from their not bearing with one another, but on the contrary endeavoring each to crush and destroy the other by methods of Persecution. *Hinc prima mali labes:* Here's the Source of all the Evil. Did each Party industriously cultivate that Toleration which I contend for, there might be the same <243> Harmony in a State compos'd of ten different Sects, as there is in a Town where the several kinds of Tradesmen contribute to each others mutual Support. All that cou'd naturally proceed from it wou'd be an honest Emulation between 'em which shou'd exceed in Piety, in good Works, and in spiritual Knowledg. The Strife among 'em wou'd only be, which shou'd most approve it self to God by its Zeal in the Practice of Vertue, which out-do the other in promoting the Interest of their Country, did the Prince protect 'em all alike, and maintain an even ballance by the distribution of his Favors and Justice. Now it's manifest, such an Emulation as this must be the Source of infinite publick Blessings; and consequently, that Toleration is the thing in the world best fitted for retrieving the Golden Age, and producing a harmonious Consort of different Voices, and Instruments of different Tones, as agreeable at least as that of a single Voice. What is it then that hinders this lovely Harmony arising from a Consort of various Voices and different Sounds? 'Tis this, that one Religion will exercise a cruel Tyranny over the Understanding, and force Conscience; that Princes will countenance the unjust Partiality, and lend the Secular Arm to the furious and tumultuous Outcrys of a Rabble of Monks and Clergymen: in a word, all the Mischief arises not from Toleration, but from the want of it.

Here's my constant Answer to that thredbare Common-place of your little Politicians, that a Change in Religion draws on a Change in Government, and that therefore special care shou'd <244> be taken to prevent Innovation. I shan't here examine whether this has come to pass as often as they pretend; I shall content my self, without inquiring into the Fact, to affirm, that supposing it true, still it proceeds from Non-Toleration only: for did the new Sect but entertain the Principles which I lay down, it cou'd exercise no Violence on those who persever'd in the old Religion; 'twou'd rest in proposing its Reasons, and instructing 'em in a Spirit of Charity. In like manner, were the old Religion govern'd by the same Maxims, 'twou'd only oppose the new by gentle and charitable Instructions, and never proceed to Violence. Thus Princes might always maintain their Authority intire, every private Person sit under his own Vine and his own Fig-tree, worshipping God in his own way, and leave others to worship and serve him as they thought fit; which wou'd be the true Accomplishment of the Prophecy in *Isaiah,* concerning the Agreement of Men under Persuasions diametrically opposite: *The Wolf also shall dwell with the Lamb, and the Leopard shall lie down with the Kid; and the Calf and the young Lion, and the Fatling together; and a little Child shall lead them,* &c.[84]

It's plain to any Man who considers things, that all the Disturbances attending Innovations in Religion, proceed from People's pursuing the first Innovators with Fire and Sword, and refusing 'em a Liberty of Conscience; or else from the new Sect's attempting, from an inconsiderate Zeal, to destroy the Religion establish'd. Nothing therefore but Toleration can put a stop to all those Evils; nothing but a Spirit of Persecution can foment 'em.
<245>

They alledg likewise I don't know how many Examples of factious Spirits, who, in order to subvert the Constitution of the State, have pretended the necessity of a Reformation in Religion; and having drawn the People into their Designs, have taken the field with Sword in hand, and committed a thousand Disorders: but this proves nothing more, than that the best things are liable to Abuse. It no way proves, that it's the Duty of Princes to suppress all Innovation in Religion by the Secular Power; for the Heathen Emperors in this case had had the justest Right of suppressing Christianity, and all their Persecutions had bin indispensable Acts of Justice: but as such a Position wou'd be impious, it follows there are Exceptions to be made to this Rule. Experience informs us, that there have bin Innovations in matters of Religion which were found to be good and holy: We know there must be Innovations for the introducing Christianity in Infidel States; we know too, that there have bin Innovations, which were only a cover for factious Designs. What course then must the Sovereign take, when he sees a new Teacher set up in his Dominions? Must he seize him at first dash, and all his Followers? By no means. He must wait a little to see where his Doctrines tend, whether to the aggrandizing himself and his Party by civil Broils: if he find this, he's to give him no quarter; he may exterminate him, tho the

84. Isaiah 11:6.

Man were never so much persuaded his Doctrine was divine. This is not the sort of Men that I plead for, since their Designs are damnable, and the Religion they preach, if they have any, is of a persecuting <246> nature; and consequently falls in with the literal Sense, which I confute. But if this new Doctor has really no design of stirring up Seditions; if his only aim be to infuse his Opinions, persuaded they are true and holy, and to establish 'em by the methods of Reasoning and Instruction; in this case we ought to follow him, if we find he has Truth on his side: and if he does not happen to convince our selves, yet we ought to permit those who are convinc'd, to serve God in this new Doctor's way. This course our King *Ethelred* took with the Monks who were sent into this Country by Pope *Gregory* the Great to preach the Gospel. But all this while we ought to omit no means, by attacking this new Doctor at his own weapon, to wit, Reason and Instruction, of bringing him back into the old way, and confirming others in it, if we judg it the best.

This furnishes me with an Answer to a specious Reason, which our Adversarys make use of: They say, that among the Blessings which God has promis'd to his Church, that of giving it Kings who shall be nursing Fathers is one of the chiefest. I grant it: Nothing is a greater Blessing to the Church, than Princes who protect and cherish it; who see it be supply'd with sober and able Pastors, who found and endow Colleges and Academys for this purpose, and spare no necessary Charge for its Maintenance; who take care to punish Ecclesiasticks for their vicious and scandalous Lives, that others may take warning, and walk in that Integrity which their Profession demands; who by their own good Lives and wholesom Laws excite all their <247> People to the Practice of Vertue; and last of all, are always ready to punish those severely who presume to invade the Liberty of the Church: For I extremely approve, and think it the indispensable Duty of Princes, if new Sects arise, who offer to insult the Ministers of the establish'd Religion, or offer the least Violence to those who persevere in the old way, to punish these Sectarys by all due and requisite methods, and even with Death if occasion be; because in this case they betray a persecuting Spirit, they break the Peace, and aim at the Subversion of politickal Laws. This I take to be the true Sense in which Princes are to be nursing Fathers to the Church: and as nothing cou'd be a greater Scourge to her than being left expos'd by the Prince to the Insults of the Laity, than being abandon'd by him to their own Lusts, without any prudential Rules or Constitutions to restrain 'em; than his neglecting to minister to her Wants and Necessitys; hence it is that God promises her the Love and Protection of earthly Kings as a special Blessing.

But, say they, this is not all. Princes don't bear the Sword in vain; they have receiv'd it from God to the intent they may punish Evil-doers; and among Evil-doers, none surely out-do Hereticks, since they affront the Divine Majesty, trample under foot his Sacred Truths, and poison the Soul, whose Life is our all, and ought to be infinitely dearer to us than that of the Body. They are therefore worse than Poisoners, than Highway-men or Banditti, who kill the Body only, and ought consequently to be more severely punish'd. *Bona verba quaeso!* Run-<248>ning on at this rate will quickly justify the Persecutors of the first Christians (I often fly to this Example, because, as we shall see hereafter, there's no fence against it) will arm the *Chinese* against the Missionarys, the Protestant Princes against their Popish Subjects, and in general every Sovereign against those of a different Religion: for each will alledg that God has commanded him to punish Evildoers, and that none are more so than those who oppose the true Religion; so each calls his own. There must therefore be some ugly Sophism at bottom; let's unravel it.

Our Adversarys don't take care in this matter to distinguish betwixt that Right with which Princes are invested, of punishing with the Sword those who exercise Violence against their Neighbor, and who destroy the publick Security which every one ought to enjoy under the Protection of the Laws; they don't, I say, distinguish betwixt this Right, and that which they falsly attribute to 'em over Conscience. But for our part we don't confound these two things. We say, it's very true that Kings are invested with a Power from God of hanging, whipping, imprisoning, or punishing in any other like manner, all such as injure their Neighbor more or less, in his Person, or Estate, or Honor; and this is so much the more just, as those who commit such Violences confess not only that they commit 'em against the Laws of the Land, but also against their Conscience, and the Precepts of their Religion: so that their Malice is perfectly wilful. I don't believe there ever was an Example of a Highway-man, or a House-breaker, or a Poisoner, or

<249> a Duelist, or a False Witness, or an Assassin, sentenc'd to death by the proper Judg, who pleaded the Instincts of his Conscience, or the Commandments of God, in justification of the Crime for which he hang'd him. So that he sins knowingly and maliciously, and offers violence to his Neighbor in contempt of his God and his King.

Here then are two Circumstances which concur not in such Hereticks as I suppose shou'd be tolerated. For, (1.) They offer Violence to no one. They tell their Neighbor indeed that he's in an error; they urge this upon him by the best Reasons they are masters of; they set before him another Faith, and support it the best they can; they exhort him to change; they pronounce him damn'd, unless he embraces the Truth which they preach to him: this is all they do, and then they leave him at full liberty. If he changes, they are glad of it; if not, there's an end of the matter: they recommend him to God. Is this treating one's Neighbor ill? Is this violating the publick Security, in the shadow of which every one ought to eat his Morsel in quiet under the Protection of the Laws, and train up his own Family as he sees fit?

In the second place, these Hereticks (I call all those so in this place, whom the Sovereign distinguishes by this name on the score of their differing from the establish'd Worship) in instructing their Neighbor, in disputing with him, in admonishing him to change his Religion on pain of Hell-fire, are far from thinking that they commit an ill Action; on the contrary, they fancy they do great service to God, and <250> it's pure Zeal in 'em, no matter whether true or false; but in fine, it's Zeal for the Glory of God, and an Instinct of Conscience, which prompts 'em: so that they don't sin from Malice, or if they do, 'tis only with regard to God; their earthly Judges can take no cognizance of it, and the Presumption lies on the side of their acting from Conscience. It's plain then, that the two grand Circumstances which authorize the punishing Highway-men and Murderers with death, do not occur in the case of Hereticks.

But, say they, the Poison shed into the Soul is much more fatal than that infus'd in a Man's Liquor: To blaspheme God and his Truths, to seduce his faithful Servants, is a higher Crime, than speaking evil of the King, or stirring up his People to Rebellion. A Heretick therefore is punishable in a higher degree than *la Voisin,* or the *Chevalier de Rohan,*[85] who spoke against his Monarch with the greatest contempt, and actually endeavor'd an Insurrection. I answer upon the two points already remark'd: *La Voisin,* and the *Chevalier de Rohan,* were conscious they committed a Crime; they acted with a formal Design of doing mischief; nor did they leave it at the discretion or choice of him whom they abus'd and revil'd, whether he wou'd be abus'd and revil'd or no: whereas a Heretick thinks he shall save his Neighbor's Soul; he talks to him with a design of saving him, and leaves him the full liberty of chusing or refusing. But besides the Disparity in both these cases, I have two things more to offer.

First, that the Prince sufficiently discharges his Duty, if he provides a proper and saving Anti-<251>dote against the Poison instill'd into his Subjects, by sending forth his Doctors and Preachers to confound these Hereticks, and prevent their seducing Men from the true Religion, and catching 'em by their fallacious Reasonings. Shou'd the Preachers not be able to prevent the falling away of some of his Subjects, yet the Prince has nothing to reproach himself with, he has done his Duty: the warping mens Souls to such or such an Opinion, is no Function of his Royal Character; in this respect Men are without the least dependance on one another; they have neither King, nor Queen, nor Lord, nor Master upon earth. A King therefore is no way accountable for not exercising a Jurisdiction in matters which God has not subjected to him.

The next thing I observe, is our giving things very hard names o' purpose to create a horror for 'em; which yet, generally speaking, are out of the sphere of our Decisions. Such a one, say we, utters insufferable Blasphemys, and affronts the Divine Majesty in the most sacrilegious manner. And what does all this amount to, when consider'd soberly and without prejudice? To this, that concerning the manner of speaking honorably of God, he has Conceptions different from our own. Our case is much the same as that of an ignorant Courtier, who upon reading a Letter written to the King by a little *Indian* Prince, suppose, in whose Country the most respectful way of

---

85. La Voisin was burned as a poisoner in 1680. Louis Chevalier de Rohan was beheaded in 1674 for conspiring against Louis XIV.

writing was in a burlesque Stile; shou'd presently, from his excess of Zeal for his Majesty, propose the sending a Fleet to dethrone this little Sovereign, who had the impudence to mock the King in his Letter. Wou'd <252> not a War declar'd against this little Prince, upon such a Provocation, be very well founded; against this Prince, I say, who quitted the serious Stile purely for fear of affronting the King, and took up the burlesque only to express the deepest respect for him? The only thing this *Indian* Prince cou'd be blam'd for, was his not informing himself of the Customs of *England,* and the Notions People there have of a respectful or disrespectful Letter; but if the Savage cou'd not possibly inform himself in this particular, whatever Inquirys he made, wou'd it not be an extreme Brutality to go and drive him out of his Dominions, on account of the pretended Irreverence of this burlesque Stile? Yet this is exactly what Persecutors do, when they punish a Heretick. They fancy his way of speaking of God is very injurious to the Divine Majesty; but for his part he speaks so only because he thinks it honorable, and the contrary next to blasphemous, and highly injurious to God. The only thing to be said against him in this case, is, that he ought to have inform'd himself better concerning that way of speaking of God, which is judg'd most honorable in the Court of Heaven. But if he answer, he has done his best endeavors to be inform'd, and that he had not taken up such a way of honoring God till after he had made all possible inquiry; and that those who charge him with Blasphemy, are, in his opinion, so ill inform'd concerning the Honor due to God, that he doubts not but they mistake one for t'other; and that he shou'd think himself verily a Blasphemer, did he talk at their rate: if, I say, he answer 'em thus, shou'd not it stop their mouths, at least till they convict him <253> of speaking against his Conscience, which none but God, the Searcher of Hearts, can do? And if they put such a Heretick to death, don't they do the very same as putting the *Indian* Prince to death, or dethroning him in the former case?

This single Example is worth the whole Commentary I am about, and must to every reasonable Mind expose the Turpitude of Persecution in its proper Colors. Examples of this kind sink our Adversarys to rights; and I make no doubt but they are touch'd to the quick as they read 'em, because they begin to be sensible their Cavils can no longer blind themselves. I'm sorry for the Smart which this is like to give 'em; but I can't avoid it, nor

forbear urging it once more as a Demonstration, that Princes have not receiv'd the Sword, to punish Irreverences of this kind to the Divine Majesty.
'Tis to these Irreverences that the saying of an Antient properly belongs,
Deorum Injuriae Diis Curae; 'tis the Prerogative of the Deity to take cognizance of these Offences, and do in them as to him seems fit: but as for
Men, they see no more in 'em than a mistake in the Judgment; they all
agree in the general, that God is to be honor'd, and that all the greatest
things shou'd be said of him which can be conceiv'd to belong to the Supreme Being: but when this is done, one determines his choice to this manner, another to that, and each condemns what the other approves. It's plain
it belongs to God alone to punish him who is in an Error; and it can never
enter into a reasonable Mind, that he'l punish an involuntary bad Choice,
I mean such as results not from an untoward use maliciously made of the
Understanding to determine us to a wrong <254> Choice. If *Alexander* the
Great, who first laugh'd at the City of *Megara*'s* presenting him with the
Freedom of their City, accepted it gratefully when made to understand,
that they judg'd it the highest Honor imaginable, and what they never had
confer'd on any one before but *Hercules;* is it not reasonable to think, that
God, who judges candidly and equitably on all things, considers not
whether the Present we make of such or such Conceptions about the Divinity, be magnificent in it self or no, but whether the greatest in our Es-
timate, and the fittest upon a due Inquiry to be offer'd to him?

As to that monstrous Medly of Sects disgracing Religion, and which they
pretend is the Result of Toleration; I answer, That this is still a smaller Evil,
and less shameful to Christianity, than Massacres, Gibbets, Dragooning,
and all the bloody Executions by which the Church of *Rome* has continually endeavor'd to maintain Unity, without being able to compass it. Every
Man who enters into himself, and consults his Reason, shall be more
shock'd at finding in the History of Christianity so long a train of Butcherys and Violences as it presents, than by finding it divided into a thousand Sects: for he must consider, that 'tis humanly inevitable that Men in
different Ages and Countrys, shou'd have very different Sentiments in Reli-

* Seneca *tells it of the* Corinthians, de Benef. l. 1. c. 13. [Seneca, *De beneficiis,* I.xiii.1,
Loeb Classical Library, p. 40.]

gion, and interpret some one way some another, whatever is capable of various Interpretations. He shall therefore be less shock'd at this, than at their torturing and <255> wracking one another, till one declare, that he sees just as the other sees; and burning by turns at a stake, those who refuse to make such a Declaration. When one considers, that we are not Masters of our own Ideas, and that there's an eternal Law forbidding us to betray Conscience, he must needs have a horror for those who tear a Man's Body Limb from Limb, because his Mind has one Set of Ideas rather than another, and because he follows the Light of his Conscience. Our Convertists therefore, by endeavoring to remove one Scandal, only fix a greater on Christianity.

I shall make no Advantage of the Parallel of a Prince, whose vast Empire comprehended several Nations differing in their Laws, Usages, Manners, and Tongues, yet each honoring its Sovereign, according to the Custom and Genius of the Country; which seems to carry more Grandeur in it, than if there were only one simple and uniform Rule of Respect: I shan't, I say, make any Advantage of this Example to shew, that all that odd Variety of Worship in the World is not unbecoming the Grandeur of a Being infinitely perfect, who has left such a vast Diversity in Nature as an Image of his Character of Infinite. No, I rather allow, that Unity and Agreement among Men were an invaluable Blessing, especially Agreement among Christians in the Profession of one and the same Faith. But as this is a thing more to be wish'd than hop'd for; as difference in Opinions seems to be Man's inseparable Infelicity, as long as his Understanding is so limited, and his Heart so inordinate; we shou'd endeavor to reduce this Evil within <256> the narrowest Limits: and certainly the way to do this, is by mutually tolerating each other, either in the same Communion, if the Nature of the Differences will permit, or at least in the same City. One of the finest* Wits of Antiquity compares human Life to a Game at Hazard, and says, we shou'd manage in this World just as Men do who play at Dice; if the Throw they want does not come up, they help out by their Judgment what is want-

---

*   In vita est hominum quasi cum ludas tesseris.
    Si illud quod maxumè opus est jactu non cadit,
    Illud quod cecidit fortè, id arte ut corrigas.
    Terent. Adel. Act. 4. *Scen.* 7. [Terence, *Adelphoe,* line 745.]

ing in their Fortune. 'Twere to be wish'd that all Men were of one Religion; but since this is never like to happen, the next best thing they can do is tolerating each other. One says it's a Sin to invoke the Saints, another says it's a Duty. Since one thinks the other in an Error, he ought to undeceive him, and reason with him to the best of his Skill: but after he has spent all his Arguments without being able to persuade him, he shou'd give him over, pray to God for him, and for the rest live with him in such a Union as becomes honest Men and fellow-Citizens. Wou'd People take this Course, the Diversity of Persuasions, of Churches, and Worship, wou'd breed no more Disorder in Citys or Societys, than the Diversitys of Shops in a Fair, where every honest Dealer puts off his Wares, without prejudicing his Neighbor's Market.

If the Church of *Rome* thinks, that a Multiplicity of Sects defaces Christianity, how can <257> she accommodate herself to that bizarre Variety in her own Communion, where the Ecclesiasticks are some Cardinals, with their Palaces, fine Gardens, and open Table; some Bishops, who are Generals of Armys, and petty Sovereigns; or who go in Embassys, pass their time at Court, at Balls, in Hunting, or who game, and live high, or who preach and publish Books; others sparkish *Abbés,* Pillars of the Play-house, Musick-Meetings, Opera's, to say no worse; others great Men at Controversy, Proselyte-mongers; some, Mumpers from door to door drest out like Harlequins, some confin'd to Solitudes and deep Recesses? How can she accommodate herself to that viler Diversity of Drunkards, Gamesters, Ruffians, Panders, Bigots, Counterfeits, Men of Probity, Men of Honor in the Notion of the World? Very well, says she, because they all profess to own my Authority. Here's the Test; let 'em be what they will, so they submit to the Church they are sure of a Toleration. And what hinders then but others may dispense with an infinite Variety of Sects in the same Commonwealth, provided they are all agreed in acknowledging JESUS CHRIST for their Head, and the Scriptures for their Rule? It shall be lawful for the Church of *Rome* to divide and subdivide into infinite Societys very opposite in Rules and in Doctrines, and which mutually charge one another, sometimes with dangerous Errors, provided they in general own the Authority of the Church; and it shan't be lawful to tolerate infinite Sects, differing from one another in Opinion, provided they all allow the Authority of the Scriptures.

If it be said, that the Church of *Rome* tolerates <258> not different Opinions in those points on which she has pronounc'd a definitive Judgment; who can hinder the tolerating Partys saying, that they allow no difference in Opinions, only as to Points in which the Scriptures are not convincingly clear?

I had forgot an Objection of one sort of Men, who skirmishing as they retreat, will so far allow, that indeed, if all the World were of a tolerating Spirit, Differences in Religion con'd be of no ill Consequence to the State: but considering the Nature of Man, and that the greatest part, especially Church-men, are apt to be transported by an intemperate Zeal, Prudence won't allow a Prince to tolerate different Sects, because such a Toleration disgusts those of his own Religion; it alienates the Hearts of his Clergy from him, who have credit enough to shake his Throne, by representing him as a Man of no Principle, a Favorer of Hereticks, and fomenting a thousand Jealousys and Resentments in the Minds of his People. I answer, The truth is, there's nothing so bad but may justly be apprehended from Men of such a Spirit as the Romish Clergy, unless proper measures were taken with 'em from the beginning: but did the Prince understand the Art of Government, he might soon put himself above all danger from 'em, by only publishing thro-out his Dominions, that he was resolv'd to tolerate no Sectarys, provided all the Clergy of the establish'd Religion wou'd but live up as became 'em to the Counsels and Precepts of JESUS CHRIST, and no longer scandalize their Neighbor by their Worldly-mindedness, by their Pride, and Ambition, and restless Spirit. This <259> Condition wou'd undoubtedly please the Laity, who desire nothing more than to see a general Purity of Manners among their Clergy: but as the Ecclesiasticks wou'd certainly chuse to continue in their disorderly Courses, the condition being not perform'd on their part, the King might dispense with his persecuting Sectarys, and the People wou'd only mock at the Clergy for exclaiming against a Toleration, which 'twas wholly in their own power to destroy by leading godly Lives. Besides this, it wou'd be requisite to chuse out a Set of moderate and peaceable Men among 'em, and prefer some to the highest Dignitys in the Church, and send others to preach about in the Country, that the only lawful way of extinguishing Sectarys was by the Example of a holy Life, and by wholesom Instruction. This wou'd soon bring the Body of the People to a better Temper; and upon the whole, a Prince who found himself importun'd to extirpate a Sect, and shou'd tell those who importun'd him, that they ought to do their part in the first place, by convincing the Sectarys of their Errors, and that as soon as he saw they were convinc'd, he wou'd expel 'em his Dominions, unless they reconcil'd themselves to the Church, might put the persecuting Convertists to a strange nonplus: for how cou'd they have the impudence to tell him, that the convincing Sectarys they were in an Error, was not necessary in order to found a Right of punishing 'em, if they knew the Prince might presently send for his Arch-Bishops, Men in favor, and able Divines withal, who might soon prove the contrary against 'em from the Fathers, and from Scripture and Rea-<260>son? It's plain then, that if ever Persecution be a necessary Evil, it becomes so wholly thro the Sovereign's fault, in delivering himself up to the Mercy of Monks and Clergymen; either thro a want of Understanding, or thro some corrupt Motive.

ʚ︎♡︎ɞ︎   CHAPTER VII   ʚ︎♡︎ɞ︎

The seventh Objection: Compulsion in the literal Sense cannot be rejected without admitting a general Toleration. The Answer to this, and the Consequence allow'd to be true but not absurd. The Restrictions of your Men of Half-Toleration examin'd.

Here our Adversarys think they have us at an Advantage. It follows, say they, from your Arguments, that not only the Socinian, but even Turk and Jew ought to be tolerated in a Commonwealth: this Consequence is absurd, therefore the Doctrine from whence it follows is absurd. I answer, and grant the Consequence, but deny 'tis absurd. The middle way in many cases is certainly the best, and the Extremes faulty; this happens very often: but here we can fix on no just Medium; either we must allow all or none; there can be no solid Reason for tolerating any one Sect, which does not equally hold for every other. It happens in this case much as in that of *Herennius Pontius,* when he advis'd one of the two Extremes, either to use all the *Romans* kindly, or to put <261> 'em all to death;[86] and Experience shew'd,

86. Livy, IX.iii.6–8: "When he learned that the Roman armies had been hemmed in between two defiles at the Caudien Forks, and was asked by his son's messenger for his

that his Son, who wou'd fain trim it, was very much out in his Politicks. *Ista quidem sententia,* says his judicious Father, *ea est quae neque amicos parat, neque inimicos tollit.*[87]

Let's endeavor to clear this matter in as few words as possible. And first as to what concerns the Jews, 'tis the Opinion even in Countrys where the Inquisition is settl'd, as in *Italy,* that they ought to be tolerated. They are tolerated in several Protestant States, and all the reasonable part of the World abhor the Treatment they meet with in *Spain* and *Portugal.* 'Tis true, it's very much their own Fault; for why will they live in those Countrys under the Appearance of Christians, and in a horrible Profanation of all the Sacraments, when they may remove elsewhere, and enjoy the free Exercise of their Religion? However, their Wickedness does not excuse the cruel Laws of *Spain,* and much less the rigorous Execution of 'em. In the second place, as for what concerns Mahometans, I see no reason why they shou'd be thought more unworthy of a Toleration than Jews; quite the contrary, since they allow JESUS CHRIST to have bin a great Prophet: nor, shou'd the Mufti take it into his Head to send Missionarys into *Christendom,* as the Pope does into the *Indies,* and shou'd these Turkish Missionarys be taken insinuating into Peoples Houses to carry on Conversions, do I see what right any one has to punish 'em; for shou'd they make the same Answer that the Christian Missionarys do in *Japan,* to wit, that a Zeal for making known the true Religion to those who are in Error, and promoting the Salvation of <262> their Neighbor, whose Blindness they lament, mov'd 'em to such an Undertaking; and without any regard to this Answer, or hearing out their Reasons, the Magistrate shou'd order 'em to be hang'd, wou'd not it be ridiculous to complain, when the *Japonese* do the same? Seeing then the *Japonese* are horribly condemn'd for their Severitys, 'twere unreasonable to treat the Mufti's Missionarys cruelly, or do any more than bring 'em to a Conference with the Priests or Ministers in order to unde-

---

opinion, he advised that they should all be dismissed unscathed, at the earliest possible moment. The policy being rejected . . . he recommended that all, to the last man, be slain"; translated B. O. Foster, Loeb Classical Library, p. 171.

87. Livy, IX.iii.12: "'That,' he answered, 'is in sooth a policy that neither wins men friends nor rids them of their enemies'"; translated B. O. Foster, Loeb Classical Library, p. 173.

ceive 'em. And tho they still persisted in their own Opinions, and protested they wou'd chuse to die rather than disobey the Commands of God and their great Prophet, yet People shou'd be very far from condemning 'em to death: for provided they do nothing against the publick Peace, I mean, against the Obedience due to Sovereigns in temporal Matters, they cou'd not even be banish'd with Justice, neither they, nor those whom they shou'd gain over by their Reasons; else the Pagans might be justify'd in banishing and imprisoning the Apostles, and those whom they had converted to the Gospel. We must not forget the Command against having double Weights and double Measures, nor that with what measure we mete it shall be measur'd to us again. Wou'd to God the Infidels wou'd truck Missions and Tolerations with us, and consent, that our Missionarys shou'd have full Liberty of preaching the Gospel, and teaching in their Parts, on condition that their Missionarys had the like Privilege among us; the Christian Religion wou'd be a great Gainer by it. The Pagan and Mahometan Preachers cou'd never make any Progress among us, and ours might <263> reap a plentiful harvest in Infidel Nations. Besides, that we shou'd be much to blame, in having such distrust of our own Reasons, as to think they stood in need of Prisons and capital Punishments to support 'em against Turkish Missionarys. Your persecuting Religions have a fine opinion indeed of what they call the pure Truth which God has reveal'd; they don't believe it capable of triumphing by its own force: They give it Hangmen and Dragoons for its Allys; Allys which have no need of the Assistance of Truth, since they can do the business without her, and bring about what they please by their own strength.

Now if in the least favorable case, such as that of sending Missionarys into a Christian Country where there are no Turks, there ought to be no temporal Punishment to restrain 'em; by a much stronger reason they may challenge a Toleration in Countrys where they have bin establish'd of old, whenever they fall into the hands of Christians by Conquest. And therefore I maintain, that unless Reasons of State require, as sometimes they do, that the new Subjects of the old Religion be dislodg'd and banish'd, Christian Princes cannot in justice expel the Mahometans out of Towns taken from the Turk, nor hinder their having Mosks, or assembling in their own Houses. All that ought to be done in this case is instructing 'em, but without any Violence or Constraint. This Justice is due to 'em, not only with regard to that eternal Law which discovers, when we consult it attentively and without passion, that Religion is a matter of Conscience subject to no controul; but <264> also on the score of Gratitude, for their having so long allow'd the Christians of their Empire the privilege of exercising their Religion. I much doubt whether they wou'd meet with the like treatment under us: The Pope wou'd never let the Emperor or *Venetians* be at rest, if they tolerated the Turks in their new Conquests; and the Imperial Court stands in no need of a spur to Persecution from that of *Rome;* she's too well enter'd at that game of old, to need a Monitor.

In the third place I maintain, that the very Pagans were entitled to a Toleration, and that *Theodosius, Valentinian,* and *Martian* are inexcusable in condemning all those to death, who exercis'd any Act of the Pagan Worship. For altho the violent Proceedings of the antienter Emperors had made the Pagans in a great measure forfeit their Right to Toleration by virtue of this Maxim, *That a Religion which forces Conscience, does not deserve to be tolerated;* yet they shou'd have given 'em quarter, when they saw 'em so low that there was no danger of their ever recovering Power enough to act over the Tragedys of *Decius* and *Dioclesian.* Beside that there is not so much to be said against the Pagan as against the Romish Religion; the Pagan was not engag'd to persecute by the Authority of Councils, and by fundamental Principles: and therefore there's no arguing from the Practice of the Emperors before *Constantine* to that of the Pagans who might, we'l suppose, have got the upper hand after *Theodosius.* Nor can it be alledg'd, that no violence was done to Conscience, by forbidding the Pagans on pain of death to worship their false Gods; for it's evident they were en-<265>gag'd to their Worship by very powerful Tyes of Superstition, and some were even ready to renounce great Advantages rather than their Paganism.*

'Tis true, few wou'd lay down their Lives for it; but if this was the only

---

* Zozim. l. 1. *speaking of* Generides *under* Honorius. [When the emperor Honorius enacted a law excluding pagans from public office, the military officer Generides resigned and remained at home. Honorius offered him a personal exemption, which he refused as an insult to all those unable to hold office because of the law. The emperor repealed the law. Zosimus, *New History: Translation with Commentary* by Ronald T. Ridley (Sydney, Australian Association for Byzantine Studies, 1982), V.46, pp. 123–24.]

cause why the Christians put no more of 'em to death in execution of the Imperial Laws, I see no reason they have to boast of their Moderation, or oppose it to the Pagan Crueltys. Now if Violence was unwarrantable in the *Roman* Empire, against the very Descendants of those who had so fiercely persecuted the Christians, it is by much a stronger reason unlawful now against those of *Japan* or *China:* so that shou'd the Emperor of either of these Countrys happen to turn Christian, or the Chief of a Crusade, like *Godfrey* of *Bulloigne* of old, become King of either; 'twou'd be very unjust in him to endeavor the Conversion of his Subjects by any other methods than those of meek Persuasion and Instruction. Yet it wou'd not be in his power to grant a Toleration; for if the Popish Missionarys converted the Emperor, or saw on the Throne the Chief of the Popish Crusade, they'd oblige him to publish an Edict next hour, enjoining all his Subjects to receive Baptism on pain of death. Which ought to be a warning to the *Chinese* to expel the Missionarys, who wou'd thus damn three parts in four of their People, by obliging 'em to profane the Sacraments, and act against Conscience.

'Twere needless insisting in particular for a Toleration of Socinians, since it appears that <266> Pagans, Jews, and Turks have a right to it: Let's therefore pass to the Limitations of our Half-Toleration Men.

These Gentlemen, either to enjoy the Comforts of Toleration without losing the Pleasure of Persecution, or from some other honester Reason, wou'd fain split the Difference, and say, there are some Sects which may be tolerated, but that there are others which deserve to be extirpated, if not by Fire and Sword, at least by Banishment and Confiscation. They add, that if Death be too severe a Punishment for the Seduc'd, it is by no means so for the Heresiarch and Seducer. *Nec totam Libertatem, nec totam Servitutem pati possunt;*[88] as was observ'd of the People of *Rome.*

When it comes to be enquir'd more particularly what kind of Heresiarchs those be who deserve to be punish'd with Death; they answer, they who blaspheme the Divinity: And because in the best-order'd Governments they bore the Tongue of a Blasphemer with a red-hot Iron, or tear it from

---

88. "They cannot bear either complete freedom, or complete slavery"; Tacitus, *Histories,* I.16.

the root, it shou'd not be thought strange, they say, that the blasphemous and horrible Outrages of *Servetus* against the Trinity were expiated by Fire. But they'l give me leave to tell 'em, they are under a gross mistake in this matter.

For to the end that a Blasphemer be punishable, 'tis not sufficient that what he says be Blasphemy, according to the Definition which one Set of Men may think fit to give this word; but it must be likewise such, according to his own Doctrine. And here's the true ground of justly punishing a Christian who blasphemes <267> the holy Name of God, and reviles that Divinity which he professes to believe in; because in this case he sins from Malice, and from a clear knowledg of his Sin. But if a Christian, who believes not a Trinity, and is persuaded in his erroneous Conscience, that there cannot be three Persons each of which is God without there being three Gods, says and maintains that the God of the Catholicks and of the Protestants is a false God, a contradictory God, *&c.* this is not blaspheming with regard to him, because he speaks not against that Divinity which he acknowledges, but against another which he disowns.

This Remark will appear more solid, when I add, That if we leave Persecutors Masters of the Definition of Blasphemy, none will be more execrable Blasphemers than the first Christians and the Hugonots. For nothing can be more reviling, nothing meaner or more scurrilous than what the primitive Christians utter'd without the least reserve against the Gods of Paganism: and it's well known, that Protestants don't spare the God of the Mass; and that sometimes their Expressions against it before their Adversarys are enough to make their very hair stand an end. I don't approve the use of odious Terms in the presence of those who are apt to be scandaliz'd: Decency and Charity oblige us to reverence Conscience, and the Respect due to Princes requires that we shou'd forbear harsh Expressions in their favor; insomuch that the primitive Christians were not always as discreet in this particular as they ought to be. But at bottom it's no more than Illbreeding and Clownishness. <268> The Protestants, if not restrain'd by these Considerations, make no scruple of speaking against the God of the Mass, such things as the Papists pronounce Blasphemy; and the primitive Christians spoke against the Idols of Paganism such things as the Pagans term'd Blasphemy. Does it therefore follow that the first Christians were

Blasphemers guilty of Death, or that the Reform'd are guilty now? Not at all, because the Blasphemy is not defin'd by a Principle common to the Accuser and the Accused, to the Persecutor and the Persecuted. Now this very thing might be pleaded for *Servetus*. The Blasphemys he was accus'd of, cou'd not be so qualify'd by virtue of any Principle or Notion allow'd on his part, as well as on the part of the Senate of *Geneva;* and consequently he cou'd not be punish'd as a Blasphemer, but it must follow that the first Christians might be punish'd as Blasphemers by the Pagans, the Reform'd by the Papists, and all who believe a Trinity by the Socinians. In virtue of this Maxim the Reform'd, call'd Calvinists, might punish with Death the Papists and Remonstrants as Blasphemers, who say the God of *Calvin* is cruel, unjust, Author of Sin, and yet the Punisher of the same Sin on his innocent Creatures. These are horrible Blasphemys in the Construction which the Reform'd will put upon these words. But as they who speak 'em don't direct 'em against that Divinity which they adore, but against what they look upon as the Vision and Chimera of another Party, they can't be justly charg'd with Blasphemy.

I know they'l tell me, *Servetus* was in reality wrong, and the Reform'd in the right with re-<269>gard to the Eucharist, and therefore there's no arguing from one to the other. But is not this the very Plea of the Papists? Were they call'd to account for saying the God of *Calvin* is a Tyrant, Author of Sin, *&c.* they'l say, they have reason to call what is spoke against the Eucharist Blasphemy, because the Truth is of their side; but that it's wrong to call their speaking against *Calvin*'s Predestination Blasphemy, because that point of Doctrine is false. So that here's nothing fix'd or determin'd, but a mere begging the Question in dispute, and a perpetual Circle. In fine, each Party will seize all the words of the Dictionary to its own use, and begin by possessing it self of this Strong-hold, *I am in the right, you in the wrong;* which is throwing back the World into a Chaos more frightful than that of *Ovid.*

Our Men of Half-Toleration say likewise, That we ought to tolerate Sects which destroy not the Fundamentals of Christianity, but not those which do. But here's the very same Illusion again. For we may ask them what they mean by destroying the Foundation? Is it denying a Point, which really and in it self is a fundamental Article, or only denying a thing which is believ'd such by the Accuser, but not by the Accused? If they answer, the first; here's the ground laid of a tedious Debate, in which the Accused will hold for the Negative, and maintain that what he denys, far from being a Fundamental of Religion, is really a Falshood, or at best but a matter indifferent. If they answer, the second; the Accused will reply, that truly he shan't stick at destroying that <270> which passes for a Fundamental only in his Adversary's brain, because it by no means follows that it is really such. And so here's a new Dispute started upon this Enthymeme[89] of the Accusers.

Such a thing appears to me a fundamental Article:

Therefore it is such.

Which is poor Reasoning. To make any thing therefore of this Dispute, 'twill be necessary to shew that such a Sect destroys what it believes to be a Fundamental of Christianity; and even then it has a right to a Toleration on the same foot as Jews are more or less tolerated: or else it must be prov'd, that the things which this Sect destroys are Fundamentals, tho she does not believe 'em such. But in order to prove this, the Accuser must not frame a Definition of Fundamentals from his own brain, nor make use of Proofs which are contested by his Adversary; for this were proving what is obscure by that which is as obscure, which is mere trifling: but come to Principles allow'd and agreed on by both Partys. If he gain his point, the Accused must for the future stand upon a foot of Non-Christian Toleration; if he does not gain the point, the Accused cannot be justly treated as one subverting the Fundamentals of Christianity.

I add, that if the subverting what we believe a fundamental Point were a sufficient bar against Toleration, the Pagans cou'd not have tolerated the Preachers of the Gospel, nor we the Church of *Rome,* nor the Church of *Rome* us; for we don't believe the Romish Communion retains the Fundamentals of Christianity pure, and with-<271>out a mixture at least of deadly Poison; and for their parts, they are fully persuaded that by denying her Infallibility, we utterly destroy the Essence and most fundamental Doctrine of Christianity.

There are some too who distinguish between Sects which are but begin-

---

89. See Appendixes, "Bayle's Use of Logic," p. 580 ("enthymeme").

ning to shew their head, and have never yet obtain'd any Edicts of Toleration, and Sects settled and establish'd either by Prescription, or Concessions duly obtain'd; and they pretend that this latter sort deserves all kind of Toleration, but not always the former. For my part, I freely allow that the second kind of Sect has incomparably a juster title to Toleration than the first; and nothing sure can be more infamous than annulling Laws religiously sworn to. But I insist that the first sort are worthy too: for if they were not, what pretence cou'd we have for condemning the first Persecutions of the Christians, and the Executions of the People call'd *Lutherans* in the Reigns of *Francis* I and *Henry* II? I say the same to that Distinction between the Head of the Sect, and the wretched People who are seduc'd. I own the Seducer, whether malicious or sincere, does more mischief than the People; but it does not follow from the People's deserving more favor, that the Heresiarch deserves to be punished: for were this a just Consequence, we cou'd not condemn the punishing *Luther* and *Calvin,* nor the putting St. *Peter* and St. *Paul* to death.

I foresee they'l tell me, for the last shift, that if *Luther,* and *Calvin,* and the Apostles had not had the Truth on their side, the Punishments inflicted on 'em had bin just. This is founding the <272> Injustice of Persecution not in the Violence done to Conscience, but on the fact that the Persons persecuted belong to the true Religion: 'Tis a considerable Difficulty, and I shall examine it particularly in the following Chapter.

∞ CHAPTER VIII ∞

Eighth Objection: Compulsion in the literal Sense is maliciously misrepresented, by supposing it authorizes Violences committed against the Truth. The Answer to this; by which it is prov'd, that the literal Sense does in reality authorize the stirring up Persecutions against the Cause of Truth, and that an erroneous Conscience has the same Rights as an enlighten'd Conscience.

It's sometimes a disadvantage to Reason with People of shallow Understandings; for be their Intention ever so honest, they shall wrangle about a thousand things solidly prov'd, for want of comprehending the Force of an Argument. Whereas there is this satisfaction in having to deal with great Wits, if they be but sincere, that taking the stress of the Difficulty at first sight, they own they are struck with it, and avow the Justness of the Consequences objected against 'em: whereupon they presently put themselves in a posture of Defence, without amusing the Bar by Disputes upon <273> a thousand Incidents and accessory Distinctions, whether resulting from their Doctrine or no. Your Disputants of a lower form fly to a world of vain Shifts and Doubles, when prest upon the Consequences of the literal Sense; the reason is, that they have not a clear Notion of the Truth, or, if they have, are loth to give their Adversary the pleasure of owning they are convinc'd: but others more sincere and more penetrating answer immediately, That how just soever the Persecutions of the Orthodox against Sectarys be, Sectarys can never be justify'd in persecuting the Orthodox, altho they shou'd believe 'em to be in a false way, and look on themselves as the only Orthodox. Let's see with what ground this can be said.

In order to confute it, I lay down this Position, That whatever a Conscience well directed allows us to do for the Advancement of Truth, an erroneous Conscience will warrant for advancing a suppos'd Truth. This Position I shall make out and illustrate.

I don't believe any one will contest the Truth of this Principle, *Whatever is done against the Dictates of Conscience is Sin;* for it is so very evident, that Conscience is a Light dictating that such a thing is good or bad, that it is not probable any one will dispute the Definition. It is no less evident, that every reasonable Creature which judges upon any Action as good or bad, supposes there's some Rule of the Seemliness and Turpitude of Actions; and if he's not an Atheist, if he believe any Religion, he necessarily supposes this Rule and Law to be founded in the Nature of God; Whence I conclude it is the same thing <274> to say, *My Conscience judges such an Action to be good or bad;* and to say, *My Conscience judges that such an Action is pleasing or displeasing to God.* To me these Propositions seem allow'd by all the world, as much as any of the clearest Principles of Metaphysicks. This which follows is equally true; *Whoever knows such an Action is evil and displeasing to God, and yet commits it, wilfully offends and disobeys God: And whoever wilfully offends and disobeys God, is necessarily guilty of Sin.* In like manner this Proposition is evident, *That whoever does a thing which his*

Conscience tells him is evil, or omits that which his Conscience tells him he ought to do, commits a Sin.

Such a Man does not only commit a Sin, but I further affirm, that all things being in other respects equal, his Sin is the heinousest that can be committed: for supposing an Equality in the outward Act, as in the Motion of the Hand which runs a Sword thro a man's Body, and in the Act of the Will directing this Motion; supposing also an Equality in the passive Subject of this Action, that is, an equal Dignity in the Person slain: I say the Murder shall be a Sin so much the greater, as the degree of Knowledg that it is a criminal Act is greater. For which reason, if two Sons shou'd each kill his Father, precisely with all the same Circumstances, except that one had only a confus'd Knowledg of its being a Sin, the other a very distinct Sense of it, and actually reflected on the Enormity as he struck the Dagger into his Father's Heart; this latter wou'd be guilty of a Sin incomparably more heinous, and more punishable in the sight <275> of God than the other. This, I think, is another Proposition which can't be contested.

But I go still further, and say, that a Sin does not only become the greatest that can be in its kind, by being committed against the greatest degree of Knowledg, but also that of two Actions, one of which we call good, the other bad, the good being done against the Instincts of Conscience, is a greater Sin than the bad Action done from the Instincts of Conscience. I shall explain my self by an Example.

We call giving an Alms to a Beggar a good Action, and repulsing him with ill words an ill Action. Yet I maintain, that a Man who shou'd give a Beggar an Alms in certain circumstances, his Conscience suggesting that he ought not to give, and he acquiescing in the good or bad Judgment of his Conscience, wou'd be guilty of a worse Action, than he who sent away a Beggar with hard words in circumstances where his Conscience suggested, from Reasons which he judg'd well of, that he ought to turn him away with this ill usage. Mark well what I lay down; I don't content my self with saying, that Conscience barely suggests either not to give an Alms, or to give hard Words; I add, that it passes a definitive Judgment in which we acquiesce; that is, we agree this Judgment is reasonable. 'Tis one thing to have Surmizes presented from Conscience, which we presently reject either as false or doubtful, and another thing to assent from our Judgment, and

acquiesce in its Representations. To commit an Action under the bare Surmizes which Conscience suggests against it, without passing its definitive
Sentence, is not <276> *caeteris paribus* so bad an Action, as doing it in
contempt of that Sentence. And that it is possible to act in contempt of
the last Judgment of Conscience, who that considers it will deny?

A Passenger looks at a Beggar; he sees he's a Cheat, or an idle Fellow that
might get an honest Livelihood if he wou'd work, a Sot who squanders all
he gets: hereupon his Reason suggests, that he ought not to relieve him,
that 'twere encouraging him in his Idleness, that 'twere better keep this
Charity for a properer Object. In a word, this Reason, or if you'l rather call
it Conscience, pronounces this Judgment, *It's a sin to give this Beggar an
Alms.* Yet after all, this very Person trifles with his own Conscience, and
bestows his Charity on the Wretch, either that he is not us'd to govern
himself by the Dictates of his Conscience, or out of mere Caprice, or mov'd
by some pitiful posture of the Beggar, or because such a one's passing by,
or for any other like Consideration working on him at that moment. If
Persons who have a thousand good Qualitys, Moral and Christian, are daily
guilty of Fornication, tho Conscience pronounces it a Sin by a formal and
definitive Judgment; shall we doubt but a Man may give an Alms in contempt of a fix'd Judgment of his Conscience that he ought not to give in
such and such circumstances?

Let's now compare the Action of this Giver of Alms, with that of another
Man who sends a Beggar away because his Conscience tells him he is a
Rogue, a Cheat, a Varlet, who is much likelier to be reclaim'd by ill usage,
than by relieving him in his necessity; and I affirm, tho <277> we shou'd
suppose each in an error as to fact, that the Action of the former is worse
than that of the latter: and thus I prove it.

The Action of the former supposing an Error of Fact, includes these
four Circumstances.

1. A Person who begs an Alms from real Necessity, and who fears God.

2. A Judgment of the Reason suggesting he's a Rogue and a Cheat, either
purely from his Looks, or because the Party mistakes him for another notoriously wicked Beggar.

3. A fix'd and definitive Sentence of Conscience, pronouncing it a thing
displeasing to God to relieve such a Varlet, since it can only serve to confirm

him in his Vices; whereas the exposing him to Want might possibly reclaim him.

4. The bestowing the Alms on this very Beggar.

Let's now consider the Action of the other. We find likewise four Circumstances attending it, supposing an Error in Fact.

The three first Circumstances already laid down, which are common to both; and in the fourth place, the hard words with which he dismisses the Beggar.

To prove that the Action of the first is worse than that of the second, it will be sufficient if I make out these two things: (1.) That there is some degree of moral Goodness in the Action of the second, but not the least shadow of it in that of the first. (2.) That the Evil on that side is much less than on this.

As to the first of these Cases, I wou'd desire those who have a mind to dispute this Point, to shew me, wherein consists the moral Good-<278>ness of his Action, who in the mention'd Circumstances gives a poor Body an Alms. It can't lie in the Judgment of his Reason, nor in that of his Conscience, which are both erroneous; it must lie then, if any such be, in the very Act of bestowing his Charity: but it's plain, there's not the least Dram of Goodness in this, because all who understand any thing of moral Actions are unanimously agreed, that giving an Alms, consider'd as it's barely the conveying a Penny from the pocket into a Man's hand, is no morally good Action; as is manifest from hence, that the Spring of a Machine accidentally jerking a piece of Gold into a Beggar's cap wou'd be an Action void of the least grain of moral Goodness.

To the end that an Alms be a good Work, it's absolutely necessary it be done by the direction of Reason and Conscience, representing it as a Duty. Now nothing of this occurs in the case in question: and therefore there's not the least degree of moral Goodness in the Act.

We can't say so of the second Act, because it's allow'd on all hands, that all Homage paid to Conscience, all Submission to its Judgment and Sentence, is an instance of his Regard to the Eternal Law, and of his Reverence for the Divinity, whose Voice he recognizes at the Tribunal of his Conscience. In a word, he who performs any Action because he believes it well-pleasing to God, testifies in general, at least that he desires to please God, and to obey his Will. And the very Desire cannot be destitute of all moral Goodness. <279>

As to the second Case, I say that the Evil of his Action, who bestows an Alms in the foremention'd Circumstances, consists in this, that he spurns the fixt and definitive Sentence of his Conscience; and that the Evil of the other's Action consists in his snubbing a poor Man. I maintain that this, in the present Circumstances, is a less Sin than the other.

For can a Man act contrary to the Dictates of his Conscience, without an intention of doing what he knows is displeasing to God? And is not this a Contempt of God, a Rebellion, upon Knowledg, Choice and Approbation, against his adorable Majesty? And willing a Sin acknowledg'd as such, willing a Transgression against God clearly and distinctly known, is it not the most crying Iniquity, and Malice, and Corruption of Heart?

'Tis quite otherwise with him who gives a Beggar hard words, taking him for an errand Mumper, and a Fellow that needs Reproof to bring him to good. The Evil he does, proceeds not from a Desire or fixt Purpose of doing evil, of disobeying God, of thwarting the Ideas of Rectitude, and trampling under foot immutable Order: It proceeds only from Ignorance, only from a wrong Choice of the Means and Manner of obeying God. He was under a mistaken Opinion, that this Beggar was unworthy of his Charity, and that Repulses and Disgrace were the likeliest means of reclaiming him. This was the Dictate of his Conscience, and he comply'd with it. The Evil which appears in this Slight of the poor Man, and which is not inconsistent with an actual Desire at the same time of obeying <280> the Law of God, is it to be compar'd with an Evil which actually excludes the Desire of pleasing God, and brings into its room an Act of known Disobedience?

I own the reviling our Neighbor is not only forbidden, and the grieving the Poor a very great Sin; but that we also suppose, the poor Man here abus'd and insulted is in fact one that fears God: I own it, yet still I maintain that this Man fearing God, not having bin insulted as such, seeing he was taken for a Vagabond, the Sin of the Person who insulted him must be resolv'd into a precipitate Judgment only, and a believing upon false appearances that this Beggar was a very ill Man. Now every one will allow, that not having temper to examine things duly, is a much more venial Sin than formally and actually willing to commit what the Party believes to be a Sin.

Some may complain, that I make very slight of the hard words given to this honest Man the Beggar. I answer, that hard words consider'd simply as consisting of articulate Sounds can't make a Sinner; else we must say that the Bulrushes in the Fable, whose ruffle and murmur disclos'd poor *Midas*'s shame, were guilty of a Sin, if what they tell of 'em were true. We must say, a Pair of Organs committed a Sin, if by any Motion of the Air or Water it shou'd happen to form Sounds injurious to a Man's Reputation, which is extremely absurd. Abusive Language from a Man in a raving Fever, or in a Tongue he does not understand, passes for nothing: It offends only in proportion to the Speaker's known Intention of giving offence by <281> it; and if he be known to mistake one Man for another, the Affront lights on him who was in his intention, and not on him whom he address'd himself to by mistake. Let any one examine the Case as I have stated it, he'l find, that all the Evil of the Action is resolv'd into too great a facility of believing upon false Reasons, that the Beggar was the Person which he really was not.

As to the Good inhering in his Action who gives the Alms, an Action which after all relieves the Wants of a poor Servant of God, whereas harsh Language adds to his Sufferings, I don't think it ought to be brought into the account; the rather, because it's at best only a physical Good or Evil, which confers no moral Worth on Actions, farther than as it might possibly have enter'd into the Intention. For example, to refuse an Alms in Circumstances where the Party knows that the bestowing it will draw on numberless Advantages, by the Combination of various Causes and Effects, and the refusing it be follow'd by a long train of Calamitys on the Person who implores it; is much a greater Sin than refusing it in Circumstances where none of these Events are in the Party's view. But it's certain, that the good or evil Consequences of our Actions avail not in the sight of God towards justifying or condemning us, when we don't act from a direct design of procuring these Consequences. It's plain then, that all things conspire to resolve the Fault of him who revil'd the Beggar, into a simple lack of Examination and Attention; and consequently, that his refusal of the Charity, and his harsh words under these Circum-<282>stances, are a less evil Action, than the other's bestowing an Alms. Which was the thing to be prov'd.

I add, that if when there's an Error in the Conscience as well of him who governs himself by its Dictates, as of him who acts directly counter to 'em, the Action of the latter is worse than that of the former, tho otherwise it had bin good, and the other bad; by a much stronger reason ought this to be so, when there's no Error in the Conscience of him who follows not its Dictates. To comprehend this, we need not go farther than the Example of our two Men, and only suppose that the Beggar who addresses himself to the first is really a Vagabond, a Drunkard, a Cheat, a Villain; and the Beggar, who addresses himself to the second, is a very honest Man. Let's leave the Supposition in all other respects exactly as it was. What will follow? Why this; that the Judgment of the Reason and Conscience of the first is just and reasonable: and then our Adversarys themselves will judg that the bestowing his Charity on a very unworthy Object, and certainly known to be such, will be much more blamable than it was before, when suppos'd to fall to an honest Man's lot.

But whither does all this long Preamble tend, these Turnings and Twistings of this Argument? To this; That an erroneous Conscience challenges all the same Prerogatives, Favors, and Assistances for an Error, as an Orthodox Conscience can challenge for the Truth. This appears somewhat far fetch'd; but I shall now make the Dependance and Connexion of these Doctrines appear. <283>

My Principles allow'd by all the World, or just now prov'd, are these:

1. That the Will of disobeying God is a Sin.

2. That the Will of disobeying the fixt and definitive Sentence of Conscience, is the same thing as willing to transgress the Law of God.

3. Consequently, that whatever is done against the Dictate of Conscience is a Sin.

4. That the greatest Turpitude of Sin, where things are in other respects equal, arises from the greatest Knowledg of the Fact's being a Sin.

5. That an Action which wou'd be incontestably good (giving an Alms for example) if done by the direction of Conscience, becomes worse by being done against its direction, than another Action done according to the

direction of Conscience, which wou'd be incontestably sinful (as reviling a poor Man for example) if not done by its direction.

6. That doing a thing which we call evil, from the Dictates of Conscience, tho in reality erroneous, renders this Action much less evil, than another Action of the nature of those which we call good, done against the Dictate of Conscience suppos'd to be truly inform'd.

From all these Principles I may reasonably conclude, that the first and most indispensable of all our Obligations, is that of never acting against the Instincts of Conscience; and that every Action done against the Lights of Conscience is essentially evil: So that as the Law of loving God can never be dispens'd with, because the hating God is an Act essentially evil; so the Law of <284> never violating the Lights of our Conscience is such as God himself can never dispense with; forasmuch as this were in reality indulging us in the Contempt or Hatred of himself, Acts intrinsecally and in their own nature criminal. There is therefore an eternal and immutable Law, obliging Man, upon pain of incurring the Guilt of the most heinous mortal Sin that can be committed, never to do any thing in violation and in despite of Conscience.

Hence it manifestly and demonstratively follows, if the eternal Law, or any positive Law of God requires that he who is convinc'd of the Truth shou'd employ Fire and Sword to establish it in the World; that all Men ought to employ Fire and Sword for the establishing their own Religion. I understand all those to whom this Law of God is reveal'd.

For the moment this Law of God were reveal'd, *It's my will that you employ Fire and Sword for the establishing the Truth,* Conscience wou'd dictate to the several opposite Partys, that they ought to employ Fire and Sword for establishing that Religion which themselves profess; because they know no other Truth but this, nor any way of executing the Order of God, but that of acting for their own Religion; and must believe they acted in favor of Falshood, and consequently fall into a Transgression of the Divine Law, if they labor'd the Advancement of any Religion but their own. It's plain then, that Conscience wou'd apply the Command of God, for the establishing the Truth, to each Party's own Religion.

Now since, as I have already prov'd, the greatest of all Iniquitys is that of not following the <285> Lights of Conscience; and since Order immutable and the Law eternal indispensably require, that we shou'd above all things avoid the greatest of all Iniquitys, and all Acts essentially evil; it follows,

That by the first, the most inviolable and most indispensable of all our Obligations, each Person to whom God reveal'd the foresaid Law, ought to employ Fire and Sword for the establishing his own Religion; the Socinian for his, as well as the Calvinist, the Papist, the Nestorian, the Eutychian for theirs. For shou'd a Socinian, after such a general Law of God, stand with his Arms folded, and not employ those means for establishing the Truth which God had appointed, he must act against Conscience; and this, *caeteris paribus,* must be the greatest of all Sins: and every one is indispensably oblig'd above all things to avoid the greatest of Sins; then the Socinian wou'd be oblig'd indispensably to employ Fire and Sword for the propagation of his Doctrines; oblig'd, I say, in virtue of an eternal Law, which enjoins every reasonable Creature to fly Sin, and especially the greatest of Sins.

The better to make our Adversarys comprehend the Force of my Argument, I desire to know what they wou'd have a Socinian do, upon a plain and express Revelation with regard to him, as well as to the Orthodox, of such a Law as this; *It is my will, that Fire and Sword be employ'd for the establishing the Truth.* Wou'd they have him, when persuaded there's no other Doctrine in matter of Religion true but that which he teaches, rest satisfy'd in the private Belief of it by himself or in his own Family, without em-<286>ploying the means Providence might put into his hands for extirpating the Religions, which he believ'd God had commanded him to destroy? But in this case he manifestly falls into a Contempt of the Law of God, and a Violation of his first and most essential Duty, which is a greater Sin than executing in behalf of Socinianism what he believ'd to be the Law of God: for here God wou'd find in his Soul a sincere regard to his Laws, and a desire of obeying him; whereas he must find quite the contrary Dispositions if he did not exert himself against the other Religions. This therefore wou'd be advising the Socinian to chuse between two States that which must render him most criminal in the sight of God. Now the very counselling this were a most wicked and abominable thought. It's plain then, that as the Socinian must make a choice between these three things, either to establish his Heresy by Fire and Sword, or not give himself the least trouble about establishing it, or in the last place favor its Ruin; he must of necessity make choice of the first, to avoid either of the other two, as being much the more sinful.

In effect, which way cou'd he excuse himself in the sight of God, if after this suppos'd Command, he shou'd sit down in a slothful Indifference, and not be concern'd whether his Religion spread or no? *Is this what I commanded you?* might God say to him; *don't you openly contemn my Authority, and become guilty of the sinful Indifference, of counting it much at one, whether you be in my Favor or Displeasure, since you won't make the least step towards obeying what Conscience tells you I have requir'd at your hands?* Reproaches much more harsh wou'd <287> still be more just, if he openly favor'd the Ruin of his own Religion; and no such Reproaches cou'd be made him if he wag'd War with all other Sects: God cou'd reproach him with nothing more in this case, than his having made a wrong Choice of the Object for which he had given him Orders to contend; the Justice of these Reproaches cou'd not obstruct God's seeing a sincere Desire in his Soul (I suppose him a Socinian from a sincere Principle) of obeying him, a regard to Order, a homage paid to the Divine Majesty. It's therefore a matter as incontestable, that the first of these three Demeanors in the Socinians, is the least Evil of all, as that a Master, who order'd his Servants to destroy all the Wolves on his Estate, wou'd think those less to be blam'd, who instead of the Wolves kill'd all the Foxes, either because they mistook one word for another, or, having forgot the Order, fancy'd he meant the Foxes; be the Reason what it will, he wou'd think 'em less in blame, than those who shou'd never disturb Wolves, or who took the way to preserve 'em, and multiply the Breed. I go further, and say, that a reasonable Master, who shou'd certainly know, that those Servants of his, who preserv'd the Breed of Wolves, were fully persuaded in their Hearts, that he had given 'em Orders to destroy 'em, wou'd think himself more affronted by their Disobedience, than by that of another Party of his Servants, who without any Malice or Design, but purely thro forgetfulness or involuntary mistake of Orders, shou'd destroy all the Rabbets and Hares instead of the Wolves. <288>

Be the Brain of the *French* Convertists ever so much turn'd, I can't forbear thinking, but there are some among 'em, who have reason enough left to agree to what I am now going to offer. That

If once it be suppos'd, that God has clearly and distinctly reveal'd a Law to Christians in general, obliging 'em to exterminate all false Religions by Fire and Sword; a Socinian, who lets the other Sects of Christianity live in quiet, who does not bestir himself to establish his own Religion, or perhaps favors those who are supplanting it, and establishing a different Sect with all their might, cannot be excus'd in his Conduct but upon one or other of the following Reasons: Either because he believes the Law in question ought not to be understood in the strictness of the Letter, but has a mystical Meaning which all the World is not oblig'd to dive into; or because he thinks, that the Execution of this Law does not belong to him; or because he is not over-certain, that Socinianism is the true Doctrine; or last of all, because believing any Religion good enough, it's equal to him which is uppermost: he'l for his part look on and let things work, resolv'd to be a Prey to the Conqueror; or perhaps favors one side, tho very opposite to Socinianism, that he may enter the Lists with a better Grace, when this has got the day. These, in my opinion, are all the ways that can be thought on for disculpating a Socinian, who is tardy in propagating his own Religion, after God had reveal'd the suppos'd Law; and consequently he must be wholly inexcusable, or exceedingly criminal, if he maintain'd this Neutrality, or if <289> he prejudic'd his own Sect, while persuaded, 1. That God enjoins propagating the Truth by Fire and Sword; 2. That Socinianism is the Truth.

Supposing him under this double Persuasion, he is inexcusably criminal if he does not persecute all other Sects; he is much more so if he favors any: he can neither forbear acting for his own Sect, nor lend his Assistance to a different Sect, without falling into a Sin against Conscience, of all Sins the most heinous. He is therefore indispensably oblig'd, by the eternal Laws of Order, to avoid this most heinous Sin, by persecuting other Christians according to the Dictates of his Conscience.

Now if once it be made appear, that a Right of persecuting, and extirpating Heresys by Fire and Sword, be common, from an indispensable Necessity founded in the Nature of things, to all Religions inform'd of this Law of God, as well as to the true; it's plain, that all the other Rights and Privileges of Truth must be common to all kind of Sects, whether true or false. Accordingly no sooner will it be prov'd, that God requires the true Religion shou'd be inflam'd with an ardent Charity for the Conversion of

the false, that she employ all her Pains, her Books, her Sermons, her Censures, her Caresses, her good Examples, her Presents, *&c.* for the Reunion
of those astray, but presently the false Religions must fall into the same
Methods of Conversion; for each Church believing it self the only true,
it's impossible it shou'd apprehend, that God commands the true Church
to act so and so, without believing it self oblig'd to do the same: <290>
and if each Sect thinks it self in Conscience oblig'd to this, it wou'd be
infinitely worse in 'em to refrain, or act quite contrary, than execute the
Command, be it of what nature it will. For unalterable Order requires, that
we shou'd avoid what we know is a heinous Sin, to do that which we know
is a good Action, and which at worse, if it be a Sin, must be of a less heinous
nature than the other; then every Church is indispensably oblig'd, and has
an inalienable right of practising all that she knows God enjoins on the true
Church.

We don't therefore, as the Objection which I examine in this Chapter
wou'd insinuate, maliciously render the literal Sense of the Parable odious,
by supposing it wou'd authorize Persecutions mov'd by the false Religions
against the true; this, I say, is no false or artificial Supposition, but the true
State of the case, as I have fully made appear.

I shall add one Remark more. That if a Religion, persecuted in a Country
where it was weakest, shou'd ask her Persecutors, why they employ such
violent Methods; and these answer, because God enjoins the true Religion
to extirpate Heresy *quocunque modo:*[90] if, I say, by making this Answer, they
shou'd happen to persuade the Persecuted that there really was such a Command, what wou'd follow? Why this same persecuted Church, finding it
self the strongest in another place, might very well say to that Communion
which had tormented it in the Country where 'twas uppermost, *You have
taught me one Lesson that I did not know before, I am oblig'd to you for it; you
have shewn me from the Scriptures, that God* <291> *enjoins the faithful to
distress false Communions; I shall therefore fall to persecuting you, seeing I am
the true Church, and you Idolaters and false Christians,* &c. It's very plain,
that the stronger the Arguments be which Persecutors bring to prove that
God enjoins Constraint, the smarter Rods they furnish their Adversarys to

90. "In whatever way."

scourge themselves in another place. Each Party will engross the Proofs, the Command, the Rights of Truth; and authorize its Proceedings by every thing which the really true Religion can offer in its own behalf.

From whence I infer anew, that it's impossible God shou'd allow the Truth's doing any thing to establish it self, which is not just, and does not belong by common Right to all Mankind: for in the present Combinations, and Situation of things, there's an unavoidable Necessity, that all Means which are permitted to Truth against Error, shou'd be lawful in Error against Truth; and hence, by the same Ordinance dispensing with the general Rule in favor of the true Religion, Crime becomes necessary, and a total Confusion ensues.

The only Starting-hole now left our Adversarys is saying, that they allow the false Religions, by an Abuse and criminal Usurpation, may appropriate to themselves what solely belongs to the true Church; but there will always remain this difference between 'em, that the true Religion constrains with Justice and lawful Authority, but the rest wickedly and without a Right. This we shall speak to in the 10*th* Chapter.

But before I make an end of this, I shall answer an Objection from a very common Topick. You did not, they'l tell me, make a fair Enumeration <292> of ways and means, when you said, the Socinian had but one of three Choices to make. There's a fourth, and that the only good one, which is changing to the Truth; and then he may follow the Instincts of his Conscience with Impunity. This I confess is the better part; but as it cannot be chosen except on one condition, I maintain, that so long as this condition is wanting, he must necessarily chuse among the other three. The Condition I speak of needs not being explain'd. All the World is satisfy'd that it is this, that the Party know the Truth to be the Truth: every Heretick accepts the Truth, provided he knows it, and as soon as he knows it, but not otherwise nor sooner; for so long as it appears to him a hideous Grotesque of Falshood and Lye, so long he is not to admit, he is to fly and detest it. The first thing therefore a Heretick shou'd be desir'd to do, is, to search after Truth, and not opinionatively pretend he has found it. But if he answer, that he has searched as much as possible, that all his Inquirys have ended, in making him see more and more, that the Truth is on his own side; and shou'd he watch day and night, that he never shou'd believe any other thing, but what's already firmly ingrafted in his Soul, to be the reveal'd Truth; 'twere ridiculous telling him to beware following the Lights of his Conscience, and think of Conversion. Every one ought to set apart some Portion of his time for Instruction, and even be always ready to renounce what he had believ'd most true, if it be made appear to him false: but after all one can't be a Sceptick or Pyrrhonist in Religion all his Life long, he must fix upon some Principles, and act according to 'em; and whether he's determin'd to true or <293> false, 'tis equally evident, that he ought to exercise Acts of Vertue and Love towards God, and shun that capital Offence of acting against Conscience. Whence it appears, that a Socinian, who has done his utmost Endeavors towards discovering the Truth, is limited in his Choice to one of the three things I propos'd. Sending him back eternally to the fourth, means, that he shou'd spend his whole Life in mere Speculation, without ever consulting his Conscience to act according to its Lights. Now this of all Absurditys were surely the greatest.

❧ CHAPTER IX ❧

An Answer to some Objections against what has bin advanc'd in the foregoing Chapter concerning the Rights of an erroneous Conscience. Some Examples which prove this Right.

I did not make use of some very pertinent and altogether unanswerable Instances to prove, that the Rights of an erroneous Conscience attended with Sincerity, are exactly the same as those of an Orthodox Conscience; because while I was actually engag'd in this Argument, someone lent me the Continuation of the *Critique Generale* on Mr. *Maimbourg*'s History of Calvinism,[91] where I found these Rights very tolerably asserted from several of these Instances, and particularly from that of a suppos'd Father, who exercises all the Rights and Functions of paternal <294> Authority as rightfully as any true and real Father. I shou'd not have expected, that an Author, who seems to aim more at diverting his Reader, and enlivening his matter, than sounding it to the bottom, cou'd have enter'd so deep into

91. Bayle, OD, vol. 2, p. 218b ff.

this. It gave me full Satisfaction, tho I'm sensible a great deal may be added to what he has said upon this Subject. Yet I cannot see how our common Adversarys will answer his Instance of a Woman, who, persuaded that a Cheat is her true and lawful Husband, can't be wanting in any Duty of a Wife towards the Impostor, without becoming as guilty in the sight of God as if she misbehav'd herself towards her real lawful Husband. They are as much at a loss to answer the Instance of a Bastard, who believing this Husband of his Mother to be his real Father, owes him the very same Honor and Obedience as if he were Bone of his Bone; nor can he fail in any point of Duty to him without incurring the very same guilt as he might incur by a failure of Duty to his natural Father. He inherits the Estate of his Mother's Husband as legally as if he were his natural Son; and consequently the false Persuasion, which as well the Son as the Husband of this Woman are under, gives both the very same Rights as a true and undoubted Persuasion. These Examples, and many more, which the Author furnishes even to profusion, demolish the Cause of our Adversarys to all intents and purposes.

For they demonstratively prove, that an Action done in consequence of a false Persuasion, is as good as if done in consequence of a true and firm Persuasion. This appears from hence, that <295> Obedience to a suppos'd Father, to a suppos'd Husband; Affection for a suppos'd Child, are Dutys, neither more nor less obliging, than if the Subjects were really what they are taken to be. On the other hand, an Action done against a false Persuasion is as sinful as if done against a true Persuasion. This appears from hence, that disobeying a suppos'd Father, abusing him, killing him; doing the same to a suppos'd Husband; hating a suppos'd Son, are Actions no less criminal than if committed against Persons who were in reality what they are only suppos'd to be. There's not the least disparity in the cases.

Yes, yes, say they, there's a great deal; for he who shou'd turn a suppos'd Son out of doors, wou'd in reality but incommode a stranger; the Person turn'd out tells a lye, if he says, 'twas his Father us'd him so ill, all the Neighborhood lyes if they say so. It is not true then, that this Man turn'd his Son out of doors; and therefore he is no more to be blam'd than if he only turn'd off a Stranger whom he was not bound to support. But if he turn out a Child sprung from his own Loins, this alters the case; and God, who judges upon all things according to their real Nature, must know, that this Man turn'd off his lawfully begotten Son, and will judg of his Action accordingly; whereas in the former case he judges that the Man had only turn'd off a Stranger.

But my Readers must needs see the grossness of this Cavil before I confute it: they must know, that the Sovereign Judg of Heaven and Earth, the Searcher of the Heart and Reins, can make no difference betwixt two Acts of the human <296> Will exactly the same as to their physical Entity, tho their Object by accident is not really the same: for it suffices, that it be objectively[92] the same, I mean, that it appear so to the two Wills which form these Acts. And how in reason can it avail the suppos'd Father, that the Person he has turn'd out of doors was not lawfully begotten by him? This Circumstance being null with regard to him, because no more known to him than if it were really not so; can it in any kind of manner affect him? Is it the Cause, that there's less Outrage, less Hardheartedness, less Inhumanity in his Soul? It's plain it is not, and that this Circumstance makes no change in the Act of his Will, or in the Modifications of his Soul; so that God must see the same Irregularity within, whether these Acts relate to a true Son, or whether they relate to a Stranger, but who instead of being reputed such is a reputed Son. In like manner, a Woman who honestly takes a Counterfeit for her true Husband, and admits him to her Bed, does not commit a less warrantable Action than if he were her lawful Husband; and if she absolutely refus'd to live with the Impostor at Bed and Board, wou'd be as much to blame as if she refus'd her real Husband. The reason is, that towards making her Action in the first case less warrantable, and in the second case less blameable, 'twere requisite she had some good reason to give for not bedding with this Cheat: now she has no such reason; therefore, &c. There's not the least color of Reason to be alledg'd, because his Character of a Cheat, the only possible just Reason, can be no Reason at all with regard to her to whom it's perfectly unknown. 'Twere therefore the most <297> groundless Illusion to say, that if this Woman refus'd to bed with this Man, she cou'd not be blameable: for her Refusal proceeding from mere Caprice, Obstinacy, Pride, or some such Failing, precisely what wou'd

92. See Appendixes, "Obsolete or Unusual Words or Meanings," p. 578 ("objectively").

hinder her bedding with the true Husband were he in place, can in no kind of manner be excus'd.

But after all, say they, this Refusal does not in reality concern her true Husband: I answer, that's nothing to the purpose, it's enough that it relates to the true Husband objectively. This is evident, because the Turpitude of an Action is not measur'd at the Divine Tribunal by the real quality of the Subjects to which it tends, but by their objective quality; that is, God considers only the very Act of the Will. Therefore a Man, who has the Will to murder another, and who thinking he is in such a Coach, fires a Musket at him, is as guilty in the Sight of God, tho he hits only a Statue someone had put in the Coach, as if he had shot him dead, because the Effects of the local Motions, which execute the Act of his Will, are wholly extrinsecal to the Crime: the willing to move his Arm, the moment he believes that Motion shall be follow'd by the death of a Man, constitutes the whole Essence of Homicide. The rest, to wit, that such a Man is, or is not really kill'd, is wholly accidental to the Sin, which God, the Judg infallible and most just, has no regard to, as a Matter which either extenuates, or aggravates the Guilt.

This may be a proper place enough to put in a Caveat, That tho I stretch Toleration in Religion as far as any one, yet I am not for giving any quarter to those who affront the Divinity <298> they profess to believe in, were it the vilest of all those Gods of Clay which the Scriptures speak of. *Grotius* is of the same mind, in the last Paragraph of Chap. 20. B. 2. *de Jure Belli & Pacis.* "They," says he, "are most justly punishable, who behave themselves irreverently and irreligiously towards those Beings which they believe to be Gods." And hereupon he makes a note, in which he says, "St. *Cyril* treats this matter very judiciously in his fifth and sixth Books against *Julian*." He likewise observes, that the true God has often punish'd Perjurys and false Adjurations of the Divinitys believ'd in, of what kind soever they be. It won't be amiss to hear what *Seneca* says on this head, in the seventh Chapter of his seventh Book of Benefits: *A sacrilegious Person can do no injury to God, who by his Nature is above all Attempts; yet he's justly punishable, because he offers the injury to a Being which he owns as God. Our Sense and his own condemn him to Punishment.* This Author joins the Sentence of the sacrilegious Person's own Mind to that of his Judges; but in one sense this Consent of Judgments is not necessary. For tho they shou'd be of a very different Religion from that of the sacrilegious Person, yet they are oblig'd to punish him for acting in this point against the Dictates of his particular Conscience. 'Tis true, the Opinion of the Judges in another sense cannot but close in with that of the sacrilegious Offender, provided they are of this opinion, that all particular Contempts of the false Divinitys rebound upon the true God. How can this be, say they? Thus, say I; 'tis no hard matter to demonstrate it. <299>

As the eternal or positive Laws of God are what makes all the difference between Vertue and Vice, between moral Good and Evil, it's the Prerogative of God to declare what Punishment is due to the Violation of these Laws; and 'tis he, as Legislator, who is the principal Party affronted by the Transgression of 'em. Now the most obliging and most indispensable of all these Laws, is that which forbids the doing of what we are conscious is wicked, criminal, and impious; all therefore who commit what they believe to be wicked and impious, violate one of the most sacred Laws flowing from the Divine Nature, and consequently offend the true God: for altho they know him not, altho the God whom they do know is a Fiction of the Brain, a most imperfect Being; yet the Persuasion they are under that this Being is God, cannot be attended with an Act which they are conscious must offend him, without the extremest Obliquity and utmost Malice in the Will. Now this Obliquity and this Malice of the Will is one of those Acts which the Law eternal has rank'd in the Class of Sin; it's therefore a Violation of the eternal Law of God: in a word, it's an Impiety.

The better to comprehend this, we need only compare the Case of a Jew who shou'd pillage the Temple of *Jerusalem,* with that of a Greek who pillag'd the Temple of *Delphos;* a Jew, I say, and a Greek equally assur'd, one that the Temple of *Jerusalem* is consecrated to God, the other that the Temple of *Delphos* is consecrated to *Apollo,* and that *Apollo* is a true God. I defy all Mankind to find any Circumstance in these two sacrilegious Actions, which can render one more <300> impious, more affronting to the true God than the other.

For will any one say, that the Jew's carrying off Vessels consecrated to the true God, and the Greek Vessels consecrated to a false God, makes any specifick difference betwixt the two Thefts? To say this, is betraying an utter

Ignorance of the formal Cause of Sin, and advancing that the Sin of the Jew consists, in part at least, precisely in this, that he has taken certain Vessels from one place, and laid 'em down in another. Now this is no ingredient in the Sin; for shou'd a high Wind cause this conveyance, shou'd a Thunderbolt, an Earthquake, a walking Machine change their local Situation, there wou'd be no more moral Evil in it, than in the twirling of a Straw, which is the sport of the Winds. The Sin therefore of the Jew consists in this, in his willing to convey away these Vessels the very moment he was near enough to reach forth his hand for that purpose; and willing this in the very moment that he believ'd 'em to be Vessels consecrated to God, and that he cou'd not convey 'em away without offending the true God. The Concurrence, or if I may so say, the Confluence of these two Acts of the Soul, to wit, of this Knowledg and this Volition, at the moment when his Hand was near enough to do its part, is that which constitutes the whole Sacrilege and Sin of this Jew. That these Vessels are really, or, as the Logicians speak, *a parte rei,* consecrated to the true God, and not to those Gods of Dung of which the Prophets so often make mention, is a thing wholly extrinsecal and accidental to the Jew's Action, and consequently < 301 > contributes nothing to the aggravating his Crime. Whence it evidently appears, that the Greek's Sacrilege is altogether as sinful as that of the Jew, because we find in it that Concurrence of a Will to steal certain Vessels, the very moment his Hand was near enough to be mov'd for this purpose; and of a clear and distinct belief that these Vessels are consecrated to a God, who shall think himself exceedingly offended at his conveying 'em from thence. *Apollo's* being a Chimera is nothing at all to the purpose; for the Greek having not the least suspicion of this chimerical Quality of *Apollo,* nothing can be drawn from it in his excuse: and it is most false, that the Reason total or in part, why he durst rob the Temple, was grounded on his believing that *Apollo* was no God. I say, and know I repeat the same things too often; but we have to deal with Adversarys impenetrable to the most forcible Arguments; their Understandings are like the Bodys of those Soldiers who have got, they say, a Charm about 'em, which renders 'em invulnerable: we must therefore work it into 'em as Water does into Stone, by saying the same things over and over; *Gutta cavat Lapidem non vi sed saepe cadendo.*[93]

---

93. "A drip hollows a stone not by its force but by falling often."

From all this I conclude, that the Conscience of a Pagan obliges him to honor his false Gods, on pain, if he reviles 'em, if he robs their Temples, &c. of incurring the Guilt of Blasphemy and Sacrilege, as much as a Christian who curs'd God, and rob'd his Churches. Wherefore I approve the Christian Magistrate's punishing a Pagan, who without a design of abjuring his Religion shou'd blaspheme his Divinitys, or overthrow their Statues. <302>

Let's now examine the Difficultys which they are ready to propose in abundance.

In the first place, they may tell us that the Examples of the Author of the *Critique Generale* prove nothing with regard to the Truths of Religion, because they relate to Questions of Fact, and not to those of Right, such as the Articles of Faith be. For which reason he who is under a mistaken Belief, that the Husband of his Mother is his true Father, shall be oblig'd to honor him as such, and wou'd be guilty of a Sin if he did not; but he who shou'd falsly believe that Murder is a vertuous Action, is not oblig'd to kill, and wou'd be guilty of a Sin if he did. Whence arises this difference? From hence; That the knowing such a Man to be the Father of such a Man is a Question of Fact, but the knowing whether it be lawful to kill is a Question of Right.

This Objection is of no great weight, and includes two Cases which we must take care to distinguish. The first is to know whether Conscience, erring in matters of Right, obliges to act according to its false Dictates; the other, to know whether he who follows these false Dictates commits a Sin. I don't see that Fact and Right in the first case beget any real difference, because the formal reason why Conscience erring in matters of Fact obliges to act, is, that he who shou'd not act betrays a Contempt of Vertue, and a Will of doing what he knows is an Evil. For example, a Man who acts contrary to what his mistaken Conscience tells him he ought to do for his suppos'd Father, formally wills a Transgression of the fifth Commandment of the Decalogue. Now as the willing this Transgression is <303> a greater Evil than willing another Action, not conformable indeed to the Law of God, but which however to us appears conformable, insomuch that its appearing so is the real Motive of our acting, and that moreover of two Evils we are indispensably oblig'd to avoid the greatest; it's plain this Person is oblig'd to honor his suppos'd Father.

Now the same Reason operates where Conscience errs in matters of Right. We can't act counter to its Dictates, without willing that which we are persuaded is a Sin; and the willing this is undoubtedly a greater Sin than willing another thing which we are convinc'd is good, altho it may not be so: the same Reason then why Conscience erring in matters of Fact obliges, takes place where Conscience errs in points of Right. The Distinction therefore is null with regard to the first Case. I add, that in reality there are but very few Questions of Right which are not reducible to this Fact, whether God has reveal'd this or that; whether he has prohibited Murder, &c. For as to the Question, whether what God prohibits is evil, and what he commands is good, no body disputes it: the only dispute is concerning this Fact, Is such or such a thing forbidden or commanded by God?

As to the second Case, to wit, whether he who follows the Dictates of a Conscience erring in matters of Right be guilty of Sin, I have no design of treating it in this place; nevertheless I shall desire my Reader to weigh the following Remark.

That the Distinction of Fact and Right is of no use, except in cases where both don't come to <304> the same thing. 'Twere making a mock of us to pretend, *Such an Action proceeding from Error is innocent, such another Action proceeding from Error is sinful; that's innocent because it concerns a Fact; this is sinful because it concerns Right:* I say, 'twere mocking the World to argue at this rate, without going farther, and without supposing other Principles. They must therefore tacitly understand, when they talk thus, that the Fact and Right are so distinct in their natures, that the Ignorance as to the first is invincible, but as to the latter affected and malicious. By supposing this Principle all will go well; and then the true reason why a Woman that beds with a suppos'd Husband, a Child who inherits the Estate of a suppos'd Father, &c. commit neither Adultery nor Fraud,[94] is, not that the Error concerns a matter of Fact (this reason supposes another previous reason) but that their Error proceeds not from Malice, and that it is not the fault of either the Wife or the Son that they are deceiv'd. I don't see how this can be deny'd; because it's a constant Truth, that if the Mistake of this Woman had its rise from any criminal Passion, which blinded her eyes to

94. For these cases, see above, p. 233, note 91.

all the means of detecting the Impostor, her carnal Commerce with him
wou'd be indeed a Sin; yet 'twou'd still be true, that this Action concern'd
a Point of Fact, to wit, *Whether such a Man be the Husband of such a Woman.*
Thus by unfolding the Circumstances, we come at the formal Reason of
moral Good and Evil. It does not consist precisely in this, That the Action
relates to Fact; but in the Party's being under an Ignorance of the Fact,
without Malice or vicious Af-<305>fectation. Now if this be the true formal
Cause of the Innocence of those Actions which proceed from Error, I maintain, that wherever this Ignorance takes place, whether in matters of Fact
or in those of Right, the Action proceeding from it is innocent; and consequently this first Distinction of Fact and Right is nothing to the purpose,
nor does it invalidate my Argument in the least: for I don't pretend to excuse
or acquit those who maliciously contribute to their own Ignorance; I speak
only for those whose Error is attended with Sincerity, and who wou'd freely
and readily forsake their Heresys, if convinc'd they were really such, and
who have employ'd the same means for discovering whether they be Heresys, as the Orthodox to discover whether their Doctrines be Orthodox.

I shan't scruple to maintain, that the Reverence and Obedience such
Men pay to their own Church, their Zeal for its Confessions of Faith, the
Care their Church takes to train up and instruct its Sons, can't be reputed
sinful Actions, but it must follow that the Obedience for a suppos'd Father,
the Commerce with a suppos'd Husband, the Tenderness for a suppos'd
Child, are likewise sinful; for in all these respective Cases there's a Transfer
of what is a just Debt to one Party, on another to whom it is not due, and
an Ignorance involuntary and void of Malice, of one side as much as the
other. And after this, it matters little that one is call'd Fact, the other Right;
as it signifies little to the justifying a Suit at Law for the Recovery of an
Estate, whether it were left the Claimant by Gift, or whether he had bought
it with his <306> Mony. A Title by Gift or by Purchase are two very different things; yet because they center in the same particular point of giving
a just Possession, they equally confer the Right of a just Possession, and of
all Claims depending thereon. This is exactly the Case before us. Fact and
Right may be as different, if you please, as Black and White; yet meeting
in the point of being equally unknown thro an involuntary Ignorance, they
confer or take away precisely the same Rights.

I shan't in this place examine whether the Ignorance of Matters of Right may be as innocent as that of Fact: I shall touch upon this Point hereafter.

The second Difficulty propos'd is, That my Doctrine does in its Consequences destroy what I wou'd endeavor to establish. My design is to shew, that Persecution is a horrible thing; and yet every one who thinks himself oblig'd in Conscience to persecute, shall be oblig'd by my Doctrine to persecute, and sins if he does not.

I answer, That the Design of this *Commentary* upon these words, *Compel 'em to come in,* being to convince Persecutors that JESUS CHRIST has not enjoin'd Constraint, I don't destroy my own Design, if I shew by solid Arguments that the literal Sense of these words is false, impious, and absurd. If I succeed in this, I have reason to hope that they who examine my Argument, may perceive those Errors of Conscience, which they may be under as to Persecution; and therefore my Design is just. I don't deny but they who are actually persuaded that 'tis their Duty to extirpate Sects, are oblig'd to follow the <307> Motions of their false Conscience; and that in not doing so, they are guilty of a Disobedience to God, because they persist in not obeying what they believe to be his Will.

But, 1. It does not follow, that they act without Sin, because they act by Conscience. 2. This ought not to hinder our crying out loudly against their false Maxims, and endeavoring to enlighten their Understandings.

The third Difficulty is, That by my Principles the Magistrate cannot punish a Man who robs or kills his Neighbor, upon a persuasion of the Lawfulness of these Actions. I have already answer'd, that this does not follow; because the Magistrate is oblig'd to preserve the Society, and punish all those who destroy the Foundation of its Security, as Murderers and Robbers do: in this case he is to have no regard to their false Consciences. He is not oblig'd to have any regard for Conscience, except in Matters which affect not the publick Welfare; to wit, Doctrines as consistent with the Liberty and Property of the Subject, as any other Doctrines.

But be that as it will, say they in the fourth place, no Violence can upon my Principles be offer'd to those who vend any speculative Doctrines; and consequently here's a door open'd for Atheists to declaim against God and Religion, as much as they please. I deny the Consequence, 1. Because the Magistrate being, by the Eternal Law of Order, oblig'd to promote the publick Welfare and Security of all the Members of the Society under his care, may and ought to punish those who sap or weaken the fundamental Laws of the State; and of this number we commonly <308> reckon those who destroy the Belief of a Providence, and the Fear of divine Justice. If this Reason won't suffice, here's another to stop the mouth of every Caviller on this head; to wit, That an Atheist, incapable of being prompted to vend his Tenets from any Motive of Conscience, can never plead that Saying of St. *Peter, It is better to obey God than Men;* which we look upon with reason as the Barrier which no secular Judg can get over, and as the inviolable Asylum of Conscience. An Atheist, void as he is of this main Protection, lies justly expos'd to the utmost Rigor of the Laws; and the moment he vends his Notions, after warning once given him, may be justly punish'd as a Mover of Sedition; who believing no Restraint above human Laws, presumes nevertheless to tread 'em under foot. I shall insist no farther upon this Answer; I'm satisfy'd, the least discerning Reader will presently perceive its force: and thus my Doctrine is intirely fenc'd against all Attempts of Impiety, because it allows that the Secular Power may in this case take what methods shall seem most fitting. But the case is different with regard to a Teacher of new Doctrines, who may plead the Glory of God, the common Lord of all Men, to the Magistrate in behalf of his teaching this or that Doctrine; and alledg that Conscience, and a Zeal for the Truth, are his only Motives. These are the Foundation of Mount *Sinai,* which can never be shaken. Such a Man must be argu'd with from the Word of God or the Lights of Reason. Add to this what I hinted before,[95] when I spoke of an Exchange of Missionarys with <309> the *Mahometans,* and the Advantages Christianity might make by such a Traffick.

But what! say they in the fifth place, wou'd he have us suffer Men to preach up Sodomy, Adultery, and Murder, as Actions praise-worthy and holy? And if they pretend that Conscience and a Zeal for the Truth had mov'd 'em to undeceive the World in these points, must not the Magistrate restrain 'em? I answer, this Objection smells strong of the Cavil; and there's so little danger of this Case's ever happening, that the Difficulty founded upon it deserves not to be consider'd.

95. See above, p. 213.

If I told those who condemn Persecution by Fire and Sword and say that one must be content to banish Hereticks, that their Doctrine tends manifestly to the Rigor of Death; because if all the World banish'd those whom they banish'd, the Wretches must inevitably perish; not finding any place of being or abode; I shou'd think I had started a pitiful Cavil, because 'twere supposing a Case which in all likelihood can never happen, to wit, that all the World shall agree to banish the same Hereticks. I say much the same to the Objection now made. There's no need of knowing what shou'd be done, in case any Person preach'd up Sodomy, Murder, and Rapine, as a Morality deriv'd from JESUS CHRIST, because there's no danger that this shall ever happen. Your Innovators in Religion never steer this course; and if they did, they must presently become the Horror and Detestation of Mankind, nor ever be able to establish any thing like a Sect. This is not the way for an Impostor, or a Man seduc'd by the Devil, to win the Multitude; Appearances of Austerity will stand him <310> much more in stead. Yet if they have a mind to know what course ought to be taken with such Teachers, I answer, that in the first place cou'd they be suppos'd persuaded of what they say, they shou'd be fairly reason'd with, and their Condemnation set before 'em from the Scriptures, and from the Ideas of natural Rectitude. Either they must be frantick, or be brought to reason by such a Catechise: and when the scandalous and execrable Consequences of their Doctrines were fairly and calmly set before 'em, Consequences which put the Lives and Estates of the Preachers themselves in the power of the next Comer; if they still persisted in their Error, and in a Design of teaching and spreading it, they shou'd be made to understand, that as they attack the politickal Laws of the Society, they are under Circumstances in which the Magistrate regards not the Plea of Conscience. Sure I am, that so many Marks of Madness and Lunacy must appear in their Conduct upon such a Dispute, unless they were reclaim'd by it, that there wou'd be ground enough to send 'em to *Bedlam*. Judg then whether such a Case (I don't remember to have met with any such in the Catalogue of Hereticks) is to be put in the ballance with that of delivering up those who err only in Points of Faith to the Secular Arm. Dutys of Morality are so clearly reveal'd in the Scriptures, that we can't justly apprehend Conscience will be deprav'd with regard to them. And Christians being besides on such a foot, that they may live Lives as dissolute as if all speculative Morality were cancel'd, they'l always leave this part intire; it furnishes <311> matter for good Books and good Sermons, and for all the fair Appearances of Piety: so that its Commodiousness in this respect, and the little or no Inconvenience it gives in the Practice, is a sufficient Guaranty that no Sect will ever revolt against it; or if it shou'd, that the Scandal will quickly give a check to its growth without the Assistance of the Secular Arm.

The Jesuits themselves, with all their Pride and all their Impudence, durst not maintain the Attempts of their Casuists; they have disavow'd 'em, and think it unjust that their whole Society shou'd suffer upon their account. They have fairly struck sail upon this occasion; and if they have done so much, of whom shou'd we despair? The antient Gnosticks, who authoriz'd all carnal Pollutions; the Adamites, and some others of the same taste, lasted but a short while: a Sense of Decency and worldly Honor is enough to reclaim all their Followers, and they can truly have none but such as are branded for their scandalous Lives; a strong Presumption that their Conscience is not deceiv'd. If they have but the least Remains of it, if they have the least Remains of Reason, they may quickly be reclaim'd by grave Conferences.

They may say in the sixth place, It follows from my Principles, that a Man who commits Murder in obeying the Instincts of Conscience, does a better Action than he who does not commit it; and that the Magistrate has no right to punish him, because he has only done his Duty. This Objection is certainly very perplexing, I don't disown it; but I persuade my self, the Answer I shall give will be satisfactory to all who <312> are not govern'd by popular Judgments. I have three things to observe upon this Objection.

The first is only a Consequence from what I have bin just saying, that there's so little danger of any number of Men's falling into the sensless and furious Persuasion of the Lawfulness of Murder, that by owning the Consequence I don't think I endanger Religion or the State. Natural Reason and Scripture are so express against Murder, and the Doctrine which maintains it has something so horrible and even hazardous, that few are capable of being so much beside themselves as really to take up this Persuasion from a Principle of Conscience. This is never to be apprehended, except from Minds over-run with Melancholy, or flaming Zealots, into whom their Directors of Conscience, flagitious Men, may possibly inspire a King-killing Principle, where the Prince is of a different Religion from theirs; whereof *France* and *England* have memorable Examples. Shou'd only a Prince in an Age fall by such Principles, still the mischief wou'd be very great; yet there's no avoiding this mischief by maintaining, as our Adversarys do, that a misguided Conscience does not oblige. For the wicked Directors, who inspire these Assassins, will never tell 'em it's a false Conscience which prompts 'em to stab a *Henry* III, or a *Henry* IV, but a very upright and orthodox Conscience. Since then the Inconvenience to be apprehended from my Hypothesis is not to be avoided by the opposite Principles, 'twere imprudence to quit it, when so useful in other respects, and particularly towards obliging Men to inform themselves thorowly of the Truth: For if once <313> persuaded that they are oblig'd to obey the Dictates of Conscience, yet without being acquitted in the presence of God on the commission of any Crime (because if their Ignorance proceeds from a neglect of the means of Information, they are liable to punishment even for what they have done from the Instincts of Conscience) they'l certainly take the more care how they bring themselves under a necessity of doing Evil: whereas if People be taught that a false Conscience does not oblige, they'l live at random, persuade themselves to what they please, except for doing nothing of what their Conscience directs; for perhaps, say they, Conscience is not rightly inform'd, and if so, I ought not to govern my self by it. See what horrible Confusions must spring from the Opinion I now confute.

Next I observe, that the reason why Murder is commonly accounted a greater Sin, tho committed from the Instincts of Conscience, than a contempt of these Instincts, is only a custom of making God judg upon human Actions, as our own Judges in criminal Cases are wont to do. That is, we imagine that Almighty God, over and above the Modifications of the Soul of Man, regulates himself in his Judgments by the Effects and Consequences of the Motion of Matter, by which Men execute their Wills, insomuch as to judg the killing a Man when there's only an intention of wounding him, a greater Sin than only wounding when there's an intention of killing him. This is a gross Abuse, and yet it is not amiss for earthly Judges to govern themselves by such Rules, because they are not Searchers of <314> the Heart and Reins. But as to God, who knows all the Degrees of Malice,

Infirmity, and Passion, which mix with our Wills, infinitely better than the best Goldsmith knows the proportions of Alloy in Metals, he judges upon our Actions most surely and most infallibly, without turning his Eye to any other Object than the bare Modifications of the Soul, and without considering whether one of these Modifications moves a Sword, and another moves it not: Such a Modification which gives it a Motion may possibly be innocenter, than such another which does not.

If it be therefore true, that God considers only the Modifications of the Soul, let's content our selves with comparing what God sees in a Man fully persuaded he ought to commit Murder, and yet refraining from it, with what he sees in a Man under the same firm Persuasion, and who at the same time commits the Murder. In the First, he sees an affected, inexcusable, and malicious contempt of the Will of God (for as I have said a thousand times over, to contemn what one believes to be the Will of God, is essentially a Contempt of the Will of God, tho the Person may be deceiv'd in believing it to be his Will.) In the Second, he sees an intire deference for what he's persuaded is the Will of God, a Homage paid to the Supreme Authority of God, in fine a Love of Order; for Order eternal and immutable joins the Idea of God as commanding a thing, to the Resolution of obeying him. We don't more clearly conceive, that the Idea of a Magnitude which exceeds that of a Part is included in the Idea of the Whole; than we conceive that the Obligation of doing any thing is included in <315> the Idea of God commanding it: So that these two Axioms are without contradiction of the same incontestable Evidence, *The Whole's greater than its Part; Man ought to do what God commands, and believe that he ought to do what he believes God has commanded him.* It's impossible therefore a Man shou'd join the Will of doing a thing to the Belief of God's enjoining it, without his willing to conform to the primary Idea of Equity, and to what we call Order eternal and immutable: and consequently God, who knows all things as they really are, sees in a Soul, which believing he enjoins him to commit a Murder commits it, a most unfeign'd desire of conforming to the eternal and natural Law; and on the contrary, in a Soul under the same Persuasion, which yet will not commit the Murder, he sees a swerving from Order, and a manifest Transgression of the eternal Law. The first Soul therefore must appear to him less inordinate than the second: because the whole Sin of the first consists in taking that for a divine Impulse or Inspiration, which really was not so; which being an Error only in Fact and Judgment, can't be a Sin near so enormous, as an Act of the Will by which we refuse to obey God.

It's fit to observe, that Homicide being an Action in some cases lawful, as in War; in the Execution of civil Justice; and from a secret divine Impulse, as in the Case of St. *Peter* who slew *Ananias;* it follows, that to convict a Man of the Sin, it is not sufficient to say he has kill'd another Man, but we must examine all the Circumstances: for there are such Circumstances as change the nature of Homicide from that of a <316> bad Action to a good, a secret Command of God for example. And therefore, when a Man from the Instincts of his Conscience kills another, we must not consider this Homicide abstracted from the Persuasion the Murderer was under, that God had enjoin'd it. Now upon considering the Murder join'd to this Persuasion, there's no more to be said, than that the Man was grosly deceiv'd in taking that for a divine Inspiration, which was nothing like it; and undoubtedly the Offence is smaller in this case, than in that of having not the least regard to what we were persuaded was the Will of God. 'Twill clear every difficulty in this matter, if we only represent the Devil accusing a Man at the Divine Tribunal, who did not commit a Murder when his Conscience prompted him to it. The Accusation must import, that this Man believing himself in such Circumstances, that God by a special Providence had thought fit to make use of him, as of *Phineas, Samuel, Elias,* and St. *Peter,* for the killing such a Man,[96] he had made a mock of the matter, and put it off to a long Day. What Answer cou'd the accus'd make? Shou'd he say that Murder was forbidden in the Decalogue; 'twill be reply'd, that God sometimes dispenses with this Precept. Shou'd he say, that he durst not stain his Hands with Blood, Judgment will be demanded against him for want of holy Resolution. Shou'd he say, that he was under some doubts whether the Command came from God, then we are no longer in the Supposition I made; and so I have nothing to say to it. It's plain then the accus'd cou'd have no good reason to alledg in extenuation of his formal Disobedience, and consequent-<317>ly that God wou'd be oblig'd to pronounce him guilty: so that what repugnance soever a Body finds at first sight to the

---

96. Numbers 25.7–11, 1 Samuel 15:33, 1 Kings 18:40, Acts 5:1–11.

owning it, yet it's certain, that a Murder committed from the Instincts of Conscience, is a less Sin than not committing Murder when Conscience dictates.

They'l tell me, that he who made a Vow to kill a Man, must sin more by performing his Vow, than by breaking it. I answer, If the breaking his Vow proceeded from a better inform'd Conscience, telling him 'twas a less Sin to violate his Vow than to accomplish it, his Conduct in this case were right. But if continuing in the Persuasion, that he was not oblig'd to cancel his Vow, he shou'd yet recede from it, my Arguments revert, and prove as in the former Case. I wou'd have People observe by the way, that shou'd God, taking pity of a Man, who bound himself rashly in a very sinful Vow, have a mind to prevent his accomplishing it, the way must be, by the interposal of a new Conscience, and by shewing him that he was not oblig'd to fulfil his Vow. This discovers to us in the Ideas of God, an indissoluble Connexion betwixt the Judgments of Conscience, and the Obligation of conforming to 'em; since God himself does not separate these two things, when he wou'd prevent the execution of a sinful Act: How does he order it then? He goes somewhat higher to the Principle of all human Actions, and reconciles his renouncing the Vow, with the Judgment of Conscience; that is, he changes the former Instincts of Conscience, and gets a new Judgment pass'd, that the Vow is no longer obliging, but <318> on the contrary that there's an Obligation of breaking it.

I conclude, by saying, that the Magistrate having receiv'd a Power from God and Man, of putting Murderers to death, may justly punish him who kills a Man from the Instincts of Conscience; for it is not his business to stand winnowing those rare and singular Cases, in which Conscience may happen to fall into Illusions in this matter.

ɷɷ CHAPTER X ɷɷ

A Continuation of the Answer to the Difficultys against the Rights of an erroneous Conscience. An Examination of what they say, that if Hereticks retaliate on those who persecute 'em, they are guilty of Injustice. Arguments to prove, that a false Conscience may sometimes excuse those who follow it, tho not in all Cases.

Having shewn, as I presume I have, that Hereticks are oblig'd to avoid whatever is not conformable to the Dictates of their Conscience as at least the greater Evil; from whence I infer'd, that they have a Right of doing every thing for the propagating their Errors, which they know God has enjoin'd for propagating the Truth: I might very well have rested here, as having sufficiently prov'd, that Hereticks have a Right of persecuting the Orthodox, supposing <319> God had any where enjoin'd the persecuting Error. However to omit nothing that can farther be desir'd, I shall here examine another very important Question, to wit, Whether a Heretick in doing what his Conscience dictates, may not only avoid the greater Evil, but also all Evil, and perform a good Action.

Before I proceed, I think my self oblig'd to remove a rock of Offence out of the way of my Readers. Some I know will be startled at my advancing, that an erroneous Conscience gives a Right of committing Evil; or to use the Terms of the Author of the *Critique Generale on Mr.* Maimbourg's *History,*[97] that Error in the guise of Truth, enters upon all the Rights and Prerogatives of Truth. This sounds somewhat harsh and extravagant; and I own I have met with other Expressions of this kind in the same Author, which to me appear'd somewhat crude and undigested at the first reading: but upon better thoughts I am clearly of his Opinion, to wit, that when Error is dress'd out in the Vestments and Livery of Truth, we owe it the same Respect as we owe to the Truth itself; just as, when a Messenger comes with a Master's orders to a Servant, the Servant is oblig'd to receive him, tho perhaps the Messenger's no better than a Cheat or Sharper at the

---

97. Bayle, *Nouvelles Lettres,* OD, vol. 2, p. 221b.

bottom, who has surreptitiously come by the Master's Orders. To say that this Sharper acquires all the Rights of a faithful Messenger with regard to the Servant to whom he delivers his Master's Orders, is a manner of expression, which in a Subject of this nature may appear somewhat confus'd to an unpractis'd Reader: but bating this the parallel is <320> just; and if the Author of the *Critique* meant no more by it, than that the Servant was oblig'd to receive this Sharper civilly, and cou'd not offer him the least Injury without becoming unfaithful to his Master, I must intirely agree with him. Yet he ought to have observ'd one remarkable Difference betwixt the Sharper and a Heresy; to wit, that the Sharper being a distinct Person from the Servant, and conscious he has no right to come with the Master's Orders, can't do this without a Sin; but the Heresy under the colors of Truth, being nothing distinct from the Heretical Soul in which it exists (for the Modifications of the Mind are not Entitys distinct from the Mind) is no way conscious of its being only the fantom of Truth, and consequently the Heretical Soul knows not that it either deceives or is deceiv'd. Now fully persuaded of her being in a good State, she has quite another Right of imposing such and such Acts on her self, which in the eternal Order of Morality are to follow upon such and such Persuasions; she has, I say, much a better right in this respect than the Sharper: For the Sharper has not the least Right or Authority, as existing outside the Mind of the Servant, but as he is objectively in the Servant's Mind; that is, to express my self more intelligibly, all his Right consists in the Idea, or in the Persuasion the Servant is under, that this Sharper is a faithful Messenger from his Master. If the Sharper usurps this Right, he is punishable beyond dispute; but the Soul modify'd by a Heresy from a sincere Persuasion, whether punishable when exercising her Right, is all the Question. There's no manner of doubt but she is when her Right is ill ac-<321>quir'd. Nor let it seem strange to any one, that I say, a Soul is liable to Punishment, when only exercising her own Right; for all agree that a Person may abuse his Right, and commit Injustice in the exercise of his Right. It's an Axiom that, *summum Jus summa Injuria,* a Man may be very unjust in stretching his Right to the utmost rigor. Have not Princes a Right of punishing and pardoning, yet don't they often make a wrong use of it? Without entring therefore into tedious Discussions, 'twill suffice to observe, that the Word *Right* or *Jus* is equivocal; sometimes it's taken for the Power of doing such a thing; and sometimes for the Justice of an Action. Children have a Right in some cases to marry in spite of their Parents, and if they do no one can molest 'em; yet this hinders not but by exercising this Right they may sometimes abuse it, physically and morally speaking. 'Twere abusing my Readers to enlarge on a matter so evident.

Having remov'd this rub out of our way, I make no scruple to say, that had God in the Scriptures commanded the propagating the Truth by Fire and Sword, Hereticks might unblameably persecute the Truth with Fire and Sword; which is a new and demonstrative Argument against the literal Sense confuted in this Commentary. My Reasons are these.

I. Let's keep to the Passage which serves for a Text to this Commentary: It's evident from what we have seen in several parts of this Work, that if the words *Compel 'em to come in,* contain'd a Command of forcing People into the Bosom of the Church, they are liable to Constraint, not <322> only by Fine, Imprisonment, and Banishment, but also by capital Punishment. We may therefore suppose, that this Passage contains a Law for persecuting to the utmost rigor. Now as this Law is conceiv'd in general terms, there can be no ground to imagine, but the Intention of the Legislator is general, and indifferently address'd to all who own the Gospel for the reveal'd Word of God. But if the Intention of God be general, all they, to whom this Law is known, are oblig'd to obey it: now this they cannot do but by persecuting those who entertain a Belief opposite to the Truth; God then it seems has commanded 'em to persecute those whom they suppose in Opinions opposite to the Truth. And if they do this, what ground is there for Complaint?

The better to perceive the force of this Argument, which seems at first sight to be far fetch'd and drag'd in by head and shoulders, 'twill be proper to observe, that all the Precepts which God has given in his Word in general terms, are obliging, not only on those who are in the visible Communion of that Church which understands the Scriptures rightest, but on those also who live in heretical Societys. This is evident from the Examples of Prayer, Alms-giving, Charity to our Neighbor, honoring our Father and Mother, renouncing our Lusts, Covetousness, Lying, Uncleanness, &c. 'Tis the Mind of God, not only that the Orthodox shou'd obey these Precepts, but those also who have the misfortune of falling into any Heresy, and even while they continue in their Errors; in the midst of all their Delusions he intends they shou'd obey these Precepts, and approves all Acts of Vertue in obedience to 'em. <323> And why shou'd not we think the same with regard to this general Order, *Compel 'em to come in?* Why shou'd the greatest part of Christians not observe it; and why do better in transgressing it? All the Disparitys which can be alledg'd, will serve only to shew, that had God given any Law at all in this matter, he had restrain'd it by some particular Expressions, by saying, for example, *I ordain, that they who believe such and such points, constrain those who do not.* Just as if it were a deadly Sin in a Protestant to give an Alms for God's sake, all the Ideas of Order incline us to believe, that the Precept of Alms-giving had bin address'd to those only, who had such or such a Mark of Christianity, those, for example, who own'd the Pope's Supremacy. But as all Men living, be they of what Religion they will, may do a good Work in giving Alms, hence it comes, that the Precept of Alms-giving is indifferently address'd to all Mankind, and so of all the other general Precepts. Seeing therefore the pretended Order for persecuting is general, we must believe, that the Intention of God is, that People of all Denominations shou'd obey it.

We are further to observe, that the Nature of all general Laws is such, that the Application of 'em must be left to the Discretion of those who fulfil 'em, unless it be otherwise prescrib'd by the Legislator. For example, the Command in the Decalogue, *Honor thy Father and thy Mother,* prescribes not to Children such or such a particular kind of Honor, nor obliges 'em to apply this Honor to such or such a kind of Person. The whole Intention of it is, that they pay to him, whom they believe their Father, the Honors in <324> use in their own Country; so that in a Country, where being cover'd in the presence of a Superior, or walking before him, were ordinary marks of respect, a Child who behav'd himself thus, not only towards him who begot him, but to him whom he believes to be his Father, wou'd as perfectly fulfil this Law of God, *caeteris paribus,* as a Child, who in this Country of ours shou'd stand always uncover'd before his Father, shou'd walk at a distance behind him, *&c.* Let's apply this to the Law, *Compel 'em to come in;* the mildest Construction we can put upon it is, that all shou'd pitch upon that kind of Constraint which makes the deepest Impression in their own Country, and make use of it against those whom they believe to be in a wrong way: and thus things being in other respects equal, a *Lutheran* who shou'd compel a Papist to turn *Lutheran,* wou'd obey the Order of God altogether as regularly as a Papist who compel'd a *Lutheran* to go to Mass.

When St. *Paul* says, *Do good unto all, especially to those who are of the Household of Faith;* does he mean, that a Papist shou'd do good unto all, but especially to the Calvinists, or that a Calvinist shou'd do good to all, but especially to the Papists? No, this were extravagant: We must therefore of necessity suppose, since the Scripture ought to be the Rule of all Christians in all Ages, that St. *Paul* commands Christians in the distribution of their Favors, to prefer those whom they believe to be Orthodox, to those whom they think to be Heterodox. We can't understand him otherwise; for the Holy Spirit, which dictated the Scriptures, with regard to the future as well as to the present time, cou'd not but foresee, that <325> Christians wou'd be divided into several Sects: so that the Rule of their Manners must have bin form'd, not upon an Hypothesis of Union and Agreement, but upon that of their Divisions and Schisms. Now since upon this second Hypothesis the Preference of the Orthodox in the distribution of our Benefits stands recommended, it follows, that the meaning of the Precept must be, that we must prefer those whom we believe to be Orthodox; this Preference is a natural Consequence of the Love of Truth: St. *Paul* therefore might well have recommended it in general; and he cou'd not have recommended it in general, had it bin a Sin in all, except one Society of Christians only. If we apply this to the words, *Compel 'em to come in,* we shall plainly find, that they justify Compulsion on the part of Hereticks as well as Non-Hereticks. Methinks I hear 'em tell me, that these words of the Parable, as well as those of St. *Paul,* imply in the first place, that People shou'd be Orthodox, and afterwards compel; and prefer those of the Houshold of Faith. But this Sense is absurd; for I may say the same of the Precepts, Honor your Father, protect the Innocent, relieve those in Distress, that they oblige not till one is converted. But while a Body is in the road of Instruction and Preparation, must not he honor his Father, relieve the Poor; and if he is so unfortunate as never to find the Truth, must he live all his Life without the Practice of these Vertues? This is so ridiculous, that there's no standing by it: we must therefore say, that God directly, absolutely, and without any previous condition, wou'd have all Men, whether <326> Hereticks or Orthodox, be charitable and vertuous.

II. Another Reason is this. Our Adversarys own that Conscience which knows the Truth obliges, and that we act right in doing what it prescribes to be done. Now this cannot be true but in virtue of some, either necessary, or positive Law of the Author of all things, which we may represent in these terms: *My Will is, that Truth oblige Men to a Necessity of following it, and they who do follow it shall perform a good Action.* Now it does not appear how such a Law cou'd be signify'd to Mankind, without its authorizing reputed as well as real Truth: so that the same Law, which tells us, we may securely follow the Dictates of a Conscience which knows the Truth, intends also, that we may securely follow the Dictates of a Conscience, which believes it knows the Truth, after having us'd all the reasonable means of not being deceiv'd. What makes me speak at this rate is, that I suppose all Men may clearly and distinctly conceive, when they seriously consider it, that this is the Mind and Intention of all Legislators.

A King, who ordains all the Judges of his Kingdom to punish the Guilty, and acquit the Innocent, authorizes 'em by the same Order, to punish all those who shall appear to them Guilty, and acquit those who shall appear to them Innocent. I don't say, that he authorizes 'em to examine the Accusations and Defences only in a slight transient way, or means, he'l excuse 'em if thro Sloth or Neglect they punish the Innocent, and acquit the Guilty; I only say, he <327> authorizes 'em to govern themselves by what, upon a thorow Examination, shall appear to 'em just: so that if after such Examination, they acquit a Man who appears to 'em guilty, tho perhaps he's perfectly innocent at bottom, or if they condemn a Man in reality guilty, but who appears to them innocent; they betray their Trust, and deserve themselves to be punish'd, their Conduct discovering a manifest Contempt of the Laws, whereof they have the Execution, and a formal purpose of disobeying their Sovereign. I might alledg a hundred Examples to my purpose of particular Laws; but I shall only add two more, and leave it to the Reader to apply my Remark to those which shall offer to his own Mind.

A General, who shou'd give his Troops Orders to shew a respect for the Ladys, and spare the Lives of all the Women in the sacking of a Town, wou'd think his Orders obey'd if the Soldiers shew'd a regard for all those they had taken for Ladys, and spar'd all they had taken for Women. No matter if there were Tradesmens Wives of a good Presence, and well enough dress'd to pass upon them for Ladys; or Youths in Womens Clothes, whom they had taken for Girls: Their respecting these Tradesmens Wives, or sparing the Lives of these Youths, wou'd be no breach of their General's Orders; whereas if they had not done so, 'tis plain, they had disobey'd him: because it is to be presum'd, that the Application of the Order to such and such Persons depends upon him who is to execute it, and who is only oblig'd to use Diligence and Sincerity in the applying it. <328>

When upon a Treaty of Peace a Prince stipulates, that all his Subjects shall enjoy a free Trade in the Dominions of another neighboring Prince, 'tis certain he does not intend to authorize the Piracys of those who might put out his Colors only to surprize the Ships of other Nations, or favor their Frauds; but 'tis as certain he means, that the other Prince shall allow full Liberty of Trade to all whom he shall take to be Subjects of that Prince he treats with: so that shou'd this other Prince make him such a Confession as this, *I expel'd such and such Merchants out of my Dominions who were indeed afterwards found not to be your Subjects, tho that was more than I knew;* 'tis plain 'twou'd be confessing he had violated the Treaty, and might actually and very justly be constru'd so by his Ally. Whence it appears, that the Intention of the covenanting Powers is to stipulate, as well for those who are really Subjects, as for those who shall appear to be such, till fairly detected.

If we carefully examine it, we shall find, that all the Examples which can be alledg'd to the contrary are either in matters so obvious, that one cannot be mistaken for the other, but it must be visible the mistake was wilful; or else these Examples suppose a mistrust of the Sincerity of others, arising from our Ignorance of the Hearts of Men. But be this how it will, as God, to whom all the Thoughts of the Heart are intuitively known, can never condemn, either from Suspicion or Distrust, those who take the Appearance for the Reality; it follows, that his Methods of proceeding can only be judg'd of by the Examples I alledg. Therefore when he de-<329>clares the Law of Constraint, the Nature of things requires by a Consequence which appears inevitable, that the reputed Truth shou'd exert it self in the same way as the real.

This will appear still more plainly, if we consider the condition of those to whom this Law is declar'd; we shall see 'twou'd be altogether useless if they were oblig'd to nothing on the score of reputed Truth: for in this case they might safely make a Jest of a thousand things, which to them appear to be Truths; and because the real Truth must appear such before they can follow it, they must often remain in a State of Suspence and Inactivity with regard to this very Truth: for thus they might say to themselves, *We are not oblig'd to follow all that appears to us real and absolute Truth; How are we sure, that we now know this Truth, or that we have so much as the Appearance of Truth?* But I shan't insist on this, I content my self with saying in this place, that Man not being able to put the Law in question in execution without a previous search after the Truth, it follows, that he's oblig'd to search after it. Now as soon as he believes he has found it, he ought to follow it; and if he cou'd not safely follow it then, his Search wou'd be to no purpose. The Intention therefore of the Legislator must be, when he establishes the Rights of Truth, and the Impunity of those who follow it, to establish this for Truth in general, that is, for that which is Truth with regard to each Person: saving always a liberty to all, of enquiring into the Causes which make Falshood appear to be Truth to such and such.

III. Let's add in this one Remark more: When God says, *It is my Will that the Truth neces-*<330>*sarily oblige all Men to follow it, and they who do follow it shall do a good Action;* either he means all sort of Truths, or only some certain Truths. It's plain he does not understand all sort of Truths, but those only which are duly reveal'd and declar'd to the Man: for how can it be imagin'd, that this Truth of Fact, *God brought the Children of* Israel *out of* Egypt, *and gave 'em a Law which leads to Salvation,* shou'd be obliging, I won't say upon the People of *America,* but upon those of the Eastern parts of *Asia,* who had never so much as heard there was any such People as the Jews? How shou'd it be imagin'd, that this other Truth of Fact, the Foundation of all Christianity; JESUS CHRIST, *the Son of God, suffer'd death to redeem Mankind, rose again, and ascended into Heaven, after having declar'd what we must believe and do, in order to eternal Salvation;* shou'd be obliging, I won't say upon the People of the *Terra Australis,* who perhaps never had a thought, that there were any other Race of Men upon Earth besides themselves, but even on the Nations of *Asia* and *Africa?* I think what *Thomas Aquinas* says very reasonable, that 'twere Imprudence to believe the Articles of our Faith propos'd unbecomingly, preach'd by Persons infamous and impious, and prov'd by ridiculous Reasons.[98] If therefore all sort of Gospel-preaching does not oblige, by a much stronger Reason may we be excus'd for not believing when no one has ever told us a word of the Matter. A Cordelier[99] of our own Nation, *Francis de Sancta* Clara,* gives us <331> the Opinions of several able Divines in this matter, he's worth consulting. Let's say then confidently, that God means not, that all sorts of Truths shou'd oblige to the belief of 'em: there are only some certain Truths which do; and which are these? Such as are reveal'd and plainly enough declar'd, to render those inexcusable who believe 'em not.

This manifestly shews, that God proposes the Truth to us in such a manner as to lay us under an Obligation of examining what it is that's propos'd, and inquiring whether it be the Truth or no. From whence we may conclude, that he requires no more of us, than to examine and search after it diligently; and that when we have examin'd it to the best of our Power, he will accept of our Assent to the Objects which to us appear true, and of our Love for 'em as for a Present from Heaven. It's impossible a sincere Love for an Object, which we receive as a Gift from God upon a diligent Inquiry, and our Esteem for it in consequence of this Persuasion, shou'd be evil, even tho there shou'd be an Error in this Persuasion.

IV. This reasoning will appear much more solid, if we consider what sort of Creatures they are to whom God reveals the Truths of Religion, by what means, and with what degrees of Light. These Creatures are Souls united to Body, which for some years have no use of Reason, nor Facultys for discerning Truth from Falshood, or suspecting, that those who instruct 'em can teach 'em any thing false; so that at this Age they believe every thing that's told 'em without bogling at any Obscurity, Incomprehensibility, or Absur-<332>dity. Then they are Creatures which carry a Body about 'em, the Cause of the Soul's being incessantly taken up in its whole Capacity,

---

* *In his* Deus Natura & Gratia, *p.* 86, &c. [Franciscus a Sancta Clara, *Deus, natura, gratia,* 1634.]

98. Not found; but see *Summa theologiae,* 1, q. 46, a. 2.

99. Franciscan, member of the Order of Friars Minor.

with a thousand confus'd Sensations, and a thousand unavoidable worldly Cares. The Passions and Habits of Childhood, the Prejudices of Education, take possession of us before we are aware what it is we admit into our Minds. All this renders the Search after Truth exceeding painful: and as God is the Author of the Union of Soul and Body, and intends not that human Society shall be destroy'd, but that every one shou'd diligently follow his lawful Calling, it's evident he ought to deal by such Creatures with allowance for those Obstacles which are involuntary, and partly of his own appointment, when they obstruct their Search after Truth, and sometimes render the attaining it impossible. To this we must add one thing more, which we all know by undoubted Experience, to wit, That God has not printed any Characters or Signs on the Truths which he has reveal'd, at least not on the greatest part of 'em, by which we might certainly and infallibly discern 'em, for they are not of a metaphysical or mathematical Evidence; they don't produce in our Souls any stronger Persuasion than Falshoods do, they don't excite any Passions which Errors do not excite. In a word, we distinguish nothing in the Objects which appear to us true, and are so in reality, beyond what we find in Objects which appear true, and yet are otherwise. This being the case, there's no comprehending how God shou'd impose any necessity on Man of loving the real Truth, without imposing the same necessity of loving the reputed <333> Truth: and to speak without mincing the matter, one can't consult the Idea of Order without distinctly conceiving, that the only Law God in his infinite Wisdom cou'd have impos'd on Man with regard to Truth, is that of embracing all Objects which appear true upon the utmost use of the Lights afforded him for discerning the Truth of 'em. The infinite Wisdom of God necessarily and indispensably requires, that he shou'd proportion his Law to the State in which he himself has rang'd his Creatures; it requires then, that he sute 'em to the condition of a Soul united to a Body, which must be fed and nourish'd, live in Society, pass from a state of Childhood to youthful Age, and struggle out of its natural Ignorance by the Assistance and Instructions of its Parents. Now this Soul is incapable of discerning when its Persuasions are false, and when true; because they have both the same Signs, and the same Characters upon 'em: it must therefore either mistrust 'em all, despise 'em all, and so never perform one Act of Vertue; or else trust to 'em all upon an inward feeling, that they appear to her true and genuin, and upon a thorow Conviction of Conscience.

I know they'l tell me, that all the Obstacles to the finding the Truth which I have here spoken of, being the Consequence of the Rebellion of the first Man, and the just Chastisement of all his Posterity, God is not oblig'd to regulate himself by a Condition which Man has drawn upon himself by his own Fault; and that he has still a Right of dealing with Man upon the old foot, that is, according to the Condition from which he is fallen by the ill use *Adam* made of his Liberty. I have a thousand things to answer to this; but <334> to limit my self to what is but just necessary, I insist on the three following Observations.

I. That it no way appears, that the Weaknesses of Childhood are a consequence of the Sin of *Adam,* no more than the continual Sensations produc'd in us by the Actions of Objects on our Organs. There's not the least probability, had Man continu'd in a State of Innocence, that his Children had come into the World with sufficient measures of Reason and Judgment, or that they had not grown up by little and little in Wisdom and Understanding as they do in Stature; the Laws of the Union of Soul and Body had, during their whole Lives, diverted the Forces of the Mind, so that the conceiving things spiritual had ever bin attended with Difficulty. Thus Man being plac'd in Circumstances which wou'd have render'd the discerning Truth from Falshood very troublesom; Man, I say, as created to multiply his Kind by the way of natural Generation; Order, which is the immutable Law of God himself, requires, that God shou'd accommodate himself to this condition of Man.

In the second place I say, that all the Consequences of the Sin of *Adam,* with regard to his Posterity, such as their being inclin'd to things sensible, their depending too much upon Bodys, being thwarted by Passions and Prejudices; all these, I say, being necessary Dependancys on the Laws establish'd by God from his mere Free-will in uniting Spirits to Matter, and in ordaining, that Man shou'd multiply by the way of Generation; Order, the unalterable Law of God, requires, that he shou'd sute his dealings with Man to that condition which Man is reduc'd to by the Fall of *Adam.* <335>

In the third place, that if notwithstanding the Rebellion of the first Man, God has, with regard to the Body, perfectly accommodated himself to the condition into which Sin has brought us, as we shall see by and by; it is much more reasonable to believe, he has accommodated himself to it with regard to the Soul.

Now he had not suted himself to the State we are reduc'd to, I mean, to the necessity we are under of bestowing a great part of our time on the Affairs of this Life, to the almost unsurmountable Subjection to the Prejudices of Education, to that continual Diversion of the Forces of the Mind, by Sensations and Passions mechanically excited in us upon the presence of other Bodys; he had not, I say, accommodated himself to this State, had he absolutely condemn'd all deference for reputed Truth, and rigorously exacted the Knowledg of absolute Truth at our hands, and the sifting it out from amidst all the false Images and Appearances of it, by that weak ray of Light which is our lot in this Life, and which resembles a faint Dawn rather than the perfect Day-light, as St. *Paul* confesses when he says, that *now we see by a Glass,* &c.[100]

He has therefore impos'd no such Laws on us, nor Duty, but such as is proportion'd to our Facultys, to wit, that of searching for the Truth, and of laying hold on that, which upon a sincere and faithful Inquiry, shall appear such to us, and of loving this apparent Truth, and of governing our selves by its Precepts how difficult soever they may seem. This imports, that Conscience is given us as a Touch-stone of Truth, the Knowledg and Love of which is injoin'd us. <336> If you demand any thing further, it's plain you demand Impossibilitys; and 'tis easy to demonstrate it.

If you demand any thing further, it's plain you demand that a Man shou'd fix his Love and his Zeal on nothing but absolute Truth, known certainly and acknowledg'd for such. Now it is impossible, in our present state, to know certainly that the Truth which to us appears such (I speak here of the Truths of Religion in particular, and not of the Propertys of Numbers, or the first Principles of Metaphysicks, or Geometrical Demonstrations) is absolutely and really the Truth: for all that can be expected from us, is being fully convinc'd we are possess'd of the perfect Truth; being sure we are not deceiv'd; that others are deceiv'd, and not we; all equivocal Marks of Truth; because they are to be found in the very Pagans, and the

---

100. 1 Corinthians 13:12.

most abandon'd Hereticks. It's plain then, we can't by any infallible Mark
or Character distinguish what is really Truth when we believe it, from what
is really not so when we believe it is. This Discernment is not to be made
by us upon any evidence in the nature of the Things; for on the contrary,
all the world agree, that the Truths God has reveal'd to us in his Word, are
deep and unsearchable Mysterys, which require the captivating our Understandings to the Obedience of Faith. Nor yet is this Discernment to be
founded on the Incomprehensibility of Things; for what can be more false,
or more incomprehensible at the same time, than a square Circle, than a
first Principle essentially false, than a God the Father by natural Generation,
such as the <337> *Jupiter* of the Heathens? Nor yet on the Satisfactions of
Conscience; for a Papist is as fully satisfy'd of the Truth of his Religion, a
Turk of his, and a Jew of his, as we are of ours. Nor last of all, on the Zeal
and Courage which an Opinion inspires; for the falsest Religions have their
Martyrs, their incredible Austeritys, a Spirit of making Proselytes, which
often exceeds the Zeal of the Orthodox, and an extreme Devotion for their
superstitious Ceremonys. In short, Man has no characteristick Mark to discern the Persuasion of the Truth from the Persuasion of a Lye. So that it's
requiring an Impossibility, to require this Discernment at his hands. When
he has done all he can, the Objects he examines shall only appear to him
some false and others true. All then that can be requir'd from him, is, that
he endeavor to make those which are true appear such to him; but whether
he compasses this, or whether those which are false still appear to him
true, he ought to be left to his own Persuasion. What follows will sufficiently illustrate this matter.

　　Ever since the Protestants have quitted the Romish Communion, the
great Objection against 'em has bin, That by destroying the Authority of
the Church, they bring themselves under a necessity of finding out the
Truth by searching the Scriptures; and that this Search surpassing the Power
of any private Person, People are left destitute of any well-grounded Certainty of their Faith, since it's ultimately resolv'd into this Foundation: *I
fancy I have reason to understand the Scripture so and so, therefore I have reason
to understand it so.* We on the other hand com-<338>plain, that after having
answer'd this Objection a thousand times over, they shou'd still propose it
on all occasions, especially in *France,* where they refine and improve it as
much as possible. But it must be own'd, they have reason in one respect to

propose it over and over, because it's never fully answer'd, and never can be answer'd upon supposing, as we commonly do, that God requires of Man the Knowledg of absolute Truth, exclusive of all apparent Truth, and requires his certainly knowing that he does know it. Let's fairly own our mistake; neither Learned nor Ignorant can ever arrive at this by any methods of Search and Inquiry: for never will these methods lead us to the Criterion of Truth, which is an Idea so clear and distinct that we perceive that the thing cannot possibly be otherwise, after having fairly consider'd all the grounds of doubting, I mean all the Objections of an Adversary. It is utterly impossible to arrive at such a degree of Certainty with regard to this single Point of Fact, that such a Text of Scripture is justly render'd; that a Word which is now in the *Greek* or *Hebrew* Copys, has bin always in 'em; and that the Sense which the Paraphrasts, the Commentators, and Translators give it, is exactly that of the Author. We may have a moral Certainty of this, and founded on very high Probabilitys; but after all, this kind of Certainty may subsist in the Soul of one who is actually deceiv'd, and therefore is no infallible Character of Truth: This is not what we call *Criterium Veritatis,* that irresistible Evidence, whereby we know, for example, that the Whole is greater than its Part; that if from <339> equal things we take things equal, the remainder will be equal; that six is half twelve, *&c.*

But the Roman Catholicks are in another respect very ridiculous in pressing these Difficultys, because it's no less impossible for them to get over 'em by their Scheme, than for us by ours; and because they have no Expedient, upon their Principles, for satisfying that Condition which they suppose God exacts, to wit, the knowing from certain and undoubted Knowledg, that what they take for Truth is not an apparent Truth, such as all other Sects take for Truth, but Truth absolute and real. The way they propose for coming at this Certainty, is a thousand times more perplext than that of Protestants, as our Authors have sufficiently shewn; since in the first place it supposes the very same Difficultys and Inconveniences in appealing to the Scriptures for an Examination of all the Texts relating to the Fallibility or Infallibility of the Church; and the searching over and above into the History of former Ages, in order to discover what is really an Apostolical Tradition from that which is only so in the vain Imaginations of a Party.

In a word, there's no possibility of attaining a certain Knowledg of the

Church's Infallibility, either from Scripture, or from natural Light, or Experience; and if there were, yet they who believe it infallible, wou'd owe their being in a true Opinion to a lucky chance, without being able to assign any necessary Cause of their Belief, or perceiving in their Souls any Criterion of Truth, which another who believ'd the quite contrary might not perceive in his: for the <340> most that a Papist cou'd perceive in his own mind, wou'd be a Sentiment of Conviction affording him a perfect Tranquillity, and great Pity, Hatred, or Contempt for his Adversarys; and these might perceive the like in themselves. They can therefore each be assur'd of no more than what each inwardly feels, to wit, that they are persuaded, these that the Church is infallible, those that she is not.

This single Consideration, duly weigh'd and thorowly meditated on, were sufficient to make us perceive the Truth of what I wou'd here establish, That God in the present Condition of Man exacts no more from him than a sincere and diligent Search after Truth, and the loving and regulating his Life by it, when he thinks he has found it out. Which, as every one sees, is a plain Argument that we are oblig'd to have the same deference for a reputed as for a real Truth. Whereupon all the Objections upon the Difficultys of examining the Scriptures vanish like so many vain Fantoms; since every Man living, be he ever so ignorant, has it in his power to give one sense or other to what he reads or hears, and to perceive that such a Sense is the true; and here's what renders it Truth to him. It's enough if he sincerely and honestly consult the Lights which God has afforded him; and if, following its Discoverys, he embraces that Persuasion which to him seems most reasonable, and most conformable to the Will of God. This renders him Orthodox in the sight of God, tho thro a defect, which he cannot rectify, his Judgments may not be always a faithful Representation of the real natures of Things; just as <341> a Child is Orthodox in taking the Husband of his Mother for his natural Father, when perhaps he is a Neighbor's Child. The main thing is living vertuously afterwards; and therefore every one ought to employ all the Facultys and Forces of his Soul in honoring God by a cheerful discharge of all moral Dutys. The reveal'd Light is so clear in this respect, I mean in respect of the Knowledg of moral Dutys, that very few can mistake, if in the Sincerity of their Minds they desire to understand 'em.

There's no need of advertising my Reader, that I don't here exclude the Operations of Grace from the Act which makes us adhere to reveal'd Truths. I'm free to own, that 'tis Grace which makes us perceive that such or such a Sense of Scripture is true, and which disposes our Mind in such a manner, that precisely the Sense which is true shall appear true to us. But I maintain, that the Grace which produces this Perception, does not however afford us any certain and convincing Argument of the Sense which we believe true. We believe it firmly; and without being able to defend it against a learned and subtil Adversary, we remain convinc'd notwithstanding that it is the reveal'd Truth. Let People call this an Effect of Grace as much as they please, God forbid I shou'd contest it: still I say, that as Faith affords us no other Criterion of Orthodoxy than the inward Sentiment and Conviction of Conscience, a Criterion common to all, even the most heretical Souls; it follows; that all our Belief, whether Orthodox or Heterodox, is finally resolv'd into this, that we feel it, and it seems to us that this or that is <342> true. Whence I conclude, that God exacts not from either Orthodox or Heretick a Certainty grounded on scientifick Search or Discussion, and consequently accepts from each their loving whatever appears to 'em true. Whether the Orthodoxy I here attribute to those who are in the main deceiv'd, will avail to their Salvation, is another Question; I shall however observe, that neither the Orthodoxy of this sort of Men, nor that of those who embrace the real and absolute Truth, is that which saves: Men may believe ever so well, but without Holiness no one shall see God. 'Tis true, one might say that God in favor of absolute Orthodoxy forgives Sins committed against Conscience, which he does not forgive to those who are in Error.

This may serve to quiet the Uneasiness of those who complain, that our Principles tend to save too many Souls. Let 'em be in no pain; there will be never the less room in Heaven for them. I can't for my part see where the great harm wou'd be, of opening the Gates of Paradise somewhat wider on the side of the Acts of the Understanding, and taking that great offence out of the way of the Profane, which makes 'em hate Christianity, and hinders their conceiving God under the Idea of a Being beneficent and loving to his Creatures: I speak of that Opinion which damns all the Race of Men from *Adam* to the Day of Judgment, except a very small Handful, who had inhabited *Judaea* before the Messias, and have made but a small part of the Christian Church ever since. But be that how it will, my Opinion saves not a Soul the more; because how innocent soever a <343> Man may be with regard to his speculative Opinions, he sins often against Conscience, he does not perform what he believes it were fit he did, and what he knows wou'd be well-pleasing to that God whom he adores: and therefore without bringing those Modifications of his Soul, which were not conformable to absolute Truth, into the account at the Day of Judgment, God will find other criminal Modifications enough in it, Desires and Wills not conformable to the Idea he had of his moral Duty. Beside that there are Opinions enough to be answer'd for, which grow up with us either thro inexcusable Sloth, or Sensuality; which Opinions I'm far from excepting out of the number of punishable Transgressions.

And here a Question offers, which it may be necessary to examine in a few words: Whether all Errors spring from a ground of Corruption, lulling Men in a neglect of all means of Instruction, or prepossessing 'em for or against such and such Opinions?

That I may not grasp at too much, I shall confine my self to the present Heresys in the Christian Church, and declare my Opinion.

I don't think there's any just reason for saying, that they who find not such and such Doctrines in Scripture, are under a wilful Blindness of Understanding, or prejudic'd by a hatred for these Doctrines; and that this is the cause of their not being undeceiv'd by the Arguments of their Adversarys, or by examining into the Scriptures. There might be some ground for this Suspicion, if the Question were concerning Doctrines which thwart the Inclinations and carnal <344> Lusts of Men; but it happens, I don't know how, that these are the Points about which Christians are least of all divided. We are all agreed about the Doctrines which teach Men to live soberly and righteously, to love God, to abstain from Revenge, to forgive our Enemys, to render Good for Evil, to be charitable. We are divided about Points which tend not to make the Yoke of Christian Morality either heavier or lighter. The Papists believe Transubstantiation; the Reform'd believe it not. This makes not for the Flesh one way or other. The Papists don't believe that this Opinion obliges 'em to live a jot better, than the Reform'd think themselves oblig'd to do, from a Belief that JESUS CHRIST in his Divine Nature, and the whole Holy Trinity, is intimately present to all their Thoughts, Words, and Actions: and shou'd we come to believe Transubstantiation, we shou'd not think Holiness and Purity more necessary to Salvation than we did before. It's a mere childish Illusion then to fancy that our carnal Lusts, or a Corruption of Heart, or any other such inordinate State, hinders our perceiving a literal Sense in the words, *This is my Body.*

Now as we are all satisfy'd that the Roman Catholicks do us the greatest injustice in imputing our Aversion for this Doctrine to a Principle of Corruption; so I am inclin'd to think, we do the Socinians an injustice in saying, that a Principle of Corruption hinders their finding the Doctrine of a Trinity in Scripture: for what greater Burden wou'd this new Doctrine lay on 'em? Wou'd their Remorse be the sharper when they fell into Sin? Wou'd they think them-<345>selves the more oblig'd by it to obey God, and resist the Temptations of the Flesh and the World? It's plain they wou'd not; and that 'tis same in this respect, whether they believe a God one in Nature and Person, or whether they believe a Trinity of Persons in the Unity of the Divine Nature.

But it's Pride, it's Vanity which hinders their submitting the Light of their Reason to Divine Authority. This is precisely what the Papists object against the Reform'd, and that in a very confident, but at the same time a most unjust manner: for were there any foundation for their Reproach, 'twou'd follow that we had the Vanity to doubt even things which we believ'd were affirm'd by God. Now this is a Thought which can never enter into any Mind, not even into that of the Devil; because every Understanding that has the Idea of a God, conceives by this word a Being which knows all things to the utmost degree of Certainty, and which is not capable of a Lye: so that the Devil, who told *Eve* the contrary of what God had reveal'd to her, yet cou'd not possibly think that he himself spoke Truth; He knew that what God had told her was true. It's therefore the most extravagant monstrous Conceit to say, that Protestants have too much Pride to submit their Lights to those of God; because it's saying they join together these two Acts in their Understanding: 1. *I know that God says so.* 2. *I know that the thing is false, and that I my self know how it is better than God.* We see to what Extravagancys of Supposition these Men are driven; and we ought to stand corrected by <346> 'em, and not impute the Socinians refusing to believe a Trinity to a like Principle. The Question between Christians is not, whether what God has reveal'd be true or false, but only whether he has reveal'd this or that: and who sees not that this Dispute concerns not either the Authority or Veracity of God, any more than our doubting whether such a one did or did not say such words, calls his Faith and Honor in question?

All that can be said with any color of Reason is, That the Prejudices of Education hinder mens seeing what really is in Scripture. But as it is true in the general of all Men in the world, except a very few who change perhaps upon rational grounds, that 'tis owing to Education that they are of any one Religion rather than another (for if we had bin born in *China,* we shou'd have bin all of the *Chinese* Religion; and if the *Chinese* were born in *England,* they'd have bin all Christians; and if a Man and a Woman were transported to a desert Island, strongly persuaded, as of an Article necessary to Salvation, that in Heaven the Whole is not greater than the Part, this at the end of two or three hundred years after wou'd be an Article of Faith in the Religion of the Country): As, I say, this generally speaking is true, there's nothing more in it than a random Reproach, which all Mankind will mutually make one another with some reason in one sense, and without reason in another, so long as it shall please God to preserve Human Kind by the way of Generation; whereby there will be a necessity of our being Children before we come to discern Good and Evil, <347> and shall learn to discern 'em asunder according as our Parents think fit; who'l always be sure to instruct us in their own way, and give us a turn which we shall think our selves oblig'd to keep, as a most precious Pledg from 'em all the rest of our life. I am of opinion, that in a Dispute between two Men, one of whom has bin bred up in the true Faith, the other in a Heresy; when they come to consult Scripture, the Prejudices of one side operate as much as the Prejudices on the other; and the Malice of the Heart, the Corruption and carnal Affection are as much suspended in one as t'other. Not that I deny but Man is sometimes answerable for his Errors; as when finding a Pleasure in Actions which he knows to be wicked, he endeavors to persuade himself into a contrary Opinion; or finding Comforts in a state which he believes right, he declines all inquiry for fear of discovering it is not.

One thing I had advanc'd which needs some further Explication, to wit, That the Disorder into which our Nature is faln, has not hinder'd God's establishing Laws admirably well design'd for the Preservation of the Body; What reason then is there to think he shou'd leave us destitute with regard to the Soul? What I wou'd be at is this:

The Condition of Man is such, that there's a necessity of his avoiding certain Bodys, and drawing near to others: without this it were impossible for him long to subsist. But he is too ignorant to distinguish those Bodys which are pernicious, from those which are beneficial to him. 'Twou'd require a great deal of Meditation, of Experience and Reasoning, to discover <348> this; yet as there's a continual necessity of his approaching some Bodys and removing from others, he might die a thousand times over, if he had so may Lives to lose, before he cou'd make one suitable Movement. To obviate this Inconvenience, God has ordain'd Laws, which readily inform him when he ought to approach and when draw off from certain Objects. This is perform'd by Sensations of Pleasure or Pain, imprest on him at the presence of certain Bodys; whereby he knows not what Bodys are in themselves, this is not necessary to his Preservation, but what they are with respect to him: a Knowledg indispensably necessary, and at the same time sufficient.

What! God shall have no regard to the Sin of the first Man, he shall provide Mankind a quick and easy means of discerning what is necessary for the Preservation of the animal Life, and yet refuse him the means of discerning what is proper for preserving the Life of the Soul? This is not probable, nor conformable to the Idea of Order.

Nor let it be alledg'd, that there's at least a select Number to whom God vouchsafes this means; for this were false on the Principle I confute: nor can it be maintain'd, without allowing that the Conscience and inward Sensation we have of the Truth, is to every particular Person the Rule of what he ought to believe and practise. In effect, if what I have bin saying is false, there is not a Man in the world who acts prudently or reasonably, when he believes that what appears to him true, merits his Love and Submission; and a Christian fully persuaded <349> of all the Mysterys of the Gospel, and perceiving in his Conscience all the Vivacity of the strongest Conviction, might still have ground enough to despise it all, if he had room to doubt whether this were the Rule of his Conduct. Now for my fifth Reason.

V. This new Reason may answer two purposes: first to shew that we are oblig'd to follow the Suggestions of an erroneous Conscience; and secondly, that we may in many cases follow 'em without Sin. Let's see which way.

If what I here advance were not true, Man wou'd be reduc'd to the strangest state of Pyrrhonism that e'er was heard of: for all our Pyrrhonists hitherto have contented themselves with barring all Affirmations and Negations upon the absolute Natures of Objects; they left our moral Actions uncontested, nor ever disapprov'd Mens proceeding in the Dutys of civil Life, upon the Judgment of Conscience. But here's a Pyrrhonism which deprives us of this Liberty, and changes us into so many Stocks or Statues which can never venture to act for fear of eternal Damnation. This I prove, because the only certainty we have that all the Acts which to us appear righteous and well-pleasing to God, ought to be practis'd, is our perceiving interiorly in our Consciences that we ought to practise 'em; but this Certainty is no Criterion according to our Adversarys, that we ought to practise 'em, or that by practising of 'em we shall not incur eternal Damnation: therefore there is not a Man in the world who ought not to apprehend that he risks eternal Damnation, by practising what his Conscience suggests as ne-<350>cessary in order to Salvation. Now no prudent Man ought to do that which he only apprehends may hazard his Salvation; he ought therefore, if he'l demean himself wisely, to live like a Statue, and never give way to the Impulses of his Conscience. Who wou'd not stand amaz'd at such horrible Notions? I'm satisfy'd that any intelligent Reader, who examines this Argument without prepossession, will find it unanswerable, and own, that if a full and intire Conviction of Conscience ben't a sufficient warrant to us that we don't commit a Sin, the most Orthodox Christians are the most imprudent, and the rashest Men alive in performing any Action from the Lights and Dictates of their Consciences.

But is there any remedy for this Evil? Yes, by saying, that God having united our Soul to a Body destin'd to live amidst an infinite number of Objects, which fill it with confus'd Sensations, lively Sentiments, Passions, Prejudices, and numberless Opinions, has given it a Guide, and as I may say a Touchstone, for discerning amidst this Croud of Objects and different Doctrines that which shou'd best sute it self; that this Touchstone is Conscience, and that the interior Sentiment of this Conscience, and its full and intire Conviction, is the final Criterion of that Conduct which every one ought to keep. No matter whether this Conscience presents to one Man such an Object as true, to another as false; is it not the same in the bodily or animal Life? Does not one man's Tast tell him that such Food is good, and the Tast of another tell him it's bad? And does this Diversity hinder each from finding his Sustenance? And is it not sufficient that the <351> Senses shew us the relation which Bodys have to our selves, without discovering to us their real Qualitys? It's sufficient, in like manner, that the Conscience of every particular Person shew him not what Objects are in themselves, but their relative Natures, their reputed Truth. Every one will by this means discern his own Nourishment. He must, 'tis true, endeavor to find the best, and employ his utmost diligence in the Search; but if when fairly offer'd, his Conscience kecks, finds an utter disrelish for it, and a longing for some other thing, let him in God's name leave the one, and cleave to the other.

This Principle is exceeding fruitful towards removing a hundred otherwise unsurmountable Difficultys, to wit, that God requires no more than a sincere and diligent Search after Truth, and the discerning it by a Sentiment of Conscience, in such a manner, that if the Combination of Circumstances hinders our discovering the real Truth, and makes us find the relish of Truth in a false Object, this reputed and relative Truth is to us instead of the real Truth; as with regard to the Nourishment of the Body, it's sufficient if by our Tast we discover the relative nature of Foods. If by this I shou'd seem to suppose that God has some indulgence for us on the score of our Opinions, I declare my Belief is, that he has none with regard to those Acts which are not conformable to the Dictate of Conscience. What *Marcus Aurelius* says in the nineteenth Article of his fifth Book, appears to me divine: "He has his Conversation among the Gods, who does what the Genius will have him do, <352> which *Jupiter* has given every one for his Guide and Guardian, and which is an* Emanation of God himself,

---

* ἑκάστῳ προστάτην καὶ ἡγεμόνα ὁ Ζεὺς ἔδωκεν, ἀπόσπασμα ἑαυτοῦ. οὗτος δέ ἐστιν ὁ ἑκάστου νοῦς καὶ λόγος. [*The Meditations of the Emperor Marcus Antonius,* ed. A.S.L. Farquharson (Oxford: Clarendon Press, 1944), V.27, vol. 1, p. 90–92.]

the Reason and Understanding of every one." There's more force in the Greek.

VI. A sixth Argument which follows from the foregoing, is, That if it be suppos'd that God absolutely requires the chusing of the real Truth in matter of Religion, on pain of eternal Damnation if the Party chuses amiss; the Conversion of an Infidel to the Christian Religion, upon Principles of Reason and Prudence, will be utterly impossible: for if it ben't sufficient that this Infidel chuse what to him appears true in Christianity, if he must of necessity light precisely on the real Truth, or else be damn'd; 'twill be fit he examine the Principles of all the different Sects of Christianity, and compare 'em together, know the Objections of all sides and the Answers, inform himself of the different Foundations they go upon; and if after all no Sect appear to him to have the essential Character of Truth to its Doctrines, to wit, demonstrative Evidence; and if for want of this Evidence he find no Security in the proofs of Sentiment, in that Relish of Truth, in that interior Conviction of Conscience, which makes it appear to him that the Truth lies in this or in that Communion: if, I say, he finds no Security from all this, because, according to the Opinion of my Adversarys, it must be own'd to him, that this Conviction is not a sufficient Guide; and that for one who is <353> sav'd by following it, there are a hundred actually damn'd; it's plain that this Infidel can never resolve to quit the Errors he is in. But according to my Principles he might forsake 'em with a reasonable Assurance of doing well, when upon a sincere and exact Research, he had, by an inward Sentiment, discover'd the Truth, either in this Communion or in that.

We see then, that in the present Condition of Mankind, a State divided into several general Religions, each of which is subdivided into several Sects, who mutually anathematize each other; 'twere putting Men upon a desperate issue, and rendring their Salvation impossible, to tell 'em they are not oblig'd to follow what appears true to them: They can't but own that that which is really Truth, when it appears such, is not distinguish'd by any infallible Criterion from that which is not true, when yet it does appear so; however, that one is oblig'd, on pain of eternal Damnation, to follow what is true altho it does not appear such, and reject what is false altho it appear true.

VII. My seventh and last Reflection is, That there are a great many important Errors, which acquit from all Sin, when believ'd true, those, who were it not for this Conviction might deserve eternal Damnation. I have given, for one example, a Woman who beds with an Impostor, sincerely believing him to be her Husband, and deceiv'd by the resemblance; and a Bastard, for another example, who succeeds to the Estate of his Mother's Husband, whom he had honestly taken for his Father, and thereby deprives the true Heirs of their Right. It must be remem-<354>ber'd, that the Impostor in the first Example is very criminal, because he commits the Sin knowingly: This is the only cause of Sin in him; for were he persuaded, tho without any ground, that the Woman he beds with was his lawful Wife, in this case he wou'd be as innocent as she. I have never read of a Case of this kind, where the Mistake was reciprocal on the part of the Man as well as the Woman. In that famous Cause of *Martin Guerre,* which a Counsellor of the Parliament of *Tholouze,* call'd *Coras,* mentions in his Pleas, the Mistake was only of the Woman's side. But after all, it is not impossible that a Husband may meet with a Wife so like his own, and he be so like her Husband, that they may make an involuntary Exchange, by which two mistaken Husbands and two mistaken Wives may bed with all the Innocence in the world.

Whence I infer, that Ignorance without Malice or Affectation acquits in the most criminal Cases, as those of Adultery and Theft, and consequently in all other Cases: so that a sincere Heretick, even an Infidel, is accountable to God only for his evil doings committed under the Conscience of their being evil. For I can never persuade my self, that Actions committed by 'em from the Instincts of Conscience, I mean a Conscience not wilfully and maliciously blinded, are really Sins. If they be, I desire to know why in the fore-mention'd Examples the Facts are not constru'd to be Theft or Adultery; when yet there's as much certainty as there can be in things of this kind, that it is as impossible for a Protestant to discover the Truth of Transubstantiation, <355> as for a Man to discover that his Mother's Husband did not beget him. This is what I shou'd offer to a Roman Catholick who believ'd Transubstantiation. As to the Distinction of Persons and Nature in God, there's reason to believe, that a Turk or a Jew wou'd find it as hard to frame their Minds in such a manner as to be intirely convinc'd of these Truths, as to discover the Intrigues that their Mother might have had. I even believe there are a great many Orthodox Peasants, who are no otherwise Orthodox with regard to these Mysterys, than as they are honestly resolv'd not to believe any thing that destroys the Doctrines of the Church: for any thing further, they have not the least Idea of 'em, that's conformable to the Truth. The *English* * *Cordelier,* whom I had cited before, observes, that the subtle *Scotus* teaches, there's an invincible Ignorance with relation to these Points, in a Man of a very mean Understanding, who comprehends not what is meant by the Terms Person or Nature; and that it's sufficient for this sort, if they believe in gross as the Church believes. This *Cordelier* requires explicit Acts of Faith only concerning things obvious and easily conceiv'd, *Quae sunt grossa ad capiendum,* says he in his barbarous *Latin;* such as that JESUS CHRIST was born, that he suffer'd, *&c.* He likewise says, That to the end an Ignorance be inexcusable and not invincible, 'tis not sufficient that it might have bin remov'd, if the Party had desir'd Instruction; but that he must also have reflected at some time or other on what he was <356> ignorant of: for if it never came into his Mind, he believes the Ignorance invincible; because it is impossible a Man shou'd inform himself of that which never came into his Thoughts. What he wou'd say is undoubtedly this, That to render an Ignorance sinful, there must have bin a Thought and Reflection made by the Party; that he was ignorant of certain things of which he might have got a thorow Information; but that he banishes the Thoughts of 'em out of his Mind. This seems but reasonable: for the State in which one is utterly destitute of the Idea of any particular thing, not depending on our Will; because to will that such an Idea shou'd not offer, this very Idea must be actually in the Mind; it follows that this State is involuntary: there's therefore no Sin in being in such a State. Now no one can get out of this State, unless the Idea of the thing in which we shou'd have bin instructed offer; and it depends not on our Will, that an Idea which is absolutely unknown to us present it self to our Understanding: the Ignorance therefore is invincible (tho in its nature easily remov'd) if the Party has never bethought himself that he was ignorant of such a thing. I cited another Author who is a† Jansenist, and who has these remarkable words: *It's very true, that the Law of Nature enjoins in general the endeavoring to*

---

* Francis a Sancta Clara, *ubi supra.* [See above, p. 258, note.]

† Traité de la Foi humane, *Par. 1. ch.* 8. [See above, p. 111, note 49.]

make a right use of our Reason, and the avoiding Error as much as possible, and Falshood of what kind soever; but it does not for all this condemn those of Sin, who are unaffectedly deceiv'd about Matters which they are not oblig'd to know; as <357> St. *Austin* expresly decides in his Book of the Profitableness of Faith.

These Words, *Which they are not oblig'd to know,* are somewhat indefinite; every one will stretch or stint 'em according as he best finds his own Account. For my part I'm of opinion, that natural Light, or the Idea of Order, shews, that we are not oblig'd to know any thing but what is sufficiently notify'd; nor to believe any thing but what has bin evinc'd by sound Reasons. But this sufficiency of Notification, this soundness of Reasons supposes an essential Proportion to the Nature of the Understandings of those who are to be instructed; for the Degree of Evidence, which is sufficient for the persuading one Man, is not so for another. And who can know these Proportions but God alone? Who but he can tell how far the Force of Education reaches, and where the ill use of our Free-will begins? The Effects of each are very different; those of the first beget Habits in us by a kind of Mechanism, which we seem not answerable for, because we receive 'em without suspecting any ill, and before we are capable of having the least mistrust of what our Parents teach us. 'Tis very probable, shou'd People agree in making all the Children of a City believe, that 'twas the Will of God they shou'd kill all the Inhabitants of another City, they wou'd firmly believe it, and never come off of this belief, unless they went thro a new course of Instruction. So that when the Decalogue were made known to them, it must be prest upon 'em with much stronger Reasons, than wou'd be necessary for others who had a better Education. Education is undoubtedly ca-<358>pable of making the Evidence of Truths of Right utterly disappear.

I have one Objection more to answer. If God, say they, contented himself with every one's embracing and loving that which was the Truth in relation to him, what need he have left us a Scripture? I answer, That this hinders not but the Scripture may be very necessary, because in matters which are perfectly clear it's an uniform Rule of Conscience to all Christians; and in those which are less clear, 'tis respected by all Partys, since all agree, that be the Sense of the Scriptures what it will, it's infallibly true. So that it serves in the general, as a Rule for all Christians; and the rankest Hereticks, who search it for Proofs of their Tenets, do even in this pay a Homage to the Word of God. Besides, that tho God is content that every one, after having search'd for the Truth to the best of his Power, shou'd hold to that which to him appears such, he yet wills and intends, that Men shou'd rectify their Opinions if they can; and that others endeavor by Reasons to the best of their Power, the setting those aright, who have not made the happiest Choice for themselves: now the Scriptures are very useful this way. St. *Jerom** makes a Remark, that as long as the *Babylonians* left the sacred Vessels of the Temple of *Jerusalem* in the Temples of their Idols, God was not offended at 'em, because after all they put 'em to a sacred and religious Use; but when once they chang'd the Property, and employ'd 'em to profane Uses, God punish'd their <359> Sacrilege. *Videbantur,* says he, *rem Dei secundum pravam quidem opinionem, tamen Divino cultui consecrasse.*[101] These words do plainly favor my Hypothesis, and prove in particular, that as long as a Heretick owns the Scripture as his Topick, and Magazin of all his Proofs, he leaves God the whole Glory of his Authority inviolate in general, tho he swerves in particular Applications, and thro mere Error, from the Mind of God: and there's something of Illusion, or at least a lack of Consideration, in pretending that of two Men, one of whom understands the Scriptures better than the other, the first must necessarily have a greater Reverence for the Scriptures and for God than the second. For I wou'd fain know from those who pretend so, whether it is not manifest, that whoever gives a Text of Scripture the true Sense, does it, not because it is the true Sense, but because he believes it so, and that God wou'd be offended at him, if he understood it in any other. I can't conceive any thing in the best Interpreter beside this that can render him well pleasing to God in this particular matter, or found the good Disposition that he is in. Then I ask 'em again, Whether they don't think, that the reason why another gives a false sense to Scripture is, not that this Sense

---

* In Cap. 6. Danielis. [Rather, cap. 5. Migne, *Patrologia Latina,* vol. 25, col. 519.]

101. "They seemed a thing consecrated to divine worship, though according to a perverted opinion of God."

is false and that he believes it false, but because he believes it really true, and believes that God wou'd be displeas'd with him if he understood it otherwise. I don't desire that this be granted with regard to every particular Heretick; yet I think it can't be deny'd with regard to some: for 'twere surely the strangest, the har-<360>diest, and even the most extravagant thing in nature to decide, that these two Acts concur in the Soul of every Heretick in the World: *I find such a Sense of Scripture false, and unworthy of God, yet I am resolv'd to maintain that this Sense is the true; and my being persuaded, that by maintaining this Sense I shall teach a Falshood which shall offend God, is a ruling Motive with me.* It must be allow'd then, that whatever begets the good Disposition of an Orthodox, with regard to his interpreting Scripture, may be found in a Heretick, and therefore that one does not necessarily love and reverence God and his holy Word more than the other.

Add to this, that from the Idea we are able to form of a Person of the most consummate Wisdom and Justice, we must conceive, that if having given his Servants Orders upon his taking a Journy into a distant Country, he found on his Return that they apprehended 'em differently; and whilst unanimously agreed that his Command was the only Rule they ought to follow, the only Dispute among 'em was concerning the Command it self; he wou'd declare they had all an equal regard for his Orders, but that some had a better Understanding than others, and took the true meaning of his Words; It's certain that we conceive clearly and distinctly that he cou'd declare nothing but this; and therefore right Reason requires, that we shou'd conceive the same of God, as to what he shall declare concerning those who are Orthodox, and Hereticks, from a sincere Principle. Now an Excellence of Understanding is not that which makes one Man more acceptable to God than another, even tho he shou'd employ it faithfully to the finding out <361> the Truth, but the good Will and sincere Intention of applying one's utmost Forces and Facultys to the finding out and practising what God requires of us.

I conclude, by saying, That what Care soever God takes to give us general Rules, whether by natural Light or by his reveal'd Word; still we each of us stand in need of a particular Rule, which is Conscience, by the favor of which we give those the Lye, who without it might tell us there was no certainty in any thing, and apply this Sentence to us:

Incerta haec si tu postules
Ratione certa facere, nihilo plus agas
Quam si des operam ut cum ratione insanias.[102]

∞ CHAPTER XI ∞

The Result from what has bin prov'd in the two foregoing Chapters; and a Confutation of the literal Sense, let the worst come to the worst.

I Enter'd upon this tedious and very abstruse Question about the Rights of Conscience, on purpose to cut off Persecutors from all their starting Holes, when ask'd, whether they themselves wou'd take it well that others shou'd persecute them. They answer, 'Twere very unjust, because they teach the real Truth, and upon this account have an incommunicable Privilege of <362> persecuting and vexing Hereticks. 'Twas necessary to sound this Answer to the bottom, and destroy all the Cavils that can be offer'd in its defence, which is the reason of my dwelling so long upon it. Let us now briefly sum up the Truths which we think have bin made out.

The Conclusion we draw from the whole is, That if God had commanded the Professors of Truth to persecute the Professors of a Lye, these apprehending this Command as directed to themselves, wou'd be oblig'd in Conscience to persecute the Professors of Truth, wou'd be guilty of an Offence if they did not, and be acquitted in the sight of God, provided their Ignorance were neither malicious nor affected.

This manifestly shews, that the Doctrine of Persecutors, founded on the words *Compel 'em to come in,* opens a door to a thousand dreadful Confusions, in which the Party of Truth must suffer most, and this without any just ground of Complaint.

But let us suppose, that the Right of persecuting belong'd in reality to the Orthodox alone; let us suppose, that the true Church has indeed that Privilege, which some wild Phanaticks have boasted of, to wit, that the most

---

102. Terence, *Eunuch*, I.61: "If you tried to turn these uncertainties into certainties by a system of reasoning, you'd do no more good than if you set yourself to be mad on a system"; translated J. Sargeaunt, Loeb Classical Library, 1920, p. 241.

criminal Actions are allowable, and cease to be Sins when committed by her; let us suppose, that the false Churches when they use the Law of Retaliation, are really in the wrong; yet what will she gain by this? Nothing more than the comfort of saying, That we shall see at the Day of Judgment which was right and which wrong. Now as this is a Remedy, which can't obstruct that dismal Torrent of Calamitys which must overwhelm <363> the World, if all those who believe themselves the true Church persecuted the rest; 'tis plain, it's a most ridiculous Conceit, that only the Orthodox are allow'd to persecute, since the very Supposition is enough to oblige each Sect to turn Persecutress, each believing it self the only true and pure Religion. The persecuted Religions might talk as long as they pleas'd, and say they are the only Party of Truth, and that God will declare as much when he comes at the last day to judg the World; the others will answer, That then will be the time they shall find their Confusion, and the Justice of persecuting 'em upon Earth, and the tyrannical Injustice with which when uppermost they durst persecute other Religions. Thus the Complaints of each persecuted tormented Party must be resolv'd into a long and tedious Debate, upon the Controversys which divide 'em; and the uppermost during the Discussion must persecute freely, which as every one sees and feels can only present the Image of the most fearful and lamentable Desolation. Whence we ought to conclude, That tho there were really grounds for interpreting the Parable in the literal Sense, yet 'twere better not, for fear of occasioning such a State of Misery in the World. 'Tis a Right which ought to lie for ever dormant, nor any Proceedings be grounded upon it, which are not warrantable in all Mankind.

I here intended to examine the Reasons which St. *Austin* has display'd with a great deal of Pomp and Industry, in defence of Persecution; but as this Commentary is too bulky already, having grown under my Pen much faster than I imagin'd, I must adjourn this part to a particular <365> Treatise on this Doctrine of St. *Austin*'s. I hope I shall be able to take in the whole in a few words, having by the way already enervated most of the Paralogisms and little Maxims of this great Bishop of *Hippo*.

FINIS.

<367>

A
Philosophical Commentary
ON
These Words of the Gospel,
LUKE XIV. 23.
Compel them to come in, that my House may be full.

The Second Volume.

CONTAINING

Remarks on those Letters of St. AUSTIN which are usually alledg'd for the compelling of Hereticks, and particularly to justify the late Persecution in *France.*

WITH

A Supplement, proving, That Hereticks have as much Right to persecute the Orthodox, as the Orthodox them.

Translated from the *French* of Mr. BAYLE,

Author of the Great *Critical and Historical Dictionary.*

LONDON, Printed by *J. Darby* in *Bartholomew-Close,* and sold by *J. Morphew* near *Stationers-Hall.* 1708.

PART III.

UPON

Those LETTERS of St. *Austin,* which contain

an Apology for the compelling of Hereticks.

As in the Entrance of the first Part of this Commentary I said,[103] I wou'd
not dwell on any particular Circumstances of the Text which I design'd to
give a Comment on, but confute the literal Sense consider'd in it self, and
attack it upon general Principles: so in the Entrance on this Third Part I
think fit to signify, that I shall have no regard to any particular Circumstances of St. *Austin,* of the Donatists, of the Century, or the Country in
which they liv'd;[104] but endeavor, from the most general Heads of Proof,

---

103. See above, p. 65.

104. During the persecutions of Christians under the Emperor Diocletian some
Christian clergy had surrendered their sacred books, the Bible, to the persecutors, who
burnt them. After the persecution ended the North African province of the Church was
divided by a controversy between those who had handed over the Bible and those who
had not. The followers of Donatus held that clergy who were *traditores* ("handers over")
could not validly baptize or ordain. This view was rejected by the Roman Church as
heresy, on the argument that the sacraments of baptism and ordination are effective by
Christ's power, independently of the character of the human minister. Augustine (in
our translation called "St. Austin") argued that the Catholics were justified in applying
to the Roman Emperor to repress the Donatists by force. The emperors Constantine (d.
337) and Honorius (d. 423) did issue edicts against the Donatists, which were enforced

to shew, that St. *Austin*'s Reasons, consider'd in themselves, and abstracted from all their disparaging Circumstances, are nevertheless false. It's nothing to me if St. *Austin* was formerly of Opinion, that no one ought to be constrain'd in matters of Religion; or if he chang'd his Opinion purely upon seeing the Successes of the Imperial Laws <370> in bringing in Hereticks, which is one of the wretchedest ways of Reasoning that can be imagin'd; it being just the same as saying, *Such a Man has heap'd up much Riches, therefore he has employ'd only lawful Means.* Nor does it concern me, that St. *Austin* was of such or such a Spirit, of such or such a Character; nor yet, that the Donatists were a ridiculous Set of Men who separated from the Church upon mere trifles. My design is to examine St. *Austin*'s Reasons as if they were drop'd from the Clouds, without regard to Persons or Partys; tho I shou'd rather incline to defend so great a Man against those who accuse him of Insincerity and Unfairness in this Dispute. I am quite of another Opinion, and believe verily he spoke as he thought: but being a well-meaning Man, and carry'd away by an overardent Zeal, he readily caught at any thing that seem'd to support his Prejudices, and believ'd he did God good Service by finding out Arguments at any expence for what he believ'd to be the Truth. He had a great share of Intelligence, but he had more Zeal; and so much as he indulg'd his Zeal (now he indulg'd it very freely) so much he fell away from solid Reasoning, and from the purest Lights of true Philosophy. This is the real state of his Case: a Spirit of Devotion and Zeal is undoubtedly a great Blessing, but 'tis sometimes at the expence of the Reason and Judgment; the Party grows credulous, he takes up with the wretchedest Sophisms, provided they advance his Cause; he paints out the Errors of his Adversarys in the frightfullest colors: and if he be of a hot Spirit withal, what ground can he stand upon, what Efforts will he not make to <371> wrest Scripture, Tradition, and all sort of Principles? He'l find his own account in all, he'l strain all; in short, he'l mar all. I don't think ever any one made a juster Judgment of St. *Austin* than one

---

by Roman officials in North Africa. Augustine had earlier held that religious dissenters should not be coerced ("A man cannot believe unless he is willing"), but he changed his mind when converted Donatists said they were glad to have been coerced. See Joseph Lecler, *op. cit.,* vol. I, pp. 53–59.

P. Adam a Jesuit, let *P. Norris* say what he please to the contrary in his *Vindiciae Augustinianae.*[105] But as I said before, it's nothing to me, whether St. *Austin* was this or that; my business is to examine his Arguments abstractedly from all Prejudices. Let's begin then and examine the two Letters of this Father, lately printed by themselves, according to the last *French* Version, by the Archbishop of *Paris*'s Orders, with a Preface at the head of 'em, part of which we have already confuted in the Preliminary Discourse; the whole is entitl'd, *The Conformity of the Conduct of the Church of* France *for reuniting the Protestants, with that of the Church of* Africk *for reuniting the Donatists to the Catholick Church.*[106] The first of these two Letters is the 93*d* of the new Edition, and the 48*th* of the old, written in the Year 408. to *Vincentius,* a Donatist Bishop, in answer to one from him, expressing his Surprize at the Inconstancy of this Father; who having formerly bin of Opinion, that it was not lawful to employ the Secular Arm against Hereticks, nor any other means besides the Word of God and sound Reason, had chang'd from white to black on this important Point. Let's hear St. *Austin*'s first Remark.

105. Henry Noris, *Vindiciae Augustinianae, quibus S. Doctoris scripta adversus Pelagianos ac Semipelagianos a recentiorum censuris asseruntur* (Augustinian Vindications, by which the holy Doctor's [Augustine's] writings against the Pelagians and Semipelagians are freed from the censures of recent writers), 1675. For Adam see *The Catholic Encyclopaedia,* http://www.newadvent.org/cathen/01134d.htm.

106. See above, p. 41, note. Bayle quotes extracts only, sometimes without indicating omissions, and sometimes paraphrases. In the modern numbering the Letters of St. Augustine he comments on are: 93, 185, 87, 105, 173, 89. All of these except 105 are available in translation at http://www.newadvent.org/fathers/1102.htm. They are all translated by Sister Wilfrid Parsons for *The Fathers of the Church* (Washington: Catholic University of America Press, 1955–), vols. 18 and 30.

ΙΟΟΙ   I. ST. AUSTIN'S WORDS   ΙΟΟΙ

*I am even much more a Lover of Peace now than when you knew
me in my younger days at* Carthage; *but the Donatists being so
very restless <372> as they are, I can't but persuade my self, that
it's fit to restrain 'em by the Authority of the Powers ordain'd
by God.*

ANSWER

Here's surely one of the scurviest Lead's that ever was seen, and the most
capable of begetting a Suspicion of St. *Austin*'s Honesty: for this plainly
is talking like a Man who had a mind to hide the true state of the Question,
who endeavor'd to change the Dice upon his Readers, who is loth to speak
out; in fine, who wou'd stick at no Artifice to gain his point. Wou'd not a
Body infer from the plain and obvious meaning of these words, that the
Reason upon which St. *Austin* believ'd it lawful to call in the Secular Arm
against Hereticks, was the Restlesness of their Temper tending to disturb
the publick Peace? If so, 'twas unreasonable applying to the Prince against
such of 'em as liv'd retir'd in their own Houses, and gave no manner of
Disturbance; this is what might fairly be collected from the words before
us; yet this was far from being St. *Austin*'s true Opinion: he was intirely
for making Laws against all Hereticks, even the most meek and inoffensive,
in hopes the smart of temporal Punishments might oblige 'em to come
over into the Unity of the Church; and had he not bin of this Opinion,
nothing wou'd be more needless or more pitiful than the Reasons which
he here lays out with so much Pomp. It's plain then he has made use of an
artificial and fallacious Preamble, or, which to me seems much more probable, fallen into a thought the wrongest, and the most opposite in the World
<373> to the Justness of one who knows how to write and reason solidly.

   For did ever any one doubt, that it was the Duty of Princes to enact
wholesom Laws against Hereticks who disturb the publick Peace, who are
of a turbulent persecuting Spirit, and so forth? Did ever any one doubt,
but the best Men may and ought to exhort Princes, who are slack in pro-
viding the proper Remedys, to restrain such Men by the Sword which God

has given into their Hands? 'Tis the Duty of Princes to repress not only Hereticks of a factious, turbulent and restless Spirit, but those of the Orthodox Party too, who fall into the same Irregularitys. What does St. *Austin* mean then when he says, he thinks it very fitting to restrain by the Authority of the higher Powers, the Boldness of Hereticks in forcing the World, and oppressing their Neighbor? Was this the Point in question? Cou'd any one have the least ground to wonder at this Father's being of such an Opinion? Is there any need of writing Apologys in defence of it? Nothing therefore cou'd be more foreign than the laying down such a Principle at the head of such a Work, in which the business in hand was to justify, not any Laws restraining the Insolences of the Donatists, but those directly and immediately enacted against their Errors; seeing they condemn'd 'em all indiscriminately to temporal Punishments, in case they persisted in their Opinions.

This the* Sieur *Ferrand,* one of the chief Ad-<374>vocates for Persecution, has own'd, and prov'd too by a Passage from St. *Austin.* He has shewn, *That the Insolence of the Donatists was indeed the Source and first Occasion of the Imperial Laws against 'em; yet that there was another, and which one may call the next and immediate Cause, or to speak more properly the principal Motive which inclin'd* Honorius *to enact severe Laws against the Donatists,* to wit, the Horror he had conceiv'd for their Heresy and Schism. The Proofs he alledges are very convincing: for he observes, that *Honorius* makes no mention of their Crueltys, that his Laws are general against all the Donatists; that he does not say, the Punishments ordain'd shall be inflicted unless they forbear their Violences; but on the contrary, declares he's resolv'd to extinguish the Sect, to condemn 'em to these Punishments unless they return to the Catholick Church, and inflict 'em as oft as they exercise any Act of Worship in their own way. These Proofs, I say, are convincing, the thing speaks it self; for when the design is only to restrain the Insolences of any Set of Men, the Lawgiver contents himself with appointing Punishments for such as offend, and ne'er means to punish even those

---

* Discours. Prelim. de sa Reponse a l' Apologie pour la Reformation. [Louis Ferrand, *Réponse à l'Apologie pour la réformation, pour les réformateurs et pour les réformez* (Answer to the apology [by Jurieu] for the reformation, the reformers and the reformed), 1685.]

who refrain. What rare Management wou'd it be, if to put a stop to the circulating Lampoons and scandalous Libels, the Government shou'd appoint Punishments for those who religiously forbore, either reading or vending 'em; or if to check the mutinous temper of a County or Province, the Prince shou'd threaten to ravage it even when it kept within Duty, and the very Citys within such a District, which never had a hand in the Rebellion? I say further, that had the Emperors meant <375> no more than just restraining the Boldness of the Donatists, and the Fury of the *Circoncellions*,[107] there had bin no need of enacting new Laws: there were Laws enough ready made to their hand, and known to every Magistrate of the Empire, against Robbers, Ruffians, against all in general who exercise any Violence on their fellow-Citizens. Nothing more was needful than giving the Judges a Charge to put the Laws in execution against the *Circoncellions;* as now in *Italy* it's sufficient to bid the Magistrates proceed against the *Banditti* according to the rigor of the antient Laws in that case. For my part, shou'd a Revolution happen suddenly in *France,* I can't think there wou'd be any need of enacting particular Laws against those Officers of Dragoons, who had plunder'd the Hugonots Houses: 'twere sufficient to look into the common Law-Books or Statute-Book, under the heads which relate to the punishing Robbers, or House-breakers; and in case they cou'd produce no Edict or Order of Court for sacking of Houses, they might legally be punish'd as Infringers of the most sacred Laws of Civil Society. So notorious is it, that every private Person, who does wrong to his Neighbor, who smites him, who robs him of his Goods, who forces him to Actions which he has an Abhorrence for, is *ipso facto* guilty of the Violation of the Fundamental Laws of the Commonwealth, and consequently obnoxious to Punishment, without any need of new Laws in his behalf. This wou'd be understood of course, tho there were no written Laws in a State; all Society essentially supposing a Disturber of the publick Peace, and whoever abuses his fellow-Citizen, justly punishable. <376>

But here it will be proper to obviate a Difficulty; to wit, that by a Disturber of the publick Peace we are not to understand those who are an

---

107. The Circumcelliones (in our translation "Circoncellions") were bands of Donatists who physically attacked Catholics, i.e. those who accepted the Roman view.

accidental Cause of mighty Combustions and Revolutions in the world: for in this case JESUS CHRIST and his Apostles had bin justly reputed Disturbers of the State, as they attack'd the establish'd Religion, and set up Altar against Altar, whence infinite Disorders must of necessity have happen'd in human Society. I mean then by Disturbers of the publick Peace only those who scour the Country, plunder Villages and Towns, and rob upon the Highway; they who stir up Seditions in a City; they who smite and buffet their Neighbor, as soon as they have got an advantage of him; in a word, they who won't suffer their Fellow-Citizens to live in the full and peaceable Enjoyment of all their Rights, Privileges, and Property. It's evident on this foot, that neither JESUS CHRIST nor his Apostles were Disturbers of the publick Peace; for they contented themselves with shewing Men the Falseness of certain Opinions, and the Iniquity of certain Actions; they whom they converted became more dutiful and more obedient to the Laws of the Empire than ever, and therefore the progress of their new Doctrine cou'd not directly prejudice the State. 'Twas lawful for every one to continue Jew or Pagan if he pleas'd, nor were they who quitted Judaism or Paganism allow'd to misuse those who did not: Thus it was wholly in the World's power to be as much at peace under these new Preachers as it was before; and consequently the Laws of the Emperors against 'em were unjustly founded. <377> From the same Principle it were easy to shew, that neither *Wickliff,* nor *John Huss,* nor *Luther,* nor *Calvin,* nor *Zuinglius,* ought to have bin treated as Disturbers of the publick Peace, tho they brought their Actions against Doctrines which had enjoy'd a long and profound Peace in the world: and unless it were prov'd, that they actually forc'd those to come in to 'em whom they found averse to a Reformation (in which case they had bin more detestable for their Character of Persecutors, than venerable for that of Reformers) the World cou'd have nothing to alledg against 'em upon this particular Article which concerns the publick Tranquillity.

The better to establish my Opinion, I observe, that we must never render a Doctrine odious which we believe false, by exposing it on such a side as is common to it, with that Doctrine which we believe true. Seeing Error therefore and Truth have this in common, that when they make their first appearance in a Country where People are settled in a contrary Religion, they equally occasion Stirs and Disturbances; 'twere absurd to maintain, that they who come to preach an erroneous Doctrine are punishable, for this reason only, that they endanger the Peace resulting before from an Uniformity of Worship and Opinion; because this Peace and Uniformity in a Country which had slumber'd in Error, had bin altogether as much endanger'd and disturb'd by sending Preachers of Truth and Righteousness among 'em: We must therefore equally acquit Truth and Error of the Consequences which accidentally attend 'em. Whence it appears, that <378> had the Donatists bin guilty of no other mischief than the making a Schism in the Church, which before was perfectly united, the Emperor's treating 'em as Disturbers of the publick Peace had bin very ill founded, and so had their compelling 'em by violent methods to return into the bosom of the Church. All the Constraint these Emperors cou'd lawfully have exercis'd on the Donatists, was the punishing very severely such of 'em as oppress'd the Catholicks, or who reducing 'em to Beggary, extorted a feign'd Consent to receive a second Baptism. If their penal Laws had had no other view than the restraining Attempts so opposite to the Law of Nature and Nations, and destructive of the most sacred and inviolable Rights of human Society; St. *Austin* might not only have spar'd himself the trouble of an Apology to justify his Approbation of 'em, but wou'd really have bin very much to blame if he had not approv'd 'em. But as Mr. *Ferrand* has fully prov'd, the Laws of these Emperors had quite another view, and aim'd at constraining the Donatists to forsake their Sect, from the apprehensions of leading a miserable and melancholy Life. Now this is it, which is not only opposite to Christianity, but even to Reason and Humanity; insomuch as St. *Austin*'s undertaking the Defence of it is scandalous to the last degree. But let's return to the Examination of the Letter.

train II. ST. AUSTIN'S WORDS train

Accordingly we have the satisfaction of seeing several oblig'd by this means to return to the Catholick Unity. <379>

ANSWER

Here's a fresh Symptom of that Something, I don't know what, which obliges Men to hide the flaws and faulty sides of a Cause. St. *Austin* durst not speak out at first dash, that 'twas very fitting to have recourse to the Secular Arm for the obliging Hereticks to sign a new Formulary; this wou'd have look'd odious, if propos'd nakedly and without any varnish: How does he order it then, I don't say from any dishonest Principle, but purely from the power of his Prejudices? He turns his Reader's eyes off of this Object, and entertains him with another; which, far from being of a shocking nature, carries its own reason with it, to wit, That it's fitting and commendable to call in the Authority of the Magistrate, for keeping the Peace against the Attempts of a pack of factious, seditious, persecuting Hereticks. But he betrays himself, or rather he owns the Fact in indirect terms, when he boasts that the Imperial Laws had oblig'd a great many Donatists to change sides. 'Twas for this end then that these Laws were enacted; and 'twas on the Donatists as persisting in their Sect, that the temporal Punishments were inflicted, and not simply as exercising Violences on the Orthodox. Now this is what he ought to have declar'd at first, and promis'd roundly to have justify'd; and then there had bin some meaning and drift in his Discourse; whereas, as it now stands, it's only a jumble of Sayings and Sentences, very ill plac'd and very ill put together, *scopae dissolutae:* He ought, I say, to have declar'd, that it's fit to <380> have recourse to earthly Powers for the obliging Men to change Religion; and then the words cited from him in the second Paragraph had had some color of an Argument either good or bad; for then St. *Austin*'s Reasoning might have stood thus:

Those Laws which oblige a great many to return to the Unity of the Church, are wholesom and good.

Now the Laws commanding the Donatists to return to this Unity, upon pain of incurring the severest Punishments, have oblig'd many to return:

Therefore they are wholesom and good.

No one will wonder for the future, that all the mercenary Pens employ'd by the modern Convertists shou'd shift and double so often, without ever daring to come to the true state of the Question; when St. *Austin,* the great Patriarch of these unhappy Apologys, is so loth to speak out, that he'l say only by halves, and as 'twere faltering, what the Substance of the Dispute is between him and the Person he wou'd confute.

∞   III. ST. AUSTIN'S WORDS   ∞

The Power of Custom was a Chain never to be broken by 'em, if they had not bin struck with a Terror of the Secular Arm, and if this salutary Terror had not apply'd their Minds to a Consideration of the Truth, &c.

ANSWER

Here's the grand Common-Place, and if I may use the Expression, the Hackny Argument of all our <381> modern Convertists. I refer 'em, if they please, to the first and second Chapters of the Second Part of my *Commentary;*[108] and promise, if they answer what's urg'd there, to confute this grand Maxim of theirs anew. But in good earnest I don't think they can ever offer any thing of weight against it: for what is there to be said against a thing as clear as Noon-day? to wit, That all who set up for making penal Laws against Sectarys, will plead with as good a face as St. *Austin* and the Convertists of *France,* that they intend no more than just rouzing the World out of that Lethargy into which it is fallen, and breaking the Chain of Error by the fear of temporal Punishment? Will they say, that they who turn this Maxim against the Orthodox miss their aim, and consequently can't make the same boasts as St. *Austin* and the booted Apostles of *France?* To this I have but one word to offer. Were the Catholicks of *England* Orthodox in the days of our glorious Queen *Elizabeth,* or not? And did they change from Inclination, or from some degree of Constraint? They dare not pretend either that they were not Orthodox, or that Queen *Elizabeth*

---

108. See above, Part II, Chapters 1 and 2, pp. 137–61.

brought 'em over purely by methods of Lenity and Instruction: They must therefore own that such Effects as their Violences have upon others, such the Violences of others have upon them. To which I might add this one Question more: The Christians whom the *Saracens* oblig'd to change Religion, were not they Believers? How then came the Armys of *Mahomet* and his Successors to make such numbers of 'em abjure? The truth of the matter is this; There are new Converts of all sides, <382> who pretend to be mightily pleas'd with their new Religion: This is one sure way of making their court, and a fair step it is to Preferment.

⥾ IV. ST. AUSTIN'S WORDS ⥾

If a Man saw his Enemy ready to throw himself down a Precipice in the Paroxisms of a raging Fever, wou'd it not be rendring him evil for evil to let him take his own way, rather than with-hold and bind him hand and foot? Yet this frantick Person wou'd look on such an Act of Goodness and Charity only as an Outrage, and the Effect of Hatred for him: But shou'd he recover his Health and Senses, he must be sensible that the more Violence this mistaken Enemy exercis'd on him, the more he was oblig'd to him. How many have we even of the Circoncellians, *who are now become zealous Catholicks, and who had never come to themselves, if we had not procur'd the Laws of our Emperors to bind 'em hand and foot, as we do Madmen?*

ANSWER

It's one of the greatest Infirmitys of human Nature, that nothing will go down with Men but popular Notions, and these prov'd to 'em from popular Topicks, which they are so powerfully accustom'd to, that no Reason which is not popular will move; and whatever is so, will perfectly run away with their Senses. Herein lies the main Strength of St. *Austin,* and of most others of his Profession: They erect themselves an Empire or Palace, inhabited only by *Swissers,* lofty Common-Places of a popular strain, Simi-<383> litudes, Examples, and Figures of Rhetorick; by these they lord it over the People, they work 'em up and lay 'em again at pleasure, as *Aeolus* did the

Sea by the Ministration of the Winds. The Comparison is very just, for it's no more than a Puff of Wind which produces all these effects o' both sides. Let 'em shut up then, and bluster in these Mansions as much as they please; *Illa se jactet in aula, Aeolus & clauso ventorum carcere regnet:*[109] still I shall endeavor to shew that there's nothing in it more than mere Wind.

Can any thing be thought on less just at bottom, or less solid, than this Comparison of St. *Austin*'s between a frantick Person bound hand and foot to keep him from throwing himself out at a window, and a Heretick forcibly restrain'd from following the Motions of his Conscience? I must repeat it once again: Had they only procur'd Laws for curbing the Fury and Insolence of the Donatists, and punishing the Injurys done by 'em to the Catholicks, for example, by condemning those to the Gallys who beat a Catholick, or rob'd him of his Goods; nothing were more commendable, nor had it bin at all necessary to fly for succor to the Comparison alledg'd: but the Question in dispute was concerning the Justice of certain Laws which decreed Servants and Laborers to the Bastinade, to Whipping, to the Forfeiture of a third part of their Wages; and the better sort to Fines which utterly ruin'd 'em, which alienated and transfer'd Estates upon the death of the Father into other Familys, with Clauses incapacitating 'em from buying or selling, or giving a night's lodging to the dearest Friend; depriving others of <384> all their Estate movable and immovable, and condemning others to perpetual Banishment. These were the Laws which ty'd down the Donatists; with these Chains they were drag'd into the Communion of other Christians, and kept from leaving: which, according to St. *Austin,* was doing 'em much a greater service than one does a frantick Person, by binding him hand and foot for fear he shou'd throw himself down a Precipice. A very lame unexact Comparison! because to save the Life of a Madman, who is ready to throw himself down a Precipice, it's wholly indifferent whether he consent or no; he's equally preserv'd from the danger with or without his consent, and therefore a wise and charitable Act it is to frustrate his Intentions, and bind him tightly if need be, how great a reluctance

109. Virgil, *Aeneid,* 1.140: "That is where Aeolus can do his swaggering, confining his rule to the closed walls of the prison of the winds"; translated David West, Penguin, 1991, p. 7.

soever he shews: but as to the Heretick, there's no doing him any good with regard to Salvation except his Consent be had. They may please themselves with bringing him by force into the Churches, with making him communicate by force, with making him say with his lips, and give under his hand while the Cudgel is over head, that he abjures his Errors, and embraces the Orthodox Faith; so far is this from bringing him nearer to the Kingdom of Heaven, that on the contrary it removes him farther from it. Where the Heart is not touch'd, penetrated and convinc'd, the rest is to no purpose; and God himself cannot save us by force, since the most efficacious, and the most necessitating Grace, is that which makes us consent the most intirely to the Will of God, and desire the most ardently that which God desires. How much Illusion then, and how much childish Sophi-<385>stry is there in pretending that a Man may be sav'd from Hell, and put in the road to Heaven, by such another Expedient, as that by which we preserve a Man in a raging Fever, when upon the point of throwing himself down a Precipice? The only way of saving a Man who drives full-speed and with a mighty zeal in the road to Hell, is by changing his Passion for the road he is in, and inspiring him with a love for the quite contrary road: and generally speaking, neither Banishment, nor Prisons, nor Fines, are of any service in this respect. They may indeed prevent his doing that outwardly which he was accustom'd to do, but never prevent his acting the same things inwardly; and 'tis in this part of him that the strongest and deadliest Poison lies. That Saying of a Latin Poet, *Invitum qui servat idem facit occidenti*,[110] is ne'er so true as with regard to Persecutors. The pains they take to prevent a Heretick's running headlong to what they call Death, and the violence they do him, are worse than if they actually slew him.

---

110. Horace, *Epistulae* II.3, l. 467: "Who saves a man against his will does the same as murder him." Translated R. Fairclough, Loeb Classical Library, 1970, p. 489.

❧ V. ST. AUSTIN'S WORDS ❧

You'l tell me, there are those on whom we don't gain an inch of ground by these methods; I believe it: but must we forgo the Medicine, because there are some incurable Patients?

ANSWER

If the Donatist propos'd this Objection as weakly as St. *Austin* represents, he was but a poor Reasoner. Why wou'd not he represent to this Father the Effects which the Persecutions of the Pagans had in St. *Cyprian*'s days, that of <386> the Emperor *Constantius,* and the Vigilance of *Pliny* the younger in his Government of *Bythinia?* Is it not well known, that very great numbers sunk under the Trials of those days; and ought not one to conclude from thence, that violent methods are very capable of making the Body comply with what the Conscience inwardly disavows, and of filling the persecuting Society with multitudes of the Worldly-minded, Covetous, Hypocrites, Temporizers, whose lot had faln in the persecuted Party? And this being incontestable when fairly reflected on, it's plain that St. *Austin*'s second Comparison is not a jot happier than the first. I shall readily grant him, that a Remedy, whose good Effects have bin often experienc'd, ought not to be laid aside because it does not recover every Patient: yet that such an Application as has turn'd a thousand times to the rankest Poison, and which is the ordinary recourse of the Enemys of Truth, by which they overwhelm its Followers, shou'd be taken up by Truth as a sovereign Remedy against Error; is certainly against all the Rules of good Sense, and the Precepts of Wisdom. Besides, that St. *Austin* supposes the thing in question, to wit, that Persecution is in effect a Remedy. The only Proof he alledges, is, that it had converted many a Donatist. But 1. how was he sure that these were all so many Donatists truly converted? 2. This pretended Medicine, had it not kill'd great numbers of the Orthodox under the former Persecutions? 3. If its medicinal Power was discover'd only by the Event, at least it must be own'd that the Experiment was rash; and yet <387> he praises those who had ventur'd to administer it, before its Effects were known.

I must offer one Remark in this place, which to me seems of some weight. He who makes but the least use of his Reason, is very capable of knowing that all Remedys ought to be adapted to the Nature of the Disease; consequently Error being a Distemper of the Soul, requires Applications of a spiritual nature, such as Argument and Instruction. Revelation, far from contradicting this Maxim, confirms and recommends it powerfully: He therefore who makes use of this kind of Remedy towards those in Error, has done his duty; and if he has not bin able to convert Men by this means, he may safely wash his hands of 'em; he has acquitted himself in the sight of God of the Blood of these Men, and may commit the whole matter to him. Now if after all Arguments and Instructions, our Reason shou'd suggest an Expedient which appear'd proper for recovering a Man from his Heresy, what must be done in this case? I answer, that if the Expedient be a thing in its own nature indifferent, and which if the worst came to the worst cou'd have no ill consequence, he ought forthwith to try it: but if it be a thing pernicious in its Consequences, and tending to force into a Crime the Person for whose sake it was employ'd, I maintain, that in this case it were a very great Sin to use it. Now all Laws condemning Men to very heavy Punishments who won't change their Religion, are of this nature: for it can't be deny'd but the taking from a Man the Patrimony of his Ancestors, or the <388> Estate he has acquir'd with the Sweat of his Brow, is downright Robbery; or that a Prince who did as much, who went for example to a Fair, and order'd all the Goods and Merchandizes to be swept away, merely because so was his Will and Pleasure, wou'd be guilty of Rapine and Robbery. The taking away a Man's Goods and Liberty then, and condemning him to Banishment, are not Actions indifferent in their own nature; they are necessarily Crimes if committed against an innocent Man: and I'm confident 'twill be granted me, that if all the Laws made against the Donatists had bin made against a Sect of Philosophers, who believing all that the Church believes as to Faith and Manners, shou'd hold this particular Opinion, *That the proper Object of Logick are Beings not real, but existing in the Mind only;* 'twill be granted me, I say, that such Laws enacted against these poor Philosophers, good Subjects and good Christians in other respects, wou'd be not only very ridiculous, but extremely criminal and tyrannical: consequently the Medicine St. *Austin* speaks of is not a thing in its own nature indifferent; and the best that can be said of it, is, that from evil and criminal, unless directed to the good of Religion, it becomes exceeding good and wholesom by being happily apply'd to this end. It's evident on the other hand, that it's a most dangerous Temptation, and that it's morally impossible but Multitudes must be driven by it to act against Conscience. It carries then the two special Characters upon it which ought for ever to exclude it from the business of Conversion; it's criminal in nature before it is entertain'd in the ser-<389>vice of Religion; and they who wou'd make use of it find it in the same class with Rapine, Robbery, Tyranny, before they do employ it: and then it's a Snare very likely to plunge the Patient from a less degree of Evil into a greater. I have* elsewhere shewn what a frightful Precipice they are led into, who go upon this Supposition, that what might be a Sin unless apply'd for the service of Religion, becomes a good Work by such an Application. So I shall insist on this no longer.

∞ VI. ST. AUSTIN'S WORDS ∞

Did we only lift the Rod over 'em, and not take the pains to instruct 'em, our Conduct might justly appear tyrannical; but on the other hand, did we content our selves with instructing 'em, without working on their Fears, they'd ne'er be able to surmount a kind of Listlessness in 'em, contracted by Use and Custom.

ANSWER

I'll allow St. *Austin,* that the joining Instruction to Threats is a lesser Evil than threatning and smiting without offering any Instruction; but here I shall stick, till the Gentlemen Apologists will be pleas'd to answer, if they can, to what was laid down in the first and second Chapters of the second Part of this *Commentary,*[111] and which amounts to this: 1. That the filling Men with the Fears of temporal Punishments, and with the Hopes of temporal Advantages, is putting 'em in a very ill state for discerning the true <390> Reasons of things from the false. 2. That joining Threats to Instruction with this condition, that if, at the expiration of a certain term of time,

---

* *In the fourth Chapter of the first Part.* [See above, p. 86.]
111. See above, Part II, Chapters 1 and 2, p. 137 ff.

the Persons under Instruction declare they'l continue in their former Persuasion, they shall suffer all the Punishments they were threaten'd with in the utmost rigor; is a Conduct which plainly shews there was a direct, tho somewhat a more remote, Intention of forcing Conscience, and plunging 'em into Acts of Hypocrisy. Now this absolutely cancels all the Merit they wou'd have us suppose in this mixture of Violence and Instruction. It's plain, what lately pass'd in *France,* where the Dragoons and the Missionarys play'd into one another's hands, those by ransacking the Houses, these by preaching the Controversy; was a very odd Medly, which savor'd much more of the Stage itinerant, or the Mummerys of a Carnival, than of the Conduct of Men in their sober Senses.

⚬ VII. ST. AUSTIN'S WORDS ⚬

All those who sooth and spare us are not therefore our Friends, nor all who chastize us our Enemys.* Faithful are the Wounds of a Friend, but the Kisses of an Enemy are deceitful. *The Severitys of those who love us are wholesomer than the soft Addresses of those who deceive us; and there's more Charity in taking a man's Bread from him, be he ever so hungry, if while he is full fed he neglects the Dutys of Righteousness, than in spreading his Table with the greatest Daintys to make him consent to a Sin.* <391>

ANSWER

Another Common-Place, and poor vulgar Conceit! All the world has heard of the difference between a Friend and a Flatterer. A Friend is not afraid of telling his Friend disagreeable Truths, of reproving him roundly, of contradicting him for his good, and of resisting his Appetites in a provoking manner; whereas the Flatterer applauds him in every thing, and so decoys him into the Pit of Destruction. All this is justly observ'd, and we have reason enough to conclude, that they who love us most are sometimes harsher with us than they who have not the least concern for us. But we must have a care of stretching this Maxim too far. I own it may in some cases be extended to Religion; nothing being more certain than that a Pastor, who is sincerely

* Prov. 27.6.

zealous for the Salvation of his Flock, will rebuke 'em sharply, and instead of sowing Pillows under their Arms, will rattle and teaze 'em out of their lives, in hopes of recovering 'em from their Vices; what a lazy luke-warm Hireling will not do, being fully resign'd as to the eternal Damnation of his Flock, and very loth to make 'em uneasy with a Representation of the Mischiefs which flow from a Corruption of Manners. But shou'd a Pastor behave himself the same way towards Strangers, with regard to their particular Tenets or Doctrines, I question whether it wou'd do so well as a milder Address and exact Civility; Men being much more apt to be embitter'd and confirm'd in their Opinions by harsh Treatment, than determin'd to change and forsake 'em. Be that how it will, still it's <392> most certain that there's no arguing from the Liberty of wholesom Reproof, for a Right of inflicting such Punishments as the Emperor's Laws ordain'd. Reproofs are allowable between Friends and Enemys; and therefore any one may make use of 'em, when he thinks he has a proper occasion: but Robbery and all the ways of Violence are of another strain; it is not lawful to make use of these either with Friends or Enemys, either directly or indirectly. We can neither take away our Neighbor's Goods by our own Authority, nor prompt others to do it, nor approve those that do; much less may we drive him from his House, and Home, and Country, or procure his Expulsion by the power of others. And therefore how allowable soever it may be in us to thwart and rudely to oppose the unlawful Pleasures of our Friends, it does not from hence follow that we ought to importune the Prince to deprive 'em of their Property, to imprison or banish 'em; and shou'd the Prince do this, we are in conscience oblig'd to look on it as a tyrannical Abuse of that Power with which God has entrusted him. For in the End I always come back to this: If the confiscating any private Party's Goods were a tyrannical Invasion, supposing him Orthodox in his Principles; and if it becomes a most righteous Action from hence only, that he happens not to be so, it follows that the same Action of a Sin becomes a Vertue from this single Circumstance, that it's perform'd for the Interest of Religion, which plainly overthrows all Morality and natural Religion, as I think I have fully demonstrated.[112] There's no ground then for maintaining that Banishment, <393> Prisons, Confiscation of Goods, and such-like Penaltys, are as warrantable on account of the Advantages we may

112. See above, p. 86.

promise our selves from 'em, as friendly Reproofs, and a want of Complaisance.

What St. *Austin* adds, that it's better in some cases to take away a Man's Bread than give him some, is a kind of a Simily which will never amount to a demonstrative Argument: for in the first place he ought to have given it this Restriction; That however 'twere a greater Sin to let a Man starve and perish, than to give him a morsel of Bread, even after we had discover'd in him an invincible Resolution of persisting in Error. 'Tis never allowable nor excusable to let a Man perish, how dissolute soever his course of Life may be; and therefore 'twere a Sin in those who had Bread to spare, if they saw him starve for want of it. But this is not St. *Austin*'s thought: his meaning is, that if Superfluity be an occasion of a Man's falling into Sin, it's friendlier to take away this Superfluity, than endeavor to procure it him. But there's still this difficulty in the case; Who shall take away this Superfluity? Not Persons in a private station; for in them to be sure it were unlawful to seize a man's Substance because he's prodigal and debauch'd. Shall the Prince then take it? but I don't find that this is customary: 'Twas never known that any Man was fin'd, or banish'd, or imprison'd for living high and at a great expence: And shou'd this really be practis'd, as I think it may, for the good of Society, it does not follow that Princes have the same right over mens Opinions as their Actions; because Opinions are no way pre-<394>judicial, as sometimes Actions are, to the Prosperity, Power, and Quiet of a State.

∞ VIII. ST. AUSTIN'S WORDS ∞

To bind one in a Phrensy, or awake one in a Lethargy, is vexatious indeed; yet it's friendly at the same time. God loves us with a truer Love than any Man can do; yet he joins the salutary Terrors of his Threats to the Lenity of his Counsels, and we find that he thought fit to exercise the most religious Patriarchs by a Famine.

ANSWER

St. *Austin* continually changes the Question; we are not now examining, whether one may love those whom he chastises, (who ever doubted it?) but whether it be lawful to take away a Man's Liberty and Property, because he does not believe with his Prince in all matters of Religion. Besides, the Example of his Frantick and Lethargick Person, with which he comes over us once more, is nothing to the purpose: We may love these Men, and yet do things which we know will vex 'em; nor do we regulate our Treatment by the Thoughts of what may be pleasing or displeasing to 'em, because we know there's no need of their Consent, in order to its being helpful and profitable to 'em. But cou'd we be sure, that all our Endeavors wou'd do 'em no good, or that whatever Methods we took with 'em wou'd only turn to their prejudice, unless done with their own Consent and Approbation; in this case so far wou'd it be from Friendship, that 'twere downright Cruelty to bind or waken 'em against their Will. And this alone utterly <395> ruins all St. *Austin*'s little Comparisons. Imprison a Heretick, pour in a Shoal of Dragoons upon him, load him with Chains; you'l ne'er promote his Salvation by all this, unless his Understanding be enlighten'd, unless he acquiesces in your Will. Now as it's scarce credible, that the Convertists are quite so stupid, as to imagine, that Prisons and extreme Misery enlighten a Man's Understanding, and make him strangely in love with the Religion of his Persecutors; one can hardly persuade himself, that these Men act from any other Principle than that of Vanity, Brutality, and Avarice. As to the Chastisements with which God is pleas'd to visit his Servants, they conclude nothing for St. *Austin*. God, who is the first Mover, as well as the Searcher of Hearts, may make his Chastisements avail to the inward Conversion of the Party: but since he has no where promis'd to send his Grace with the Persecution we inflict on Hereticks, to afflict 'em with sundry temporal Punishments in order to convert 'em, is not only a Temerity and notorious tempting of God; but the proposing the example of God in this case to Princes, is moreover a Degree of Impiety. Wou'd the Convertists take it kindly, that as God exercis'd the Patriarchs of old by a Famine; so the most Christian King wou'd exercise his Clergy, seize their Revenues, and diet 'em with Bread and Water in order to convert 'em? Ridiculous! The World wou'd laugh at us shou'd we say, in case the King of *France* seiz'd all the Treasure of the Churches, that 'twas an instance of Tenderness for his Clergy, and that he treated 'em at this rate only to make 'em live more becoming <396> their Christian Profession. The World wou'd say, we insulted over the Miserys of our Neighbor; and yet our reasoning wou'd be just the same as St. *Austin*'s. Another ridiculous thing is, that Opinions only are what Men must be fin'd for in order to make 'em change; but they alledg no Laws, nor instance any Dragoon Crusade for the Reformation of Manners. It is a Scandal and sore Disgrace of Christianity, to tyrannize over Men on account of their Opinions, to call in the Secular Arm against 'em, whilst they think it sufficient to preach against Vice; for never was a profest Convertist of Manners heard of, who sollicited Edicts against Luxury, Evil-speaking, Gaming, Fornication, Leud Discourse, &c. or call'd for the help of the Soldiery to make Catholicks change their Manners.

⚘ IX. ST. AUSTIN'S WORDS ⚘

You are of opinion, that no one shou'd be compel'd to do well; but have you never read, that the Father of the Family commanded his Servants to compel all they met with to come in to the Feast? Han't you seen with what Violence Saul was forc'd by JE-SUS CHRIST *to acknowledg and embrace the Truth? . . . Don't you know, that Shepherds sometimes make use of the Rod to force their Sheep into the fold? Don't you know that* Sarah, *according to the Power committed to her, subdu'd the stubborn Spirit of her Servant by the harshest Treatment, not from any hatred she bore to* Agar, *since she lov'd her so far as to wish that* Abraham *wou'd make her a Mother, but purely to humble the Pride of her Heart? Now you can't be igno-<397>rant, that* Sarah *and her Son* Isaac *are Figures of spiritual, and* Agar *and* Ishmael *of carnal things. Notwithstanding, tho the Scripture informs us that* Sarah *made* Agar *and* Ishmael *suffer a great deal;* St. Paul *does not stick to say, that 'twas* Ishmael *persecuted* Isaac, *to signify, that tho the Catholick Church endeavors to reclaim carnal Men by temporal Punishments, yet it is they persecute her, rather than she them.*

ANSWER

There are four things to be consider'd in this Discourse. 1. The Words of the Parable, *Compel 'em to come in.* 2. The Violence which JESUS CHRIST exercis'd on St. *Paul,* taking away his Eye-sight, and throwing him on the

Ground. 3. The Conduct of Shepherds sometimes to their Sheep. 4. The Conduct of *Sarah* towards her Servant *Agar*. I have said enough to the First of the four, in the former Parts of my Commentary. The second is sufficiently answer'd by what I have lately said,[113] that God, being the first Mover as well as the Searcher of Hearts, seconds the Punishments he inflicts on us with the Efficacy of his Grace as often as he sees fit. He thought fit to manifest his Power particularly in the Conversion of St. *Paul;* he appear'd to him in Person, he flung him on the Ground; in a word, he conquer'd this Soul by a mighty Hand, and a stretch'd-out Arm. But does it hence follow, that Men ought to imitate this Method when they wou'd convert a Heretick? Let 'em in God's Name, provided they have the Gift of turning the Heart, as the Al-<398>mighty may, at the same time that they afflict the Body; but as they are not thus qualify'd, they shou'd take care how they meddle in so nice an Affair. Punishments in the Hands of God himself, don't always produce the Conversion of Sinners; they only serv'd to harden *Pharaoh*'s Heart, tho God manifested his Power on him in the most extraordinary manner. The Punishments he dispenses in an ordinary way, either by the Mediation of Men, or of other created Beings, operate very differently; they very rarely change Mens Opinions about the Worship of God: on the contrary, they rather make the better sort more zealous in their own Religion; for which reason there being such a Probability, that temporal Punishments shall ne'er persuade a Man of the Falseness of his Religion, but rather of his want of Zeal for it, nothing can be more absurd than proposing the Conduct of God in chastising his Children for their good, as a rule for Princes. Besides that if once we stick by this example, 'twill follow, that Princes may from time to time set fire to Fields of Corn, to the Hay and Vines, and Woods of their Subjects, and send their Officers thro all their Dominions to decimate the Children, and send away their Fathers and Mothers to the Mines and Gallys. For as God sometimes makes use of Pestilence and Famine, those Scourges of his Wrath, to express his Love towards his Children, in order to bring 'em to Repentance; so Kings, who are his Vicegerents on Earth, may by the advice of their Clergy do all I have said within their Dominions, out of stark Love

113. See above, p. 302.

and Kindness to their Subjects; and from a Prospect of making 'em <399> look home to themselves, and awake out of that Lethargy and Death of Sin in which they lie bury'd. Did Kings really do this, wou'd not they find their Justification ready drawn to their hands in St. *Austin,* and in the Examples of Emperors, who have shackl'd their Sectarys with Penal Laws; not, say they, from any hatred to their Persons, but out of pure Charity, and in hopes of converting 'em? It's plain then, that the Result of this Doctrine of St. *Austin* is the turning all Morality into ridicule, since it offers Expedients for justifying the most criminal and the most extravagant Actions.

The Example of the Shepherds, who sometimes drive their Sheep into the Fold with Rods, is as unhappy as that of the frantick Person; for to make it of any weight, 'twere necessary that the counterpart of the Comparison shou'd relate to Creatures void of Liberty, and whose Conversion depended not essentially on a Consent of the Will. They alledg the constraining of Sheep into the Fold, to save 'em from the Thief or the Wolf; the Shepherd, who sees 'em refuse the Door, or not in a hurry to get in, acts very wisely in pressing 'em forward either with his Foot or with his Crook, and even dragging 'em in if there be need. Why is this Conduct wise in him? because it fulfils all the Dutys, and answers all the Ends the Shepherd can propose. His only aim is to save his Sheep from the Jaws of the Wolf, or any other outward Danger; and provided he can but get 'em into the Fold, the Work is done; the Sheep are safe whether they come in freely or by force. But the case is very different with regard to a Shep-<400>herd of Souls; he does not save 'em from the Power of the Devil, he does not heal 'em of the Scab, by transporting the Heretick into a certain House call'd *Notre Dame,* St. *Peter'*s, St. *Paul'*s, *&c.* or by sprinkling some Drops of Holy Water on his Face. This is not the thing which decides his Destiny; he must have a sense of his Errors, he must be willing to abjure 'em, and embrace wholesomer Doctrine: thus he may be rescu'd out of the Clutches of the Devil. But if these means be wanting, they may drag him with a Cord about his Neck at the Feet of the Altars, they may cram a hundred Hosts down his Throat, they may guide his Hand to sign a form of Abjuration; they may force him, on pain of the Boot, or of having his Flesh torn off with red-hot Pinchers, to declare a hundred times over, that he believes all the Church believes, and renounces *Luther* and *Calvin:* Still he's in the suds as much as ever, notwithstanding all this Cookery; and what's yet worse, of an Orthodox Christian, as he was in my Opinion before, he becomes a perfidious Hypocrite, and a Slave of the Devil, unless God in his Mercy recover him from his Fall. It's prodigious to me that there shou'd be so many Men of good Sense in the Church of *Rome,* who can't see the monstrous Absurdity of all these Similys.

Let's endeavor to give 'em one on our part, which may help 'em to a juster Idea of this matter. Shou'd I see a Man standing at my door in a heavy Shower, and from a sense of pity shou'd desire to shelter him from the Rain or Storm, I might make use of one of these two means; either I might invite him civilly into my House, and pray < 401 > him to sit down, or if I were stronger than he, I might pull him in by the Shoulder. Both these means are equally good with respect to the propos'd end, to wit, the preventing this Man's being wet to the Skin: it signifys very little how he comes under my Roof, whether freely or by force; for whether he comes in of his own mere Motion, or upon a civil Invitation, or whether he be pull'd in by main force, he is equally shelter'd from the Rain by one way as much as t'other. I own, were the case exactly the same as to our being sav'd from Hell, the Convertists might justify their forcible Methods; for if the getting under the Roof of a Church were sufficient to this end, 'twere not a pin matter whether the Party came in of his own accord, or whether he were thrust in by head and shoulders: and in this case the best way wou'd be to have a Set of the brawniest Street-Porters in town always at ready hand, to seize Hereticks the moment they appear'd in the streets, and heave 'em away upon their backs into the next Church; nay, burst open their doors with Petards if need were, and take 'em out of their Beds piping hot into the next Church or Chappel. But by ill luck for our Gentlemen Convertists, they are not quite so extravagant, nor so much out of their Senses, as to say, this is all that's requisite to the saving a Soul: They confess, that the Heretick's consent to his being brought over from one Communion to another is so necessary, that without it not a step can be made towards saving him. And if so, how absurd is it to compare the Violence done a Man who falls < 402 > into the Fire or Water, and whom we drag out by the very hair of the head, without the least scruple, with the Violences exercis'd on a

Calvinist, by holding a Dagger to his Throat, or quartering a hundred Dragoons on him till he abjure his Religion: this, I say is extremely absurd, not only because it's naturally to be suppos'd, that a Man who falls into the Fire or Water desires nothing more than to be sav'd at any Price whatsoever; but also because the danger is of such a nature, that his consent is no way necessary in order to the preserving him from it: the Man is equally preserv'd, tho drag'd out against his Will and in spite of him.

But to shew the Impertinence of those who pretend, People are extremely oblig'd to 'em for tearing 'em from a Communion in which they were bred and born, and which they believe much the best, tho the Convertists think it stark naught; I must desire 'em to imagine a Man enjoin'd by his Father Confessor to stand two hours by the Clock at such a door, in a soaking Shower of Rain, and this by way of Penance. If the Master of the House, not content to invite him in, shou'd send out his Footmen to pull him in by head and shoulders, wou'd he do him a Kindness pray, or a Pleasure in this? It's plain he wou'd not; but on the contrary, do him a very ill Office by interrupting his Devotion: *Invitum qui servat idem facit occidenti.* The case is the same with regard to those violent Convertists who tear Men from the Exercises of their own Religion. I'm tempted to think, that the cursed Maxims of these Quacks of Conscience spring in-<403> tirely from this ridiculous Opinion, that in order to be intitl'd to the Grace of God, one must be indispensably matriculated in such a certain Communion, and that this is all that's requisite. In consequence whereof they deal by Hereticks just as Men do with their Cattel when they wou'd save 'em from a storm of Rain or Hail, and with regard to whom it's all one, whether they go into the Hovel or Stable of themselves, or whether they are drub'd in with a Wattle.

As to St. *Austin*'s Conceit about *Sarah,* and her Maid-servant *Agar,* for my part I think it can serve no other purpose than exposing Scripture to the Railerys of the Profane. For in fine, if, in the way St. *Austin* intends, *Sarah* be a Type of the Children of God, and *Agar* a Type of the Children of the World, what will follow, but that the Children of God may constrain the Children of the World to seek for Refuge in Desarts, unable to bear the Rigor of their Discipline; and yet the Children of the World shall be they who persecute the Children of God. Was ever any thing in Farce or Droll more a Bull than this? I say nothing of St. *Austin*'s unaccountable mistake in representing, purely to make out the Wedlock of Charity and Persecution; *Sarah* as treating *Agar* in a very harsh manner, and at the same time loving her with so much tenderness, as even to desire she shou'd share her Husband's Bed. The Scripture represents this matter quite otherwise;[114] nor does it speak of *Sarah*'s ill humor to *Agar,* till the latter finding her self big with Child, grew saucy upon't, and slighted her Mistress. <404>

114. See Genesis, c. 16.

∞ X. ST. AUSTIN'S WORDS ∞

The Good and the Bad do and suffer very often the same things; nor ought we to judg of the nature of their Actions by what either does, or what either suffers, but from the Motives on which they act or suffer. Pharaoh *oppress'd the People of God with excessive Labor.* Moses, *on the other hand, punish'd the Transgressions of the same People by the most severe Punishments. The Actions of each side were much alike, but their Ends very different: One was an errant Tyrant, bloated with Pride and Power; the other a Father, fill'd with Charity.* Jezabel *put the Prophets to death, and* Elias *the false Prophets; but that which put Arms into the hands of one and t'other, was no less different than that which drew on the deaths of each. In the same Book, where we find St.* Paul *scourg'd by the Jews, we find the Jew* Sosthenes *scourg'd by the Greeks for St.* Paul; *there's no difference between 'em if we only look at the Surface of the Action, but there's a great deal of difference if we look at the Occasion and Motive. St.* Paul *is deliver'd to the Jailer to be cast into Irons, and St.* Paul *himself delivers the incestuous* Corinthian *to Satan, whose Cruelty much exceeds that of the most barbarous Jailers; yet he delivers this Man to Satan only that his Flesh being buffeted his Soul might be sav'd.*[115] *When the same St.* Paul *deliver'd* Philetus *and* Himeneus *to Satan to teach 'em not to blaspheme,*[116] *he did not intend to render Evil for Evil, but judg'd it an Act of Goodness to redress one Evil by another.* <405>

ANSWER

Here's another new Flight of those little Reasonings which pass well enough in a Croud, where not one of a thousand has the Skill to distinguish where the Comparison holds, and where it does not. St. *Austin* breaks his heart to prove what no body living denys, That the same Action may be good or

---

115. 1 Corinthians 5:5.
116. 1 Timothy 1:20, 2 Timothy 2:17.

bad, according to the difference of Circumstance. If a Prince punishes a seditious Province to the rigor, from no other design than just to hinder its revolting anew, this is an Action of Justice; but it's an Act of Cruelty and Avarice, if he rigorously punishes a slight Offence in the same Province, in hopes an unreasonable Severity may make it rebel, and give him a Pretence of reducing the People to Beggary. I'l allow St. *Austin* then, that *Moses* did well in punishing the *Israelites,* and *Pharaoh* as ill in oppressing 'em; a difference which arose not purely from *Moses*'s proposing, as his end, the Reformation of this People, and *Pharaoh* its Ruin; but from their being punish'd without any demerit by *Pharaoh,* and not by *Moses.* But to unhinge St. *Austin*'s Comparisons all at once, I need only shew, that he instances on one hand in certain violent Proceedings arising from Aversion, or some other unjust Passion, and compares these with other Actions, afflictive indeed to our Neighbor, but at the same time enjoin'd by a special Revelation from God, and consequently operating under Circumstances, in which the Agent or instrumental Cause might be sure of their producing a good Effect. I speak with relation to *Moses, Elias,* and St. *Paul.* These were all Pro-<406>phets, who understood by an immediate divine Inspiration that 'twas proper to proceed in a way of Punishment; and in this case 'twas allowable in them to exercise Severity, because there was no room to doubt but God, who ordain'd the means, had a purpose of turning it to his own Glory in a singular and extraordinary manner. In this case one has an assurance both of the Justice of the Action, and of the right Disposition of the Circumstances, and of the good Success. Can any one say as much for *Theodosius*'s persecuting the Arians, or *Honorius* the Donatists? What assurance had either, that God wou'd give a blessing to their Violences, or make 'em an efficacious means of enlightning the Understanding, or turning the Hearts of those in Error? It's evident they had no such assurance, and that the Probability was much stronger on the other hand, that these methods wou'd rather rivet 'em in their Errors, and produce false Conversions rather than any real Change; so that 'twas the highest Temerity to venture on the ways of Violence in such a posture of Affairs. As to the Case of *Sosthenes,* I can't imagine what St. *Austin* wou'd infer from it; since 'twas an Act of the Rabble, who without the least regard to the Proconsul there present, or the place they were in, rush'd in a tumultuous manner on the Head of the Synagogue.[117]

I have one Remark more at hand, which will absolutely demolish all these Arguments of St. *Austin*. It's plain that the whole force of his Reasonings turns on this Supposition; That when Men treat Hereticks hardly in hopes of converting 'em, they act from a Principle of Charity, a <407> Motive which changes the nature of hard usage in such a manner, that it presently becomes a Good-work; whereas it's downright Sin, if proceeding from Hatred, Insolence, or Avarice. It's plain likewise, that the reason which makes Men imagine there's a Motive of Charity in the case, can be no other than this, or something very near it, to wit, That they look on ill usage as a very proper means for making a Heretick think of getting instructed, and entring on a Search after Truth and the right way to Salvation. So that St. *Austin*'s Reasoning amounts to this:

Treating one's Neighbor ill, from a Principle of Charity, is a Good-work.

Now it's treating him ill from a Principle of Charity, to give him such ill Treatment of any kind, as may oblige him to get instructed and heal the Diseases of his Soul.

It's therefore a Good-work to give him this sort of ill Treatment.

This is one of the most dangerous, and at the same time the most absurd Sophism in Morality that e'er was fram'd; for by this rule one might justify the most execrable Actions. Shou'd I see my Neighbor puff'd up with Pride, shou'd I see his Vanity fed by a vast Estate, and by an extraordinary Esteem and Respect for his Person; I might safely endeavor to lessen his Fortune and blast his Reputation: To this end I might set fire to his House, invent and raise a thousand Calumnys of him; and if one in a private station might not lawfully do this, yet the Prince may; as St. *Austin* maintains he may justly keep a Heretick poor, in hopes of awakening him out of his slumber. The Prince, I say, might justly beggar <408> this proud Man, and eat him up with his Soldiers, or get him falsly impeach'd of High Treason, declare him attainted in his Blood, and brand him as a Traitor. Shou'd any one murmur at this hard usage of the Man, we might tell him upon St. *Austin*'s

117. Acts 18:17.

Scheme, that truly it wou'd be unjust, if proceeding from any other Motive than that of Charity; but since it's only design'd to rescue the Man from Damnation, into which his Vanity, founded on his Opulency and Honors, drove him head-long, it was perfectly just. I desire no more of my Readers, than calmly and impartially to compare the Effects which Jails, Fines, Chicanes, and a continual Anxiety of Life, might produce on a Heretick, in order to make him renounce his Opinions from Heart and Mouth; with the Effects which the taking away his Substance and Good Name might have upon this proud Man: and I persuade my self they'l allow, that if the Treatment in the first case be capable of changing the Heart of a Heretick, the Treatment in the second case must likewise change the Heart of this proud Man; and consequently he may be rob'd of his Goods and Good Name from a Principle of pure Charity (according to the Minor of my Syllogism) which will become a Good-work according to the Major of the same Syllogism. So that here's a Sophism for justifying the most execrable Actions; which was the thing to be prov'd.

The more one examines this matter, the more he discovers the Illusion good St. *Austin* was under. He imagin'd, that as those things which are absolutely indifferent, and left to our own discretion, become good or evil according to the <409> Motive or Intention; so those which are expresly commanded or forbidden are subject to the same alteration, by virtue of the different Motives upon which we act. But as from hence it wou'd follow, that Robbery, Murder, Perjury, Adultery, wou'd cease to be Sins, when practis'd with a design of humbling our Neighbor, and bringing him to Repentance, or in general when practis'd from any Motive of Charity; it manifestly follows, that we must distinguish between Dutys of Obligation, and those which are left to our own Choice. Now refraining from the Goods or Good Name of our Neighbor, not swearing a false Oath, not debauching our Neighbor's Wife or his Daughter, not smiting, reviling, or insulting him, are all matters of Obligation; and therefore whatever Benefit he may be suppos'd to reap from our calumniating, or from our smiting him, &c. what Benefit soever, I say, he may reap from hence with regard to Salvation, it's by no means allowable to treat him after this manner. God does not require us to endeavor the Salvation of our Brethren at the expence of his Laws; and we wou'd do well to leave it intirely to his Providence to reclaim 'em if he sees fit, either by Poverty, or Sickness, or Shame, and make 'em sensible of the ill use which they have made of their good Fortune. This altogether shews how much of Illusion there is in this pretended Charity, which prompts us to do evil to our Neighbor with a design of bringing him to good; and consequently, that Princes are grosly misled when they ruin their Subjects, when they banish, imprison, and expose 'em to <410> a thousand Straits and Vexations, under pretence of obliging 'em to get themselves instructed. An Apology therefore for Persecution, built on so rotten a Foundation, can never stand.

There's only one Case, as I can think of, in which a Man may dispense with the Precepts of the Decalogue in hopes of procuring the spiritual Good of his Neighbor; and that is, where the Party finds himself favor'd with the Gift of Prophecy and that of Miracles, and led immediately and extraordinarily by the Spirit of God. In this case he may kill a Man, as St. *Peter* kill'd *Ananias* and *Saphira* his Wife; he may maim him, he may cover from head to foot with Leprosy and Ulcers, get the Ship cast away in which he has all his Effects, *&c.* because, as I have already observ'd,[118] he acts from the express Order of God, who by the transcendent Eminence of his Nature is exempted from all Rule, and by his Quality of Searcher of the Heart and Reins is able to perceive the Sutableness and Congruity of Circumstances and corporeal Actions, to the Inflexions and Modifications of the Soul; insomuch as there's no room to doubt of the good Success of these violent and acute Remedys. And therefore it is that St. *Paul* positively assures us he deliver'd the incestuous *Corinthian* to Satan, only in order to save his Soul; and *Himencus* and *Philetus,* that he might teach 'em not to blaspheme. But as for any Underling, or mere common Man, confin'd within the Sphere of human Knowledg, and incapable of foreseeing what effects Poverty and Anguish may have upon the Mind of a Heretick; for him, I say, to take upon him to spurn the Commands against Stealing, against smiting <411> his Neighbor, *&c.* upon a pretence that the Party, to deliver himself from Hunger and Pain, will set about examining his Errors, and o' course perceive 'em; is undoubtedly the greatest Presumption, and the most ridiculous Pretension in the world.

118. See above, p. 310.

By the way 'twill be useful to observe, that in the case of *Moses*'s punishing the *Israelites* he had to deal with a People who were under no Error of Conscience; for they well knew that the Actions for which they were punish'd, were evil and unjustifiable. St. *Paul* in like manner did not excommunicate Persons who believ'd they had acted aright. The incestuous *Corinthian* was no such Fool as to maintain, that Incest was an Action commanded or indulg'd by JESUS CHRIST; and as for *Himeneus* and *Philetus,* the Apostle affirms they had not only cast away the Faith, but also a good Conscience: consequently their Error was not attended with Sincerity, as the Errors of those are whom Princes take upon 'em to persecute, at the abominable instigation of Priests and Monks.

I wou'd likewise have People once more to observe what I have said in other Parts of this *Commentary,*[119] to wit, that Men having receiv'd a standing Rule of their Actions from God, are by no means allow'd to depart from this Rule, on pretence of imitating the ways of God himself, or the Methods he makes use of either by the Intervention of natural Causes, or of Men endu'd in an extraordinary manner with the Gift of Miracles. For example, God shall make use of Tempests, Earthquakes, Infections, Hail, Mists, Locusts, *&c.* for punishing the People of a Coun-<412>try, and awaking 'em to Repentance; or perhaps he shall commission a *Moses* to inflict all these Plagues. Does it therefore follow, that Kings or other Men may set whole Fields of Corn on fire, poison the Fountains, and create as much as in them lies a Dearth or Sickness, in a Country whose Inhabitants are wicked and impenitent? Another Example; God sends his Apostle a Thorn in the Flesh, he permits a Messenger of Satan to buffet him, and this for the good of his Servant, and most certainly knowing that his own Power shall be manifested thro the Apostle's Infirmity. Have we now any right of imitating this Conduct towards those whom we see puff'd up with the great Talents which God has vouchsafed 'em? Is there a King upon earth, who hearing of a famous Doctor in his Dominions, admir'd for his Learning and Eloquence, and holy Life, has a right of sending him a Thorn in the Flesh to humble or to mortify him; such as suborning false Witnesses to blast his Reputation in some inferior Court, or giving him a Potion to

119. See above, p. 152, p. 302.

weaken his Body and Mind? We make no doubt but there are Women in the world, who, thro the special Favor of God, have had the sad mortification in their Childhood of losing their Beauty by the Small-Pox. God who has a love for 'em, and who knows they wou'd make an ill use of their Beauty, and that the loss of this Jewel will engage 'em more intensly to the solid Contemplations of the World to come, disfigures 'em most justly, and from a Motion of pure Grace. May a King lawfully imitate this Conduct? And when he sees a fair Lady pride her self in her Beauty, <413> catching all the Men in her way, and caught her self in the Snares of Love, may he without a crime destroy all her natural Charms? May he in charity hire a Ruffian to mangle her Face; may he send her a Box, which in the opening shall set fire to a Preparation of Sulphur or Gunpouder, and for ever ruin her Bloom and lovely Complexion? May he bribe her Physician to prescribe her a Pouder or Potion, which shall throw her into a languishing Sickness, end in a frightful Jaundice, ghastly Looks, and an offensive Smell? It's plain he cannot; and that this Prince wou'd make himself ridiculous to all the World, shou'd he gloss such a Conduct with the specious pretence of Charity; as that he design'd to preserve this fine Woman from the Dangers to which her Soul was expos'd, and sequester her from the Vanitys and Pleasures of the World to think only upon things above. There's infinitely a greater probability, that the disfiguring such a Woman, and throwing her into a languishing Sickness, wou'd mortify her Vanity, and accomplish her Conversion, than that the quartering a hundred Dragoons on a *Hugonot* shou'd put him in the right way of perceiving he is a Heretick, and of sincerely embracing the Romish Faith. Yet the World wou'd hiss such a Prince, or his Directors of Conscience, who took these methods of converting the Ladys; and yet they applaud his endeavoring to convert Protestants the same way.

I shall conclude this Article with the following Remark; That nothing is more groundless than St. *Austin*'s Distinction of those Cudgellings, ransacking of Houses, and other ways of Violence <414> which proceed from a Motive of Charity, and those which are exercis'd without this Principle of Charity. True Charity is that which inclines us to keep those Laws of God which forbid Robbery, Blood-shed, and Battery: for by the same Distinction a Prince might innocently set fire to all the Citys in the Kingdom, and every year destroy a great part of the Harvest; still pretending that his Design was to humble his Subjects, who don't think enough upon God in convenient Houses and great Plenty.

XI. ST. AUSTIN'S WORDS

If the being persecuted were always a sign of Merit, JESUS CHRIST *wou'd only have said,* Blessed are they who are persecuted, *and not have added,* for Righteousness sake. *In like manner, if persecuting were always a Sin,* David *wou'd not have said,** Whoso privily slandereth his Neighbor, him will I persecute.

ANSWER

I am very unwilling to believe what I see with my own eyes, that St. *Austin* shou'd apply some Scripture-Passages so much amiss. Who disputes but the whole Merit of Persecution depends on its being suffer'd for Righteousness sake? Who doubts but a vain Man who chose to be eaten out of house and home, rather than acknowledge his Error, and who in his heart convinc'd of the Badness of his Cause, shou'd notwithstanding < 415 > persist in it in hopes of gaining a Reputation of Constancy and Steddiness of Soul; who doubts, I say, but such a Man loses all the Fruits of his Sufferings, and is besides in a very ill state? To what purpose then shou'd this Father stand to confute so trifling an Objection? There is not a Man of tolerable good Sense, but knows that to be blessed in Persecution, the first and main Condition is the suffering it from a love of Truth and Righteousness; which is very consistent with an Error of Sincerity and an honest Mind. But how wicked soever he may be who draws Persecution on himself, because he's too proud and stately to retract, or to own to his Persecutors that their Cause is best; still it's certain, that they are both wicked and unjust. Here then is a Distinction of somewhat a better kind than that which St. *Austin* gave us just now. It's possible the persecuted Party may be wicked, but it's certain

* Psalm 101.5.

the Persecutor is;* for the Passage from *David* alledg'd to prove there may be pious Persecutors, proves nothing in the Case before us, where the Question is only concerning Persecutions for Religion. *David* sets forth in this Psalm, that he'l have no Fellowship with the Wicked; and names in particular that Pest of Civil Society, worthy of the Execrations of all honest Men, to wit, those poison'd Tongues which wickedly slander their Neighbor. If *David* speaks here as a King, he can say nothing more becoming the Wisdom and Justice which belongs to <416> his station, than declaring he'l employ the Authority of the Laws, and the Sword which God has given into his hands, for the chastizing those vile Slanderers, these idle Poisoners of human Society. If he speaks here only to give us the Character of a righteous Man, he means to inform us that we ought to have no fellowship nor dealing with the Backbiter and Slanderer. But how does this tend to authorize the Convertists, who won't suffer Folks either to die or live in Peace, good Subjects, good Citizens in the main, only because, they have certain Opinions different from theirs? On the whole, can it be suppos'd that St. *Austin* thought before he spoke, when in this matter he alledges Punishments ordain'd by a King against Slanderers and false Accusers, where he ought to have given examples of Punishments inflicted purely on the score of speculative Doctrines or Opinions.

---

* *Here, and it may be on some other occasions, we must take things without regard to the Author's particular Opinion concerning an erroneous but justifying Conscience.*

ঙ XII. ST. AUSTIN'S WORDS ঙ

*The Wicked have never left persecuting the Good, nor the Good
the Wicked: but these act unjustly herein, and only to do mischief;
those charitably, and so far as the necessity of correcting requires. . . . As the Wicked have slain the Prophets, so the Prophets
have sometimes slain the Wicked; as the Jews were seen with
Scourge in hand against* JESUS CHRIST, *so* JESUS CHRIST
*was seen with Scourge in hand against the Jews. Men deliver'd
the Apostles to the earthly Powers, and the Apostles deliver'd Men
to the infernal Powers. What then ought we to consider in all these
Examples? only this, which side acts for the Truth and Righteousness, and* <417> *which for Iniquity and a Lye; which acts only
to destroy, and which to correct.*

ANSWER

Here's a rare Maxim of Morality indeed, the most detestable in its Consequences that e'er was broach'd: for provided you act in favor of the true
Opinion, and have no other design than that of correcting your Neighbor,
you may lawfully, as to any thing else, imitate the ways of the Wicked; and
whereas these shall have committed a Sin, you shall have perform'd a heavenly Action. Accordingly let's imagine two Persons, the one an Orthodox,
and the other an Heterodox. The first sees a great Lord in the opposite Party,
very zealous in its cause, and supporting it by his great Riches, his Credit,
and good Sense. The second sees such another great Lord in the Orthodox
Party. The first contrives how to ruin his great Lord, and starts so many
scurvy Affairs upon him, that running the risk of his Honor and Estate, he
has not the leisure to mind the Interests of his Party. All this while he has
no intention of doing this great Lord the least mischief; he only wou'd
prevent his Lordship's doing any, and bring about his Conversion. Here's
an Action now fit to be canoniz'd, or at least perfectly innocent, if we judg
of it by St. *Austin*'s Principles. It's no matter if he ruins this honorable
Person, by setting fire to his Barns, to his Mills, to his Castles, by poisoning
his Cattel, and involving him in Law-Suits, which he's sure to lose: All this

is very fair, provided it's from no other Intention than that of working on him to get himself instructed, and forsake <418> his Errors. Yet if the other acts against his great Orthodox Lord the same way, he's a Villain and a Monster. And why so? Is it because he commits Actions repugnant to the Decalogue? No, but because he commits 'em with a design of doing prejudice to the Orthodox Party, and to his Orthodox Neighbor. This, without my mentioning it expresly, must appear to all the World to be a Confirmation of what I have so much urg'd against the literal Sense, at the fourth Chapter of the first Part;[120] to wit, That it overthrows that holy and fundamental Barrier, which God has fix'd betwixt Virtue and Vice; and leaves us no other Character of Vertue than the Gain of those who follow certain Opinions, and no other Character of Vice than their Loss. I wou'd not willingly charge St. *Austin* with having seen this Consequence; but it is plainly contain'd in these Words: *What then ought we to consider in all these Examples* (that's to say Murders, Scourgings, Captivity) *only this; which side acts for the Truth and Righteousness, and which for Iniquity and a Lye; which acts only to destroy, and which to correct?*

One can hardly here avoid thinking of some Maxims of loose Morality, condemn'd by the Court of *Rome,* under the present Papacy; and truly St. *Austin's* Distinction is not a jot better than that of these wicked Casuists, who teach, 1. *That one may, without the guilt of mortal Sin, be sorry and repine at the Life of another, provided he carrys it with Decency and due Moderation; and even rejoice at his death, desire and wish for it by a Wish which has no effects, provided this proceeds not from any prejudice to his Person, but from a* <419> *Prospect of some temporal Advantage to himself.* 2. *That it is lawful to wish the death of one's Father by a positive Wish, not as an evil to the Father, but as an advantage to him who wishes, and as it lets him into the Possession of a fair Estate.* 3. *That it's lawful for a Son to rejoice even in a Parricide committed by him when drunk, if upon the misfortune of killing his Father he succeeds to great Hoards and a noble Estate.*[121] These Casuists, we see, make so great a difference between two Persons who rejoice at the death of their Fathers, or even at Parricide if committed in drink; that one's

---

120. See above, p. 86.
121. See Denzinger, *Enchiridion Symbolorum,* Rome, edn. 31, 1957, p. 370, nos. 13–15.

innocent, if his Joy proceeds not from any motive of Hatred to his Father, but from a Love for himself; and the other sinful, where his Joy is founded on the evil befaln his Father. Is this very much worse than the difference St. *Austin* makes between two Persecutors: one of which, gives his Neighbor a hundred Strokes of a Cudgel, with a mischievous design; the other lays him on as many, not to do him a Mischief, but purely with a design to convert him? Must not we, to reason consequentially, say in like manner, that of two Men, each of which kills his Neighbor, one from a Principle of Malice, the other to deliver him from Want; the first is guilty of a Sin, and the second not? Or rather, to avoid all Cavil by putting one case more, must not we maintain, that of two Men who kill'd each his Neighbor, one out of a personal dislike; the other, because seeing him in a State of Grace, just after confessing and receiving the Sacrament, he considers, that dying in such a State his Neighbor must go strait to Heaven, and that if he liv'd any longer he might possibly relapse and <420> die in his Sins: must not we, I say, maintain, that the first is guilty, and the second innocent; and consequently, that 'twere a pious and charitable part in the Priest, to knock his Penitent on the head, as soon as he has absolv'd and given him the Sacrament, provided he does not act from any Malice or Rancor, but purely to make sure of his Predestination, by delivering him from the Temptations of the World, which he might afterwards sink under, and possibly not rise again by Repentance. Upon the same Principle, a Nurse or Maid-servant, who strangl'd or over-laid all the Children in her Care, not from any Ill-nature or Cruelty to the Children, but o' purpose to send 'em infallibly to Heaven, at an Age in which they have not yet forfeited the Benefits of Baptism; wou'd perform a good Action. So that St. *Austin*'s Distinction over-throws all Morality, and makes the Decalogue the Sport of our Distinctions, our Intentions, and our Caprices.

Two Sons wish the Death of their Fathers; they are therefore sinful and wicked. I deny the consequence, says any one who'l go upon St. *Austin*'s Distinction: One of 'em wishes the death of his Father, because he is a Pillar of the Orthodox Party, or because he bears a strict hand upon his Son; this is a wicked Child: The other wishes it, because his Father favors Hereticks, or because he wou'd have his Father enjoy the Felicitys of Heaven, which are incomparably beyond those of the present Life; here's a good and an innocent Child.

Two Men kill each of 'em a Passenger; they are therefore each guilty of a Crime. Hold there, <421> may any one say on St. *Austin*'s Foundation, not so fast; we must examine, whether they have kill'd in behalf of the Truth, or in behalf of Heresy, to hurt or to reclaim their Neighbor. For if one has kill'd a Passenger, who was an Enemy to the Truth, or purely with a design of delivering him from a languishing Distemper, which might hang upon him for several Years, he has done well; but if the other has kill'd a Passenger, who was a Promoter of sound Religion, or from any personal Malice, he is guilty of a Crime.

Two Men have taken a Purse on the Highway; they are therefore a couple of Robbers, and deserve to be hang'd. I deny the consequence, may any one still insist, I distinguish: for if they have taken it from any of the Orthodox, such especially as freely contribute to carry on the Interest of the Party, or with a design of vexing those they took it from, I allow they are punishable; but if they have stript a Heretick, who was going to see his Lawyer or Attorny in a Law-suit against an Orthodox, which now happens to be lost for want of a Fee, they have perform'd a Good-work: or if they have not taken it out of any Ill-will to the Owner, but on the contrary to ease him of the Burden; or in hopes, by this Disaster, to make him retrench his superfluous Expences, and abate his Vanity.

Thus one might elude all the Dutys which the Law of God prescribes; and before we cou'd say, that a Man taken in a flagrant Adultery were guilty of a Sin, it ought to be known, whether he had bin induc'd to this, not to satisfy his own brutal Lust, but to assuage a craving Ap-<422>petite in the Woman, and assist the Husband to fulfil the too weighty Functions of his Duty to such a Wife: for shou'd it appear, that he had acted not from any formal Intention of prejudicing either the Wife or Husband, or from his own sensual Inclinations, but purely to correct a craving Constitution, and for the common Benefit of the marry'd Couple, 'twere a truly Christian Act of Charity in him.

Is it not very strange, that our Gentlemen Convertists, who so clearly perceive the abominable Absurdity of these Consequences, and the necessary Connexion between those Principles and them; shou'd notwithstanding be eternally telling us, That smiting, imprisoning, pillaging, and vexing a poor Christian, are good Works, provided the Party acts not from any personal Malice, but purely to recover 'em from their Errors? Confess then, say I to 'em, that the same Discipline, how repugnant soever to the Decalogue, shall be warrantable in order to reclaim a Coquet, or rich Beau; such as, seizing their Revenues and Equipage, taking away their best Clothes and Jewels, fleaing or mangling their fine Faces, enlanguishing and weakning 'em by poisonous Potions, provided it be done from a Motive of Charity; or, which is all one in this place, with a design of recovering 'em from their evil Courses.

I might here take notice of St. *Austin*'s Inaccuracy, in making use of the general and indefinite Terms of annoying and correcting, to denote the different Characters which distinguish the good Persecutors from the bad. For what, pray, does he mean by this? Does he mean, that <423> the good Persecutors persecute only to work Hereticks to an Abjuration of their Errors; whereas the purpose of your wicked Persecutors is to ruin and grieve their Neighbor: Or does he mean, that the pious Persecutors punish in Measure and Moderation; whereas your wicked Persecutors put to death those whom they persecute. If we are to take his Terms in the first sense, 'twill follow, according to him, that Hereticks who persecute the Orthodox don't act with a design of making 'em change Opinion, and abjure what to these Hereticks appears a capital Error. Now this is manifestly false: for, not to mention the very Pagans, who put a stop to all violent Proceedings against those who pretended to renounce the Jewish or the Christian Religion; is it not well known, that the Arians, and all others in general, whom the Church of *Rome* brands as Hereticks, never did exercise any Violence on other Sects, but with a design of obliging 'em to embrace their own? If he understands 'em in the second sense, he's mistaken again, because it's plain, not only that there are Persecutors of that Stamp which he calls good, that is, which he believes Orthodox, who inflict death; but also because the Heterodox Persecutors most commonly content themselves with Punishments, as moderate as those of the other Class of Persecutors. So that upon the whole, I can see but one reasonable meaning in these Words of St. *Austin,* to wit, That the end of the Heterodox Persecutors, being constantly that of bringing Men over to an Error; and the end of the Orthodox Persecutors, the bringing 'em to the Truth; these promote only <424> the Advantage, those the Damage of such as they persecute. But this again is characterizing things amiss, and pointing principally at what is only accidental in 'em. It's purely by accident, that Persecutors who are themselves in error do any prejudice, or that those who are Orthodox do good: each Party have equally a design of delivering his Neighbor from what they deem amiss, and of instructing him in what they believe the Truth. So as we can't justly say, That the first have a design of prejudicing their Neighbor; their declar'd purpose being manifestly, that of saving him from Hell: and if it happen, that by turning an Orthodox, they put him in the strait way to Hell, it's purely accidental, and wholly beside their Intention. They are both then upon an equal foot with regard to the Intention; and if sometimes the success of the Orthodox Party's Persecutions, be better than that of the Heterodox, 'tis purely by accident, and for the most part tends only to make the State of the Persecuted worse, by leading to Hypocrisy and Sins against Conscience. So that, strictly speaking, the Character which St. *Austin* proposes for distinguishing the good from the bad Persecutions, amounts only to this; that the Orthodox Persecutors persecute for Orthodoxy, and the Heterodox for Heterodoxy: a ridiculous Tautology, of no manner of Service for coming at the Knowledge of that which is under Enquiry!

∞ XIII. ST. AUSTIN'S WORDS ∞

But, say you, it no where appears from the Gospel, or from the Writings of the Apostles, that they ever had recourse to the Kings of the Earth <425> *against the Enemys of the Church. True; but the reason is because this Prophecy,* Be wise now therefore, O ye Kings: be instructed, ye Judges of the Earth. Serve the Lord with Fear, and rejoice with Trembling; *was not as yet accomplish'd.*

ANSWER

This Passage of St. *Austin,* and his *Nebuchodonosor*[122] Type of the Christian Church persecuted, as he ordain'd the worshipping his Image; and Type of

---

122. Bayle's extract from Augustine stops just short of the mention of Nebuchodonosor: "If past events in the prophetic books were a figure of future ones, in the king named Nabuchodonosor both periods were foreshadowed: that under the Apostles, and

the same Church persecuting, as he ordain'd the punishing those, who blasphem'd the God of the *Hebrews:* is pretty much the same with what the Canonists tell us, That if the first Christians did not take up Arms against the Pagans, 'twas because they were too weak to make the Attempt. It's certain, St. *Austin* does plainly insinuate, that had *Tiberius* embrac'd Christianity, the Apostles wou'd have gone directly to him, and demanded Edicts of Constraint and Vexation; such as those of *Honorius* against the Sect of the Donatists. And one must forfeit common Sense to pretend that the Apostles, in this case, wou'd not have proportion'd the Rigor of the Penal Laws to the Resistance they shou'd meet with: for it's absurd to suppose, that Confiscations, Banishment, Dragoonery, Cudgelling, Prison, Gallys, shou'd be agreeable to the Spirit of the Gospel; but not the death Penalty, where the Obstinacy of the Distemper requir'd a desperate Remedy. I shan't repeat what I have already sufficiently urg'd, against the Inequality of Conduct ascrib'd to the Son of God, by those who imagine his Intention was, that there shou'd be <426> no Constraint, till after such a period of time: I refer my Readers back to the latter end of the fifth Chap. of the first Part.[123] There they'l see that this wou'd be exactly the Original of Pope *Boniface* VIII, of whom 'tis said, that he riggled himself in like a Fox, and reign'd like a Lion: *Intravit ut Vulpes, regnavit ut Leo.*

---

the present one in which the Church is now living. Thus, in the times of the Apostles and martyrs, that part was fulfilled which was foreshadowed when the king forced devout and upright men to adore an idol, and, when they refused, had them thrown into the fire; but, now, that part is fulfilled which was prefigured in the same king, when he was converted to the true God, and decreed for his realm that whoever blasphemed the God of Sidrach, Misach, and Abdenago should suffer due penalties . . . the latter part of that king's reign signified the period of later faithful kings under whom the impious suffered instead of the Christians"; translated Sister Wilfrid Parsons.

123. See above, pp. 100–101.

∞ XIV. ST. AUSTIN'S WORDS ∞

As it is not impossible, but that even among those Christians, who have suffer'd themselves to be seduc'd, there may be some of the true Sheep of JESUS CHRIST, *who soon or late shall come back to the Fold, tho ever so far gone astray; for this reason we mitigate the Severitys appointed against 'em, and use all possible Lenity and Moderation in the Confiscations and Banishments, which we are oblig'd to ordain, in hopes of making 'em enter into themselves.*

ANSWER

Observe St. *Austin*'s Language, while he is only to make the Apology of certain Laws, which did not carry things to an Extremity against the Donatists! Had it bin the Emperor's Will and Pleasure to condemn 'em to death, he had undoubtedly alter'd his Note, and invented Excuses for it altogether as plausible. And in effect, if once it be suppos'd lawful to exercise any Violence at all, we have no Rule left of more or less, but what the Circumstances of Time, and Place, and Persons do constitute; as I have fully prov'd in the third Chapter of the second Part:[124] and a Man shall sin altogether as soon by not carrying the Punishment to the last Extremity, <427> as by not stopping short of this Severity. What St. *Austin* says in this Place, concerning those stray Sheep which soon or late shou'd come back to the Fold, makes nothing for him; because if they stand in need of Fines, Prisons, Gallys, and such other Punishments to make 'em enter into themselves, and seek Instruction, there's no manner of doubt but the fear of Death wou'd be still more conducive to this end.

124. See above, p. 161.

❧ XV. ST. AUSTIN'S WORDS ❧

There is not a Man among us, nor yet among you (Donatists) but approves the Laws of the Emperors against the Sacrifices of the Pagans; yet these Laws ordain much severer Punishments, and punish those with Death who are guilty of these Impietys: whereas in the Laws enacted against you, it's visible they have study'd much more how to recover you from your Errors, than how to punish your Crimes.

ANSWER

'Twere a hard matter to reckon up all the Errors in point of Judgment, which occur in these words. Let's remember that St. *Austin* had said not long before, 1. That the good Persecutors differ from the bad in this particular, that those keep within the Bounds of Moderation, these abandon themselves to Rage and Fury; those aiming only at the Health and Recovery of their Patients, have a care what they cut away; these aiming at his Destruction, ne'er mind where the Stroke lights: those have a design only upon the Gangrene, these against the Life. 2. That altho the Pro-<428>phets have slain the Wicked, as the Wicked have frequently slain the Prophets; and tho *Nebuchodonosor* Type of the different States of the Christian Church, denotes that Christians under believing Kings, shou'd inflict the same Punishments on the Wicked, as they inflicted on the Christians under unbelieving Kings; yet they mitigate the Severity, and use all possible Moderation: because *among even those Christians,* who suffer themselves to be seduc'd, it's possible there may be some who are predestinated. Let's think, I say, on this, and see how St. *Austin* will be able to reconcile it with what he says in this place, that all sort of Christians approve the Laws which punish Pagans with Death for exercising their Religion.

In the first place, What will become of this differencing Mark of ungodly Persecutors, that they strike at the Party's Life, that they lay about 'em without Fear or Wit, and ne'er mind where they cut and slash; and this other distinguishing Mark of godly Persecutors, that they aim only at the Cure, that they only attack the Gangrene: what, I say, will become of these differencing Marks, if the good Persecutors, the Persecutors approv'd by St. *Austin,* and by the whole Body of Christians, put those to death without Mercy who adhere to Gentilism? In the second place, if the reason why they don't exercise the whole of that Severity prefigur'd by *Nebuchodonosor* Type of the Christian Church persecuting, as also of the same Church persecuted, be, that even among those Christians, who are drawn away into Schism or Heresy, there are Sheep who shall soon or late return to the <429> Fold: if, I say, this be their reason for mitigating the Punishments, why shou'd they not mitigate 'em towards the Pagans? Is't because there can be none of those predestin'd Souls among them; those Sheep which God has given to his Son, and which shall soon or late be brought home to the Fold? But this were strange Doctrine indeed; a Doctrine which must destroy all Endeavors in the Ministers of the Gospel of converting Infidels: For according to the System of Predestination, commonly ascrib'd to St. *Austin,* 'tis only for the sake of the Elect that the Gospel is preach'd to Mankind; so that its Ministers wou'd not preach it at all to a People, they were assur'd, had none of those predestin'd Souls among 'em. Now it's plain, 'twas not impossible but Paganism might have had some of those Predestin'd; since 'tis to them principally, that the Apostles preach'd the Gospel: and what are we our selves, but the Posterity of those Pagans who were converted to the Gospel? Besides all which, St. *Austin,* in this very Letter confesses, that the Laws of the Emperors against Idolaters had converted great Numbers of the Pagans, and converted others daily.

It looks, says such a one, as if St. *Austin* made use of this Expression; *It is not impossible, but that even among those Christians, who have suffer'd themselves to be seduc'd, there may be some Sheep of* JESUS CHRIST; only to signify, that those Christians who forsake the Communion of the Church, are in a more deplorable state than the Pagans. This is what Divines generally pretend: They'l needs have it, that a Man, who having once known and profess'd the Truth, falls <430> afterwards away, is in much a worse condition than he, who having never heard of the Gospel, has likewise never made profession of it. And for this reason it is, that St. *Austin* ranks it in the number of things barely not impossible, that there shou'd be any of the Predestin'd in a Society of Schismaticks or Hereticks; but won't speak of it as a thing very likely, or very reasonable, much less as certain. Now if this be a thing which at best is only not impossible, St. *Austin* must have believ'd it much more reasonable, that there shou'd be Sheep among the Pagans, who might one day come into the Fold, and to whom the Particle *even,* which he here makes use of, has a relation. But *that such a one,* who shou'd talk at this rate, wou'd talk too refin'd. St. *Austin* himself declares a little lower, that they look on the Donatists at a less distance from the Church than Idolaters, and that this is the reason of their punishing 'em less rigorously. But waving all these Subtiltys, who sees not that nothing can be more void of the Justness of a Man of good Sense, than saying on one hand what St. *Austin* remarks concerning the Character of ungodly Persecutors, and the Reasons for mitigating the Punishments of the Donatists; and on the other hand to approve all the Laws which condemn'd the Pagans to death, for sacrificing to their Gods, according to the immemorial Rites of their Ancestors.

A modern* Author, after having cited a great many Passages from St. *Austin,* shewing, that he <431> us'd all his Interest with the higher Powers to prevent their punishing Sectarys with death; says, *That the Character of the most humane and the best-natur'd Man, can't be deny'd him without Injustice.* But it's most certain it may, without any Injustice; seeing he openly approv'd the murdering such Pagans as wou'd persevere in the Religion of their Fathers. I say nothing of his approving a world of other Laws, which, tho they did not come up to the spilling of Blood, and to Death, were yet exceedingly hard, exposing to Infamy, Banishment, Confiscations, and Forfeiture of all the Privileges and Advantages of Society; but I must say, he reason'd not the most consequentially, and that there is not the least Justness or Consistency in his Principles. Better tho he shou'd be guilty of reasoning unconsequentially, than of carrying the Cruelty so high, as to demand the punishing Hereticks with death no less than Pagans. Be that how it will,

---

* Thomassin de l' Unitè de l' Eglise, I *Part. Ch.* 1. [Louis Thomassin, *Traité de l'unité de l'Eglise et des moyens que les princes chrestiens ont employez pour y faire rentrer aux qui en estoient séparez* (Tract on the unity of the Church and the means Christian rulers have used to cause those who have separated from it to rejoin), 1693. Reviewed by Bayle, NRL, OD, p. 688.]

one of the* Apologists of the modern Convertists has bin simple and un-advis'd enough to publish, that all the Maxims of Moderation, with regard to the converting Men, concern the Pagans only, and by no means those Christians who have rent the Unity of the Church; and at the same time to quote St. *Austin,* with regard to that Constraint which is to be made use of towards those in Error. The poor Man cou'd not see, that if he has reason of his side, St. *Austin* knows not what he says, and consequently his Authority in these matters deserves to be hiss'd; but that if <432> St. *Austin* has reason, he himself deserves to be hooted. St. *Austin* approves Violence with regard to Hereticks, and with regard to Pagans; but with regard to these he approves it even to death, as being farther off from the Church, whereas he won't allow Hereticks to be punish'd to that Extremity: On the contrary, the *Sieur Brueys* pretends, that the Church ought to make use of no other means than Instruction and Persuasion with the Pagans, but may punish Hereticks as rebellious Children with death, over whom she has infinitely a greater Right than over Strangers and Infidels; without reckoning, adds he, that the Pagans keep off only because of the Incomprehensibility of the Church's Doctrines, whereas Hereticks separate from pure Aversion.

What a strange Idea do the Clergy form of Lenity and Moderation? *P. Thomassin* extols the Gentleness and Lenity of St. *Austin,* as something very transcendent, because he wou'd not have People dye their Hands in the Blood of the Donatists, but only punish 'em smartly some other way: and it's well known, that† St. *Bernard,* who passes for Meekness it self, approv'd the Zeal of a heady Rabble, who fell upon a parcel of Hereticks, and dispatch'd 'em out of the way. *Approbamus zelum, sed factum non suademus; quia Fides suadenda est, non imponenda:* We approve their Zeal, says

---

* Le Sr. Brueys Reponse aux Plaint. [*Réponse aux plaintes des Protestans contre les moyens que l'on employe en France pour les réunir à l'Eglise, où l'on réfute les calomnies qui sont contenuës dans le livre intitulé: La Politique du clergé de France, et dans les autres libelles de cette nature* (Answer to the complaints of Protestants against the means being used in France to reunite them with the Church, refuting the calumnies contained in the book called "The policy of the French Clergy" [by Jurieu] and other libels of the kind), 1686. Reviewed by Bayle, NRL, OD, p. 611.]

† Sermo. 66. in Cantic. [Migne, *Patrologia Latina*, vol. 183, col. 1101.]

he, but don't advise the Practice; because Faith ought to be infus'd by Persuasion, and not by Constraint. The good Abbot had a <433> Sense on his Mind of the Truth and Holiness of this Maxim, yet cou'd not forbear praising the Zeal of those who violated it most barbarously; and he scarce utters this Maxim, when, as tho he had gone too great a length, he seems willing to recal his words: for he tells us in the very same breath, *Quanquam melius proculdubio Gladio coercentur, illius videlicet, qui non sine causa Gladium portat, quam in suum errorem multos trajicere permittantur: Tho there's no doubt but 'twere better restrain 'em with the Sword, of him, I mean, who bears not the Sword in vain, than suffer 'em to seduce many other Souls to their Errors.* In another place* he says, 'twere better indeed overcome Hereticks by Reason; but if this won't do, they ought to be banish'd or imprison'd. Are not these very illustrious Instances of a Spirit of Lenity and Moderation? Yet let's rather wonder, that a Doctor bred up in the Romish Communion, tho naturally meek and tender-hearted, shou'd preserve the least Remains of Humanity, than that he shou'd mingle such Lessons of Injustice and Harddealing with his Clemency. A modern† Author has handl'd the Ecclesiastical Clemency as it deserves.

---

* Serm. 66. in Cantic. [*Ibid.* See DHC, art. "Bernard."]

† Nouvelles de la Repub. des Lettr. Fevr. 1686. Art. de Mr. Maimbourg. [Bayle, OD, vol. 1, pp. 493–98.]

✂ XVI. ST. AUSTIN'S WORDS ✂

As to the solliciting the Emperors to make Laws against Schismaticks or Hereticks, or to enforce 'em, and enjoin their being put in Execution; you'l be pleas'd to remember the Violence with <434> *which the other Donatists egg'd on, not only the Maximinasts,* &c. *but above all, you won't forget how in the Petition, by which they implor'd the Authority of the Emperor* Julian *against us, they tell this Prince, whom they knew to be an Apostate and Idolater,* That he was wholly mov'd by Justice, and that nothing else had any Power over him.

ANSWER

These words don't at all concern me, seeing they are only an *Argumentum ad hominem,* or a Recrimination.[125] The Donatists may have done all the irregular things he pleases, still this won't excuse the Catholicks, except Sin is to be authoriz'd by Examples. Besides, as I propos'd to examine only the general Question, and the Arguments which St. *Austin* offers for forcing the Conscience; I have nothing to do with these Retorsions, or Reasons founded on Retaliation. I shall only say, that if I were not under some sort of Engagement to my self, not to charge St. *Austin* with Insincerity, I cou'd hardly forbear saying, that he here wou'd slur not only little Artifices of Rhetorick, but even downright Sophistry, upon us. For how else can we qualify his saying, that the Donatists, by giving *Julian* the Praises alledg'd, were either guilty of an abominable Lye, or own'd Idolatry to be a righteous thing? How little does this look, how strong does it smell of the Cavil! Had the Popish Priests, in a Petition to the late King, told his Majesty, that he hearken'd only to Reason and Justice; common Sense wou'd tell us, they did not hereby mean to say, the Church of *England,* which the King <435> was a Member of, was the rightful and true Church; but only, when the Question was about Settlement of a Dispute, that his Majesty consider'd the Rights of the Parties without any respect of Persons. So nice was the

125. See Appendixes, "Bayle's Use of Logic," p. 580, note 3.

Emperor *Julian* in this particular, and in all other moral Dutys, that he might very safely be prais'd in a Petition, without the Partys touching upon the string of Religion, or importing, that even in this respect too, he suffer'd not himself to be struck by any other Light than that of Justice. Had St. *Austin* seen the Elogys of Pope *Gregory* the Great, on the Emperor *Phocas*, and the Queen *Brunehaud*, he'd perhaps have compounded with the Donatists, and engag'd never to reproach 'em more with their Petition to *Julian*, on condition they wou'd spare the great Flatterer St. *Gregory*.

Another Quibble of St. *Austin*'s, at least something very like it, is his arguing, *A dicto simpliciter ad dictum secundum quid*.[126] His Adversarys complain'd of the methods of flying to the Secular Power, and oppressing 'em with the Imperial Penal Laws; and as it is usual to talk in general, or at least in indefinite Propositions, where we take a thing ever so little to heart, there's no reason to doubt but their meaning was, that it was not proper to appeal to the Secular Power in Disputes about Religion, and that the Church ought not to have recourse thither. St. *Austin*, willing to ruin this Principle by the Absurdity of its Consequences, takes the Proposition in the strictness of the Letter, and the very utmost Extent; and from it wou'd conclude, that we must never appeal to the Secular Power, not even in criminal Cases, or for the determining Causes <436> purely Ecclesiastical: and as the Donatists themselves had had recourse to it in like Cases, he charges 'em with confuting their own Maxim. But with Submission to this great Bishop of *Hippo*, he takes the matter wrong; for tho the procuring an Order or Law for punishing a Bishop or Minister who abjures not his Belief, is a very bad Practice, yet it is very proper to apply to the temporal Power for the preventing any Man's intruding into Ecclesiastical Preferments, and keeping 'em by wicked means; or appealing in any difference arising upon a matter of this nature, which cou'd not be decided by the ordinary course of Law. In a word, it's lawful to desire the Prince, that he wou'd not suffer a Bishop, whether guilty, or only suspected of a Crime, to be exempted from clearing himself by due course of Law.

---

126. The fallacy of arguing "from something true in general to something said of a particular case," which may be an exception.

ଓ XVII. ST. AUSTIN'S WORDS ଓ

By this time you must, I'm sure, be sensible, that we ought not so much to consider, whether People are forc'd, as what they are forc'd to; that is, whether to Good or to Evil. Not that any one becomes a better Man by mere Force; but the dread of what People are loath to suffer, makes 'em open their Eyes to the Truth.

ANSWER

And I, for my part, shall tell my Readers, that by this time they must, I'm sure, be sensible, we ought never to examine what People are forc'd to in matters of Religion, but whether they are forc'd; and from this very Circumstance declare it a wicked Action, and most opposite to the <437> Nature and Genius of all Religion, and especially of the Gospel. But after all, was St. *Austin* simple enough to imagine that the Adversarys he then had to deal with, and those which he might have in after-times, wou'd all be weak enough to be impos'd on by this kind of Reasoning? Here it is drawn up in Mood and Figure.[127]

People don't do ill in forcing others, unless when they force those, who are in the Interests of Truth, to pass over to Error.

Now we have not forc'd those, who were in the Interests of Truth, to come over to an Error; (for we, who are the Orthodox, have forc'd you, who are Schismaticks or Hereticks, to come over to our side.)

Therefore we have not done ill.

And you only wou'd have done ill, if you had forc'd us.

Is not this manifestly that kind of Sophism, which the Logicians call *Petitio Principii?*[128] To which I can think of no shorter an Answer at present, than converting the Minor in the Syllogism from a Negative to an Affirmative, and concluding the direct contrary. 'Tis in this view of it, that one may justly say of Christianity what Mr. *de Meaux* wou'd infer from the Supposition of Protestants, concerning the Fallibility of the Church; to wit, *That it is assuredly the most helpless Society upon earth, the most expos'd*

127. See Appendixes, "Bayle's Use of Logic," p. 580 ("syllogism").
128. Ibid. ("petitio principii").

to incurable Divisions, the most abandon'd to Innovators and factious Spirits:[129] For if they who have the Truth of their side may lawfully exercise Violence against all other Religions, behold a Right in being which shall be challeng'd by all the Sects, and which each shall exert with precisely the <438> same Reason and Excuses for so doing, without a possibility of ever applying any other Remedy to such an Evil, than the discussing all the Controversys between 'em from the very Source and Beginning; a Discussion which wou'd take up the Life of *Methusalem* upon any one Article. So that if, under an Impossibility of mutually convincing each other, they won't consent to the common Laws of Society and Morality; I mean to abstain from Robbery and Murder, and other ways of Violence with regard to one another; it's impossible but Christianity shou'd be a Scene of Blood, and a continual Source of Civil War and Violence.

As to that Fear which makes Men open their eyes to the Truth, I refer to the first Chapter of the second Part of my *Commentary*.[130]

౧౦ఠ XVIII. ST. AUSTIN'S WORDS ౧౦ఠ

I cou'd instance you not only in private Persons, but intire Citys, which of Donatists, as they formerly were, are become good Catholicks, and detest the diabolical Sin of their old Separation; who yet wou'd never have bin Catholicks, but for the Laws which you are so displeas'd with.

ANSWER

This kind of Reasoning is so very unworthy of any Confutation in a Philosophical Commentary, that I shou'd truly be asham'd to expose it by all its weak sides: and in good earnest St. *Austin* moves my pity by his Ingenuousness, in confessing that his Collegues had brought him off from his first Opinion, which was that which I maintain, by alledging to him the

129. This and a passage quoted below come from a letter by Bossuet to a resident of his diocese, April 3, 1686, appended to the first of Jurieu's *Lettres pastorales addressees aux fideles de France qui gemissent sous la captivite de Babylon* (English translation: *Monsieur Jurieu's Pastoral letter, directed to the Protestants in France*, 1688; see pp. 27, 29).

130. See above, p. 137.

good Successes of Con-<439>straint. Just so we find Ecclesiasticks and bigotted Laicks in *France,* who imagine that all the infamous Practices of the Dragoons have bin amply rectify'd and compensated by the accession of so many thousands of Souls, who are re-united to Popery. These Men must needs be very short-sighted, since they can't perceive that they reason on this Principle, That every thing which is attended with good Success is just. Whence it will follow, that *Mahomet*'s Religion and his Constraints were just; whence it will also follow, that a Roman Catholick ought to conclude, that the Laws under *Edward* VI and Q. *Elizabeth* were as just as those in Q. *Mary*'s Reign: and consequently, that Utility being the sole Rule of Justice, things diametrically opposite shall be equally just.

I take no notice of the account St. *Austin* gives of what the re-united Donatists us'd to say touching the Causes which had hinder'd their Reunion, nor of the Gratitude which they profess'd for those who had bin Authors of the Constraint. Mr. *Arnaud* has made the Application of this to the Protestants of *France,* who had abjur'd before the Dragooning: And a certain* Author, whom I have cited in another place, has made his Remarks on him. For my part I wave it, because I only propose to confute the general reasons and grounds of Constraining, not such as are peculiar to the Donatists: if any one will take the pains of applying 'em to all who yield under Constraint, he shall form from 'em a Set of Common-places which shall confute one <440> another; serving as an Argument for the good Persecutors here, and for the wicked Persecutors there, and as a Jest to all the rest of the world, who look on things without prejudice.

* Suite de la Critique de Maimbourg. [*Nouvelles letters critiques sur l'Histoire du Calvinism,* Lettre XI, sec. 2, in Bayle, OD, vol. 2, p. 236.]

⋈ XIX. ST. AUSTIN'S WORDS ⋈

Ought I to prevent the confiscating what you call your Goods,
while you with impunity proscribe JESUS CHRIST? *The barring*
you the liberty of disposing 'em by your last Testament, according
to the Roman Law, while you by your slanderous Accusations
tread under foot the Testament which God himself has made in
favor of our Fathers, &c.?

ANSWER

St. *Austin* runs on here in seven or eight Antitheses or Clenches of this
kind, which may be alledg'd by all sort of Persecutors more or less; for each
supposes that the Party it persecutes are Enemys to God: so that if this
Supposition is a sufficient ground for persecuting, we are all ready arm'd
at all seasons against one another, and always with the same pretence. To
say, that only they who can reasonably make the Supposition, have a right
to persecute, is saying nothing; because till such time as the ungodly Persecutors are made sensible that they believe they act upon a sure bottom,
but really do not, they'l persecute without remorse: so that this will be only
wrangling about the main thing in dispute, and not assuaging that horrible
Storm which shall overwhelm here the true Church, there the false, and
every where occasion a Concatenation of Insult, Cruelty, Sacrilege, and
Hypocrisy: <441> Not to insist, that one may turn all these fine Antitheses
upon the Catholicks who lead wicked Lives, upon the Slanderers, the Covetous, the Tiplers, &c. Shou'd Princes think fit to seize their Estates, or
hinder their disposing of 'em to their Children, might not any one say in
defence of such a Proceeding, *Why shou'd you think it hard to be deny'd the*
Privilege of making your last Will and Testament, when by your disorderly
courses you shew so little regard for your heavenly Father's Testament?

∞ XX. ST. AUSTIN'S WORDS ∞

If there be any among us who abuse the Laws which the Emperors have enacted against you (Donatists) and who make 'em a handle for exercising their private Spite, instead of employing 'em as an instrument and means of Charity to rescue you from Error; we disapprove their Proceedings, and think of 'em with grief. Not that any Man can call this or that thing his Property, at least unless entitled to it by a divine Right, by the which all belongs to the Just; or by a Right founded on human Laws, and which depends on the Pleasure of the temporal Powers: so that you, for your parts, can call nothing your own, because not entitled to it, as being of the number of the Just, and because the Laws of the Emperors deprive you of all: consequently you can't properly say, This thing is ours, and we have got it by our Industry; *since it is written,** The Wealth of the <442> Sinner is laid up for the Just. *Notwithstanding, when under color of these Laws men invade your Possessions, we disapprove the Practice, and it troubles us exceedingly. In like manner, we condemn all those who are mov'd more by Avarice than Zeal, to take from you, either the Funds for your Poor, or the Places of your Assemblys; tho you enjoy neither one nor t'other but under the Notion of the Church, and tho only the true Church of* JESUS CHRIST *has a true Right to these things.*

ANSWER

This Passage contains Paradoxes so mysterious, so odious, and so absurd, that it will not be improper to range my Reflections on it in some kind of order.

I. I affirm then in the first place, That it's a vain Excuse, and a pitiful palliative Remedy, to tell People persecuted and molested in their Persons and Estates, that we disapprove the Proceedings of those who abuse the Prince's Laws; for beside, that tho no one strain'd or abus'd these Laws, the

---

* Prov. 13.22.

poor People under Persecution must be expos'd to a thousand Distresses, and the Authors no way disapprov'd by the Gentlemen Ecclesiasticks; so that the Persecuted have no such mighty Obligations to 'em, for their disapproving only the Abuse of these Laws: besides this, I say, is it not mocking the world, to sollicit Laws with Earnestness and Ardor, the Execution of which we know must inevitably be attended with a thousand Excesses; and then think to come off by saying with a grave Air, That we disapprove these Abuses? And if you really <443> disapprove 'em, why, wretched Men as you are, don't you demand the proper Redress with the same Earnestness as you demanded the Laws themselves? Why are you the foremost in dissembling, in disowning these Abuses, in publishing thro a whole Kingdom, that there were none committed? This I thought fit to remark by the by, against those base mercenary Pens, who speak so soothingly of the late Dragoon-Conversions in *France*.

II. In the second place, Is it not an abominable Doctrine, tho veil'd with a big mysterious Air, that all belongs to the Godly by a Divine Right? What Nonsense is this? What, the Effects which a Jew has bought and paid down his Mony for, and which he has transported from *Asia* to *Europe* with a deal of hazard, and at a vast expence, don't belong to him; no, it's downright Robbery in him, and an Usurpation in prejudice of the Members of the true Church? It shou'd seem now quite contrary, that as JESUS CHRIST had not the common Privilege of Foxes and Fowls, which have Nests and Holes to lie down in, while he had not a place wherein to lay his head, his Members ought not to have had all the Good things of the World shar'd amongst them; yet by this Theology, no less chimerical than the Stoicks' wise Man, a small Handful of Men, call'd Catholicks, are put in possession of all the Earth, and of all the Goods and Estates, movable and immovable, personal and real, of Jews, Turks, Pagans, and Sectarys. In good earnest these are strange Visions; and at the same time here's a plain foundation laid for the Pretensions of the Pope over the Temporals of Kings; <444> for if every thing belongs to the Church by divine Right, the Monarchys and Principalitys of the Earth must o' course fall to his share; and accordingly he may dispose of 'em in the old Continent, with the same Authority as in the new.

III. Yet even this destroys the Alternative which St. *Austin* proposes: for if every thing be suppos'd the Property of the Godly by a Divine Right, it follows that Princes cou'd not dispose of the Goods of the World in favor of the Profane and Ungodly, without the notorious Invasion of a Right vested in the Godly by the Donation of God. It's false then, that what a Jew enjoys by his Prince's Gift or Permission belongs properly to him: for the Prince's Grant being only a Robbery or Pillage committed upon the Godly, renders not a Jew the rightful Possessor; and consequently St. *Austin* blunders inexcusably, when he allows there are two ways of becoming the lawful Possessor of an Estate, one when the Party is of the number of the Godly, the other when the Prince makes a Grant of it, or suffers the Party to enjoy it. All he cou'd in good reason allow, was, that the Godly not having force enough to put 'em in possession of all that belongs to 'em, permitted those Usurpers whom Princes had vested to enjoy the mean Profits. And are not the Jews now finely met with for their chimerical Pretensions, the Original and Model of those of St. *Austin!* Their Doctors maintain, that none but *Israelites* possess any thing rightfully, and that the Estates of all others are like a Common, which the next Comer may seize on, and become the lawful Possessor; they mean, provided he's a Jew. <445>

IV. In the fourth place, Let's not lose the benefit of this Father's Talent at finding out Expedients: he's for having all the Godly let their Rights sleep, and be so complaisant to their Princes, as not to take ill that they confirm that Partition, which has taken place in the World from Time immemorial. What will follow from hence? why this, That any Prince who destroys this Partition, without a very cogent Reason, is a Tyrant and a Robber. Every one will allow, that 'twere Robbery, strictly speaking, in a King, to take away a Merchant's fine Stuffs and Silks, and not pay him the full value. I except one Case, where a whole Kingdom may be in danger, unless some particular Person's Effects were seiz'd and made use of: But once more 'twill be granted me, that 'twere Robbery in a King to sweep away all the Mony out of the Bankers Shops, and all the Jewels from the Goldsmiths, for his own private use, or for his fancy, without ever making restitution. 'Twere Robbery likewise and Tyranny in him, to take away his Estate from *John o' Nokes* or *John o' Stiles,* to annex it to the Crown-Revenues, or bestow it upon Mistresses, Favorites, or Buffoons: 'Twere the same, shou'd he do the like upon the pretext of such a Disobedience, suppose, as this; to wit, That the Prince having enjoin'd by a solemn Edict, that all his Subjects shou'd be of such a Stature at such an Age, shou'd have blue Eyes, a hawk Nose, black Hair,

shou'd love Musick, Hunting, Books, like such a Dish better than such a
Dish, believe firmly that Snow is not white, nor Fire hot, in the sense of
the Peripateticks, and that the Earth moves round the Sun, &c. several of
<446> 'em shou'd not conform to his Will: I say then, that shou'd a Prince
punish Disobediences of this nature by Confiscation, Fines, or by a general
Change in the Settlements and Freeholds within his Dominions, he'd be
a most unjust Tyrant, and might be said to rob his Subjects of their lawful
and rightful Property. Whence it follows, as I have prov'd at large in another* place, that to the end a Disobedience be justly punishable by loss of
Goods, it's necessary the Law disobey'd be just; at least that it be of such
a nature, that the disobeying can only proceed from Perverseness or inexcusable Neglect. Now as all Laws ordaining the Belief of this or that in the
Worship of God, or of doing this or that in discharge of the Dutys of
Religion, are not of this nature; for it's manifest, that a Man persuaded he
ought not to believe concerning God otherwise than he already believes,
nor honor him otherwise than as he had bin taught to do in his Father's
House; and who, do what he will, finds himself irresistably convinc'd, that
by believing or acting otherwise he must draw on himself eternal Damnation, disobeys not such a Law from inexcusable or unreasonable Neglect:
it follows then, that a Prince who punishes a Disobedience to such Laws
by Confiscations, Prisons, Banishment, makes a tyrannical use of the Power
lodg'd in him; and consequently St. *Austin* has no ground for saying, that
where a Man conforms not to his Prince's Laws, condemning the Estates
of those to his own use who won't conform, he has no longer any Right
vested in him, either to <447> what he enjoy'd by Descent, or to what he
has acquir'd by the Sweat of his Brow. He ought at least to have added this
Proviso, that the Laws be such as the Subjects might in Conscience comply
with. But this is what cannot be affirm'd of those Laws which relate to
Religion, and which enjoin one Party of the Subjects to abjure what they
believe to be the true and divine Faith. They therefore, who might disobey
'em, continue lawful and rightful Possessors of their Goods as much as they
were before, nor can they be outed any fairer than those may be, who obey'd
not their Prince enjoining to believe, that such a Sauce was better than such

* *Chap. 6. of the first Part*, p. 110, &c.

a Sauce, that Mr. *Des Cartes* had assign'd the true Cause of the Phenomena of the Loadstone, *&c.* or rather let's say, they'd be outed with exactly the same Justice, as *Naboth* was turn'd out of his Inheritance.[131]

This Example carries something awful in it. *Achab,* as wicked a King as he was, wou'd come by *Naboth*'s Vineyard no otherwise than in a way of fair Bargain between Man and Man, that is, by Purchase or Exchange; and even offer'd the Proprietor a better Vineyard in another place, in case he lik'd that better than ready Mony. So far the Conduct of this King was perfectly reasonable; nor is it besides unfair in a Prince, who has built him a Seat for his Pleasure, to desire a larger Garden to it than ordinary, for which it seems *Naboth*'s Vineyard lay very commodiously: Yet this Man had not the least Complaisance for his King; he told him very drily, that he cou'd not part with the Inheritance of his Fathers; wherein, it's pretended, he acted from Reasons <448> of Conscience, and from a fear of breaking some Precepts of *Leviticus*. Nothing less cou'd have clear'd him from the height of Brutality. *Achab* had no more to say, but left him, and took on heavily. His Queen, tho much the hardier Spirit of the two, yet durst not advise him to seize the Vineyard by his mere Authority; but got *Naboth* sentenc'd to death upon another pretext, to wit, that of blaspheming God and the King: and so the Vineyard fell to *Achab*. There's no doubt, had the King, upon the refusal of the Proprietor to comply with his Proposal for an Exchange or fair Purchase, confiscated this Vineyard, but the Prophet *Elias* wou'd have censur'd it as a very unjust Action. An Example which serves to shew Princes, that they ought never to disturb any one in the possession of that Estate which he's come honestly by, and which he's entitled to by the municipal Laws, at least unless the urgent Occasions of the State require; but by no means as a Punishment on those who follow the Motions of their Conscience, without doing any injury to the Publick, or to their Fellow-Citizens.

There are very great Men who maintain, that Kings are so far from having a Right of alienating or transferring Estates at pleasure from one Family to another, or impoverishing those to enrich these, that they can't justly lay

---

131. 1 Kings 21.

even a Tax upon their People without their* Consent. Hear how the famous *John Juvenal des Ursins,*[132] Archbishop of *Rheims,* speaks in a Remonstrance <449> to *Charles* VII. *Whatever any body may tell you of your ordinary Power, you have no right at all to take away any thing of mine. What's mine is not yours: In matters of Civil Justice you are indeed supreme, and the last Appeal is to you; you have your Domain, and every private Person has his. John*† Gerson says, *It's an Abuse, to tell a King he has a right to make use of the Estates or Persons of his Subjects at discretion, without any farther pretence of the publick Good or Necessity, imposing Taxes as he thinks fit: for to do this without any other reason, were playing the Tyrant, and not the King.* The Author of the Maxims, cited in the Margin, proves in the same place, *That Princes not only sin grievously, when they don't prevent, by all kind of means, the Rapines and Oppressions of the Soldiery; but also that they are in Conscience oblig'd to repair the Losses and Damage which their Subjects sustain by the Army. And truly,* continues he, *I wonder this Point shou'd be so much neglected, and that Confessors and Directors of Conscience shou'd have so much Complaisance; as in matters of such importance, and so very notorious, to be loth to grieve the Souls under their direction, by injoining the proper Penance.* A fine Lecture, not only for the Molinist Confessors of Kings, but also for St. *Austin, Molina's* Antipode![133] St. *Austin,* I say, who vends the most corrupt Morality that can be imagin'd, to wit, that whenever a Prince thinks fit to issue Edicts relating to Religion, and constraining the Conscience of the Subject by Fines and Confiscations, they who don't obey forfeit all Right to their Estates and Inheritances; <450> which consequently may become as much a Prey to the Soldiers, if the Prince delivers it into their hands, as to any other.

---

* *See a Book entitled,* Recueil des Maximes veritables & importantes pour l'Institution du Roi, *ch.* 11. [Claude Joly, *Recueil de maximes véritables et importantes pour l'institution du roi contre la fausse et pernicieuse politique du cardinal Mazarin, prétendu surintendant de l'éducation de Sa Majesté* (Collection of true and important maxims for the instruction of the king, against the false and pernicious policy of Cardinal Mazarin, self-styled supervisor of his majesty's education), 1652.]

† Contra Adul. Prin. confid. 6. [Joannes Gerson, *Opera omnia,* ed. Du Pin, Antwerp, 1706, vol. 4, col. 623.]

132. Jean Juvenal des Ursins, ecclesiastic and writer of the fifteenth century. Passage not found.

133. On Molina and Augustine see Appendixes, "Grace, Original Sin, Predestination," pp. 585–87.

V. But in the fifth place, Who can forbear admiring this Father's Application of Scripture-Passages, as if *Solomon,* in foreshewing that the Riches of the Wicked shou'd not long abide in their Familys, but become the Possession of the Righteous, had meant this in a way of Seizure and arbitrary Confiscation? Does not every one see, that all these fine Sentences of Scripture relate not to those who err in matters of Religion, but to those who are guilty of Immoralitys; else what had become of all the Riches out of the Borders of *Judea,* since no one abroad was in the true Religion, to whom, according to the Principles of these Convertists, they ought to be bestow'd. What Godly were there in *Persia,* in *Greece,* in *Italy,* &c. to possess the Wealth which the Ungodly in these Countrys had heap'd up? It's a mere Chimera then, to appropriate to what they call Orthodoxy, that which is promis'd only to Uprightness and Honest-dealing. Is it that there's no sound Morality out of the Pale of that Society which St. *Austin* believes the Orthodox? Another Chimera! We believe the Papists in an Error, and they believe the same of us; yet they and we wou'd be errand Fools to fancy, they, that there were no vertuous People among us, and we, that there are none among them.

VI. In the sixth place, Let's admire St. *Austin*'s Good-nature: He approves with all his heart the Laws which deprive the Donatists of their Estates, and disapproves the Proceedings of the Catho-<451>licks who seize upon these Estates. This is pleasant enough, to blame him who executes, and praise him who enjoins the Execution of the Law.

VII. What he says in the last place, That the Churches of the Donatists, and the Funds for the Maintenance of their Sick and Poor, belong'd to the true Church, is so wretched, that I scorn to confute it. Is not there a Right of Nature and Nations for founding Hospitals; is it not a necessary Emanation of all Society, and an inseparable Appanage of incorporated Humanity? May not every State, Kingdom, Commonwealth, consecrate certain Sums for the Subsistence of their indigent Poor, and of all other Poor; and certain Places for celebrating the Ceremonys of Religion: and must these Endowments belong o' course to the Christian Religion? What, do all the Mosks of *Constantinople* belong to the Christians? And had they power enough to seize 'em in spite of the Turks, might and ought they to do it, together with all the Revenues of the Mahometan Religion? In good truth, this is rendring Christianity justly odious; and on such Maxims as these, Infidels ought to look on the Christian Missionarys only as so many Spys, thrusting in to prepare the way for an Attempt on their temporal Possessions, upon a persuasion that all the rest of Mankind are Usurpers, who with-hold their Birthright from 'em, tho they very often have not as much as heard that there are Christians in the world. <452>

∞ XXI. ST. AUSTIN'S WORDS ∞

But tho you will always be complaining of this kind of Treatment, you find it a hard matter to prove it upon any one; and tho you shou'd, it is not always in our power to correct or punish those you complain of, and we are sometimes oblig'd to tolerate 'em.

ANSWER

This is the very Answer now-adays to the Complaints of the *French* Protestants. Let 'em prove, say they, from the Tenor of the Edicts or Injunctions, that they were pinch'd, cudgel'd, kept awake, *&c.* they can't do it: But why? because the Convertists gave only verbal Instructions on these heads. They were not such Fools, as to leave it in any one's power, to preserve publick Monuments, to all Generations and all Ages to come, of their pernicious Maxims, ever impregnated and stain'd thro with Insincerity and Perfidiousness. But there are other as authentick Proofs, besides those taken from an Act of State enrol'd and recorded. As to the necessity of tolerating those Excesses, I say it over and over, that the Excuse is frivolous: They might have prevented 'em if they wou'd, or if they cou'd not, they might at least have punish'd some of the Authors for a terror to the rest; nothing had bin easier than this. *Lewis* XIV is so absolute in his Dominions, and so punctually obey'd, that we may truly apply to him in an eminent manner that Saying of the Historian *Nicetas: Nihil est quod ab Imperatoribus emendari non queat, nec ullum peccatum quod vices eorum su-* <453> *peret, & quicquid permittunt facere videntur.*[134]

Henceforward let's see what is to be seen in St. *Austin*'s Letter to *Bon-*

---

134. "There is nothing that cannot be corrected by the Emperors, nor any fault that overcomes their office; whatever they are seen to do is permitted." Passage not found.

iface. It's the 185th in the new Edition, and was the 50th in the old. 'Twas wrote about the Year 417.

∞ XXII. ST. AUSTIN'S WORDS ∞

When Nebuchodonosor *ordain'd, That whoever blasphem'd the Name of the God of the* Hebrews, *shou'd be destroy'd with his whole House; had any of his Subjects incur'd the Punishment, by the violating this Law, cou'd they have said, as these (Donatists) do now, that they were righteous, and alledg'd the Persecution by the King's Authority, as a Proof of their Innocence.*

ANSWER

Since an occasion fairly presents of speaking of this Edict of *Nebuchodonosor*, St. *Austin*'s favorite Model, and the Type, as he imagines, of the Christian Church, under the Christian and under the Persecuting Emperors; it mayn't be amiss in this place to shew, that this is not a fit Model to be follow'd. In order hereunto, it is necessary we observe these two things; first, That the Pagan Religion admitting a plurality of Gods, and supposing, that those which were never before ador'd or known, might make themselves so conspicuously known in due time, that it wou'd be for the Interest of the establish'd Religion to take 'em in; the Pagan Princes had not the same Reasons against making Laws, for obliging People in matters of Religion, as the Christian Princes had: and when <454> they did make such, they had much juster grounds to believe, that the Dissenters were Men of factious Principles, who differ'd not upon any Motives of Conscience. I'l suppose, that the *Babylonians* had a contempt for the Divinity which was worship'd in *Judea;* but after this Divinity had once manifested its Power in the Miracle of the fiery Furnace, 'twas very highly probable, that they wou'd make no scruple of speaking of it with Esteem, and of thinking, that it had a Sway in the World as well as the rest, and the means of protecting its Votarys. So as the Court might reasonably judg, that whoever comply'd not with these Sentiments when notify'd by the Royal Injunctions, was a seditious Spirit, and a Brute who deserv'd to suffer the threaten'd Punishment. In the second place we are to observe, that the Law of the King of *Babylon* impos'd not a necessity on People, of paying any Worship to the God of the *Hebrews;* but only of abstaining from all reviling and blasphemous Expressions against him, which it is very easy to conform to, how much persuaded soever the Party may be of the Falseness of his Worship; for no sober Man is in Conscience oblig'd to ridicule or sing Ballads in the Streets, or elsewhere, upon the Divinity of the Country where he is tolerated: all that he is in Conscience oblig'd to, is offering his Reasons against this or that Worship with Modesty, Calmness, and Honesty.

By this we perceive the great difference between this Law of *Nebuchodonosor,* and the Laws lately enacted in *France,* and in a hundred other Countrys for several Ages past; forasmuch as these concern Christians instructed in the Unity <455> of one holy Religion, and persuaded that God will damn all those, who shall depart from the way which he has mark'd out in his Word; and ordain, not only that all Men demean themselves fittingly towards the establish'd Religion, but likewise make open Profession of it, and declare it the only true.

But I shall make no scruple to say, pursuant to what I have so often prov'd and explain'd, That had any *Babylonian,* convinc'd in his Conscience, that the God of the *Hebrews* was a false God, declar'd so much before the proper Judges, who enjoin'd him upon Oath, to speak his Thoughts; or had he done this from a Persuasion, that this Religion requir'd his making such an open Declaration, and bin punish'd for it with Death: the King of *Babylon* had actually committed an unjust Action, seeing that he had usurp'd a Right over Conscience, which did not belong to him, and for the exercise of which he had no special Vocation, such as that of *Moses.* And this more and more discovers St. *Austin*'s want of Judgment in the choice of so many Examples, which he has collected with so happy a Memory. But to answer the drift of 'em in this place, and to confine my self precisely to the point under Consideration in this passage, I shall repeat what I have already insinuated in another place;[135] to wit,

That if he has any ground for censuring the Reasonings of the Donatists, upon their pretending, that the Persecutions they endur'd were an Argument of their being the People of God, we have ground enough at least to

135. See above, pp. 316–17.

say, that they who persecuted 'em were guilty of an ill Action, <456> and so far were estrang'd from the Nature and Essence of all true Religion, and principally of the Christian.

ଅଟ XXIII. ST. AUSTIN'S WORDS ଅଟ

Was not Agar *persecuted by* Sarah? *Yet she that persecuted was holy, and she who suffer'd Persecution was wicked.*

ANSWER

Still the same Illusion, of confounding Punishments inflicted for Crimes of a moral Nature, with those inflicted for Opinions of Religion! What shou'd we say to one who went about to prove the Lawfulness of persecuting Protestants, from the Practice in all well-order'd Commonwealths of persecuting Highway-men, and raising the Country upon 'em; and who shou'd add, that as in this instance the Persecuted are wicked, and the Persecutors the Ministers of Justice, so likewise are the persecuted Protestants wicked, and their Persecutors good Men and true? We shou'd only laugh at such piteous Reasoning. To be frank, the example here alledg'd of a good Woman, pious indeed and vertuous in the main, but not altogether free from Fits of Jealousy, and domestick Ill-humor, or the Freaks which a too saucy Maid might easily work her to; is not a jot more to the purpose. *Sarah* was a Saint, I allow, but not as she persecuted *Agar:* 'twas not her Goodness which operated in this occasion, but her Jealousy, her Chagrin, her Spite, her Spleen; in a word, the Failings of the Sex, supported, if you please, by a Right she had of not keeping a Maid in her Family, who had us'd her ill. <457>

I have already taken notice of an Equivocation which runs thro St. *Austin*'s Letter, while he confounds the Accusations given in against a Bishop for his Vices, or want of Ordination, with Punishments inflicted for Opinions. He makes use of this Equivocation, to prove Injustice upon the Donatists from their own Principles; for, says he, they had persecuted *Cecilian,* and yet they say it's never lawful to persecute. A weak Retorsion,[136] con-

---

136. See Appendixes, "Bayle's Use of Logic," p. 581 ("retorted").

sider'd in the general; since there's so vast a difference between accusing a Man, or endeavoring to convict him of Crimes, which he denys; and punishing him for Opinions, which he does not deny, and which he rather glorys in. But having spoke to this point already,[137] I shan't insist on it any longer, tho St. *Austin* wou'd beat it into us by saying the same thing over and over.

∞ XXIV. ST. AUSTIN'S WORDS ∞

If the Good may not persecute, and if they are only to suffer Persecution, he was neither a good Man nor a Saint, who speaks thus in the 17th *Psalm,* I will persecute my Enemies, I will pursue them and attack them and will give them no Rest *&c.*

ANSWER

Still a falser Application than any of the former! for *David* speaks in this place only of his Military Exploits, and of a Victory gain'd by him over his Enemys. I must own, that if once *Abraham* pursuing the four Kings who had spoil'd *Sodom, Joshuah* destroying the *Canaanites, David* winning the Battel against the *Philistines,* <458> *&c.* be Precedents for Persecution in Religion, we shall every where find enough ready to our hand; but at the same time, who can forbear mocking or murmuring, to see Scripture wrested at this rate, or apply'd so very injudiciously.

St. *Austin*'s Description of the Fury of the Donatists, and the strange havock they made among the Catholicks, is perfectly surprizing, when one considers that the Laws for which his Apology was wrote, condemn only to Banishment, Fines, *&c.* but what he subjoins, *The Church then being reduc'd to these Extremitys, with what reason can any one pretend, that we ought to suffer all, rather than implore that Protection, which God has afforded us by means of the Christian Emperors; or how cou'd we excuse our selves towards God for such a neglect?* This, I say, is imposing on us a second time the Sophism, *Ignoratio Elenchi,*[138] which I have confuted at the beginning

---

137. See above, pp. 203–5.
138. See Appendixes, "Bayle's Use of Logic," p. 581.

of this third Part.[139] For was there a Man upon Earth who cou'd pretend, that they were to blame in desiring the Emperor to restrain all the Murderers and Incendiarys in the Sect of the Donatists? Was not the whole Complaint concerning those Laws alone, which reach'd the peaceable Party among 'em, and which punish'd 'em purely on the score of Religion? Why then wou'd he change the Dice so grosly, upon all intelligent Readers, tho with slight enough for those who were strongly prepossess'd or void of Penetration?

I don't know whether I might venture to say, that there's ground to think the Catholicks exaggerated things very much, when they describ'd the Fury of the Donatists; for one can hardly comprehend how *Honorius,* with all his Softness, <459> shou'd be quite so patient, especially when sollicited so earnestly by the Churchmen. But this is constantly the way of those who are the strongest Side, and of those who persecute: They extenuate their own Severitys as much as possible, and even ballance 'em with Accounts of the Long-suffering and Patience, which they pretend they had exercis'd. They describe the Persecuted with all the Arts of Rhetorick, as guilty of an insupportable Insolence, unheard of Crueltys, furious Rebellions. I'm much mistaken, if there ben't something of this nature in the Account of the Donatists and their Sufferings. The Authors set forth the Behavior of the *Circoncellions* in very tragical Expressions; and instead of telling, that they were punish'd according to their Demerits, speak only of Corrections, and moderate Chastisements of the Donatists in general. What a disproportion is there in these things? We don't see in 'em the Highways and publick Places full of Gibbets and Faggots for the *Circoncellions,* who richly deserv'd these Punishments, if they were really such Men as they are represented; but we see Confiscations, Banishments, and a thousand other ways of Punishment for the Donatists of sober Life and Conversation. How rare a thing is a faithful History among Convertists and their Apologists!

139. See above, p. 286.

∞ XXV. ST. AUSTIN'S WORDS ∞

*The Service which Kings perform to God as they are Men, is one
thing; and that which they perform as Kings, is another. As Men
they serve him, by leading Lives as becomes the truly Faithful; but
as Kings they serve him, only <460> by enacting righteous Laws,
which tend to the promoting Good, and punishing Evil; and by
maintaining these Laws with Firmness and Vigor.*

ANSWER

This Passage may be all allow'd, if taken in an equitable sense; but the
Mischief is, that it abounds with Equivocations towards the latter end: for
by righteous Laws, St. *Austin* understands Laws in favor of his own Party;
and by Good, he understands whatever's conformable to his own Ideas; as
by Evil he understands what's repugnant to 'em: So that Maxims so indefinite, and capable of a thousand different Interpretations, according to the
different Notions of Partys, offer nothing which is capable of enlightning
Mens Understanding, or of putting a stop to the reciprocal Persecutions
of the uppermost Sects in the several Countrys. To make these Maxims of
any use, 'twere necessary to agree upon some common Principle, for the
definition of righteous Laws, for that of Good, and of Evil; and this can
only be found in the Hypothesis of Toleration: because then we might say,
that righteous Laws are such as tend to the Advantage of the State and of
Religion, by means suited and proportion'd to the Natures of each.
Whence it will follow, that Religion shall be promoted only by Instruction
and Persuasion; and the publick Good of the State only by the Punishment
of those, who won't suffer their Fellow-Citizens to live in quiet. It's certainly
the Duty of Kings, as such, to maintain Laws of this nature with Firmness
and Vigor; and as to the promoting the Practice <461> of moral Good, as
they can't with all their Power be instrumental this way, unless they promote
the Practice of that which is apprehended as Good, it's evident that their
Duty is limited to the making this Good understood by the Methods of
Instruction. Nor can they prevent Evil, unless they previously take care to
make it understood to be such: for so long as a Soul takes that to be Good

which is really Evil, it will embrace this Evil; and if it be outwardly con-strain'd to renounce it, the consequence will be its committing two Faults instead of one, because it must fall o'course into Hypocrisy: So that no other Hypothesis, but that of Toleration, can put Princes in a way of re-ducing this Maxim of St. *Austin*'s into Practice. The Reader will find the full Solution of this Passage of St. *Austin* in the sixth Chapter of the second Part of our Commentary.[140]

ঙ XXVI. ST. AUSTIN'S WORDS ঙ

One must be void of common Sense, to tell Princes, Take no thought whether People trample upon, or whether they revere, within your Dominions, the Church of him whom you adore. What, they shall take care to make their Subjects live according to the Rules of Vertue and Sobriety, without any one's presuming to say, that this concerns 'em not; and yet they shall presume to tell 'em, that it is not their business to take Cognizance within their Dominions, whether Men observe the Rules of the true Religion, or whether they give themselves over to Profaneness and Irreligion? For if from hence, that God has given Man a Free-will, Pro-faneness were to be permitted, why shou'd Adultery be punish'd? <462> The Soul which violates that Faith which it has plighted to its God, is it therefore less criminal than the Wife which violates the Faith she owes her Husband? And tho Sins, which Men thro Ignorance commit against Religion, are punish'd with less Sever-ity; must they therefore be suffer'd to subvert it with Impunity?

ANSWER

This is all very specious, and deserves so much the more to be consider'd with Order and Exactness.

I. I'l allow St. *Austin,* that one must be void of common Sense, to think it amiss in Princes to concern themselves, whether Men trample upon, or whether they revere, within their Dominions, the Church of him whom

140. See above, p. 199.

they adore. So far ought they to be from being wholly unconcern'd about the Church, that on the contrary, it's their Duty to keep a watchful eye over it; but after what manner? for here's the whole Difficulty, and the sole ground of the difference. Why, if their Religion be attack'd by Arms, they ought to defend it by Arms; if attack'd by Books and by Sermons, they ought to defend it by the same Weapons. So that if a Sect springs up in their Dominions, which wou'd seize the Churches, and take People by the Collar to force 'em to follow 'em; they ought to dispatch their Missionarys of the short Robe against 'em, their standing Troops and Militia, to fall foul on these Sectarys, to restrain their Insolences, and chastise 'em according to the nature of their Offence. But if this Sect employ only Arguments and Exhortations, they ought only to get 'em confuted <463> by better Arguments, if they can, and endeavor to inform 'em of the Truth: For it's plain to any Man who considers this matter aright, that if they employ Wheel and Scaffold against Men who back their Arguments and Exhortations with Scripture-Proofs, they violate the Reverence due to Reason and Scripture: and that if they extort Subscriptions from 'em by a dread of Death, they constrain 'em to deny with their Mouth, what their Heart adores as Truth; which is plunging 'em into much a greater Sin than their Error.

II. From hence it appears, that it is their Duty to enquire, whether People observe the Rules of the true Religion within their Dominions, or whether they are guilty of Profaneness and Irreligion. But the great Question is, how they ought to behave themselves when they are inform'd, that a Party of their Subjects follow not that Religion which their Princes believe to be true, but exercise another Worship which they look on as impious and damnable. I think I have already most evidently prov'd,[141] to all who are not utterly blinded by their Prejudices, that Princes ought in this case to content themselves with letting the Controversy play, and convincing 'em, if it be possible, by sound Arguments and Instructions. Having done their Duty this way as much as in them lies, they ought to think themselves acquitted before God; and for the rest take care, that this Sect, which differs from their own, contain themselves within Bounds, and live like good Subjects,

141. See above, p. 205.

and good Citizens. But, say they, this Sect is daily committing the horriblest Impietys and Profanations. Yes, say I, <464> if you define things by your Notions of 'em, but not if you consider 'em according to the Definitions of the Sect; for they pretend, that the Impietys and Profanations are all of your side, and that their own is the only true and perfect Worship of God. This brings me again to the applying a Thought of the Bishop of *Meaux,* as I did once before;[142] That if each Sect of Christianity assumes a Right of defining Blasphemy, Impiety, Profaneness, by Principles peculiar to themselves, and decree Punishments on Men as Blasphemers, and Profaners of holy things, convicted upon a Definition of the Crime which they don't allow; *Christianity is the weakest of all Societys, and the most obnoxious to incurable Evils:* For whilst the Protestants burnt the Catholicks in *England* as Blasphemers and Profane, these might burn the Protestants in *Italy* and *France* as Blasphemers and Profane: the same Opinions being treated at the same time as pious and impious, as holy and blasphemous; and what's the very Excess of Horror, we shou'd see Men expire in Flames as Blasphemers of God and his Truth, who protested with their last words, that they died only because they cou'd not say any thing that they believ'd displeasing to God; and to testify, that the Truth reveal'd to Mankind, in his Holy Word, was dearer to 'em than Life. The only means for preventing all these Confusions wou'd be, to define Blasphemy and Profaneness, by Principles common to the Accuser and the Accused; and then a Man fairly convicted of Blasphemy or Profaneness, might be hang'd out of the way, or burnt, or broil'd; and they, who delight in the death of Hereticks, have Content. Thus a Christian is <465> justly punish'd who renounces God, or robs the Vestry, the Poor-box, *&c.* because by his own Principles he is guilty of Blasphemy and Sacrilege. But the truth is, it were too hard upon St. *Austin,* to desire he wou'd qualify things otherwise than from the Instinct of his own Prejudices.

III. My third Remark arises naturally from the second. 'Tis all the reason in the world, that Princes shou'd ordain Penaltys and Chastisements for the obliging Men to the Observation of the Laws of Honesty and Sobriety, because all their Subjects acknowledg the Justice of these Laws, and con-

142. See above, pp. 333–34.

sequently every Transgression against 'em is malicious, wilful, and under the Conscience of its being displeasing to God. But as to the Tenets of Religion, and the Laws enacted by Princes concerning the Worship of God, all their Subjects acknowledg not the Justice of 'em alike; there are those who believe 'em impious and abominable: so that their disobeying 'em proceeds not either from Malice, or a Spirit of Rebellion, or a Contempt of their Sovereign, but from a fear of disobeying God, the great Lord and common Master of Prince and People. This, this is the great and capital Circumstance which makes the difference between Civil Observances, and Religious, with regard to the Prince's Jurisdiction; and the reason why he may justly enforce the Laws concerning those, with temporal Punishments and Rewards, but not punish the Infringers of such Laws as determine concerning these.

IV. The Answer is now very plain to St. *Austin*'s Comparison between Profanation and Adultery. Why, says he, shou'd they punish Adultery and < 466 > not Profaneness? Because, he who commits Adultery is agreed with his Accuser and his Judg, that it is Adultery and a wicked Action; but far from agreeing with 'em, that he is guilty of Impiety or Profaneness, in serving God according to the Principles of his own Sect: he thinks he's in the Discharge of a pious Work, and shou'd think himself guilty of Impiety and Profaneness, shou'd he worship God according to the Principles of his Judg or Accuser. The Judges find nothing, in the case of an Adulterer, that challenges their regard. They find the Motive evil, and a Sense and certain Knowledg in him of his acting wickedly; consequently that he had not any manner of regard in it to God, or to his Neighbor, so that every thing crys for Vengeance against him. But when a Catholick Judg wou'd punish what he calls Impiety, Blasphemy, and Sacrilege in a Calvinist, maintaining that the consecrated Host is no more than Bread, and refusing it Adoration; he discovers a Motive in the Soul of this Heretick which merits his regard, to wit, a fear of offending God, a horror of Idolatry, and a stedfast purpose of incurring the Detestation of Men rather than do that which he believes God has forbidden. A Disposition of Mind like this, ought it not to be an inviolable Asylum against all human Jurisdiction; and is it possible, there shou'd be Men of Blood and gigantick Boldness enough, to put a Man to

death, because he makes that the Rule of his Actions, which he takes to be
the Law and express Will of God?

V. As to the Parallel between a Wife who violates her conjugal Faith, and
a Soul which per-<467>severes not in a rightful Persuasion (and this St.
Austin calls, violating the Fidelity which we owe to God) I have little more
to say than that this Father cou'd not possibly mark out his Camp in worse
ground; he cou'd not maintain this Post a moment against a modern* Author, whom I have cited elsewhere,[143] and approv'd in part, and in part
disapprov'd. I refer him therefore to this Author; he'l shew him, by the
Example of a Wife, who, deceiv'd by the Likeness, and persuaded that an
Impostor, who personates her Husband, is her lawful Spouse, receives him
into her Bed without offending God in the least; that a Heretick, who mistakes a Falshood for the Truth, ought to pay it the same regard as if it really
were the Truth, and is answerable in the sight of God only for the Neglect
or Malice, by the means of which he might be led into the Mistake. So that
one can never enough blame St. *Austin* for his want of Exactness and Ac-
curacy in all these Parallels. He runs on with his Comparison very demurely,
and as if he had to deal with mere Ideots; between a Wife who lies with a
Man whom she knows not to be her Husband, and a Soul which entertains
false Opinions, but entertains 'em only because it's fully persuaded they are
true; insomuch that the whole Influence and Power they have over the Man,
proceeds from no other Cause, than the firm and sincere Disposition of
his Soul to the loving and reverencing the Truth. <468>

* Nouv. Lett. de l' Auteur de la Crit. Gen. de Maimbourg, *Tom.* 1. [Bayle, *Nouvelles
Lettres,* OD, vol. 2.]

143. See above, p. 233.

∽ XXVII. ST. AUSTIN'S WORDS ∽

We must own, that Children, who are drawn by Gentleness and Love, are much the best; but these don't make the greatest number: there are incomparably more of another sort, whom nothing will work upon but Fear. Accordingly we read in Scripture,* That a Servant will not be corrected by words; for tho he understand he will not answer: *which supposes a Necessity of employing some more powerful Means. It informs us in another place, that we must employ the Rod, not against evil Servants only, but untoward Children. It is true, says the Scripture again,*† Thou shall beat him with a Rod, and shall deliver his Soul from Hell: *and else-where,*‡ He that spareth his Rod, hateth his Son; but he that loveth him, chasteneth him betimes.

ANSWER

Pergis pugnantia secum, frontibus adversis componere,[144] may one in some measure tell St. *Austin;* for surely never was any Man more unhappy in Comparisons than he, tho he finds a power of 'em, fit enough to impose on Understandings which look no farther than the Surface of things. Let's see now, whether the Education of Children, and the Conversion of Hereticks, ought to be carry'd on the same way.

I say not; and I ground it on this substantial Reason: That Children being unable to form any deliberate or reasonable judgment upon their <469> own Actions till such a certain Age, but obeying the Impressions of the Machine, and those Sensations of Pleasure or Pain which Objects produce in 'em; what we are principally to require at their hands, is the Practice of certain Actions: but as they are very little sensible of any Motives of Honor, and can't see far enough into the depth of a Reason to give it the preference

---

* Prov. 29.19.

† Prov. 23.14.

‡ Prov. 13.24.

144. Horace, *Satires,* I.102: "You go on to set opposites in head to head conflict with each other"; translated R. Fairclough, Loeb Classical Library.

to their Passions, they must be threaten'd, and sometimes whip'd, before they can be brought to perform these Actions. Now it answers our end sufficiently, if they only perform 'em, even tho we shou'd not just then enlighten their Understandings to know the benefit of 'em, nor endue 'em with any one just Notion of things. For example, a Father has a mind that his Son shou'd learn to write, and orders him to write so many hours a day; the Son wou'd much rather play, whatever Lectures his Governors may read him to the contrary: What must be done in this case? He must be whip'd if he does not write. 'Twere better, I own, to possess his Mind before-hand with this Point of Knowledg, *It's my Interest and Advantage to write, for such or such a reason;* and give him this as the Rule of his Obedience to his Father's Will, who desires he shou'd write: but if his Mind be not at a maturity to take the impression of this Idea, he must notwithstanding be made to write; because whether he thinks Writing an Accomplishment, or whether he does not, the Father equally gains his point, which is the teaching him to write: For it's sufficient to this end, if he only practises Writing, and if for fear of a whipping he endeavor to write a fair hand: there's no great need of any <470> Thought or Opinion of his own as to this particular Design; the whole matter lies in his being under the fear of a whipping, unless he finishes his Task.

We are to say the same of the Actions of Servants, always making the due Allowances and Abatements. A reasonable Master wou'd be very glad he cou'd make 'em understand the Obligations of their Station, and quicken their Diligence by Motives worthy of human Nature; but if this won't do, he employs his Threats and Stripes, and makes 'em get the knowledg of their Duty well enough, in the ordinary and vulgar way. Why does the Master do well in this? Because with regard to the Actions which he requires of his Servants, 'tis all one to him, whether they perform 'em from such or such a sense of the Reasons of 'em, or whether they perform 'em without any such sense at all. Accordingly let a Cook persuade himself as much as he please, that his Master is not fit to live, and that he deserves to have his Dinner spoil'd; yet if the Dread of a Horse-whip hinders his dressing it ill, is not this all his Master aims at? Wou'd his Ragoo be better or more savory, if the Cook had better thoughts of him? We see the reason then for threatning and chastising untoward Children and Servants, because we are not concern'd about their Opinions, but about their Actions; and that it signifies very little, whether these Actions be conformable to their Opinions or no, provided they be done.

But the case is quite different in the Conversion of Hereticks: We do nothing at all, unless we change their Opinions; and consequently attain <471> not the end we ought to propose, if we only prevail with a Heretick to frequent such and such Assemblys, assist at Divine Service, and conform outwardly to the King's Religion. Our propos'd End ought to have bin the delivering him from the Power of Prejudice and false Persuasions, and filling his Mind with the Knowledg of the Truth; and nothing of this kind is done: we have only outward Actions in the room of it, which in the order of Nature shou'd have bin the Result and Consequence from the main End and principal Design. I shan't lose time in proving over and over, that Menaces and Blows are not a means of enlightning the Understanding, and that all they can do is agitating the Machine by the Passions of Fear or Pain arising from 'em in the Soul. What remains then, but saying that St. *Austin* join'd things together which are intirely different in that point at least, wherein they shou'd exactly have answer'd, to ground a just Parallel?

They'l undoubtedly tell me over again what I have sufficiently confuted elsewhere,[145] That Stripes are intermediately instructive, by making the Mind apply more intensly to the Consideration of the Truth: and I, in answer, shall refer 'em to my former Solutions.

If Fear of any kind be necessary in order to a Man's Conversion, 'tis certainly that of the Judgments of God; but as no body apprehends that God will chastise him for things which he believes to be good, and every one believes his religious Opinions such, it follows evidently, that the threatning a Heretick with the Wrath of God, is of no manner of service towards unde-<472>ceiving him; he never will believe that this Wrath shall be reveal'd on him for any other cause than his Indevotion and disorderly Life: so that all the effect it can naturally have, is the confirming him in his Heresy. Yet St. *Austin* has taken care not to omit, among his many faulty Parallels, that of some rebellious Children of God, who have profited by the Afflictions with which God has visited 'em. I believe there may be many

145. See above, Part II, Chapter 1, p. 137.

such cases, but then it's with regard to Manners only; or if Opinions have
ever bin the cause, 'twas only where God interpos'd in a very singular manner. Now we must not presume to make those particular Cases a Rule for
our Conduct, nor tread under foot the most sacred Laws of the Decalogue,
on so vain an Imagination.

∞ XXVIII. ST. AUSTIN'S WORDS ∞

Jesus Christ *himself exercis'd Violence on St.* Paul, *and forc'd
him to believe: let these Men then never say more, as their custom
is,* Every one is at liberty to believe or not to believe.

ANSWER

It truly tires one's Patience, after having met with so many Sophisms already, still to meet with more. For is it not an Illusion unworthy this great
Doctor of Grace, to imagine that because Jesus Christ converted not
St. *Paul* till after he had flung him on the ground, blinded, and fill'd him
with astonishment; therefore *Honorius* might convert the Donatists, by depriving 'em before-hand of their Liberty, and Property, and Country? But
had *Honorius* Grace <473> at hand, as well as Jesus Christ, to give his
Chastisements the wish'd Success? Did he know the critical Seasons and
Circumstances for tormenting and vexing? Had he any assurance that his
Violences wou'd be efficacious? 'Tis nonsense, from all that God does, to
conclude that Princes may do the same. God made use of Afflictions for
the converting of *Pharaoh*'s Heart, and yet *Pharaoh* harden'd in his Sin:
but his Chastisements produc'd quite a contrary effect on the Persecutor
Paul. This shews us, that all kind of Instruments are good in the hands of
God, whensoever he pleases; yet Men must not presume to imitate this
Conduct: else why might not they imitate God's sending St. *Paul* a Thorn
in the Flesh, to hinder his being puff'd up? Why not force those, who make
an ill use of their Youth and Beauty, to take Pouders or Potions to destroy
their Complexion and Vigor, or get defamatory Libels against 'em publickly
dispers'd, that they might never dare shew their faces abroad? Why not slay
the Children to punish their Parents, and wean 'em from the World, as
God often does; and so go on in all the other ways of Plague and Affliction

with which he promotes the Salvation of his Elect? Had Princes the two Characters with which JESUS CHRIST is invested, they might in God's name disquiet and grieve People as much as ever St. *Paul* was griev'd. But have they the same Prerogative as JESUS CHRIST, of afflicting whom they think fit by Sickness, Shipwreck, Loss of Children and Substance? And can they, like him, assure and inwardly convince those whom they afflict on the score of their Opinions, that these Opinions <474> are displeasing to God? The Prerogative of Kings in this respect is the lowest in the world: for shou'd they tell a Heretick a hundred times a day, *Your Opinion is stark naught,* this were not so good a reason to him as a Priest's telling him so; because it's to be presum'd, that a Priest has examin'd into the ground of different Religions much more than a King. Consequently, the Punishments he inflicts are no way likely to create the least Doubt in the Mind of the Persecuted, tho they may produce a Desire of conforming unworthily to the Time and Season.

⚇ XXIX. ST. AUSTIN'S WORDS ⚇

Why shou'd not the Church have the Privilege of employing Constraint for recovering her lost Children, and bringing 'em home into her bosom; when these wretched Children make use of the same means for bringing others into Perdition?

ANSWER

This Question is easily answer'd by saying, that Examples don't authorize Sin, and that a Mother who committed an Indiscretion, because her Daughter was guilty of the same, wou'd make her self much more ridiculous than if she had not used that reason. If the Donatists committed any Outrages on their Brethren, were not there Laws enough in the Roman Code for trying 'em, and Courts of Justice enough in the Empire for condemning 'em to the Punishments which their Crimes deserv'd? Must the Church, instead of exhorting the Judges to discharge their Duty against these Persecutors, <475> become her self a Persecutress of those who had no hand in their Crimes? St. *Austin* was at first for requiring no more than Security and Protection for the Catholicks, but he chang'd his mind.

⌘ XXX. ST. AUSTIN'S WORDS ⌘

*Shou'd we, for example, see two Men in a House that we knew
was ready to fall down about their ears, and that whatever pains
we took to warn 'em out, they shou'd obstinately resolve to abide
in it; wou'd it not be a degree of Cruelty, not to drag 'em out by
main force.*

ANSWER

This, with a very small alteration, is the Objection of the Frantick or Lunatick, hinder'd by main force from throwing himself out at a window. We
have shown[146] so unanswerable a Disparity between the Cases, that there's
no danger of its ever rising in judgment against us. The Sum of it is this:
When a House is ready to fall, we equally prevent a Man's being crush'd
to death by it, whether we persuade him to get out, or whether we drag him
out by main force. But we don't save a Man who is in a false Religion, unless
we rationally persuade him to quit it. Do with him what you please, yet
without this you do nothing; consequently all Constraint, all dragging as
by a halter into the Churches of the Faithful, is lost labor, and the most
unprofitable Attempt in the world, with regard to Salvation. <476>

146. See above, pp. 294, 302.

‡ XXXI. ST. AUSTIN'S WORDS ‡

As to what they say, that we have a design upon their Estates, and wou'd fain have the fingering of 'em; let 'em turn Catholicks, and we assure 'em they shall not only enjoy what they call their own Estates, but also come in for a share of ours. Passion has blinded 'em to such a degree, that they don't perceive how they contradict themselves. They reproach us with exerting the Authority of the Laws for constraining 'em into our Communion, as if it were the most odious Action: and shou'd we take this pains, if we had a design upon their Estates?

ANSWER

This is a very fine Turn; but it can never prevent People's believing, that a great many of those who advise Kings to confiscate the Estates of Sectarys, are acted by Avarice; because they are sure a great many will always be found, who'l chuse to part with their Estates rather than their Religion. Many an Officer and Soldier, during the late Dragoonery in *France,* was vex'd at the heart to find that their Landlords wou'd sign so soon, and not give 'em time to make up a small Purse. How many of the Catholicks of that Kingdom wou'd be e'en distracted, shou'd the Refugees return, and take possession of their Estates? Wou'd any one collect accounts of all the Collusions and pick-pocket Innuendo's, which have operated in the procuring 'em private Passports to depart, he might have plenty of matter. <477>

✂ XXXII. ST. AUSTIN'S WORDS ✂

The Canaanite *shall ne'er rise in judgment against the People of* Israel, *tho these drove them out of their Country, and took away the Fruit of their Labor; but* Naboth *shall rise up against* Achab, *because* Achab *took away the Fruit of* Naboth*'s Labor. And why one, and not the others? Because* Naboth *was a just Man, and the* Canaanites *Idolaters.*

ANSWER

This is the last Article I shall examine in this Letter of St. *Austin* to *Boniface.* The Passage before us is very remarkable: He advances this Principle in it, expresly and without disguise, That Hereticks in seizing the Goods of Catholicks commit a Sin, and that Catholicks seizing the Goods of Hereticks perform a Good-work. Did ever any one see a more Jesuitical Morality?[147] Is not this the very Chimera and Frenzy of several abominable Sects, who have boasted that what was a Sin in other Men, was lawful and innocent in their Communion. For my part I own, I know not whereabouts I am, when I find Men annex such Privileges of Impeccability to the Profession of the Orthodox Faith. I always thought that the more one was Orthodox, the more he was oblig'd to be just towards all Men; but here's St. *Austin's* Authority, that invading the Property of our Neighbor, and seizing the Fruit of his Labor, is a Good-work, provided the Seizer is an Orthodox, and the Sufferer a Heterodox. I can see no reason for stopping here; for why shou'd Robbery be more privileg'd than Murder <478> and Calumny? We must therefore say, that smiting and slaying Men, blackning 'em by all kind of Calumny, betraying 'em by false Oaths, are all good Actions in a Member of the true, against a Member of a false Church. If a Man were dispos'd to make moral Reflections, might not he here say, that God in his Justice permits those who depart so egregiously from the ways of Righteousness, and the Spirit of the Gospel, in favor of Persecutors, shou'd fall from depth to depth into Maxims of Morality, whose Impiety

147. See above, pp. 245, 319.

gives the utmost horror. By this rule the Sin of *David*, in taking away the Wife of *Uriah*, was no farther a Sin, than as *Uriah* was a Jew; and if by chance he had bin a Native of *Tyre*, who had sought for Refuge in *Judea*, the Action had bin lawful: at least, in case *David* had only taken from him what Mony and Jewels, or other Effects he had sav'd from *Tyre*, or Lands purchas'd by him at the usual Value with the King's Consent. What Sanctions are there, in the Law of Nature and Nations, that the Christian Religion won't cancel at this rate? that Religion which ought to support and strengthen 'em!

Here's all I have to say to these two Letters of St. *Austin*, printed apart by the Archbishop of *Paris*'s Orders, to justify his own Conduct by the Sense of this Father. And here I might stop, justly believing that this is all the Convertists have to say for themselves of any great weight: however, as there are some other Letters of St. *Austin*, in which he has treated the same matter, I think it mayn't be amiss to answer these likewise, that we may leave no Enemy in our Rear. <479>

↞ XXXIII. ST. AUSTIN'S WORDS ↞
Letter 164,[148] to *Emeritus*.

If the Temporal Powers stretch forth their hand against Schismaticks, 'tis because they look on their Separation as an Evil, and that they are ordain'd by God for the Punishment of Evil-doers, according to that Saying of the Apostle, Whosoever therefore resisteth the Power, resisteth the Ordinance of God; and they that resist, shall receive to themselves Damnation: For Rulers are not a terror to Good-works, but to the Evil, *&c. The whole Question then lies here, whether Schism be an Evil, and whether you have not made the Schism; for if so, you resist the Powers, not for any Good, but for Evil. But, say you, no one shou'd persecute even bad Christians. Allow they ought not; yet how can this secure 'em against the Powers ordain'd by God for the Punishment of Evil-doers? Can we cancel that Passage of St.* Paul, *which I have just now cited?*

ANSWER

One can hardly imagine what St. *Austin* cou'd be thinking of, when he applies his Scripture so very wrong. Cou'd not he see, that he gave it a strain beyond what the Apostle ever dream'd of? For at his rate of quoting St. *Paul,* he makes him plainly affirm, that Subjects who conform not to the Prince's Laws are wicked and worthy of Punishment, and Resisters of the Ordinance of God; the most impious Falshood that ever any one advanc'd! since it charges all the <480> Martyrs and Confessors with Rebellion against God, and a punishable Untowardness, and in general all the Christians of the primitive Church, and the Apostles in the first place, who obey'd not the Heathen Emperors forbidding by their Laws the Profession of Christianity. We must of necessity take up with this abominable Consequence, or own there are Limitations essentially understood in St. *Paul*'s words; such as except those Cases at least, wherein we can't conform to the

---

148. In the modern numbering, Letter 87.

Prince's Laws, without deeming it better to obey Man than to obey God. Now he who conforms to the Prince's Laws, when persuaded in Conscience that God ordains the contrary, chuses to obey his Prince rather than God (there's no cavilling against the Evidence of this Proposition, for those who weigh the Terms of it ever so little) consequently St. *Paul* must be understood to except all those Cases, wherein one is persuaded that God ordains the contrary of what Princes ordain. And so the Schismaticks, which St. *Austin* had to deal with, being within this case, the alledging this Passage of St. *Paul* cou'd be of no force against them, without proving, as it must if taken in this latitude, that one ought to be a Turk at *Constantinople,* an Arian under *Constantius,* a Pagan under *Nero,* a Protestant in *Sweden,* a Papist in *Rome,* &c.

If the temporal Powers stretch forth their hand against Schismaticks, 'tis because they look on their Separation as an Evil, and that they are ordain'd by God for the Punishment of Evil-doers. Let's put this Argument of St. *Austin's* in form. <481>

If it were* a Sin in Princes to stretch forth their hands against Schismaticks, 'twou'd be a Sin in 'em for this reason only; That they did not look upon Schism as an Evil, or that God had not ordain'd 'em for the Punishment of Evil-doers.

But they do look upon Schism as an Evil, and God has ordain'd 'em for the Punishment of Evil-doers.

Therefore it is not a Sin in 'em to stretch forth their hands against Schismaticks.

We now perceive how this formidable Syllogism shrinks to a wretched *begging the Question;* I persecute you justly, because I am Orthodox: and by the same rule I kill, I slander, I cheat, I betray you justly, because I am Orthodox.

Let's suppose an Arian Bishop under *Constantius* reason the same way.

If it were an ill thing in the Emperor, to stretch forth his hand against those who hold the eternal Divinity of JESUS CHRIST, the reason must

---

* *That no one may suspect this Argument is not put into due form, the Reader is desir'd to consult the* Logick of *Port-Royal, Part* 3, Chap. 12. [Antoine Arnauld and Pierre Nicole, *Art de penser, ou logique* (The art of thinking, or Logic), 1659.]

be, that he did not look on this Opinion as an Evil, and that God had not ordain'd him for the Punishment of Evil.

But he believes this Opinion Evil, and that God has ordain'd him for the Punishment of Evil.

Therefore it's no ill thing in him to stretch forth his hand against the Patrons of this Opinion.

Suppose, I say, an Arian Bishop reason'd thus, what cou'd St. *Austin* say for himself? Nothing <482> but this, That *Constantius* look'd upon that as Evil which really was not so, and that God had not ordain'd him for the Punishment of that which is no Evil. Nor must he henceforward say a word more of the Passage from the Apostle, which he had cited as an invincible Argument. The whole Dispute for the future will turn upon the ground of the Separation: and if either convince t'other, well and good; if not, each must stand upon his own bottom, and serve God according to his own Principles. This Remark alone is sufficient to shew, that the Secular Power has no right to interpose in religious Differences, so far as to constrain any one to the Belief of this or that: The getting all contested Points stated and explain'd, is the most that Princes ought to do; or taking care, that the publick Peace is not disturb'd by the Differences in Opinion.

To return to the Arian Bishop's Syllogism, I say that whoever wou'd effectually answer it, must deny that the Emperor, because he looks on a thing as evil, has a right to punish it, or to exercise that Authority which St. *Paul* speaks of, when he says, God has ordain'd the Powers which are, for the Punishment of Evil-doers. But the denying of this, puts St. *Austin* quite out of sorts, and lays him under a necessity of changing his first Proposition into this which follows; *The Emperor stretches forth his hand against you, because your Separation is an Evil, and because God has ordain'd him for the Punishment of Evil.* Now this is manifestly supposing the thing in question, because the Donatists maintain'd that their Separation was very just; and consequently St. *Austin*'s Argument amounts to no more than this, <483> *You are wrong, and I am right;* which the long Passage he has cited from St. *Paul* has undoubtedly nothing to do with, one way or other.

He well saw, that what he had bin all along urging amounted to no more, since he adds; *The whole Question lies here, whether Schism ben't an Evil, and whether you have not made the Schism.* If this be all the Question, it ought to be decided by Reasoning; and if St. *Austin* offers Arguments of weight enough to convince the Donatists, there will be no more need of Fines or Prisons, they'l re-ingraft on the old Stock with all their heart. But if St. *Austin*'s Reasons convince 'em not, the Question and Contest will still subsist; and consequently 'twill be manifestly begging the Question, if St. *Austin* reasons at this rate:

You have committed an ill Action.

The Emperor is oblig'd to punish those who commit ill Actions.

Therefore the Emperor is oblig'd to punish you.

Now it's absurd arguing upon a bare begging the Question,[149] and much more absurd to inflict Punishments, banish, imprison, pill and pillage Folks on a bare begging the Question: consequently St. *Austin*'s Cause is stark naught in this part of it.

For since the whole Question, as he himself owns, amounts to this; *Is Schism an Evil, and have the Donatists made the Schism?* the Laws of good Order and right Reason require, that the Partys examine this Point, and dispute it fairly, before either condemns what either affirms or denies. What will be the issue of this Discussion or Dispute? Why one of these three things <484> must necessarily happen; either each Party will persist in its own Opinion; or one of 'em, convinc'd it's in the wrong, will comply with what the other proposes; or, last of all, tho convinc'd of its Error, will yet obstinately refuse to change sides. If we suppose the Donatists, or any other Sect accus'd of Heresy, within the first Case, the Question and Ground of the Dispute is still on foot; and consequently St. *Austin* ought not to fly to the Prince's Authority, because he can't suppose the Right of his own side, but by manifestly begging the Question, and because there's no common standing Rule between him and his Adversarys, by which he may justly pronounce 'em Evil-doers. If we suppose 'em under the second Circumstance, there's no need of calling in the Secular Power against 'em. In the third Case we may very justly have recourse to the Authority of the Prince, provided we have a certain and undoubted knowledg of their persisting contrary to the Lights of their Conscience: but how shall we come by this Knowledg; we have not the Gift of searching the Heart, and we ought to

149. See Appendixes, "Bayle's Use of Logic," p. 580 ("petitio principii").

suppose that a Man is not convinc'd of his Error as long as he protests he is not: and whatever Conjecture we may have to the contrary, we have no right to act by him according to our Conjectures, rather than according to his own Protestation. So that we can't possibly imagine a Case, which, in pure Disputes about Religion, authorizes our arming the Secular Power against Schismaticks, and solliciting penal Laws.

But I can't well comprehend what St. *Austin* means in this place, when he says, *That allowing* <485> *no one ought to persecute even the worst Christians, yet this cou'd be no Protection to them against the Powers ordain'd by God for the Punishment of Evil-doers.* To me it looks like a Contradiction: for if bad Christians shou'd not be persecuted, this is a strong Reason in their favor against those Princes who wou'd bring 'em to Punishments from which they are exempted; I mean such Punishments as the Powers ordain'd by God may inflict on Evil-doers. But to pass over this want of Consistency in our Author, I shall only observe, that Christians who are no otherwise bad than as they believe and mistake certain false Doctrines for Divine Revelation, are not to be reckon'd among those Evil-doers, for the Punishment of whom Princes have receiv'd the Sword from God. This Sword concerns only such as are guilty of Crimes, and of violating the politickal Laws of the State, Murderers, Robbers, False Witnesses, Adulterers, *&c.*

This Passage of St. *Austin* is, I suppose, the Fountain from whence the Bishop of *Meaux* has drawn his Query to one of his Diocesans; *Tell me,* says he, *in what place of Scripture do you find Hereticks and Schismaticks excepted out of the number of those Evil-doers, against whom St.* Paul *tells us, God himself has armed the Princes?*[150] There was no need of an Exemption: for it's plain to any one who consults the Genius of the Gospel, that this sort of Evil-doers ought not to be treated like the rest. What they do, they do with an intention of serving God more perfectly, and of avoiding what they think displeasing to him; they therefore ought only to be undeceiv'd and better inform'd: and none but Brutes and <486> Savage Natures, or stupidly blinded by senseless Prepossessions, can have the cruelty to punish Misdemeanors committed involuntarily, or from such an intention. Beside, that all the Arguments which I have urg'd at large in my *Commentary* on

150. See above, p. 334, note 129.

the words, *Compel 'em to come in,* are so many demonstrative Proofs, that God design'd not to arm Princes with the avenging Sword, *Gladio Ultore,* against Errors of Conscience.

And here I can't but call to mind a Passage of St. *Paul,* which I have elsewhere[151] made my use of; *Do good unto all, but especially to those who are of the Houshold of Faith:* and I maintain it's a sufficient Answer to the Bishop of *Meaux*'s Query. For it's plain, this Precept of the Apostle concerns all Christians, and consequently Sovereigns; and that by it Princes are oblig'd to do good unto others beside the Houshold of Faith, otherwise 'twere absurd to bid 'em do good *especially* to the Houshold of Faith: but if from the time that one ceases to be of the Houshold of Faith, he commences an Evil-doer of that kind which human Justice is oblig'd to pursue, and for the Punishment of whom Princes have receiv'd the Sword from God; it's as plain, against the Precept of the Apostle, that they can do good to none but those of the Houshold of Faith. Whence we infer, that the Apostle design'd they shou'd make an essential difference between their Nonconformist Subjects; and Murderers, Robbers, False Witnesses, Adulterers, and all other Disturbers of the publick Tranquillity, on whom God won't have Magistrates exercise any other good than that of punishing their Crimes. So that this single Passage of St. *Paul* is demonstration that < 487 > God exempts Hereticks and Schismaticks, demeaning themselves civilly otherwise, and living according to the Laws of the Land, out of the number of those Evil-doers, whose Punishment is enjoin'd on Princes upon their receiving the Sword from God.

151. See above, p. 254.

✹ XXXIV. ST. AUSTIN'S WORDS ✹
Letter 166,[152] to the Donatists.

Must not he be abandon'd to all shame, who won't submit to what Truth ordains by the Voice of the Sovereign?

ANSWER

I own, he must be abandon'd, that refuses submitting to a Sovereign when persuaded he enjoins nothing but the Truth: yet, if I may presume to say it, he exposes himself on the other hand to the Laughter of all reasonable Men, who censures, as abandon'd to shame, such as refuse to submit to what Emperors, in his opinion Enemys to the Truth, ordain against the Light of his Conscience. Now this is the case of all the Persecuted; it's therefore ridiculous to tell 'em, they refuse submitting to the Truth, speaking by the mouth of the Sovereign. This can properly reach only those who, persuaded of its being the Truth, refuse obstinately to submit to it.

✹ XXXV. ST. AUSTIN'S WORDS ✹
Ibid.

If the care we take to rescue you from Error and Perdition be what inflames your Hatred so much <488> against us, you must lay the blame upon God, who has given this terrible Reproof to the slothful Pastors, Ye have not brought back the Stray or looked for what was lost &c.[153]

ANSWER

St. *Austin* is so fond of Persecution, that he chops upon it in infinite Passages of Scripture, which yet have no more relation to it, than they have to the Interests of the *Great Mogul.* The lowest of all Mankind might easily apprehend that God, in this passage, complains only of those Pastors who neglecting the Salvation of those committed to their charge, interpos'd not

152. In the modern numbering, Letter 105.
153. Jeremias 23:2.

by their Instructions, Censures, and Exhortations, to check their evil Courses, and preserve 'em from Heresys, into which fallacious Reasonings, Ambition, a Marriage, &c. might have betray'd 'em. But it's a palpable Chimera, to imagine that God addresses those fearful Threats to Pastors who implore not the Assistance of the Secular Power, or don't bring into the field a Force of Provo's with their Archers, Dragoons, Cuirassiers, and the rest of the awful Tribe, to croud their Sheepfolds for 'em. If so, the Pastors of the Church of *Rome,* and those who have best discharg'd the pretended Duty towards the Calvinists of *France* in this last Dragoon Crusade, wou'd still be answerable to God, and chargeable with Connivance and wicked Neglect, in not prevailing with the King to dragoon the Covetous, the Unclean, the Evil-speakers, the Gamesters, the Tiplers, the Gluttons, the Uncharitable, and the rest of the Children of this World, so inti-<489>mately known to 'em, by the means of Confession. According to this fine Maxim of St. *Austin,* a Confessor who saw a Lady relapse into the Sins of Lasciviousness, and who did not take care to have twenty Dragoons quarter'd on her more or less, according as she was more or less rich, to break her Looking-Glasses, spoil all her fine Furniture, and eat her out of House and Home, till she sign'd an Instrument renouncing all her Vanitys and Vices; wou'd deserve the terrible Reproof, in Scripture, against those Pastors who fulfil not their Duty. What Dreams are here!

∽ XXXVI. ST. AUSTIN'S WORDS ∽
Letter 204,[154] to *Donatus.*

If you think it unlawful to constrain Men to do good, pray con-
sider that a Bishoprick is a good Office, since the Apostle has said
as much; yet there are a great many on whom Violence is actually
exercis'd to oblige 'em to accept of it. They are seiz'd, they are
hurry'd away by main force, they are shut up and confin'd till they
are forc'd to desire this good thing.

ANSWER

Here's an Argument drawn from the days of yore, and which there was no
great danger, that either the Archbishop of *Paris,* or any other Prelate of
France, wou'd publish with the rest of St. *Austin's* Sophisms; they don't
desire, the People shou'd know they attain to the Episcopacy, by Methods
so unlike those of the unaspiring Antients, whom 'twas necessary to <490>
force; that they run headlong to it, rise by Intrigue, and by making their
Court, Year after Year, to *P. la Chaize,* or some other Idol of the cringing
Tribe. But say they, be that how it will, heretofore at least there were those
whom 'twas necessary to constrain to be Bishops. Now a Bishoprick is a
good thing; therefore they were constrain'd to do good: Such Constraint
therefore is not always unlawful.

To dispel the Illusion of this Parallel, I have only one Remark to make,
to wit, That they who refus'd a Bishoprick, did not act from an Opinion
of its being evil; but from an Opinion of their own Insufficiency and Un-
worthiness. Such was their Humility and Modesty, that they cou'd not perceive they had Strength enough to support the weight of this Office; and
as they knew, that the Glory of God, and the Good of the Church, depended on the filling this Post with fit Persons, they believ'd, that by accepting it they shou'd only obstruct a greater measure of good and greater
Benefits from a worthier Hand. They likewise believ'd, that the Person
ought to feel an inward Call to this Office, or otherwise not accept of it;

---

154. In the modern numbering, Letter 173.

but wait God's Time, till he declar'd himself, either by a Vocation clearly communicated to the Ears of the Soul, or a Conjuncture of Circumstances, by which one might safely conclude, that such was the Will of God. These Circumstances might either be the persevering of those who offer'd the Dignity, in exhorting and pressing to accept it; an Earnestness that he wou'd comply, express'd by Compulsions, and little obliging Captivitys; repeated Commands on pain of Disobedience, and <491> other things of a like nature; which, far from grieving or violating the Conscience, might and ought to deliver it from all kind of Scruple: For it's matter enough of Comfort, upon accepting a Charge which one believes above his Strength, if he accepts it only to give way to repeated instances, and in some measure to the Commands of his Superiors and Directors. He may rest satisfy'd, that by doing his best Endeavors, he shall have no cause to reproach himself on the thoughts of occupying a Station, which might be fill'd by a more deserving Person. So that the Parallel between a Man who is made a Bishop, as it were by force, and a Person constrain'd to abjure his Religion, won't hold.

1. He who was forc'd to the Bishoprick, was persuaded 'twas an excellent thing: whereas a Heretick constrain'd to abjure, believes the Religion he's compel'd to exceeding bad.

2. He who refus'd the Bishoprick, refus'd it only from a Principle of Humility and Modesty: whereas the Heretick refuses from an Aversion to the thing propos'd: Accordingly in such a degree as it's obliging to press the one to accept the good thing, who trembles at the Thoughts of it; in such a measure, is it rude and brutal pressing the other to throw himself headlong into a Pit, which gives him a horror. St. *Austin* compares these two things together (judg you whether the Comparison be just) the Action of a Man, who keeps another to dinner, seats him at the upper end of his Table, and constrains him to submit to a thousand Civilitys, which he modestly refus'd; and the Action of a Man, who <492> goes to another's House, and drubs him with a Cudgel out of his own Home.

3. The constraining to a Bishoprick, was a proper means of quieting all Scruples upon the Point, and did effectually remove 'em: whereas the constraining a Heretick, does but afflict him in Body and Mind, without af-

fording the least Ray of Light; and exposes him to a thousand distracting Thoughts and criminal Devices.

4. Last of all, there's this further difference between the two Cases: that he who shou'd peremptorily refuse a Bishoprick, and plead, that the Experience of his own Infirmitys wou'd not in Conscience permit him to undertake such a Charge; that another might sustain it much more gloriously for the Honor of God and the Church; wou'd be sent home again in Peace, and admir'd for his Humility: whereas a Heretick sees no end to his Miserys unless he abjure.

∞ XXXVII. ST. AUSTIN'S WORDS ∞
Ibid.

We well know, that as nothing can damn Men but an evil Disposition of Will; so nothing but their good Will can save 'em: But how can the Love, which we are oblig'd to bear our Neighbor, permit our abandoning such numbers to their own wicked Will? Is it not cruel to throw, as I may say, the Reins loose on their Necks; and ought we not, to the utmost of our Power, prevent their doing Evil, and force 'em to do Good. <493>

ANSWER

Undoubtedly we ought to endeavor it to the utmost of our Power; but as it's impossible to compass this by any other means than Persuasion and Instruction; drubbing and cudgelling having indeed a Power over the Soul, of making it cast the Body into what Posture the Convertist pleases, but not of changing the corrupt Will: it evidently follows, that we ought never to employ such means for the Conversion of Souls. We sufficiently express our bounden Duty towards our Neighbor, and oppose his wicked Will, if we expostulate and reason with him the best we can to make him perceive his Deviations and Errors: if this won't do, we must commit the Care of him to God, the great Physician of Souls. And if the Heretick endeavors to pervert others, we must encounter him with all our Might; that is, we must oppose an Antidote of sound Reasonings, to the Poison of his: and if he proceed to Violence, we must bring him to condign Punishment, in the ordinary way, as we wou'd any other Malefactor who oppresses his Fellow-Citizen. To force a Man to do good is a contradiction, as much as *Cogere voluntatem,*[155] unless understood of Good resulting from a Machine, like that of a Fountain, which runs Wine for the Rabble's drinking. This kind of Good may be fetch'd out of a Miser, by forcing him to give an Alms; yet he does not do a good Work for all this.

∞ XXXVIII. ST. AUSTIN'S WORDS ∞
Ibid.

If we must always leave an evil Will to its natural Liberty, why so many Scourges and pier-<494>*cing Goads to force the Children of* Israel, *in spite of all their Murmurings and Stiffneckedness, to move forward toward the Land of Promise,* &c?

ANSWER

St. *Austin* here resumes the formerly-confuted Examples of St. *Paul* flung to the Ground,[156] of a Father whipping his Children,[157] of a Shepherd running after the lost Sheep, and bringing it home by fair or by foul means;[158] on the neglect whereof God reproaches him with Sloth and Unfaithfulness. I have confuted all this so often, that I am e'en tir'd of it. Will Men never comprehend the essential Difference between Acts where the Good-will and Consent is indispensably necessary, and those where it is not; between Acts committed under a sense of their being displeasing to God, and those perform'd from an Opinion of their being agreeable to his Will? The *Israelites* who murmur'd, and refus'd to proceed towards the Land of *Ca-*

---

155. "To compel the will." It was held that the idea of compelling the will is self-contradictory, since compulsion is the opposite of choice, and to will is to choose. See Aristotle, *Nicomachean Ethics,* III.1, Augustine, *The City of God,* V.10, Thomas Aquinas, *Summa theologiae,* 1, q. 82, a. 1, and 1–2, q. 6, a. 4.

156. See above, p. 303.

157. See above, p. 356.

158. See above, p. 303.

naan, were not so brutish as to think their Behavior approv'd by God, or that their Conscience and Religion exacted this Refusal and these Murmurings; therefore they justly deserv'd to be punish'd: and the Punishments God inflicted on 'em were a proper means of reclaiming 'em from their Sin, because they were persuaded, that 'twas God who punish'd 'em for this very Sin. But a Schismatick or Heretick, whom the Convertists load with Chains and Dragoons, is far from believing, that 'tis God afflicts him on the score of his Opinions. On the contrary, he imagines, that God punishes him for his former want of Zeal for those very Opinions; and <495> therefore Dungeons, Dragoons, and Galleys can never redress that Evil, which the Convertists wou'd propose by 'em; as the Punishments inflicted on the *Israelites* might quell their Murmurings and Impatience.

Besides, with regard to the Conquest of the Land of *Canaan,* 'twas all one, whether the *Israelites* mov'd freely to it, or whether they mov'd from a Fear of Punishment. And therefore all lay in their marching on, and moving towards it. The Case of the General of an Army will illustrate this: He is not displeas'd, that his Men move to the Assault cheerfully, and with a sense of Honor; but cou'd he be assur'd, that the Fear of Punishment wou'd make 'em braver than their Love and Affection for him, he cou'd easily comfort himself upon their conquering with an Ill-will. If it hinders not their marching up to the Enemys Fire with equal Briskness and Ardor, it's all that he desires. To consider then only the journying towards the Land of *Canaan,* and the attacking the *Canaanites;* 'twas equal to God, whether the People acted freely or from Fear: and therefore 'twas reasonable to punish 'em when they refus'd to march. But the Case is different, with regard to Religion and the Worship of God: here the Persuasion, the Affections and Good-will are essentially requisite; and St. *Austin* will find no example to the contrary.

I cant see his Reason for bringing St. *Paul*'s Conversion so often upon the Stage: Perhaps he imagines (which were a very poor Illusion) that if it were not for the Violence, which JESUS CHRIST exercis'd on his Body, his Mind had not <496> bin enlighten'd with the Knowledg of the Gospel. An Error! JESUS CHRIST cou'd have converted him without the least Bustle, and, as I may say, in his very Sleep. If he thought fit to do it in so remarkable and so signal a manner, 'twas that the Fame of it might have a good Effect and Influence on many others. But what's all this to the Laws of *Honorius,* and the Dragoons of *Lewis* XIV?

If *Solomon* advises Fathers to chastise their Children, 'tis not with a Design of infusing into 'em such or such Opinions in Religion; (there's no need of a Rod for this, Children believe all that's told 'em) but to correct their naughty Humors, their Truancy, their over-eating themselves, their Love of Play; which if suffer'd to grow up to confirm'd Habits, might become incorrigible.

St. *Austin* writes this Letter to a Donatist, who had attempted to kill himself, but was prevented by some of the Myrmidons of the Convertists: and tells him, that since they had exercis'd a just Violence on him to save the Life of his Body, by a much stronger Reason they might do so, to save the Life of his Soul. To make way for my adding a word or two more in this matter, to what has bin said in another place;[159] I shall consider this Donatist, as designing to kill himself from a Principle of Conscience. It's plain, say they, on this Supposition, that there was a just Violence exercis'd on Conscience; therefore all constraining of Conscience is not unjust.

I answer, That Conscience may be forc'd two several ways; one way, as when a Catholick is hinder'd from falling on his Knees, as the Host <497> passes by, three or four Fellows seizing and holding him in a standing Posture by main force; or else seizing one of the Reform'd Religion, and bending his Knees to the Ground, as the Host passes: The other way, as when the Alternative is set before him of abjuring his Religion, or undergoing such and such Punishments. In the first Case, the Person constrain'd is not made to sin. In the second, he's brought into a violent Temptation, and the Constraint is very often the occasion of his sinning. They who prevented the Donatist's killing himself, exercis'd a Violence on his Conscience, in the first way only; and consequently laid him under no Temptation to Sin, so that they ought not to be blam'd for what they did: yet their Case is not to be put in comparison with the Case of those who constrain in the second way, as St. *Austin,* ever unhappy in his Comparisons, wou'd do. If any one wou'd know my Opinion concerning those, who in the way first repre-

159. See above, pp. 294, 302.

sented, shou'd hinder a Catholick's adoring what he believes his God; or who shou'd force a Protestant on his Knees as the Host passes by: I shou'd tell him, they'd do very ill, tho they did not constrain their Neighbor to the Commission of a Sin; for there's no Sin in kneeling before an Idol, when this Genuflexion is not an Act of the Will.

∞ XXXIX. ST. AUSTIN'S WORDS ∞
Ibid.

While JESUS CHRIST *was upon Earth, and before the Princes of the World worship'd him, the Church made use only of Exhortation;* <498> *but ever since those days she has not thought it enough to invite Men to Happiness, she also forces 'em. These two Seasons are prefigur'd in the Parable of the Feast: The Master of the Family was content, for the first time, to order his Servants to bid the Guests to his Dinner; but the next time he commanded 'em to compel 'em to come in.*

ANSWER

The Reader will find the Confutation of this Passage in the two first Parts of the *Commentary.*

ಜಾಗ XL. ST. AUSTIN'S WORDS ಜಾಗ
Letter 167,[160] to *Festus*.

*If any one will compare, what they suffer thro our charitable Se-
verity, with the Excesses to which their Fury transports 'em against
us; he'l easily judg which are the Persecutors, they or we. Nay they
might justly be denominated such, with regard to us, without all
this; for be the Severitys which Parents exercise over their Children, to bring 'em to a sense of their Duty, ever so great; yet they
can never properly be call'd Persecution: whereas Children, by
following evil Courses, become Persecutors of Father and Mother,
tho possibly they may'nt be guilty of any personal Violence
against 'em.*

ANSWER

St. *Austin* does all he can to excuse the Violences exercis'd by his own side,
on those exercis'd by the Donatists; but this is a very ill < 499 > Justification:
the rather, beside that Example is no Authority for sinning; because they
were not content to retaliate on those who had bin the Aggressors, but also
involv'd the Innocent in the Punishment of the Guilty. They shou'd have
bin satisfy'd with punishing the *Circoncellions,* and all others who had murder'd or rob'd their Neighbor; treated 'em as Ruffians and Banditti; and
endeavor'd by Gentleness and calm Reasoning to bring over the rest, and
not lay a Tax on Religion, nor use it as Farmers do certain Provinces, where
they exercise their Depredations without Control. As the knowing whether
a Son, who follows ill Courses, persecutes his Father and Mother; or
whether the Father and Mother, who turn their Son out o' Doors, who
disinherit him, get him lash'd at a Whipping-Post to make him resume the
Doctrines of his Catechise, which he began to suspect were naught, persecute the Son: As this, I say, turns into a Dispute about meer Words, I
shan't bestow any of my time in considering it. I'm persuaded my Readers,
if they examine it, will find that a Father and Mother in several Cases de-

160. In the modern numbering, Letter 89.

serve the Title of Persecutors, be their Intention in chastising their Son, on the score of any Heresy which he may fall into, ever so sanctify'd. St. *Austin* was not quite so delicate on this Head, in a former Letter,[161] where he owns, that the Righteous have always persecuted the Wicked, and the Wicked have ever persecuted the Righteous.

161. See above, p. 318.

A <501>
SUPPLEMENT
TO THE
Philosophical Commentary
ON
These Words of Jesus Christ,
Compel 'em to come in.

Where, among other things, the last Subterfuge of our Adversarys
is utterly destroy'd, by shewing, that Hereticks have an equal Right
of persecuting with the Orthodox. The Nature also, and Origin of
Errors, is here treated.

Containing the Reasons for suppressing a large and particular Answer to the *Treatise of the Rights of the two Sovereigns,* &c. The chiefest of which Reasons is this; That one may in five or six Pages, as shall be seen anon, draw up an unanswerable Defence of what has bin censur'd in the *Philosophical Commentary.*

Two things might have induc'd me to believe, that I shou'd quickly see an Answer to my Philosophical Commentary: *First, if I had allow'd this general Thesis, That Princes ought to proceed in a way of Authority, and by temporal Punishments, against Schismaticks or Hereticks; next, if I had handl'd this matter as jejunely as* Castalio *did in the last Age, under the name of* Martinus Bellius. *It must* <504> *be own'd, the true* Topick *of this Question was not known in those days; I mean, the Principles and Source of the Arguments, by which the Doctrine of Non-Toleration, either total or partial, is to be overthrown. Accordingly it happen'd, that poor* Castalio *was presently run down at a strange rate, and very roughly handled by* Theodore Beza;[162] *who, were he now to come into the World, durst not attempt answering today's Writings in defence of Toleration: so much are they beyond those of former days!*

---

162. Sebastian Castellio, *De haereticis an sint persequendi* (Whether heretics should be persecuted), 1554; see DHC, art. "Castalion, Sebastian," and Lecler, *op. cit.,* vol. 1, pp. 336–59. Theodore Beza, *De haereticis a civili magistratu puniendus libellus* (Concerning heretics, who should be punished by the civil magistrate), 1554; see DHC, art. "Beze, Theodore de," and Lecler, *op. cit.,* vol. 1, pp. 325–32.

But as I took care not to lay my self open on the side of Recrimination, the only thing which gives the Romish Apologists for Persecution an Advantage over our Divines, ever since the great Lights of the present Age have discover'd the true Topick of this Question[163] *(those Divines I mean, who assert, that Princes are bound as Guardians of Religion, by their temporal Authority, to extinguish Heresys, and that my Opinion, touching the Rights of Conscience, leads to Deism) I believ'd my Work wou'd hardly be attack'd, especially with regard to what had bin advanc'd in it concerning the Obligations of acting according to the Lights of Conscience. For tho some Objections, 'tis true, may be made against this, and have actually bin propos'd to my self a hundred times in Conversation; yet it was not probable, that any one wou'd appear in print against a Doctrine which seems to be one of the first Notices of Reason, and suppos'd as a Principle in all Treatises of Morality; all having adopted it, even* Hobbs *himself, in several places of his Treatise* de Cive.

Notwithstanding, I had scarce receiv'd the Account of my Commentary's *being publish'd, when the Post from* Amsterdam *brought me a Treatise con-* <505>*cerning* the Rights of the two Sovereigns;[164] *wherein the Author advances, that Princes are bound to maintain Religion by destroying Sectarys, and that denying this, as I have done, is* an Extreme, vicious to a degree of Folly; *that besides, my Opinion concerning the Rights of Conscience, leads directly to Deism. The Author of this Treatise seem'd to be a very good Protestant, which makes the matter so much the worse; as it gives ground to suspect, that we are still of the Mind of the first Reformers, as to the punishing of Hereticks, which must needs enervate and pall the greatest part of our Remonstrances against the late Proceedings in* France.

At the same time I was inform'd by several Persons here, that before I had quite finish'd my Commentary, *a famous Divine of* Holland, *in an Answer of his, to a Book entitl'd,* The pretendedly Reform'd convicted of Schism,

---

163. This is irony.

164. Pierre Jurieu, *Des droits des deux soverains en matière de religion, la conscience et le prince, pour détruire le dogme de l'indifférence des religions et de la tolérance universelle, contre un livre intitulé 'Commentaire philosophique'* (Rights of two sovereigns in matters of religion, conscience and the prince; to destroy the dogma of the indifference of religions and universal tolerance, against a book [of Bayle] entitled "Philosophical Commentary," 1687.

had* attack'd my Opinion about Toleration, and the Rights of Conscience; which 'twas but fit I shou'd know, that I might satisfy all his Difficultys. I was of the same Mind, but their Advice came too late.

The first Page I look'd into, upon opening the Rights of the two Sovereigns, *let me understand, that he imputed it to me as my declar'd Opinion, that nothing a body does, in following the Instincts of Conscience, can be sinful; and happening to cast my eye slightly over it, I can safely say, I never lit upon a Page, having open'd it in several places, where I did not find this false Supposition reign, evidently contrary to the plainest and most express Declarations in several Passages of my* Commentary; *as,* <506> *not to cite all, particularly* pag. 241, 242, 251, 266.

Upon this I took leave of the Treatise of the Two Sovereigns, *and contented my self with writing, for the whole Reply, a short Letter to my Bookseller, which was publish'd before the third Part.*[165] *As to what concerns the Author of the*

---

* Ch. 22, 23, 24. of a Book entitl'd, *The True System of the Church,* &c. by Mr. *Jurieu.* [Pierre Jurieu, *Le vray système de l'Église et la véritable analyse de la foi . . . sur la nature de l'Eglise, son infaillibilité et le juge de controverses* (The true system of the Church and true rule of faith . . . on the nature of the Church, its infallibility and the judge of controversies), 1686, an answer to Nicole, "The self-styled Reformed convicted of schism." Reviewed by Bayle, NRL, OD, p. 525.]

165. Not included in the 1708 translation. See OD, vol. 2, p. 444. Translation: "I have just been reading the treatise *Of the Rights of Two Sovereigns, etc, against a book entitled 'Philosophical Commentary'* [above, p. 386, note 164] and have found it a false and very weak attack on that Commentary. From the beginning the author avows that in spite of himself and nature, anger and the will of one of his friends make him step forward as an author. To avow such a thing shows little judgment. Anger should not enter into the composition of a work; one should look with a serene eye on the objects, and not through a cloud that confounds them and jumbles them as much as anger does. One must not, I say, look at them thorough such a cloud when one wishes to refute a man, and he had done much better if he had followed the counsels of the nature that discouraged him from turning author. In fact his work is faulty in the places where it ought to be the most essentially solid, because it goes only on a false position on the state of the question and combats a phantom, I mean an opinion that he imputes to me falsely. He labours to prove that one very often sins and offends God in acting according to the lights of conscience. Who denies this? Have I not said so, in more than one place? He accuses me also of introducing religious indifference, and on the contrary there has never been a doctrine more opposed to that than the doctrine that one should always act in accordance with one's conscience. Similar illusions reign in the place where he speaks of the legislative power of the sovereign in religious matters. As for citations from Scripture, they are very frequent in his book, but mostly misunderstood and in the style of St.

True System, *I carefully read over all he had said upon this Question; and tho I found he had manag'd the Argument like a Man of Sense, and practis'd in Dispute, yet I cou'd not see he had offer'd any one Argument which I might not have confuted solidly, and which an intelligent Reader might not answer of himself, by the help of the Solutions, which I had given to most of this Author's Objections, which are the very same that had bin propos'd to my self a thousand times over in Conversation; for they offer at first sight to whoever meditates on this matter.*

Accordingly I thought it needless to write a new Treatise, and pass'd some Months in this Disposition.

But the Advice I soon after receiv'd from Holland, *that the Author of the* Rights of the two Sovereigns *was not, as he pretended, and as I might well have believ'd on his own Word, a young Volunteer, and this his first Exploit; and that the contrary appear'd from some Expressions in his Advice to the Reader, where he tells the World, that he's afraid he shall be look'd on as a Man posted Centinel to challenge and stop all bad Books, which gives us an Image of an old Stager who has often appear'd in print:*[166] *this Advice, I say, together with some Objections propos'd to me, which were borrow'd from this Book, and with which I saw some were struck, oblig'd me to read it over with more than ordinary Care; and I own, it then appear'd <507> to me much more tolerable than I had judg'd it at first sight. Yet still I dare not affirm, as a great many do, that this is a Work of the Author of the* True System of the Church. *He had done better, in my Opinion, upon such a Subject as this.*

But be it whose it wou'd, I resolv'd to answer the Treatise, and to divide my Book into three Parts. The first to contain some Supplements, which to me

---

Augustine. In a word, this author meddles with things he has not considered, and continually commits the fallacy of not proving what he ought [*ignoratio elenchi:* see Appendixes, 'Bayle's Use of Logic,' p. 581]. I believe this proceeds less from bad faith than from inexperience in the composition of polemical works, or from a bad habit of judging things precipitately and without much thought, and of reading new books cursorily and intermittently. Such a way of reading should be allowed to anyone who does not wish to become a critic, but when one wishes to refute people it is quite unpardonable. In fact able readers never pardon anyone who examines so negligently what he refutes, that he dares to attribute to his adversary, and refute on that footing, the opposite of what he taught."

166. The author was in fact Pierre Jurieu.

seem'd proper for utterly silencing Compellers. The second to be an Answer to the three Chapters of the True System of the Church, *cited before in the Margin, and to all the Objections of the Author of the* Rights of the two Sovereigns, *which consist either in Texts of Scripture, or in horrible Consequences, flowing, as he pretends, from my Opinion; and which, like a Man of Skill in Controvertist Tactick, he has posted in the Outworks of his Book, to startle the Reader at first glance, and put him upon his Guard against me. The third to destroy his whole System, Root and Branch, his Maxims, his Aphorisms, and all he has said directly for his own Opinion.*

I press'd the Execution of this Design with so much Ardor, that I had as good as finish'd it by the Latter end of December, 1687. *and to redeem the lost time I gave my Translators, or rather, Paraphrasts (for to tell the Truth, they made a full use of the Liberty I allow'd 'em, of accommodating my Thoughts to their own Sense and Stile) my Sheets, fresh from the Pen; and as soon as the first Part was render'd into* French, *they sent it away to the Printer, with Orders to work it off as soon as possible.*

But mark what happen'd, and which I think my self oblig'd to mention in this place, that the World may know the Reasons why only a small part of this Work is like to appear. <508>

Having finish'd my three Parts, and the Translators their Version, I had the Curiosity to look it over, and see all the Sheets together; and then it was, that I began to think they must never see the Light, for in reality they made a Pile which even astonish'd me.

This Prolixity proceeded, I. *Partly from my not keeping the Sheets by me as I was writing this Work, so that I cou'd not perceive its swelling to such a prodigious Bulk.* 2. *Partly from a way I have of endeavoring to bring things to the greatest Evidence possible; which requires the confuting all the little Cavils which an Adversary can be suppos'd to think of, and the strengthening the main Argument by several Proofs, firmly supported and link'd together: a great Variety presenting to my Mind in the heat of the Argument.* 3. *Partly from my Matter's having a necessary Connexion with a thousand Incidents which engag'd me in new, profound, and nice Discussions; the want of which might bring an Author under a Suspicion of Disingenuity or Unfairness.* 4. *Partly from the Circumstances of Time, which have produc'd a great Variety of Arguments here among our selves, for and against the Penal Laws, the taking off the Test,* &c. *all which*

I was oblig'd to examine. 5. Partly from hence, that they who translated the Work from the English, *cou'd not, as they pretended, purge off its native Air without running into a diffuse Stile; besides, that they were pleas'd to divert themselves with mixing several Notions of their own, sometimes borrowing from one System, sometimes from another, and imitating here one Author's manner of Thinking, but not his Stile; there the Stile of another, but not his way of Thinking: thus affecting an Inequality in the whole, which makes, say they, the Readers* <509> *ascribe the* Commentary *to several different Persons, without ever guessing, either at them, or at me; overjoy'd they cou'd disguise so artfully, and puzzle your Finders out of the Fathers of Anonymous or Pseudonymous Books.*

The length of the Work, the three Parts of which had each made a Volume of 25 Sheets, was a just Reason for suppressing it; and how was it likely there shou'd be Readers found, much less Buyers, for so bulky a Work, at a time when one can hardly read over the Mercurys, Journals, and stitch'd Pamphlets, which swarm every where in the Booksellers Shops. But when I came to consider the Nature of the Matters treated, and which I have sometimes push'd a little too far, I found a second, and much a stronger Reason for condemning my Work to the shades of the Closet.[167] *Accordingly the Bookseller was order'd to put a stop to the Impression; and, as good luck wou'd have it, he was not got so far in the first Part, as the Reflections on the Disposition of this Country, in relation to the Test. A Subject which was not perhaps so seasonable at this juncture, considering the Train which our Affairs seem to take.*

What I had said in the third Part,[168] *touching the Dispute betwixt us and the Church of* Rome, *about the Rule of Faith,*[169] *startl'd my self when I came to consider it all together; for I have shewn, that the Charge of Temerity, which the Author*[170] *of the* Pretendedly Reform'd convicted of Schism, *pushes so home, and in short, the insuperable Difficultys in examining Scripture which*

---

167. Explained in the next section.

168. Not the third part of the *Philosophical Commentary* (p. 283), but the third part of the answer to *The Rights of Two Sovereigns* (see above, pp. 388–89), of which only the first part was published, as this "Supplement" to the *Philosophical Commentary*.

169. See Appendixes, "The Rule of Faith," p. 591.

170. Pierre Nicole, *Les prétendus Réformés convaincus de schisme* (The self-styled Reformed convicted of schism), Paris, 1684.

*have bin all along objected against us; are never to be answer'd but by a way
of Retorsion, and by putting the same Arms into the hands of Infidels against
Christianity: which tending either to Pyrrho-<510>nism,[171] or to lull Men in
an ill-grounded Assurance of Salvation, there's a necessity of coming into my
System. And without this I make appear, that the next and only surest way is
to turn* Psychopannichist,[172] *if one cou'd in this World, or at least* Omphalopsyche,[173] *or perfect Quietist; and not such as* Molinos, *who approves, as they
say, the most agitating and most polluting Operations of Soul and Body. This
likewise had bin somewhat unseasonable.*

A Short and Peremptory Answer to all that has bin publish'd
against the Rights of an erroneous Conscience.

But what most of all determin'd me to suppress my large Work, was this:

*I consider'd, that the chief Reason which shou'd oblige me to reply, was the
justifying my self against the odious Imputations with which my Opinion was
loaded; as tending to an Indifference for all Religion, and a hundred other
wicked Consequences of the same kind. Whoever gives heed to Aspersions of
this nature, quits all Claim to the Character of an Intelligent Reader, who
judges for himself, and from an attentive Examination of what may be said o'
both sides; and must be content to be rank'd with another sort of Readers, who
are govern'd by a way of Prejudice, and who having observ'd, that a Reverend
Divine,[174] in very high Esteem for his Zeal, for his Orthodoxy, and for his Capacity too; and another Author,[175] who describes himself as posted on the Pass
to challenge all Books, and stop the bad; have treated my Doctrine as pernicious:
have ground enough, without informing themselves further, to conclude, that
the matter must be so. These are the Men* <511> *with whom I am and ought
to justify my self, good Refugees for the most part, and worthy that all occasion*

---

171. See Appendixes, "Philosophical Controversies," p. 596 ("Pyrrhonism"). See also
DHC, art. "Nicolle," rem. C.

172. Psychopannichist: maintained that the soul sleeps between death and the resurrection of the body.

173. Omphalopsyche: mystics who practiced "navel gazing."

174. Jurieu, in *The True System.* See above, p. 387, note.

175. Jurieu again, in *Rights of Two Sovereigns;* see above, p. 386, note 164.

of Scandal be taken out of their way; especially considering, that nothing had determin'd me to write the Commentary, *but a Sense of the sad Hardships they have undergone.*

But what service cou'd a vast Collection of Arguments and Authoritys do me with them; a tedious Train of Reasonings, sometimes a little too abstracted and metaphysical; Clusters of Reflexions on Passages of Scripture, founded on good Sense much more than on the usual beaten Common-places? Wou'd they read a word of 'em, when they saw the Book so bulky? Wou'd they read my Arguments and Discussions all together? Cou'd they always comprehend 'em with that Clearness which is necessary for perceiving the weight of 'em? No, there's not the least likelihood of this: So that all my pains cou'd be of use only to those who were able before to decide upon this Dispute from the Pieces I have already publish'd, and which to me appear more than sufficient with regard to them. My business therefore was to find out the shortest Proof of the Innocence of my Opinion, and the most obvious to every Understanding; and having had the good fortune to light on it, I thought it best to drop my long Defence.

This Proof is drawn from a Passage of the True System of the Church, *whereby it appears that the Author and I are exactly of a mind: Therefore to reason now after this manner.*

My Opinion is the same as that of the Author of the True System of the Church.

Therefore it's Orthodox.

There's not a Man to be found, among those Readers with whom I stand in need of a Justification, <512> *who won't receive the Consequence with open arms: and as to our Conformity, which serves for the Principle, here's an instance of it, obvious enough to every Capacity.*

The Words of the Author of the True System of the Church, *p.* 307.

Nay, tho we were actually in the wrong, as to all the Points which keep up the Separation betwixt us and the Church of *Rome,* yet we shou'd be oblig'd in Conscience to separate from her, and persist in our Separation, till persuaded she has Reason of her side. We are convinc'd in our Consciences, that the Bread in the Eucharist is not the true Body of our Lord;

and this being the case, we shou'd be Idolaters, Hereticks, and Hypocrites, shou'd we re-unite with the Church of *Rome,* and submit to the Decisions of its Councils in this matter. This Principle is self-evident to all who have the least Freedom of Thought, and who know what the Empire of Conscience is, and to what a degree one offends whene'er he resists it.*

He afterwards examines some Objections; the first of which is, That Hereticks who believe themselves <513> *unjustly condemn'd by a Church, sin not in separating from her: To which he answers, that this does not follow;* "because," *says he,* "one always sins in following the Motions of a Conscience either ignorant, or surpriz'd by the Illusions of Error." *Then he shews how these two things may be reconcil'd: first, that one is oblig'd to separate from the true Church when he believes it false; next, that he sins in so separating.* "This," *says he* p. 308. "happens, because Conscience always obliges, in whatever state it is, to do that in which there's manifestly less Sin: Now there's less sin in a Heretick's separating, than in his persevering in the Orthodox Church, while he believes it Heretical and Idolatrous."

I shan't examine how it's possible to reconcile this to the three Chapters cited above; this is none of my business: I only say, that the words which I have now quoted being subsequent to the three Chapters, are to be reputed the true Sense of the Author, as a Will of a latter date passes for the true Will of the Testator preferably to all former Wills. To which I add, that these very Words contain in substance all that I have said concerning the Rights of an erroneous Conscience.

For it follows from these Passages, that if Luther *and* Calvin *were persuaded of what they spoke against the Church of* Rome, *they were oblig'd to act as*

---

* Take notice, that this is an excellent short Argument to the Roman Catholicks, without entring into a dispute upon the main of the Controversy betwixt us, that our Fathers were necessarily oblig'd to quit the Romish Communion. Mr. Daillé has handled it very solidly in Chap. 8. of his Apology; and since him, the Author of the True System has made use of it, to get clear of a very perplexing Objection of Maimbourg, in his Book against Dr. Lewis du Moulin. [Jean Daillé, Apologie des Eglises réformées où est monstré la necessité de leur séparation d'avec l'Eglise romaine contre ceux qui les accusent de faire schisme en is Chrestienté (Defense of the Reformed Churches, showing the necessity of their separation from the Roman Church, against those who accuse them of making a schism in Christianity), 1633 (English translation 1653); DHC, art. "Daillé, Jean." On the *True System* see above, p. 387, note.]

they did, even tho we shou'd suppose the Church of Rome *to be really what she pretends, to wit, the Holy Catholick Church mention'd in the Apostles Creed, the Spouse of* JESUS CHRIST, *his mystical Body, his Dove, the Ark out of which there is neither Grace nor Salvation.* <514>

An erroneous Conscience then lays a Man under an Obligation of revolting against the true Mother Church, of raising the Rabble upon her, seducing as many of her Children as he can, and drawing Citys, Provinces, Kingdoms, into Rebellion against her, spoiling her of her Temples, breaking down her Altars and Images, and defaming her throughout the world for an errand Prostitute, &c. If an erroneous Conscience lays under this Obligation, it lays one by the same rule under that of erecting a new Form of Church-Government and Worship, of establishing Pastors and Consistorys, and all the other Institutions which are necessary for the maintaining Societys, enlarging 'em, making 'em prosper, &c.

Here then we find the very Maxim, against which such a Cry has bin rais'd, contain'd in the Doctrines of the Author of the True System, *to wit, That Error in the guise of the Truth enters upon all the Rights and Privileges of Truth; or, which is the same thing, lest any one shou'd take exception at a word, That a Man who's persuaded such a Doctrine is the pure Truth reveal'd by God, is oblig'd, tho absolutely in an Error, to have all the same Regard and Sollicitousness for this Doctrine, as he ought to have for the celestial Truth who has the good fortune to know it.*

For what shou'd it proceed from, that a Heretick is oblig'd, according to this Author, to separate from the true Church; but from hence, that an Orthodox is oblig'd to separate from an Heretical Communion? All the Right the Heretick enjoys is borrow'd, without doubt, from that which belongs to the Truth, for which he's persuaded he is acting; or, which is the same thing, all his Right consists in this, that he ought to avoid the shock which he must give to Truth and Order, if he did not act according to Conscience; <515> *which shock is a greater Sin, than that which he may fall into by following his false Conscience.*

Now as it's impossible to grant, that Heresy disguis'd in the colors of Truth obliges to make a breach with the true Church, without granting at the same time that she obliges to all the natural Consequences of Schism, that is, to the establishing in the schismatical Society the properest Regulations that the Scripture prescribes for the maintaining the true Church; it follows, that Heresy en-

gages every one to all that Luther *and* Calvin *had done, that is, to endeavor, as much as in him lies, to gain over from the Church he has quitted those who still persevere in it, by maintaining with Zeal and Power, as well in Preaching as in Writing, what he takes to be the Truth: and if the Scriptures warrant the making use of corporal Punishments and Armys for the converting of Men, Heresy obliges to these methods also; for the building up her self on the Ruins of the true Church.*

The Author cannot deny these Consequences; for he that may do the greater, may do the lesser. A Province which has a right to revolt, has that of chusing a Leader, of establishing a Civil Judicature, and in general of following all the Lights of true Policy, for maintaining the publick Peace, and for helping those to shake off the Yoke of Tyranny, whom she believes Reason, and Piety, and Charity, oblige her to have a compassion of.

And this alone destroys what the Author of the Defence of the Reformation,[176] *and that of the* True System,[177] *have advanc'd as a Maxim; That nothing but the Truth has a right to be preach'd: a Principle which they themselves have contradicted, one in a Memoir presented to the King, on occasion of the Declaration making the Conversion of Children of seven <516> years of age valid; the other, in the second Volume of the* Politicks of the Clergy,[178] *on occasion of the same Declaration. They have both laid down as constant Principles, that the Education of Children belongs to the Parents, and cannot be deny'd 'em, without violating the most sacred Laws of Nature. They are in the right; but from hence follows,*

That Error has a right to be preach'd and taught: for if it had not such a right, the Orthodox might have a just ground for hindring Infidels and Hereticks to instruct their own Children; and then the taking these Children out of their hands wou'd be a most just Action: whereas both these Authors brand it, when practis'd with regard even to Jews, as a very great Abomination.

Now if Heretical Parents have a right to instruct their Children in their

---

176. Jean Claude, *La défense de la Réformation contre le livre intitulé: Préjugés légitimes contre les calvinistes* (Defense of the Reformation against the book [of Nicole] entitled "Lawful presumptions against the Calvinists"), 1673. See DHC, art. "Claude, Ministre de Charenton."

177. Jurieu; see above, p. 387, note.

178. Jurieu; see above, p. 37, note 3.

Errors, they have a right to have Schoolmasters of their own, Catechists, Pre-ceptors, Preachers, as well to teach their Children, as to improve themselves more and more by the Conversation of Persons more learned than they.

But here's something stronger still; to wit, That if an erroneous Conscience obliges to make a Schism, as the Author of the System *owns, there's no Action so enormous, which it does not oblige to the commission of; for we can't conceive a Crime more heinous than that of* Luther *and* Calvin, *upon a supposition that the Church of* Rome *were really what it pretends. If* Luther *then and* Calvin *were oblig'd to do what they did, as this Author owns, tho their Con-sciences shou'd in reality be as erroneous as the Papists suppose, they ought by a stronger reason to commit any lesser Sin than Schism from the Instincts of their Consciences; for he that may do the greater, may the lesser in all these matters.*

<517>

Now I don't know where we can find out Crimes, which are not of a less heinous nature than that of rending the mystical Body of JESUS CHRIST, *that Spouse which he has redeem'd with his Blood, that Mother which begets us to God, which nourishes us with the Milk of that Wisdom which is without guile, which leads us to everlasting Bliss. What fouler Crime can we think of, than rebelling against such a Mother, than defaming her all the world over, en-deavoring to stir up her Children against her, tearing 'em from her bosom by Millions, to drag 'em as much as in us lies into everlasting Flames, they and their Posterity from Generation to Generation? Where can we find the first-rate High Treason against the Divine Majesty, unless in Instances of this kind; con-sidering it's notorious, that a Spouse who tenderly loves his Wife, and perfectly knows her Vertue, judges himself much more affronted by Libels, which make her pass for a Punk prostituted to Dog and Cur, than by any Scandals rais'd of himself?*

Of all the Crimes that a Subject can fall into, none is more horrible than that of rebelling against his lawful Prince, and stirring up as many Provinces as he can, with a design of dethroning him, tho by the ruin of all the Provinces which continue faithful.

Now as much as the Divine, the Supernatural, the Heavenly, exceed the Human, the Natural, and the Earthly; so much the Church, the Spouse of our Lord JESUS CHRIST, *surpasses all Societys, Kingdoms, and Commonwealths: And so much all Rebellions against the Church exceed those against the State in Sin. Mr.* Daillé *has touch'd this matter very worthily in the beginning of his* Apology.

Hence one might insist, that were the Church of Rome *what she boasts her self,* Luther *and* Calvin <518> *had sin'd beyond all comparison more heinously in making a Schism, than if they had, I won't say, cut a couple of Travellers throats in the skirt of a Wood, or bin cutting of Purses for ten years together at a Church-door; but if they had poison'd or stab'd* Charles *V or* Francis *I from an Instinct of Conscience, and a false Persuasion that they had an extraordinary Impulse from on high to such a Work.*

So that the Author of the System *cannot reasonably deny but* Luther *and* Calvin, *since they were in his opinion oblig'd to act as they did against the Church of* Rome, *even tho their Conscience had bin erroneous, and the Church of* Rome *bin what she pretends; were likewise oblig'd to reach forth their hand against their lawful Prince, if they had felt an inward Impulse of Conscience to such an Attempt: and so of every other evil Action; for, once again, he that may do the greater, may the lesser.*

'Twill behove him then, if he please, to answer all the Difficultys, which he and the Author of the Rights of the two Sovereigns, *have offer'd against the Doctrine I have advanc'd; for I shall trouble my self about it no further, seeing I may rely on another, who for the future is as much concern'd as I; there being no one ill Consequence imputable to me, which results not from what he has precisely establish'd in* Pag. 307. *of his* System.

I admire the Author of the Rights of the two Sovereigns, *wou'd bring* Ravillac[179] *so often upon the stage, without taking notice of these two things; first, My answering, that 'twas a folly to press me with Consequences of this kind, since the opposite Opinion cou'd not remedy the Evil; it being a Contradiction, that a Man shou'd be persuaded his Conscience obliges him to this or that, and that his Conscience is de-*<519>*ceiv'd. Thus every one is persuaded his Conscience is true; and since all the World's agreed, that one ought to follow the Instincts of a true Conscience, don't they say enough to encourage* Ravillac *in his execrable Design? Is it pardonable to trump up an Objection a hundred times, which has bin invincibly confuted, and not offer the least word in answer?*

---

179. Ravaillac assassinated Henry IV, contrary to the generally held tenet that no ruler, not even a tyrant, should be assassinated. See Appendixes, "Church and State," p. 589.

The next thing is, That People imagine, without any good grounds, that a Man who believes himself inspir'd by God to excite one Prince to make war upon another, and destroy him root and branch, and cries out till he's hoarse again for the execution of his Commission; is not as great a Villain, if deceiv'd, as he who believing he has had an Inspiration to kill the same Prince, and, yet deceiv'd, does actually kill him. Let's suppose Drabicius[180] *to have taken for Inspiration what was only a Crack or Disorder in his Brain; did not he design, pray, to cause as much mischief in the world as* Ravillac? *The latter govern'd himself by the High-Priest's Maxim,* It's expedient that one Man shou'd die for a great many: *On the contrary,* Drabicius *never thought of finding out the One who shou'd be a Price for the Many, but chose to arm a hundred thousand Men against the Emperor, who in four Campagns must have committed a hundred thousand millions of Sins, Profanations, vain Oaths, Pilferings, Burnings, Rapines, Murders, and utterly ruin'd the Lord knows how many innocent Familys. Yet my Adversarys, do they doubt, if this good Man was sincere, as 'tis very probable he was, but that all the Extravagances of his Imagination, all his Efforts, in following the Instincts of an erroneous Conscience, to stir up a bloody and destructive War, pass'd for very venial Sins in the sight of God.* <520>

This is truly what we may call weighing things with unequal Weights, looking only at the Surface, swallowing a Camel, and straining at a Gnat: or if this be not so, let 'em assign a good Reason, I shall be oblig'd to 'em, so it be really a good one; that is, founded on the Reality and intrinsick Nature of Objects, more than on the first Impression, which things make from Custom, and a Contagion of Imaginations: Let 'em, I say, assign such a Reason as this, to shew that a Man falsly persuaded he's inspir'd, and call'd forth by God to avenge his Church, and who sounds to War by his Writings, by his Sermons, imitating Isaiah *and the other antient Prophets to get Leagues and Confederacys form'd, who wishes from his Soul, he had the Power that* Pompey *the Great once boasted, to raise an Army of a hundred thousand Men with a stamp of his Foot, that he might send 'em away, with his holy and paternal Benediction, into the persecuting States, there to ravage and do their worst; sins less than another deluded Soul, who imagining he has such another Inspiration, to avenge the*

---

180. Drabicius was a violent fanatic. See DHC, art. "Drabicius."

Church by the Death of his Prince, steals into his Palace, and dispatches him with a Dagger.

Whoever thorowly considers this, will find it hard to justify the first of these, rather than the second: the former designing to involve an infinite number of innocent People, in the Punishment of the guilty; and not being able to alledg in excuse, without exposing himself for a dastardly poor Wretch, who wou'd do mischief at a distance, and without hazarding his own Skin, or putting himself to Trouble (even tho it did not follow, that he must hereby resist a divine Inspiration) that if he had been under the Persuasion of the second, he wou'd not have made the Attempt. <521> Happy for one and t'other, might they both appear before the Throne of God, as distemper'd in Brain; having, for Example, each the Pinal Gland set athwart in his Noddle, or expos'd from time to time to the Distillations of a petrifying Humor; which, as overwhelming Cause, might occasion those Paroxisms, and Fits of their pretended Inspiration: their Crimes in this case cou'd no more be imputed to 'em, than to a Frantick or Lunatick; supposing 'em forc'd into 'em by an overwhelming Physical Cause.

Whatever it be, my Opinion and that of the Author of the True System *are exactly conformable.*

For if I hold, that one is oblig'd to do what his Conscience suggests, as fit to be done; he holds the same.

If he says, that the reason of this is, that hereby he avoids at least the greater Sin; I say the same.

If he says, that it does not from hence follow, that the Party commits an Action void of all Sin; I say so too: and have repeated it so often, that I wonder, how an Author, who has taken upon him to confute me, can pretend any cause of Ignorance.

If I say, that Conscience erring from an invincible Ignorance excuses; he says the same: for I don't think, he'l disown what his Second, the Author of the Rights of the two Sovereigns, *lays down at Page* 238. *to wit,* "That all invincible Ignorance excuses, as well in points of Right as Fact"; *and shou'd he disown this, can he disavow what's to be read at the* 189th *Page of the System,* "That the Truth obliges not, unless where reveal'd and preach'd." *Which plainly imports, That they who obey not a Command, which is neither reveal'd nor preach'd to 'em, are blameless; and by consequence,* <522> *that an Action committed from an invincible Ignorance is exempt from Sin.*

All the difference that can be between us in this matter, is, That I have advanc'd several Remarks, by way of Conjecture, to insinuate, that there are abundantly more in an invincible Ignorance, than we imagine. But this makes no difference at all in the Substance of our Doctrines; since it's evident, I can have nothing particular on this Head, but bare Conjecture: God alone knowing who are, or are not, maliciously in Error. And I shall never be asham'd of being more favorable in my Opinion, to the Salvation of Men, than others are in theirs.

These last Reasons might likewise have determin'd me to suppress my Answer to the Rights of the two Sovereigns; *it being notorious, that all the Difficultys and Objections there offer'd against me, all the Authoritys of Scripture, prove no more, than that it does not follow, a Man is acquitted of Sin, on the score of doing what his Conscience suggests. And having shewn, that I don't maintain the contrary; there's nothing farther in it, that can touch me. But if these Objections, these Texts of Scripture, import, that a Man is never acquitted of Sin, by following an erroneous Conscience; it must be allow'd me, that this likewise proves, either there's no such thing as invincible Ignorance, or if there be, yet that it does not excuse. In either case, this Author proves nothing more against me, than against himself, and against the Author of the* True System. *I have therefore but one Word more to say upon this matter. You'l alledg Examples of some who have bin severely punish'd, for having done things, which they thought were well-pleasing to God. Be it so: What can we infer from this, but that their* <523> *Error was insincere; for you your self allow, that sincere or invincible Ignorance (for I take these two Terms to be synonymous) excuses as well in Fact as Right. Let the following Example serve for all.*

In the 116*th Page, the Author objects the Example of the Worshippers of the Golden Calf, to prove, that a Man, tho sincerely believing he does God great Honor, and acting from an honest Intention, may yet grievously offend him. To this I shall only ask this short Question, in Answer: Were those* Israelites, *who worship'd the Golden Calf, under an invincible Ignorance, or were they not? If they were, you were very wrong in affirming, Page* 238. That invincible Ignorance excuses as to Fact and Right; *and you have contradicted the Author of the* True System of the Church, *if as publick Fame informs us, he and the Author of the* Apology for the Reformation against *Maimbourg's* History of Calvinism,[181] *be one and the same Person; for he asserts,* Chap. 10. of the second Recrimination, n. 6. *That the Idolatry of the Jews cou'd not proceed from Ignorance; that the Words of the Law were not subject to various Interpretations; that there was no Ambiguity in 'em: and therefore that their Rebellion proceeded purely from Malice and Obliquity; and therefore deserv'd no Indulgence. One might have seen a great many curious Reflections on this point in my second Part.*[182] *Yet if the Ignorance of the* Israelites; *who worship'd, was affected and vincible, I shan't hinder the Judges, in Ecclesiastical Causes, to condemn 'em as culpable.*

I had drawn a strong Confirmation of all the Remarks I now make, in Chap. 27, & 28. of my third Part,[183] from the famous Distinction of Points fundamental and non-fundamental: which besides the <524> good Reception it meets with from all Protestants, is so necessary to the Author of the True System of the Church, *that one may say, it's the very Corner-stone or Pedestal of his whole Work. Here's an Abstract of what I had very much enlarg'd on there, and which I have suppress'd, together with a hundred other things.*

Non-fundamental Points, according to the Author of the True System, *and the rest of the Reform'd, are of such a Nature, that things being in other respects equal, one is as certainly sav'd by erring in 'em, as by believing the Truth; without the least need of repenting, or asking Forgiveness of God for these Errors at the Moment of Death: for were there any such necessity, the distinction of Fundamental and Non-fundamental wou'd be null. In the number of these Non-fundamental Points, they reckon the real Presence of* JESUS CHRIST *in the Eucharist,*[184] *and the five contested Points between the Remonstrants and the*

---

181. Pierre Jurieu, *Histoire du calvinisme et celle du papisme mises en parallèle: ou apologie pour les réformateurs, pour la réformation, et pour les réformez, divisée en quatre parties; contre un libelle intitulé l'histoire du calvinisme par M. Maimbourg* (The history of Calvinism and that of papism put in parallel: or defence of the Reformers, the Reformation and the Reformed, divided into four parts; against a book entitled "History of Calvinism" by M. Maimbourg), 1683.

182. Of the unpublished answer to *The Rights of Two Sovereigns.* See above, p. 390, note 168.

183. Of the unpublished answer to *The Rights of Two Sovereigns.*

184. See Appendixes, "The Eucharist," p. 589.

Anti-Remonstrants, ever since the Synod of Dort.[185] *You may err in these Points, as the Lutherans and Remonstrants do, according to the Calvinists; or be Orthodox in 'em, as these are; it's all one as to eternal Salvation: for we make no doubt, and the Author of the* True System *makes less than others, but one may be sav'd in the Lutheran or Arminian Communions, without the least need of retracting upon a Deathbed. Yet if we consider the Matter and Substance of the Errors of these two Sects, we can't but qualify 'em with the Name of horrible Blasphemys, outrageous Lyes given to God, grievous Calumnys against the reveal'd Truth. In effect, if it be true, as we believe, that* JESUS CHRIST *does not give us his Body to be eaten, the Lutherans who affirm, that we depreciate the Eucharist, that we rob Chris-<525>tians of the strongest Pledg of the infinite Love of* JESUS CHRIST, *and his adorable Flesh of the glorious Prerogative of being the Instrument of all our heavenly Gifts and Graces; blaspheme God himself most outrageously, by charging the Truth, which he has reveal'd us in his Word, with these three notable Defects.*

Likewise, if it be true, that God damns the greatest part of Mankind, without having afforded 'em the necessary means of Salvation, and by leaving 'em under an irresistible necessity of sinning; which God thought fit, that the Sin of the first Man shou'd lay 'em under: they who maintain, that this Doctrine makes God the Author of Sin, and on a Supposition of his punishing this Sin eternally, represents him as a cruel unjust Being, and consequently leads to Atheism; it being impossible and a Contradiction in Terms, that God shou'd be God, unless exempt from every thing that we conceive to be a moral Imperfection, by the clearest and most distinct Ideas: These, I say, who maintain this, affront God himself in the most outrageous manner, rendring that which he judges most worthy his supreme Perfection, incompatible with his Nature, and destructive of it. Yet all these Outrages and Blasphemys hinder not, according to the Author of the True System, *but the Lutherans and Arminians are in as fair a way of Salvation as we. He must therefore of necessity own, that Errors, which, consider'd in the matter of 'em, are direct Affronts to the Majesty of God, and Blasphemys against his holy Truth, become most innocent from hence alone, that they are entertain'd from a sincere Persuasion of the Truth of 'em; and from a Persuasion, that the not maintaining 'em, wou'd be injurious to*

---

185. See Appendixes, "Grace, Original Sin, Predestination," p. 588.

the divine Nature. Add to <526> *this, that no one is so unjust, as to impute to those he believes in an Error, all the frightful Consequences which are chargeable on it; nor to maintain, that if they were convinc'd their Errors necessarily led to 'em, they wou'd notwithstanding persist: The most that any one does, is shewing 'em, what, in his Opinion, they tend to, hoping, if they cou'd perceive it as he does, that they wou'd immediately forsake it.*

This invincibly proves, that if the Author of the True System *reasons consequentially, as an Author of good Sense shou'd do, he ought to acknowledg, that there are altogether as many unaffected Errors in Christianity, as there are Non-fundamental Points, and consequently a very great number; and that Sincerity absolves the Erroneous, even where they are most opposite at bottom to what God has reveal'd, concerning his Attributes and Perfections. For let no one deceive himself, an Error's not Non-fundamental because of its being small, but because of the Obscurity or Ambiguity of the Proofs, which shew the opposite Truth is contain'd in the reveal'd Word. Nor is there any Error which ought not to be reputed Fundamental, how insignificant soever the opposite Doctrine may be towards Salvation, how slight and trifling in its own nature; if it boldly strikes at the clear, and plain, and express Authority of Scripture: as saying, for example, that* Noah *entred the Ark with four Persons only, or that St.* Paul *was never a Persecutor of the Christians.*

I had almost forgot one short Proof, and possibly more convincing than any other, of the Conformity of my Opinion with that of the Author of the System; *by virtue of the Passage already cited from him;*[186] *to wit, that the Author of the* Rights *of the two Sovereigns had so fully perceiv'd, that no exception* <527> *cou'd be taken at what I have said, by any one that had taught the Substance of that Passage, that he has taken special care not to make the same Confession:* "A conceal'd Heretick," *says he,* "who is in the Bosom of the Church, is not oblig'd to separate; because his Separation wou'd be a new Sin added to Heresy: and tho his Conscience shou'd tell him, he ought to separate, yet he is not oblig'd to obey this Conscience, because it's erroneous." *This is plainly contradicting the Author of the* System, *and yet there was no avoiding it.*

I have one Observation more to make concerning what I had somewhere

186. See above, p. 392.

advanc'd,[187] *rather to strengthen a bare Conjecture, or as an Objection for my Adversarys to bite upon, than a formal Assertion; to wit, that after one has sincerely and diligently sought the Truth, he ought to embrace that which appears Truth in his eyes, and that this is instead of absolute Truth to him. This is often cry'd out against in the* Rights of the two Sovereigns. *But that it might appear to all my Readers, who stand in need of as short a proof of my Orthodoxy (that is, of the Conformity of my Opinions with those of the Author of the* True System of the Church) *as this which I have now given; I have shewn in my third Part,*[188] *by a great number of Observations, which are very close to my purpose, that all this Author has answer'd the Objections of Messieurs* de Meaux *and* Nichole, *concerning the Rule of Faith, amounting to this:* We must give due Attention to the Word of God, and the Truth will by this means draw near to us, and make it self felt to the Soul: *it's plain, all the Distinctions he has invented, unknown to all our Controvertists before him, and consequently a sign he has bin beaten out of the old Track, and forc'd to seek <528> for new cover from the storm, contains in Substance no more than this; to wit, that a Christian does his Duty, if he seeks Knowledg with Sincerity and a teachable Mind, and if he holds by that which he feels to be the Truth; and that this Feeling, even as the Tast, with regard to Foods, ought to amount to a Proof to us of what is the the good and wholesome Nourishment of the Soul.*

That Christians, who persecute, are more inexcusable than the Pagans who persecuted the Primitive Church.

It remains, that I now say a word or two concerning the following Supplement. *I have some reason to fear this Subject, being so very much beaten ever since the late Persecution in* France, *that my Readers may be tir'd with it. But beside, that I have occasionally handl'd some* Matters *which are worth the examining, I thought nothing cou'd be more seasonable, than a Dissertation which overthrows the* Ne plus ultra[189] *of Compellers, to wit, their pretending,*

187. See above, pp. 258, 261, 271, etc.
188. Of the unpublished answer to *The Rights of Two Sovereigns.*
189. "The ultimate."

that God will one day punish the Persecutors of Orthodoxy, and reward the Persecutors of Heresy. I shew, that this Hope is vain, and that the Doctrine of compelling grants an Impunity to Hereticks, who believing they shall do great Service to God, root up his Church like so many wild Boars: And this, together with the many other Enormitys, which, as I prove anew, are inseparable from this cursed Doctrine, may, and ought to inspire Protestants with a just Horror, and necessary Distrust of that Church, which for so many Ages past has made it the invariable Rule of its Conduct, and still will practise by it here and else-where, unless depriv'd of the Means and <529> Power. This is the only Security of the Church of England, *as Monsieur* Fagel[190] *has justly observ'd, in that polite and wise Letter of his, worthy the Pen of the first Minister of a well-govern'd Commonwealth, in which he discovers the Sentiments of their High-nesses of* Orange, *whom we look on at present as the tutelar Angels of the Reformation: A Letter which gives new Life and Spirit to all good Patriots; who moreover wou'd do well continually, to read the Historys of those Persecutions, which Popery has stir'd up in the World, and the Treatises which confute its abominable Theory; or, in Imitation of that King of* Persia *of old,[191] order one of their Domesticks to come to 'em every Morning, with this Lesson;* Remember what has lately bin done in *France.*

Nothing's more true, than that Popery is chargeable with whatever's most odious and infamous in Persecutions; and that of all those she has hitherto stir'd up, none is more inexcusable than this last Persecution, mov'd amidst all the shining Lights which set the present so much above all former Ages.

Say the Pagans persecuted the first Christians, I don't wonder at it: 'Twas in a great measure pardonable in Men, who cou'd not but look on Christianity as the strangest, the most unaccountable Innovation; to see a parcel of little Fellows, scatter'd thro the Roman *Empire, treat their Religion as abominable (a Religion which had subsisted for so many Ages) and pretend to nothing less than the intire Destruction of their Temples, Statues, and Sacrifices. No body*

190. Gaspar Fagel, Grand-Pensionary of Holland, *Their Highness the Prince and Princess of Orange's Opinion about a general Liberty of Conscience, etc. Being a collection of Four Select Papers, viz., I. Mijn Heer Fagel's First Letter to Mr. Stewart. II. Reflections on Monsieur Fagel's Letter. III. Fagel's Second Letter to Mr. Stewart. IV. Some extracts out of Mr. Stewart's Letters, which were communicated to Mijn Heer Fagel,* London, 1689.

191. Herodotus, *Histories,* V.105.

cou'd give an instance, how great soever his Reading might be, of any thing like it, either since the Foundation of Rome, *or before.*

Laws they might have found, and Injunctions made from time to time, to prevent the introducing new <530> *Ceremonys; but this cou'd mean no more, than that there were sometimes those, who without derogating from the establish'd Religion, had endeavor'd to insinuate the Rites of other Countrys, and practise 'em clandestinely in* Rome. *An Attempt so new and impious, according to the Prejudices of Pagans, as that of the Christians, how cou'd it chuse but enrage the Emperors and Ministry?*

Besides, the Emperors, for the most part, had never handl'd any thing but the Sword, they were utter Strangers to Politeness and Literature; nor had their Ministers of State ever consider'd the Nature of Religion seriously, any more than the Pontiffs, Priests, and Augurs. They were in this respect, and in all others (I speak of the Churchmen) under the grossest Ignorance; those among the Pagans, who had any Knowledge of the Arts and Sciences, being generally of the Laity. On the whole, both sorts contented themselves, as to what concern'd Religion, with following the Doctrines deliver'd from Father to Son, and were of Opinion, that no one Religion ought to destroy another.

What cou'd be expected from such a sort of Men, but the persecuting those who shou'd tell 'em, the Religion of the Empire ought to be abolish'd as ridiculous, infamous, execrable; and that of a God, crucify'd between two Thieves, adopted in its room?

But today, as is known by a hundred Experiences, that the World is divided into various Opinions about the Gospel, and that Conscience won't allow one's making Profession of the Doctrines of a Sect which he believes naught; now that it's known, the Protestants are not wedded to their Opinions by any vain Motives, because, without mentioning other Countrys, the Reform'd Ministers of France *have, for more than a* <531> *hundred Years past, held tack with the learnedest of the Romish Communion, in verbal Conferences and controversial Writings; that they have often had the better in these Disputes; that few considerable Books have bin publish'd against 'em, which they have not confuted; that they have publish'd some which have not bin answer'd; that they daily publish new ones, loading the Church of* Rome *with so many Scandals and Reproaches, and with such loud and insulting Defiances, that since no one appears in its Vindication, there's a strong Presumption, their Cause won't bear it; this Communion having too many good Pens, and too much Pride to pass over Injurys: I add, that they have of late Years offer'd such Reasons against the Authority of the Church, that no one can answer 'em directly, nor any other way, than by offering in return as great Difficultys against the Examination of private Judgments: Now, I say, that all these things are well known, it's altogether inexcusable to ruffle and dragoon 'em.*

What I have bin just saying, is enough to shew, that the Question about the Authority of the Church, and the Rule of Faith, are a Rock which they must for ever split upon, as well as we; and I own, this had furnish'd me, in the third Part of this Work,[192] *with an Argument for Toleration, which I cou'd not suppress without regret, tho forc'd to sacrifice it to other Considerations. Here's a small Sketch of it:*

The Protestants wou'd be absolutely to blame in compelling Catholicks (I mean, upon any other account than their particular Doctrines of dispensing with Oaths of Allegiance, and extirpating Sects) shou'd these represent, that they cou'd not depart from that Foundation of their Faith, which they find in the <532> Authority of Councils, unless a better were propos'd; and that they can't bring themselves to believe, that a private Interpretation is better than that which, for so many Ages together, has bin given by all those who have govern'd the vast Body of the Romish Communion.

You may fancy this Reason as weak as you will, it's at least a specious one; the rather, because the Ministers are driven by it to a particular Grace of the Holy Spirit, to compound a greater Certainty of their Faith, than that which the Church of Rome *proposes.*

This is evident from the Example of two Ministers, who have answer'd to two Works of Port-Royal, *about the Rule of Faith.*[193] *They have bin forc'd, at the very opening of the Scene, to do what the antient Poets did only in the extremest intricacy of the Plot; have recourse* ad Deum ex Machina, *to the Grace of the good God.*

Yet this hinders not but the Papists are very unjust in compelling us, as long as we offer Difficultys against their Rule of Faith, which they can never abso-

192. Of the unpublished answer to *The Rights of Two Sovereigns.*
193. Claude and Jurieu. See DHC, art. "Nicolle," rem. C.

lutely satisfy; all that they can say in direct Defence, and without Retorsion, not amounting to a quarter part, I won't say of a Proof, but of a good Color.

Now since we are oblig'd to fly to Grace for an Answer to the Objections of Rome, *we can no longer pretend to constrain any other sort of Christians; since they may equally fly to the same Asylum, when unable to answer the Arguments of the opposite Party.*

The Papist, the Socinian, the Anabaptist, the Quaker, the Arminian, the Labadist, will answer, when hard prest; I own, the Opinions which I entertain do not carry in 'em a convincing Evidence: But God has had the Goodness to lead <533> me into this Sense, either by a subjective Grace, or by the favorable Dispositions of my Temper and Constitution, or by a happy Concurrence of Circumstances, or by turning aside those Objects which might have warp'd me to the wrong side, *&c.*

Thus Grace might be a Plaister for what it does not touch, and for what it does; it might become a Principle of Concord and charitable Forbearance: whereas there are no kind of Controversys so inextinguishable, as those which Grace has given Occasion.

It's easily seen that this Demonstration, which I have carry'd very far, comes up to the Remark in the English *Preface to* Lactantius, De Mortibus Persecutorum; *That the Persecutions of Christian against Christian can't chuse but be unjust, because they have no demonstrative Evidence whereby infallibly to decide who is right and who wrong.*

And because this has never bin so clearly discover'd as in our days, therefore I conclude, that the late Persecution in France *is more inexcusable than that of the antient Pagans.*

Who is not in a Sweat, at reading what a Bishop of France, *and two Reform'd Ministers of the same Country, and Heads of the Party, have wrote concerning the Faith of Children: Who, I say, is not in a Sweat, to think what a swadder these Authors must be in, when laboring to prove, either that Children believe the Gospel by Acts of Faith exerted on the Authority of the Church, or that they begin to exert Acts of Faith upon the Evangelick Truths themselves, and in virtue of the Truths themselves.*

They may look long enough for what's never to be found: Children have no Motive of Belief, that has <534> *any relation to the Objects themselves; for they who believe the Gospel, wou'd swallow the Alcoran, and all the Storys in*

Amadis de Gaul, *if propos'd in the same manner. The Ground of their Belief then at most (for many of 'em know not explicitely why they believe at all) is an Opinion they have, that their Father or Mother tell 'em such and such things in serious earnest, and know very well what they say when they explain the Catechise to 'em; and there's reason to believe, that of a hundred Men who live to a good old Age, fourscore die without any other reason for their Belief, but a preconceiv'd Opinion of the Capacity and Honesty of their Instructors: They, good People, wisely relying on what the Book-Learned tell 'em, more than on what themselves might judg of matters, not being bred either to write or read, and living almost all their life long among Cows and Sheep, or with the Hammer, or some other such Tool in hand, from morning till night.*

What a twirl has the Church-Controversy had! and how wou'd Beza *look (were he to come again into the World, with that little Poem of his printed before the singing Psalms, and which the Protestant Children were all oblig'd to get by heart,* Petit Troupeau)[194] *to find that Extent is now-adays such a Mark, according to us, of the true Church, that we dispute the Church of* Rome's *Pretensions, on this very account among others, that it is not extended and universal enough. I speak thus, because I'm assur'd from the mouth of several Refugee Ministers, tho only two of their Body have written upon this new Notion,[195] that for thirty years past the most knowing have held, that the true Church must include either all, or very near all Christian Communions.*

<535>

How many of our People have died in the Lord heretofore, with an incredible Consolation, to think that the Church of Rome *not being the* Little Flock, *as the Reform'd seem'd to be, the Kingdom of Heaven must belong to these alone? Behold 'em launch'd into the Ocean of Eternity with a hopeful Cargo!*

A Thought upon *Molinos*.[196]

I'm at last come to an end of this long Preface, if yet I ought to make an end of it without saying a word or two to Molinos. *They instance this Man black*

194. "Little Flock," implying that the true Church is a small group.

195. Probably Claude and Jurieu; see above, p. 407, note 193, and p. 395, notes 176, 177.

196. Miguel de Molinos, whose teachings on mysticism and morality were con-

as Hell, and still reeking with the Anathema's of the Inquisition, as an Objection, he and his Disciples, against what I had positively asserted; That the Truths of Morality are so plain in Scripture, that all Christians discover 'em without any Difficulty or Controversy upon these Points. I answer, either that Molinos *must be one of those Visionarys, who, when they are not asleep, reason after the manner of those in Dreams, without the least Coherence in their Words, Principles, or Consequences; or else that he was an errand Impostor, who out of mere Vanity or Singularity (to say no worse) wou'd persuade his Votarys to the strangest and most accommodating of all Paradoxes, to wit, That the most sensual Pollutions are a great Advancement in the purgative, and even in the illuminative way. But besides, the little progress his Doctrine has made, and the pains which a world of People take to prove he never taught such Abominations, sufficiently justify me. Add to this, That having ask'd several why they believ'd* Molinos *innocent, I found the best reason they cou'd give me, was, because he was condemn'd at* Rome: *so that they have in a manner own'd to me, that if he had* <536> *bin clear'd there, they shou'd have thought him guilty.**

Proh Superi quantum mortalia Pectora caecae
Noctis habent![197] ———

---

demned by Rome in 1687; see Denzinger, *ed. cit.,* p. 375. See article in the *Catholic Encyclopedia,* http://www.newadvent.org/cathen/10441a.htm.

* The Reader shou'd take this along with him, That at worst *Molinos* allows carnal Desires and impure Motions to be Sins, when they proceed from our selves; and that he does not justify 'em, but when excited by an external Agent, to wit, the Devil or unclean Spirits. So that he does not properly err as to the Right, but as he assigns a false Cause of certain inordinate Motions. He does not therefore deny the Substance of that Morality which other Christians are agreed in.

197. Ovid, *Metamorphoses,* VI.472: "Ye gods, what blind night rules in the hearts of men"; translated Frank J. Miller, Loeb Classical Library.

<537>

A

SUPPLEMENT

TO THE

Philosophical Commentary

ON

These Words of Jesus Christ,

Compel 'em to come in.

ЮↃ CHAPTER I ЮↃ

General Considerations on St. Austin's *Argument in defence of Persecution; shewing, That he offers nothing which may not be retorted, with equal force, upon the persecuted Orthodox.*

Persuaded, as I always was, that the literal Sense of the Words, *Compel 'em to come in,* is indefensible, impious, and absurd; I did not doubt St. *Austin*'s defending it weakly enough, but never cou'd <538> imagine that he'd have help'd it out with so much fallacious Reasoning. Nor did I perceive this, till I was actually in confuting him; and I'm now more sensible than ever, that one's struck with the false glare of a Paralogism when he reads over a Book only for an Amusement, infinitely more than when he sits down with a design to consider and answer it. I have a hundred times admir'd, while I was writing the third Part of my *Commentary,* how a Man cou'd have so much Wit as St. *Austin,* and yet reason so wretchedly; but I'm come at last to this, that nothing is more rare than a Justness of Judgment, and a sound logical Head. Every Age produces uncommon Genius's, bright and pregnant Wits, who have a rapid Imagination, who express themselves with a deal of Eloquence, and have inexhaustible Sources for maintaining what they please: This was exactly St. *Austin*'s Character. But we find very few, who have a talent at taking the stress of a Difficulty, and who, when they go about to solve it, suffer not themselves to be dazled by Reasons, as they fancy, of their own finding; and which, far from a satisfactory Solution, are liable to be retorted, prove too much, are wide of the point, or subject to some defect or other of this kind. What wretched things are most of St. *Austin*'s Comparisons! He cou'd not perceive, that the Counterparts of his Parallels clash like a couple of Loadstones presented by their opposite Poles. This is a mighty Oversight, especially where the Point to be defended is destitute of all direct Proof, for otherwise the use of Comparisons is not blameworthy. Possibly I may often make use of 'em: but beside that they shall be always just, I'l take care not to bring 'em in, <539> till after I have fairly prov'd my Thesis from evident Principles. The Reader may see how they lie in my *Commentary.*

I have all along endeavor'd to keep close to St. *Austin*, I have follow'd him step by step, and verily think I have not left a place about him, that does not want a Plaister, which 'twill be a hard matter to find: But tho I had offer'd nothing more in answer, than that all his Reasons may equally be employ'd by Heretical Sects, who in the parts where they are uppermost shou'd persecute the Catholicks; this alone were enough to expose the Vanity of his Pretensions. For what more is requisite to convince any reasonable Person of the Vanity of 'em, than shewing that by only changing the Climate or Parallel, one may find twenty times, in the space of a year or two, the same Arguments true and false; true in the Countrys where the Orthodox persecute, and false in those where they are persecuted. Ask a Jesuit of *England,* whether supposing the Episcopal Party in that Kingdom have the right of their side, as they pretend, they do well to deny the Nonconformists[198] Liberty of Conscience; and whether they might not very well defend themselves by alledging St. *Austin*'s Reasons? He'l answer you, No: That Conscience shou'd never be forc'd; that we ought only to inform it, and in all cases leave it under the Dominion of God. Cross the Seas, and come over into *France,* the Jesuits there will tell you quite the contrary: and if you alledg the fine Maxims which their Brethren o' this side the Water

198. Including Roman Catholics.

alledg for the Immunitys of Conscience, they'l laugh at you. What will any unprejudic'd Person say to this? With-<540>out doubt he'l say, he never knew a People so void of common Sense as the Christians; because even in matters of Morality, in which they boast of vast Improvements beyond the rest of the World, they have not any one fix'd Rule or Principle, but explode in one place what they maintain in another. Once more, to use the Bishop of *Meaux*'s Words, let's say, That if the forcing Conscience be a Good-work on the part of the Orthodox, *the Christian Church is of all Societys on earth undoubtedly the most helpless, the most expos'd to incurable Divisions, the most abandon'd to the Caprice and Cruelty of indiscreet Zealots, and violent ambitious Spirits.*[199] It's plain then, that since St. *Austin* cou'd not offer an Apology for Persecution without building on Principles authorizing all Heretick Persecutors as well as himself, without a possibility of destroying their Claim, but by appealing for a fair Discussion of the main Ground of the Differences (a Work of much time, and too too slow a Remedy for so imminent and so real an Evil as the Mischiefs of Persecution) or else to the Valley of *Jehosaphat,* when God at the last day shall declare which side is right and which wrong, in the Interpretation of his Oracles: It's plain, I say, that St. *Austin*'s Apology being subject to all these terrible Inconveniences, drops o' course. For to say, that Hereticks in this case wou'd misapply the Principles which were rightfully employ'd of his side, is telling, for example, a Troop of Dragoons ready to ravage a Protestant Town, to force all the People to Mass; *Oh! Gentlemen, you little consider that the Violence exercis'd on your part, is as abominable in you who believe a false Religion, as it wou'd be good and* <541> *holy in us who believe the Truth. Forbear vexing us, at least till your Missionarys in Conference with our Ministers have explain'd to you these three or four huge Volumes of your own* Bellarmin, *and the* Panstratie *of our* Chamier;[200] *and afterwards plague*

---

199. See above, p. 334, note 129.

200. Robert Bellarmine, Jesuit, *De Controversiis christianae fidei adversus huius temporis haereticos* (Concerning the controversies of Christian faith, against the heretics of the present time), 1586–89; Daniel Chamier, Calvinist minister, *Panstratiae catholicae sive controversiarum de religione adversus pontificios corpus* (Panstratiae catholicae or body of controversies concerning religion against the papists), 1626–30. See DHC, art. "Chamier, Daniel."

and persecute us as much as you please, if you don't find that we have reason of our side. Every one sees that such a Discourse, whether address'd to the Executive Power, or to the Ordainers of Persecution, must needs appear ridiculous, at least very useless; because these might reply upon 'em after this manner: *Good People, since you are agreed that the Orthodox may justly employ the sharpest methods, you shou'd not think it strange that we, who are undoubtedly the Orthodox, persecute you who are wretched Hereticks. As to* Bellarmin *and* Chamier, *we are not now at leisure to hear 'em explain'd; this were drinking up the Ocean: You might die and perish in your Unbelief, before the Missionarys and Ministers cou'd dispatch a quarter part of the first Volume. You must therefore take your Resolution forthwith, with free leave however to complain that we treat you unjustly, if your Ministers hereafter happen to convince us they have the Truth of their side. The Justice of your Complaints depends wholly on the demonstrating this Point; so that while it's actually in dispute, you only suppose the thing in question, when you complain you are unjustly treated.* Is it possible St. *Austin,* with all the Fruitfulness of his Imagination, shou'd not have seen how extremely improbable it is, that God shou'd have left his Church destitute of any other Remonstrance, than that of praying their Persecutors to examine into a boundless Ocean of Controversys, so entangled with Cavil and Illusion, thro the Knavery and <542> false Zeal of Controvertists, that there's no Patience but must be quite tir'd out with hearing and weighing the Answers, Replys, and Rejoinders of both Partys upon the minutest Point in contest? Is it, I say, to be conceiv'd that St. *Austin* shou'd think all those fine Maxims of Morality, Principles of Equity and upright Dealing, precious Relicks and inestimable Ruins of the Innocence of the first Man, render'd unserviceable to the Cause of true Religion; and that besides the Patience of its Martys, it ought not to claim any benefit (the better to convince the World of the injury done it) from those Rules of Justice and Humanity, which all Nations of the Earth, tho ever so little civiliz'd, have always respected? Now it is evident, the Church cou'd claim no benefit by 'em from the time she thought herself oblig'd to persecute the Heterodox, by virtue of the Precept, *Compel 'em to come in;* because beside that* she herself wou'd be oblig'd to dispense with these

---

* *We have prov'd in the fourth Chapter of the first Part of the* Philosophical Commen-

Maxims whene'er she persecuted, and to despise 'em when alledg'd by the Persecuted to move her Compassion, and therefore wou'd deserve to be hiss'd in her turn, if when the day of her own Persecution came she shou'd wish to use 'em: beside this, I say, is it not plain, that all Christian Sects wou'd believe they offended God, if in prejudice to JESUS CHRIST's Command of compelling, they shou'd shew any regard for those Principles of Righteousness and <543> Humanity which right Reason inspires. Thus you see the Orthodox fairly and deservedly stript of the Protection of these Principles; and accordingly instead of saying, as JESUS CHRIST himself did, *That he was not come to destroy the Law and the Prophets, but to fulfil 'em;* we must affirm, if St. *Austin* be right, That JESUS CHRIST is come not only to destroy the Law and the Prophets, all the Precepts of the Decalogue, and the holiest Maxims scatter'd in the Psalms, in the Books of *Solomon,* &c. but likewise that natural Religion, those Irradiations of the Law eternal, those Illapses of unalterable Order, which have shone forth among all Nations, tho ever so little civiliz'd.

There's no need of any thing further to destroy this wretched Apology of St. *Austin,* or that of any other Patron or Abettor of Persecution.

ɷ CHAPTER II ɷ

A Confirmation of the foregoing Chapter, chiefly by a new Confutation of the Answer alledg'd at every turn against my Reasonings; to wit, That the true Church alone has a Right to dispense with the natural Rule of Equity, in her Proceedings against Hereticks.

Possibly some may tell me, That God might have wise Reasons for depriving his Church, even of the Benefit of the most humble Remonstrances to her cruel Persecutors, founded on the <544> general Laws of Equity; because, say they, this is a means of letting us see, that his Church is preserv'd purely by the invisible and extraordinary methods of his Providence, when

---

tary, *and shall prove farther hereafter, that the Command of compelling wou'd overthrow all Morality.* [See above, p. 86.]

wholly, as 'twere, abandon'd, or left intirely to the passive Constancy of its Children in the midst of Persecution. But to reason at this rate, People must give very little heed to two things, which yet are very certain:

1. That the holiest Men, and the most zealous Defenders of the Cause of the Son of God, have never omitted all lawful and modest ways of making their Persecutors understand, that they trod under foot the most sacred and inviolable Maxims of Equity. Thus St. *Peter* remonstrates, on that great and universal Maxim, *That it is better to obey God than Men:* and in general, we find by all the Apologys which the Christians of the first Ages presented to the Emperors, that they insisted principally on the Innocence of their Morality, and the Injustice of not letting 'em enjoy that Security which the Laws of the State, and those of Nature and Nations, provided in common for all the Subjects of the Empire. Is not this manifestly appealing to the common Right, and claiming the benefit of all the natural and positive Laws observ'd in the State? It's false then, that God intended the Orthodox shou'd encounter their Persecutors only by one or other of these two ways, either a dumb Patience, or a bare Declaration at most, that they had the Truth o' their side. We find 'em often reasoning on Principles common to them and the Gentiles: my meaning is, that they urge the Gentiles to think of those universal Dutys, <545> which bring Men under a mutual Obligation to each other, and which were not observ'd towards the Christians. This was the speediest way of moving 'em: for while they reason'd only on Maxims deny'd by their Pagan Adversarys, such for example, as telling 'em they paid a false Worship to the Divinity; they cou'd gain very little against an Edict for Persecution, at least unless they prov'd their Assertion by some sensible Argument, founded on Principles evident and allow'd by Pagans as well as Christians. *Tertullian* is admirable this way. Who knows not that bright Passage of his, in the second Chapter of his *Apologetick?*[201] "You overturn (says he to the Persecutors) all Methods of Justice with regard to us. You torture other Criminals to make them confess what they deny, and you torture Christians to make them deny what they confess. If the being a Christian were really a fault, we shou'd deny it, and you wou'd force us by Torments to confess it. In the mean time, you can't abide a Christian

201. Tertullian, *Apologeticum,* II.10; T.R. Glover, Loeb Classical Library, 1977, p. 13.

shou'd tell you what he really is, and you wou'd have him tell you what he is not. You, who are specially appointed for extorting the Truth from the mouths of other Criminals, leave no means unessay'd to draw a Lye from the mouths of Christians; and whereas you won't easily give credit to what others say, when they deny what you ask 'em, you'l take us at half a word, if it happen that any of us are wretched enough to deny what we are. Let this so uneven, so preposterous a Conduct, become suspect to your selves, and possess you with a Dread of some hidden Malignity at <546> bottom, which tempts you thus to violate all the Rules of Justice in your dealings with us."

This was giving the thing a right turn, and was an Argument *ad hominem,*[202] or Representation importing that they did not act consistently with their own Principles: in which, by the way, the Authors of the *French* Dragoonerys may see some of their own Lineaments.

The second very certain thing which the Authors of the Answer in question don't give heed to, is their manifestly contradicting themselves. For if JESUS CHRIST has enjoin'd Constraint, and the extorting the signing a Formulary; if he authorizes all the ways of Violence, employ'd from the days of *Constantine* down to our own, for enlarging the Borders of the Church: it is not true, that God had a purpose of preserving this Church by the invisible and miraculous Assistance of his Holy Spirit, without the intervention of human means.

I come now to another Engine, which we may properly call the Perpetual Motion, because no sooner is it dash'd on the ground, but it presently rises again with a jerk, and plays with as much activity as ever. God, say they, never meant to deprive the Truth of a right of urging, when persecuted, all the Principles of natural Religion in its own defence, and compassing it self about with 'em as with a Wall of Brass; he only intended that Falshood, when persecuted, shou'd not have the same right. I have answer'd this Exception so often, that I am perfectly tir'd of it. However, because they'l still be repeating it, without taking the least notice of my Confutations, I shall offer 'em a new Answer, which <547> lies more on a level with mean Understandings.

202. See Appendixes, "Bayle's Use of Logic," p. 580, note 3.

I say then in the first place, That it is equally depriving a Man of the benefit of his Arms, whether they be taken clearly away from him, or whether they be left in his hands, when his Adversary is fitted with a Buckler that's perfect Proof against 'em, and which comes out of the same Forge with the Arms themselves. Now this is precisely the Case. Prove stoutly that JESUS CHRIST has enjoin'd constraining Conscience, and put this Command in execution on all occasions, you shall infallibly produce these two dismal effects: First, Infidels will look on you as the Pest of human Society, and the infamous Violators of those Laws which are most essentially necessary to the Welfare and Preservation of Human Kind; and consequently will think themselves oblig'd to treat you like so many wild Beasts, when or wherever they are uppermost. Secondly, Christian Schismaticks and Hereticks, thinking themselves no less oblig'd than you to execute the Orders of JESUS CHRIST, will give you no Quarter, in hopes hereby of forcing you to come over to that Communion which they believe the true: thus each will become inexorable and impenetrable to all your Remonstrances and Apologys; and the beseeching your Persecutors to observe the universal Dutys of Equity and Humanity towards you, will serve only to make you ridiculous as well as miserable.

What kind of Right then, is this you pretend God has especially left you, of urging the common Ideas of Equity in the presence of Tyrants and Persecutors? A Right indeed of no man-<548>ner of use or advantage, a pure Chimera!

What wou'd any Man of good Sense say of *Virgil,* if having fetch'd his Hero from the *Taurick Chersonesus,* where 'twas the custom to cut the throats of all Strangers at the foot of *Diana's* Altar, he shou'd have put that moving Complaint in his Companions mouths, which we find 'em make, when just sav'd from a Shipwreck on the Coast of *Africk,* the Natives immediately assaulted 'em:* *Good God,* say they, *what a barbarous inhospitable Nation is this, that won't allow us the privilege of the Sands on the Seashore!*

As proper and reasonable as this Complaint is in the mouths of Men

---

* Quod Genus hoc hominum, quaeve hunc tam barbara morem Permittit Patria? Hospitio prohibemur Arenae; Bella cient primaque vetant consistere Terra. [Virgil, Aeneid I.539.]

who had themselves observ'd the Rules of Humanity, just so ridiculous wou'd it be in the mouths of Persons belonging to the *Taurick Chersonesus.* So true is it, that the Violators of Faith and Humanity have no reason to take it ill, if they are paid in their own coin.

What will you get then, my Gentlemen Orthodox Persecutors, by saying that God has restrain'd the Right of compelling to the side of Truth alone? Will the ill effects of this pretended Right be hereby render'd less fatal and destructive? As to the bloody Consequences of your Persecutions, from all the Laws of Retaliation and Reprisal, they'l be much the same, whether you say that Falshood has not in reality the same Right in this respect as the Truth, or whether you maintain the contrary. Whence it ma-<549> nifestly follows, that had God commanded the Orthodox to force the Heterodox, he had done the most unjust thing in the world on one hand; and the most likely, on the other, to expose the true Church to incurable and insupportable Evils, perpetrated at least with such a plausible appearance of Right, that she cou'd not find a disinterested Judg upon Earth, who wou'd not affirm this Right against her.

But the Church will at least have the Consolation, at the Day of Judgment, of hearing her Persecutors condemn'd. Here again we justle with the Engine of perpetual Motion, the last Resource of our Adversarys, their Sheet-Anchor. What answer can be made? We shall see.

◊ CHAPTER III ◊

The new Confutation of the fore-mention'd Answer continu'd, and supported by two considerable Examples.

I say in the second place, That it is a matter much to be doubted, on a supposition that JESUS CHRIST had given orders to constrain, whether Hereticks of sincere Principle wou'd be condemn'd by God, at the last Day, for having put 'em in execution. There are a good many Arguments on this head in the second Part of my *Commentary;*[203] but I shall add one more, which possibly may make a greater impression on most part of my Readers.

203. See above, Part II, Chapters 8–11, p. 219 ff.

I say then, and maintain, That a Man who is in an Error, but who, when <550> that's done, does religiously observe all the Laws of God, shall be punish'd at most on the score of his Error only. This appears from these two Examples.

A Conqueror who possesses himself of a great Kingdom by the expulsion of the lawful Prince, and who after this governs according to the Laws which God has given to Kings, promotes Righteousness and Religion, dispenses exact and speedy Justice, punishes the Wicked, and protects the Innocent, the Fatherless, and the Widow, &c. shall he be condemn'd at the Tribunal of God, not only for his having usurp'd a great Kingdom, but also on account of his religiously observing the Laws of God in the governing the conquer'd Country? It's plain, he shall not; and that his Obedience to God in this particular shall rather efface the Crime of his Usurpation, than become an aggravation of his Sin. If so, I desire to know, why a Man who banishes the Truth from his Mind, and puts an Error in possession; and who, after this, exactly observes all that God has commanded in his Word, and that Precept among the rest, which they pretend is given by JESUS CHRIST, of exterminating Sects: shou'd be guilty before God of any more than the first false step, to wit, his forsaking the Truth which appear'd to him an Error, and adopting that which appear'd to him the Truth? If JESUS CHRIST has enjoin'd the forcing Conscience, as he has Almsgiving, Prayer, &c. has not this Man done very well, if he has had the knowledg of all these Laws, to fulfil 'em all alike to the best of his power? <551>

Another Example. If *Solomon* had not bethought him of that Stratagem, which so happily discover'd the false Mother, and had she had more Eloquence and a happier Behavior than the true, so as to carry the point, and get the Child adjudg'd to her; we may make the supposition, that about fifteen or twenty years after, a new Contest arose between 'em. The true Mother happening to find out some further means for justifying her Claim, cites the pretended Mother before *Solomon*, and accuses her of a long Catalogue of Crimes; as, 1. That she had laid claim to a Child that was not her own. 2. That she had nurs'd him with the best Milk. 3. That she had educated him with great care; chiding and caressing him on the proper occasions; in a word, doing every thing for his good, that Nature and Religion teaches a Mother to do for her own Child. Cou'd *Solomon* in equity or reason pass Sentence in favor of the true Mother, on all these Accusations; and must not he, on the contrary, have pronounc'd the Accus'd quit of every other Offence, but that of setting up a false Title, and rather to be commended in all other respects; since among all the methods of fulfilling the Dutys of a true Mother, she had manifestly chosen the best, by taking the Law of God in this point for her Rule and Model?

To acquit this Woman intirely, we need only suppose a very possible Case, to wit, that she had bin sincerely persuaded at the time of the Contest, and even after, that the Child in reality belong'd to her. *Solomon*, wise and judicious as he was, had undoubtedly declar'd, knowing the Sincerity of this pretended Mother, that she was <552> clear before God and Man; and had condemn'd her no farther, than by adjudging the Child to her, who shou'd prove herself the rightful Mother.

From hence it appears, that they who err in any particular point, are not therefore absolv'd from their Obedience to the Laws of God; but on the contrary, that they do well to observe 'em faithfully, and that they may hereby in a great measure redeem or expiate the Evil, which may possibly be inseparable from their Error. Why then shou'd we damn Hereticks of sincere Intentions for executing the Order of compelling in, together with those of being charitable, chast, sober, and all the rest of the Commandments of God.

✄ CHAPTER IV ✄

Another way of considering this second Example.

One may come at the knowledg of the Truth by Cases suppos'd at pleasure, as well as by the most real Facts: For which reason, I desire my Reader to consider this false Mother pleading before *Solomon;* in whose Case I demand the changing of two Circumstances: one, that she in good earnest believe the Child her own; the other, that after the Child was formally adjudg'd to her, she had nothing more at heart than the bringing him up according to the Commandments of God. This gives us a true and very just Image of a sincere Heretick, who does his best endeavors to practise the Gospel-Morality. Education, Prejudices, if you will, a physical Defect or Want of Address in the Understanding, <553> adjudg him a false Religion instead of the true. He looks upon this Religion as a Jewel, which he ought to have as tender a regard for, as a Mother has for her Child; that he ought to love and cherish it, settle it in the World, and not thinking it possible to make choice of fitter means for discharging all his Dutys towards it, than those which God himself has prescrib'd, he consults the Scripture, and presently finds (if our Persecutors are in the right) that JESUS CHRIST has enjoin'd converting Men by Violence, going out into the Highways and publick Places, to compel all those he shall meet with to come into the Church. This Command he obeys; and if he has the Sovereign Power in his hands, he sends forth his Soldiers to force in all who he thinks are not of the true Religion. What has any one to say against all this? Does not he fulfil the Will of JESUS CHRIST, as much as when he bestows an Alms on a Cheat, who begs it in CHRIST's Name, and whom he believes to be truly poor: and at worst, does not his whole Offence lie in taking that for the Child of his Bosom, whom he's bound in Duty to rear and promote, which really is not; as the false Mother's only Sin wou'd be, her not knowing that the Child she nurtur'd belong'd to another Woman?

The Comparison wou'd still be juster, if we consider'd the Heretick under the Emblem of a natural Son, and his Religion under that of a Mother; but the Author of the *Critique Generale* having made the most of these Examples, and it being an easy matter for my Reader to metamorphose the Mother into a Son, I shall let it stand as 'tis. Let's now only try whether the Cases hold. <554>

❧ CHAPTER V ❧

An Answer to the first Disparity which may be alledg'd against my Examples; to wit, That Hereticks, in giving an Alms, do well, because they give it to those to whom God intended it shou'd be given; but do ill, in compelling to come in, because this Command relates only to those who are in Error. *I here shew, by just Examples, that Heretick Judges wou'd obey God in punishing the Orthodox, if the Principle of Persecutors hold good.*

I Fancy my Reader will be pleas'd at seeing this Objection, since he might very well expect, that in Imitation of my Brethren, the Gentlemen Authors, I wou'd content my self with proposing two plausible Examples, without ever taking notice of the strongest Exceptions, which might be offer'd against 'em. But he shall quickly see, that I don't conceal the best sides of the Cause of my Adversarys. They may tell me very plausibly, that since the Persons, to whom Hereticks give an Alms, are in that rank of Men to which God in his Word has destin'd it; they obey the Law of God: but that as the Persons compel'd to come in, are not in the Circumstances of those whom God design'd shou'd be compel'd; we ought to conclude, that they don't obey the Will of God in compelling them. This at first sight appears <555> somewhat perplexing: let's see tho, whether it be really as knotty as it appears.

No one can reasonably contest this Maxim, that when God commands us to do such or such an Action to such or such of our Neighbors, he leaves us the liberty of examining, whether they are under the requisite Circumstances: For example, he commands us to relieve the Needy, to visit the Sick, to assist the Orphan; yet it is our part to examine, whether they, who say they are Needy, Sick, Orphans, are really such: and if, upon a diligent Enquiry, but at the same time subject to Error, we believe we have discover'd an Imposture in their Case; it's certain, our Obligation of assisting 'em as such ceases. There are even Cases, in which our refusing to assist wou'd be no Sin, altho we shou'd be deceiv'd as to the matter of Fact. For shou'd the Confessor of a great Prince represent to him, that a Storm of Hail having laid fourty or fifty Parishes in his Country wast, 'twou'd be an Act of Charity to send some Relief to the ruin'd Peasants: we may suppose, that this Prince wou'd appoint Commissioners to inquire upon the spot into the Damage sustain'd; who betraying the Trust repos'd in 'em, shou'd, from a malicious Partiality, and respect of Persons, make their Report, that such or such a Parish had no need of Relief, having suffer'd little, and having good Stocks before-hand. The Fact may be false; yet it being impossible for the Prince to see every thing with his own Eyes, he may very innocently rely, as to the Distribution of his Charity, on another's Preference and Choice of the Persons: Whence it will follow, that they, who are really needy, shall go unre-<556>liev'd; and they, who had sufficient before, run away with that which belong'd only to the Poor. Yet will any one pretend, that the Prince has herein disobey'd the Precept of relieving the Poor and Needy?

The Case is the same, as to a Widow with a great Charge of Children, who shou'd bring 'em day after day into Court, to move the Compassion of her Judges. It's very lawful for Men in their Post to examine, whether this ben't an Artifice or Cheat; and it might possibly happen, that the Plaintiffs in a Law-Suit with this Woman may have Credit enough to possess the Mind of the Judges against her, tho otherwise well-intention'd, but subject to surprize from an inseparable Infirmity of human Nature; to possess 'em, I say, with a thousand false Storys, as if this Widow liv'd at a topping rate in her own Country, was very rich, and had but few Children, insomuch that they may afterwards have no Consideration for her Circumstances or Charge of Children, nor consequently be as favorable to her as the Law of God requires. Wou'd they in this Case be answerable for any thing more, than their not having penetrated thro all the Clouds and Darkness industriously spread around 'em? On the whole, it's a mistake to think, that in order to fulfil the Precept of Charity, those who are the Objects of it must of necessity be Needy or Orphans; it's enough, if we believe 'em such: and shou'd they happen to be errand Cheats, yet JESUS CHRIST will accept of the Charity bestow'd on 'em for his sake, upon a Persuasion of their being really what they pretend, that is, Fatherless and Indigent. <557>

What now follows, will satisfy my Reader still more; I'm sensible he is not thorowly satisfy'd with what has bin yet offer'd. One of the most essential Obligations that Magistrates and Sovereigns lie under, is that of punishing the Guilty, and delivering the Innocent; *He who justifys the Wicked, and he who condemneth the Righteous, are an Abomination to the Lord,* saith the Scripture.[204] Yet is it not for all this incontestable, that the Laws of God, about punishing the Guilty, and acquitting Persons falsly accus'd, oblige not to punish precisely the Guilty, and acquit the Innocent; but only to punish those who shall appear to us Guilty, and absolve those who shall appear Innocent? All that the Judg is oblig'd to in this Case, is carefully to examine the Facts, and to endeavor, that they, who are in reality guilty or innocent, may appear so to him; but if after all his Endeavors, the Guilty cannot be convicted, nor the Innocence of the Accus'd made appear, I say, and say it over again, that he is not oblig'd to punish the Guilty, nor to discharge the Innocent from Prosecution.

It undoubtedly happens much oftner than it shou'd, that a Person, guilty of several heinous Crimes, Murder, Poisoning, Plundering, *&c.* being brought before his Judges, nothing can be alledg'd against him but Appearances or violent Presumptions, either that there are just Exceptions in Law to the Evidence against him, or because they are bought off by the Friends of the Accus'd, and prevail'd with to unsay or contradict themselves upon Re-examination. If the Accus'd has the Question[205] given him, he has sometimes the strength to outbrave it, and not confess a tittle. <558> What must be done in this case? Must he be condemn'd? No, the Judg cannot exceed his Commission; he can't condemn a Man to the Gallows upon any Presumptions, how violent soever: the Party must either confess his Crime, or be fairly convicted by Witnesses, of good Reputation, persisting and agreeing in their Evidence against him. Where these Circumstances are wanting, the greatest Malefactor upon Earth must be acquitted, and the Judg not wanting in the least to his Duty: consequently the Command of God, for punishing Malefactors, amounts to this; *You shall punish those, who are convicted of the Crimes they stand charg'd with.*

Let's now consider the other Branch of the Judg's Function, to wit, the acquitting the Innocent. Does this import, that a Person perfectly innocent

204. Proverbs 17:15.
205. The rack.

of a Murder charg'd on him, but accus'd by several Witnesses, who play their Game admirably to the last, without contradicting one another in their Evidence, or faltering in the least, ought to be discharg'd? By no means; provided the Judg has had a sincere Will to discover the Truth of the Fact, and to the best of his Skill has endeavor'd to invalidate the Evidence, and set the Proofs of the Innocence of the Accus'd in the best light: he may sentence him to death without the fear of offending God; and if he did not, wou'd discharge his Duty very ill, since he is to judg *secundum allegata & probata*.[206] The Supposition may be made, that the Presumption is against the Innocent accus'd, that the Judg gives him the Question, and that he is so sensible of Pain, that to get off at any rate he confesses the Fact. One might add, that <559> having produc'd Witnesses to prove his *Alibi,* the false Witnesses have more Firmness than they, and fairly outface 'em, or that secret Enemys engage 'em to declare, they were suborn'd to swear for the Accus'd (our Country affords but too many Examples of this kind). In all these Cases, it's evident, an innocent Person may be sentenc'd to death without the least blame on the Judg's part: consequently I have ground to conclude, that the Command of acquitting the Innocent is restrain'd to this Proposition; *You shall acquit those, whose Innocence is clearly prov'd to you.*

It's plain then, that a Judg, who studys nothing more than the fulfilling the Law of God, may, without the least Violation of it, acquit the Guilty, and condemn the Innocent, provided always, that he acquit only such Malefactors as appear not guilty to him, and condemn only such innocent Persons as appear not innocent to him.

It is no less certain, that the Obligation of obeying God, as well with regard to this Law as to that of Almsgiving, of defending the Cause of the Fatherless and Widow, rises and falls, or stands still and remains suspended, according to the degrees of our Knowledg, concerning the Subjects upon which these Laws are to be exercis'd; I mean, even a mistaken Knowledg, but attended with Sincerity.

For the Magistrates or Governors, who shou'd turn out of their Hospitals, or even out of their Towns, in order to make 'em work, a certain

206. "In accordance with the testimony and proofs."

number of Poor, whose Recovery and Fitness for Labor were certify'd by the Physician; wou'd not transgress the Precept of Almsgiving, <560> altho it shou'd happen, that the Physician were mistaken in some Cases, judging on such and such equivocal signs of Health, that such and such Beggars were thorowly recover'd. Much less wou'd they transgress, tho they maintain'd the merest Vagrants, while persuaded they were not able to earn their Living.

The Judg who, deceiv'd by fair Appearances, and by false Certificates, but carrying an Air of Probability, shou'd not shew a Widow with a great Charge of Children all the Favor she deserv'd, and which he certainly wou'd do, were he not prepossess'd against her, that she is a sly Hypocrite, who sues her Adversary at Law, only to run headlong to a second Marriage, with greater Advantages of Fortune: The Judg, I say, plac'd in such Circumstances, might in a great measure suspend the natural Obligation he is under, of being more indulgent to the Fatherless and Widow, than to any others. And on the contrary, this Obligation wou'd subsist in its full Force, if a Widow, who really liv'd in Splendor, shou'd find a way of persuading her Judg, by Certificates, and other Credentials, in appearance authentick, that her Innocence was oppress'd; insomuch as any Judg, who, under this Persuasion, shou'd shew favor to a Widow, in reality unworthy of it, wou'd nevertheless fulfil the Law: Whereas in the first case he might dispense with this Favor, without derogating from the Law, unless People will have him answerable for his not being infallible; which is a Pretension so ridiculous, that even those of the Church of *Rome,* who believe an Oecumenical Council, wherein the Bishop of *Rome* presides, either in Person, or by his Legats, in-<561>fallible in its Decisions of Faith, dare not, notwithstanding, attribute to it a Prerogative of never being surpriz'd, or impos'd on by false Informations; which is never constru'd a Disobedience in the Church, or a Deviation from the Law of God.

Now if the Obligation of giving an Alms, of protecting the Fatherless and Widow, supposes, as a necessary and fundamental Condition, a sincere Persuasion of the Partys being in reality Poor, Fatherless, and Widows; that of punishing the Guilty, and acquitting the Innocent, supposes this Knowledg much more: because, as I have already prov'd, where a Malefactor happens not to be legally convicted of his Crime, the Judg is *ipso facto* oblig'd to treat him as Innocent; as, on the contrary, he's oblig'd to treat an innocent Person as a Malefactor, if he happen to be legally convicted of the Crimes he stands accus'd of.

I was willing to set this Matter in the clearest light, at the hazard of being thought verbose and given to Repetition, needless indeed for those who have a ready Apprehension; because here I find the true Decision of the Cause before us, and because 'twas necessary to make it obvious to those who are somewhat slower of Understanding. We shall now see the Application of my Examples. <562>

✿ CHAPTER VI ✿

A Parallel between a Judg who shou'd punish the Innocent, and acquit the Guilty, from an Error in point of Fact, and a Heretick Judg who shou'd condemn the Orthodox.

I Desire my Reader to weigh well this Enthymeme.[207] The Precept of Alms-giving, of defending the Fatherless and Widow, of punishing the Guilty, and delivering the Innocent, leaves us such a Latitude of examining, whether the Party be Poor, Widow, Fatherless, Guilty, Innocent; that when our Lights and Means of Information, sincerely and diligently apply'd, lead us into Judgments and Practices, which sute not the real Condition of the Subjects with whom we are concern'd, but only with that Condition which we believe 'em in, we by no means transgress the Law of God.

If therefore it were true, as St. *Austin* pretends, that God has given the Sword to Princes, in order to compel Hereticks into the Church by dint of Punishment; they might fulfil the Command, altho the compel'd Partys were Hereticks, not really, but in the Opinion of their Judges only.

Let's remember, that St. *Austin* has* prov'd the Right of persecuting from that Passage of <563> St. *Paul,* which imports, that the Powers which are, are ordain'd by God for the Punishment of Evil-doers: in consequence

---

* Comment. Part 3. p. 365.
207. See Appendixes, "Bayle's Use of Logic," p. 580 ("enthymeme").

whereof Mons. *de Meaux* challenges[208] the Protestants arrogantly enough, to shew him a Text of Scripture, in which Hereticks are excepted out of the number of those Evil-doers, against whom God has arm'd the Powers ordain'd. Let's grant 'em their Demand for a while, we shall see they'l be no great Gainers by it.

Because, as a Prince is oblig'd to no more, with regard to the Administration of Justice, than the appointing throut his Dominions, Judges of Integrity and Understanding ('twere ridiculous to pretend, he's oblig'd to judg all Causes himself in Person, this were absolutely impossible) and hearing the fair Appeals, if such shou'd be, of his Subjects from the ordinary Courts of Judicature; it's plain, he discharges his Duty in this respect towards God, if he enjoin his Judges to dispense exact Justice to all his Subjects, and to punish Offenders, that is, according to St. *Austin,* Murderers, Robbers, Sodomites, Sorcerers, Hereticks, *&c.* insomuch as a Prince, who gives such Injunctions, has done his part. Consequently, as it is not the Prince's Fault, if his Judges, Men of Integrity and Capacity, happen to condemn a Man as a Murderer, who, tho at bottom innocent of the Fact, is yet legally convicted of it; or acquit a Murderer, where the Crime cannot be fairly prov'd upon him; so, neither will it be his Fault, if the same Judges punish a Man as a Heretick, who, tho not really such in the Judgment of God, is yet fairly convicted of Heresy, according to the Principles and Religion of the <564> Judges. Here then we find a Heretick Prince free from all blame, tho the Orthodox throut his Dominions be punish'd as Evil-doers.

But what will become of the Judges? I'm of Opinion, they may be justify'd upon these two Accounts: 1. Because they do not ordinarily judg upon the Fact; they refer that Judgment to the Ecclesiasticks, who, after the necessary Examination and Interrogations, pronounce the Party a Heretick, and deliver him over to the Secular Arm; that is, to the Magistrates, who hereupon condemn him to such Punishment as they see proper. 2. That if they do judg upon the Fact, and declare the Party a Heretick, they proceed upon Depositions of credible Witnesses, or upon his own Confession (for tho he won't own himself a Heretick, yet he'l confess that he holds such

208. See above, p. 334, note 129.

and such Opinions, which his Accusers damn as Heresy) and by the Principles and Laws of their Religion and Country. So that the same Sincerity of Mind, which makes 'em assert the Truth of their own Religion, obliges 'em to declare and brand as Hereticks, all those who impugn it.

Upon the first of these two Accounts, the Judges are perfectly blameless, and have no more to answer for, in condemning a Heretick (St. *Austin's* Notion once presuppos'd) than the Judges of this Kingdom wou'd have, for condemning a Criminal, upon the Verdict of a Jury legally chosen and impannel'd: The Judges in this Case, being only the Mouth of the Law, to declare what Punishment is due to the Crime, and to order the inflicting of it. It matters not whether the Party be innocent; let the Jury < 565 > look to that if they have brought in their Verdict without sufficient Proof. But the Judges have nothing to answer for; it being most certain, that whoever is under the Circumstances, in which they are oblig'd to suppose the accus'd, deserves the Punishment to which they sentence him.

The Case is exactly the same, when a Man being accus'd of Heresy, the Magistrates refer the Inquest upon the* Fact, to those who have properly the Cognizance of matters of this Nature, to the Doctors in Divinity, to the Universitys, the Synods, the Chapters, the General Assemblys, the Councils, to the Tribunals of the Inquisition, the natural Judges of what is Orthodox and what not. If these, who are the proper and competent Judges, declare the Heresy; the Secular Arm can do no less than sentence the Evil-doer to the Punishment which the Law of God ordains; nor shall it be answerable before God, for any Error of Judgment, in those whose Province it is to declare, what is Heresy and what is not.

Let's represent this whole reasoning in a Syllogism:

Hereticks are punishable;

John Huss is a Heretick,

Therefore *John Huss* is punishable. < 566 >

The Major is clearly and expresly contain'd in Scripture, according to St. *Austin,* and all the other Apologists for forcing of Conscience. The Mi-

---

* Take notice, that I here call the inquiring whether an Opinion be heretical or no, a Question of Fact. I'm not ignorant, that in some Cases, this is a Question of Right; but I speak thus, the better to square the Examination of this Question, Is such a one a Heretick? to the Examination of this, What Punishment do Hereticks deserve?

nor is a Fact attested by the natural Judges in this case; the Magistrates therefore must pronounce the Conclusion, and can never go upon two surer grounds than the two Premises of this Syllogism.

They don't condemn upon quite so sure Grounds, when they themselves judg of the Fact; I mean, when they judg that the Opinions of the Party accus'd are heretical: yet even here they are blameable on no other account, than believing themselves in the true Religion. Now this is what all the Men of Worth and Honor in the World are guilty of; since they continue in the Religion they profess, on no other account, than because they believe it the best. So that judging such or such a Man to be a Heretick, can only be Ignorance, or an Error at most: and consequently all the Malignity and Turpitude attending the Persecution of the Orthodox, resides, properly speaking, in the pretended Command of Persecuting. I had reason then to maintain, that the condemning the Orthodox to Death, wou'd become warrantable and lawful, if God had in general commanded the putting Hereticks to Death.

For we can find no Subject to lodg the Crime in: since Sovereigns, who enjoin their Judges to punish Evil-doers (and in this number God reckons Hereticks, according to my Adversarys) are not answerable for the Conduct of their Judges, in extending their Punishments to Persons, who tho not in reality Evil-doers, are convicted <567> however by due Course of Law; and because these Judges either don't take cognizance of the Fact, or try it according to the most authentick Rules and Forms in use: whereupon they have the Scripture for a clear and positive Rule for the punishment of the Offence.

✿ CHAPTER VII ✿

Whether Heretical Ecclesiasticks may be blam'd for having a hand in the Trials and Condemnation of the Orthodox.

We have seen in the foregoing Chapter, that neither the Prince, nor Courts of Justice, are any way to blame on the score of persecuting the Orthodox; On whom then does the Blame fall? Does it fall on the Doctors and other Churchmen, who only pronounce such a Man a Heretick? But so far the

Fault they are guilty of is not what we call Persecution, Murder, Crime; 'tis at most but Ignorance or Error, or the wrong qualifying an Opinion. Every Man who thinks his own Religion true, is oblig'd if requir'd, to declare it such: Now it's the same thing to say, *my Religion is true;* and to say, the Religion which is opposite to mine is false. Therefore when an Assembly of the Romish Clergy, requir'd to declare what they think of the Tenets of Protestants, affirm they are Hereticks; they do no more in the main, than declare that the Church of *Rome,* which these directly oppose, is Orthodox. Now I wou'd fain know, whether <568> Persons, sincerely persuaded of this, can dispense with declaring, when duly cited by the Magistrate, that Protestants are Hereticks. And as they don't precisely, by this Declaration, do any Injustice to Protestants; I mean, don't disturb 'em in their Persons or Estates: we can't reasonably fix the Fault on them. If the Magistrates, pursuant to this Declaration, order Fires to be kindled for burning Protestants, or condemn 'em to any other kind of Punishment; it's only an accidental consequence of what the Doctors were in Conscience oblig'd to declare.

Is it not plain, that a Casuist who's of Opinion, that a Woman's forcing Abortion before her Fruit's quick, is actual Parricide; and who declares this as his Opinion before the criminal Judges; can't justly be charg'd with Cruelty, or reputed the Cause of their hanging a Mother convicted of a Crime of this kind, which they pronounce a Parricide? I maintain, tho he knew the Judges waited only for his Opinion to condemn this Woman, that he is oblig'd in Conscience to declare it Parricide. And for the same reason, tho the Inquisitors know, that the Judges, upon their pronouncing such a Man a Heretick, will certainly put him to Death; yet they ought not to be reputed the Authors of his Punishment; because it's only an accidental Consequence of their Decision: inasmuch as the Law of God ordains, according to the Notions of Persecutors, that Hereticks be punish'd.

But I'l suppose further, that the same Ecclesiastical Judges, who declare such a certain Opinion Heresy, declare also, that they who obstinately maintain it are punishable; still I don't <569> see how they can be branded with Cruelty. For on a supposition, that the Scripture makes Hereticks obnoxious to the Sword of the Magistrate; an Assembly of Ecclesiastical Hereticks errs not in forming this Decision or Canon, *Hereticks are punishable by the Secular Arm,* because the Position is really a reveal'd Truth. This being the Case, the conditional Proposition, *If* John Huss *be a Heretick, he is punishable by the Secular Arm,* is as true, as if it were to be met with in so many Words in Scripture; since it's certain, that where any universal Proposition is express'd in Scripture, all the particular Propositions contain'd under it are Scripture. Implicitly and virtually, say you; however it be, they are Scripture in such a sense, as satisfys us of their Certainty, no less than if we read 'em explicitly in the sacred Text.

But what will follow, when an Assembly of Hereticks pronounces absolutely; John Huss *is a Heretick, therefore he deserves to be deliver'd over to the Secular Arm to be punish'd?* I answer once again, That if the Assembly act from a sincere Principle, 'twill at most be answerable only for its Persuasion of the Truth of a false Religion; and if they can get over this in the Sight of God, they'l hear no more of the matter; they may safely punish *John Huss.*

The reason is, that upon a supposition of St. *Austin's* Doctrine, there's an indissoluble Connexion made by the very Finger of God, between being a Heretick, and being punishable. It's certain too, there's an indissoluble Connexion, and which no way depends on us, between believing a thing to be true, and believing that <570> which contradicts it false. So that when you once suppose a Man persuaded firmly of the Divinity of his Religion, he must of necessity be firmly persuaded, 1. That they who impugn it are Hereticks. 2. That they are punishable. And if you remonstrate, that there's Cruelty in their believing 'em punishable; I answer, That you can't reasonably blame 'em, because they have found the Connexion of these two things, *Heretick* and *Punishable,* ready made to their hand and fated in Scripture; as well as the Connexion of these two, *Homicide* and *Punishable.* As therefore there is no Cruelty in declaring, that such and such deserve Death, after they have bin convicted of Murder by due Course of Law; so there is none in declaring, that they who are convicted of Heresy by the ordinary Forms and Practice of the Country, are likewise punishable.

'Twill now appear, That I have perform'd more than I at first propos'd; for I perceive, that my reasons, if good, will serve to acquit even those, who shou'd take on 'em the whole Process of Persecution, from beginning to end; a King, for example, who shou'd himself interrogate the Party accus'd of Heresy, hear his Defence, weigh and examine it, take the Advice of his Council, and in the Issue pronounce him guilty and convict of the Crime he stood accus'd of, and consequently punishable. St. *Austin* cou'd not reasonably have any thing more to say against a Prince, who dealt thus by the Orthodox, than that he was in an Error; for the Error once suppos'd, it is not the *Arian* Prince punishes the Orthodox, but the Gospel-Law. <571>

Is it not a horrible thing, that so great a Saint shou'd maintain a Doctrine, which discharges the whole Odium of the Persecutions and Sufferings of infinite numbers of the Faithful, immediately on the Divinity? For 'tis plain from this Doctrine, that nothing were blameable in a Heretick Persecutor, but his being born in a false Religion, and having receiv'd from it almost invincible Impressions by Education; things upon which he was not consulted, and for which he cannot be answerable.

ꙮ CHAPTER VIII ꙮ

An Abstract of the Answer to the first Disparity.

But to give an Abstract and Recapitulation of this long Article, I desire my Readers to consider these two short parallel Cases.

1. An honest Citizen, who gives an Alms every Morning to an old Beggar, who plies at a Church-door, and who has laid up a considerable Sum by begging, obeys the Precept of Almsgiving; and shou'd he refuse an Alms to a really poor Man, but who he was assur'd, by sober People and such as he always found sincere, cou'd do without his Charity, and beg'd only out of mere Covetousness and Idleness, he wou'd not disobey this Precept.

Then it is not true, in order to obey this Precept, that they we give our Alms to be necessarily in the Circumstances of those to whom <572> JESUS CHRIST directs 'em; and that they to whom we refuse our Alms be not.

Then it suffices, that we sincerely believe, they are in such Circumstances, or that they are not; and 'twere ridiculous to pretend, that by the Intention of God, the richer Beggars are in these Circumstances preferably to the poorer.

Then the Disparity of my Adversarys is null.

Then one may obey the Precept of compelling, tho those he compels shou'd not be really Hereticks, but such only in the sincere Persuasion of the Compeller.

Shou'd they tell me, that in giving an Alms to a rich Beggar we do him no hurt, but by compelling an Orthodox we do him a prejudice; whereas by compelling a Heretick, we do him a Kindness: they'l run themselves into several new Difficultys. For, beside that this is losing Ground, and quitting the first Disparity to find out a new Retreat; it's certain our bestowing an Alms on a counterfeit Beggar, makes him guilty of a moral Evil: since it's an actual Robbery in him, of the real Poor. And besides, by letting a Heretick live in quiet, we do him a Physical Good; as we do a rich Beggar, by giving him an Alms: but by the very Act of forcing his Conscience, and hereby driving him to Hypocrisy, we do him at the same time a moral Evil.

On the whole, what will they say of the refusing an Alms, to one whom the Party believes to be a mere Mumper and errand Cheat? Won't this be altogether as pardonable, as compelling one whom the Party sincerely believes to be a Heretick? <573>

Now for my other Comparison.

2. A Judg, who to the best of his Skill examines the Case of a Person accus'd of Murder, and who seeing him fairly convicted according to the most exact Forms of Justice, condemns him to Death; obeys the Law of God concerning the punishing of Murder; altho this Person be really innocent, and dies by the wicked Contrivances of his Enemys, who come prepar'd with a well-concerted false Evidence.

A Judg then, who honestly guides himself by the best Lights afforded him, and the best means of Information; and who upon hearing the Defence of a Person accus'd of Heresy, and having taken the best Advice he possibly can, finds him convicted by due Course of Law, and sentences him to Punishment; obeys the alleg'd Law of God, for the punishing of Hereticks, altho it shou'd happen, that the condemn'd Person was really Orthodox at bottom.

ಚಿ CHAPTER IX ಚಿ

That a Judg who condemns an innocent Person, and acquits a Malefactor, sins not, provided he act according to Law.

There wou'd be no need of discussing the Proposition which makes the Title of this Chapter, if Readers were always reasonable. But some there are so very difficult and so prepossess'd, that rather than own, either directly <574> by a sincere Confession, or indirectly and* interpretatively by not being able to answer a syllable, that they are convinc'd of their Error, they'l stand it out against the most evident Truths. It's possible then, there may be those who'l maintain that a Judg in the Case before us sins mortally; and therefore that I prove nothing, in favor of those who shou'd condemn and punish the Orthodox, imagining in the Sincerity of their Souls, tho falsly, that they were Hereticks.

To give any kind of plausible color to this paultry Exception, they must needs suppose, that the Judg has fail'd of discovering the Fact, only because he's under the power of some inordinate Passion, which obscures the Light of his Understanding; or at least is blamable in taking a charge upon him, which he knew, or ought to have known, that he was not thorowly qualify'd for. So that I am now oblig'd to make good these two things: first, that a Judg may very well be deceiv'd, tho free from all those inordinate Passions suppos'd in the Objection; next, that he may have a sufficient Capacity for the discharge of his place, tho he may not always be able to penetrate the Truth of a Fact.

Whether a Judg's not discovering the Truth, be an argument that he is under the power of some wicked Passion?

With regard to this first Point, I wou'd fain know from my Adversarys, whether they believe <575> that all Ignorance and Error is a Consequence

---

* *We must not understand this in the rigor; for I'l allow there are those who don't know how to answer an Objection, and yet are as much persuaded as ever, that they have reason o' their side.*

of Sin. If they answer me, Yes; I shall quickly shew 'em, that they are under the grossest Mistake.

Was not *Adam*, in a state of perfect Innocence, ignorant of infinite things; and did he not pass a false Judgment before ever he had sin'd? It's manifest he had not actually committed Sin, when he first began to sin. Now he began to sin, by judging that what was reveal'd to him by God, was not more certain than what was told him by his Wife, or by affirming some other matter which was false. He therefore pass'd a false Judgment, which was not preceded by any Sin. It's false then, that all Ignorance or Error proceeds from Sin. Why then shou'd we suppose, that all the wrong Sentences and Decrees of Judges proceed from some Sin?

Besides, if JESUS CHRIST, who was perfectly without Sin, was yet capable of seemingly doing what he had no design to do; *Adam* and his Posterity, tho they had preserv'd their Innocence, might undoubtedly have bin capable of sometimes making use of Signs, which had not bin certain Indications of their Thoughts. Now who doubts, but in these cases they might have led their Acquaintance or Friends into Judgments concerning 'em very wide of the Truth; just as JESUS CHRIST led those, who saw that he made as if he wou'd go on farther,[209] into a belief that such was his intention? It's certain then, that Men in a state of Innocence might deceive, and be deceiv'd in one another on several occasions, where no evil Motive might intervene; nor can this be contested, without <576> falling into this absurd Consequence, that nothing but Sin cou'd deprive us of the Gift of searching the Heart and Reins. A manifest Error! Neither Man nor Angel can know the Thoughts of the Heart, otherwise than by Signs of Institution, or some such other occasional Cause; and 'tis very possible for any created Intelligence to deceive another, by falsly employing these Signs. God alone, as he has a direct and intuitive Knowledg of the Modifications of Minds, cannot be deceiv'd by false Appearances.

From hence I conclude, that a Judg, tho ever so free from Passion, may yet fail of discovering a Truth of Fact. For as he is not able to read in the Hearts of the Accus'd and the Witnesses, he must have recourse to those Signs by which Men mutually discover their Thoughts: but all these Signs

209. Luke 24:28.

are equivocal, and Man has a thousand Folds, a thousand dark Corners in his Heart, and knows how to cover these over by a thousand Artifices and a thousand Lyes. They may therefore happen to deceive not only the most righteous Judges, but those also who have the greatest Talent at catching the Witnesses and the Accus'd in their own snare: and so far is an honest Man from being the best qualify'd to see thro all the wily Dissimulation of this sort of Men, that, on the contrary, a Person who from his own Experience were acquainted with all their Cheats, wou'd make much the abler Judg. *Adam,* as he came out of the hands of God, was a great deal easier impos'd on, than one who had liv'd a profess'd Rogue all his life long. < 577 >

I can hardly conceive, how almost all sort of Christians have suffer'd themselves to be drawn into this Notion, That nothing but Sin is the cause of our Ignorance. Because if we ever so little reflect on the manner in which our Soul is united to the Body, we may be convinc'd that there's a downright necessity of its being mightily stinted, and very defective in its Attainments in Knowledg: for beside that this Union makes it depend, for its Thinking, on the Impressions made by outward Objects, and left in the Brain; there's a necessity, on other accounts, of the Soul's having numberless Thoughts which relate to the Preservation of the Body only: and these being only confus'd Sensations, or Passions which bear not a just Idea of any Object, such as it is in it self, here's consequently the greatest part of our time taken up by Modifications which enlighten not, which enlarge not its true Knowledg, and which tempt it to judg of Objects upon false Appearances, without troubling it self to know what they really are in themselves. And on the other hand, its Dependence, as to its acting, on certain Impressions made in the Brain, stinting it still more by reason of that Limitation essential to all occasional Causes; there's a further reason why its Lights shou'd be very narrow and indistinct. And what fills up the measure of its Ignorance, is, that we live to fifteen years of Age, and sometimes more, before we make the least use of our Reason, with regard to any real Improvement of the Understanding. For how is it with us before fifteen? We feel Hunger, Thirst, Heat, and Cold, or some other Inconvenience: We < 578 > have the pleasure of sucking the Breast, of being dandl'd in our Nurse's Arms, of playing at Ball, of eating and drinking, *&c.* Then we learn our Mother Tongue, which gives those who rear us an opportunity of making us believe all the Nonsense they please. We learn to read and to write *Latin* and *Greek,* if you please: but all this does not take off our minds from a thousand little idle Pastimes, nor hinder our swallowing every silly Story that's told us. Reason has not yet Strength enough to stand it out against any thing, or oppose the introducing of Error, unless where it concerns some Interest of the Flesh, or contradicts our own small Experience; as if any one shou'd go about to persuade us, that there's no pleasure in drinking when a body is a-dry. By this we see, that Man before he's aware is under the power of infinite Habits, which shrink his Soul to nothing, how great soever his Desire may afterwards be, of furnishing it with a vast Knowledg.

I am willing to believe, that if *Adam* had preserv'd his Innocence, things wou'd have gone better; but still Man had bin very much stinted in his Knowledg, because of the Union of the Soul with this portable Machine, and of the mean state of Reason for the first years of Life.

Shou'd any one not yield to these Reasons, I desire he wou'd tell me how he knows, that Sin and Ignorance are two things which naturally follow each other. Does he find any thing in the History of the Temptation, that induces him to think this; and wou'd not one much sooner infer from it, that the Fall of *Adam* rather increas'd his Knowledg? Or does he judg so, because he's persuaded that the Devils have lost their Know-<579>ledg with their Holiness? But this is directly against the general Notion. We are told strange things of the Craft and Subtlety of the Devils, of the great Power of the Demons of the Air, in forming Thunder, Tempests, Hail, Pestilence; of their rendring themselves visible under all kind of Forms, and their imprinting several Motions in the Brain for the exciting our Passions. In a word, they who treat of the heavenly Hierarchy make no scruple to affirm, that a good Angel of an inferior Order engag'd with an evil Angel of a superior Order, wou'd be constantly worsted and overcome, if God did not interpose in an extraordinary manner. Which shews that the evil Angels are not by their Fall become inferior to the good, in point of Knowledg or Power, if taken in the same rank of the Hierarchy.

But not to go so high as the Angelick Nature, is it not well known, that *David* and *Solomon* lost not the least degree of Understanding, by falling into the most enormous Sins? Nor is there any better ground for thinking that *Adam,* after his Sin, had forgot a tittle of what he knew before, unless thro Length of Time, or the Infirmitys of old Age. Last of all, have we not daily Examples, that they who have the greatest share of Piety and Vertue, are for the most part incomparably more simple than the wickedest in their Generation? I can't therefore see what ground there is, for this natural Connexion betwixt Sin and Ignorance.

Be that how it will, I don't think any reasonable Man can deny what I am now to offer; to wit, That there are criminal Trials, in which the Charge and the Defence are sometimes <580> supported by such Probabilitys, such Proofs and Counterproofs, that a Judg who, far from inclining to favor the Accus'd, may have a mind to see him convicted, and even a suspicion of his Guilt, can't however find ground enough to condemn him; but is oblig'd, against his Inclination and against his Suspicions, to acquit him, tho the Person is really guilty of the Fact. Now if when even Passion and Suspicion help to discover the Truth of Facts, we can't notwithstanding come at it; how will it be, when we stand perfectly Neuters between the Accuser and the Accus'd? It can't be deny'd, but there are Cases, in which the Judg is perfectly in such an Equilibrium.

And are not Civil Causes sometimes so puzzl'd by the Variety of Pleadings and Laws differently interpreted, that the most learned Judges in the Law, and the freest from all Partiality, can do no more than split the difference, or give it o' that side which their Conscience tells 'em has the Right; tho the Court perhaps is far from being unanimously of their opinion, some thinking the Right in *John o' Nokes,* and others in *John o' Stiles?*

Sure I am, that whoever considers this matter aright will come into my sense of it, and allow, that in many cases where the Judg does not discover the true State of the Case, whether it be concerning Fact or Right, nor hit it to the exactest nicety; this proceeds not from any Obliquity in his Will, but from the Obscurity and Perplexity of the matter it self under examination.

Not that I wou'd hereby pretend, that there are not too many Judges, who not only betray the Lights of their Conscience, but who are also <581> Bubbles to their Passions; I mean, who by mere dint of wishing, from human Considerations, that such and such may or may not have the Right on their side, come at last to persuade themselves that it is really so.

Whether he who perceives not in himself a profound Knowledg, and very clear Understanding, is oblig'd to decline the Office of a Judg?

I now proceed to my second Point. We'l allow, say they, that a Judg who has not known how to convict a Person really guilty, might not have bin blinded by any unjustifiable Passion; yet you must allow us, that he wants a Capacity, and is therefore an ill Man in taking such an Office upon him, when conscious of his Unfitness for it.

I answer, and say this is a Cavil, which if People were govern'd by, the whole World must run into Anabaptism:[210] no body wou'd be a Judg, and consequently Mankind must be left without the Administration of Justice; what they cou'd somewhat less dispense with than Religion. We must not therefore require so much from those who dedicate themselves to the Bench. I own, these two kinds of Qualifications are, generally speaking, indispensably necessary; in the first place, Integrity of Heart, a good Conscience, and clean Hands; and in the next place, a Skill in the Laws, and a sound Judgment: But of these Talents, the first sort is much more necessary than the latter, because there are a world of Causes in which common Good Sense and Judgment will suffice, with a moderate Skill <582> in the Laws; whereas there is no Cause, in which Uprightness and Integrity of Heart are not absolutely necessary. Provided then that a Judg, or Candidate for the Office, find that the ground of his Heart is right, and that he has a stedfast purpose of rendring to all their Due, and a steddy Resolution to go thro with the hearing and examining all Causes which come before him, and getting the best means of Information that he can; he may be assur'd he's well enough qualify'd for the Office. And tho it might happen, that he has not quite so much Skill as another, in sifting by his Questions and Interrogatorys into the Truth of a Fact, obscure in it self, and boldly deny'd; yet is he not oblig'd in Honor or Conscience to resign his Place: because if so, there is not perhaps a Man in the world, who cou'd take the Office upon him with a good Conscience; since no Judg can be assur'd, that the Witnesses and Accus'd, which he interrogates, cou'd have conceal'd the Fact

210. Some members of the Anabaptist sect taught that Christians should not hold civil authority. See Lecler, *op. cit.,* vol. 1, p. 204.

from another, if they had stood his Examination, with as good success as they have from him. This kind of Scruple wou'd reduce Men to very strange straits: for he who had the Law at his fingers ends, who had a clear Head, and was provided with a thousand Stratagems, for descrying the Truth thro all the Folds in the Heart of Man; must put off his Instalment, till morally assur'd there was not a Man upon earth who excel'd him in these Talents, and to whom he ought to make a tender of his Place, as the Objection I confute insinuates. All this is so absurd, that it wou'd not deserve a Confutation, were it not of some consequence to cut off my Adversarys from all their Retreats and Starting-<583>holes: Beside that it opens a way to some other things, which I shall have occasion to speak of hereafter.

One thing it mayn't be amiss to observe; That good Sense and a sound Judgment are much better Qualifications in a Judg, than a lively, subtle, imaginative Wit, abounding with all the Flourish and Volubility of the Bar: We rarely see a Judg with these last Qualitys, who does not overshoot the Mark, and one way or other fall wide of the true pinch of the Difficulty. It shou'd also be remember'd, that no Judg can possibly be so *adroit,* but that those who have Causes before him, or their Abettors, may by their Contrivances, by their Knights of the Post and Ruffians, raise such a mist, as the most upright and most understanding Judges shall never be able to dispel. On the other hand, no Law, either human or divine, obliges any Person whatever, upon pain of mortal Sin, to have a vast deal of Wit, an extraordinary Memory, an incomparable Penetration, a noble Erudition. St. *Paul* does not require this, in him who desires the Office of a Bishop, tho the most difficult of any, seeing its Province is the Salvation of the Souls of Men; he requires in him several excellent moral Qualitys, and that he be fit to teach and to instruct, which imports Gentleness and Patience, and Clearness, much more than a Vastness of Understanding. And can we in reason require that of any Man, which is not in his own power; and which is not acquir'd either by Fasting, or Prayer, or Pains: the greatest part of Mankind being born with such Facultys, that if they study'd twelve hours a day, <584> they cou'd never acquire those extraordinary Talents? 'Tis true, every one ought to know his own Strength, and not take an Office upon him which he is not qualify'd for; but still he whose Attainments seem equal to what the Sphere he is in requires (and this is no such mighty matter in subaltern Judicatures, in which notwithstanding the Judges are oblig'd to take as much care, as if their Judgments were never to be rectify'd at a higher Tribunal) and who withal is conscious of his own Probity and Strength to apply himself diligently to his Function, ought not to deem himself unqualify'd.

A Confirmation of what has bin just now said, from a Parallel between Judges and Physicians.

To set this Answer of mine in a clearer light, I shall add one Remark more. Tho Physicians are not so necessary in a State as Judges, yet it's certain we can't do very well without 'em. There must therefore be great numbers of 'em in chief Citys, and some in the smaller: and consequently a Man may be a Physician with a good Conscience, tho he has not all the Skill and Judgment of *Hippocrates* or *Galen;* because 'twere impossible to find the thousandth part of the Physicians which the World has occasion for, if they must all be such Oracles as those two. For which reason, let a Man be ever so great a Wrangler, he can't deny but where a Person has gone thro his Studys in the Schools, and commences Doctor of Physick after the requisite Forms, and has a sincere Design of improving himself by Study and Experience; he is fitly <585> and duly qualify'd to practise Physick. By a much stronger reason we may affirm, That in order to be a Judg, it's sufficient if he has obtain'd his Certificates, or is arriv'd at such a Degree or Formality, after having pass'd thro the necessary Studys; and if he afterwards apply him, with a clear Conscience, to the examining the Causes which come before him to the best of his Skill. It was not without just grounds, that I made use of the Terms, *by a much stronger Reason;* because the State has much more need of Judges than Physicians, and because Judges are not so often call'd upon in Cases of Life and Death as they.

Neither is this all. The ablest and honestest Physician may happen sometimes to prescribe Remedys which kill his Patient; the nature of the Distemper being such, that by the course of the general Laws of the Communication of Motion, the Patient might have recover'd if he had not taken such a Potion, or if he had taken of a different kind from that which the Doctor prescrib'd. The famousest Physician perhaps in *London* or *Paris,* who has practis'd for many years, and with great Reputation, has happen'd to kill a hundred Patients in his time: Hereupon I appeal to the Conscience of any reasonable Man; Does he believe, these hundred Patients will be heard in a Charge of Murder against this Physician before the Throne of God, supposing they shou'd learn, by some Revelation, how the prescrib'd Remedy had occasion'd their Death by a Consequence of the Laws of Motion? Does he not on the contrary believe, that provided the Physician acted from a sincere Inten-<586>tion, and according to the Rules of his Art, and to the best of his Knowledg and Observation from Experience and Study, he shall be declar'd perfectly innocent of the Blood of these hundred Accusers, in the face of the World? I can't conceive that a Man is so unreasonable, as to imagine that a Physician is accountable to God for the ill success of a Remedy, which he has prescrib'd upon the solidest Reasons in his Judgment: for saying, that if he had understood his Business better, he wou'd not have prescrib'd such a Remedy, is in effect banishing Physick out of the World; since 'tis impossible but the ablest Physician must be very often mistaken, as to the Consequences of his Prescriptions: and even *Galen* or *Hippocrates,* or in general the best Physician that ever was or ever shall be, might by this rule be condemn'd to Hell-flames, if he prescribe a Remedy which happens to kill the Patient. For, say they, according to this fine Notion, it is not enough that he has gone according to his Lights and his Conscience; if he had understood his Business, he had never prescrib'd such a Remedy. Nothing therefore being more ridiculous than this Reasoning, it follows, that a Physician kills his Patient innocently in the sight of God and Men, provided he does all in his power to recover him.

The reason of this undoubtedly lies in the profound Obscurity of human Distempers, and of Accidents resulting in the Machine of the Body from the Operation of such and such Remedys, in consequence of several inward Dispositions, which are not discoverable till the Physick takes place, nor cou'd be judg'd of by any out-<587>ward Symptom or Indication. These unforeseen Accidents, this Concurrence of several unlook'd for Causes, is that which renders Physick in the hands of the ablest Doctors no better than a conjectural Science, which often deceives; and Men may read over Volumes, improve in Anatomy, add new Discoverys and Experiences to those of former Ages, Nature will still be incomparably more exquisite in forming new Distempers, than the Art of Man in curing 'em: just as the crafty Malice of Men will, as long as the World lasts, get sometimes the better of all the Sagacity of the ablest Judges.

I don't by this Parallel pretend, that civil or criminal Causes are as hard to be judg'd of as Distempers; but I think I may without rashness say, that the Fact is in some Cases as hard to be discover'd as the Distemper. For we have natural Signs and Symptoms of Distempers, which depend not on the Artifices of the human Mind, nor can possibly be render'd equivocal; and Physicians can besides borrow great Lights from the Answers of the Patient, who in his Sickness will hide nothing: whereas the Accus'd and the Witnesses falsify and pervert the Use of the most sacred Signs, and give no Answers to the Judg's Interrogatorys, but what are enough to puzzle and confound him. So that I see no reason why a Judg may not sometimes be as excusable before God, in putting the Innocent to death, and acquitting the Guilty, as a Physician in prescribing a Remedy which kills his Patient.

Thus I have, beyond all exception, asserted the Innocence of Judges, whom I had pitch'd upon for my running Comparison; and consequently <588> have sufficiently supported my Proof. But to give it the finishing stroke, let's examine another Disparity which our Adversarys insist on.

⬥ CHAPTER X ⬥

An Answer to a second Disparity; to wit, That when a Judg gives Sentence against a Person falsly accus'd of Murder, it's an Ignorance of Fact; whereas if he condemns as Heresy what is really Orthodox, it's an Ignorance of Right. *I shew that it's as hard to discover the Truth in Charges of Heresy, as in those for Murder.*

A Marginal Note, which I had taken care to insert by the way,[211] might inform my Readers, that I don't take a Charge of Heresy to be in every sense a Question of Fact. I'm sensible there's a Question of Right contain'd under it in one respect. For example, in the Action for Heresy against

211. See above, p. 430, note.

Michael Servetus,[212] there was first a Charge of his denying the Trinity. This was a Question of Fact, which might be prov'd either by the Writings of this Heretick, or by the Depositions of those who had heard him teach, or by his own Confession. When this Question of Fact was clear'd, the next thing was to find out the Qualification or Nature of his Doctrine, whether rash, scandalous, erroneous, heretical, impious; and this was properly the Question of Right: which yet cou'd not be prov'd, but by <589> resolving it anew into the Class of matters of Fact, seeing *Servetus* was agreed with his Accusers and Judges in this Thesis, *That if his Doctrine was contrary to the Word of God, it was false and impious.* Now, as he alledg'd that it was not contrary, but very agreeable to Scripture, 'twas necessary to examine the Passages, which he pretended did either not favor the Doctrine of a Trinity, or did favor the Doctrine of the Unity of God, as well in Person as Nature: whereby any one may see, that the Question now is only concerning this Fact, to wit, whether such a thing be contain'd in the Book call'd Holy Scripture.

But not to draw out my Discussion of the second Disparity to too great a length, I am willing to quit the Advantage of this Observation, and for the present allow my Adversarys these two points: First, that all Prosecutions for Heresy are properly matters of Right. Secondly, that there's good Reason for not excusing an Ignorance of Right at human Tribunals: for tho it may possibly happen, that a Man is honestly and innocently ignorant of what the Laws of the Land ordain; yet, as the Judges can't discern, whether he speaks sincerely or no, they can't take up with his Excuse, for fear of the Disorders which might happen upon it; since a world of Malefactors and Disturbers of the publick Peace might make use of the same Justification: therefore, to prevent a general Evil, they'l make no exception to this general Rule, *Ignorantia Juris non excusat.*[213] This may possibly be unjust, and very hard upon particular Per-<590>sons; but 'tis necessary to sacrifice something to the publick Good of the Society.

This is undoubtedly the Reason why human Tribunals admit no Excuse

212. See above, p. 198, note 83.
213. Translation: "Ignorance of the law does not excuse." See A. Friedberg (ed.), *Corpus iuris canonici* (Leipzig, 1879; reprint Graz: Akademische Druck-u. Verlagsanstalt, 1959), vol. 1, col. 422, para. *Notandum.*

upon an Ignorance of Right; but let's beware imagining, that God proceeds by the same Reason: as he is the Searcher of Hearts, he knows most assuredly, whether such or such a Person be under an invincible Ignorance of Right; and if he be, absolves him as freely as if the Ignorance were only of Fact.

I have ruin'd this Distinction of Fact and Right to such a degree, by shewing,[214] that where the discovering the Truth is as difficult in one Case as in the other, our Ignorance is no more culpable in one Case than in the other; that the Author of the *Treatise of the Rights of the two Sovereigns,* who has wrote against the two last Chapters of the second Part of my *Commentary,* has quitted this Post, and granted that there may be an invincible Ignorance of Right, and that invincible Ignorance excuses as well with regard to matters of Right as of Fact.[215] We shall hereafter see what Advantages this Concession gives me; at present I shall not insist on it: 'Twill suffice for accomplishing what I'm now upon, if I can shew, that it is not more difficult to discover, whether a Person, accus'd of Murder, Adultery, Poisoning, be guilty (these are Questions of Fact) than to discover, whether such or such a Doctrine be Heretical, which is properly a Question of Right. If I can make this out, I totally overthrow the second Disparity, and my Comparison will have its full and intire effect. Let's try what can be done. <591>

It is not necessary to make a tedious Enumeration of Causes, which sometimes render the Ignorance of Facts invincible to human Judicatures. 'Tis well known, that the Heart of Man has depths unfathomable to the clearest-sighted Judges; that there are false Witnesses of a consummate Experience, ready at Evasions, steddy, intrepid; that true Witnesses may have short Memorys, and sometimes differ in their Evidence; and last of all, that Circumstances sometimes conspire in such a manner, by an unaccountable Juggle and Combination for the puzzling an Affair, that there's no Light to be seen thro it: and then it happens, either that it's put off to a longer day, or that the Judges determine themselves to that which the Proceedings observ'd in all the due Forms conduct, to wit, the pronouncing such a Man

214. See above, p. 240.
215. See above, p. 399.

guilty, who yet is not, or pronouncing him innocent, when perhaps he is not. Will any one say, that the examining of speculative Doctrines is encompass'd with as many Difficultys? Yes, without doubt.

Considerations on the Dispute of Jansenism, as to what regards the Fact.

There has arisen in our own days a very famous Dispute about a Book of *Jansenius*.[216] His Enemys drew five Propositions out of it, which were condemn'd at *Rome*. The Jansenists own'd, that these Propositions were capable of receiving a Heretical Sense, but in that sense they were not found in *Jansenius;* they own'd 'em heretical in the Sense the Pope had condemn'd 'em, but deny'd that *Jansenius* understood 'em in that Sense. Upon this <592> we had nothing but Book after Book concerning this particular Fact, whether these Propositions were really contain'd in *Jansenius*. The Pope declar'd for the Affirmative, but the Jansenists refus'd to submit to his Decision, because, in matters of Fact, neither the Authority of the Pope, nor that of Councils, is infallible. Upon this they condescended to treat with the Gentlemen of *Port-Royal;* and not being able to obtain of 'em the believing by a divine Faith, what the Pope had decided concerning the Fact, they insisted at least on their believing it by a human Faith:[217] but the Jansenists shew'd the Injustice of this demand, by so many invincible Reasons, that at last the opposite side were contented with their Promise of a respectful silence upon the Point. Who can avoid making two Observations upon this, one in appearance against me, the other really favorable to my Position?

1. That Disputes about Fact are the hardest in Nature to be decided, since so small a Party had, for so many Years together, bin able to maintain against the whole Body of Jesuits, favor'd by the Pope, and by a world of Doctors and Prelates besides, that what was imputed to *Jansenius,* was not really in his Book; without their being able in the issue, to bring it to a fair decision.

216. See Appendixes, "Grace, Original Sin, Predestination," p. 587.
217. Ibid., p. 588.

2. That Disputes upon this Question, *Whether such a Doctrine be Heretical,* are the hardest in nature to be clear'd: for if in a strife depending on a single Book, as this of *Jansenius,* compos'd within a few Years, and whose Stile and Phrase must consequently be more intelligible than if written some Ages ago, the <593> two contesting Partys cou'd never be brought to agree, that certain Propositions were contain'd in this Book; how will it be, when, to prove any Proposition Heretical, we must shew the contrary Proposition from the Scripture and Fathers; the Scripture, I say, and the Fathers, which make up a vast number of Volumes, written a long time ago, and in a Stile very different from the Tast and Manner of our Age?

Considerations on the same Dispute as to Right.

To set this matter in still a clearer Light, it won't be amiss to dwell somewhat longer on the Dispute about *Jansenius.* I know his Disciples were loth to jump over the Barrier of the Council of *Trent,* or maintain, as perhaps they had the Skill and Capacity to do, had they judg'd it proper, that this Council had not decided upon the Doctrines which *Jansenius* was accus'd of having deny'd in the five Propositions; my meaning is, that they own'd these Propositions Heretical in the Sense that *Rome* had condemn'd 'em. But my Reader will easily conceive, had a Set of able Calvinist Advocates taken up the Cause where the Jansenists drop'd it, and insisted on a Reexamination of these Propositions, maintaining they were Orthodox in the Sense in which the Pope had declar'd 'em Heretical; that this wou'd have open'd a Field for endless Broil and Contention, which 'twere impossible to make an end of, but by a way of Authority, much as in civil or criminal Causes, where the Right is determin'd by a Majority of Voices, and as to <594> which the Judges, after having carefully weigh'd the Allegations, think they have nothing to answer, provided they condemn only what appears to them fit to be condemn'd; tho they don't think it impossible, but that what they do condemn may at bottom be wrongfully condemn'd. 'Tis true, the Church of *Rome* has found out a particular Secret, which other earthly Judges have not; for she pretends, that God never permits what is really false to appear true, to the Majority of the Fathers assembl'd in an Oecumenical Council: but this is another Question.

As I may take occasion in the third Part,[218] to enlarge on the Difficultys which attend the Discussion of Controversys, I shall be as short on it in this place as possible; and therefore shall content my self with shewing my Reader, that in order to know, whether the five Propositions of *Jansenius,* understood in the Sense at *Rome,* were Heretical or no, it had bin necessary,

1. To be profoundly skill'd in Metaphysicks, in order to know whether the Attributes of a Being infinitely perfect, are better reconcil'd to the Free-will of Man, than to an irresistible Necessity of his doing Evil without Grace, and doing Good with Grace. This Study might likewise be of great use for settling the Sense of several obscure Scripture-Passages.

2. To be Master of the *Greek* and *Hebrew* Tongues, Biblical Criticism, and of the Customs of the Jews in our Saviour's Days; for, beside that the Sense of Texts, alledg'd by the contending Partys, may sometimes depend on the force of Particles, and this again on a certain Disposition of the Words, 'twou'd be of consequence to <595> be assur'd, that no Faults had crept into the Copy, and to know how the antient Versions and Paraphrases are agreed on this head. Then how many Phrases are there in the New Testament, which are purely Allusions to Proverbs, or Customs of the Jews of those times? Some learned Men pretend, that to understand what St. *Paul* says concerning Predestination, Vocation, and Election, it were necessary to know what Prejudices the Jews of that Age were under.

3. To read over the Fathers of the four or five first Centurys with great Care and Application, in order to know how they understood those Texts of Scripture, which seem to prove or condemn the five Propositions of *Jansenius.* This is of Consequence, whatever some may think to the contrary; because, if the Scripture, for the first four or five hundred years after JESUS CHRIST, was understood in such a certain Sense, this were a strong Presumption, that God design'd we shou'd hold to this Sense. Now the reading over so many Volumes, so as to understand 'em, is no such easy matter; you may understand your *Demosthenes* and *Cicero* perfectly well, and yet be often at a loss in reading the Fathers for want of some new *Greek* and *Latin* Vocabularys, because the Fathers have Words in each of these

218. Of the unpublished answer *The Rights of Two Sovereigns.* See above, p. 390, note 168.

Languages, which you might look out long enough in *Stevens* and *Callepin.*[219] You must know their Opinions before you can well understand their Terms; and whereas the ordinary way of understanding an Author's Opinions, is to understand his Words, you must here sometimes be acquainted before-hand with your Author's Opinions, before you can understand his Words. Nor is it enough to exa-<596>mine the Passages themselves, alledg'd *pro* and *con,* in the Dispute about Jansenism: Very often to understand the Sense of two or three Lines only, one must read over a large Treatise; he must be acquainted with the Stile and way of his Author, and his particular View and Design in such a Work.

4. In the last place, maturely and impartially to weigh the Reasons, which each Party alledges, to justify the Sense it gives the Passages from Scripture and the Fathers, the reciprocal Objections, the Solutions, the Replys, the Rejoinders, *&c.*

I now make bold to ask my Reader a Question or two; first, Whether it is not absolutely necessary to do all this, if one wou'd fulfil the Duty of an exact Judg? For if the Judges, in mere Civil Causes, ought to examine all the Deeds and Parchments of the Partys, and the Pleadings of the Advocates; by a much stronger Reason, ought they to be careful in examining 'em all when the Dispute is concerning the Truths of Religion, and the inflicting of Punishment on a world of People, in case they be convicted of Heresy.

The next thing I'm to ask my Reader is, Whether he thinks there ever was a criminal Cause (tho puzzl'd and banter'd as much as the late Popish Plot[220] among our selves) harder to be trac'd and brought to a fair Decision in the very critical point of Truth, than that in which it were necessary to perform the four Requisites just now mention'd, in order to find whether the five Propositions be Heretical. Shou'd any Reader be capable of answering me, that the deciding these five Propositions is much easier than clearing the most perplext, civil, or criminal Cause, I own I have not a word more to say; for all I <597> cou'd say wou'd be of no use, to one who did

219. Robert Estienne, *Dictionarium seu Latinae linguae Thesaurus,* Paris, 1531; Ambrosii Calepini, *Dictionarium latino-graecum,* Lyons, 1681.
220. The Catholic plot to kill Protestants and burn London, an invention of Titus Oates.

not perceive, that the four premis'd Requisites surpass the Strength, the Patience, and Parts of most Judges in the World.

From whence I conclude, either that there can be no Tribunal upon Earth for judging of Heresy, and inflicting Punishments on the Convict; or else, that God requires no more from them, than he does from those who are to judg and condemn upon Murder; that is, to examine the Cause as diligently and conscientiously as they can: And shou'd it after this unfortunately happen, that they inflicted the Punishment due to Heresy on an Orthodox Person, or the Punishment of Death on a Man falsly accus'd of Murder; God will never judg 'em for the Mistake. Now if this be so, there's an end of the Dispute; Heretical Princes are as much authoris'd to punish the Orthodox, as Orthodox Princes to punish Hereticks; which is the Consequence I had bin laboring all this while.

I might have added, in favor of what I maintain'd, that in criminal Causes the Judg has the advantage of interrogating living Witnesses, of laying Trains for 'em, and catching 'em by Surprize, of taking hold of what they say one day, and by it wresting the Truth from 'em the next; in fine, of making 'em answer ay, or no, to every short peremptory Demand, that he's pleas'd to make, and turn'd as he thinks fit: whereas the Witnesses to be consulted in a Cause of Heresy, are dumb and dead Witnesses, unable to plead or protest against those who make 'em say what perhaps they never dream'd of. I own the Judges and Partys torture these <598> Witnesses, much more than they do those in criminal Causes: but this, if I may be allow'd the Expression, is acting the part of Father *Martin*,[221] and making the Question and the Answer out of their own Head; for he who tortures a Text of Scripture, or a Passage from the Fathers, till it gives a favorable Answer, forges the Answer out of his own Brain: And thence it is, that while one Side, by dint of Torture, forces such a Sense from a Text, the opposite Side wrings out a quite contrary Sense by the same Methods. So that the Judges are much more gravel'd here, than when they have a Criminal at

221. "Faire le Prêtre Martin" and "Prêtre Martin qui chante et qui répond" were apparently proverbial expressions referring to someone who answers his own questions. See http://www.amicale-genealogie.org/Les_Saints_Patrons/Les_Saints_Patrons_novembre .htm.

the Bar, desperately bent on denying the Fact, or Witnesses sworn to conceal the Truth.

Whether the discussing the Fathers may well be dispens'd with.

Let People talk as long as they please, that there's no need of troubling one's Head to know, what was the Faith of the first Ages of the Church; this won't lessen the Difficulty: because if the Accus'd, in the first place, shou'd boast that his Opinions are agreeable to the Sense of the first Fathers; the Judges cannot dispense with the examining 'em. Dare they condemn a Man, whose Faith was really agreeable to that of the primitive Church? This were unrighteous, and hard to be digested; they must therefore, before they pronounce Sentence of Condemnation, let the Accus'd see, that the Fathers are against him, which brings the tedious thorny Discussion fairly about. <599>

In the second place, shou'd the Accus'd make a mock of the Authority of the first Ages of Christianity, and their Adversarys suggest thus; That the Scripture having its Obscuritys, which St. *Peter* himself, as obscure at least as St. *Paul,* owns in his Judgment on the Epistles of St. *Paul:*[222] it's very probable, that Difficultys were started in the very days of the Apostles, about the Sense of their Writings, as the same St. *Peter* insinuates; which Difficultys the Apostles themselves, or their immediate Disciples, might have satisfy'd by word of Mouth: whence it follows, that the Sense, which the Fathers of the first Ages gave to some obscure Texts of Scripture, might be founded on these verbal Explications, which had not as yet bin vary'd or corrupted. If, I say, the Accusers shou'd suggest thus, must not the Accus'd of necessity make their Defence, and maintain, that the Fathers of the first Ages err'd in many points; which brings about by a Backdoor that Discussion which they wou'd decline, and gives a Trouble over and above to the Judges, of examining the Reasons on which the Accuser wou'd appeal to the Authority of the Fathers?

222. "So also our brother Paul wrote to you according to the wisdom given him, speaking of this as he does in all his letters. There are some things in them hard to understand, which the ignorant and unstable twist to their own destruction, as they do the other scriptures"; 2 Peter 3:15–16.

In the last place, suppose they were to proceed upon the Testimony of Scripture only, won't there still remain three of the four above-mention'd Requisites for qualifying a Judg; and might not any one very reasonably cry out upon these three Requisites only, *Who is sufficient for these things?* <600>

Whether it be easy to give the Definition of Heresy.

Methinks I hear some Body suggest, that in order to know whether an Opinion be heretical, there needs no more than considering it by this Definition, *Heresy is an Opinion, maintain'd with Obstinacy, against the Decisions of the Church.* But what a wretched Expedient is this? for here you are presently stop'd; first upon the Notion of Obstinacy; next upon that of Church: where you'l quickly find your self in the most boisterous Ocean in the World. For by the Church, you understand the True; but the Question is, How to find this True Church? 'tis sought for in the Scriptures, and purest Tradition; but this is matter of long and tedious Brawl. To say, that the Church of *Rome* is the true Church, is saying nothing, unless it be prov'd; and to prove it so, in effect, all sorts of Discussions present.

Shou'd another pretend to mend the matter, by giving a juster Definition, and saying, That a Heretick is he who denys a fundamental Article of the Christian Religion, he'l find himself no less mistaken: for as no Christian will acknowledg, that what he denys is a Fundamental; 'twill be necessary to prove it upon him, by shewing, from the Word of God, the characteristick Mark of a fundamental Truth. And here's a new source of endless Discussion.

I shall say no more upon this Head; I fear I have said too much for any intelligent Reader, who undoubtedly must have perceiv'd, <601> from the first Pages of this Chapter, that it's much harder to discover the Truth in Trials for Heresy, than in those for Murder, Adultery, or Poisoning: whence they might justly conclude, to the Ruin of the second Disparity, that if a Judg is not answerable before God for having, in some Cases, acquitted the Guilty, and condemn'd the Innocent; neither will that Judg be answerable, who protects a Heretick and punishes an Orthodox, supposing God had enjoin'd the punishing of Hereticks.

ιΟΟι CHAPTER XI ιΟΟι

An Answer to a third Disparity; which is, That in Criminal Trials, the Obscurity arises from the thing it self; whereas in those
of Heresy, it proceeds from the Prepossession of the Judges.
I answer, That even disinterested Judges, as the Chinese *Philosophers for example, wou'd find our Controversys more intricate,
and harder to be decided, than Civil or Criminal Causes.*

I'll allow those who propose this Disparity, which is very different from the
Objection confuted in the ninth Chapter; that Prepossession is a mighty
Obstacle in a Search after Truth. For it's very certain, that where the Party
is once possess'd in favor of an Opinion, he looks very graciously on all the
Reasons brought to support it, and is as ready to despise those which support the contrary Opinion. It even < 602 > happens, that our Prepossessions,
inspiring a Love for the Doctrines we embrace, and an Aversion to those
which oppose, puts us upon studying, with Earnestness and Zeal, a thousand Reasons in their Justification; and turning these Reasons all manner
of ways, to make 'em avail; upon framing Answers to the Objections of
our Adversarys, and finding Flaws in all their Arguments in behalf of their
own Opinions: Whence it comes to pass, that we are infinitely better acquainted with what we call our own best Reasonings, than with those in
which they place their greatest Strength; whereby our own Cause appears
to us clear and incontestable, while we look upon all that's alledg'd o'their
side, as so much vain Subtilty and Cavil.

This is most remarkably exemplify'd in Lawyers. Excepting some few,
who love Cavil as they do their very Life, and who'l engage against their
Consciences in any Cause, either out of Covetousness or mere Malice; they
all fancy the Right is of their Side, and never speak of their Cause but as
a Matter clear and incontestable, whereas they look on that of their Adversarys as destitute of any Color. The reason is, that they are continually
turning their own Pretensions in their Heads, and all the Expedients which
can offer for defending 'em, till the Object by continual thinking on it

becomes so familiar, and so easy to be discuss'd, that they really find a World of Reasons for it, which no body living besides can descry. Now as they never think of the Reasons on the other side, but in a Spirit of answering and confuting 'em; they can't perceive their Force; and believe, <603> the Judges will find 'em as weak as they do, if they design to act fairly. Mean time it often happens, that the Judges can't see, either of one side or t'other, all that pretended Clearness in the Cause which the opposite Lawyers fancy; and therefore make each Party bate of their Pretensions: and it very rarely happens, that they who have lost the Cause, don't accuse the Judges either of Partiality or Ignorance.

But tho I agree as to all these ill Effects of Prepossession, which lets us see, to the exceeding Scandal of Human Kind, that the most ridiculous sensless Sect in the World will pretend all the rest are in the most palpable Errors; and that the Truth of its own side is most apparent and obvious: yet I can't think, but as there are sometimes Civil Causes, in which the Judges cannot clearly discern which side is right and which wrong; it is still more true that there are particular Controversys among Christians, which if submitted to the Decision of disinterested Persons, the *Chinese* Philosophers for example, wou'd puzzle 'em to such a degree, that they wou'd e'en abandon us to our Disputes; and perhaps do just what the Judges did before whom *Protagoras* a Sophist of *Greece* summon'd one of his Disciples: 'Twere needless relating the matter here, since it's to be met with in all our Logicks, at the Chapter *de Dilemmate*.[223]

If I did not consider, that this were more a Philosophical than a Theological Treatise, I shou'd here say, that God from a secret, tho adorable Providence, hinders the Protestants sending Ministers into the Eastern World, to labor in the Conversion of Infidels; for to speak my <604> Thoughts freely, since the Pope's Missionarys are before hand with 'em, it's more expedient for Christianity to let 'em go on by themselves, and make some Christians there, such as they can make, than go thither to disclose the Shame and deplorable Lot of the Christian Religion, divided into a thousand Partys, who pull each other to pieces like so many wild Beasts.

223. See Aulus Gellius, *The Attic Nights,* V.x, Loeb Classical Library, vol. 1, pp. 406–9.

For what does any one think must be the consequence, if thro the Credit of the *East-India* Companys of *London* and *Holland,* our Ministers shou'd obtain Permission to sojourn in *China,* and to form Catechisms? Why this, that they must at first word let their Disciples know, they had bin wickedly abus'd, if told, that the Christian Religion allow'd Images: whereby they must presently understand, that the *Romish* Missionarys taught Doctrines which those of *Holland* condemn'd as abominable, which must equally expose both Partys to the publick Contempt; and make the *Chinese* hear neither, since they cou'd not turn Christians, without being damn'd in the Judgment of one Party of the Christians themselves.

> *A suppos'd Conference between the Ministers and Missionarys, in the Presence of the* Chinese *Philosophers.*

The Ministers and Missionarys might possibly, upon this occasion, desire the Emperor of *China,* that he'd be pleas'd to name Judges, before whom they might fairly plead their Cause. And now (at least, unless Miracles step'd in to the Assistance of the Christian Religion) now were the time to hear it terribly hiss'd. For the first <605> thing the Ministers of *Holland* wou'd set forth to the Judges wou'd be, that the Book which all Christians call the *Bible,* is the Rule for determining those Differences between them and the Missionarys, for the debating of which they are now assembl'd. But the Missionarys wou'd presently represent on their part, that this Book is not the only Rule of Christians; and that besides this written Word of God, there's another unwritten Rule, which must likewise be consulted; as the Episcopal Party in *England,* a Protestant Sect, does in some Respects allow. Here then we find our Gentlemen enter'd into a most nice Dispute about the* Rule for judging of all others; they never can get clear of it, without running down, one side Scripture, charging it with Obscurity, with Insufficiency, with being a Nose of Wax; the other Tradition, calling it the Bulwark of Ignorance, a Field of endless Contradiction and Darkness. The Dispute about the Authority of the Church must come next after:

---

* *In a Conference at* Ratisbon, *in* 1601, *they spent fourteen Sessions on this single Point, without being able to come to any Resolution.*

one Side alledges, that we don't know the Scripture is Divine, but because the Church assures us so; the other maintains the contrary, that this is known, either by those Characters of Divinity which shine in the very Text, or by a particular Grace of God; and that moreover the knowing and discerning the true Church, depends on every private Person's comparing the Doctrine of the Church with Scripture: which brings about all the Difficultys in examining Articles of Faith by <606> Peasants and Tradesmen. Six Sessions cou'd not well pass, before the Disputants came to Invective and personal Reproach; the Ministers wou'd twit the Jesuits with *Ravillac's* Exploit, reckon up all their Conspiracys against our good Q. *Elizabeth,* the Gun-pouder Plot, *&c.* The Missionarys wou'd confront 'em with the Civil Wars of *France,* the formal Arraignment of *Charles* I and the beheading him on a Scaffold. Those again wou'd reply, that this was the Work only of a Fanatick Sect of Independents, had in detestation by all the true Reform'd; and these wou'd likewise say, That the Plots against Heretick Kings ought not to be charg'd on their whole Society: so the Controversy turns to a Dispute of Facts.

In what a Condition can we suppose the *Chinese* Judges by this time, they who are to decide upon these Differences? In a strange Puzzle no doubt. They cou'd not but think, what the Ministers observ'd about the uncertainty of Tradition, very reasonable: but when the opposite Side represented all the Inconveniencys which must needs attend the allowing every private Person a Right of examining Scripture, in order to judg whether the Sense which Councils give it be right, and without being oblig'd to stand by that Sense which has prevail'd all along for fifteen or sixteen hundred Years; then indeed the Arbitrators wou'd in all likelihood change Opinion: for all profane Religions look on it as a Principle of common Sense, that they who have the Superintendency of the Divine Worship, are the natural Judges and Interpreters of all Difficultys, either by themselves, or in conjunction with those who <607> govern the State; and that private Persons ought to acquiesce in their Decisions. I wou'd not be understood, as if I thought the *Chinese* right in making this Maxim their Rule; I only say, they wou'd in all probability govern themselves by it, and put it in ballance against all that the Ministers cou'd offer of greatest weight for their

Cause. And there's ground to believe, if they resolv'd to pass Judgment only on what appear'd to 'em very certain, that they wou'd drop their Commission, and intirely decline the determining this Dispute.

Some may perhaps tell me, that I make the Ministers very silly, in beginning with the Church of *Rome* on her strongest side, which undoubtedly lies in the Objections she makes against the Capacity we suppose in our Peasants, of sifting out the Truth in a boundless Ocean of Controversy: whereas she sticks by that Principle, which makes the Security of all Societys, Communitys, and Bodys Politick; to wit, that every particular Person ought to submit his own Judgment to that of the greater number, and especially of those who are intrusted with the Administration of Affairs. Let's suppose then, the Ministers prudent enough to attack the Church of *Rome* by some weak side; and certainly that of Transubstantiation, and its Consequences, is one.

There's no manner of doubt, but that after they had play'd all their Batterys of Sense and Reason against this whimsical extravagant Doctrine, alledg'd a thousand excellent Arguments which Scripture furnishes, a thousand solid Answers to the Reasonings of the Papists; there's no doubt, I say, but the *Chinese* Commissioners <608> wou'd find themselves powerfully dispos'd to adjudg 'em the Victory on this point, and to believe that the opposite side, to whom they wou'd however give the hearing, had not a word to say for themselves. But have a little Patience. They shall no sooner have heard the Missionarys represent, that their Adversarys renounce the most evident Principles of Reason, when they are to maintain the Mystery of the Trinity, the Incarnation, *&c.* against the Socinians; that our Senses ought not to carry it against an express Text of Scripture, those Senses which deceive us daily in the most obvious matters; in fine, that all Christians in general, from the days of JESUS CHRIST to the Calvinist Schism, had held the literal Sense of the words, *This is my Body:* They shall no sooner, I say, have heard out all this Plea, but they'l be at a strange loss which side to turn themselves; for if we suppose 'em to have ever so little Sense, they must comprehend, that if they who convers'd with the Apostles, who were immediately instructed by 'em, who receiv'd the Communion from their hands, had taken this Passage in the Strictness of the Letter, this is Presumption enough that the Apostles themselves understood 'em so: So that the Difficulty will soon be at an end, unless the Ministers stoutly deny the Fact.

But they do deny it, we'l suppose; and then what a new Forest of Discussion rises before 'em, at the sight of which it is probable the Judges may order the Partys to give in their Reasons in writing? The best thing the Catholicks cou'd do in this case, wou'd be to produce all that *Port-Royal* has publish'd against Mr. *Claude*.[224] <609> For as there never was a Man, in the Catholick Party, of Mr. *Arnaud*'s Force in Polemicks; what he has written upon the Eucharist, is perhaps the best-manag'd Piece of Controversy that has yet appear'd. The Ministers wou'd oppose the Writings of the foresaid Mr. *Claude;* and as to the two* Volumes of Mr. *Arnaud* which remain unanswer'd, they might find Protestant Authors enough, who had furnish'd Answers to 'em before.

Now I maintain, that the subtlest Philosophers of the East wou'd utterly lose themselves in these tedious Controversys; in which there's a deal of Barratry, and not one Objection which is not answer'd. Possibly they might tell the Missionarys, That tho all the Christians before *Calvin* might have taken the words, *This is my Body,* in the literal Sense, yet nothing more cou'd be concluded from it, than that the Apostles had understood 'em the same way; which they had no great reason to glory in, since they were a

---

* *Mr.* Lortie *wrote against the first, but never answer'd to Mr.* Arnaud*'s Reply; and therefore these two Volumes are look'd upon as unanswer'd.* [Possibly: André Lortie, *Traité de la Sainte Cène, divisé en trois parties, où sont examinées les nouvelles subtilitez de Monsieur Arnaut, sur les paroles: Cecy est mon corps* (Treatise on the Holy Supper, divided into three parts, in which are examined new subtleties of M. Arnauld on the words, "This is my body"), 1674.]

224. Antoine Arnauld, *La perpétuité de la foi de l'Eglise touchant l'Eucharistie défendue contre le livre du Sr Claude, ministre de Charenton* (The perpetuity of the faith of the Church concerning the Eucharist, defended against the book of M. Claude, Minister of Charenton), 1669–74 (with Nicole and others, arguing that Catholic doctrine concerning the Eucharist could be traced back to the belief of the early Church); DHC, art. "Arnauld, Antoine." Pierre Nicole, *La Perpétuité de la foi de l'eglise catholique touchant l'eucharistie* (The perpetuity of the faith of the Catholic Church concerning the Eucharist), short version 1664 (written by Nicole and Arnauld in controversy with Claude); *La défense de l'Eglise* (Defense of the Church), 1689 (a reply to Claude's *Défense de la Réformation;* see above, p. 395, note 176); DHC, art. "Nicolle, Pierre."

Company of simple illiterate Men, void of all the Improvements of Philosophy or the Sciences. But tho we shou'd suppose they made this Remark, it cou'd be of no service to the Calvinists, who own the Infallibility of the Apostles: consequently the *Chinese* Judges, who might alledg this, if appointed Judges in a Cause against all Christians in general, must be oblig'd to suppose the Infallibility of the Apostles as the Rule of their Judgment; it being a Principle common < 610 > to the Partys which had accepted 'em for Arbitrators of their Differences.

If any one shou'd wonder at my supposing the *Chinese* Judges at such a puzzle about this Point, I must desire him to take one thing of consequence along with him; which is, that this does not suppose that I my self find any difficulty in the Controversy about the Eucharist. I am clearly convinc'd that the figurative is the true Sense, and the Objections of the Catholicks give me no manner of Uneasiness. All the Reform'd are of the same mind. The Lutherans and Romanists think on the other hand the literal Sense most true, and make no great matter of all our Objections. Undoubtedly Education in those who are deceiv'd, and Education together with Grace or without Grace in those who are not deceiv'd, is what produces these opposite firm Persuasions; whereupon it naturally follows, that the Reasons for the affirmative appear solid and convincing, those for the Negative mere Sophism, Cavil, and poor Stuff. Whatever it be, let us not imagine that Persons not engag'd or prejudic'd of either side, must relish our Reasonings, and those of our Adversarys, just as we our selves or as they do. Such Men wou'd never see in ours all that Evidence which we see in 'em, nor in those of the opposite side all that Weakness which we fancy in 'em. Neither wou'd they find in the Arguments of the Missionarys all that Force which these feel in 'em, nor in our Objections that want of Solidity which the Missionarys think they perceive in 'em. They wou'd certainly find Appearances of Right and Wrong, of Truth and of Falshood, of both sides: And this is what < 611 > wou'd puzzle, what wou'd hinder their giving a definitive Judgment, and make 'em desire to be deliver'd as soon as possible from such intricate Wrangles, as fearing they shou'd never be able to decide 'em aright.

Gentlemen Christian Convertists (wou'd they say to the contesting Partys) *who come so very far to inform us that you are not agreed among your selves, we have not leisure enough to hear out all your Disputes; and since you have mention'd Socinians, Independants, an Episcopal Party, as so many other Sects among you, 'tis but reasonable that we hear them too: Write to 'em to send their Deputys hither; it may be they can help us to some Lights in this matter. In the mean time we fear you not; you can never gain over one Chinese, if you employ no other means than Reason, provided the Emperor forbids all his Subjects to receive the Christian Religion, unless from the hands of a Minister and Missionary, keeping a strict eye on one another.*

I must say it then positively once more, that it's much better we shou'd lie still, than go as far as *China* to become a Rock of Offence to the Infidels; who if they had a mind effectually to frustrate the Endeavors of the Convertists, who are already settled there, without any violence, ought to send over at their own charge and expence for Reform'd Missionarys, to set the Christians together by the ears. If much such another Stratagem had succeeded with the Cardinal of *Lorain,* who had slily concerted, by the advice of *Baldouin,* to invite some famous Lutheran Divines to the Conference at *Poissy;*[225] he had mortify'd *Theodore Beza* by it, and his Collegues, much more than by all his own great Learning and <612> Eloquence, and that of the Flower and Cream of the Popish Chivalry, who disputed at this Conference, and yet did not gain an inch of ground of the Ministers. But *Theodore Beza*'s Good Fortune spar'd him the Confusion. The Lutheran Divines having touch'd the Sums before-hand which the Cardinal was to pay 'em, arriv'd a little late at *Paris;* and one of 'em dying presently of the Plague, the rest made what hast they cou'd home again, without proceeding a step farther to *Poissy. Sic me servavit Apollo,*[226] might *Theodore Beza* then have said.

225. See Joseph Lecler, *op. cit.,* vol. 2, p. 55–67. "Poissy, Colloquy of" in *The Oxford Encyclopedia of the Reformation,* vol. 3, pp. 281–82. See DHC, art. "Baudouin, Francis," rem. C; art. "Bèze, Théodore," rem. H.
226. Horace, *Satires,* I.ix.78: "Thus Apollo saved me!"

◌◌ CHAPTER XII ◌◌

A particular Consideration of one of the Causes which renders the Controversys of these times so cross and intricate; to wit, That the same Principles which are favorable against one sort of Adversarys, are prejudicial in our Disputes with others.

I Shall add one Consideration more, which is, That Controversys are become intricate, not only because there's no Objection which one Party can make against another, which that other Party has not some Answer to ready coin'd; but also because the Principles which one Party may make an excellent use of on some occasions, become prejudicial in others. I shall give two Examples of this.

It's a mighty advantage, when we dispute against the Real Presence, to say, that it destroys < 613 > the purest Ideas of natural Reason, and the most incontestable Principles of Philosophy. The Patrons of this Doctrine answer, that Reason shou'd be silent when God speaks, and that we shou'd not presume to set bounds to the Power of God. We reply, that God has not given us Reason as a useless piece of Furniture; and that whatever implies a Contradiction, is impossible. Every one sees what a stress we now lay upon natural Light: But if we have to deal with a Socinian a little after, who disputes against the Trinity and Predestination upon the same Principles, we presently fly to the Incomprehensibility of the Divine Nature, to the Darkness of our own weak Reason, to the Duty of captivating our Understanding to the Yoke of Faith. So that the same Principles which we make use of against the Roman Catholicks, are turn'd against us by the Socinians: And the Catholicks themselves renounce their own Principle when they attack us on the Article of absolute Predestination, and that of the Servitude of our Will. For when we answer, these are incomprehensible Mysterys, *O Altitudo Divitiarum!* [227] they press us the harder on Reason's

227. Romans 11:33: O altitudo divitiarum sapientiae et scientiae Dei, quam incomprehensibilia sunt iudicia eius et investigabiles viae eius. "O the depth of the riches both of the wisdom and knowledge of God! how unsearchable are his judgments, and his ways past finding out!"

finding the Goodness, and Justice, and Holiness of God wounded by these Doctrines.

A second Example. When the Roman Catholicks, to raise the Authority of the Church above Scripture, tell us, the Scripture is obscure, subject to a thousand Interpretations, a dumb Judg, a dead Letter which may be turn'd which way one pleases, and which stands in need of the authoritative Testimony of the Church, in order to its being acknowledg'd as Divine; <614> we maintain in opposition to 'em, that the Scriptures have so many conspicuous Characters on 'em of Divine, all which we draw up in a kind of martial Order, that one need only read 'em over with Humility and a teachable Mind, to be fully convinc'd they are the Word of God. But if a Stander-by steps forth, and maintains that these Marks of Divinity are conspicuous enough to produce the Vertue of Faith in a well-dispos'd Mind, presently the Tables are turn'd; we oppose, and affirm that these Marks or Characters are not distinct enough to produce Faith, and that one stands further in need of an immediate Grace for inclining the Will, the natural Man not discerning what's sufficient to enlighten. It's manifest this weakens the Reasons we object against the Papists, when they run down Scripture: for it's no way necessary it shou'd be better than they allow it, nay it might be much worse, and yet neither more nor less profitable for all that; Grace being sufficient to make us believe its Doctrines, since nothing can resist Grace.

The Church of *Rome* might afford us a hundred Examples of this kind. For as soon as she presses us on the Obligation that private Persons are under to submit to the Church, on the score of its Antiquity, Universality, the Succession of Sees and Bishops, *&c.* we let loose Jews, Pagans, Mahometans, Greeks at her, who may make use of the same Arms against her, that she does against us.

One might bring under this Head of Difficulty what several have made their Observations of; That there's no Christian Sect, all the Writers of <615> which are agreed in the same Proofs. For you shall find some among the Orthodox alledg several Texts of Scripture in proof of the Mystery of the Trinity, which others reject as proving nothing; one this Text, another that, a third Author some other Text: so that there remain but very few, which in the Judgment of some Orthodox or other don't fall short of what they are brought to prove. The same has befaln those of the Church of *Rome:* for the sixth Chapter of St. *John,* which is eternally objected to us as the great Bulwark of the Real Presence,[228] does not appear a sufficient Proof to all their own Doctors; some having even held, that that place of Scripture had no relation to the Sacrament of the Eucharist. How then can they have the confidence to reflect on us for not finding in that Chapter a Proof of their Doctrince, since one may be a good Catholick according to them, without being able to find it there? This represented to the *Chinese* Judges, wou'd incline 'em to believe, that the Evidence which seems to be in the Expressions of this sixth Chapter of St. *John* in favor of the Popish Missionarys, is liable to exception, and even to suspicion, since it is rejected with impunity even by some of those whose interest it is to maintain it.

But what need is there of going about the Bush, to prove that our Controversys wou'd appear very intricate to the *Chinese* Philosophers? Is not the Confession of the contesting Partys a sufficient Proof of this? The Roman Catholicks contend with all their might, that no private Person is capable of discerning Orthodoxy from Heresy, and that the Councils themselves <616> might err, did not the Holy Ghost assist with a special Grace. The Protestants own as much; nay, they go something farther, since they not only hold, that Councils and Synods stand in need of the Assistance of God's Spirit, in order to find of which side the Orthodoxy or Heresy lies between the contending Partys, but also that after the Decisions of the most Orthodox Councils, a private Person still needs a most efficacious Grace to be convinc'd of the Truth of these Decisions. And as for those who won't have recourse to efficacious Grace for the Belief of Evangelick Truths, they reduce these Truths to a very small number, and oblige to the Belief only of such Points as are too clear and evident to admit of any dispute.

Let's conclude then, to the ruin of the third Disparity, That our Controversys are difficult and very hard to be decided, not only on account of the Prejudices which those who examine 'em may be under, but also in themselves: Whence it follows, that if a Judg does honestly take that for Heresy which really is not so, and afterwards punishes it in obedience to

228. John 6:48–58.

the Command of JESUS CHRIST, he's no less excusable herein, than he who condemns an innocent Person to death, when convinc'd upon the strictest Examination that he is guilty of Murder. <617>

♥♥♥   CHAPTER XIII   ♥♥♥

An Answer to the fourth Disparity; which is, That when a Judg is deceiv'd in a Cause of Heresy, he is guilty in the sight of God; because the Error in this Case proceeds from a Principle of Corruption, which perverts the Will: an Evil not incident to a Judg, who is deceiv'd in Trials for Murder or Adultery. *I shew, that were this the Case, each Sect wou'd be oblig'd to believe, that those of other opposite Sects never pray'd for the Assistance of God's Spirit to direct 'em in reading his Holy Word.*

As this is the nicest part of the whole Dispute, I have defer'd giving my Reader a Word of Advice till now; which may serve, if need be, for what has bin said already, but is especially necessary with regard to what remains to be said.

A Preliminary Observation, which the Reader is desir'd to remember in due time and place.

I don't properly consider, in what I advance in my Answers to the Disparitys of my Adversarys, any other Errors than those of Heterodox Christians; I'm concern'd no further. Notwithstanding, as I may sometimes happen to make use of Expressions of a more extensive and ge-<618>neral nature, or which however may appear somewhat dark and confus'd, I must desire my Reader always to understand my Terms by the following Propositions, and to explain 'em by this precise Declaration of my own Opinion.

1. That no Error in Religion, of what nature soever we suppose it, is a Sin when purely involuntary.

2. That the same degree and kind of Ignorance suffices to render an Error, be it of what nature it will, involuntary, as suffices to render human Actions involuntary, in the sense that we find this matter explain'd in all

the moral Treatises of our scholastick Philosophers. See *Heerebord* in particular, a Professor in the College of *Leyden*.[229]

3. That a great many Men live and die, after they have arriv'd at an Age in which they might and ought to have made use of their Judgments, in very strange Errors in Religion, but involuntary by that kind of Ignorance which excuses; and in this case the Error is properly an Error of Sincerity.

4. That a great many others live and die, after they have arriv'd to the same Maturity of Age, in Errors which cannot be call'd involuntary unless in an improper sense, inasmuch as they don't proceed from that kind of Ignorance which excuses, but from an affected Ignorance springing from a Principle formally evil. This is properly an Error of Insincerity.

5. That Men may make various Conjectures more or less probable, and sometimes almost to a degree of Certainty, concerning those who err in this last manner; yet that none but <619> God alone can know and affirm it positively.

Let's now return to the Subject of the Chapter, and examine this new Retreat, which I suppose my Adversarys may fly to, when convinc'd of the Nullity of the Evasion, which has bin render'd altogether useless to 'em in the ninth Chapter. They'l tell us, that he who is in an Error persists in it from an evil Principle, because he never makes use of the means of Information which lie ready to his hand; whereby his Error becomes a wilful Sin: just as the Ignorance of a Scholar is acounted voluntary, tho he has ever so great a desire of being learned; if on the one hand he knows that 'tis absolutely necessary to study in order to become learned, and on the other hand is idle and refuses to study. But what are those means of Information which lie ready at hand? One Party answers, that it's giving heed to what that Church has defin'd, which has Universality and Antiquity of its side, and an uninterrupted Succession of Bishops ever since the Apostles days, adhering to the Apostolical Chair of St. *Peter*. Others tell us, that it's reading the Word of God with a teachable Mind, and a sincere Desire of finding that Light which its Author has diffus'd in it; recommending one's self to

---

229. Adriaan Heereboord (1614–59), Dutch Cartesian. The reference is perhaps to his *Meletemata philosophica,* 1665. On the ignorance that makes actions involuntary, see Thomas Aquinas, *Summa theologiae,* 1–2, q. 6, a. 8, and q. 76, a. 2–4.

God while he reads; praying to him for that Wisdom from on high, which he never refuses to those who ask in Faith; not stifling those Rays of heavenly Light which this Holy Word darts thro the Souls of its Readers, from any Love or Fondness for preconceiv'd Opinions: but guiding our selves by 'em as by a Lamp shining in <620> a dark place. Let's first examine* the last of these two Answers.

One must be utterly void of all Sense of Religion, to doubt that what is propos'd in this last Answer is every Man's Duty, and a means highly pleasing to God; but on the other hand, they who suppose that all those Christians who don't surmount their Errors, act counter to this method, run themselves into very frightful Consequences.

For if they be Calvinists, they must suppose that no Papist, who dies in his Religion, had ever read the Scriptures but with an intractable perverse Disposition of Mind; not desiring to find out the Truth, but seeking all pretences for strengthening his old Prejudices; never imploring the Assistance of God's Spirit to render his reading profitable, but industriously stifling all Motions and Beginnings of Instruction afforded him by perusing this Divine Book. Now what madness were it to say, that for so many Ages together, in which Christianity and the Church of *Rome* were in a manner but one and the same thing, at least while it was much the most numerous and the most flourishing Part of the Christian Church, there shou'd never be either Priest, or Prelate, or Monk, who died in his Errors, that had not all along read the Scriptures in that extravagant Disposition of Mind which has bin just now describ'd? Yet this is what we can't avoid affirming upon the Supposition which I now examine, and accordingly concluding, that any Man who had pray'd earnestly to God for his en-<621>lightning Grace, and perus'd his Holy Word with a teachable Mind, and a sincere Desire of being instructed; must have discover'd the Falseness of Monastick Vows, of Celibacy, of Fasts, Invocation of Saints, Images, Relicks, Real Presence, *&c.* From whence it follows, that whoever did not perceive these to be Errors, must never have pray'd to God to make his reading and perusing the Scriptures profitable to Salvation. So here's the whole Eastern, as well as the Roman Church, in the same predicament.

---

* *The first Answer is examin'd in Chap.* 16.

Nor will the Lutherans come off a jot better than they; for according to this Supposition we must maintain, that not only all the Lutheran Clergy, but the Laity also, have ever read the Scriptures, and still read 'em, with an untractable stubborn Disposition, obstinately resolv'd never to depart from what they have once taken up, never recommending themselves in Prayer to the Grace of the Holy Spirit; and so on. This of necessity must be their case: For very far from being corrected, during the space of above 150 years, from their prodigious Error of *Consubstantiation*,[230] not less absurd, or but very little less than that of *Transubstantiation*, they have departed from several Truths which *Luther* had establish'd, to build up in their room the Doctrine of Free-will, with its Consequences. Now how can any one conceive, that for above an Age and a half past, during which the Lutherans have bin possess'd of intire Kingdoms and Provinces, with fine Colleges and famous Universitys, there shou'd never be one Minister or Professor among those numbers who have written upon <622> the Scriptures, no devout Woman, or honest House-holder, among such multitudes as read a Chapter in the Bible every day of their life, who had read the Word with an honest Heart and a sincere Intention, and after having recommended himself in Prayer to God? What a monstrous Supposition is here?

But the Calvinists themselves must not expect a more favorable Lot. For according to the foremention'd Supposition, the Greek, the Romish Church and the Lutheran, will all agree in condemning them as having never read the Scriptures but in a proud opiniater Disposition, without any previous devout Prayer, to draw down a Blessing upon their reading. They'l make this Judgment in a more particular manner on the famous Synod of *Dort*;[231] because, far from profiting by those Hints and Gleams of Light, which the Arminians furnish'd the Calvinists for discovering some part of that which the three fore-mention'd Churches call their Error, this Synod confirm'd it by an authentick Decree. Must not they likewise on this Supposition conclude, that all the Members of this Synod consulted the Scriptures without the least sincere Intention, and that the Prayers they offer'd

230. See Appendixes, "The Eucharist," p. 589.
231. On the Arminians and the Synod of Dort see Appendixes, "Grace, Original Sin, Predestination," p. 588.

up to God at every Session were but as *a sounding Brass and a tinkling Cimbal?*[232]

Let's beware then giving into an Hypothesis so unreasonable; for beside what has bin already said, it must draw each Party into a belief, that its own Members have obtain'd of God either by their Prayers, or by the holy Dispositions with which they have read the Bible, the true Sense of the contested Passages. We, for example, <623> ought to believe that all the Reform'd have obtain'd by these means the Knowledg of all the Truths which distinguish us from Roman Catholicks, Lutherans, Arminians, Socinians. But how cou'd we have the face to say this, while there are so many wicked Wretches among us, void of Piety and Vertue, who yet are as much persuaded of these Truths as the most righteous Men?

All that can with any reason be said in this matter, is assuredly this; That the imperious Force of Education is what has given the Wicked in our Communion a Persuasion of these salutary Truths: And shall not the same Power avail to the persuading a Roman Catholick and a Lutheran of the Truths which they hold? Will any one dispute, if Education can fix a very wicked Man in a Belief of the Truth, but it may fix a very sincere Man in the Belief of a Lye? Why always recur then to the Malice of the Heart, as the Principle of all Error; why pretend, that no one continues in Error, but because he does not read the Scriptures with Humility, Sincerity, and the requisite Devotion?

I pass over this farther convincing Argument against my Adversarys, to wit, That if the Roman Catholicks and Lutherans persisted in their Errors for want of perusing the Scriptures duly, it wou'd follow, that they read the Word of God with the proper Dispositions for finding out the true Sense, and with the Dispositions which hinder the finding it, almost in the same breath: because they may almost in the same breath light upon Passages proving the Trinity and Incarnation, and on those wherein the Eucharist is men-<624>tion'd; and thus take the Sense of the first right, and of the latter wrong. Can any one say, that their Intention is not equally good with regard to both?

232. 1 Corinthians 13:1.

∞ CHAPTER XIV ∞

Examples shewing that Men continue in their Errors against the Interests of Flesh and Blood, and their own Inclinations.

Did error always spring from a Corruption of Heart, Men wou'd come off of it when this Corruption found its account in the Change. Now this, we see, does not always happen. And there be those who are under an invincible Persuasion of a Falshood, even where they wish for the Interest of Truth in general, that they cou'd disbelieve such and such Points.

For who knows not that *Luther* wish'd passionately, that he cou'd disbelieve the Real Presence, judging that as long as he believ'd this Article, he depriv'd himself of the greatest Advantages for battering the Papacy to the ground? His Wishes, founded on the greatest Interest that he cou'd propose himself, were all vain; he never cou'd, tho he endeavor'd with all his heart, find out the figurative Sense, which is so obvious to all of us in the words, *This is my Body.* He had therefore as hearty an Intention to discover the Truth with regard to this Point, as with regard to several others, in which he happily lit on it; and he pray'd with as much fervor, that God <625> wou'd direct him as well in this as in the rest. And yet he miss'd it here: consequently it is not always for want of Application, of Zeal, of Sincerity, of Good-will, that Men continue in Errors, but from too strong Impressions made on us by Custom and Education.

Such another Instance may be drawn from what I remember to have heard several of the Reform'd say in *France,* when press'd to change their Religion, and reproach'd as if their Unwillingness to re-unite proceeded wholly from Stubbornness, Obstinacy, a sinful Shame, or an unreasonable Aversion to the Church of *Rome.* They answer'd judiciously, that 'twere for their eternal and temporal Interest that the Church of *Rome* were really the true Church, and that they cou'd believe it such; that they wish'd it with all their heart, and that all kind of Reasons inclin'd 'em to wish so, since hereby they might conscientiously quit a Religion under disgrace, which depriv'd 'em of the Comforts of Life, and go over to another, in which they might enjoy the Good Things of this World and of that which is to come:

Common Sense might teach 'em this. It's plain then, the Reform'd of *France* had bin very glad that God had done 'em the Grace and Favor of discovering to 'em, that the Church of *Rome* was the true Church; they had hereby bin preserv'd from all those Storms which have since overwhelm'd 'em. Yet the greatest part of 'em remain persuaded of what they had bin taught to believe from their Childhood: a plain Argument, that Men can't alway believe what they wou'd, and that neither our natural Proneness to Evil, nor the Advan-<626>tages of this World, are able to efface the Impressions of Religion.

By the Law which banish'd the Socinians out of *Poland,* 'twas provided, that if any of 'em wou'd turn Catholicks they might freely continue; yet they almost all chose to undergo the Inconveniences of a Pilgrimage, rather than quit their Religion. Was it not their Interest, on all manner of accounts, to believe that the Church of *Rome* was the true Church? Is it not sometimes the Interest of Roman Catholicks, to believe that Protestantism is the true Religion? How comes it then that so few change? We must perceive in this, not a Malignity of Will which hinders the asking with due Humility God's Assistance towards coming at the Truth, but a firm Confidence of its being already found; for when People are under this full Persuasion, the Order of Nature requires that they believe every thing false that's opposite to it, and consider whatever wou'd draw 'em from this Persuasion, as the Suggestion of an evil Spirit, or their own corrupt Nature. Now can any Man in Conscience tell me, that this is the effect of a Corruption of Heart, an Obliquity of Will, a Perverseness of Spirit, and not rather an infallible sign of our loving the Truth?

But what shall we say to the Jews, who for so many Ages past have bin the very Scum and Off-scouring of the World, without an abiding City or Country in any part of the Earth, without Places or Preferments, frequently banish'd and persecuted from City to City, the ordinary Game of the Inquisition, and oblig'd even in the Countrys where they are tolerated to enlarge <627> their Phylacterys, to be humble, and put up with a thousand Indignitys? Does Ambition, Voluptuousness, a vindictive Principle, find its account in such a way as this? Are they ignorant, that as to this World 'twere infinitely better for 'em to be Christians or Mahometans, according to the diversity of Place, than Jews? Yet nothing is more rare than the Conversion of a Jew. From whence can this proceed, but from a strong Persuasion that they shou'd offend God, and be eternally damn'd, if they chang'd the Religion of their Fathers? But whence does this strong Persuasion generally speaking proceed, but from Education? for the same Jew, who is so obstinate now in his Errors, wou'd have bin a Christian to Fire and Faggot, if taken from his Father at two years old, and educated among conscientious zealous Christians. Now will any one say, that the Malice of his Heart was the cause of his being bred up not by a Christian, but by his Jewish Father? And yet I shall soon shew, that had he become a Jew of himself by Education, yet this cou'd not prove that his Heart was evil. <628>

⁙ CHAPTER XV ⁙

That the Persuasion of the Truth of a Religion, which Education inspires, is not founded on a Corruption of Heart.

This is a Point which to me seems worthy our Consideration. I don't doubt but every reasonable Man, if he weighs it well, will allow, that the Children of Christians are not Christians at such a certain Age because their Fathers are so, but because they are bred up and instructed in the Christian Religion: and shou'd Christians and Turks, living in the same Town, make an exchange of their Children on the Breast, those of the Christians wou'd be certainly Mahometans, and those of the Turks Christians. From whence I draw this Conclusion, That not only the same Soul which becomes Christian by being united to the *Foetus* of a Christian, wou'd have become a Turk if it had lit a House or two shorter or farther off into a Turkish Family; but also that the same Soul which has bin ingrafted into Christianity by Baptism, wou'd infallibly become of the Jewish Religion, the Mahometan, Siamese, Chinese, &c. according as it were bred from its first Infancy among Jews or other Infidels. We sometimes see Hereticks and Orthodox live together in the same Buildings, with their Wives and Children, and distinct Familys apart. Cou'd it be suppos'd, that a Soul which was destin'd for the *Foetus* of an <629> Orthodox Mother, shou'd straggle, or missing its way ever so little, shou'd mistake one Chamber for another, it wou'd as certainly become Heretical; as another Soul, which went strait to its appointed place, to wit, into the *Foetus* of a Heretical Woman: so that according as it lights a Story higher or lower, at No. 3. or No. 4. the Man is either a Heretick or an Orthodox.

What are we to understand by all this, but that all the Souls, which God unites to human Bodys, wou'd be in the Party of the Orthodox, at the Age of ten or twelve, if none but the Orthodox had a hand in their Education? No body, I suppose, can deny this Consequence; but from hence it necessarily follows, that a Soul's adhering for the first ten or twelve Years of Life to false Doctrines, in which it is instructed, proceeds not from its being corrupted, or infected by Original Sin. For since the Ground-Plot, in which the true Religion takes root, is numerically the same, in which the false Religion, if sown, wou'd take root too (this is the Result of my former Remarks) we must of necessity allow, either that the Soul embraces not the true Religion, but because it's infected by Original Sin; or that it embraces not a false, inasmuch as it is infected with this same Sin. If you deny the latter Proposition to advance this,

The Soul becomes not tinctur'd with a false Religion, but because it contracts the stain of Original Sin from the moment of its Union with Matter:

Of necessity you must allow the following Proposition too;

The Soul becomes not tinctur'd with the true Religion, but because it contracts the stain of Original <630> Sin the moment of its Union with Matter.

Now 'twere the greatest Extravagance imaginable to advance this last Proposition, and yet it must of necessity follow if we admit the former: we must therefore reject both, and say, that the Soul receives all the Doctrines infus'd into it, as it is a spiritual Substance, susceptible by its Nature of all sorts of Ideas and Opinions, even as a Copper-plate receives all kind of Gravings indifferently: The Canons of the Council of *Trent*[233] no less readily than those of the Synod of *Dort*. Original Sin[234] has nothing to do here; it may very well be the Cause of our depraving those Notions which we suck in with the Milk; but it never is the Cause of our sucking in, or adopting 'em.

---

233. The Council of Trent (1545–63) defined Catholic orthodoxy against teachings of the Protestant reformers.
234. See Appendixes, "Grace, Original Sin, Predestination," p. 588.

The better to comprehend this Truth, it will be proper to observe, that altho the Soul, by its Union with the Body, contracts an odious Leprosy, call'd Original Sin; yet it does not always act as affected with this contagious Distemper: for example, a Child who's hungry, and desires Food, does not form this Desire, because he bears the Punishment of *Adam*'s Sin; much less can we impute to this Sin his drawing a just Consequence from any thing that he has heard, as Children will sometimes do at four or five Years of Age. Let no one go about to wrangle, on pretence of our not knowing what Children might do in the state which we have forfeited by the Fall of *Adam;* for don't we find, in the History of the Passion of JESUS CHRIST, that he call'd for Drink when he was a thirst? A demonstrative Argument, that this sort of Desires are consistent with perfect Innocence, and <631> therefore that we don't form 'em as infected with the Leprosy of Sin. Let's say the same, by a much stronger Reason, of our believing honestly in our tender Age all that is told us concerning God. If we don't deserve Praise on the score of it, because our Consent to these Instructions depends not on a free and reasonable Choice; neither do we deserve Blame for the very same Reason. It's pure Chance, not with regard to God, but with regard to our selves, that we rather consent to the Truth than to a Falshood; and with the same natural Force wherewith the Mind embraces a Falshood, if it be presented to it, it wou'd have embrac'd the Truth if that had bin offer'd: just as the different Determination of Motion, according to the Remark of the new Philosophy,[235] supposes not that the Motion it self is different; it being most certain, that a Body shall tend from East to West, and back again from West to East, with the very same quantity of Motion, if the meeting with some other Body changes its Determination.

This brings to my Mind another Remark of the same Philosophy, to wit, That all Motion impress'd by God on Matter, tends by its first Destination, constantly in a strait Line; so that if it ever describes a circular or curve Line, 'tis only because of invincible Obstacles, which it meets with: whence it follows, that the same Force which produces Motion in a strait Line, produces that in an oblique also; and that the same Motion, which is oblique, had bin actually strait, if it had not met with some unsurmount-

235. On the "new philosophy" see Appendixes, "Philosophical Controversies," p. 595.

able Obstacle. Here's a faithful Representation <632> of what happens to our own Souls. They receive a continual Impression which carrys 'em by its first Destination directly towards Truth; but a thousand particular Circumstances hinder their moving by this strait Line, and cast 'em off by one side or other, a thousand different ways. Yet it's still the same Force, the same Impression, the same Tendency towards Truth which moves 'em; as is plain from hence, that our Souls never entertain any Opinion unless cloth'd in the Robes and Colors of Truth. The Devil may play all his Engines long enough, he shall never be able to get Error receiv'd into our Souls as Error; they are incorruptible and infallible in this respect, and utterly incapable of adopting any Opinion which presents as false. But here's what happens; this Force, and this Motion towards Truth, is, by those who train us up, determin'd sometimes to the right hand, and sometimes to the left, according as they tell us, that here or there lies the way which leads to the End that all Men naturally incline to. They are not therefore two different Impressions or Motions, distinct in Nature, which carry us, one to Truth, the other to Error; this latter is only the first Motion turn'd out of its own natural course, and determin'd anew by the Opposition of a kind of reflective Bodys, to wit Education, and the Pedagogy of a School-Master or Mistress. Let's beware then flying at every turn to the stain of Original Sin, and I don't know what Corruption of the Will; Is this the Cause of our being born in the House of a Heretick, or any such Miscreant, rather than in that of a faithful Child of God? <633>

But to give the common Readers, as well as Philosophers, a Comparison within their Sphere, let's suppose a great Monarch pitches on a Gentleman, whose Fidelity, Activity and Diligence, he has often experienc'd, to carry a Message of Consequence, and which requires the utmost dispatch, to another great Prince. This Courier remembring his Master had hinted to him, that Expedition's all in all, that *in mora periculum;*[236] and born on the Wings of Zeal for his Service, rides night and day, changes Horses as oft as possible, and gets the best Guides he can, to lead him by all the shortest ways: If it happen unfortunately, that an ignorant or roguish Guide puts him in a wrong Road, and that following it with all his Ardor and Zeal, he

---

236. "There is danger in delay."

loses himself, and the faster he rides the farther he goes from the City whither he was bound; will any one say, that the Speed and Dispatch, with which he follow'd this wrong Road, was owing to a Principle different from that which carry'd him on before in the right Road? One must be an errand Fool to imagin, there's the least difference in the Principle, Obedience and Fidelity on one hand, Rebellion and Perfidiousness on the other; or not to see, that his moving in the wrong Road, is only a Continuation of his Motion in the right, and that his Speed in one as well as t'other, proceeds wholly from Fidelity, and a Zeal for his Master. The Application of this to Children is very obvious: for who sees not, that if a Child, bred by his Father in the Orthodox way, and who has felt a great Zeal for Truth, fall at nine or ten Years old into the hands of a Heretical Tutor, who persuades him that the way of Truth lies not as he has bin told, but quite con-<634>trary; who sees not, I say, if this Child proceeds in this new Path, which his Tutor puts him in; with the same Ardor and Zeal as before in the true, that these are not two Actions different in Kind, and proceeding from a different Principle, but a Continuation of that Motion which first carry'd him towards the Truth?

Consequently so far is corrupt Nature from influencing our Zeal for an Error before we come to a full use of our Free-will; for Error, I say, recommended to us as heavenly Truth; that on the contrary, this Zeal can proceed from nothing else than the Remains of Good in our Nature ever since the Fall of *Adam,* to wit, an invincible and irresistible Determination toward Truth in general, a Determination which suffers not the Soul to adhere to any thing which appears false. Can any one deny, but this is a very excellent Perfection? I own, the being subject, as we are, to mistake Truth for Falshood, is a great Infirmity; yet this never happens but when we are deceiv'd by a superior Power, as is that of Education, till such a certain Age: we love that which appears to us Truth, we love it only because it appears such, and reject it for no other reason than that it appears to us an Error, and a Lye. But the Corruption of our Heart begins then to work in us, when the Soul, persuaded that a Doctrine comes from God, does notwithstanding reject it, and regulate its Actions on quite another Model. Then the Disorder is great indeed, whether the Doctrine we reject be in reality true, or whether it be false: nor wou'd it be a less Sin in us to labor in propagating Orthodoxy, while firmly persuaded of its being <635> a Heresy, than having no regard for a Heresy, while firmly believing it to be the Truth.

✂ CHAPTER XVI ✂

That the strong Belief of a Falshood, attended even with the rejecting those Suspicions which sometimes arise in our Minds, that we are in an Error, does not necessarily proceed from a Principle of Corruption.

I Persuade my self, that those who weigh what I now offer with a settl'd Judgment, will readily agree to it; as for others, I doubt whether they will or no: but most of all I mistrust your Readers of a pert Wit and gigantick Imagination, because they have generally the Misfortune to take things wrong, and eternally misunderstand 'em; either that the Author's Reasoning hinders their weighing things with that Disinterestedness which is requisite, or that before they have quite read over a Chapter, they have fram'd in their own thoughts several Answers to it, which can't chuse but be very defective, as having in view only a piece or skirt of an Objection. But by those who have more Application of thought, and who are able maturely to examine the strong and the weak sides of a Cause, 'twill always for the future be reckon'd, I think, a constant Truth.

In the first place, that the Soul of a Child adheres not to the first Religion taught to it, either as adorn'd with Sanctity, or stain'd with Sin; but <636> simply as it is a Spirit, susceptible of all kind of Ideas and Opinions, and limited to some rather than to others by its Union with Matter.

2. That the Facility with which this Soul receives whatever is offer'd to it in matter of Opinion, is neither a good nor a bad moral Quality, but a physical Imperfection at most, and a very great Limitation arising from the Laws of the Union of Soul and Body.

3. That the Docility of the Children of the Orthodox, and the Love they have for Orthodoxy, is not a Quality any way different from that of Heterodox Children; because the same Children, who now are all Zeal for Orthodoxy, wou'd have bin just the same for Heterodoxy, and *vice versa,* if

they had bin bred up in another set of Opinions: whence it follows, that if Docility and Devotion were an effect of Original Sin in either sort, it must be so in both. Now 'twere impious maintaining this. Let's think of the Courier I spoke of a while ago.[237]

4. That tho it's somewhat strange, that Children shou'd with Joy and Transport embrace the most important Truths of a Paradise, Hell, Trinity, Incarnation, Original Sin, and all the other Doctrines propos'd to 'em, some according to *Rome,* others according to *Geneva,* &c. that they shou'd embrace 'em, I say, upon the Authority of a little School-Mistress or Master, or at most on that of the Curate or Minister of the Parish (for here's their whole Rule of Faith) yet one may easily account for this; it being but fit that a Child shou'd have Humility enough, not to presume on his own Lights more than on those of his Father, Mother, or Pedagogue, and <637> consequently shou'd believe 'em without reserve. Beside, that 'tis but reasonable he shou'd have a good Opinion enough of 'em, not to call their Sincerity in question; so that if on one hand he believe their Light to be greater than his own, and that they teach him what they believe to be true, he ought by all means to conform to their Opinions; and 'tis impossible but he shou'd, because to call their Opinions in question, and guard against 'em, 'twou'd require a great stock of ready Ideas, and this he is not Master of; the few he has, are afforded him by slow degrees, and at second-hand, and only to fortify one another thro the great Care of those who instruct him.

5. But whether that Facility in Children, of adopting all Opinions taught them in matter of Religion, be reckon'd Good or Evil, still it's certain, that 'tis a physical Perfection at least (if it be improper to call it a moral one, because antecedent to any free and reasonable Choice) to love what they take to be Truth, and hate what they take to be an Error. No matter whether their Guides deceive 'em or no; still the loving what one believes comes from God is conforming to Order, and the hating it wou'd not, altho it shou'd happen, that the thing hated was really displeasing to him: 'twere only by Accident, and beside our Intention, that we shou'd hate what God prohibits. And whoever loves that which he thinks approv'd by God, altho

237. See above, p. 476.

perhaps it is not, wou'd, by the same Motion of his Soul, love what is really approv'd in his sight, did he know it as such; as he who despises what he believes come from God, altho it comes not from <638> him, wou'd by the same Act of his Soul despise what really came from God, did he know it as such. This I think is what no one will deny me, who has the Sense to take this matter aright, and does not mistake my thought.

6. That since the great Facility of Children, in believing every thing told 'em without distinction, whether true or false, is a Quality, which morally speaking is neither Good nor Evil; it follows, that their embracing a Heresy with the firmest Persuasion, and which excludes all shadow of doubting, is no Sin in them: for, beside that this may proceed in a great measure from the Temper and Constitution, and from the way in which they have bin educated; we are moreover to consider the principal Reason already assign'd, to wit, that the same Child, who embraces a Heresy with the most obstinate and tenacious Belief, wou'd embrace the Truth altogether as firmly, if propos'd with the same Advantages as Error. So that one can no more say, that the opiniatre Spirit of an Heretick Child is a Mark of the depravation of his Soul, than that the Constancy with which the same Child wou'd have believ'd the Truth, if propos'd as the Lye was, was the Consequence of his Perverseness and Pravity of Heart. Now who dare advance such an Extravagance?

7. That if a Child may be strongly (or obstinately, if you will, for I shan't stand upon the Propriety of Words) persuaded that his Heresy is a thing perfectly well-pleasing to God, without the least mixture of Malice in his Persuasion, or Corruption of Heart; he may also, by the same Rule, be obstinately persuaded, that Ortho-<639>doxy is a Fundamental Error, more to be avoided than Plague or Leprosy. This is not believing two different Doctrines, but one and the same, propos'd in different terms; consequently the first cannot be innocent without the second, nor this without the other.

This alone is sufficient to make out the Position in the Title of this Chapter. For if once it's allow'd, that a Man may be under a full and intire Persuasion, that the Doctrines opposite to our own are false and detestable; if, I say, there may be such a Persuasion, without the least mixture of Malice or Corruption of Heart, it follows, that without the least tincture of the same Malice, one may believe all that flows naturally, and according to the inviolable Laws of Order, from this Persuasion: as first, That all the Arguments, in favor of Opinions contrary to our own, are mere Sophism and Cavil. Secondly, That we must take special care not to be ensnar'd by 'em, and remember the saying, *That Suspicion's the Mother of Security.* Thirdly, That if any Scruples or Doubts happen to be suggested to our Minds upon hearing the Reasons for the opposite side, we must encounter 'em with the Shield of Faith, as so many Temptations of the World or the Devil; and in general, be as deaf as the Adder, which stops her Ears to the Voice of the Charmer. Fourthly, That we must continually pray to God, that he wou'd give us Grace to persevere to our Lives end in the Faith to which we have bin call'd; and strengthen our selves in it more and more by reading his holy Word, and by Meditation. <640>

When once we come to this, and are resolv'd to lose no ground, there's neither Disputer nor written Controversy, that can persuade us out of what we have bin taught in our Childhood. For we slight all kind of Explication and Instruction that's offer'd to us; and are not at all startl'd at the Arguments of a subtle Adversary, which we are not able to answer. This, say we to our selves, is a Poisoner, who knows how to sweeten and gild his Pill. But what Judgment must we now make of those, who by this means are never to be recover'd from their Errors? Must we, according to the first Answer propos'd at the beginning of the thirteenth Chapter,[238] say, That they err thro Malice, because they refuse to consult an Oracle, which wou'd set 'em right, to wit, the Definitions of the Church of *Rome;* or because they read not the Scriptures with an humble teachable Disposition, zealous of the Truth, which was the second Answer propos'd in the same place? Neither I think can be pleaded; I have already given the reason with regard to the second Answer,[239] and here's something further to be offer'd upon it.

They who refuse to consult what may have bin defin'd by that Church, which has most Universality and Antiquity to plead, and the most invariable Union to the Chair of St. *Peter,* do this, either because they are afraid,

238. See above, p. 466.
239. See above, p. 468.

that by consulting it they shou'd find something to convince 'em they are in an Error; or else, because they are persuaded they shou'd get no good by consulting it, but rather expose themselves to the Snares of the Devil. In the first Case I'll allow, that if they be in an Error, they may be <641> deem'd to err wilfully and maliciously: for the Truth is not that which they love, seeing they are afraid to find it; they are only willing to believe, that the State they are in, and which they are loth to forsake, is reconcilable to Truth. In the second Case, every one sees, without my Help, that the Error is neither wilful nor malicious. Now as on one hand, there is none but God the Searcher of Hearts can know who they are, that continue in Error from the first alledg'd Motive, which is undoubtedly sinful, even tho they believ'd their own Religion good in the main; so I believe, on the other hand, that a World of People persevere in their first Opinions, and won't trouble their Heads with Disputes, Examinations, and nice Discussions, purely from the second alledg'd Motive: and all that can be said against those is, that their absolute Acquiescence in the Doctrines they imbib'd in their tender Years, is not so excusable when they are grown up to Mens Estate, as it was during their Childhood, and while under a Physical Inability of examining different Religions, and comparing what can be said *pro* and *con;* yet that they are not chargeable with the least degree of Hatred or Contempt for the Truth.

I repeat it too often perhaps; but 'tis because my Readers are not us'd to Explications of this kind: so that to work 'em into their Consideration, it's absolutely necessary to renew and represent 'em afresh from time to time; I shall therefore say it over again, That it is the greatest Illusion in the World, to imagine, that an Act of Love, which tends towards an Object in reality false, <642> but objectively[240] true, or, which is the same thing in plainer terms; which appears true to us, is not an Act of Love for Truth, in the utmost Rigor and Propriety, when we are mov'd to it from no other cause than a sincere Persuasion, that the Object on which it terminates is the Truth. Shou'd this be deny'd me, this Extravagance must of necessity follow; to wit, That a Heretick, thorowly persuaded that what he believes, is

240. See Appendixes, "Obsolete or Unusual Words or Meanings," p. 578 ("objectively").

the Truth, and loving what he believes, only from a firm Persuasion of its being the Truth, and which is much the same, ready to forsake and abhor it, if once convinc'd 'twas not the Truth, wou'd not love Orthodoxy, if he knew it distinctly such as it is in it self. I say, this is maintaining an Extravagancy, of which Man, unaccountable as he is, does not afford an Original; there are Combinations of Acts in this Supposition, which are in nature impossible.

Let's therefore say, when a Man is once come to this pass, as to love his Opinions only because he believes 'em true; 1. That he has a general most sincere Disposition to love the Truth wherever he finds it, which is a very excellent moral Quality; and that in effect he does love it: for will any one pretend, that a Miser who takes counterfeit Broad-pieces for true, and sets his Heart upon 'em, does not love Gold? 2. That the real Falseness of his Opinions, is not the Cause of his loving 'em. 3. That if what is really true appear'd such to him, he wou'd love and prefer that. 4. That he not only exceeds in the Love of Truth, him who knows the Truth, and does not love it; but may <643> even dispute this Love with him, who really knows and loves it.

Let's say further, that a Heretick who shews no regard for what he believes to be the Truth, wou'd shew as little for real Truth if he had happen'd to know that; and is consequently as guilty of despising the Truth, as if he were one of those Orthodox, who have a perfect indifference for the Truth which they do know. The Reason of this is obvious enough; because with regard to a Heretick indifferent for Religion, the Falseness is only an accidental Cause of his Indifference: just as with regard to a Heretick zealous against Orthodoxy, the Truth is only an accidental Cause of his Hatred to it. Now that which is a Cause only by Accident passes for nothing, when the Question is concerning an Action's being morally good or evil.

All this might be illustrated by the Case of two Men, who are to shoot at a Mark with a single Ball, and each to have a piece of Plate, if he hits at such a distance. We'l suppose one of the Plates chang'd, and a piece of Block-Tin laid in its room; they'l certainly shoot with as earnest an Intention of hitting the Mark, as if both were Sterling: and the real difference of the Object, and which they 'tis suppos'd are strangers to, abates not in the least of the ardency of either's desire to succeed. Is not this a faithful

Representation of two Men, sincerely zealous each for his own Religion, one really true, the other only in appearance? they move with the same Ardor towards the Prize and the Mark: and had the false bin presented to the first, so as he shou'd believe it true, he'd act just as he <644> did before; and the second, in like manner, if the true were presented to him, so as that he might believe it true.

But to return to the strong Persuasion which Education inspires, I shall add, that in places where there are two Religions which dispute the ground; the chief Care of Fathers and Mothers is to possess their Children betimes, that God has bin very gracious to them above a World of other Children, in ordering by his Providence that they shou'd be born in the true Religion. They accustom 'em to thank God Morning and Night for this particular Favor, and to beg him earnestly, that he wou'd not suffer the sacred Pledg of his Truth to be snatch'd from 'em, either thro the Wiles of the Devil, or the Deceitfulness of this World. There are some Parents whose Zeal carrys 'em to the making use of several little pious Frauds, as frighting their Children with Hobgoblins, or some Deformity of Body; unless they detest the opposite Communion. The natural and almost infallible Consequence of which is, that these Children, when come to Man's Estate, are most firmly convinc'd of the Truth of their own Religion, or which is the same thing of the Falsness of the other; that when they read the Scripture, or any Treatise of Controversy, 'tis with a design of confirming themselves in their first belief; and if Doubts or Difficultys arise, tending to weaken their Persuasion, that they look on 'em as Suggestions of Satan, Temptations which the World and the Flesh lay in their way, to surprize 'em into the Paths of Perdition. I'l even allow, that when they read the Scriptures, they don't expresly <645> pray to God to enlighten 'em, if the way they are in be erroneous. What can be infer'd from it? that they despise the Truth and love a Lye? By no means, but only that they overfirmly believe themselves in possession of the Truth. And is there in Conscience any thing more in this than Credulity, and want of an enlarg'd Philosophical Mind? Is there the least Trace of any Malice of Heart in it, or of that corrupt Source from whence Sin is deriv'd? Can one reasonably say, that a Heretick who refuses to confer with a learn'd Orthodox, whom he looks on as an artful Poisoner of Souls, and a dangerous Emissary of Satan, and who refuses this Conference on no other score but for fear he shou'd be seduc'd, hates the Light of Truth?

I have seen a great many Books of Devotion in my time, and Collections of Prayers on all Occasions, and for all States and Conditions, several preparatory Offices for the Lord's Supper; but never met in 'em with any such Request as this, That shou'd it be our misfortune to be mistaken concerning Images, Invocation of Saints, Real Presence, the Authority of the Church, Antichrist, &c. God wou'd be pleas'd to enlighten and recover us from our Error. No Religion or Church prescribes its Children any such Form; and shou'd any one from his private Authority begin it, he'd be look'd upon as weak in the Faith and wavering, and pity'd as a bruis'd Reed which ought not to be broken, or smoking Flax which ought not to be quench'd.[241] A Heretick therefore can't justly be requir'd, when persuaded from probable Reasons that he is in the right way (and the Persuasion of an Orthodox <646> is built on no surer grounds) to desire of God, that he wou'd enlighten him if he errs in such or such Points; since this can't be exacted from a Heretick, but it must be exacted from an Orthodox too, there being room enough for either to believe, that 'tis very possible he may be deceiv'd.

∞ CHAPTER XVII ∞

An Answer to what is objected, That all Errors are Acts of the Will, and consequently morally evil. *The Absurdity of this Consequence shewn; and a Rule offer'd for distinguishing Errors, which are morally evil, from those which are not.*

I Have bin longer upon this Question than I design'd, for I had resolv'd to reserve it to another place; but finding my self once enter'd, I cou'd not forbear enlarging on it, tho I don't pretend to have said all that the Matter might bear. I have pass'd over several Difficultys, which I know will be objected, and which may be better discuss'd elsewhere; what I have said being more than sufficient to destroy the pretended Disparity, which was

---

241. Cf. Isaiah 42:3.

to be confuted in this place. Let's now consider, what is to be answer'd to the Objection inserted in the Title of the Chapter.

I must allow those who make the Objection, that the new Philosophers[242] teach with a great <647> deal of Reason, that what was formerly call'd the second Operation of the Understanding, is truly an Operation of the Will; that's to say, all the Judgments we make upon Objects, whether by affirming concerning 'em that they are such and such, or by denying, are Acts proceeding from the Soul, not as capable of perceiving and knowing, but as capable of willing. Whence it follows, that since Error consists in our affirming concerning Objects what does not belong to 'em, or in our denying what does, therefore every Error is an Act of the Will, and consequently voluntary.

But so far is this from being any way favorable to the Cause of my Adversarys, that I desire nothing more to confound 'em, and deprive 'em of the only Arms they had left, after having yielded up their three first Disparitys. For the only thing left for them to say was, that a Judg who is deceiv'd in absolving the guilty and condemning the innocent, is under an involuntary Error, and consequently innocent: whereas if he be deceiv'd in taking an Orthodox Person for a Heretick, his Error is voluntary, and consequently sinful. All this falls to the ground, if it be true, as there's no room to doubt, and as the Authors of this Objection themselves suppose, that all Error is an Act of the Will: and therefore it's their business to fly if they can to the Asylum, which was taken from 'em in the ninth Chapter;[243] to wit, that all Error proceeds from a Source of Corruption, and consequently deserves Hell-Punishment.

Here then we find 'em reduc'd to a sad Alternative. They must of necessity say, either <648> that all Error being voluntary is sinful; or that there are Errors which are innocent, altho voluntary. If they chuse the first, Good Lord, what a Load of Absurditys do they draw down upon their own poor Backs! for as there are a great many Criticks, who maintain that the *Iliad* is preferable to the *Aeneid,* and that *Plautus*'s Comedys exceed those of *Terence;* and a great many others, who maintain, that the *Aeneid* surpasses

242. On the "new philosophy" see Appendixes, "Philosophical Controversies," p. 595.
243. See above, p. 438.

the *Iliad,* and that *Terence* is preferable to *Plautus;* it must of necessity follow, that one Party or other of these Criticks passes a false Judgment; that's to say, commits a Sin, according to the first Member of the Alternative. Besides, what shall we say to invincible Ignorance, an Ignorance of Fact, which excuses in the Sight of God and Men? What to Children sprung from the adulterous Embraces of their Mother; and who nevertheless, knowing nothing of that, inherit her Husband's Estate, in prejudice to his lawfully begotten Children, or his Relations? What if these poor Creatures die without making Restitution, and doing the proper Penance for all the Sins they have committed, as often as they thought their Mother an honest Woman, and that they had a natural Right to the Estate of her Husband, their reputed Father? Shall they be eternally damn'd? This single Circumstance were enough to overthrow this extravagant Hypothesis; to wit, that it tends to introduce the rankest Quietism[244] that ever enter'd into the Brain of the most expert Phanatick in the extatick Mysterys: for who dare affirm, without the fear of offending God by an erroneous Judgment, that a Man who has fasted three days has an Appetite? <649> Who dare believe, that the Dinner which his Cook sends him up is not poison'd? Where's the Judg who dare try any Cause, or the Physician who dare prescribe a Remedy, for fear of sinning in Judgments of this kind?

They must therefore stand by the other Member of the Alternative: but when once I have gain'd this Point, that there are Errors which are innocent tho voluntary; they must compound for the exclusion of some, and the including of others in the Class of Sins; they must find a Rule for determining such a thing is a Sin, such a thing is not. And till such time as they can furnish me a better, I have a right to make use of the following Rule, to wit,

That since there are some false Judgments, neither morally good nor morally bad, (such for example, as the Judgment of those who prefer the *Iliad* to the *Aeneid,* or of those who prefer the *Aeneid* to the *Iliad*) there's no false Judgment which precisely as false has any thing of a moral Qual-

---

244. "Quietism" is the name given to a version of religious mysticism condemned by the Catholic Church, but here Bayle seems to use it in a broader sense for any doctrine that implies that persons should give up choosing and acting on their own choice.

ification; but that to make it of an Act purely indifferent become morally evil, we must necessarily be determin'd to it from some wicked Motive: as if we judg *Homer,* for example, excels *Virgil,* purely to have the Satisfaction of contradicting one we have a dislike for, whom we have a mind to vex, or be reveng'd on; or because we hope to gain the Reputation of a Superiority of Genius, and be rank'd above others in competition with us. This is one sure way of making an Error, in its own nature perfectly indifferent, become a Sin.

But here it will be fit to observe, that not only they who err'd in preferring *Homer* to *Virgil* <650> from any such Motive, wou'd be guilty of a Sin; but they likewise, who did not err in giving him the Preference. So that by ill luck for my Adversarys, Truth has no more Privilege here than Error; for if the *Iliad* in reality excels the *Aeneid,* they who hold the Affirmative judg right, and they who hold the Negative judg wrong: yet the Judgment of the first sort, better indeed physically than that of the latter, is not however morally better, both being Acts which morally speaking are neither good nor bad; consequently if what renders the Act of those who are deceiv'd evil, occur in the Act of those who light on the Truth, the Act of the latter becomes morally evil, no less than that of the former. So that on supposition, that the *Iliad* is a better Poem than the *Aeneid;* they who are determin'd to judg it so, by any Motive of Hatred, Envy, Revenge, or Vanity, sin as much as they, who from the same Motives* affirm, the *Aeneid* excels the *Iliad.* I don't enlarge so much on this Remark without some Reason; it has a Relation and Influence on other Matters.

Hence I think we may be able to form a Rule for distinguishing Errors sinful and not sinful; to wit, That all Error is sinful, when the Party is led into or entertain'd in it by any Principle of which one knows the Disorder, as a Love of Ease, a Spirit of Contradiction, Jealousy, Envy, Vanity.

For example, if a Man who is at an age to make use of his Reason and Liberty (for there's no Case to be put before this Age) continues in <651> the Errors he has suck'd in with the Milk, because he won't examine whether the Religion in which he has bin educated is the true, as judging

---

* *Take notice, that I all along here mean mental Affirmation, for the verbal without the mental is not Error but Lying.*

the Inquiry too painful, and chusing to take his pleasure rather than this trouble; or rather because he's afraid of finding it erroneous, in which case his Conscience wou'd teaze him to forsake a Religion he's intirely pleas'd with, and hinder his enjoying quietly the Comforts it affords: if, I say, a Man persist in his Errors from such Motives, they become criminal; for then he plainly shews, that he loves his Pleasures more than the Truth, and instead of persevering in his Religion because he believes it true, is willing and industrious to believe it true, because it sutes with and indulges the Desires of the Flesh.

A Man also who persists in his Errors, because having maintain'd 'em by word of Mouth, or by Writing, or Messages, or otherwise with great Reputation, dreads declining in his worldly Glory, if he shou'd come to embrace the contrary of what he had once believ'd and taught, and follow this new Opinion: such a Man, I say, errs not in the Sincerity of his Mind; his Error is attended with Sin.

Nor he who is loth to give his Enemys the satisfaction of being able to reproach him, that he had bin a long time a Heretick, and under an extreme Blindness of Understanding.

Nor, lastly, he who shou'd be sorry the Religion his mortal Enemy preach'd and defended with great applause, shou'd prove the true.

These and such-like Motives, whose Obliquity is notorious from natural Light and Conscience <652> (for no one dare own that he suffers himself to be led by such Motives) and which are capable of hindring a Man's forsaking his Errors, render 'em wilful and criminal.

As to those, who being born in the true go over to a false Religion, in a Persuasion that they forsake Error for Truth, and who had bin led into this Persuasion either by some Affront receiv'd in their first Religion, or by the Unlikelihood of passing their time as agreeably in it, according to the Opinion of this World, as in another; or by the occasions which another Sect might afford 'em of gratifying their Revenge, or from any other Principle of this kind: I say in like manner, that these err, and shou'd be reputed to err voluntarily, according to the Sense of this Word in the old Philosophy;[245] and that they come under the Condemnation of Divine Justice.

245. See Thomas Aquinas, *Summa theologiae*, 1–2, q. 6, a. 8, and q. 76, a. 2–4.

But I dare not make the same Judgment on a Man, who without any secret Reserve, or hidden Motive whose Obliquity he perceives or knows; but purely because naturally his Turn of Understanding is such, that he's struck much more by one sort of Reasons than by another; quits the best Sect of Christianity, to embrace one with a thousand Errors in it: for we must consider that this Sect, as erroneous as it is, has its offensive and defensive Arms, puts the Orthodox sometimes to a very strange puzzle, and supports it self by Reasons, which some here and there, by an odd Turn of Understanding, and I don't know what sort of Proportion between certain Objects and certain Complexions, shall relish much more than the Arguments of the Ortho-<653>dox, and think 'em much more solid, and tending more to the Glory of God. I can't for my part see, that there must necessarily be a criminal Passion at heart, to make a Man prefer the Reasons which are to be alledg'd against some Points of Orthodoxy, to the Reasons which support 'em.

What Judgment is to be made of those who won't enter into Disputes.

As to those who continue in their Errors of Birth and Education, purely from this Reason, that they won't examine into the Doctrines or Principles of any other Sect, as well because persuaded their own Religion is the true and all the rest false, as because they have heard say, that this Research is the business neither of a Day nor a Year, but an almost infinite Labor, beset with a thousand Snares which Satan has cunningly interwove with it, and in which the greatest Genius's have bin catch'd and brought to perdition; I dare not for my part tax 'em with a Contempt for the Truth, and wilful Error. This I will say, that philosophically speaking they are guilty of a great piece of Imprudence; because it's most certain, as *Seneca* says, that a great many wou'd become really wise, if they did not fancy themselves so already; *Multi ad Sapientiam pervenirent, nisi jam se pervenisse putarent:* and because their Persuasion not arising from a free and reasonable Choice, upon a fair comparing the Reasons of both sides, favors more of the Machine than the rational Creature; but further I don't see in it either Malice or the Will <654> to err. The Case is not the same here as when a Scholar refuses to study; his Ignorance, I own; is wilful, for he knows he's ignorant, and ever shall be so unless he study: but the Heretick now before us believes he's already possess'd of the Truth, and refuses to examine, only because he believes there's no need of it.

I desire any Minister wou'd tell me, what Judgment he wou'd make of any of his Flock, who shou'd tell him he had always bin so firmly persuaded of the Doctrine of the Trinity, that he never cou'd enter into a Dispute upon it with any Socinian, nor hear their Reasons with any patience: He wou'd praise him for't without doubt.

So that the refusing to examine is not morally evil in it self; for if it were, 'twou'd be always evil.

Oh! but, say they, it's always evil where the Party is in an Error. This is easily confuted by my fore-going Remarks; for can any one deny me this, That the firm Belief of a false Doctrine precisely as such, is neither a good nor a bad Quality, morally speaking? Can any one deny me, for example, but the same Force (I say numerically the same) which acts on the Understanding to apply it to Objects, and which has made a Turkish Child believe that the Alcoran is a Divine Book, wou'd have made him believe the same concerning the Bible, if directed on this Object? Whence it follows, that if this Force was evil in the Turkish Child, it must likewise be evil in the Christian Child; and if good in one, it must be good in the other too: which ought to instruct us, that morally speaking it's <655> neither good nor bad; and whether it beget in a Child the Belief of a Falshood, or that of the Truth, still it's an Act which thus far is neither morally good nor evil: and consequently to become an evil moral Quality, the Soul which has this Force must direct it by Motives, whose Obliquity it knows, rather on this Object than on that; as to become morally good, the Soul must direct it, from Motives whose Rectitude and Goodness it knows, rather on one Object than another. Accordingly I shan't stick to say, that all the Morality which enters into the Acts of our Soul, proceeds from the Motives which determine it, with the Knowledg of the Cause, to direct these Acts towards certain Objects; and that the Nature of the Objects makes no alteration, consider'd as it is in it self, but only as envisaged in the Understanding.

From whence I shall draw this Conclusion, That the refusing to examine not becoming a good moral Quality, precisely because they who do refuse it have the Truth of their side, but rather because believing they have the Truth they won't give themselves a needless trouble, and which might throw 'em into Illusion; it's not material towards knowing whether they who do refuse act morally well or ill, to know whether they are in an Error or no; all lies in knowing by what Motive they make this Refusal: and if this Motive be exactly the same in those who err, but who are under a strong Persuasion that they hold the Truth, as in those who are so persuaded upon good grounds; 'twere absurd to pretend that it's sinful in the first and righteous in the latter; the nature of <656> the Objects, as I have already said, having no influence on the Morality of our Actions, consider'd as they are really in themselves, but only as reputed such or such by our Understandings.

'Twill now be easily conceiv'd, that according to these Principles a Man born in the true Religion, but who continues in it from corrupt Motives, is not one jot a better Man than he who from the same Motives continues in the false Religion in which he had bin bred; and that he who goes over from a false Religion to the true upon wicked Motives, is not a jot more righteous than he who goes over from the true Religion to a false on the same Motives.

If it be true, as a great many have believ'd, that the Duke of *Guise* and the Prince of *Conde*'s Interests were so diametrically opposite, that had either chang'd his Religion, the other wou'd certainly have done the same;[246] I shou'd not for my part chuse the Condition of one rather than t'other at the Tribunal of God: tho as for any thing else, one of 'em might always have done great service to the good Cause, and the other to the bad; but as each wou'd have made his own Glory his chief End, each may read his Doom in that Saying of JESUS CHRIST,* *Verily they have their Reward:* or in that Answer which at the last Day shall be given to those who shall plead that they have prophesy'd in his Name, and in his Name have cast out Devils and done Miracles; *I never knew you, depart from me ye that work Iniquity.*† 'Tis <657> being a Worker of Iniquity, to cleave to the better

* Mat. 6.
† Mat. 7. 23.
246. See DHC, art. "Guise, Francis de," rem. A.

Church not from a Love for the Truth, but from worldly Interest, or any other human Consideration.

In the mean time, I won't deny but there may be those who have rectify'd in the sequel what had bin amiss in the Motives which first induc'd 'em to embrace the good Cause, God sometimes making use of our Passions to convert us: but to this end it's necessary that whatever was inordinate in these Motives cease acting on us, in which case likewise the continuing in an Error may become sincere; for Men shou'd once for all be undeceiv'd in this Point, which was confuted in the foregoing Chapter,[247] That when one loves Error purely because he believes it the Truth, he does not love the Truth. This is making a wrong Judgment in this matter; it is actually a Love of Truth: for leave a Man who is in this Disposition exactly as he is, only substitute in the place of the Object which he loves, tho false, that Object which is really true, and you shall see him love this new Object just as he lov'd the other.

How much it concerns us, in the Acts of our Understanding, not to confound the Physical and Moral.

I shall conclude the Chapter with this Remark, That nothing has led the World into greater Mistakes in judging of false Opinions, than the little care Men take of distinguishing between that which is physical in the Acts of our Soul, and that which is moral. I hope the hint <658> I have given may be useful towards making 'em beware confounding these two Things; and for my part I shall never repent having contributed to hinder the multiplying Sins without necessity: for if the multiplying real Beings without a necessity, be condemn'd as a Breach upon good Sense and the Ideas of Order, by a much stronger Reason may we condemn the multiplying Sins without need, which are only Monstrositys, and Fantoms of Being rather than real Beings, and of which we have too many already in the World.

Let's say then, that all Error, of what kind soever, is a Defect, or physical Imperfection; and every true Judgment, of what kind soever, a physical Perfection: for every true Judgment is a faithful Representation of Objects,

247. See above, p. 482.

such as they are in themselves, and outside of the Understanding; whereas all Error is a false or unfaithful Representation of Objects as they are outside the Understanding. Now as 'tis a physical Imperfection in a Painter, to paint a Man so ill that 'tis the hardest thing imaginable to find him in his Picture, and that a Looking-Glass which shews the Objects naturally and just as they are in themselves, is more valuable than another Glass which transforms or disfigures to such a degree, that they are not to be known; so it's an ill physical Quality in the Soul, to form an Idea of Objects, which does not represent 'em such as they are in themselves: and that Understanding which takes 'em exactly to the life, is without doubt preferable to another, in which the Images are all overturn'd or strangely distorted. But on the other hand, as *Apelles, Michael Angelo,* or any other famous Painter, <659> excels not in the least as to the moral part, those wretched Painters who are forc'd to write at the bottom of their Pieces, *a Bear, a Rose,* &c. as, I say, these two sorts of Painters have not the least advantage one over t'other in point or moral Good precisely from hence, that one copys Nature to a wonder, the other after a very vile manner; and that to the end some excel the others, morally speaking, it's necessary they shou'd propose for themselves some morally better end, and paint from some morally better Principle; so those Souls which believe the Truth, and those which believe an Error, are not so far either morally better or worse one than t'other: and the only advantageous difference of either side, as to moral Good, must arise from one Set's believing what they believe from a Motive whose Rectitude and Goodness is known to 'em, the other's believing what they believe from a Motive in which they have perceiv'd some Obliquity.

I shan't here consider what the Cartesians teach,[248] that one is guilty of a great Temerity in affirming things which he does not distinctly comprehend, and which he has not examin'd with the utmost Exactness and Nicety, whether it be his good fortune to succeed in his Inquirys or no; that is, the Temerity is no less in those who light on the Truth by chance than in those who miss it: I shan't, I say, stand to consider this, because it's manifest this Maxim transplanted to Religion and Morality wou'd not do near so well as it does in Physicks. <660>

248. See Appendixes, "Philosophical Controversies," p. 595.

꙼꙼ CHAPTER XVIII ꙼꙼

A Discussion of three other Difficultys.

First Difficulty. *Knowing the Obliquity of the Motive, is not necessary towards denominating an Action evil.*

You have all along argu'd, say they, that to make an Error become Sin, it is necessary not only that the Motive which leads to it be evil, but also that we know it to be evil.

But this is a false Supposition; for how many wicked Springs are there in the Heart of Man, which are utterly unknown to him? Who is it that knows himself thorowly enough, to spy out that hidden Poison which Self-love and natural Corruption mixes with all our Actions and Judgments?

I answer, that as nothing were more capriciously unjust, than to require that an Officer plac'd Centry at the Gate of a City to hinder the coming in of Man or Goods, or any visible thing, from places suspected of a Plague or Infection, shou'd likewise hinder the pestiferous Atoms which mix imperceptibly with the Air being brought in by a Blast of Wind; so it were notoriously unjust to require that the Soul shou'd defend it self not only against all sensible Temptations, but also from Enemys absolutely unknown to it, hidden Springs of Action, and blended Poisons, the Names, and Place of Abode, <661> and Qualitys of which are utterly unknown to it. To reduce all this then to something reasonable, we must say, that he who does not narrowly examine himself is a Bubble to his own Heart, and imagines he acts from a Love of God when he is principally mov'd by Self-love; but still it must be suppos'd that it's no hard matter, if a Man will deal plainly with himself, to discover these pretended invisible Springs of Action. Certain it is, that a body may sift 'em out, may perceive, and may know 'em if he endeavor it with some degree of Application: but here's what happens to a world of People; They find a deal of Satisfaction from the Testimony of a good Conscience, and find that this Satisfaction is so much the more comfortable, as they fancy they have acted intirely from a Motive of Religion and Piety. However they perceive that perhaps some human Considerations mix with it; and this Conjecture, which is far from groundless, disturbs their Peace of Mind. What's to be done in this case? They won't examine themselves too rigorously, for fear of discovering what can't chuse but fill 'em with Confusion; so they suffer the Force of these corrupt Principles, these secret Passions, to grow upon 'em. But in reality they are not unperceivable: and if People don't discover 'em clearly enough, 'tis because they are resolv'd, from Motives which they perceive are none of the most justifiable, to conceal 'em from themselves; and in this case the Ignorance or Error is not attended with a thorow Sincerity. So that my Doctrine suffers nothing by this Difficulty. <662>

Second Difficulty. *If we were not Sinners, we shou'd not mistake Truth for Falshood, and contrariwise.*

This second Attack is still weaker than the former; it imports, that Original Sin is the Original Cause of all the false Judgments which Men make.

But from hence it follows, that if Men had remain'd in a State of Innocence, they might have known the moment they were born that Colors don't subsist in the Objects; and as soon as they saw the Sun rise and set, they cou'd infallibly have decided whether that turns round us, or whether the Earth turns round daily on its own Center; and so upon all the other Problems of Physicks: They had always most certainly declar'd the Truth, or they had religiously have forborn judging upon things which they did not certainly know; but neither is very probable. On the contrary, it's very probable that the Angels themselves of the highest Order of Seraphims are ignorant of most of the Secrets of Nature, and don't see a jot into the Questions of Continuity, or Motion in general, or into the Causes of the Velocity and Slowness of the Motion of certain Bodys, *&c.* And if Men in a State of Innocence had suspended their Judgments of things until they had a scientifick Certainty, 'tis probable they had bin Pyrrhonists upon most Questions of Physicks all their life long.[249]

But all this makes little against me, and I have already said enough to it

249. See Appendixes, "Philosophical Controversies," p. 591.

in the ninth Chapter.[250] What's most perplexing in it to my Adversarys, <663> is, that their Objection proves too much; for either they prove nothing against me, or else they must mean, that since Man if he were not a Sinner wou'd never take Truth for Falshood, this is an Argument that he sins when he's deceiv'd: A Consequence which I have already confuted in the foregoing Chapter,[251] and which wou'd prove,

1. That a Man who is deceiv'd in judging that the Colors which he sees are really in the Objects, or that *Lucretius*'s Lines are finer than *Virgil*'s; or that there's neither Void, nor imaginary Space, nor substantial Forms, or that there are; and so of all other Questions on which the Criticks and Philosophers are divided; commits a Sin.

2. That a Judg who acquits a Person in reality guilty, but against whom there has not bin sufficient Evidence; or who condemns a Person innocent in reality, but who has bin convicted according to due Course of Law; violates the Law of God concerning the punishing the Guilty, and acquitting the Innocent.

3. That a Physician who following the Rules of his Art, and the best Lights his Experience furnishes him, prescribes his Patient a Potion that kills him, is guilty of Murder.

4. That a Woman, who deceiv'd by the Resemblance of Persons, and a thousand other Circumstances, mistakes another Man for her Husband, is guilty of Adultery.

5. That a Child sprung from his Mother's adulterous Embraces, of which neither her Husband nor he have the least suspicion, who comes in for Heir to her Husband, is guilty of Fraud and Usurpation. <664>

6. That a Lunatick, a Demoniack, a Frantick Person, a Woman who has had so strong a Love-Potion given her, that she's deflower'd without her perceiving it, commit as many Sins as they suffer or act things contrary to the Law of God.

7. Last of all, that there wou'd be no such thing in the Universe, which yet has bin acknowledg'd by all Casuists, Lawyers, and Philosophers, as

250. See above, p. 438.
251. See above, p. 486.

invincible Ignorance, which renders Actions involuntary, and excuses at the Tribunal of God and Man.

For concerning all these Errors and Actions I might say, as my Adversarys do, that one wou'd not fall into 'em if he were not a Sinner; and conclude as they conclude. But this is a Doctrine so sensless and extravagant, that the bare shewing it is enough to make any one drop this second Difficulty, who shou'd ever have thought it worth the proposing.

They have only one poor Evasion now left; to wit, That in Matters Civil and Philosophical Error has nothing that favors our corrupt Nature; so that if we prefer it to the Truth, 'tis not from any corrupt Principle: But that in matters of Religion the Case is otherwise; the Truth there combats our Vices, the Error favors 'em, and therefore we refuse to believe that what is true is Truth from a Principle of Corruption and Concupiscence, and are carry'd to judg that Error is the Truth from the same Principle.

This I shall have a great many things to say to, when I come to examine[252] the eleventh Chapter of the *Treatise of the Rights of the two Sovereigns.* At present I shall content my self with these three Remarks. <665>

First, It's false that Errors in matters of Religion are for the most part more favorable to a Corruption of Heart than Truths; for we shall find, if we consider this matter, that false Religions are much more encumber'd with burdensom Observances and painful Superstitions than the true. We shall find, that almost all the Heads of Sects have drawn Crouds of Followers after 'em, purely by preaching a severe Morality, and by crying out against the Remissness of the Church. It's even true, that they who in the last Age restor'd the pure Worship of God in the West, ow'd their Success chiefly to a Reformation of Manners, which they insisted on with a wonderful Zeal; and 'tis very probable they had had still greater Successes, if their Enemys had not fram'd a pretence for running 'em down as a sensual Generation, on their declaiming with an astonishing Force against Lent, Vows of Celibacy, and other Institutions which in reality are grievous to Flesh and Blood. Whence one may infer, that let Man be ever so corrupt, he's generally speaking more inclin'd to believe a thing comes from God, when it does not flatter his natural Inclinations, than when it gratifies 'em.

252. Not found in the work as published. See above, p. 390, note 168.

My second Remark is, That in what Communion soever we place the purest Orthodoxy, still there will be Sects which will reproach it, as disapproving certain Doctrines only because they are too severe. Thus when *Tertullian* became a Heretick, he reproach'd the Catholicks, as if from too great a Love for the World and the Flesh they had condemn'd the Abstinences and the *Xerophagys* of the Montanists.[253] Might not the Jews tell those who turn'd Christians, that <666> Judaism appear'd to 'em false, only because it impos'd too hard a Yoke of Ceremonys, grievous and disagreeable to Nature; and Christianity true, because it destroy'd this heavy Yoke? But this had bin a poor Cavil in the Jews, because the new Christians were no sooner deliver'd from this petty Servitude, but they enter'd upon much a heavier, to wit, that of continual Persecutions, and the Practice of the pure Gospel-Morality.

Which brings me to my last Remark. There's no Christian Sect which does not know for certain Truth, that the Gospel forbids Revenge, coveting our Neighbor's Goods, his Wife, or his Daughter; that it commands us to love our Enemys, to pray for those who persecute us, to live soberly, chastly, humbly, and religiously. These are Truths which grate corrupt Nature, and are much harder to be practis'd than the Abstinences of *Pythagoras* or *Montanus;* these are what lie heavier upon our Hearts than the most sublime speculative Mysterys. Whence comes it then, if the Objection of my Adversarys hold, that the most extravagant Hereticks, who refuse to believe these Mysterys, believe firmly all these other Truths so hard to Flesh and Blood? There's no answering this, but by giving up the second Difficulty, and by owning that if these same Hereticks had bin educated in the Belief of these Mysterys, as they have bin in a Belief of the Precepts of Gospel-Morality, or if they found these Mysterys as clearly reveal'd in Scripture as the moral Dutys, that they wou'd believe one as firmly as the other. And 'tis a very strange thing, that they will have Men reject certain Doctrines as false from Sensuality and <667> Corruption, who yet admit several oth-

---

253. Tertullian joined the Montanist sect. The Montanists advocated strict fasting and abstension from wine (xerophagy). See Tertullian, *On Fasting. In Opposition to the Psychics, Ante-Nicene Fathers,* ed. A. Roberts and J. Donaldson (Edinburgh: Clark, 1867–97), vol. 4, p. 102ff.

ers as true, which expose 'em to a thousand Miserys and Persecutions, as I have shewn in the fourteenth Chapter.[254]

Let 'em turn then as many ways as they please, the pretended dependance of false Opinions on the Malice of our corrupt Nature, either as set forth in the ninth Chapter, or in the thirteenth and following,[255] or as urg'd here; they shall never be able to offer any thing whereon to form a good general Reason. I don't deny, but Errors in particular Persons proceed from a corrupt ground of Heart; but who can detect and single out these particular Persons? And who dare deny, if he think better of it, but they are incomparably a smaller number than the others?

I refer my Readers to what I have remark'd in my *Commentary,* Chap. 10. pag. 266. and the following.

> Third Difficulty. *St.* Paul *in the fifth Chapter to the* Galatians, *reckons Heresys among the Works of the Flesh, which damn those who commit 'em.*

This third Difficulty is of greater weight than the other two, yet it's far from being beyond a satisfactory Answer.

I shan't insist in this place, that when JESUS CHRIST reckons up the evil Works which proceed from the Heart, such as* Adultery, Fornication, Murder, *&c.* he does not mention Heresys, for this wou'd prove nothing: as well because <668> St. *Mark* introduces the Son of God giving a longer Catalogue of this kind than St. *Matthew,* whence one may infer, that if the latter had omitted some, the former might likewise have omitted others; as because St. *Paul*'s affirming any thing is a sufficient Authority, tho he were the only inspir'd Writer who did affirm it. Let's proceed therefore to some more solid Remark on this matter.

I say then, that the Term which St. *Paul* here makes use of, is extremely equivocal, and one might write a Book on the different Fates of this Word, and the different Significations it has born, as well among the Greeks as

---

* *St.* Mar. *ch.* 7. *v.* 21. *St.* Mat. *ch.* 15. *v.* 19.
254. See above, p. 471.
255. See above, pp. 436, 495.

among the Romans, Pagan and Christian. The Scripture does not always make use of it in an ill Sense; sometimes indeed it does, and this alone were enough to render the Notion of it hard to be determin'd or fixt to a nicety. This being the Case, who can bar my saying, that by Heresy in the cited Passage, St. *Paul* understands the Attempt of a Person, who, to make himself Head of a Party, and to gratify a restless, turbulent, and ambitious Humor, sows Discord in the Church, and rends its Unity; his Conscience at the same time telling him, that the Doctrines he opposes are good, at least very tolerable; or who's induc'd to doubt 'em from mere Vanity, and a desire of distinguishing himself, and contradicting some great and holy Doctor of the Church, for whom he had conceiv'd an extreme Prejudice or Jealousy? I own, and all the World will be of my mind in this point, that Heresy thus understood, is a Sin which cries for Vengeance, and deserves Hell-fire. <669>

One might maintain with great probability, that St. *Paul* has an Eye in this place only to the Authors of Schisms and Divisions, and to those who oppose the current Doctrine, not from any Zeal for the Truth, or a Reformation, but purely to make a Sect apart. Such Men very rarely act from a sincere Principle, and seldom prefer the Instincts of Conscience to those of Ambition, Jealousy, Spleen, or some other criminal Passion, which they themselves know to be wicked, and which they dare not avow. Sometimes too they who declare for their Party, act more from personal Feelings, Family Quarrels, Jealousy, Vanity, than any godly design of advancing wholesom Doctrine. It may even happen, that they who have Reason at bottom to cry out against the current Doctrines, are tempted to separate from the main Stock by corrupt Motives; and tho they may be Instruments of good, by erecting an Orthodox Communion, are nevertheless extremely wicked, and altogether as inexcusable as the Heads of a Heterodox Sect. Be that how it will, the Heresys St. *Paul* here speaks of, are, in my Opinion, an Attempt to advance particular Doctrines, and form a Party in the Church, proceeding from a Spirit of Pride, Contradiction, Jealousy, &c. and not from any Zeal for the House of God.

But as these very Men may impose on others by an orderly outward Behavior, and a mighty Appearance of Zeal; defend their Opinions with a deal of Eloquence, and specious Reasoning, and give the contrary Doctrines an odious turn: 'tis very possible, that many of their Followers may act from a sincere Principle; and 'tis very evi-<670>dent, their Posterity may, as I have shewn already in this *Commentary.* Thus the very same Opinions may be those Heresys which St. *Paul* speaks of, and may not. In those who broach 'em from Motives which they know to be sinful, they shall; and they shall not in those who hold 'em only because they sincerely believe 'em true.

I might confirm this Explication by that famous Passage of St. *Paul* to his Disciple *Titus,* where he exhortes him to avoid a Man who is a Heretick after the first and second Admonition; *Knowing,* says he, *that he who is such, is subverted and sinneth, being condemn'd by his own Judgment.*[256]

Words, which shew as clear as Noon-day, that the Character of Heresys damnable and sinful, according to St. *Paul,* is the resisting the Truth, known as such by the very Person who broaches the Heresy; and consequently, that those who err from a sincere Principle come not under the Charge of Heresy. But I think I have another kind of Argument at hand, which perhaps may be more convincing than any Inferences or Observations from this Passage, in the last Chapter of the Epistle to *Titus.*

It's certain, that St. *Paul,* in that Passage of the Epistle to the *Galatians,* does not speak worse of Heresys, than of Murder, Adultery, Theft, Poisoning, Drunkenness; he says of all these, and of a great many more, that they are Works of the Flesh, and that they who commit such things, shall not inherit the Kingdom of God. Does not common Sense, and natural Light inform us, supposing the Real Presence were the Truth, that they who believe it not upon a Persuasion of its being a Falshood, injurious to JESUS CHRIST, <671> are not guilty of a greater Sin than they who commit Murder, who poison, rob, or defile their Neighbor's Wife? There's no Foundation then, either in Scripture or Reason, for believing, that Heresy is a much greater Sin than Murder, Adultery, Robbery; and consequently I have ground to say, that whatever is necessary to render the three last Actions sinful, is likewise necessary to render Heresy sinful; and that what excuses with regard to the three, ought also to acquit with regard to the fourth.

Now, is it not true, that Murder, Adultery, Robbery, *&c.* cease to be Sins,

256. Titus 3:10–11.

when committed involuntarily, that's to say, when the Party is ignorant that he kills, commits Adultery, or robs? This can't be deny'd, because it's allow'd by all the World, 1. That a Physician, who does his Endeavors to recover his Patient, and who nevertheless prescribes him Remedys which are the Cause of his Death, is not guilty of a Sin; nor a Judg, who sentences a Man, innocent indeed but convicted by due course of Law, to the Gallows; nor one, who in hunting shoots into a Thicket, where he believes he hears some wild Beast stir, and kills a poor Creature, who had bin hiding there from his Creditors or the Bailiffs. 2. That a Woman who, honestly deceiv'd by the Resemblance, takes a wrong Man for her Husband, or one that her Husband himself introduces into her Bed while she is asleep, commits no Sin. 3. That a Person who possesses himself of the Estate of his reputed Father, in prejudice of the true Children or Relatives, sins not. 4. That a Servant who fills his Master a Glass of poison'd Wine (which he knows nothing of) and drinks of the <672> Bottle himself, is neither his Master's Murderer, nor his own. 5. Last of all, that a Man, who calling for a Glass of Wine or Ale to quench his Thirst, receives a Glass of some Potion, which makes him drunk and mad, is not answerable for what Mischief he does in his Madness, as he wou'd be if he had known the Nature of the Potion.

It's a constant Truth then, that the greatest Sins, when involuntary, cease to be such, and that an honest Ignorance renders 'em involuntary, as we have it very justly explain'd in all our Courses of Philosophy.[257] Heresy therefore has the same Privilege, for no Reason can be assign'd why it shou'd not; and consequently those Heresys, which are Works of the Flesh, and which exclude from Heaven, ought to be attended with a knowledg of their being evil Works, as well as Murder, Adultery, Robbery, otherwise they'l become innocent as well as these.

'Tis impossible for my Adversarys to get clear of this, but by denying there are any sincere Heticks, or which is all one, by maintaining, that when People err in points of Faith, 'tis because they have maliciously refus'd Instruction. But besides what has bin urg'd already in this matter,[258] who sees not how absurd it is to imagine, that 'tis in the power of a Lapland Boor,

257. See above, p. 467, note 229.
258. See above, p. 467.

converted to Christianity by a *Swedish* Minister, to discover, in spite of all this Minister's Reasons, the Falshood of Consubstantiation, and become intractable on this head, after he had fairly submitted to that of the Trinity? 'Twou'd undoubtedly be a mighty source of Tranquillity, and Peace of Heart and Conscience to the Boor, that he had follow'd his own Lights in this single <673> point, rather than those of his Minister, whom he had follow'd in all the rest.

> *That the Love of what appears true, without its being so, is not a*
> *Love of Falshood.*

What deceives the World most in this matter, and I'm amaz'd People shou'd be so generally carry'd away by a mere childish Illusion, is, Their supposing as a thing incontestable, that the adhering to a Doctrine, false in it self, but in appearance true, and embrac'd purely on account of its appearing so, is an Act, not of Love for the Truth, but of Love for Falshood. What a stupid Judgment is this, and how very far from just? This Adherence, in the Circumstances I have suppos'd, is as much a Love for Truth, as an Adherence to the truest Doctrine. They'l oblige me (and therefore, to provoke those who think they are able, I defy 'em too) to shew me a difference (I'l be satisfy'd with any, be it ever so little) between this Adherence to Error, and adhering to the Truth, as to the moral part.

Who ever doubted, that a Man, extremely fond of antient Medals, but a bad Judg, and who, having purchas'd a great many false ones, which yet he thinks true, is ravish'd at the thoughts of his possessing such a Treasure; has as great a Passion for antient Medals as another equally fond of such things, but who has Skill enough to collect none but the true? There's a vast difference between the two Men in point of Judgment and Capacity, but none at all as to their Passion for antient Medals. <674>

What shall we say of two Men, who being to chuse the beautifullest among several Sisters, shou'd pitch, one upon the eldest, the other on the youngest, each imagining he had chosen the Beauty; tho the youngest, in the Judgment of the World, is but so so, and the eldest perfectly handsom? Can any one pretend, strictly speaking, that these two Men differ, not only in their Fancy, but also in their Love of Beauty in general? Is it not on the contrary plain, that both are equally Admirers of it, and that the younger Sister's Lover adores Beauty as much as the elder Sister's; and that were Beauty a reasonable Being, it wou'd owe as much good Will to one as to t'other, on account of the Homage paid by each, equally her faithful and devoted Servants?

Have People never consider'd this old Maxim, *There's no Love without Knowledg, Nullum volitum quin praecognitum,* as plain as Noon-day? If People reflected on it, wou'd they say, that a Heretick loves a Lye; he who does not perceive the least shadow of Falshood in the Religion he loves, and which he loves under no other Notion or Idea but that of true? Can he love a Falsity that he does not know? Truth then is what he believes he beholds in the Opinions which he loves, and not the Falshood of 'em, which he's perfectly blind to. In a word, he who wou'd talk in a Philosophical Strictness, must say, that the Center of Love, or its direct and immediate Object, is always that Quality which determines our Love, whether it subsist really outside us, or only in our own Idea.

In like manner 'twere absurd to say, that a Roman Catholick, who shou'd write against the Real Presence, and going up and down like a <675> Knight-errant, shou'd act the part of a Hugonot Convertist, lov'd the Truth. I suppose him a Man of that kidney as to love only forbidden Pleasure, and perverse enough to be pleas'd with the figurative Sense, purely because he believes it false. He must, on this Supposition, love a thing in reality true; yet the central Point, and proper Object of his Love, wou'd be only Falshood. *Bonitas voluntatis a solo pendet objecto,* as *Thom. Aquin.* has very justly said, *quaest. 9. art.* 2.[259] Now the Logicians teach, when they treat of the first Operation of the Understanding, that it is never false, not even when it represents to us a Dog as a Wolf, because its Object then is not the Dog, which reflects the Rays of Light to our Eyes, but the Wolf in our Imagination.

---

259. "The goodness of the will depends on its object alone." Reference incorrect. It should be to Thomas Aquinas, *Summa theologiae,* 1–2, q. 19, a. 2.

∞ CHAPTER XIX ∞

The Conclusion of the Answer to the fourth Disparity.

It's full time to return to the principal point of this Dispute, after having follow'd our Adversarys thro all their starting-holes, and all the Barriers they cou'd possibly lay in our way. Let's now resume the Comparison[260] of a Judg in a case of Heresy, with a Judg for Murder; and say,

That just as the Fact that the Judges are not always able to distinguish the Innocent from the Guilty, and, with the best Intention of doing Justice, sometimes absolve the latter and punish the former, shews their Knowledg is limited, and their Understandings subject to Illusion, the unavoidable Infirmity of human Nature; but not that they hate Righteousness, and resolve to be unjust from a Principle of Corruption: so the Fact that <676> Heretick Judges, examining the Orthodox Opinions with all Sincerity, yet judg 'em false, shews indeed, that their Understandings are not perfectly enlighten'd, but not that their Heart is corrupt, their Will canker'd, or less of a general Disposition in 'em to protect and cherish Truth, than in those whom their Birth has made Orthodox. The same Argument may be drawn from hence, that the honestest and skilfullest Physicians kill a great many of their Patients, without being accountable for it, either at the Tribunal of God or Man.

And thus I think the fourth Disparity is fairly overthrown, as well as the other three.

∞ CHAPTER XX ∞

The Conclusion and Summary View of the general Considera-
tion, hinted at in the Title of the first Chapter.

I have now offer'd every thing that I think cou'd possibly be invented by my Adversarys, to elude the Force of the Arguments which I had advanc'd

---

260. Beginning at p. 466.

against 'em in this general Consideration of the Weakness of St. *Austin,* the great Apologist for Persecution; and this is the Reason why this single Consideration has held me so long, and bin drawn out to such a length: but I can hardly repent of it, having heard good Judges say, and experienc'd it my self, that one never convinces his Readers by the Arguments he offers, unless he take care <677> to foresee all the Difficultys they may raise upon 'em, and unless they spare 'em this trouble, by solidly confuting all that 'tis probable they can invent, or imagine against 'em. I can't therefore ask pardon for being so prolix, since I persuade my self, that nothing less cou'd have decided the dispute with St. *Austin,* and with all the other Adherents and Patrons of Persecution, on the Sense of these Words, *Compel 'em to come in,* so clearly to my Advantage; for now my Argument stands thus.

That Sense of these Words which enjoins a Conduct, that no tolerable Reason cou'd be assign'd for when employ'd against the Partizans of Falshood, which might not equally justify those when they thought fit to keep the same Conduct with the Orthodox Believers, is false.

Now such is the literal Sense of these Words.

Therefore it's false.

The Major of this Syllogism is evident: for what wou'd become of the Wisdom, the Goodness, and the Justice of God, shou'd he have had an Intention of putting into the hands of the Persecutors of his Truth, the same Arms which he had given the Protectors of this same Truth? The whole difficulty then lies in the Minor, but to remove this I have done as follows.

I have in the first place[261] suppos'd as a thing incontestable, that shou'd the Protestants, whereever they were uppermost, think fit to proceed against the Church of *Rome,* in the manner that she has lately treated the Reform'd in *France;* they might say, in answer to the Complaints and Remonstrances of the Catholicks, all the same things that St. *Austin* has answer'd to the Dona-<678>tists, and the *French* Writers to the Protestants. No one will deny the Supposition; but what they will say is this, that the same Arguments which are true in the Mouth of a Catholick, are false in that of a Protestant. To overthrow this Answer,

261. See above, p. 412.

I have shewn in the second place,[262] that 'twou'd be absolutely of no effect towards putting a stop to the oppressing of the Truth; that 'twou'd be only a begging the Question, and an Appeal to an endless Discussion of the Controversys between 'em; that the Justice of the Complaints, turning on a Determination of the Dispute, 'twere ridiculous in the Orthodox to complain, so long as this Dispute were continuing. And,

In the third place,[263] that from hence it might be concluded, this Answer was false at bottom; that it's repugnant to all the Ideas of the Divine Wisdom and Equity, that God shou'd leave his Church in such a condition, that all the most inviolable Maxims of natural Righteousness shou'd not only become useless to her with those who were the most inclin'd to be equitable, but her claiming the benefit of 'em, even render her ridiculous to all the World. But because, in opposition to this, they answer, that God will at last justify his Church in the Face of the World, by shewing she follow'd his Intention, in treading under foot all the Rules of natural Equity with regard to Hereticks, whereas these have merited eternal Death, by presuming to act the same way against the Orthodox;

I have shewn in the fourth place,[264] that supposing there were a Command from God, for persecuting those in Error; Hereticks, who perse-<679>cuted the Orthodox, cou'd not on this score be said to do ill, any more than a Conqueror can be said to do ill in governing the Kingdoms he has usurp'd, according to the Laws of God; or a false Mother, who piously educates a Child that she has stoln, can be said to do ill in this particular. In a word, I have shewn, that as Hereticks shall not be blam'd at the last day for having obey'd the Precept of Alms-giving, so neither shall they be blam'd for having in the Sincerity of their Souls obey'd that of compelling. But because it might be objected, that the Poor, to whom they give an Alms, are the proper Objects, and those for whom JESUS CHRIST design'd it; whereas they whom they compel are not the Persons against whom he intended Constraint:

I have shewn in the fifth place,[265] that it is not necessary, in order to obey

262. See above, p. 413.
263. See above, p. 414.
264. See above, p. 419.
265. See above, p. 423.

the Precept of Alms-giving, that the Persons to whom we give be really and actually poor, or that they to whom we refuse be not; but that 'tis enough, if we sincerely and upon probable Reasons believe, that they whom we refuse are above want, and that they to whom we bestow our Alms are not. But, lest Examples of this kind shou'd not be convincing enough,

I have shewn in the sixth place,[266] by the Example of Magistrates, that we obey the Precept of punishing the Guilty and delivering the Innocent, even when we acquit the Guilty and punish the Innocent, provided this be done according to the Forms of Law, and from an Ignorance which cou'd not be surmounted by the strictest Inquiry. This is a Case in point, because the pretended Command of compelling Hereticks is directed to <680> Sovereigns, and the Civil Magistrate: so that Trials for Heresy must undergo the same Fate as those for Poisoning, Murder, Adultery, in which the Judg is only oblig'd to examine the matter with due care; nor is he further answerable for its happening that the Innocent is punish'd, and the Guilty deliver'd. But because it might be objected, that the Ignorance in these Causes is invincible, but not in those of Heresy,

I have prov'd in the seventh place,[267] that it is at least as difficult to discover, whether a Person, accus'd of Heresy, is really a Heretick, as whether a Man, accus'd of Murder, Robbery, or Poisoning, be guilty of the Fact. And because it might be alledg'd, that the Ignorance in these Cases proceeds not from a malicious corrupt Heart, whereas in Trials for Heresy it does;

I have shewn in the eighth and last place,[268] and that beyond all Contradiction, that nothing is more false or more absurd than this Supposition, taken in the general, or restrain'd to such and such.

This, as far as I cou'd conceive upon the maturest thought, is all that can possibly be objected to elude the Force of my Reasonings: So that I have ground to hope, that it's building with Lime and Stone to answer as I have done. Shou'd my Adversarys hereafter start any new Cavil, or even a sound Difficulty, I dare engage to answer it; in the mean time I may, on so solid

266. See above, p. 425.
267. See above, p. 445.
268. See above, p. 466.

a Foundation as this before us, be allow'd to superstruct the following
Conclusion,

To wit, That if God had enjoin'd the persecuting of Hereticks, Hereticks
might perform a good Work by persecuting all such, as, on a thorow < 681 >
Examination of the Cause, and from a sincere Principle, they deem'd
heretical.

I hope my Readers will pardon my insisting so much on this Point: for
since this was the only Hold which the Patrons of Compulsion had left,
and which how pitiful soever they were not asham'd to boast of on all Occasions; 'twas but fit to drive 'em clearly out of it, and deprive 'em of every
Shift or Shadow of Defence.

How weak and wretched St. Austin's *Apology must now appear.*

My Readers will likewise, I hope, be convinc'd I had good grounds for
saying in the first Chapter, that to confute St. *Austin's* Apology for Penal
Laws, I needed only to shew, that all his Arguments might be turn'd upon
the Orthodox, when under Persecution from Hereticks. In effect, retorting
the wretched Justifications for forcing Conscience, sinks all Apology for
Persecution to rights: and if St. *Austin* has judiciously remark'd in some
part or other of his Works, That in all Disputes,* *We ought to wave those
general Mediums, which may be offer'd of each Side, tho not with Truth by
each;* how much more ought we to follow this excellent Rule, where the
contending Partys have an equal Right of employing the same Arms; as, I
think, I have unanswerably prov'd, that Hereticks and the Orthodox have
with regard to Persecution, sup-< 682 >posing JESUS CHRIST had enjoin'd
Violence, and the constraining Men to come into his Fold?

Now if nothing be more ridiculous in all Disputes, than ecchoing to our
Adversary's Words, and pleading, *I am right and you are wrong;* in answer
to his saying, *He is right and we are wrong:* if this be a mere Childish Play,
tossing the same Ball backwards and forwards; if begging the Question be

---

* Omittamus ista communia quae dici ex utraque parte possunt, licet veré dici ex
utraque non possunt. *See the Art of Thinking,* ch. 19. [Cf. Augustine, Migne, *Patrologia
Latina,* vol. 44, col. 641.]

the lowest and sillyest of all Sophistry; if we are guilty of this, not only when we offer, as a reason, the very Thesis which our Adversary impugns, but also when we urge a Doctrine in proof against him, which we know he rejects, no less than the main Thesis; how will it be for the future, when we may not make use even of this weak and pitiful Subterfuge, *You who are an Heretick, have no right to persecute me who am Orthodox; but I may justly persecute you, because you are in an Error, and I am not:* How extravagant, I say, will it be for the future to plead, *Compel 'em to come in;* when 'tis manifest, that even supposing a Man a Heretick, there's no denying him a right to persecute with Impunity, even before the Throne of God, if he is sincere in his Error, and if the persecuting Orthodox may hope for Impunity at the same dreadful Tribunal?

I have one word more to add, before I quit this Matter. For as my principal Design was only to justify those in Error, who don't therefore cease to be Christians, as has bin shewn at the beginning of the thirteenth Chapter;[269] it remains still a Question, Whether Infidels might justly persecute Christians, on a supposition that JESUS CHRIST had enjoin'd the forcing Conscience. <683> I say, that their right of treating Christians as Enemys of Mankind, is incontestable; because they might have just ground to imagine, that the Gospel is the Production of the evil Genius of Human Kind, which seem'd to have instructed Men in a purer Morality, and enhanc'd Conscience, only to plunge 'em hereby into the most enormous Iniquitys, and the most deplorable State of Woe: Since it's certain, that the more a Soul knows the Obligation it lies under of loving God above all things, and with the utmost Purity of Affections, the more guilty it becomes, and the sharper Remorses it feels when it sinks under the Trials of Persecution. Add to this, that the Command to compel, importing that the greatest service we can render to God, is that of extending the Borders of his Church, the greater the Zeal of Christians is, the more they'l ravage the World, and lay wast Towns and Countrys, in hopes of making Converts. So that the Pagan Nations, who once understood this Doctrine, might very justly be prais'd for endeavoring to maintain natural Religion, the Principles of Humanity, and Reason, and Equity, against the Attempts of such

269. See above, p. 466.

Convertists, by expelling 'em. See the fifth Chapter of the first part of the *Commentary,*[270] where this Matter is treated at large.

None cou'd justly be condemn'd, but such Persecutors only as were void of all Religion themselves, or who from mere Sloth or wickeder Motives, living in a confus'd and loose Belief of the Goodness of their own Religion, wou'd yet authorize their Violences, by the pretended Pre-<684>cept, *Compel 'em to come in.* But this can be of no manner of service to St. *Austin,* because it's an Arrow which equally pierces Persecutors outwardly Orthodox (or those resting in a loose general Belief) who are Orthodox from no sincere Principle, and Persecutors who are Hereticks outwardly and from no sincere Principle.

⋈ CHAPTER XXI ⋈

An Answer to a new Objection: It follows from my Doctrine, that the Persecutions rais'd against the Truth are just; which is worse than what the greatest Persecutors ever pretended.

I Shou'd now pass to a particular Consideration of the Weakness of St. *Austin,* in comparing Princes to Shepherds, who in case of danger thrust their Sheep forcibly into the Fold, when they won't freely go in; I shou'd pass, I say, to this matter at present, if I did not find my self stop'd by the Objection propos'd. Your Opinion, says such a one, is more pernicious than that which you confute; for by justifying Hereticks, you endeavor to prove that their Persecutions are just. So that all kind of Persecutions are just in your account; whereas your Adversarys bestow this Privilege only on those which are manag'd by the Partizans of Truth.

I answer, That my Argument is one of those which we call *Reductio ad absurdum,*[271] and which <685> has always bin reckon'd one of the most effectual for undeceiving such as suffer themselves to be impos'd on by false Principles. Nothing is properer for this, than shewing 'em by unavoidable Consequences that they lead to manifest Absurditys. Now this is what I

270. See above, p. 92.
271. See Appendixes, "Bayle's Use of Logic," p. 581 ("reductio ad absurdum").

have done, by shewing after an invincible manner, that if God had enjoin'd the constraining Conscience, it wou'd follow that Hereticks might justly and piously compel the Orthodox; that is, that the Persecutions stir'd up against the Truth, and carrying in 'em a Complication of Crimes, and drawing after 'em a total Subversion of Morality, wou'd be an Act of filial Obedience to the Laws of God. Now as nothing can be more impious than such a Consequence, it's impossible I shou'd prove it without its following that the Principle from which it flows is impious; and therefore, that the pretended Command of compelling is the falsest and the most abominable Doctrine that can be propos'd to Christians.

But, adds he, if they who are in this Error be only sincere, 'twill follow according to your Principles, that neither this nor their persecuting actually is any Sin in 'em. This, I own, is the most perplexing Difficulty that can be propos'd to me. But in answer to it I say,

In the first place, That if there be Errors, as without doubt there are, to which we our selves are accessary, thro an inexcusable neglect of Information, and too great a Complaisance for criminal Passions; the Error of those who are persuaded of the literal Sense of the Words, *Compel 'em to come in,* is very obviously of this kind: so necessary is it to tread under foot a <686> thousand Ideas of Reason, and Equity, and Humanity, which present daily before our Eyes, e'er we can persuade our selves that God has enjoin'd such a kind of Violence. From whence it must follow, that all the Mischiefs done to the persecuted wou'd be so many actual Sins.

I say in the second place, that humanly speaking, 'twere impossible not to sin in executing what this Error prompts to, by reason of the Passions of Hatred and Wrath which must needs be excited in the Souls of the Executioners: Not to mention that the Persecuted wou'd be brought into a Temptation of sinning several ways, as I have shewn in the sixth Chapter of the first Part.[272] And this strengthens the Presumption, that they who persecute err not from a sincere Principle; and shews, that tho they had the extraordinary good Fortune to err involuntarily, yet they must sin in the Execution and Practice of their false Principle.

Last of all, I say, that tho this Error and its Consequences shou'd be

272. See above, p. 102.

suppos'd to enjoy the Privilege of those Evils which are committed involuntarily; yet all possible Care shou'd be taken to correct it in those who are deceiv'd: for the greater Right it gives to 'em of persecuting, the more fatal it becomes to human Society, and the more fruitful in Calamity and Sin. It therefore behoves us extremely to labor in the undeceiving those who are bewitch'd to this Doctrine; and this is what I have propos'd to my self by this whole Commentary, and particularly by shewing, as I have all along done, in order to convince Men more effectually of the Falsness of the literal Sense, that this Doctrine if < 687 > true wou'd very often justify, even at the Tribunal of God, those who afflicted and ravag'd the true Church. See my *Commentary* second Part, p. 242.

⚬ CHAPTER XXII ⚬

That what has bin lately prov'd, helps us to a good Answer to the Bishop of Meaux *demanding a Text, in which Heresys are excepted out of the number of those Sins, for the punishing of which God has given Princes the Sword.*

I have spoke to this Demand before in the third Part of my *Commentary*, p. 369. But I have some other Reflections to make upon it here.

The grand Defect of this Query is, that it is up to the Bishop of *Meaux* to find a Scripture Passage, in which Hereticks are reckon'd in the number of those Evil-doers who are punishable by the Sword.

For in effect, the Spirit of all Laws tending more to Mildness than Rigor, and being liable to the favorablest Construction, where it's doubtful whether a Matter be punishable or no; Heresy ought to be deem'd exempt from all Punishment, if the Legislator has not specify'd and declar'd it punishable expresly and by name. Now that it's at least doubtful whether Heresys are cognizable by the Civil Magistrate, we < 688 > need bring no better proof than the Sense of the first Ages of the Church, and that of several grave Authors of different Sects, Ages and Nations, without reckoning on any of the Reasons I have hitherto alledg'd. And it even happens, that many of those who write Apologys for Persecution, let fall several Expressions in favor of Forbearance and a Liberty of Conscience, when caught unawares and not actually thinking on the Engagement they are under of writing for the persecuting Sect. So true is it, that Reason and natural Light revolt against the Doctrine of Persecution. Consequently, till the Bishop can produce an express Passage of Scripture, comprehending Hereticks among the Evil-doers whom Princes are bound to punish, we shall have ground enough to believe 'em excepted.

But I have a further peremptory Answer to Mr. *De Meaux*'s Query. If Princes had receiv'd the Sword from God, for the Punishment of Hereticks no less than for the Punishment of Assassins, Poisoners, Robbers, False Witnesses; all Princes must give it in charge to the Judges appointed by 'em in their several Dominions, to take cognizance of Causes of Heresy, as they do of all other Causes Civil or Criminal, with Liberty to take the Advice and Opinion of Divines, as they shou'd see fit. Consequently Trials for Heresy must undergo the same Fate as all other Trials; I mean, they must be examin'd into with Care, the Defences of the Accus'd heard, and after the exact Observance of all due Forms of Law, the Suffrages or Opinions of the Judges counted, and Sentence pronounc'd <689> against the Accus'd; upon a Plurality of Voices. Now all the World must agree, provided the Judges act conscientiously, and do their utmost Endeavor to discover the Merits of the Cause, and the Rights of the Partys, that their Judgments are righteous, as well in the sight of Man as of God, altho they shou'd happen to be deceiv'd. Then Sentences pronounc'd against Persons accus'd of Heresy, whether in effect Hereticks or no, must be just in the sight of God and Man, provided they were pass'd conscientiously, and after Examinations in due form, and a legal Proceeding in the whole Trial.

The meaning whereof, in one word, and without disguise, is this, That God, acting the equitable part, as no doubt he always does, cou'd not require at the hands of Heretick Kings, the Blood of those Orthodox, which they might on occasion spill; because, in quality of a righteous Judg, he wou'd hear the Reasons of these Kings, who might alledg the Command they had receiv'd in his Holy Word, to punish Hereticks with the same Care as Murderers, Ravishers, False Witnesses, &c. whereupon they had done no more than obey the Will of God, in ordering their Judges to proceed against Hereticks: That if the Judges were deceiv'd in taking those for Hereticks who really were not so, this cou'd not be a greater Fault in 'em than sentencing a Man as a Murderer or Felon, who really was not so; that not being infallible, nothing more cou'd reasonably be requir'd of 'em, than examining all Causes diligently, and always declaring for the side that seem'd to them true and just: That when, thro the artificial and impenetrable Contrivances of a knot of <690> False Witnesses, or Abettors of Villany, they had condemn'd the Innocent to death, and acquitted the Guilty; their Integrity, tho attended with an Error, which might lead 'em into Actions materially unjust, was sufficient to justify 'em; it manifestly follow'd, that having acted with the same honest and upright Intention in the Trials of those accus'd of Heresy, they were not to blame in having condemn'd 'em, since they saw 'em fully convicted of the Crime.

I desire my Reader, if possible, to lay by his Prejudices for one moment, and consider, whether Equity will permit God to condemn a Heretick Judg who has sentenc'd an Orthodox; when this Judg can alledg in his defence,

1. The Holy Scriptures, which according to the Bishop of *Meaux,* has rank'd Hereticks among those Evil-doers whom the Magistrate is bound to punish.

2. The full and intire Conviction which he found himself under, upon a thorow Examination of the Cause, that such a one was a Heretick.

3. Several Instances, in which he, and a world of Judges besides him, had condemn'd a Person as guilty of Murder, who really was not, and deliver'd him that was guilty, yet without its being chargeable on 'em as an Iniquity, or making 'em liable to Punishment; provided they went *secundum allegata & probata,*[273] sincerely and from a good Conscience, and upon a strict Examination of the Cause.

These three Points, known by God to the utmost degree of certainty, must undoubtedly jus-<691>tify Heretick Judges, who shou'd with Zeal and Vigor punish the most Orthodox; for it's impossible to alledg any new Disparity after those which have bin already dispers'd like so many vain Mists rais'd before our sight.

Now, as from hence it follows, that the punishing the Orthodox wou'd become an Act excusable at the Throne of God, were there a Command in Scripture for punishing Hereticks; I have just ground for answering Mr.

---

273. "According to the testimony and proofs."

de Meaux, that nothing is more repugnant to Reason and Religion, than the pretending there's any such Command in Scripture.

It's in vain to fly for Examples to the Old Testament, because here there's no possibility of confounding the Orthodox and Heterodox; nothing being clearer, or more express, than the case of those who were punishable on the score of Religion. They were such as work'd upon the Sabbath-day, or who maintain'd in express terms, that the God of the Jews was not the true God; or in general, whose* Impiety was, in some respect or other, manifestly repugnant to the Law, as they themselves wou'd have own'd. And we don't find the Jews had any Power to punish those, who acknowledging the Authority of the Law, had perhaps particular Notions of their own about the Sense of Passages, which were doubtful or capable of different Interpretations. <692>

But see what a pass Christians have brought themselves to. They all are agreed, if JESUS CHRIST or his Apostles had design'd to say so or so, that we ought to believe it; but maintain, one Party that they have said this, another Party that they have said that; and alledg so many Reasons of each side to puzzle the Cause, as alone might serve to convince us that the penal Laws which took place under the old Dispensation are abolish'd under the new: for as the Case has all along stood, these Laws cou'd never be safely put in execution, but at a time when the Christians had really no Jurisdiction. My meaning is, that in the days of the Apostles, or their first Disciples, it had bin easy to discover those who gave the Scriptures a wrong Interpretation; because the Infallibility of the Apostles, who might have bin consulted by word of Mouth or by Letter, and the fresh Remembrance of the verbal Instructions they had given their Disciples, and Pastors whom they themselves had consecrated, was a ready means for clearing any Doubt or disputed Point. But the Christians had not the power of the Sword at this time; nor did they receive it, till the different Sects and Disputes among themselves had darken'd the Understandings of all those who might have bin inclin'd to judg without partiality.

This Evil has bin increasing ever since, whence one of these four things

---

* *They, who from hence wou'd conclude, that we may punish Infidels at least, will find the Answer in* Part 2. ch. 4. [See above, p. 174.]

must necessarily follow: Either that God has given no Command for punishing Heresys, like those he has given for punishing Murders, Thefts, &c. Or that the Idea he has given of Heresy is as clear and as generally agreed in as that of Murder and Theft: Or <693> that he has made a Law which became impracticable as soon as People began to have the power to put it in execution (an Imprudence not to be pardon'd in any Legislator who cou'd see but the length of his nose): Or last of all, that in case of Obscurity he design'd Men shou'd govern themselves as they do in all other Matters, Civil or Criminal, where the Cause is decided by a Majority of Voices, and where the Judges are no way answerable if they act with Integrity and a good Conscience. Sure I am, that neither the second, nor third, nor fourth of these Suppositions will be admitted, and consequently the first must hold good.

Let any Man consult himself a little. Will he find any thing more unequitable in that low State of Knowledg which Men are doom'd to, and in those Circumstances to which their Malice has reduc'd the Functions of the Judicature, than a Law of God importing, that a Judg who gave a wrong Vote shou'd be damn'd? I understand by giving a wrong Vote, not his voting against Conscience, or at random, without a disinterested and attentive Examination of the Cause, but his being of an Opinion which agrees not with the Judgment of God upon the same Cause; God who knows the critical precise point, from which whoever varies ever so little, swerves from that which is right, and passes to what is wrong. Cou'd the ablest and most upright Judg upon earth keep his place for one day, without a mortal Sin, were such a Law as this reveal'd to him from on high? And wou'd not a King sin mortally only in naming and appointing Judges, when the Charge were such as no Man cou'd <694> with a good Conscience undertake, without risking eternal Damnation by deciding the very least Cause; nothing being so easy for a Man who is not infallible, as missing the fix'd and critical Point which separates Right from Wrong? How then must it be, when they are to judg in weightier Causes, where the Advocates quote of each side a vast number of Laws, Precedents, and Decrees given in like cases? For we find in the Reports and Common-place Books of Lawyers, Texts of contradictory Laws, a hundred different ways of reconciling these Contradictions; we find Decrees in 'em made either in different Courts of the same

Kingdom, or in the same Court, some of which are *for*, others *against* the Partys impleading: for the same Court does not always give the same Judgment in similar Causes. In fine, these Decrees, these Laws, these Customs variously interpreted, suffer nothing to appear evident or demonstrative, and at most but very probable. Now when a Man, who knows he's not infallible, is determin'd only by that which to him carries the greatest probability, he may very well believe that he is not deceiv'd, but he does not know it by a certain Knowledg of Science: for according to the Remark of Philosophers, our Assent to a Conclusion, prov'd from Premises which are only probable, is not Science, but Opinion; and Opinion does not exclude all fear of being deceiv'd.

That Judg then must be the rashest, and the foolishest Man alive, who stakes his eternal Salvation on the Persuasion he's under, of not swerving in the least from the precise Point on which the Merits of the Cause turn; the rather, be-<695>cause he often sees other as able Judges as himself differ from him in Opinion: which shews that what appears to us most probable, does not always appear so to others; and that therefore 'twere imprudent hazarding eternal Happiness on a Certainty, which is founded only on a great Appearance of Truth.

This helps me to a new Argument against Mr. the Bishop of *Meaux:* for it's plain, that in this Conflict of Decrees, this inextricable Labyrinth of the Laws, in a Complication of cross Incidents which very often entangle Civil Causes, God requires no more of Judges than that they examine the matter carefully, and vote according to their Consciences; nor shall it any way affect their Salvation, that what appear'd to them right and just, did not appear so to him who sees the most hidden things exactly as they are in themselves. Consequently, if he had enjoin'd Princes to punish Hereticks, he wou'd require no more of their Judges than carefully to examine and vote according to Conscience, without intending that their Salvation shou'd be endanger'd by their making a judgment of what is Heresy, different from that which he himself makes by his omniscient Knowledg. Now as this were granting Heretical Judges a full Impunity, who in pursuance of their own Notions of Heresy shou'd put the most zealous Orthodox to death by wholesale, it follows, God never intended that Princes shou'd exercise any Jurisdiction in Cases of Heresy. <696>

A new Turn given to the Examination of the Objection, founded on the Clearness of Controversys.

The only Defence now remaining is to say, That Trials for Heresy are not so perplex'd as the more perplex'd Civil Causes. To which I answer, That this is very true, provided the Judges have the liberty of defining Heresy according to the Prejudices of their own Religion; for then nothing is easier than convicting a Man of Heresy. They have no more to do in this case than just ask him whether he believes all the same Articles of Faith which they believe; and if he answers No, there's an end of the matter: he's convicted of Heresy in due form. But as the Orthodox and Heretick Judges wou'd by this means be upon an equal foot, and as it wou'd hence follow that the same Doctrine was true and false at the same time, 'tis plain there's no standing by this way. There's an absolute necessity that the Judges and the Accus'd agree upon some common Rule, and go by it, instead of holding by Principles which divide 'em. Now whether this common Rule be the written Word of God alone, or whether it comprehends an unwritten Word besides, every one may perceive, from the Reflections already made in the Answers to the second and third Disparitys,[274] that the finding the critical Point which separates the True from the False, the Probable and the Seemingly True, is no small Difficulty; the finding it, I say, with such a Certainty as leaves no room to doubt that we have found it, and <697> that every other Opinion different from our own is necessarily false. For after all, in matters contested between Christians no body pretends to carry his Proofs to a Metaphysical or Geometrical Evidence; they must ever remain in the Class of probable Propositions: and therefore from hence alone, that Man owns he's not infallible, he must confess that he may be deceiv'd in preferring one probable Proposition to another probable Proposition: Consequently the Judges in Trials for Heresy can have no greater assurance that they have voted right, than those may have who are Judges in Civil Causes.

To render this more plain and obvious to all the world, I shall only remark the Conformity between disputable obscure Points of Divinity, and

274. See above, Chapter 10, p. 445, and Chapter 11, p. 455.

Matters of Law or Physick. Distempers have this peculiar to 'em, that whenever they come to any height, you can hardly get a Consultation of three or four Physicians who are not divided in Opinion, both as to Fact and Right: one will have it that the Distemper proceeds from the Liver, another that it proceeds from the Stomach; one defines it one way, another another way; and they might dispute the Point till the Patient's dead, unless they put it to the Vote: but they decide it by a Majority of Votes to be one Distemper rather than another; and sometimes it happens to be such a one as the Doctors said not one syllable of in the whole Consultation. The same kind of Difficultys divide 'em as to the Right, I mean the way by which this Disease is to be cur'd, when agreed on: some will have such a Remedy, others quite the contrary; and after a great many Ar-<698>guments, they are forc'd to put it again to the Vote. It's the same in Civil Causes: Shew your Case to different Lawyers, you shall almost always find 'em disagree in their Opinions, and one Person has perhaps ten or twelve Advices upon the same Law-Point, which hardly agree in any one instance.

The same thing happens in Theological Questions: Be they ever so little obscure, you can't find three Professors of the same University who'l give you the same Answer upon 'em; and when they happen to meet in a Visit, if any of the Company consult 'em seriously on any Point, they presently go together by the ears about it, without being ever able to clear the propos'd Doubt. From thence have arisen so many different Explications of the same Passages of Scripture, so many different ways of reconciling Passages which seemingly contradict one another; and what's nearer to my purpose in this place, thence the great Conformity between Civil and Theological Causes. In law Cases each Advocate has Texts of Law on his own side, Interpretations or Answers of antient Judges or Lawyers, Decrees given in like Cases, Objections ready fram'd, and Solutions to those which are made against him: In theological Controversys each Party has Texts of Scripture on his side, antient Fathers, Opinions of the most famous Universitys, Arguments, Objections, Distinctions, Solutions; not a Book being written by any Sect, to which the opposite Sect does not presently reply.

How comes it then, that each Party boasts that his own Cause is as clear as Noon-day? This must of necessity be owing to the Force <699> of Prejudice and Education: for those we call your *Esprits Forts, a Generation of*

little Faith and slow of heart to believe, unfortunately too much unprejudic'd, scarce see any thing convincing in all our Books of Controversy,
but the Objections and reciprocal Retortions of the contesting Partys; and
make the same judgment of 'em as that Elector of *Cologn* did, mention'd
by Father *Paul,*[275] who in the Disputes between the *Thomists* and *Scotists*
protested, he cou'd perceive nothing solid in 'em of either side when each
spoke for his own Cause, but cou'd abundance when either spoke against
the other.

Let's conclude then, that the necessity there wou'd be of permitting
Judges to decide Causes of Heresy, as they do Civil Causes, upon the greatest appearances of Reason, and by a Majority of Voices; or in other words,
according to the Lights, whether great or small, of the Judges, and the Prejudices of the prevailing Religion; is a convincing Argument, that God has
not made Heresy liable to the Sword of the Magistrate.

But we must not make an end of this Chapter without remarking one
thing which is a certain Truth, tho nothing can be further from popular
Notions; to wit, That if Hereticks were indeed made obnoxious to the
Sword of the Magistrate, and that Heretical Judges who condemn'd the
Orthodox to Punishment sin'd, 'twou'd follow that the Orthodox Judges
who condemn'd Hereticks wou'd sin too. For the Fault of the first cou'd
consist in nothing else than the Temerity they had bin guilty of, in condemning Persons whose Crime was prov'd upon 'em only <700> by probable Reasons. Now the Orthodox Judges wou'd come under the same imputation; since it's notorious, that the Proofs of Orthodoxy not amounting
to Demonstration, can at best be but probable: Then, *&c.* I own these two
sorts of Judges, perfectly alike in that of their following the greatest Probability in the respective Judgments of each, wou'd differ very much in this,
that one sort wou'd have the misfortune of taking that for true which was
not so, and the other the good fortune of taking that for true which really
was so. But as this good and ill fortune supposes no difference of Merit,
but a Disparity in their Lot, one being born by ill chance in a Heretical
Town or Family, the other in an Orthodox Town or Family; it can't be

---

275. Paolo Sarpi, *The History of the Councel of Trent,* Book 4, 1551; tr. N. Brent, 2nd
edn., 1629, p. 329.

imagin'd that this shou'd make any difference in the Destinys of Men. In this World the having Merit without being happy, is less than being happy without having the least Merit; but in Heaven things are measur'd out and weigh'd by the Ell, and Ballance of Reason: there's nothing given by mere Chance; and in truth 'twere winning Heaven at cross and pile, if he who was sav'd differ'd from him who is damn'd only in this, that neither having any better Evidence for what he affirm'd than the other, one of the two shou'd have the good fortune to hit on the Truth. <701>

ⅩⅩ CHAPTER XXIII ⅩⅩ

A Summary Answer to those who fly to Grace for a Solution of these Difficultys.

I had once resolv'd not to meddle with the Objection before us, till I shou'd come to sound this whole matter to the bottom; but I don't see that I can well avoid saying a word or two upon it in this place. Most of my Readers wou'd think hardly of me, if they did not find something in this first Part concerning a Difficulty which they must o' course make in their own minds. As thus:

They'l object that the Grace of the Holy Spirit, which interposes in our Conversion, gives us the Gift of discerning Truth from Falshood; and as this might become a Principle for directing the Orthodox Judges in Trials for Heresy, their Decrees wou'd be render'd by it as pleasing to God, as those of Heretical Judges wou'd be displeasing: they[276] being neither mov'd nor led by his Grace, but remaining in the Darkness of their corrupt Nature.

I answer in the first place, That where the business is only to persuade Men that such and such Doctrines are true; those, for example, which are really contain'd in Divine Revelation; there's no necessity of flying to a particular Assistance of the Spirit of God. Education alone is sufficient for this purpose, or the natural Qualitys of the Understanding, which are such, that <702> upon reading, examining, and comparing what can be said for

276. The heretics.

and against two opposite Opinions, we see more reason of one side than the other; and even without weighing the Reasons of both sides, are sometimes by the first Impression of the Object determin'd to embrace it.

This Answer bears upon Pillars which can never be shaken, since the most Augustinian Christians are agreed, that the Devils under the greatest destitution possible of the Grace of God, are yet most firmly persuaded of the Truth of the Doctrines of Christianity; which therefore proceeds intirely from the natural Force of their Understandings, for the discerning in all Objects the sound Proofs from the false. Beside, that we all allow there's such a thing as an historical Faith, by which we believe the Gospel in general to be true, and thus particular Mysterys reveal'd in it; which Faith is yet by no means suppos'd to be a Grace of the Holy Spirit: Consequently a Man can't be deem'd converted, or endu'd with Grace, precisely on the score of his being persuaded of the Gospel Truths. This simple Persuasion is only the effect of Education or natural Sagacity. And how can any one pretend, that all who are persuaded of the Mysterys of the Christian Religion, are gifted for this purpose by a particular Favor of the Holy Spirit, when the greatest part of those who are so persuaded live most ungodly Lives, and are damn'd at last?

This Supposition wou'd utterly ruin the Thomistical Doctrine of efficacious Grace, and that of the Inamissibility of Grace according to the Calvinists; and reduce the Molinists[277] to this grand Absurdity, That the most execrable Sects, and <703> the most infected with Heresy, have their share in the particular Influences of Grace, for the believing one part of the Mysterys, while they obstinately combat others, and lie bury'd in the most sensual Enormitys.

This Absurdity wou'd be likewise common to all those Sects which mutually damn each other. In fine, those who are bred up from their Infancy in the Belief of a certain Catechism, Jews, Pagans, Mahometans, Romans, Lutherans, Calvinists, Arminians, Socinians, being all firmly persuaded of the Truth of it at a certain Age, and almost all of 'em all their life long; recurring to a spiritual and supernatural Principle for the producing a bare Persuasion, be it of what Religion it will, is manifestly against good Sense.

277. See Appendixes, "Grace, Original Sin, Predestination," p. 587.

In the second place I answer, That according to the most general Hypothesis of Protestants, that Faith which passes for one of the three Christian Vertues, and is praised under the Term justifying, is that which makes us love God, obey his Commandments, and cherish the Truths of which it begets in us a firm Persuasion; in a word, 'tis that Faith which works by Love. This is what they call Grace properly speaking; but the simple Persuasion of the Truths of Faith, which is to be met with in a world of sensual perverse Christians, and who die impenitent, is not the Grace of the Holy Spirit, according to this Hypothesis.

I say in the third place, That whether they'l have it that all Persuasion of Evangelick Truths is the effect of a supernatural Grace, or whether they restrain it to a Persuasion <704> attended with Charity, I don't see how they can get clear of the Difficultys here propos'd. My reason is, that the business now is either to render the Conduct of those Judges just and blameless, who shou'd condemn such as were accus'd of Heresy at their Tribunals, or else to render it evil. To this end it is not sufficient that one sort declare those Hereticks who are really such, and the other declare those Hereticks who are really Orthodox: for if this were all, we ought to approve the Conduct of a Judg, who having nodded all the time of the Pleading, and starting out of his sleep the minute his Judgment was demanded, shou'd answer, *Hang him by the Neck;* but the Trial's about a Meadow, my Lord, says the Court; *Let it be mow'd then,* says he: We must praise, I say, the Conduct of this Judg, shou'd it happen that the Trial was about a Murder which really deserv'd the Gallows, or a Meadow which the lawful Proprietor desir'd, with all the reason in the world, he might be suffer'd to mow. An accidental stumbling then upon the Truth not being sufficient to render the Conduct of a Judg just, let it be said, if you please, that certain Judges act prudently, and others imprudently; that those have gone by such Proofs, as upon a strict Examination appear'd to them best, and that these had no regard to the Quality of the Proofs alledg'd of one side or t'other: for if once it be suppos'd that the Judges of both sides have inquir'd into the Merits of the Cause with all possible Application and Sincerity, and govern'd themselves by the Proofs which appear'd to them most solid, they must be allow'd to have acted pru-<705>dently o' both sides, tho their Judgments are contrary. There shall be no difference between 'em as to the moral part, tho there may be as to the natural Qualitys of the Understanding.

For the Confirmation of this, I cou'd wish the Reader wou'd only think of my preceding Remark;[278] which is, That the Proofs of Heresy or Orthodoxy never amount to more than a strong Probability: so that the Judges can't have recourse to that way for avoiding the Imputation of all Temerity which the new Philosophers prescribe,[279] to wit, never affirming any thing but what we clearly and distinctly conceive cannot be false, after having maturely consider'd it over and over without prejudice. This Rule being impracticable in matters of Religion, it follows that a Judg may declare what is Orthodoxy and what Heresy, upon Reasons which are only probable, without incurring the Charge of Temerity. But if so, there will be no more Temerity in a Heretick Judg's pronouncing Sentence against Orthodoxy, upon Proofs which appear to him the most probable upon mature and sincere Deliberation, than in an Orthodox Judg's pronouncing with the same Conditions against Heresy.

The Result on the whole is, That Grace can be of no service towards removing the Difficulty; because he who shou'd be led by this Grace, wou'd not therefore perceive the Objects clearer, the Arguments, the Force of the Objections, and the Solutions.

Experience is incontestable in this Point. Assign Orthodoxy in its utmost Purity to what Communion you please, three parts in four of <706> the good Souls in it, Souls predestinated, and ready to suffer all rather than abjure, shall not be able to give a reason of their Belief to a subtle Controvertist, after a first or second Reply of his to their first Defences. All the World must own (and who can dispute it against daily Experience?) that the most efficacious Grace improves neither the Understanding, nor Memory, nor Imagination; teaches us neither *Greek* nor *Hebrew,* neither the Rules of Argumentation, nor the way of solving Sophisms, nor historical Facts: so as one may safely answer, that a Person void of all Grace and Vertue, but who at the same time has a world of good Sense and studys hard, shall in a year's time be Master of more Argument, more Knowledg,

278. See above, p. 519.
279. See Appendixes, "Philosophical Controversies," p. 595.

and Skill for silencing one that's an Adversary to his Religion, than the holiest Person in the same Communion, who neither reads nor studys, who has but a moderate Understanding, and a worse Memory. Consequently a Judg who were endu'd with Grace, and shou'd pronounce that such a Text of Scripture ought to be taken in the literal Sense, and a Judg void of Grace, who shou'd declare for the figurative Sense of the same Passage; wou'd be either equally guilty of Temerity, if they gave Judgment before they had faithfully consulted the Originals, and acquir'd all the Improvements of sound Learning; or equally exempt from Temerity, if each of 'em sincerely determin'd that to be the Sense which to the best of his Judgment seem'd most certain and reasonable: for as to that *Cartesian* Evidence, by means of which a Judg pronounces without a possibility of imagining that he can be mista-<707>ken, that an Order of Court issu'd within these four days contains a certain Thing (for example, that any new Convert who refuses the Sacrament at his death, shall have his dead Body drawn on a Sledg) and that neither the Words nor Expressions ought to be understood in any other Sense but this; it's plain, that Grace bestows it not, with regard to several obscure Passages of Scripture, on a Man who knows neither *A* nor *B*,[280] or even to a Lawyer, who's a stranger to *Hebrew,* to *Greek,* to Divinity, to the Prophetick Stile, *&c.* They who are Masters of all these things, seldom arrive at such a certainty about obscure Points.

From hence it appears, that the Temerity of the Judges diminishes only in proportion to the Force which they perceive in the Arguments and Proofs which determine 'em. Now so it is, that Grace does not make 'em perceive a greater Evidence in the Proofs and Arguments than they might perceive in 'em without it: for a Peasant abounding with Grace, or an Advocate who understood neither *Greek* nor *Hebrew,* shall know no more whether the Version of *Louvain* or that of *Geneva* has translated such a Text truest, than if they were utterly void of Grace, other things being equal; or which is the justest Exposition of the Epistle of St. *Paul* to the *Romans,* on which the Doctors make new Discoverys daily: an Argument that former Ages had not hit upon the true Key for explaining it, tho assisted by a saving Grace. 'Tis vain then going about to condemn or absolve the Judges, on pretence

280. I.e. the alphabet.

that a Principle unknown to themselves inclin'd 'em imperceptibly of one side rather than another; a Principle, I say, unknown, which on this very account is incapable <708> of affording a just and well-grounded Assurance, that what they pronounce to be Truth is more to be rely'd on, than that which others assert in opposition to 'em.

Did Grace operate now as heretofore in the miraculous Gift of Prophecy, the Objection I examine wou'd hold good; for when once a Prophet was fully assur'd by unequivocal Signs from God that he was a Prophet, he might reasonably securely rely on what he himself spoke as true, tho perhaps he might not be able to comprehend or understand all the reasons of it: but as the Case stands today, Christian Certainty with regard to our being in possession of the Truth, cannot be otherwise well grounded (for as to the Love of God, and a Sincerity of Intention, it's quite another thing) than in proportion to our Knowledg of the respective Arguments, Proofs, Solutions, and Objections. And therefore unless we give a little, or rather very much, into Quakerism and Enthusiasm,[281] there's no getting off by the way which I examine; the exploding of which ruins the Pretensions of Councils, or Pope speaking *ex Cathedra,* by the very same Arms which Mr. *Nicole* makes use of, for shewing that the Assurance of private Persons, founded on their own proper Examination, is rash.[282] For as the Debates and Examinations which precede the Decisions of Pope or Councils never carry matters to that degree of Evidence, in which it distinctly appears to 'em impossible they shou'd be otherwise than they conceive 'em; it follows, either that the Assurance they have of not being deceiv'd is rash, or that they found it on Enthusiasm, I mean on an immediate Direction of the Spirit of <709> God, which makes 'em utter the Truth by way of Mechanism, or at least without discovering to 'em the necessary Proofs of it.

I own, if we allow'd 'em their Hypothesis, to wit, that God never permits the Reasons which favor Error to appear to them as probable as those which favor the Truth, they might get over the Difficulty: for then this Conse-

281. "Enthusiasm" here means the belief that the divine Spirit directly forms thoughts in one's mind, which one can recognize intuitively as being from God and therefore certainly true. The Quakers believed that every human being is immediately open to an inner light guiding them to truth. In their religious meetings Quakers sat in silence until the Holy Spirit gave one of them something to say.

282. See Appendixes, "Philosophical Controversies," p. 595.

quence wou'd hold good; *We have founded our Decisions on the Reasons which to us appear the most probable, after having maturely weigh'd what can be alledg'd o' both sides; therefore we have lit upon the Truth.* But it fares with this Hypothesis as with that of *Epicurus:* Grant him his Atoms and his Vacuum, and he shall account extremely well for abundance of Phenomena, and avoid a thousand Objections which lie against infinite Divisibility, Motion, Gravitation, Hardness of certain Bodys; but if you don't allow his Hypothesis, if you make an immediate attack upon the very Foundation of his Doctrine, you sink him to rights under Mountains of unanswerable Objections. Just such is the Strength of the Roman Catholicks.

From what I have bin now saying one may easily collect, that a Judg who were assur'd of his being possess'd of the Grace of the Holy Spirit, in such a measure as might preserve him from Error, might condemn those accus'd before him of Heresy, altho he went upon Reasons which were only probable: but as he has no necessary Proof of his possessing this Grace, or, which is the same thing, no Proofs whose Force he perceives more clearly than another Heretical Judg perceives that of his own Proofs, by means of <710> which he believes himself assisted by the Holy Spirit in condemning those accus'd of Heresy; any Man may comprehend, if he thinks attentively on it, that the Charge or Exemption from Rashness equally fits both Orthodox and Heretical Judges, provided they condemn those accus'd of Heresy only on a fair Hearing, and upon Reasons which shall appear to them respectively the best.

And this brings me to my fourth and last Answer: That there's no assigning any sure Mark and Character, a Character free from all Equivoke, of those Opinions into which God leads us by his special Grace. So that neither to ground a difference between Judges who shou'd condemn real Hereticks, and those who condemn only reputed Hereticks, nor to answer Mr. *Nicole*'s Objections concerning the Temerity with which he charges the Illiterate among us, who believe they hold the pure Truth of the Gospel; is it to any purpose to have recourse to the extraordinary Grace of the Holy Spirit. For how wou'd you have a Peasant rationally assur'd, that he believes his own Religion true from this Principle, when he sees other Peasants of the opposite Religion maintain in like manner, that they believe their own Religion thro the influence of the same Grace?

Does not a Lutheran pretend, that it's owing to the Mercy and Favor of

God that he believes several Doctrines which the Calvinists and Socinians reject as false; the latter that concerning three Divine Persons in the God-head, the former those touching the Real Presence, Free-Will, the <711> Universality of Grace? A Calvinist shall allow, that the Lutheran is right in ascribing his Persuasion of a Trinity to Grace, but not that of the other Doctrines. Yet the Lutheran can neither outwardly express, nor does he inwardly feel any difference between the Motive which binds him to the Doctrine of the Trinity, and that which binds him to the others. Consequently the being persuaded that God reveals to us certain Doctrines, is no certain Proof of the Truth of 'em; and for this very reason the Objection which I confute is of no force: for if I have not a certain and necessary Proof, that I am directed by a special Grace towards the Truth, my fancying I am directed will be rash, and without any reasonable grounds, even tho it shou'd be true that I was actually directed by it.

Two Men, one of which shou'd say that the Parts of a cubick Inch of the Body of the Moon were even, and the other that they were odd; wou'd they not be equally rash whether they spoke at a venture, and as if they were at Cross and Pile, or whether they spoke upon some Geometrical Calculations absolutely false and erroneous: since no one can exactly tell what are the Inequalitys of the Surface of the Moon; and in a word, that it's affirming what cannot be evidently known? Yet one of these Men must be right. Then a Man may affirm a Truth without being less rash than he who tells a Falsehood. Nor wou'd it signify any thing, that he who hit on the Truth was persuaded of what he said; his Temerity wou'd be never the less, <712> so long as the Reasons and Grounds of his Persuasion are neither* solid nor convincing.

Here's what People don't give heed to: They imagine, provided a body speaks the truth, that he's very knowing and prudent, or at least is more so than he who does not speak it. To shew the Emptiness of this Conceit, we need only promise a Crown to any Peasant of a Village that shall find out the exact distance from hence to the Moon. Shou'd the first Peasant say fifty thousand Leagues, and the second raise it a thousand, and the third as many, and so on; one of 'em will o' course hit on the Opinion of some

* The Reader will see in another place what use I make of this, in my System of Conscience. [See above, pp. 262 ff.]

famous Astronomer: and it might even happen, that by bidding whimsically upon each other so many or so many Leagues, one of 'em hits precisely on the true Distance, or on that at least which the best Astronomers are agreed in. Wou'd he for all this have any better grounds for what he said than his Neighbors? Yes undoubtedly, say you, since the Object is such as he affirms it, and not such as the rest say it is. But how poor an Answer is this? For was it the real Truth of the Object, known to this Peasant, which determin'd him to affirm it? Not at all: consequently it cou'd communicate no Vertue to his Act, which shou'd render it better than that of the other Peasants.

It's manifest then that neither the real Truth of Objects, when we don't perceive it by solid Proofs, nor an invisible Principle directing, yet without discovering to us these solid Proofs, or <713> making us feel its direction by any certain and necessary Signs; are capable of founding a difference between Orthodox and Heretical Judges, when suppos'd in other respects equal as to Sincerity, Application in examining the Cause, and a Purpose of following the Proofs which to them shall appear the strongest.

⚘ CHAPTER XXIV ⚘

Whether the Arguments for the Truth are always more solid than those for Falshood.

To consider things absolutely, the Affirmative of this Question is most certain; but to consider 'em with regard to Man in common Life, I think there's a distinction to be made.

Let's say then, that there are necessary Truths, and Truths contingent.

Among the necessary Truths there are some so evident, either immediately, and these carry their own Reason along with 'em which no one contests; or mediately, that is, which may be resolv'd into some first Principle by a well-link'd Chain of Consequences and Demonstrations: so that the Proofs of 'em are not only more solid in themselves than those of the opposite Falshoods, but are also stronger even with regard to Man; it being easily perceivable, that nothing of any weight can be offer'd in favor of these Falshoods.

But when a necessary Truth is not evident, either in it self, or by means of a Train of <714> Demonstrations running it up to a first Principle upon incontestable Premises; then indeed it may be attack'd in such a manner, that it's hard to distinguish, whether those who deny or those who affirm are most in the wrong.

With regard to Truths of a contingent nature, whereby I understand not only historical Facts, but such Truths also as depend on the free Decrees of God; I'm of opinion that we shou'd keep to the same distinction, to wit, either that they are evident, at least mediately, or that they are not. If the first, their Proofs ought to be deem'd more solid, with regard to Man, than those of the opposite Falshoods; so that there's ground enough for suspecting, that all who maintain these Falshoods are either insincere, or extremely disorder'd; under a gross Ignorance, or a slavish Engagement to their Prejudices.

But when these Truths are of such a nature, that the Principles by which we endeavor to run 'em up to a common Notion, or to such a Combination of Circumstances as amounts to a moral Demonstration, are doubtful and uncertain, or clash with contrary Principles, which we sometimes make use of as true, so that our own Arguments are liable to be retorted; I say, it's very possible in this Case, that the opposite Errors may be defended as solidly, in all appearance, as these Truths.

I shall confirm this Explication by some Examples.

These two contradictory Propositions, *There's a Space distinct from Body; There's no Space distinct from Body;* [283] are of such a kind, that neither can <715> be true without its being necessarily, absolutely, and unalterably true, and without the other's implying a Contradiction. So that there's either in the first, or in the second, a necessary Truth, or an impossible Falshood. Yet each of these Propositions is supported by Reasons so strong, or rather encounter'd by Difficultys so perplexing and inextricable, that it's very hard to determine, whether the Reasons alledg'd for the true be more solid, with regard to us, than those alledg'd for the false.

These two Propositions, *God wills that all Men shou'd be sav'd, and affords 'em Aid sufficient for this purpose; God wills not that all Men shou'd be sav'd,*

---

283. For arguments for and against the reality of a vacuum (space distinct from bodies) see DHC, art. "Zeno of Elea," rem. I.

and does not afford 'em all Aid sufficient for this purpose;[284] contain one or other of 'em, a contingent Truth, since it depends on the Free-will of God: but if one be true, the other must be necessarily false. Yet each is supported by so many Arguments from Philosophy, Divinity, and Piety, and by so many Passages of Scripture, that one wou'd be at a loss which side to chuse, if he were not apt to be determin'd by Temper and Complexion to some Notions rather than others.

Nor can there be a surer sign, that two Opinions, tho contradictory, and consequently one true the other false, are founded each upon solid and very probable Reasons, than to see, that each have had their Patrons and Partys in different Countrys, and different Ages of the World, Persons distinguish'd by their Knowledg, and Vertue, and Piety, who have carefully examin'd the Question; or likewise to see, that if one of the Opinions has crush'd and overwhelm'd the <716> other in one place, this has sprung up again in another.

Must not a Man be very much prepossess'd to maintain henceforward, that the Doctrine of particular Grace, and some others, so warmly defended by *Luther* and *Calvin,* have not only the Advantage of being supported by several very probable Reasons, but also that the contrary Doctrines are not supported by any? This, I say, were somewhat out of season, considering that all the Lutherans have departed from their Master's Mind in this point; that those who reform'd themselves in *Holland,* according to the Confession of *Geneva,* have long since bin divided into two great Bodys, on occasion of these Doctrines; and last of all, that most of the able Protestant Divines of *France,* and almost all the Church of *England,* run counter to *Calvin* on this Article.

Philosophy affords us a hundred Examples of contradictory Propositions, which are each so strongly supported by Reasons equally specious, that difficult nice Understandings don't know, upon a fair hearing, how to chuse the best from the less good Opinion. Don't we see contradictory Thesis's maintain'd in the very same Day, and before the same Audience? Does not a Rhetorick Professor make two of his Scholars declaim, in the same hour, one *for,* the other *against* the same Question in Morality, Pol-

284. See Appendixes, "Grace, Original Sin, Predestination," p. 586.

iticks, &c? Are not there large Volumes printed of this sort of Orations, so plausible o' both sides, that if the Reader inclines to one, 'tis more from some Prevalence of Temper than that of the Arguments, or because he always thinks the last he reads the best, and that only because he remembers it best? <717>

Let no one therefore pretend to tell us more, that the Arguments for a Falshood are never to be compar'd to those in favor of Truth.

They who say so, are far enough from believing it; for it's observable, that all the Christian Sects dread one another. The Romish indeed plays the Poltron more egregiously than any of the rest, because she burns all the Books written against her, and won't suffer, without the greatest regret, the Laity within her Jurisdiction to cast an eye upon the Books of Protestants. But these, on the other hand, are not altogether free from their Fears; the Ministers of *France,* in these latter days, were not at all pleas'd that their People shou'd converse with the Popish Clergy, or amuse themselves with reading over their Controversys: and 'tis certain, a young Divine wou'd take a wrong way of recommending himself to the Professors, shou'd he often come to borrow Socinian Tracts from 'em, and let 'em know, that he study'd 'em with great Application. They wou'd from thence forward conclude, he had a leaven of Socinianism in his Soul, and gravely tell him, that such Books were dangerous reading for young Men. I don't see that our Divines will suffer the Writings of this Sect to be printed or publish'd, where they have Credit or Power enough.

Nor yet do I believe, that the Socinians advise their young People to read over the Books written against themselves; they are well pleased that they know the Objections by which the Orthodox confound 'em only in the Writings of Socinian Authors: where, as in all the controversial Writings of each Sect, the Objections of the oppo-<718>site Party lie scatter'd up and down like the Movements of a Clock taken to pieces; without any Force or Significancy.

Whence can this proceed, and what every one may observe, that even Men of Wit and good Learning boast of it as a very prudent and pious Conduct in 'em, that they never wou'd read those Writings of the opposite Party, which have the most Reputation for Subtilty and close Argument?

Whence, I say, can this proceed, if it be an inseparable Fatality of all Error, to have no Proofs on its side, but what are weak and very improbable, in comparison of those which are to be offer'd in behalf of Truth?

Human Life affords us a hundred Examples to the contrary, which we shou'd wonder at the less, because Facts, in reality false, are often as possible, if not more so than the true. Ask a couple of *Reasoners,* whether a golden Globe shew'd 'em at a distance in a strange Country might be worth so much; one tells you no, because he believes 'twas hollow; the other, yes sure, because he believes 'twas solid: They shall maintain their Conjectures by a hundred Arguments, and it shall often happen, that the first is in the wrong, and yet shall make his Opinion much more probable than the other makes his.

Has not some Author or other advanc'd in his Book, that pitch upon what Action you please, he'l assign you fifty different Motives for doing it, and all very probable?

In general, it's possible enough that there may be Arguments more specious and more affecting for an Error than for the Truth, not only with regard to those who are ingag'd in this Error by < 719 > Birth and Education; but even with regard to a Stranger, who, without the least Prepossession *pro* or *con,* shou'd examine this Error, and the opposite Truth. But this is more especially true with relation to Facts.

It happens here much as it does in the case of History and Romance.

Sometimes a Romance has a greater Air of Probability than the most sincere History; and nothing again appears more natural, or more undoubted than the Motives assign'd by a Historian of such a Prince's Conduct: yet these Motives are only a Fiction of the Historian's Brain, the widest in the World from the Truth, which if he had faithfully related, the Readers might very often look upon as flat, absurd, and void of the least shadow of Reason or Probability.

Wou'd you have an Instance nearer to those very matters on which the Controvertists try their Skill? The Criticks have restor'd Passages in the antient Authors after very different manners. One will have us read it thus, another will have us read it quite the contrary, the Affirmative instead of the Negative. It very often happens, that he who's widest of the Author's

Meaning, wins the Prize in the Judgment of Readers of the best Tast, as having given the antient Author a turn of perfectly good Sense, of very plausible and very judicious Reasoning.

How it comes to pass that Falshood is sometimes prov'd by sound Reasoning.

I think I had insinuated the true Reason of all these things, when I said above, that Facts in rea-<720>lity false, are altogether as possible, or perhaps more so than the true: for in this case we are not to wonder, that the Reasons for denying, are equally if not more probable than those for affirming a Fact, so long as its Existence does not come up to what we call *Publick Notoriety,* a Combination of Circumstances which amounts to Demonstration; such as this Fact at present, *The Pope has resolv'd to deprive Embassadors of their Privileges.* Upon which, if we shou'd suppose two great *Reasoners* in *Japan* arguing the point, on the Receit of Letters from *Rome,* importing no more than that there was a talk the Pope wou'd soon publish a Bull to this effect, they might bandy the matter in such a manner, that to this day a great many of their Hearers wou'd believe that the Report was come to nothing, so many and such probable Reasons appearing to them against it.

But I shall now make an Attempt towards dissipating all those Fantoms and pannick Fears which have exercis'd Divines for so long a time on the Article of Errors. It's plain, the Reason why the Mind of Man finds so many Arguments, equally solid in all appearance for maintaining Truth and Error in religious Controversys, is, that most of the Falshoods advanc'd in 'em are altogether as possible as the Truths. In effect, we all suppose, that Revelation depends intirely on the Free-will of God; for he was not under a necessity by nature, of making either Men or other Creatures. Consequently he might, if he wou'd, either have produc'd nothing, or have produc'd a World intirely different from this; and in case he had thought fit to have a Race of <721> Men in it, he might have conducted him to his own ends, by methods directly opposite to those he has chosen, and which had bin altogether as worthy of an infinitely perfect Being: for infinite Wisdom must have infinite ways of manifesting it self, all equally worthy of it. This being the case, we are not to wonder, if Divines can find out as good Arguments for maintaining Man's Free-will, as for impugning it; for we are not destitute of Ideas and Principles for conceiving and proving, that God might make Man free, or might not make him free with a Freedom of Indifference, and so of a hundred other contradictory Propositions.

What happens then when Revelation is obscure or doubtful upon any point? Why this, that one Party explains it by one System, and another Party by another. I'l suppose, that the System of one Party is really agreeable to what God has really chosen: this hinders not but that of the other Party may be conformable to what God might have done with as much Glory to himself as can accrue to him from what he has actually done; since we conceive, that God might have form'd things otherwise than they are form'd, and after a hundred different manners, all worthy of his infinite Perfection; else he wou'd be an Agent void of Liberty, and no way different from the God of the Stoicks, chain'd down by unavoidable Fate, a Doctrine very little better than Spinozism.[285] Consequently there's no Sin in following a false System, but when a Theologist frames it on an Idea, which he thinks repugnant to what God himself has reveal'd, and Injurious to the Divine Majesty. Now I can't <722> believe there are any such Theologists in the World. Add to this, so far as is needful, what I have observ'd before[286] concerning Errors voluntary and involuntary.

One must be an Ideot to believe, that the Schoolmen,[287] whose System *Luther* and *Calvin* had destroy'd, fram'd this System upon an Opinion, that the rigid Predestinarians in St. *Austin*'s way gave God too great an Authority, and that 'twas necessary to retrench it, as our Parliaments here in *England* clip the Prerogative of our Kings upon occasion. In like manner one must be an Ideot to believe, that *Luther* and *Calvin* fram'd another

285. The Stoics were "fatalists," i.e. they believed that whatever was fated would happen, and nothing else—i.e. that there was no such thing as free choice. See DHC, art. "Chrysippus," rem. H; A. Long, *Hellenistic Philosophy,* 2nd edn. (London: Duckworth, 1986), pp. 163–70; A. Long and D. Sedley, *The Hellenistic Philosophers* (Cambridge: Cambridge University Press, 1987), vol. 1, pp. 333–43. Spinoza also held that whatever happens, happens of necessity; see DHC, art. "Spinoza."

286. See above, p. 486.

287. See Appendixes, "Grace, Original Sin, Predestination," p. 586.

opposite System, upon an Opinion that the Schoolmens System represented the Deity as too equitable, and that 'twas fit to abate that exceeding Praise which it gave to God.

Let's do both Partys Justice. Neither had a thought of wounding the Supreme Majesty of God, or his infinite Perfections: but they conceiv'd, one side, that such and such Notions were inconsistent with the Divine Nature, and accordingly treated 'em as false; the other, that such certain Notions tended more to his Glory, and hence believ'd 'em true, and explain'd the Scriptures in favor of 'em: that's to say, not having the same Idea of Perfection, but what one side judg'd a Perfection worthy the Divinity, appearing to the other side a Defect and Imperfection unworthy the Sovereign Being, they took two different Paths for explaining what the Scriptures say of him. And so far I can't see any more Sin in those who are deceiv'd than in those who are not. <723>

Wou'd to God Men had always look'd on Controversy with such an eye, there had bin no such thing as Schism or Excommunication; but Men had employ'd in living well, and in eschewing what all the opposite Partys are agreed is Sin, Slander, Theft, Fornication, Murder, Uncharitableness, &c. that time which they have mispent in Disputation and mutual Persecutions.

But I insist too long on a Question which I design'd only to glance at in this place, proposing to examine it with the utmost nicety in the sequel of this Work.

Having thus given a full and invincible Answer to Mr. *de Meaux*'s Query, by solidly asserting an Equality of Right, in Heretical and in Orthodox Judges, as to the condemning and punishing Persons accus'd of Heresy; let's return upon St. *Austin* once more, and then take leave of his wretched Apology for Persecutors, a Blot on his Life and Memory. <724>

ᗡᗡ CHAPTER XXV ᗡᗡ

A new Confutation of that particular Argument of St. Austin, drawn from the Constraint exercis'd by a good Shepherd on his Sheep.

First Defect of this Comparison, *That the Evil from which they wou'd preserve the Heretick by constraining him, enters with him into the Church; whereas the Wolf does not enter the Fold with the Sheep that's thrust in by main Force.*

The Comparison of the good Shepherd, who to save his Sheep from the Jaws of the Wolf, thrusts 'em into the Fold, if need be, by main Force, has appear'd so dazling to the Gentlemen Convertists; that not content to have preach'd it a thousand times over to their People, and publish'd it to the World in imitation of St. *Austin,* they have taken it for the Fancy, or Design, before the Books which they had dedicated to the King of *France* on this Subject. For which reason, because I have two Thoughts against the un-justness of this Comparison, over and above what I have already said in my third Part, p. 305. I hope my Readers won't take it ill, if I edg 'em in here by way of Supplement.

The first of these Thoughts is, That the Shepherd never uses this Con-straint, when he sees his Sheep already in the Wolf's Power: all his En-<725>deavors then amount to driving the Wolf away, and depriving him of his Prey; and he'd think he had committed a gross Fault, if he drove the Wolf towards the Fold, and forc'd him in along with the Sheep that he has fast in his Clutches. Yet this Imprudence wou'd be more excusable than that of Persecutors who extort the signing a Formulary; because a Wolf shut into the Fold may possibly be knock'd on the head there, nor wou'd it be a hard matter to find a sure way to dispatch him: But a Heresy shut into the Church along with a false Convert, is a lurking Distemper which it's no easy matter to cure. Be that how it will, the Comparison is still de-fective. The good Shepherd forces his Sheep into the Fold, not when they are seiz'd by the Wolf, but before they are fal'n into his Clutches. The Convertists force Hereticks into the Church when actually of a piece with the Error, and there shut 'em in with the Enemy, who holds 'em, as they pretend, in Thraldom.

A Confutation of those who say, That since a Heretick must be damn'd unless he is constrain'd, it can do no harm to constrain him.

And here I can't forbear expressing my astonishment at what I have heard some Catholicks say, and even read in Letters written from *France,* That People shou'd not be troubl'd, to think that the Dragoons made numbers of the Hugonots sign, who were persuaded that what they sign'd was false; because at worst these false Converts cou'd but damn themselves, and they <726> wou'd be damn'd without this: so that since either way they must be damn'd, better chuse that which puts a stop to the Scandal, of having a multiplicity of Sects in the same Country.

I own, this makes me question whether I am in a Christian Country; for what becomes of all the Morality of the Gospel, if we authorize so monstrous a Thought? Are we ignorant, that Holiness requires we shou'd do our utmost to prevent God's being offended, and his Holy Name dishonor'd; and that Humanity, and much more Christian Charity, forbid us to enhance the Guilt, or enflame the Account of our Neighbor? Yet these two sacred Obligations are destroy'd by the Maxims of these wicked Convertists, who having it in their Power to let the Heretick rest in his first Sin, to wit, his Heresy according to them, force him to add Hypocrisy, and a Sin against Conscience, to his Error: whence it follows, that he offends God in more ways than otherwise he wou'd have done, and treasures up for himself a more insupportable degree of Hell Torments, than simple Heresy cou'd have merited.

According to this fine Maxim of Morality, it might be lawful to tempt Hereticks, by the powerfullest Sollicitations, to get drunk, to cut one another's Throats, calumniate each other, live promiscuously: Men and Women in all carnal Pollutions, rob, filch, and steal from one another. For if the stopping a visible Schism, be a Good which counterballances those Sins of Hypocrisy, into which Hereticks are thrown; the Good which might accrue to the Church, from this Peoples living the most <727> dissolute

Lives, and thereby becoming a Foil to the good Lives of Catholicks, wou'd ballance all the Sins which they might be tempted to commit.

Let's now proceed to my other Thought.

> Second Defect of the foresaid Comparison; *That it proves invincibly, either the Pretensions of the Court of* Rome *over the Temporal Rights of Princes, or that the Church may depose Princes who persecute her.*

One's strangely surpriz'd, and can hardly forbear laughing, when he reads in *Bellarmin* or *Suarez*,[288] that these Words of JESUS CHRIST to St. *Peter, Pasce oves meas, feed my Sheep,* mean, that the Pope may depose Heretick Kings, or absolve their Subjects from their Oaths of Allegiance.

But it's most certain, if once the Conduct of Shepherds be made the Rule for Pastors of Souls, and it be proper to argue from one to the other, that nothing can be more convincing, within the Borders of the Church of *Rome,* than the Reasons of these Jesuits: for in fine, there's a natural Right in Shepherds, a Right inseparable from their Charge, of defending their Sheep against the Attempts of the Wolf, by every kind of way that they can devise, either by letting loose their Dogs at him, or by setting Traps or Snares to catch him, or by laying poison'd Flesh or other Baits in his way, or by shooting him dead with a long Gun. Seeing then the Roman Catholicks are agreed, that the Pope is the Vicar of JESUS CHRIST, the Supreme Pastor of <728> Souls; and since they can't but own, that a Heretical persecuting Prince, who by his Wiles and his Violences draws the Children of his Kingdom after him into Perdition, is a destroying Wolf with regard to the Church; they must, if they reason consequentially, agree with *Bellarmin* and *Suarez,* that the Pope ought to make this Prince away, by the shortest way that he can think of, *quocunque modo potest*,[289] either by letting loose the neighboring Princes and Potentates against him, or by stirring up his own Subjects to Rebellion, or by Poison or Assassination.

It's pleasant enough to see, how Mr. *Maimbourg* answers this Similitude

---

288. See Appendixes, "Church and State," p. 589.
289. "In whatever way he can."

of the good Shepherd, in Chap. 27. of his *History of the Church of* Rome. *This,* says he, *is a Sophism not only false and opposite to all the Rules of right reasoning, but impious also and detestable, which leads directly to Parricide, and is a just ground for burning the Books which advance it.* He might reasonably have judg'd so, if he were of my Principles; but approving Compulsion, as he did, and supporting it by the Example of the Shepherd, it had bin impossible for him to shew, that the Ultramontans reason'd amiss. He had bin harder set here, than by another Comparison of theirs, taken from the States General of *France,* to shew, that as the King of *France* has the whole Monarchical Power vested in him, even when for the Good of his Kingdom he thinks fit to call together the three Estates; so the Pope, who can't follow a juster Model for governing the Church than that of the Kings of *France,* is always superior to a Council.[290]

Poor *Maimbourg* was at a loss to answer this Difficulty. <729>

But let the Command, *Feed my Sheep,* be address'd to whom it will, it must be own'd that it confers a right of making away persecuting Princes, if the Conduct of Shepherds be a Rule for Imitation.

಄ CHAPTER XXVI ಄

A small Sketch, representing the Enormitys attending the Doctrine of Compulsion by some new Views, as the destroying the Rights of Hospitality, Consanguinity, and plighted Faith.

In a marginal Note towards the beginning of this Continuation of my *Commentary,* I promis'd to go back once more to the Argument made use of in the* fourth Chapter of the first Part,[291] the sum of which is; That the Execution of the Command, *Compel 'em to come in,* obliging the Orthodox to pill and pillage the Houses of Hereticks, drive 'em out of their Country, confine 'em to Prisons or Monasterys, the Fathers and Husbands of one

---

* *See also the Answer to St.* Austin'*s twelfth Argument,* P. 3. [See above, p. 318.]

290. On the Ultramontains and Gallicans see Appendixes, "Church and State," p. 590. Maimbourg was a Gallican, so held that a Church Council is superior to the pope.

291. See above, p. 86.

side, the Wives and Children of another, send 'em away to the Gallows or Gallys; it must necessarily follow, that the same Actions which wou'd be a formal Violation of the Decalogue, if the constraining Hereticks to change Religion, were not their true End and Aim, become good Works when perform'd from such a Motive. Now from hence it manifestly <730> follows, that all sorts of Sins cease to be such, when committed from a design of forcing those into the Communion of the Church who are gone astray; and consequently, that the Interest and Aggrandizement of the true Church, is the surest Test of discovering, whether an Action be just or unjust: so that the more an Action is capable of crouding the Church with Infidels and Sectarys, the more easily it passes from Iniquity to Piety.

If so, behold all the Bands burst, and all the Dutys broken which tie Men to each other; either by the general reason of their partaking all of the same specifick human Nature, or by particular Reasons of Consanguinity, or mutual Contract.

I. On the bare score of Humanity, Reason requires, if a Tempest casts Men away on a strange Coast, that the Inhabitants shou'd endeavor to save 'em from the Billows of the Sea, and afford 'em some refreshment of Food and Raiment. But this Obligation, according to the Principles of our modern Convertists, is no more than a Chimera: for if they follow the Doctrine of Compulsion, they must, instead of going forth with Food and Clothing to these miserable Creatures, who are laboring to save themselves the best they can, by swimming, or on broken Planks, meet 'em with a Formulary or Profession of Faith ready drawn, and with Pen in hand require 'em to sign incessantly, or declare in case of refusal, that they'l drive 'em out again to Sea, or let 'em perish with Cold and Hunger on the bleak Sands. The best Terms they can expect, is allowing 'em three or four days to get instruc-<731>ted; but no Quarter after that, unless they sign. Who'd have imagin'd, that Christianity countenanc'd so barbarous an Inhospitality? which the Companions of *Eneas* complain'd of so movingly before, Chap. 2.[292] Yet as it might be an infallible means of propagating the Faith, the Inhumanity is metamorphos'd into a most charitable Work; as in all like Cases, the

---

292. See above, p. 418.

refusing an Alms to a perishing starving Beggar, unless he promises to come over into the Bosom of the Church.

I don't pretend to advance it as Fact, that this Inhumanity is practis'd in the Countrys of the Inquisition; I know there have bin Refugees of *France,* who forc'd by stress of Weather into some Ports of *Spain,* have got off at a cheaper Rate, by suffering some few Insults and Indignitys, and promising to embark as soon as possible, after having satisfy'd the Avarice of those who threaten'd 'em with the Inquisition. Yet who doubts but the Quality of disaffected *Frenchmen* was of great Service to 'em in *Spain?* Who doubts but the necessity the *Spaniards* are under of keeping fair with some Protestant States, obliges 'em to abate of their usual Rigor on the Article of Compulsion? Finally, the Question is not so much about what is actually practis'd, as what their Doctrine inspires, and will naturally lead to, when they don't apprehend ill Consequences from it.

II. As to the Rights or Obligations of Blood and Consanguinity, they can't on these Principles be a jot more sacred than those of Humanity: it shall be lawful in a Father, if his Son, either by his own reading or the Instructions of others, thinks himself oblig'd to change Reli-<732>gion, to treat him like a Scullion, diet him with Bread and Water, turn him out of Doors, and absolutely disinherit him; till these temporal Afflictions make him resume his former Belief. A Son on the other hand, who changes to the true Religion, and sees his Father persist in his Heresy, may refuse him in his old Age all the Offices and Assistances of natural Duty; and which is worse, threaten him unless he abjure. A Daughter may insult her Father and Mother who won't change as she has done, and even tell 'em she'l turn Whore, unless they give her the Satisfaction of coming into the Bosom of the Church; and if Threats fail, she'l do well to be as good as her word, and lie with every Fellow in her way, as long as her Father and Mother persist in their Obstinacy. And if by this means she shou'd happen to bring 'em over, she fulfils that Scripture which the Convertists keep such a stir with, *Imple faciem eorum ignominia, & quaerent nomen tuum Domine; Fill their Faces with shame, that they may seek thy Name, O Lord.* Shou'd any one pretend to tell me she commits a Sin: Yes say I, if she had not in view the converting her Father and Mother from their Heresy; but this being her end, the Action loses its sinful Quality, as well as Robbery, Imprisonment, Death, ordain'd and inflicted on innocent Souls, with a design to compel 'em in.

III. As to the Religion of an Oath or solemn Contract, the thing in the World that's strongest founded on the first Principles of Morality, and the most necessary to the Being of human Society; it shall no more escape uncancel'd, than the other Dutys of Humanity, <733> wherever there's a probability that the violating our Word or Oath may bring Hereticks into such a Pinch, that they shall be oblig'd to sign a Formulary. This is so true, that as the Church of *Rome* has signaliz'd it self more than any other Religion in Acts of Violence upon Conscience, so none has weaken'd the Obligation of keeping Faith and Promises so much as she: And asking t'other day a Friend of vast reading, for my own is very small, whether he ever met with an Example of a Catholick Sovereign who had kept his Word concerning Religion with his Subjects of a different Religion; he answer'd, he never had, and that he did not believe there was one such instance in Story; and therefore he never was surpriz'd at the late Proceedings in *France,* having always expected 'em: whereupon he told me, he mightily approv'd a Passage at the seventy third Page of a small Treatise entitl'd, *Ce que c'est que la France toute Catholique,*[293] which says, *'Twere Charity not to put Catholicks to their Oath.*

A Sample of this Matter taken from the late Persecution in France.

The Truth of what I have bin just saying, has bin sufficiently experienc'd in *France,* within a few Years last past; all the Tyes of Blood and Affinity, good Neighborhood, old Friendship, and Hospitality trod under foot: and bating that they did not cut Peoples Throats, 'twas the perfect Image of the terrible Proscriptions under *Marius* and *Sylla,* and the Triumvirate in *Rome;*[294] when 'twas Death for a Father or Mother to conceal their own Son, or help him to make <734> his Escape; and when the best Friend, or Slave, or freed Servant who had receiv'd the greatest Benefits from his Master, was requir'd to discover his Friend or Master, on pain of Proscription.

293. Bayle, OD, vol. 2, p. 346b.
294. See above, p. 55, note 24.

It's notorious to all in *France,* that the Inns or Hotels were forbid at their Peril to entertain those of the Reform'd Religion, to give 'em a Night's Lodging, to receive or secure any of their Goods, or contribute in any kind of manner to their avoiding the Vexations of the Dragoon Crusade. A Landlord who did not turn his Protestant Guests out of Doors, or give in their Names to the Directors of the Conversions, was liable to the heaviest Punishments; so that this was truly the Emblem of the Iron Age, *non hospes ab hospite tutus.*[295] A near Relation, a Friend convicted of concealing his Friend, his Relation, his Children, or his Goods, in a Vault or Cockloft, was liable to the same Punishment; and what's still more strange, 'twas made a Crime in a Husband to send his Wife out of the way, in a Father not to hinder his Children's making their Escape: and hence it was that after a Man, quite weary of his Garison, had sign'd the Formulary, and hop'd thereby to enjoy some respite, he found himself in a few days after crouded with new Lodgers, upon pretence that all his Children were not forthcoming, and that his Wife lay conceal'd. The holding a Correspondence by Letters with Brothers, Sisters, Children, Father or Mother fled for Refuge into foreign Parts, is a matter of no small danger in *France,* for those who have sign'd; and this is the reason why they dare <735> not write directly to 'em, nor express themselves but in Enigmas, for fear their Letters shou'd be intercepted and open'd.

If there be Children who hearken more to the Voice of Nature than to that of the wicked Religion, which they have at least outwardly embrac'd; I mean, such as endeavor to make private remittances to their Fathers and Mothers, who are in an indigent Condition in foreign Parts; this is a Crime which seldom goes unpunish'd if discover'd. Did ever any one read or hear of a more odious, a more crying Violation of all the Dutys which Nature and right Reason enjoin?

I don't touch upon that Breach of Faith, and that Contempt of the most solemn Engagements, which has bin so notorious in the whole course of this Persecution, and particularly in the Edict of Revocation;[296] because

295. Ovid, *Metamorphoses,* I.144: "Guest was not safe from host"; translated Frank J. Miller, Loeb Classical Library, p. 13.
296. See above, p. 195, note 82.

this Matter has rung sufficiently all over *Europe*. I shall only say a word or two on the ungrateful returns made to the important Services of Mareschal *Schomberg*,[297] which I hope will not be thought a Digression; this Vice of Ingratitude being the Violation of a tacit and implicite Contract, which challenges as religious an Observation from every well-born Soul, as those which are sign'd and seal'd before a Notary and Witnesses.

A short Reflection on the Dealings with Mareschal Schomberg.

This Mareschal merited so much the greater regard from the Kings of *France,* and *Portugal,* as having bin born a Subject to neither, he had <736> the Fortune of doing 'em both the most important Services, with the utmost Fidelity.

Yet he was forc'd in his old Age, by an Order from the first of these Princes, to quit *France* his adopted Country; where he had marry'd a Wife, and purchas'd a considerable Estate in Lands. This same Order having specify'd *Portugal* for the Place of his Retreat, he there hop'd to pass the remainder of his Life in Peace, on account of the long and very great Services he had done that Court; yet nothing was capable of securing him from the Persecutions of the Inquisition, neither the remembrance of the Obligations which they had to him, nor the Regard which the *Portugueze* ought to have had for any thing recommended to 'em by the King of *France,* to whom they owe the Honor of not being a Province of *Spain,* and who sustains 'em with a high Hand, even at a time when he cannot do it without violating one of the most express Articles of the *Pyrenean* Treaty; which has expos'd his Reputation, and drawn on him a thousand Reproaches of Breach of Faith in a world of Libels. So the Mareschal was forc'd to decamp once more, and seek an Asylum far enough out of reach of the Wolf's Paw, I mean the Countrys in which Popery reigns. <737>

297. Friedrich de Schomberg, 1615–1690, German soldier who served in various countries including France, Portugal, and England; killed fighting on the Protestant side in the Battle of the Boyne.

∞ CHAPTER XXVII ∞

That Sodomy might become a pious Action, according to the Principles of our modern Persecutors.

Let's always remember, that according to these fine Maxims, Crimes are metamorphos'd into good Actions, provided they make a great many Hereticks sign. This being the case, we may bid fair for sanctifying the most odious, the most beastly Sin, and which deserves burning the most of any Crime that can be nam'd, I mean Sodomy: for there's no manner of doubt, but a great many who stand it out against Threats of Imprisonment, Pillory, Banishment, Gallys, and Death, wou'd sink under the Threat of being abandon'd, they their Wives and their Children, to Prostitution. St. *Epiphanius* relates,[298] that *Origen,* who from his tenderest Age had a most fervent Passion for Martyrdom, and was all along a great Example of Intrepidity, and Inflexibility under all the Rigors of Persecution, had not for all this Force enough to withstand the Threats of being deliver'd to an *Ethiopian,* brought before him for the purpose. The Horror he conceiv'd at being given up a Victim to this Brute, made him consent to incense an Idol, which was the same in those days as signing a Formulary now, or writing one's Name in the Parish Roll. Such an Effect, and the very great Probability of Success, founded on the Idea of so <738> shocking, so execrable an Act, might be a just ground to hope for a plentiful Harvest of Conversions; if instead of ordering the Dragoons to throw the House out of the Windows, the Directors of the Conversions shou'd command 'em to try what preposterous Lust might do; and mix as many Negroes among 'em as they cou'd find.

What, in such a case, wou'd that Sex do, which is not only the fairest Moiety of human kind, but the piousest and the chastest, that Sex to whom Modesty and Shamefacedness is fal'n in Lot? How bear the Thoughts of Prostitution against Nature, and according to Nature (for undoubtedly they'd leave the Choice to the Dragoons) so many Wives and Virgins of

298. Epiphanias, *Panarion,* 64.2.1–5, in Migne, *Patrologia Graeca,* vol. 41, col. 1071.

Estate and Honor, to whom the least obscene Word, the least Indecencys in a Picture, or any other Object seem insupportable? The most satyrical against the Sex won't deny that of all the Punishments and Indignitys which it's possible to inflict on a Woman of Honor, none can be severer than that of running the Gauntlet naked thro a numerous Rabble; and what then wou'd it be, if so hard a Procession shou'd end in her being deliver'd to the beastly Lust of the Persecutor's Assistants? There are few Women, even of those who have most Religion, and have perhaps the Courage to die for it, who to be deliver'd from a Punishment so ignominious, and so insupportable to a modest Nature, wou'd not sign any Formulary that was offer'd 'em. So that this were a most effectual way of Constraint, the surprizing Progress whereof wou'd rectify and recompense with Usury and Overmeasure what-<739>ever may be irregular in the means. All the World knows, that the Women of *Miletum* being seiz'd with a kind of Melancholy, which put 'em upon killing themselves, nothing cou'd be thought on for preventing it, till the Magistrates made a Law, That they who kill'd themselves shou'd be expos'd naked in a place where several Highways met.[299] The Thoughts of their being view'd naked made such an impression on 'em, tho they were not ignorant that in Death they shou'd be insensible of Shame, that they chose to live rather than be made such a Spectacle.

✣ CHAPTER XXVIII ✣

An Examination of what may be answer'd to the foregoing Chapter.

First Answer. *This way of Compelling wou'd scandalize the Publick.*

I don't suppose they'l answer me simply, that these Actions are evil; for this were saying nothing, since they maintain that pillaging the Houses of Hereticks, condemning 'em to Death or to the Gallys, of very wicked, as they are in themselves, become good Actions by being destin'd to the compelling

299. See Plutarch, *Moralia, Mulierum virtutes,* 249b–d.

Men in. We must say the same of every other Crime, if some particular Circumstance bar it not. Let's see whether the Answer alledg'd in the Title be of this kind. <740>

I say not: For if the Publick can bear the Din and Roaring of a Rabble of Dragoons, who live at discretion on the Hereticks, who turn every thing topsy-turvy, thresh their Landlord, toss him in a blanket, beat Drums at his ears to keep him from sleeping; if the Publick can bear the sight of a world of People of both Sexes drag'd to Torture and Death, as during the Crusade against the *Albigenses* under the Auspices of St. *Dominick,* and during the Government of the Duke *D'Alva* in the *Low Countrys,*[300] and upon several other occasions: if it can be pleas'd with seeing those burnt alive, who are condemn'd by the Inquisition, when it performs what it calls *Autos de Fe* with so much pomp; 'twou'd soon be reconcil'd to this other kind of Punishment. The Novelty might shock a little at first; but the Scandal wou'd soon be remov'd, by shewing the good effect which these Threats, executed now and then only on the more Obstinate, might produce.

Second Answer. *Sodomy is essentially sinful, whereas Murder is sometimes warrantable.*

To show the Invalidity of this Exception, I shall only consider Murder not in a general manner, but restrain'd to a certain Murder actually sinful; as that, for example, of a Citizen of *Paris,* a perfectly honest Man, a good Subject, a good Commonwealths-man, a good Catholick; but who shou'd believe, contrary to the Opinion of the King and Court, and all the Scholars of the Kindom, that the *French* Tongue in the days of *Francis* I was purer and more elegant <741> than that which is spoken now-a-days. I say, that shou'd the King order him to be hang'd purely for this reason, he'd be guilty of a crying Murder; and that this Murder is of an essentially sinful nature, it being impossible that any Murder thus circumstantiated and qualify'd

---

300. Dominic founded in 1215 the Order of Preachers to convert the Albigenses, against whom Pope Innocent III had launched a crusade; Dominicans were active members of the Inquisition. The Duke of Alva was sent in 1557 by King Philip II of Spain to punish the rebellion of the Protestant heretics in the Netherlands; see above, p. 168.

shou'd be warrantable. Let's leave this Person just the same in all other respects, only make him of a Catholick, as he was, a Hugonot; such as *Anne du Bourg*:[301] We'l suppose the King orders him to be hang'd for this reason alone, that he is not a Catholick; the Convertists maintain that this is not a sinful, but a good Action. Consequently the same individual Murder, which might be essentially evil if it had not bin committed for the advantage of Religion, ceases to be a Sin when committed for the destroying of a Sect. In like manner then the unnatural sex Act, which were wicked if it had not bin design'd to bring over those in Error to the true Church, shall become a good Action when proceeding from this Motive.

> Third Answer. *Kings have not the same power over Pudicity, as over Life.*

And why then wou'd the *Romans* order, that Virgins sentenc'd to death shou'd be first deflower'd by the common Hangman, as was actually executed on the Daughter of* *Sejanus?* However it be (for as I don't set up for much <742> Reading, I can't tell whether this Question has bin treated by the Canonists, and I leave the discussing it to any one that has a mind to shew himself) I think it strange, that Men who give Sovereigns a Right over Conscience, shou'd not allow 'em the same Power over the Parts of Shame as they have over the Tongue, the Hand, the Head, the Life of a Subject; for they may order the Hand to be cut off, the Tongue tore out, the Head sever'd from the Body, and the Life to be taken away by any other means. I see no reason why, if they can order the Hangman to tear a Virgin's Tongue from the root, cut off her Arm or Nose, pluck out her Eyes, they mayn't as well command him to deflower her; if they think this kind of Punishment, which wou'd be no Sin in her provided she did not consent but

---

* Tradunt temporis ejus Auctores, quia Triumvirali supplicio affici virginem inauditum habebatur, a Carnifice laqueum juxta compressam. *Tac. Ann. l.* 5. [Tacitus, *Annales,* V.9: "It is recorded by authors of the period that, as it was an unheard-of thing for capital punishment to be inflicted on a virgin, she was violated by the executioner with the halter beside her." Translated J. Jackson, Loeb Classical Library, pp. 150–51.]

301. See above, p. 160, note 69.

yielded to superior Force, likely to turn to a better account than any other Mark of Infamy.

Fourth Answer. They who executed this Command, wou'd commit a great Sin on account of the pleasure they might take in it.

But if this reason holds, the Dragoons shou'd not be allow'd to live at discretion on the Hereticks; for undoubtedly they take a deal of pleasure in getting drunk with their Wine, in domineering, in vilifying 'em, in squeezing out of 'em day after day all the Pence they have left. <743>

♙ CHAPTER XXIX ♙

The surprizing Progress which the Doctrine of Compulsion has made in the World over many Centuries, tho so impious and detestable. Reflections on this.

They who reflect with any attention on the Arguments I have made use of in the fourth Chapter of the first Part, and which I have touch'd upon in other places, particularly in these last foregoing Chapters,[302] will stand amaz'd that the Doctrine of compelling Conscience shou'd ever be attributed to the Son of God; a Doctrine which, in a kind of poisonous Extract, contains in it all the Ferments, the Quintessence, and impregnate Seeds of all Sin and Iniquity, and which, as is said with much less reason of Predestination, is the very Spunge of all Religion: for it not only renders all the most sacred Rights of Humanity, Consanguinity, Affinity, Contract, and Gratitude, so many vain Fantoms, and Rebus's with regard to those of a different Religion, but even with regard to those of the same Faith; since no sooner is a Catholick persuaded that a King, a Judg, a Bishop, a Priest, or any other Catholick, is in a Post which another might fill much more to the advantage of Religion, but he may attempt any thing against 'em with-

---

302. See above, Part I, Chapter 4, p. 86 ff., especially p. 88; Part II, Chapter 3, p. 161; Part III, Chapter 12, p. 318; Part IV, Chapters 26–28, p. 542 ff.

out Sin; the Utility and Interest of the Church being the grand Rule of good and evil Actions. <744>

And what's still more deplorable in this matter, is, That Princes who are but too well inclin'd already to follow no other Rule in their Actions than their worldly Grandeur, will make no scruple of it for the future: for it depends only on their holding that the Prosperity of their State and the Advantag of their Religion are inseparable, so that the Rule of their Ambition and that of Conscience becomes the same, and thus, whatever they undertake for advancing their own Greatness being able to redound to the Advantag and Propagation of their Religion, it will be perfectly conformable to that Rule of Equity which our Convertists lay down; which by a direct Consequence authorizes all the perfidious Ways and Violences of Princes, whether exercis'd on their own Catholick Subjects, or on the neighboring Catholick States, provided they are attended with success.

All these Consequences, together with a great Variety of other Arguments, which may be seen in my *Commentary,* compound such a Demonstration against the literal Sense of the Parable, that I'l defy all the Missionarys, who now are or ever shall go to *China,* to answer a *Chinese* Philosopher, who shou'd attack 'em with my *Commentary* in his hand (and how wou'd it be, if he were provided with a better Book on this Subject, which an abler Pen than mine might easily furnish him?) to answer him, I say, if he undertook to prove that JESUS CHRIST, had he design'd by this Parable to enjoin the crouding his Church by fair or by foul means, either did not know what he said, contradicted himself grosly, or was an errand Impostor: *Absit verbo Blasphemia.*[303] Let's hold then <745> by that wise Maxim of natural Religion, *Quod tibi fieri non vis, alteri ne feceris;*[304] which he so earnestly recommends to his Disciples, *Mat.* 7. 12. in much the same words: *What you wou'd that Men shou'd do unto you, that do ye also to them; for this is the Law and the Prophets,* adds he: A remarkable Saying, which shews that this single Rule comprehends the Substance of all Christian Morality.

---

303. "May there be no blasphemy in the word[s]," i.e. in speaking of Jesus Christ as possibly an impostor, etc.

304. "Do not do to another what you do not wish done to you."

Since therefore it's certain that no one wou'd have his Conscience forc'd, let's firmly believe, that JESUS CHRIST never design'd that his Followers shou'd compel; because they cannot act thus, without doing that to another which they wou'd not have done to themselves. We are oblig'd to expound the Words of the Parable by this Rule.

But the great Subject of Wonder, is not that there shou'd be a Set of Men found to derive the Doctrine of Violence and Persecution from these words of the Gospel, *Compel 'em to come in:* It's infinitely more amazing, that a Doctrine of this nature shou'd prevail to such a degree over the Christian World, that there shou'd not be one considerable Sect which does not maintain it vigorously, either in whole or in part. There are particular Persons here and there in every Christian Communion who inwardly condemn, or even publickly brand the Use of all violent Methods for making Men change their Religion; but I don't know any, except the* Socinian <746> and Arminian Sects, who professedly teach that all other means for converting Hereticks or Infidels, but those of Instruction, are unwarrantable. And pray what are these two Sects? The first is scarce more visible than the Church of the Elect; the Socinians are blended imperceptibly with other Christians, and don't make a visible Body apart, except in a very few Places of the World: and as for the Arminians, they are known only in some Towns of *Holland.* So that the Doctrine of Toleration is receiv'd only in a few dark Corners of Christianity, while that of Non-Toleration goes about every where, and is not asham'd to shew its face.

In effect, this is the favorite Doctrine of the Church of *Rome,* and practis'd by her in all places where she has the power in her hands. And the Protestants, who, to do 'em justice, have in a great measure pluckt out its sting, do nevertheless reduce it to practice where they are uppermost. It's not many months since none but the Episcopal Party had a full Liberty of Conscience here. There are some of the *Swiss Cantons* who will tolerate no other Worship but the Calvinist, and who within our own memory have exercis'd great Violences on the Anabaptists; the Men in the World who best deserve a Toleration, since renouncing the Profession of Arms, and the

---

* *One might add the very small Sect of Quakers and the Anabaptists; but beside that they scarce write any thing, this latter Sect will readily join with the Arminians.*

Magistracy, from a Principle of Religion, there's not the least danger of their rebelling, or interfering with those who sue for Posts in the Government: and as to their refusing the Oath of Allegiance, it is not that they are more averse to Government than other Subjects, but that they take the Precept against <747> swearing in the Strictness of the Letter, and believe themselves as much bound by their bare Word as others are by Oaths. The Lutherans in some Imperial Towns, where they are uppermost, don't tolerate the Calvinists without reluctance; they are oblig'd to have their Meetings without the Walls (like People infected in the Lazarets) and sometimes their Churches are remov'd at a greater distance. The Queen of *Denmark,* who's a Calvinist, is allow'd no more Ministers than are just necessary; to which we may add a few others who have bin allow'd the *French* Refugees of late years, and who are lookt on with an unkind eye by the Lutheran Pastors. The Dutchess of *Zell,* a Calvinist too, cou'd not obtain a Minister of her own Communion, till very lately: Not that the Duke her Husband was rigid in his own Principles, but that he was loth to disoblige his Clergy. The *French* Refugees in the Country of *Wirtemberg* were deny'd the Lutheran Sacrament, till they subscrib'd a Formulary, containing the Doctrine of Ubiquity, and the Communication of the other Propertys of the uncreated Word to the Humanity of Jesus Christ; as also that of the Real Presence, Oral Manducation, and the rejecting the Doctrine of particular Grace, and absolute Reprobation.[305] The Calvinists might as soon obtain the free Exercise of their Religion in the Hereditary Countrys of the House of *Austria,* as in those of the Electorate of *Saxony.*

The Papists are not tolerated either in *Sweden* or *Denmark;* and as for the Greek Church under the Turkish Government, no matter what their Conduct is, because it depends not on them to <748> tolerate or compel any. The Greek Churches, where they have the power, as in *Muscovy,* tolerate no other Communion.

Nor is the spreading of this Doctrine over the whole face of Christianity, except the few Spots that I have spoke of, a thing of a late date: it has universally prevail'd ever since the Christians got the Power of the Sword

---

305. Apparently the Formula of Concord (1577); for text see http://www.bookof
concord.org/fc-ep.html.

into their hands, from *Constantine* the first Christian Emperor to *Leopold,* who now sits on the Imperial Throne. This has bin demonstrated so amply, so clearly, so exactly, and with so much care, by *Lewis Thomassin* a Father of the Oratory at *Paris,* in the two Volumes lately publish'd by him concerning the Unity of the Church;[306] that a Man must put out his eyes, to have the least doubt on this head. He has prov'd the Perpetuity of the Faith of the Church[307] as to this Doctrine from the Time of Constantine until the Present to such a degree of Evidence, that if the Jansenists cou'd have done as much on the Perpetuity of Faith concerning the Real Presence, I mean by Testimonys so free from all Equivoke and Exception, so irrefragable as those of *P. Thomassin,* there had not bin room left to offer a tittle against it.

And here I think my self oblig'd to take notice of the Ingenuity of the Person who wrote of the Rights of the two Sovereigns,[308] against what I had advanc'd concerning Toleration and Conscience. He owns, *pag.* 280. *That Paganism had still subsisted, and three parts in four of* Europe *had bin Pagans at this day, if* Constantine *and his Successors had not employ'd their Authority to extinguish it.* What he says of Paganism holds as true of Arianism, Manicheism, Monothelism, <749> Wicliffism, Albigeism, *&c.* And therefore I am surpriz'd, that a celebrated *French* Author,[309] and who has the Reputation of great Skill in Antiquity, shou'd tell us in a Treatise of Controversy, publish'd by him about eight or nine years ago; *That one must be very little skill'd in Ecclesiastical History, to be ignorant that in all the Differences with the Arians, the Eutychians, and other Hereticks, the Church employ'd only Exhortations, or Reasoning, or Councils, or other such-like Arms.* But perhaps 'twill appear more surprizing, that after *P. Thomassin* had so

---

306. See above, p. 328, note.

307. This is an allusion to the work of Nicole and Arnauld on the perpetuity of faith in the Real Presence, above, p. 460, note 224: if their argument proves the orthodoxy of that doctrine, Thomassin's proves the orthodoxy of the doctrine of persecution (an *argumentum ad hominem*).

308. Jurieu; see above, p. 386, note 164.

309. Not identified.

clearly prov'd the contrary, the Author of the *Seduction éludée*,[310] another *French* Writer, shou'd say, addressing himself to the Bishop of *Meaux: I must tell you, my Lord, that in all History, as well antient as modern, all Ways of Violence exercis'd by Princes on the score of Religion, have never bin otherwise lookt upon than as Spectacles of Horror; and that the Names of these Princes are not mention'd to this day without execration.* What, the *Constantines,* the *Theodosius's,* the *Honorius's,* the *Marcians,* the *Justinians,* who order'd the putting so many penal Laws in execution against Sectarys, and condemn'd those to death who continu'd in the Pagan Idolatry *&c.* or those who wou'd read or keep by 'em Heretical Books; Names not mention'd to this day without execration! How will he make this out? These two Authors agree moreover in saying, that Hereticks never establish'd themselves but by the Terrors of Death, by Fire and Sword; and the latter affirms this principally of the Arians. I refer 'em both to the following Chapter. <750>

The Scandal wou'd be less indeed, cou'd they prove that in reality the Names of those Princes who had establish'd the Truth by ways of Violence had bin always odious: But alas, to the Scandal of the Christian Name, the same *Lewis Thomassin,* who has so clearly demonstrated the Perpetuity of penal Laws against Sectarys, has prov'd with the same Evidence, that Councils, Bishops, or the most eminent Doctors, were they who always sollicited these Laws, or honor'd with Elogys, Acclamations, Benedictions, or most humble Addresses of Thanks, the Princes who had enacted those Laws, and put 'em vigorously in execution. So that we find in this matter a Combination of two or three Circumstances, which amount in truth to a Prodigy: One is, the enacting penal Laws against such as shou'd not have certain Opinions concerning the Truths of Religion, practis'd in every Corner of the Christian World, and reiterated as oft as occasion presented for above twelve hundred Years past.

310. *Séduction eludée* was reviewed by Bayle, NRL, OD, vol. 2, p. 741. *La Séduction éludée, ou Lettres de M. l'évêque de Meaux* [J.-B. Bossuet] *à un de ses diocésains* [Pierre de Vrillac] *qui s'est sauvé de la persécution avec les réponses qui y ont esté faites et dont la principale est demeurée sans réplique* (Seduction eluded, or letters of Bishop Bossuet to a resident of his diocese who was saved from persecution, together with answers that have been made, the main one of which has remained without reply). This book is attributed to Jean Rou in Bibliothèque Nationale catalogue.

Next, the exact and sometimes very bloody Execution of these same Laws on every occasion. And the last and most monstrous of all, is the Approbation of the two first by Prelates, Councils, Popes, and most of the individual Doctors.

I repeat it once more, This is what looks most monstrous in the whole Affair; for it's no such wonder, that Christian Princes shou'd abuse their Power to the oppressing those Christians who differ'd from themselves in Worship or Opinion: They have so often abus'd it, to the involving their Subjects in most unjust, and sometimes most destructive Wars, and to the loading 'em with <751> Taxes and Imposts, that Persecution might very well be lookt on as an ordinary Failing in 'em. One might make a Genealogical Table with as little Interruption in the Lines, and with many more Branchings, of Princes, their Concubines, and their Bastards, as of them, their Queens, and their lawful Progeny; we are accustom'd to this, and don't wonder at it: Why then shou'd we cry out on their Injustice against those who differ from 'em in Religion? But as we might justly deplore an universal Corruption, if we saw Divines and Pastors of Souls excite Princes to enter into unnecessary Wars, to lay heavy Taxes on their People, to carry on scandalous Gallantrys, bless 'em for these things, thank 'em publickly from the Pulpit, extol 'em in Harangues, in Epistles Dedicatory, &c. so is it the height of Iniquity and utmost Depravation, when the Depositarys of sound Doctrine, the most Venerable Part of the Christian Church, instantly sollicit unrighteous Laws, press the Execution of 'em, and load those with Thanks and Praises from the Chair of Truth, who grant and enforce 'em. Blindness and Flattery never carry'd it to such a height, with regard to the Adulterys and Concubinages of Crown'd Heads. The Church, the Priests, the Preachers, in the most complaisant Times, have contented themselves with keeping a respectful Silence; and undoubtedly Christianity must be suppos'd in a much more deprav'd State, if Murder, Rapine, Fornication, were publickly taught and recommended, than we can judg it to be from hence, that several Christians commit these Crimes. It's therefore the excess and utmost strain of Iniquity and Blindness, when so <752> mad a Doctrine as that which authorizes the punishing those who from a Motive of Conscience refuse to sign a Formulary, spreads thro the Christian Church with the Approbation and Applause of almost all its Doctors; and is so thorowly establish'd, that one passes for little better than a Heretick, even in the Judgment of Protestants, if he speaks with some force for Toleration, as I have ventur'd to do.

It's undoubtedly a great Scandal to those who exercise their Reason, to find that such a Doctrine as this; *The Truths of Religion ought to be planted in the Understanding and Heart of Man by means of Instruction, and none compel'd by main Force to the Profession of what their Consciences don't approve:* it's, I say, a very great Scandal, that such a Doctrine, agreeable to the Lights of common Sense, to the most refin'd Reason, to the Spirit of the Gospel, to the Sense of the Christian Church for the three first Centurys, shou'd be so intirely worn off over the whole face of Christianity, that it is no where now to be found except in a very few small Sects, some of which are abhor'd by all other Christians, and others consider'd as Schismaticks, with regard even to Protestants, and lookt on with a very ill eye.

The Scandal enhances, when we consider all the Horrors of that Doctrine which has bin adopted in its room.

As also when we consider, that they who have detected so many other Falshoods of the Church of *Rome,* shou'd see nothing of the* Enormity of this. They judg'd very right, that she acted un-<753>justly in persecuting them, but not that themselves did ill in compelling others; and this was indeed retaining all the Falshood of the Doctrine.

Might not we justly apprehend, that this Scandal may make some Men doubt, 1. Whether God has not once more rejected his chosen People (for the Promises made to the Jews of an everlasting Covenant were no less express than those of the Gospel.) 2. Whether the Christian Religion, over and above its part in the general Providence, is still govern'd and specially protected by a Head sitting at the Right Hand of God; which Head is endu'd with infinite Wisdom, and Goodness, and Power. 3. Whether these small Sects, who have retain'd the Doctrine in question, may not be as happy with regard to other parts of the Faith of the first Ages, as with regard to this Article. This was the Point which shou'd have expir'd last: Since therefore it has not subsisted among those who have given themselves over to violent ways, who can ensure us that they have not stifled several other

---

* *The Proof of this is to be seen in Chap.* 31.

Truths? 4. Whether, let the worst come to the worst, these Sects so run down on the score of their speculative Heresys, are not at least as good as those who boast themselves Orthodox, even tho we allow their Pretensions; considering that their Doctrine of compelling is a Heresy in Morality, a practical and most pestilential Heresy, and which, with the Crimes it produces, does more than ballance any mere speculative Falshood. <754>

⚬ CHAPTER XXX ⚬

That the Spirit of Persecution has reign'd, generally speaking, more among the Orthodox, since Constantine's *days, than among Hereticks. Proofs of this from the Conduct of the Arians.*

I confine my self to the Consideration of the Arians,[311] because the other Hereticks either had no Kings, or but very few of their own Sects; so that they were not in a condition to discover by the effect, whether the first fire of their Zeal being spent, they wou'd have follow'd the Maxims of Toleration. But the case of the Arians is different, they reign'd a long time in several parts of the World. Now as we have none of their Writings preserv'd to us, we can't better judg of their Theory on the Article of Toleration, than by the Conduct of their Princes towards those of a different Religion. This is a sure way enough: for if once it appear, that these Princes tolerated other Sects, the Consequence will hold good, that the Arian Clergy were much more moderate than the Orthodox; it being scarce possible, that a King, press'd by his Clergy in season, and out of season, to extirpate Sects, shou'd long preserve a Spirit of Moderation, especially when made to understand, that his eternal Salvation, and the Tranquillity of his Kingdom depended on it, and that besides he shall acquire by it the greatest Glory a Monarch can aspire <755> to, and that nothing is properer for expiating the Irregularitys of Morals which he may have fallen into. These are the Brands with which the Faggot of Persecution is set a fire; and 'tis moreover an easy matter for Churchmen to impose on Kings in matters of Religion, and to

---

311. See Appendixes, "Trinity and Incarnation," p. 584.

represent to 'em as monstrous and abominable, whatever they have a mind shou'd be persecuted.

Kings, for the most part, are very ignorant in these points, and take up with popular Notions. However it be, let's consider a little the Conduct of the Arians.

It can't be deny'd in the main, but Hereticks have sometimes proceeded cruelly against those who remain'd united to the main Stock; but it must be own'd too, that the Orthodox were the Aggressors, for 'twas they implor'd the Secular Arm under *Constantine* against Arianism, before the Arians had exercis'd any Violence on them.

It's true, *Constantine* did not go such lengths as perhaps they wou'd have had him; and towards the latter end of his Life, he was indulgent enough to the Followers of *Arius:* but his Son *Constantius,* a rank Arian, prompted by his natural Temper, and by the Resentment of the Arians, who no doubt remembred the Hardships which the Orthodox had endeavor'd to bring 'em under by the Secular Authority; and perhaps provok'd by the too little regard that the Catholick Party had shewn for his Commands, exercis'd great Violence on the Orthodox, as did also the Emperor *Valens.* But bating this, I don't think it can be prov'd, that the Arians departed from the Gospel Spirit of Moderation so much as the Or-<756>thodox, or from that Toleration which is due to those who are not to be convinc'd by Argument: and this falls in with the foremention'd Motives of Scandal, for if some Party of Christians has retain'd any thing of a Spirit of Equity and Moderation, and avoided propagating it self, and growing by Violence and the Spoil of others, it is that which is look'd on as most corrupt in the Faith; whereas, they who pass for most Orthodox have all along oppress'd, by the temporal Power of their Princes, those whom Reason, corroborated by the Gospel, requires that we shou'd not bring in by any other way than that of brotherly Instruction.

I might prove this Moderation of the Arians by the Conduct of *Theodorick,* one of their* Kings, who, hearing that the Emperor *Justin* had depriv'd this Sect of their Churches in the East, sent Embassadors to him,

---

* See Maimb. Hist. de l' Arr. *l.* 10. [See Louis Maimbourg, *Histoire de l'Arianisme* (History of Arianism), 1673.]

and the Pope at the head of 'em, to let him know, he shou'd be oblig'd to make terrible Reprisals, unless a stop were put to the Persecution of the Arians. This was an Instance of great Moderation in a King sprung from a warlike and barbarous Nation, and who had never molested the Catholicks of his Dominions; to make use of the peaceable way of Embassage, and send him at the head of it, who of all the Orthodox Prelates was the likeliest to make it succeed, on the score of that great Veneration paid to the See of *Rome* in those days. A Prince who was a zealous Persecutor wou'd not have acted thus, he wou'd have snatch'd at the Occasion <757> of distressing his Subjects of the other Religion, and not hazarded the losing it by an Embassy of such a nature.

The Conversion of the Arians in Spain.

But I shall give another Instance of much greater Force. The Arian *Goths,* having conquer'd *Spain* towards the beginning of the fifth Century, were govern'd there by Kings of their own Religion till towards the latter end of the sixth. Yet when *Recared,* one of their Kings, resolving to change his Religion, had a design of making all his Subjects abjure with him, there were but seven or eight Arian Bishops found in the whole Kingdom, and five Lords; whereas the Catholick Bishops, who appear'd on this occasion in the third Council of *Toledo,* made up about three-score and ten.

This is an incontestable Argument, that the Catholick Bishops, who had bin settl'd in *Spain* at the time that the *Goths* conquer'd it, were suffer'd to continue there with their Churches and Flocks; which proves unanswerably, that the Arian Kings, under whom they liv'd for near two hundred Years, were none of the fiercest Persecutors: for had they ordain'd Confiscation, Banishment, Dragooning, Imprisonment, and other such like Punishments, for those Catholicks who refus'd to change Religion, with great Rewards for those who turn'd Arians; every one will agree, that they had not in less than a Century, left a Soul in their Dominions who had not profess'd Arianism. <758>

Here then we find a Succession of Kings, who for the most part granted their Subjects of a contrary Religion full Liberty of Conscience, and who did not believe, that any other way but that of Persuasion made sincere and faithful Converts. And this single Fact is of greater weight than all the little Flourishes of *P. Maimbourg,* and all that he wou'd fain make us believe, with the usual Blindness of his Prejudices, touching the Barbarity of these Arian Princes.

But see the Reverse of this Conduct in these *Gothick* Kings, as soon as they embrac'd Catholicism. *Hermenegilde,* Son of King *Lewigilde,* having bin taken by his Father into a share of the Government, had no sooner abjur'd his Heresy at the Sollicitations of the Princess his Wife, but he refus'd to obey his Father, not only as to his Command of returning to Arianism (so far a very commendable Disobedience no doubt) but also as to his Command of coming to Court; and as soon as he had acquainted his Father with this Resolution, he prepar'd for War, and enter'd into a Confederacy with the greatest Enemys of his Father's Crown, faithfully supported by the Catholicks of the Kingdom. He had the Misfortune to be worsted in the War; and being forc'd to surrender himself, was clapt in Prison, and put to death by his Father's Orders. We can't refuse him the Praises of Martyrdom, because it lay in his own Breast to regain his Liberty and Crown by turning Arian; yet we must not, after the Example of St. *Gregory* the Great, extol him for this, without condemning him on the other hand, for rebelling against his Father: one Instance among many of the false Oratory of <759> several Ecclesiastical Writers, who praise those they are pleas'd with, and mention all the good things they have done, but suppress whatever they have done amiss. The Roman Martyrology at the 13*th* of *April* says, that *Hermenegilde* dy'd of Poison for the Catholick Faith; now this is false, he was poison'd for his Rebellion.

One might venture to say, without indulging ill-natur'd Conjectures, that had he liv'd he'd have labor'd in the Conversion of the Arians by a way of Authority, as his Brother *Recared* did, who, as soon as he mounted the Throne, apply'd himself intirely this way, and the better to compass his ends, practis'd the Reverse of the *Latin* Proverb, *Ubi leonina pellis non satis est vulpina est addenda,*[312] as was lately practis'd in *France:* for as he had

---

312. Plutarch, *Lysander,* VII.4: "Where the lion's skin will not reach, it must be patched out with the fox's"; translated Bernadotte Perrin, Loeb Classical Library, p. 251.

an artful insinuating way,[313] he manag'd the chief Lords, and Persons in greatest Authority with the People and Army, so well, as to get their Word, that whenever he shou'd think fit to declare, they wou'd second him: 'Twere needless telling, he gain'd 'em by Caresses and Promises, that's understood. When he had made sure of such a Party as was sufficient for the Attempt, he summon'd the Arian Bishops to Court, and declar'd to 'em, that he was resolv'd not to have two Communions in his Kingdom any longer, and therefore that they must prepare for a Dispute with the Catholick Bishops, and the conquer'd side, which ever it was, unite with the Conqueror. He himself assisted at the Disputes; and as he wish'd that the Catholicks might prevail, it is not to be doubted, but his Presence and Influence contributed very much to their Victory, much as the <760> Bias of *Henry* IV, I wou'd say, his Interest to be thought a good Convert, was a mighty Disadvantage to the Sieur *du Plessis Mornay,* in the Conference of *Fountainbleau.*[314] *Recared* not content to let the Catholicks dispute with that haughty and confident Air which the Presence of a King, whose kind Intentions they cou'd not be Strangers to, must needs have inspir'd, reckon'd up I don't know how many Miracles which he himself had observ'd; and having stun'd these wretched Arians by so open a Partiality, declar'd for the Catholicks, and got himself publickly rebaptiz'd.

I'm not ignorant, that the Reasons of the Catholicks were true at bottom, and those of the Arians false, but this was not the thing which caus'd the Change; for the King himself declar'd in the Council, that he brought 'em the *Goths* and *Sueves* ready converted, and that the Bishops had nothing more to do than just to instruct 'em, *Catholicis eos dogmatibus instituere:*[315] which shews, they had, at the Sollicitation of the Persons gain'd over by the King, promis'd, without examining the two Religions, to do what his Majesty desir'd. I'm apt to think the Bishops did instruct 'em afterwards, and try'd the ways of Lenity as far as they wou'd go; but where these fail'd,

313. One can gather this from Maimbourg's narration, *History of the Arians,* book xi. [Author's note in the French edition. See above, p. 561, note.]

314. This was the debate on 2 April 1600 between Duplessis-Mornay and du Perron. See "Duplessis-Mornay, Philippe," in *The Oxford Encyclopedia of the Reformation,* vol. 2, pp. 11–13.

315. "To instruct them in Catholic doctrines."

Recared employ'd Force: whence I conclude, that the first steps he made were a Trial of the Fox's Skill, and that my Application of the Proverb is just. Let's hear *Mariana,* at the fifth Book, Chap. 14.[316] *Recared,* says he, upon changing his Religion, happen'd to meet with some Disturbances, as 'twas scarce possible but he shou'd; yet they did not last long, nor were they <761> considerable: *And the Severity of the Punishments which he inflicted was not odious, because 'twas absolutely necessary;* 'twas even popular, and applauded by the better sort, and by the common People.

These last words seem to me confus'd; for one does not readily know, whether he means, that the chastiz'd Arians themselves were they who applauded the Severity, or the opposite side only. If the first, that wou'd say much; if the latter, it's saying nothing: for there are few Punishments which don't please the common People, when only those whom they abhor as obstinate Hereticks suffer. However, we may see from this Passage of *Mariana,* how the Historians of *Louis* XIV will speak hereafter; they'l say, there was sometimes a necessity of using severe Methods for reducing the Hugonots, but that this did not last long, and was besides conducted with so much Wisdom, that all *France* admir'd the Hand which cou'd so divinely temper the weight of its mighty Power. I only paraphrase or comment on *Mariana;* the intelligent Reader will easily see what he wou'd be at, this Passage of him being one of those pieces where more is to be understood than seen. However it be, it's plain enough from the unsuspect Testimony of this famous Historian, that *Recared* exercis'd the Severity of Punishment wherever there was a necessity. Had we the Writings of the Arians who disapprov'd this way of converting, we shou'd undoubtedly find in 'em a Detail of all the Violences exercis'd on the Sect; but we have none of their Books left, they have bin all burnt long enough ago. Now, as it never will be known from the Catholick Writers of <762> *France,* that the Hereticks were dragoon'd at such and such a rate, that they'l only mention in general, and in two or three Lines as *Mariana* does, that there was sometimes need of a little Severity, and that the Particulars of these Violences will never be preserv'd, but by the Pens of the persecuted Party; we have ground enough

---

316. Probably: Juan de Mariana, *Historiae de rebus Hispaniae libri XX,* 1592 and later editions. See DHC, art. "Mariana," rem. D.

to believe, either that there was a very smart Persecution in *Spain* under *Recared,* or that the Arians were so effectually made to understand, that the King wou'd stick at no kind of vexatious Usage unless they freely comply'd, that they had not the Courage to expose themselves to the hazard. We shall see towards the latter end of this Chapter, whether we can reasonably suppose, that they understood the Truth at first.

I shall add this peremptory Reason, That since he employ'd Severity where 'twas found necessary, his Design was to convert his Heretick Subjects by Gentleness and Instruction if that wou'd do; but if not, to make 'em abjure by Force. Now this purpose in a Person firmly resolv'd to execute it in case of need, comprehends at least virtually all the Horrors, all the Crimes, and all the Sacrileges of the Doctrine of Compulsion set forth thro-out this *Commentary.* So that it's of little Service towards justifying King *Recared* to say, that he did not long make use of Severity, of an odious Severity; it was not owing to his good Intentions, or to his Notions about the sound Doctrine of Toleration, but to the readiness of the Arians in escaping the Persecution which was preparing for 'em at the expence of their Profession. Consequently the Conversion of the Arians in *Spain,* without Cru-<763>elty and criminal Vexations, was purely accidental.

The modern Catholick Writers can't disown this, if they think on what they themselves remark, That the Arians had no Zeal for their own Religion, and that this was the Reason of their quitting it by shoals. *The little Reluctance,* says one of 'em,* *with which People quit all these false Religions, is a Mark of their Falshood, and of the Impossibility of having a true Zeal for 'em: Truth alone is strong and eternal, a Lye dies away almost of it self. The Resistance the Arians made was so short and faint, that one might judg from this alone, that they strove for a Lye, and not for the Truth, which only is capable of engaging reasonable Minds, and inspiring 'em with Constancy.* Another†
mentioning an Arian Embassador, who pray'd *Gregory* of *Tours* not to speak ill of the Arians, since the *Visigoths* did not speak ill of the Catholicks; the *Visigoths,* adds he, who have a saying, *That in passing between a Pagan*

---

* Thomassin de l' Unité de l' Eg. *par.* 1. *p.* 448. [It does not seem that his discourse strikes all the papist peoples who reformed themselves during the last century (Author's note in the French edition). See above, p. 328, note.]

† Maimb. Hist. de l' Arr. *l.* 11. [See above, p. 561, note.]

Temple and a Christian Church, it's no Sin to bow before one, and before the other; presently subjoins this Reflexion, *So natural is it for Heresy to inspire by little and little an Indifference in Religion, and so certain, that whoever forsakes the true runs a risk of having no Religion at all.*

I wish these Gentlemen wou'd reconcile all these fine Maxims with what so many others of their Brethren, and they themselves, have undoubtedly often advanc'd, *That Pertinaciousness is the Character of Heresy.* Father *Simon* has <764> taken it for the Lemma of a Book which he has lately publish'd against our Mr. *Smith.*[317] If I were not loth to make a Digression, how easily cou'd I expose the Extravagance of this vile little Aphorism! and how heartily cou'd I second the Blow which the small Pamphlet, *France intirely Catholick,* has struck so home at the Convertists, *pag.* 22.[318] But this is not so much the Business in this place.

Another Comparison between Catholick and Arian Princes.

Let us therefore make one Remark on somewhat better grounds, and in a matter of Fact; to wit, That the Arians having subdu'd or possess'd several Provinces of the *Roman* Empire, under the name of *Visigoths, Ostrogoths, Burgundians, Vandals, Lombards,* never disturb'd the Catholicks in these Provinces, nor hinder'd their continuing and multiplying in 'em; as appears from hence, that at the very time, when either the Emperors recover'd these Provinces, or the Arian Princes chang'd Religion, there were always found Catholick Churches in 'em ready form'd, and in a good number. On the contrary, as soon as the Emperor had recover'd these Provinces, or the Princes themselves abjur'd, there was scarce an Arian to be heard of. I say then, that none but those who are blinded by childish Prejudices, in which Historians of the same stamp entertain your half-witted silly Readers; I maintain, I say, there's only this sort, but must conclude, from a Fact so notorious, that the Arians, generally speaking, were more moderate, and more <765> tolerating than the Catholicks, and less capable of having re-

317. Probably: Richard Simon, *Créance de l'Eglise orientale sur la transubstantiation avec une reponse aux nouvelles objections de M. Smith* (Belief of the Eastern Church on transubstantiation, with an answer to new objections from Mr Smith), 1687.
318. Bayle, OD, vol. 2, p. 339b.

course to the impious methods of coactive Authority, to make what they call Conversions.

And in effect, who can reconcile persecuting Cruelty with that Indifference for Religion with which they are charg'd?

Why can't we see, that if they sometimes pillag'd the Monasterys, and exercis'd other Violences on the Catholicks, 'twas more from a Spirit of War and Plunder, which drew their Fathers from the extremest Peak of the North to ravage the *Roman* Empire, than from a Spirit of Conversion. This is evident from hence, that the *Lombards* converted from Arianism, made as frequent Incursions into the Territorys of *Rome,* and plunder'd all before 'em as much as when they were Arians.

An Answer to some Difficultys.

Methinks I hear some body tell me, that instead of wondering as I do, that none but the Hereticks in all Ages shou'd be moderate and forbear Constraint, I ought rather to acknowledg in it the Wonders of the Power of God, who has inspir'd Hereticks with Moderation, and the Orthodox with coactive Principles, the better to propagate and preserve the Truth. But for my part, I own, this sort of Miracles are above my Comprehension; and if we will suppose particular Volitions in God, or miraculous Operations in favor of his Church, I think leaving Hereticks to violate all the Laws of Equity and righteous dealing, yet without their being capable <766> of hurting the Cause of Truth, were more agreeable to the Divine Nature than putting the Orthodox in this unfortunate Predicament, and bringing the Good of the Church out of their most unrighteous Practices.

There's no eluding the Consequence which I had drawn before from a reported historical Fact, by saying, that a Lye gains no ground by Persecution; whereas Truth extinguishes the Followers of a Lye if it ruffle 'em ever so little. For to say nothing of the Jews, proof against all the Attempts that have bin made upon 'em at several times, is it not well known, that the *Irish* and the *Vaudois* of *Piedmont,* one or other of which must be Followers of a Lye, are yet so tenacious, that it's impossible to purge the Place of their Opinions, unless you put 'em every Mother's Child to death, or transport and blend 'em with other Nations? Add to this, that there being several Examples of true Churches which have sunk under Persecution, no one can universally affirm, either that persecuted Falshood is easily destroy'd, or that persecuted Truth is never overcome. What we may venture to say in general is, I think, this, That a Church which subsists under Princes of a different Religion has not bin violently persecuted; and that a Church, which vanishes all at once under a Prince of a different Religion, sinks under Constraint; whereby the Arian Kings will still carry it from the Catholick, in point of Equity and Moderation.

To leave my Adversarys no kind of Subterfuge, I must desire 'em to give me a good Reason why the *Saracens,* when they invaded *Africk,* shou'd extinguish Christianity to such a <767> degree, that there are not the least Footsteps of it remaining on these Coasts, where 'twas formerly so flourishing: Why, if the *Vandals,* when they invaded the same Country, had exercis'd the same Violence on the Catholicks as the *Saracens* did soon after, they might not as well have extinguish'd Catholicism. They ought in all Reason to have compleated its Ruin much sooner than the Disciples of *Mahomet* cou'd have done, because the Passage is incomparably longer from the Catholick Faith to Mahometism than to Arianism. The only good Reason then that can be assign'd is, that the *Vandals* persecuted in Measure, and by Intervals.

One may even say, that that which next under God preserv'd Christianity in the first Ages, was the Pagan Emperors persecuting it only by fits, and sometimes more violently in one Country than another, after which came long Periods of Calm; so that they who had a mind, might find Retreats till the Storm was over. The Emperors had generally one Rival or other to deal with, some Revolt or Sedition to pacify, and too much other business upon their hands to make the Extirpation of a Sect their principal Care. The Empire chang'd Masters frequently: besides, that they and their Ministers were but Novices in comparison of the Christian Princes, who have apply'd themselves to the extinguishing Sects; had those had the managing of what *Decius* and *Dioclesian* undertook, they had in all probability done the Work.

For it's a Folly to pretend, for example, that *Recared,* or the Bishops of his time, gave the Arians such evident and palpable Demonstrations of the Falshood of their Tenets, that they quitted <768> their Heresy unanimously and of their own motion. The Consubstantiality of the Word, a Trinity of Persons in the Unity of the Divine Nature, are not so clearly conceiv'd as the Unity of God, the Incommunicability of his Essence, the Identity of Natures and Persons: consequently when a Man has bin bred up to believe these last Articles as most worthy of God, for the first twenty years of his Life, and to reject the others as destructive of the Divine Nature, it's a hard matter to reconcile him to the Belief of 'em be they ever so true. He might be apt to think, that 'twere hazarding his Salvation too much, to acquiesce in Proofs which his Reason cannot comprehend. It's very improbable then, that the whole Body of Arians throout a Kingdom were converted by Argument and Persuasion.

It's much more likely they comply'd, because they were not the most zealous People in the World for their own Opinions; but it must be own'd too, that they had a prospect of temporal Detriment, if they persisted obstinately in their own way, and consequently were made to understand, that they must do that by force which they refus'd to do by fair means: for let one's Indifference for his own Religion be ever so great, he'l scarce change when he has the full liberty to live and die in it. <769>

❧ CHAPTER XXXI ❧

That the first Reformers in the last Age retain'd the Doctrine of Compulsion.

I have already represented it as a matter of great Scandal, that Persons rais'd up extraordinarily for retrieving the Church fal'n into utter Ruin and Desolation, to use the Words of the *Geneva* Confession,[319] shou'd not have consulted the sacred and inviolable Immunitys of Conscience; and that having rejected so many Follys and Heresys of the Church of *Rome,* they shou'd retain the Doctrine of Constraint; a Doctrine in virtue of which she had made her self drunk with the Blood of the Saints, and fal'n into the principal Enormitys, which oblig'd a good part of the Christian Church

---

319. For the text, see http://www.creeds.net/reformed/gnvconf.htm.

to disown her for a Mother. There's no need of many words to prove the Charge against the first Reformers, for the Fact is but too notorious.

All the World knows, that at *Geneva,* the Mother Church and Center of Unity of the Calvinists, the Party for the Reformation having prevail'd over the other, the Republick in 1535 forbid the Exercise of the Romish Religion, and order'd those who wou'd not renounce it to depart the City in three days, on pain of Imprisonment or Expulsion. It's well known too, that in other Countrys where the Prince or Sovereign embrac'd the Reformation, he not only authoriz'd the publick Exercise of Protestantism <770> (which so far was very just and laudable) but also abolish'd the Mass, and carry'd it to that Extremity at last, as not to suffer those who persever'd in their old Religion to live in the Country. Now this was plainly exceeding the Bounds of Justice: for the Ministers of those days did not found the necessity of abolishing the Mass, on the political Reason which I shall touch anon, nor on the non-tolerating Principle of Papists; but on the Idolatry of the Church of *Rome,* which Kings and Princes, said they, were bound to destroy, in imitation of the ancient Godly Kings of *Judah,* who destroy'd the high Places, and the false Worships introduc'd by their Predecessors, who had done what was not right in the sight of the Lord. All the Arguments, which I have so much press'd against the literal Sense of the Parable, strike directly at every Law or Injunction of the Supreme Power, requiring People to abjure the Mass, on pain of Imprisonment, Banishment, Confiscation of Goods, *&c.* For it's by no means respecting the Empire of Conscience, to annex Punishments to her refusing to embrace or reject any particular Religion.

Let the Mass then be an Idolatrous Worship, as much as you please: A Prince who having once believ'd it the true Worship of God, comes afterwards to look on it as Idolatry, is not to attack it in his Dominions by carnal and temporal Arms, but by Instruction; and if the way of instruction fail, the only lawful pretence that he can have for expelling his Popish Subjects, is, not that their Opinions are false, and their Worship half Pagan, but that they want the <771> requisite Qualifications for making a part of any Society, whereof the Prince is a Protestant; in which case it's plain, they may be justly depriv'd of all the Rights and Privileges of this Society. Let's explain this a little more clearly, and by a Thought perfectly new, and different from what has bin offer'd in the *Commentary* Part 2, ch. 5. and in the Preliminary Discourses p. 47.

A Political Reason for not tolerating Papists.

It's plain that all human Societys are a Confederation of a certain number of Men, who mutually engage themselves to be aiding and assisting to each other against the common Enemy, to observe certain Laws necessary for maintaining the publick Tranquillity, and to obey him or them on whom they confer the Sovereign Power, for the putting those Laws in Execution, which individuals have consented to; or even for reforming 'em. It follows then that the Sovereign is oblig'd to maintain the publick Peace, by putting the Laws in Execution; and that the Subjects on their part are oblig'd to obey him.

But the better to be assur'd of their Obedience, it's necessary he have a double. Tye upon 'em: one of which consists in the Fear of being punish'd by the Criminal Judg, if they transgress their Duty; the other consists in the fear of incurring the Wrath of God, if they disobey the higher Powers. It follows then, that* Subjects must <772> take an Oath of Fidelity and Allegiance, as a Security and Test of their Obedience to the Prince, who hereby sees 'em subjected to the severe Laws of Providence, which beholds and avenges all the most secret Crimes, and especially those for the Punishment of which God is solemnly appeal'd to.

From whence I conclude, that he who can't give the Sovereign these two Securitys, is unqualify'd to be a Member of the Commonwealth, and may be justly expel'd on this score, and banish'd, with Permission however to withdraw, and retire whither he please, he, his Wife, his Children, and Effects, *&c.* Now such is a Roman Catholick, with regard to a Protestant Sovereign, since he may without shocking his Religion, make a mock of all Oaths of Fidelity sworn to him.

I don't say (and this is what I desire may be remark'd) that his Religion necessarily obliges him to look upon his Oath as null; I only say, that it

---

* *This touches not the Quakers or Anabaptists, for the reason hinted before.* [See above, p. 554, note.]

permits him to do this, and furnishes him a Spiritual Sovereign, who can absolve him from this Oath, if he will have recourse to him, and who offers him withal the Felicitys of Heaven, and the Crown of Martyrdom, if he suffers by the Hand of his Prince for any Enterprize against him in favor of Catholicity; which weakens the Fear of the Civil Laws, and thus dissolves both the Tyes which the Subject was under. This is ground enough for a Protestant Sovereign's never having an intire Confidence in a Catholick Subject. Yet I can't think, unless there be other particular Reasons, that they ought to be banish'd out of Places where they <773> behave themselves quietly, and where their Numbers or Force give no Jealousy.

There being therefore only this one political Reason, which can render the Non-toleration of Roman Catholicks excusable; and the first Reformers not having this in View, it follows, that they were not quite so deep as the Papists, but however that they were in this fatal Error, *That it is lawful to compel into the true Church;* or which comes in the end to the same thing, *That it's lawful to condemn those to certain Punishments, who refuse to come into the true Church from a Principle of Conscience.*

They cou'd not fairly alledg, in defence of their Non-Toleration, that the Roman Catholicks tolerated none; for had this bin their reason, they ought to have tolerated those Sects which do tolerate, but this they were far enough from. For not to speak of the Exploits in several Places against the Anabaptists, it's notorious to all the World, that *Servetus* was punish'd with Death at *Geneva; Valentine Gentilis* imprison'd there, afterwards expel'd, and then beheaded at *Bern; Ochin* and *Laschus* ignominiously thrust out of *Geneva* in the depth of Winter:[320] Men who undoubtedly held great Errors, but by no means that of Non-Toleration.

Before I come to make some Reflections on these things, it mayn't be improper in this place to anticipate a Word or two of the Confutation of the *Treatise of the two Sovereigns,* and shew what a gross Mistake this Author is guilty of in his thirteenth Chapter. He pretends that my Principles destroy our Answer to the Popish Writers, when they object, that the Reforma-<774>tion was made in a tumultuous manner, by two or three

---

320. On Servetus, see above, p. 198, note 83. On Jean Gentilis and Bernadin Ochin see articles on them in DHC.

Monks stirring up the People to shake off the Jurisdiction of the Church of *Rome,* by their own Authority: Our Answer, I say, that in *Scotland, England, Swisserland, Geneva,* and in several other Places, the Business of Reformation was carry'd on by the Authority of the Supreme Power, who order'd the inspecting into the State of Religion, and the examining it maturely by learn'd Men, and chang'd the Worship, and restor'd the Purity of God's Service with the greatest Regularity and Order. He pretends, that by my Principles 'twas unjust in the Secular Authority to interpose, and that it renders the Reformation vicious in the manner of it; but he's mistaken, and hides from his Reader the principal part of the Cause, as if he had lost his Minutes or green Bag. All that he says was transacted by the Sovereign Power, is very just, according to my Doctrine; my Principles assert the Authority of the Magistrate in Matters of Religion up to this Point: but that which I condemn, and he suppresses, is, That not content to establish the Reform'd Religion in their Dominions, and give it the Preheminence as they might justly do, they abolish'd every other kind of Worship, and condemn'd those to Punishments who cou'd not in Conscience depart from the Religion of their Fathers, or conform to that Plan of Reformation which had bin approv'd by their Princes,

FINIS.

APPENDIXES

The Language of the Translation

The spelling of the 1708 translation follows sensible conventions not quite the same as those that have since become current:

· Every noun is capitalized (as in modern German).

· Some words are combined, with omission of sounds marked with an apostrophe ('Tis, t'other, let's, it's, here's).

· Silent letters are replaced by apostrophes (wou'd, can't, alledg'd).

· An apostrophe is used to form the plural of some foreign words (Anathema's, Opera's, Provo's, Genius's, Thesis's).

· Sometimes the apostrophe is omitted from possessives (mens Souls).

· Singulars ending in "y" are made plural simply by adding "s" (Qualitys, Deputys, Absurditys).

· The silent terminal "e" of modern spelling is usually omitted (Tast, Judg, Pledg).

· "Virtue" is sometimes spelled "Vertue."

· "Though" is "tho"; "been" is "bin"; "thorough" is "thorow."

· "Them" is almost always abbreviated to "'em."

· Words spelled "-our" in modern British English are spelled without the "u" (Honor, Author, Harbor, Ardor, Rigor).

· Some proper names are spelled differently: "Louis" is often (not always) spelled "Lewis."

· There are variations of spelling that should not trouble the reader: "justle" for "jostle," "Sadduces" for "Sadducees," "plaister" for "plaster," etc.

Punctuation is excessive by modern standards. Many colons and semicolons should be read as commas; many commas should be ignored.

The modern convention that a defining clause should not be preceded by a comma is not followed: "For to render a Punishment just, which is inflicted for Non-compliance with a King's Injunctions, it's necessary these Injunctions be founded on some good reason."

There are some old-fashioned idioms.

"The -ing" without "of," where in modern English we would say "the -ing of." Examples: "for the killing such a man"; "repugnance . . . to the owning it"; "a right of doing everything for the propagating their errors."

A possessive governs an "-ing" word used as a noun (gerund). Examples: "God's enjoining it"; "their being put in Execution"; "any one's presuming to say"; "one Party's refusing to conform." This is still good practice in British English, but perhaps obsolescent.

"Of X becomes Y" means "from being X becomes Y." Example: "It follows that the same Action of a Sin becomes a Vertue."

"These"/"those" means "The latter"/"The former." Example: "The wicked have never left persecuting the Good, nor the Good the Wicked: but these act unjustly herein, and only to do mischief; those charitably. . . ."

Obsolete or Unusual Words or Meanings

The translation uses many colloquialisms to express scorn. Their precise meaning is often uncertain, but unimportant; their general meaning is clear enough from the context: "no better than a Cheat or Sharper at the bottom"; "a band of Ruffians, Cut-throats, Hell-hounds"; "Who, I say, is not in a Sweat, to think what a swadder these Authors must be in":

· "Acted" may mean "actuated," "motivated." Examples: "Persons acted by an indiscreet Zeal"; "many of those who advise Kings to confiscate the Estates of Sectarys, are acted by Avarice."

· "Admire" may mean "marvel," without any suggestion of approval. Example: "one can never enough admire, that in a Country where there are so many good Pens, so many vile Justifications shou'd be suffer'd to pass."

· "Austin" is the old-fashioned English form of St. Augustine's name.

· "Barratry" means stirring up or perpetuating disputes or quarrels. Example: "these tedious Controversys; in which there's a deal of Barratry" (meaning argumentative ingenuity misapplied to keep a controversy going when it should be settled).

· "Catechise" means "catechism." Example: "to make him resume the Doctrines of his Catechise."

· "Challenge" may mean "claim." Example: "a Man, who might otherwise challenge some regard, forfeits all Pretence to it when he shews himself an errand Opiniater."

· "Competency" may mean "sufficiency." Example: "it's as absurd to say, that such an Explication is a Competency for the Conviction of such an Understanding" (i.e. that such an explanation is enough to convince such an understanding).

· "Complexion" may mean "temperament." Example: "the Gnawings of Hunger which a Mother . . . sees her Children suffer before her eyes, are altogether as sharp as the Pains of the Rack, and sharper perhaps in some Complexions than the Rack it self."

· "Conceit" may mean "concept" or "conception." Examples: "a very odd medly of contradictory Conceits"; "it's a most ridiculous Conceit, that only the Orthodox are allow'd to persecute."

· "Demean" may mean "behave." Examples: "if he'l demean himself wisely"; "demeaning themselves civilly otherwise."

· "Doubt but" means "doubt that." Examples: "Tho I don't doubt but there are still brave Spirits"; "there's no manner of doubt but they will introduce"; "I make no doubt, were there such another Process before the Magistrates of Geneva at this day, but they wou'd be very cautious."

· "Elogy" means not "elegy" but "eulogy." Example: "honor'd with Elogys, Acclamations, Benedictions, or most humble Addresses of Thanks."

· "Expedient" as an adjective means "useful," as a noun "a means," not necessarily with any suggestion of lack of principle. Examples: "if they conceive it expedient for the Peace of the State"; "if the Expedient be a thing in its own nature indifferent, and which if the worst came to the worst cou'd have no ill consequence, he ought forthwith to try it."

· "Illapses" means "gentle influences." Example: "those Irradiations of the Law eternal, those Illapses of unalterable Order."

· "Jealousy" may mean "suspicion." Example: "and where their Numbers or Force give no Jealousy."

· "Just" may mean "accurate," "well-adjusted," "appropriate," or "well-founded." Examples: "to settle its just and proper Sense"; "does not always reason justly, because his Notions in one place do not perhaps nicely fall in with his Notions in another"; "computing the just Proportion between the Crueltys of antient and modern Persecutions"; "who can't say three words together with any Justness"; "the Consequence follow'd justly and necessarily from their false Principle"; "I here shew, by just Examples."

· "Objectively" means *not* "in reality," but almost the opposite, "as an object in the mind." Examples: "it suffices, that it be objectively the same, I mean, that it appear so"; "For the Sharper has not the least Right or Authority, as existing outside the Mind of the Servant, but as he is objectively in the Servant's Mind; that is, to express my self more intelligibly, all his Right consists in the Idea, or in the Persuasion the Servant is under, that this Sharper is a faithful Messenger from his Master"; "but objectively true, or, which is the same thing in plainer terms; which appears true to us."

· "Obnoxious to" means "liable to." Example: "if Hereticks were indeed made obnoxious to the Sword of the Magistrate."

· "Physical" may mean "natural" (as opposed to voluntary), without the thing necessarily being material. Examples: "it's at best only a physical Good or Evil, which confers no moral Worth on Actions"; "can make no difference betwixt two Acts of the human Will exactly the same as to their physical Entity"; "'tis a physical Perfection at least (if it be improper to call it a moral one, because antecedent to any free and reasonable Choice) to love what they take to be Truth"; "distinguishing between that which is physical in the Acts of our Soul, and that which is moral."

· "Prejudice" may mean "injury," or it may mean "initial opinion" or "presumption" without implication of unfairness. Examples: "an Usurpation in prejudice of the Members of the true Church; in prejudice of the true Children"; "a Treatise intitled, Proofs and Prejudices in favor of the Christian Religion"; "an Argument, or a very strong Prejudice at least."

· "Pretend," "Pretension" may mean "claim," often without any suggestion of untruth; "supposing the pretensions" means "assuming the truth of the claims." Examples: "not by a bare Pretension"; "you have not prov'd your Pretensions as yet"; "these are the Protestants, or at least pretend to be"; "to pretend this, is so far from being a Sign that one is lost to all shame, that not to pretend it, one must have lost all his Senses"; "But by supposing the Pretensions of the Protestants, their most extreme Rigors are in the order of human things."

· "Resume" may mean "recapitulate." Examples: "St. Austin here resumes the formerly-confuted Examples"; "to make him resume the Doctrines of his Catechise."

· "Topick" means "a source or underlying principle of arguments." Examples: "as long as a Heretick owns the Scripture as his Topick, and Magazin of all his Proofs"; "the true Topick of this Question was not Known in those days; I mean, the Principles and Source of the Arguments."

Bayle's Use of Logic

Seventeenth-century French education included a more or less thorough training in logic, the art of thinking. Medieval logic textbooks were rivaled by new texts, notably the famous work of the Jansenists Arnauld and Nicole, *The Logic of Port-Royal.*[1] Bayle frequently comments on the logic of his arguments, using the terminology common at the time. Argument was thought of as disputation, an "adversary procedure" with opposing parties (though sometimes the opponent might be imaginary).

An argument, inference, or "consequence" (see p. 75) is a set of premises from which a conclusion "follows." The premises of a valid argument

---

1. Arnauld, Antoine, and Pierre Nicole, *Logic or the Art of Thinking* (first edition 1662). Translated into English by Jill Buroker (Cambridge: Cambridge University Press, 1996).

"necessitate" or "compel" the conclusion: if you accept the premises as true, you must also accept the conclusion. This characteristic of a valid argument is sometimes called its "consequence"; see p. 186. (Thus "consequence" has two meanings: the argument and its validity.) A valid argument with true and accepted premises is "cogent" or "compelling."[2]

Various kinds of arguments were distinguished, including the *syllogism* (with two premises, called in order the "major" and the "minor," arranged in "mood and figure"; see p. 333, pp. 430–31), the *enthymeme* (an argument with one or more of its premises not expressly stated; see p. 186, p. 218, p. 428), and the *dilemma* ("either p or q, if p then r, and if q then s, therefore either r or s," and other variants; see p. 142).

The premises of an argument were called "antecedents" (p. 75). The fundamental premises of a chain of arguments, or of all reasoning in a field, were called its "principles" (p. 72), or "common notions" (p. 68), or "maxims" (p. 416). It is pointless to try to convince people by an argument the principles of which they do not believe. Since the proposer of the argument (normally) also believes its premises, its principles must therefore be "common" to both parties (p. 43).[3] Bayle often insists that discussion cannot achieve persuasion unless the issues are traced up to "common principles" (p. 134). Premises likely to be acceptable to almost anyone were called "commonplaces."[4] A "topic" is as it were a pigeon-hole in which commonplaces are stored, a magazine of premises (p. 276).

An argument that fails by using a premise that no one will believe unless they already believe the conclusion was called a "petitio principii" (p. 333), literally a "begging of the principle" (p. 23), usually called in English "begging the question" (p. 54, p. 510), or "assuming" or "supposing the

2. If one or more of the premises is not asserted but merely "supposed" ("for the sake of argument"), the argument is hypothetical, useful for showing what would follow from what, but not proving anything.

3. If the arguer does not believe one or more of the premises but supposes that the other party does, the argument is "ad hominem"—not a proof, but an argument suitable for shaking the other party's current belief, or, as Bayle says, a "Representation importing that they did not act consistently with their own Principles" (p. 417; see also pp. 124, 331).

4. However, this term (as also "maxims") was often used contemptuously, since what some people think is obvious to everyone may be just prejudice; see p. 147.

thing in question" (p. 42, p. 45). (Note that "begging the question" does not mean raising a question, but assuming as premise something that will not be believed by anyone the argument is meant to convince.)

A "direct" proof argues positively from premises which imply the desired conclusion (p. 150, p. 199, p. 412). An "indirect" proof shows that a proposition is true by assuming "for the sake of argument" the truth of the proposition that contradicts the one you wish to prove, and then on that assumption constructing a hypothetical argument to a conclusion the other party will admit is absurd or impossible. Such indirect proof was called "reductio ad absurdum" (p. 72, p. 211, p. 512).

The other party's argument could be undermined by showing that it "proves too much" (p. 175), that it implies "inconveniences," conclusions that the other party cannot accept (p. 134). Or the argument can be "retorted," i.e. adapted to prove conclusions inconsistent with the position of the party using it (p. 347). Or a counter-argument can be "objected" (literally "thrown up against") its premises or its conclusion. The other party might well reply to such "difficulties," and the reply might provoke a counter-reply; the reply might be characterized as an "evasion" (p. 37), meaning an unsuccessful attempt to avoid the force of the objection.

Some arguments are faulty because the conclusion they lead to is simply not relevant or "not to the point." In such a case the arguer is accused of "impertinence" (see p. 42), of "changing the question" (see p. 301), or of "ignoratio elenchi" (not knowing what a proof is); see p. 348.

If an argument is unsuccessful, not because its premises are false or not accepted, but because even if they were accepted its conclusion would not follow, it is said to be a fallacy, paralogism, or sophism (p. 54, p. 411). Often Bayle is at pains to point out that *even if* something is accepted that in fact might well be challenged, still the opponent's conclusion will not follow. One virtue of such an analysis is that it clears the ground, brings into sharper focus the issues in dispute: there is no need to argue about various things the parties might in fact disagree about, because they make no difference to the point in question. For examples of Bayle's passing over disagreements that do not need to be pursued, see p. 88, p. 200, p. 480.

On moral questions a common method of argument is by example, parallel, or analogy. "If you accept that in situation X one ought to make moral judgment J, then you must also accept that in this similar situation one ought to make the same judgment." The counter to such an argument is to point out a "disparity" between the two situations (p. 361). The practice of comparing situations and analyzing similarities and disparities was called "casuistry," the analysis of "cases" (p. 70). Though this was recognized as a legitimate activity in principle, it was often felt that casuists were "too clever by half." Jesuit casuists, in particular, were accused of working to make the demands of morality less exacting than they really were (pp. 245, 319).[5]

The fierce contests fought with the aid of the art of logic were often carried on unfairly, in Bayle's opinion. Hence his warning that he will not accept that his book has been "answered" if opponents merely find various minor faults of reasoning—they must come to grips with his main and best arguments for toleration; see p. 38, p. 478. On the other hand, he claims that he himself does not treat his opponents unfairly (pp. 175–76, p. 423). Compare DHC, art. "Chrysippus," rem. G.

Religious and Philosophical Controversies

During the sixteenth and seventeenth centuries the various denominations and schools of thought among Christians fought out their differences in "conferences" or debates before some influential audience and in print. (See Bayle's remarks, pp. 406–7.) For example, the Catholic Jacques-Bénigne Bossuet, bishop of Meaux, published a record of his conference with Jean Claude, a prominent Protestant theologian, held before a noble lady who was considering which denomination she should belong to; in reply, Claude published his *Réponse au livre de M. de Meaux intitulé: Conférence avec M. Claude* [Answer to a book by M. de Meaux entitled *Debate with M. Claude*], 1683. The Catholic Antoine Arnauld published *La perpétuité de la foi de l'Eglise touchant l'Eucharistie défendue contre le livre du Sr Claude, ministre de Charenton* [The perpetuity of the faith of the Church concerning the Eucharist, defended against the book of M. Claude, Minister of Charenton], 1669; Claude replied with *Réponse au livre de M. Arnauld 'De*

---

5. The reputation of the Jesuit casuists was attacked especially by Blaise Pascal's *Letters of a Provincial,* for which material was provided by the Jansenist Antoine Arnauld; it was later translated into Latin by Arnauld's colleague Nicole.

la perpétuité de la foi' [Answer to a book by M. Arnauld on the perpetuity of the faith], 1670. To every attack there was a reply, to every reply a reply, almost without end. There was a widespread belief, at least before Bayle had his say, that religious disagreements could be resolved by reasoning.

In the course of the *Philosophical Commentary* Bayle often mentions or analyzes these debates between the denominations or schools of thought among Christians. He mentions Roman Catholic, Orthodox (i.e. Greek and Russian Orthodox), and Protestant. The Protestants included the Episcopal (meaning Church of England), the Lutherans, the Calvinists (also called the Reformed, sometimes Huguenots), the Arminians (also called Remonstrants), the Socinians, Anabaptists, and others. If readers find the differences among them confusing, that suits Bayle's point that the controversies among Christians are extremely difficult to decide. However, he does not intend to suggest that they cannot possibly be decided, that no one can reasonably make a decision. He indicates that he is himself a Calvinist and that he is not a "Pyrrhonist" (i.e. a sceptic, one who holds that one should suspend judgment). His point is not that we should throw up our hands and believe none of the conflicting versions of Christianity, but that Christians should be ready to acknowledge one another's sincerity in holding conflicting beliefs.

Faith and Heresy

Christians of all denominations believed that being a Christian involved holding various beliefs, the "articles of faith." The correct beliefs are "orthodox," beliefs inconsistent with them are "heresy." Some differences of opinion were regarded as tolerable. On many religious questions the Catholic Church had not "defined" an answer, and Catholics were at liberty to hold different beliefs. Catholic religious orders (Jesuits and Dominicans, for example) sometimes espoused conflicting answers to some questions (see p. 209). Similarly among Protestants some distinguished between "fundamental" and "nonfundamental" articles and did not regard as heretics those who disagreed with them on nonfundamentals (see p. 217, p. 401, p. 403). (See article "Fundamental Articles" in *The Catholic Encyclopaedia,* http://www.newadvent.org/cathen/06319a.htm.)

To be a "heretic," however, was not a matter merely of believing a false doctrine; in addition one must hold it in a "pertinacious" way, i.e. stub-bornly, opinionatedly, obstinately, with *opiniâtreté* in Bayle's French—i.e. refusing to abandon the false belief even when one could see, or should have been able to see, that it was false. (On the definition of *heretic* see p. 454.) Bayle maintains that only God can tell whether someone is opin-ionated in religious belief: we must assume that others' religious beliefs are held sincerely, in good faith.[6]

Trinity and Incarnation

Christians of most denominations agreed that the doctrines defined by the first four General or Ecumenical (i.e. World-wide) Councils of the Church[7] were essential to orthodoxy. These councils formulated the doctrine of the Trinity, i.e. the doctrine that there are three divine "persons," namely the Father, the Son, and the Holy Spirit, really distinct (i.e. the Father is not the Son, etc.), and equal in all respects, but there is only one God. They also formulated the doctrine of the Incarnation, i.e. that one of the three divine persons, the Son, became a man, Jesus Christ, so that Jesus is both God and man. In Bayle's day all Christians believed in the Trinity and the Incarnation, except for the Socinians, who rejected both doctrines as ir-rational (see p. 66). In ancient times various dissenters disputed some aspect of these doctrines; Bayle mentions the Arians, Eutychians, Monothelites, Nestorians, and others; none of these ancient sects had survived in Europe into his own time, and he does not discuss the content of their beliefs.

6. Among medieval theologians William of Ockham probably came closest to ar-guing for freedom of thought and speech among Catholics. (See A. S. McGrade, J. Kil-cullen, M. Kempshall, *The Cambridge Translations of Medieval Philosophical Texts:* vol. 2, *Ethics and Political Philosophy* (Cambridge: Cambridge University Press, 2001), pp. 484–95.) However, in Ockham's view there may come a point when it is reasonable to judge that another person is pertinacious, namely when the correct doctrine has been explained to him and proved with sufficient evidence, so that if he still does not accept it, it is because he is not willing to be corrected by the rule of faith. Bayle holds that this point never comes, since it is impossible to know whether something has been shown sufficiently to someone, and he goes further than freedom of thought and speech among the orthodox, arguing for toleration universally.

7. The first four ecumenical councils were Nicaea (A.D. 325), Constantinople (381), Ephesus (431), and Chalcedon (451).

Grace, Original Sin, Predestination

In Bayle's time Catholics and Protestants all held some version of a doctrine of "grace," i.e. that God gratuitously gives to human beings something additional to ordinary human nature, to make them holy and capable of acting well and believing rightly, and that without this grace it is impossible to be saved. Even without grace it may be possible to arrive at correct religious beliefs, based on the probability of human testimony (for example, a persuasion that the gospels are reliable historical documents and that their testimony establishes this or that). But this is merely "human" or "historical" faith (p. 524), as distinct from "divine faith" effected by grace. Human faith is not sufficient for salvation; to be saved it is necessary to have the divine faith that is caused by grace.

The doctrine of grace was developed mainly by Saint Augustine in his writings against Pelagius and the Pelagians (see Augustine, *Nicene and Post-Nicene Fathers, Series I,* Vol. V). Pelagius tried to encourage efforts to live well by saying that anyone who wished could act rightly. Augustine attacked this optimistic teaching, saying that living well requires special help from God at every stage—the initial wish to live well, actually doing the right thing, and persevering in right action to the end of one's life. God's help is "gratuitous," it cannot be earned. God does not give his grace to everyone; he does not give anyone grace to act rightly on every occasion, and he may in the end not give the grace of "final perseverance" to someone who has lived a substantially good life up to the moment of death. Anyone who dies in a state of sin will be damned, even though he has lived well until then. Only those "predestined" for salvation receive the grace of final perseverance; predestination cannot be earned, it is not based on the quality of a person's life before the time of death. The difficulty of living well, according to Augustine, has been increased by "Original Sin." The first human beings, Adam and Eve, by their first sin against God ("the Fall"), brought punishment on themselves and on all their descendants. Part of the punishment is a weakening of the will to act rightly and a clouding of the mind, producing ignorance and error. (Bayle argues at length that error is not always due to Original Sin; see p. 260, p. 473, p. 496.) Since all mankind are guilty of sin—they share the guilt of Adam's sin, at least—there is, according to Augustine, no injustice in the fact that God does not give his grace to everyone, since he is under no obligation to help anyone.

During the middle ages Augustine's teaching was followed by most theologians, and the Pelagians (and the semi-Pelagians or Massilians) were regarded as heretics. However, in the fourteenth century William of Ockham and other theologians modified Augustine's doctrine by suggesting that, while it is true that God is absolutely under no obligation to any creature, he has of his own free choice adopted the rule that he will give grace to those who do their best. (This free choice is nothing accidental: it is identical with God's goodness and with his being—it is God himself.) Grace cannot be earned, but those who do their best can be confident that grace will not be withheld. In effect, Pelagius's optimism is reinstated, thanks to God's free choice of a policy or rule governing his own conduct.[8] Bayle refers to this theory at p. 537, as that of "the Schoolmen."[9]

Against these Schoolmen Luther and Calvin reasserted the strict Augustinian doctrine. According to Calvin predestination and its opposite ("reprobation") are determined by God's eternal decrees, which relate to individuals, not to classes of people who satisfy some condition, and have no reason that human beings can discern. Some features of Lutheran and Calvinist doctrines were condemned by the Catholic Church in the Council of Trent (1545–1563), which, however, reaffirmed a version of Augustine's doctrines.

Among both Catholics and Protestants there continued to be some uneasiness over some aspects of Augustine's theory. According to Augustine, the wish to live well, and the acceptance of God's help, must be already the effect of grace. Since the effects of grace include willingness to accept it, it would seem that grace is irresistible. To some this seemed to give too little room to human free choice. Also, since not everyone is saved, it would seem that God does not give grace to everyone, which seems to conflict with the idea that God's benevolence is universal, and it seems inequitable that God

8. See Obermann, Heiko, *The Harvest of Medieval Theology: Gabriel Biel and Late Medieval Nominalism,* 2nd edition (Grand Rapids: Eerdmans, 1967).

9. Many, if not most, scholastic theologians rejected the theory, which had been put forward by Ockham.

should give grace to some and not to others just as deserving (or undeserving). Bayle refers to these disputes in several places (see pp. 530, 532–33, and 402).

The Jesuit Luis de Molina made another attempt to modify Augustine's doctrine to make more room for human free will and ideas of equity in his *Harmony of free will with the gifts of grace, and with God's foreknowledge, providence, predestination and reprobation,* Lisbon, 1588. This book led to controversy between Thomists (followers of Thomas Aquinas, who followed Augustine) and Molinists who included most Jesuits). Bayle mentions these schools of thought at p. 342 and p. 524. Toward the end of the sixteenth century, the pope established a commission "De Auxilliis" ("Concerning Helps," grace being help from God) to decide the debate between Thomists and Molinists. It was unable to decide, and allowed both doctrines to be taught; see *The Catholic Encyclopaedia,* "Congregatio de Auxiliis," http://www.newadvent.org/cathen/04238a.htm.

Molina's work also provoked *Augustine: or the Doctrine of St Augustine on the health, sickness and medicine of human nature, against the Pelagians and Massilians,* by the Louvain Catholic theologian Cornelius Jansen. Pope Innocent X condemned five propositions drawn from Jansen's book: (1) Some of God's precepts are, given their present abilities, impossible for just persons willing and trying to fulfil them; (2) in the state of fallen nature, interior grace can never be resisted; (3) for merit and demerit in the state of fallen nature, freedom from necessity is not needed, only freedom from compulsion; (4) the heresy of the semi-Pelagians was to hold that human will could resist or obey grace; (5) it is semi-Pelagian to say that Christ died for absolutely all human beings. The main issues here are whether grace is irresistible (propositions 2, 3, and 4) and whether God's will to save mankind is universal (proposition 5). See *The Catholic Encyclopaedia,* "Jansenius and Jansenism," http://www.newadvent.org/cathen/08285a.htm.

Jansen's followers (including Antoine Arnauld, Pierre Nicole, Blaise Pascal, and others associated with the Convent of Port-Royal) distinguished between the question of right (whether the five propositions in the sense the pope took them in were heretical) and the question of fact (whether certain words are to be found in the pages of Jansen's book, and if so whether Jansen intended them in the sense the pope intended to condemn).

The Jansenists acknowledged the pope's power to decide questions of theological principle, and therefore acknowledged that, in whatever sense the pope had taken them, the five propositions were indeed heretical. However, they maintained that as a matter of fact these propositions either were not in Jansen's book at all or were there in some sense other than the one the pope had condemned. Church authorities insisted that clergy and nuns suspected of Jansenism subscribe to a formulary stating that the condemned propositions were in Jansen's book in the condemned sense. Many Jansensists signed subject to various qualifications—that the statement of the formulary did not deserve "divine faith," that it did not deserve even "human faith" (see p. 524). When Church authorities refused to accept signatures with such qualifications and insisted on subscription "pure and simple," the Jansenists signed with "respectful silence," with the implication that they would qualify if they could, and in the end the papacy tolerated this. In various places Bayle alludes to the controversy over Jansenism and the distinction between the question of right and the question of fact; see for example pp. 448, 449.

While the controversies over Molinism and Jansenism divided Catholics, a similar controversy took place in the Reformed churches. Calvin's version of Augustinianism was criticized by the Dutch theologian Jacob Arminius, who affirmed the universality of God's benevolence toward mankind and human freedom in accepting or rejecting God's grace. The Arminians in 1610 published a "Remonstrance" (protest) in which they asserted five propositions, which may be summarized as follows: (1) that God's decree of Predestination is to save anyone who, through grace, believes and obeys (this is a general policy, rather than a decree relating to individuals); (2) Christ died for the forgiveness and redemption of all men (not only for the predestined); (3) no one can do anything truly good without God's grace; (4) grace is not irresistible; (5) it is not certain that those who once have true faith can never fall away. Strict Calvinism was reasserted by the Synod of Dort (Dordrecht), 1618–19, which condemned the Arminian propositions. Bayle refers to the controversy between Arminians (also called Remonstrants) and strict Calvinists at various places; see for example pp. 217, 401–2, and 469.

Bayle himself was a Calvinist, but he does not argue in favor of the

Calvinist doctrine of grace. He refers to these disputes as illustrations of the difficulty of deciding which position is correct.

See DHC, art. "Augustine."

The Eucharist

About the Eucharist (Holy Communion), Catholics and Lutherans held that Jesus Christ is *really* present in the bread and wine, Calvinists held that the bread and wine are only *symbolically* the body and blood of Christ. Catholics held that in the Eucharistic ceremony the substance of the bread and wine is transformed into the substance of Jesus Christ ("transubstantiation"); the Lutherans held that the substance of Jesus Christ becomes present along with the substance of the bread and wine ("consubstantiation"). For references to these controversies see p. 459.

Church and State

Since the middle ages the Catholic Church had claimed that the rulers of Christian states should come to the aid of the Church when the Church requested it, for example by repressing heresy. The pope claimed the power to remove an unsatisfactory ruler either by directly deposing him, or (this was the more usual doctrine) indirectly, by absolving subjects from their obligation of obedience and calling on them to replace their ruler. Catholic writers also argued that, apart from any dissatisfaction the Church might have with a ruler, the ruler's subjects might in some circumstances be entitled to disobey or rebel. Almost all (but not quite all) Catholic theologians disapproved of the assassination of a tyrannical ruler, and argued that a rebellion should be carried on by someone with a right to act on behalf of the people. These theories can be traced back to medieval writers such as Thomas Aquinas, John of Paris, and William of Ockham; their chief exponents in the sixteenth century were the Jesuits Francisco Suárez and Robert Bellarmine.[10]

10. Q. Skinner, *Foundations of Modern Political Thought* (Cambridge: Cambridge University Press, 1978).

Protestants usually held that Christians have a duty to obey the "powers that be" no matter how irreligious or tyrannical they may be, but not by doing anything contrary to the commandments of God; if the tyrant commands an immoral act, the Christian must refuse, but still not rebel. This is called the doctrine of "nonresistance" or, sometimes, "passive obedience" (passive in contrast to active—a Christian would not actively obey an immoral command, but would submit to the punishment for not obeying). Protestants denied the pope's claim to direct and depose rulers and disclaimed such powers for their own religious bodies. But although obedience and nonrebellion were their usual doctrines, some Protestants (notably Pierre Jurieu and John Locke) adopted something like the Catholic doctrine of the subject's right to rebel, especially when the true religion was being persecuted.[11]

Among French Catholics there was a tendency, usually called "Gallicanism," that aimed at protecting the interests of the French monarchy and of the parish clergy and bishops against the pope. This tendency originated during the thirteenth-century controversies at the University of Paris between the secular clergy and the mendicant friars (Franciscans and Dominicans), in the controversy between King Philip and Pope Boniface, and in the attempts to heal the Great Schism that came to fruition in the Council of Constance. The "Gallican Articles" of 1682 affirmed that kings are not subject to the authority of the Church in temporal and civil matters or to deposition by the ecclesiastical power, that their subjects cannot be dispensed by the pope from their allegiance, that a General Council has authority over a pope (as the Council of Constance asserted), and that doctrinal decisions by a pope need the consent of the Church. Gallicans also affirmed that royal officials could not be excommunicated for anything they did officially. The "ultramontanes" rejected Gallicanism, and maintained that the pope's authority held undiminished "beyond the mountains," i.e. the Alps, i.e. in France. The historian Maimbourg was a Gallican, and for this reason was expelled from the Jesuit order (which made a special point of obedience to the pope). For a reference to the controversy between Gallicans and Ultramontanes see pp. 541–42.

Bayle adheres to the view common among the Huguenots before Jurieu began to advocate rebellion, namely that a king's right to rule was not conditional upon his behavior. See, for example, p. 48. He therefore rejects the Catholic doctrines that the pope may depose a ruler for heresy or for failure to repress heresy and that the people may rebel against a tyrant. Like most Christians at the time, Catholic and Protestant, he held that a ruler should foster religion (see p. 202). However, in opposition to Catholics and to many of his Protestant contemporaries, he argues that the ruler must not use coercive measures to favor any religion—this is the thesis of the *Philosophical Commentary*. Although Catholics of Gallican tendency say that the pope cannot depose a king, Bayle thinks that the Ultramontane claim is a more authentic expression of Catholic doctrine (see pp. 48, 91, 541); and the Gallicans themselves were active persecutors of heretics. Bayle therefore says that Catholics, whether Gallican or Ultramontane, cannot safely be tolerated. But the "nontoleration" he advocates means, not persecuting Catholics, but taking precautions to make sure that they do not acquire the power to overthrow a heretical ruler or to persecute (see pp. 47–48, pp. 192–93, and p. 572).

The Rule of Faith

The various disputes about the Christian faith outlined above gave rise to another dispute, over how to resolve disputes about questions of faith (see pp. 457–59). According to Catholics, the "rule of faith" was the teaching of the Church, based partly on the Bible and partly on Catholic tradition. The teaching of the Church was formulated authoritatively by popes and General Councils (though there was some disagreement over whether a pope could decide questions of faith without reference to a Council). Catholics held that in deciding questions of faith a General Council was infallible. For Catholics important witness to tradition was to be found in the writings of the "Fathers" of the Church, i.e. the Christian writers of the first three or four hundred years after Christ. (See p. 121.)

According to the Protestants, the rule of faith is the Bible (not tradition), to be interpreted by each individual (not authoritatively by popes or councils). This did not mean that any individual interpretation would do—some interpretations would be correct and others not, but each individual had to arrive at the correct interpretation in person. From time to time Protestant churches published "confessions of faith," but these were supposed to be summaries of correct interpretations of the teaching of the Bible, without independent authority.

Catholics argued against what they called the Protestant doctrine of "private judgment" (i.e. judgment by a private individual), urging that ordinary people would not be able to carry out all the difficult inquiries needed to arrive at a correct interpretation of the Bible—how could they be sure what books belonged to the Bible, how could they be sure that the text transmitted to them was authentic, that the translation was faithful, etc.? See p. 262. The Catholic controversialist Pierre Nicole, assuming that it is wrong (an instance of temerity or rashness) to believe anything without adequate evidence, argued that no one could without temerity arrive at any conclusions by way of private judgment.

Protestants "retorted" these arguments against the Catholics. How could an individual know whether the currently recognized list of popes and General Councils were true popes and true Councils, how know which were authentic decrees, etc.? See p. 263. The Calvinist Jean Daillé applied the same topics to the appeal to the fathers of the Church—if it is difficult to find out the teaching of the Bible, it is just as difficult to find out the doctrine of the fathers.[12] (However, Bayle argues that Protestants cannot avoid inquiring into the opinions of the Church fathers; see p. 453.) Protestants often pointed out that Catholics must use private judgment in coming to the conclusion that they should believe the teaching of the Catholic Church.

Bayle comments that Nicole's principle that faith should not be without sufficient rational foundation was damaging not only to Protestantism but also to Catholicism, since popes and councils will be guilty of temerity in

---

12. Jean Daillé, *Traité de l'employ des saints Pères pour le jugement des différends qui sont aujourd'hui en la religion* [Treatise on the use of the holy Fathers for judging differences that exist today in religion], 1632 (English translation, London, 1675).

arriving at their decisions (see p. 528). In fact it is damaging to all forms of religious belief and favorable to Pyrrhonism, i.e. scepticism (see pp. 390–91). He argues that grace cannot meet the difficulty. Even if true believers are led to their beliefs by God's grace, grace cannot provide a criterion of correct belief, since there is no way of distinguishing between having grace and merely thinking that you do. See p. 529, p. 526.

Bayle argues that the rule of faith must be conjoined with the clear judgments of reason, since reason is also God's voice; see p. 68. Anything the Bible seems to teach that conflicts with basic moral principles must not in fact be the teaching of the Bible. Reason must therefore be used in interpreting what the Bible seems to say; see Part 1 chapter 1, p. 65ff. It is in this sense that his commentary interpreting the words of the Gospel is "philosophical." Bayle insists that he does not take this idea as far as the Socinians did (p. 66), though he does not explain how to draw the line.

Reason the Fundamental Rule

There was a long-standing tradition in Christian thought that presented faith in the Church and in the Bible as reasonable.[13] We should accept guidance if we have *reason* to believe that the guide knows and is truthful. Hence the fundamental rule of belief and action is reason, though in some situations reason may lead us to see that we should follow some other guide, which will then provide a "secondary" or "derivative" rule—once we have been convinced by reasons that some guide is reliable, it is rational to follow that guide.

This is the idea behind the opening chapter of the *Philosophical Commentary:* Reason or the "light of Nature" is a "Standard and original Rule" (p. 69), a "standing Test of all Precepts . . . not excepting even those which God has afterwards reveal'd in an extraordinary way" (p. 70). Adam thought himself obliged to obey God only "because that inward Light . . . continually presented the Idea of his Duty, and of his dependence on the Sovereign Being" (p. 70), so that for Adam "the reveal'd truth was sub-

---

13. See for example Étienne Gilson, *Reason and Revelation in the Middle Ages* (New York: Scribner, 1952).

ordinate to the natural Light in him" (p. 70). A theologian would treat
the Gospel as the first rule of morality, but "writing as a Philosopher, I'm
obliged to go back to the original and mother Rule, to wit, Reason or natural
light" (p. 80); the Gospel is "a second standing Rule collated with the
Original" (p. 81). Similarly, for the Jews the law of Moses was a secondary
rule recommended by reason: For the Mosaic Law, "once vouch'd by the
natural Light, acquir'd the Quality of a Rule and Criterion, in the same
manner, as a Proposition in Geometry once demonstrated from incontestable Principles, becomes it self a Principle with regard to other Propositions" (p. 72).

One of the major cultural changes in Europe since Bayle's time is widespread loss of the conviction that there is any reliable secondary rule, so
that even many Christians these days go back directly to reason in considering controversial questions of morality. But like Christian fundamental-
ists of today, Bayle believed that the Bible, though not the Church, is indeed
a reliable secondary rule, and he looked for a way of reconciling the Bible
with morality in cases of apparent conflict. He calls on the idea that God
may dispense with his own laws in special cases to explain such passages as
Numbers 25:7–11, where God might seem to have approved murder; see
pp. 85, 248.

The Bible

Both Catholics and Protestants in Bayle's time held that the Bible contains
no errors whatever, having been written at the dictation or "inspiration" of
the Holy Spirit. The Bible is a collection of originally separately circulating
"books" (Genesis, Matthew, Apocalypse, etc.). The set of books currently
included between the covers of one book, the Bible, is called "the canon."
Catholics and Protestants disagreed (to a minor extent) over the list of ca-
nonical books, and they also disagreed over how the canon was to be arrived
at. Catholics argued that no one would know which writings made up the
Bible, or would know that these writings were absolutely free from error,
except from the teaching of the Church. Calvinists claimed that qualities
of the writings that made up the Bible were clear to anyone aided by grace,

which would also guide the predestined to a correct interpretation. See pp. 458 and 464.

Philosophical Controversies

Bayle was an admirer of the philosophy of Nicolas Malebranche; he makes constant use of Malebranche's key moral concept, "order" (see for example pp. 100, 129, and 259). "Order" is equivalent to the medieval idea of the "eternal law," binding on God himself; see p. 130. Malebranche was in turn an admirer of Descartes, as were also the Jansenists Arnauld and Nicole. These "Cartesians" (and others) were exponents of the "new philosophy," so called in contrast with medieval Aristotelianism. According to the new philosophy material things have only the qualities recognized by mathematics; other apparent qualities such as color, taste, etc. ("secondary" qualities) exist only in the perception of a human being on whom the mathematical qualities impinge. Descartes attempted to reconcile our tendency to suppose that secondary qualities exist in material things with his principle that God would not deceive us by postulating (a) that assent is voluntary, and (b) that there is a duty to withhold assent from anything that is not absolutely clear (see Descartes, *Meditations on First Philosophy,* "Meditation VI"). God gives us sensation of secondary qualities, for example taste, not to reveal the real natures of things but to guide us in preserving our bodies. Thus it is our fault of precipitate judgment, and not God's deception, if we think that secondary qualities are real, since their reality was never absolutely clear, and we ought to have withheld assent. Nicole argued that this duty implies that Protestants' beliefs are illegitimate (rash, temerarious), since they cannot be based on evidence that meets Descartes's standard.

Bayle refers to these tenets of the new philosophy in various places. He comments that Descartes's postulated duty to withhold assent in the absence of indubitable evidence is useful in natural science, but not in religion (see p. 494). He models his account of conscience on Descartes's account of the function of the senses, such as taste: conscience does not necessarily reveal the true moral qualities of things, but is given to us as a practical guide for the preservation of our souls (see pp. 270–71). He remarks that the new philosophy's thesis that assent is voluntary should not obliterate the distinction between culpable and nonculpable error, which the Aristotelian philosophy made in terms of a distinction between voluntary and involuntary error: even if all error is in some sense voluntary, some errors are nonculpable (see pp. 486, 487).

Bayle points out on several occasions the great difficulty of reaching reasonable conclusions on many important questions (see, for example, Supplement, chapter XXIV, p. 531). In his *Historical and Critical Dictionary* the arguments for skepticism became a major theme; see for example the article "Pyrrho." (Pyrrhonism is the assertion—if a Pyrrhonist can assert anything—that nothing can be asserted even as merely probable, at least on speculative questions.) Bayle points out that skepticism and Christian faith are inconsistent, since a Christian must assent to doctrines on some of these difficult questions (see HCD, art. "Pyrrho," rem. B, and art. "Nicolle," rem. C; see also RQP 770 b51–771 a48, EMT 42 a40–61). Arguments for skepticism are therefore objections to Christianity, but Bayle, though he presents the skeptical arguments, rejects Pyrrhonism (e.g. p. 75) and affirms the doctrines of Calvinist Christianity. He objects to Nicole's arguments on temerity that they lead to Pyrrhonism and destroy Christianity (see pp. 390–91).

For more on these topics see the relevant articles in *The Oxford Encyclopedia of the Reformation* (New York: Oxford University Press, 1996), *The New Catholic Encyclopedia* (New York: McGraw-Hill, 1967–79), and *The Catholic Encyclopedia* (New York: The Universal Knowledge Foundation, 1913–14; on-line at http://www.newadvent.org/cathen/).

Alterations to the 1708 Translation

The following are the places where the translation has been altered (references are to the 1708 edition): p. 2, line 10; p. 2, line 25; p. 4, line 18; p. 8, lines 8–9; p. 9, line 32; p. 12, line 12; p. 14, line 17; p. 14, line 34; p. 16, lines 3–6; p. 16, line 33; p. 17, lines 2–6; p. 18, lines 25, 27; p. 19, line 26; p. 21, lines 9–10; p. 23, line 29; p. 24, lines 18–19; p. 25, line 25; p. 25, line 15; p. 26, lines 15, 20; p. 32, line 31; p. 34, lines 13, 14; p. 35, lines 9, 19; p. 37, line 12; p. 40, line 28; p. 46, line 32;

p. 52, line 7; p. 54, lines 1, 6, 18; p. 55, lines 18–19, 23, 33; p. 56, line 23; p. 57, line 34; p. 59, lines 16, 27; p. 60, line 6; p. 61, lines 1, 13; p. 62, lines 2–3; p. 63, line 21; p. 64, line 1; p. 65, lines 15, 20; p. 68, lines 1–2, 29–30; p. 69, line 19; p. 71, line 20; p. 77, lines 10–11; p. 78, line 35; p. 81, lines 19, 25, 30, 32; p. 82, line 7; p. 83, line 3; p. 85, lines 5, 18, 19, 24–25; p. 86, lines 4, 7; p. 87, lines 6, 17; p. 88, line 26; p. 89, lines 5, 22–23; p. 90, lines 4, 20, 21; p. 91, lines 9, 20; p. 92, line 18; p. 93, line 13; p. 94, line 3; p. 96, line 5; p. 97, line 34; p. 100, lines 2, 34; p. 101, lines 1, 12, 13; p. 102, line 12; p. 103, line 11; p. 104, line 24; p. 106, line 7; p. 107, line 33; p. 108, line 21; p. 109, lines 7, 13; p. 111, line 14; p. 112, line 20; p. 113, lines 28, 34; p. 114, lines 9, 12; p. 115, lines 7, 12; p. 116, line 8; p. 117, lines 1–3; p. 120, line 11; p. 123, line 13; p. 124, lines 4–6; p. 125, line 1; p. 129, lines 8–9, 18, 20; p. 133, line 1; p. 136, line 14; p. 137, line 31; p. 138, line 15; p. 140, lines 5, 7, 11; p. 146, line 4; p. 149, line 21; p. 153, lines 11, 34; p. 155, lines 8, 21; p. 156, lines 23–24; p. 158, lines 5, 7; p. 160, lines 7, 25; p. 164, lines 11, 26–27; p. 165, lines 23, 26, 31; p. 166, lines 13, 20; p. 172, line 10; p. 174, line 3; p. 176, lines 30–31; p. 179, lines 3–4, 10, 26; p. 180, line 16; p. 181, line 16; p. 184, line 27; p. 186, line 18; p. 187, line 6; p. 190, lines 1–2, 23; p. 191, lines 17–18; p. 194, lines 14, 28–29, 30; p. 196, lines 12–13; p. 197, lines 2, 14, 16; p. 198, line 26; p. 202, line 5; p. 209, lines 20–21; p. 211, line 15; p. 212, lines 17, 21; p. 214, lines 33–34; p. 217, line 35; p. 218, lines 2, 31; p. 219, lines 19–20, 22–23; p. 222, line 11; p. 225, lines 1, 5–6; p. 228, lines 8–9; p. 229, line 10; p. 230, lines 10, 33; p. 231, line 14; p. 234, lines 17, 19; p. 236, lines 13, 24; p. 237, line 7; p. 240, line 18; p. 247, lines 3, 12–13; p. 252, line 12; p. 254, lines 15–16, 27; p. 256, line 21; p. 257, lines 1, 14; p. 258, line 32; p. 260, line 22; p. 264, line 20; p. 265, lines 23–25; p. 266, line 7; p. 267, lines 7–8; p. 268, lines 4, 23, 32; p. 269, line 9; p. 271, line 28; p. 272, lines 2–4; p. 273, lines 7, 10; p. 274, lines 25–26; p. 278, lines 25–26; p. 283, lines 20–21; p. 286, lines 9–11; p. 291, lines 15, 18, 22; p. 292, lines 11, 13, 30; p. 293, lines 24–25; p. 295, lines 22–23; p. 296, line 33; p. 297, lines 11, 16, 20; p. 300, line 22; p. 301, line 7; p. 304, lines 2–3, 4; p. 305, lines 3, 35; p. 306, line 11; p. 309, lines 14–15, 22; p. 310, lines 17–18, 28; p. 313, line 13; p. 314, line 33; p. 319, lines 6–7, 22–26; p. 320, lines 4, 10, 25; p. 321, line 4; p. 324, line 24; p. 325, line 9; p. 326, line 17; p. 329, lines 29–30; p. 330, lines 6, 19; p. 335, line 32; p. 336, lines 7–9; p. 338, lines 15–16; p. 339, line 16; p. 340, line 6; p. 341, lines 34–35; p. 345, lines 17–18; p. 347, line 17; p. 348, line 5; p. 349, line 25; p. 350, lines 20, 25–26; p. 351, lines 6–7, 28, 30; p. 352, lines 24–27; p. 353, line 7; p. 357, line 3; p. 358, lines 6, 21, 23; p. 359, lines 8, 18; p. 360, lines 19, 27; p. 370, lines 22, 25; p. 379, line 27; p. 383, lines 22–23; p. 384, lines 5–6; p. 386, line 32; p. 387, lines 28–29, 31; p. 388, lines 8, 23; p. 392, lines 24–25; p. 393, lines 7–8; p. 395, lines 18–21; p. 396, line 8; p. 403, line 15; p. 411, line 25; p. 412, line 4; p. 414, lines 20–21; p. 417, line 31; p. 424, line 23; p. 425, line 29; p. 430, line 27; p. 435, lines 3–4; p. 436, lines 7, 11; p. 438, line 30; p. 442, line 11; p. 442, lines 1–2; p. 445, line 4; p. 452, line 21; p. 454, line 31; p. 455, lines 5, 18; p. 456, line 21; p. 457, lines 22–25; p. 465, lines 28–29; p. 466, line 11; p. 474, lines 23–26; p. 480, lines 9–10; p. 483, lines 9, 22–25; p. 484, lines 26–27, 28; p. 485, lines 11, 18, 27; p. 488, lines 3–5, 25; p. 490, lines 1–2; p. 492, line 2; p. 496, lines 2, 15; p. 504, lines 9–10; p. 507, lines 4, 16; p. 514, line 17; p. 518, line 5; p. 519, line 1; p. 520, lines 29, 34; p. 521, lines 6, 9; p. 524, lines 14, 21; p. 527, line 23; p. 528, lines 4–6; p. 530, line 28; p. 531, line 23; p. 533, lines 11–12; p. 534, line 25; p. 535, line 23; p. 538, line 33; p. 540, lines 15–16; p. 541, lines 2, 10, 27; p. 542, lines 25–26; p. 544, lines 9, 25–26; p. 546, line 9; p. 553, lines 20, 21; p. 556, line 14; p. 572, line 1; p. 573, line 18; p. 586, line 22; p. 589, line 19; p. 591, line 30; p. 593, line 15; p. 594, line 30; p. 595, lines 27, 33; p. 597, lines 33–34; p. 601, line 4; p. 603, line 19; p. 612, line 8; p. 621, lines 7, 23; p. 622, line 2; p. 623, line 7; p. 624, line 25; p. 625, line 12; p. 627, line 1; p. 633, line 32; p. 635, line 29; p. 636, lines 2–3, 8; p. 637, lines 6, 17; p. 638, lines 7, 25; p. 643, line 31; p. 647, line 19; p. 648, line 19; p. 650, line 28; p. 655, lines 18, 25; p. 658, lines 2, 18, 21; p. 659, lines 8–10, 13; p. 660, lines 8–9; p. 661, lines 19, 26; p. 663, lines 27, 29; p. 664, lines 7, 26; p. 665, line 24; p. 667, lines 8, 9; p. 668, line 21; p. 669, line 13; p. 670, line 13; p. 671, lines 24, 29, 33; p. 674, lines 24, 25, 31; p. 675, lines 26–28, 33; p. 676, line 2; p. 677, line 12; p. 678, line 15; p. 680, line 34; p. 681, lines 20, 24; p. 683, line 26; p. 685, lines 16, 34; p. 687, line 17; p. 688, line 9; p. 689, line 34; p. 694, lines 16–17, 25; p. 695, line 7; p. 696, lines 28–29, 30–31; p. 698, lines 22, 27; p. 700, line 23; p. 702, lines 12, 18; p. 703, lines 4, 21–22; p. 705, line 24; p. 706, line 5; p. 707, lines 2, 25; p. 708, lines 8, 9, 12; p. 711, lines 4, 31; p. 717, lines 31–34; p. 721, line 20; p. 723, line 20; p. 725, lines 12, 33; p. 726, lines 10, 31–32; p. 728, line 23; p. 729, line 14; p. 731, line 25; p. 737, line 27; p. 738, lines 26–27; p. 740, line 1; p. 741, line 19; p. 742, line 17; p. 743, line 3; p. 744, lines 5–13; p. 748, line 19; p. 750, line 27; p. 751, lines 25–26; p. 755, line 2; p. 756, lines 3, 4, 5, 8; p. 758, line 9; p. 759, line 31; p. 760, lines 1, 2; p. 761, line 9; p. 762, line 32; p. 764, line 10; p. 766, lines 7, 29; p. 767, lines 19, 21; p. 771, line 18; p. 774, line 22. In addition we have corrected misprints and in some places supplied omitted headings and heading numbers.

INDEX

abortion as parricide, 432

Abraham, 178, 181, 182, 303, 348

Absalom, 44

abuse of laws against heretics for private ends, 337–38, 344

accidental (per accidens), 108, 128, 235, 236, 238, 289, 290, 322, 323, 432, 479, 483, 525, 566

accidental *vs.* willed use of coercion, 127–31

actions, whether to be judged by motives, 309, 311–13. *See also* interest of the True Church

A(c)hab, 341, 363

Acts 5:1–11, 248n

Adam (Biblical figure), 70–71, 437–39, 593. *See also* original sin

Adam, John, 285

Adamites, 245

ad hominem argument (recrimination), 124, 331, 417, 580n

a dicto simpliciter ad dictum secundum quid, fallacy, 332

Adrian VI, Pope, 118

adultery, heresy compared to, 354–55

advancement or advantage. *See* temporal advantage

advantage of the True Church. *See* interest of the True Church

Aeneid (Virgil), 294n, 418–19, 486–88, 497, 543

affected ignorance. *See* ignorance

Africa, Islamic invasion of, 569

Agar (Hagar), Sarah's persecution of, 303, 307–8, 347–48. *See also* Sarah

agreement of all Christians as to certain tenets, logical consequences of, 499–500, 520–30

Ahab. *See* A(c)hab

Aix de la Chaiz(s)e, François d', 373

Albigenses, 169, 550, 556

Alcoran (Koran), 408, 491

Alexander, Natalis, 169n

Alexander the Great, 207

alienation of property of heretics. *See* property, confiscation of

alms-giving, 252–53, 420, 423, 426, 428, 434, 508–9

Alphonso, King of Castile, 118

Alva, Duke of, 168–69, 171, 550

Amadis de Gaul, 409

Ambrose of Milan, St.: burning of Callicin, 187–89

Amelote, Denis, 85

Anabaptists, xv, 408, 441, 554–55, 572n, 573, 583

analogy of faith, 163. *See also* Spirit of the Gospel

analogy or parallel, argument by, 581–82

Ananias, St. Peter's slaying of, 248, 313

ancient authors, different restorations of passages of, 535

Anglicans (Episcopalians), 457, 462, 533

504–5; beauty, motive for deliberate destruction of, 315; love-potions, victims of, 497; seduction *vs.* rape of, 173; sexual coercion of, 548–52; supposed husbands, right of conscience evinced in faithfulness to, 234, 355, 497, 503 (*See also* Right of conscience). *See also* mothers

works of the flesh, heresy reckoned among, 500–4

worship of God consists principally in acts of the mind, 76

Wyclif, John, 289

xerophagy of Montanists, 499

Zell, Duchess of, 555
Zeno of Elea, 532n
Zozimus, 214n
Zwingli, Ulrich, 289

This book is set in Adobe Garamond, a modern adaptation by Robert Slimbach of the typeface originally cut around 1540 by the French typographer and printer Claude Garamond. The Garamond face, with its small lowercase height and restrained contrast between thick and thin strokes, is a classic "old-style" face and has long been one of the most influential and widely used typefaces.

Printed on paper that is acid-free and meets the requirements of the American National Standard for Permanence of Paper for Printed Library Materials, z39.48-1992. ⊗

Book design by Louise OFarrell
Gainesville, Florida
Typography by Apex Publishing, LLC
Madison, Wisconsin
Printed and bound by Worzalla Publishing Company
Stevens Point, Wisconsin